# THE MEANING
# OF SOCIOLOGY

## A Reader
## Sixth Edition

# Joel M. Charon, Editor

*Moorhead State University*
*Moorhead, Minnesota*

PRENTICE HALL, *Upper Saddle River, New Jersey 07458*

**Library of Congress Cataloging-in-Publication Data**

Charon, Joel M.,
    The meaning of sociology / Joel M. Charon, editor. - - 6th ed.
      p  .cm.
    Includes bibliographical references and index.
    ISBN 0–13–906066–9
    1. Sociology.  I.  Charon, Joel M.,  1939-
HM51.M325  1999
301- - dc21                     98-33680
                                     CIP

Editor in Chief: Nancy Roberts
Sr. Acquisitions Editor: John Chillingworth
Managing Editor: Sharon Chambliss
Marketing Manager: Christopher DeJohn
Production Liaison: Fran Russello
Project Manager: Ray Robinson, Douglas & Gayle Ltd.
Interior Design: Susan Finkelstein
Copy Editor: Alice Martina Smith
Art Director: Jayne Conte
Cover Design: Joe Sengotta
Cover Illustration: Doree Loschiavo, *Market Prices*, 1997
Manufacturing and Prepress Buyer: Mary Ann Gloriande

This book was set in 10/11 point Electra LH by D & G Limited, LLC
and was printed and bound by Quebecor Printing—Fairfield.
The cover was printed by Phoenix Color Corp.

©1999, 1996, 1993, 1990, 1987, 1980 by Prentice-Hall, Inc.
Simon & Schuster/A Viacom Company
Upper Saddle River, New Jersey 07458

Printed in the United States of America
10  9  8  7  6  5  4  3  2  1

ISBN 0-13-906066-9

Prentice-Hall International (UK) Limited, *London*
Prentice-Hall of Australia Pty. Limited, *Sydney*
Prentice-Hall Canada Inc., *Toronto*
Prentice-Hall Hispanoamericana, S.A., *Mexico*
Prentice-Hall of India Private Limited, *New Delhi*
Prentice-Hall of Japan, Inc., *Tokyo*
Simon & Schuster Asia Pte. Ltd., *Singapore*
Editora Prentice-Hall do Brasil, Ltda., *Rio de Janeiro*

# Contents

# Preface

The purpose of this reader is to share the excitement of sociology. Each selection has been chosen carefully according to the following criteria: Is it interesting? Is it a good example of sociology? Does it illustrate an idea or concept that is central to the sociological perspective? Is it written at a level that can be understood by a student who does not have an extensive background in sociology?

Sociology can be applied to every aspect of our lives. It is the study of society and the individual, interaction and organization, social patterns and institutions, social issues and social problems, social order and social change. The selections in this reader attempt to capture this diversity.

Some selections are written by professional sociologists, and some are written by people who think like sociologists. Some are very recent; whereas some happen to be older. Some are theoretical; whereas, some are empirical. Diversity and balance have been my aim.

I also have tried to take selections from a wide variety of sources. Included are selections from *American Journal of Sociology*, *Symbolic Interaction*, *Society*, *Esquire*, *The Atlantic Monthly*, *Social Policy*, *Time*, *Journal of Social Issues*, *Gender and Society*, *Social Theory*, *American Sociological Review*, and *Psychology Today*. As you will see, most of the selections are taken from books rather than journals. Always, my concern was to include what I consider to be good representatives of how sociologists think about the human being and to include articles that students can understand and apply to their lives.

This is the sixth edition of this reader. It is always difficult to know which selections should be kept and which should be replaced. In making decisions for this edition, I relied heavily on a poll of several users of the fifth edition. Although I did not always take their suggestions, they caused me to question my choices, and they gave me good leads. In the end, I decided to use 41 selections from the fifth edition. Twenty-three selections are new.

This reader is organized logically. I have made an attempt to tie the selections to a central concept in sociology and to illustrate what the sociological perspective means. In my opinion, it is not easy to think sociologically, and a book such as this should be used to examine some of the possibilities.

The introductions to the sections have been carefully written. Difficult selections are introduced with a brief outline that should prove helpful to many students. Usually, the introductions give a rationale for including the selection, which helps tie the selection to a central concept or idea.

I would like to thank Nancy Roberts, Sharon Chambliss, and the staff at Prentice Hall for their confidence in me and for their encouragement and advice.

I would like to dedicate this book to David Cooperman—advisor, sociologist, teacher, and friend.

Joel M. Charon

# Part I
# THE MEANING OF SOCIOLOGY

The first two readings in Part I are classic statements about the discipline of sociology. Peter Berger calls sociology a "passion," a "demon" that captures those interested in understanding the human condition. C. Wright Mills calls it a very special "imagination," a creative and important way of understanding the human being and his or her relationship with the larger society. Both statements reveal an excitement that many of us feel about the perspective of sociology, and both also reveal the ultimate purpose of sociology: to understand the human being in a social context, carefully and systematically.

Berger emphasizes that sociology is misunderstood, and that it is often confused with social work and social reform. His point is basic: Sociology is an attempt to **understand society**, it is a **science**, and it is a **unique way** of looking at a familiar world.

Mills argues that more than just understanding our social life, sociology must be concerned with human problems. It must sensitize the individual to the fact that society exists and is important for what we do—that our individual lives and our personal problems are part of a much larger history and are embedded in a society. Our problems, in large part, are created in history and in the patterns of society.

The third selection is by Alan Wolfe, who reminds us of the importance of society to understanding the human being, and, therefore, the critical reason that sociology is an important perspective to nurture in the intellectual community. It is fragile, he maintains, because we take society for granted.

Jessie Bernard gives us a personal essay on sociology: How she became a sociologist and what it has meant to her.

Harold Kincaid presents to the reader a case for the importance of sociology as a science. Rosabeth Kanter's study from **Men and Women of the Corporation** is the final selection, and its purpose is to show how some sociologists "do" science. Note that her approach uses many techniques, and that she carefully describes these techniques so that others, if they wonder about her conclusions, can criticize how she went about doing her work.

# 1. SOCIOLOGY AS A PASSION TO UNDERSTAND

PETER L. BERGER

*"The sociological perspective is more like a demon that possesses one, that drives one compellingly, again and again, to the questions that are its own."*

This first reading is Chapter 1 from the excellent book by Peter Berger, **Invitation to Sociology**. There, the chapter is entitled "Sociology as an Individual Pastime," but Berger's point is that it is much more than that—it is an exciting passion, a perspective that truly helps us understand our social world. In this selection, Berger shows us the many misunderstandings about sociology, emphasizing always that it is a scientific attempt to understand. "The sociologist," he says, "is someone concerned with understanding society in a disciplined way." It "will be satisfying, in the long run, only to those who can think of nothing more entrancing than to watch men and to understand things human."

1. What are the misconceptions people have about sociology? Why are they misconceptions?
2. What is sociology? What do sociologists do?
3. Why do sociologists do what they do? What drives them?

(By the way, you might notice that Berger uses the term **he**, not **he or she**. Things have changed a great deal in society and in sociology since 1963, when this article was written. Today, few people would attempt to publish a work in sociology that makes it appear that only men contribute to the world. This problem reappears in many other selections in this book too. It is very difficult for me to change other people's work in this book for the purposes of inclusion—sometimes, it is impossible. Please do not let this detract from your enjoyment or learning.)

If one asks undergraduate students why they are taking sociology as a major, one often gets the reply, "because I like to work with people." If one then goes on to ask such students about their occupational future, as they envisage it, one often hears that they intend to go into social work. Of this, more in a moment. Other answers are more vague and general, but all indicate that the student in question would rather deal with people than with things. Occupations mentioned in this connection include personnel work, human relations in industry, public relations, advertising, community planning, or religious work of the unordained variety. The common assumption is that in all these lines of endeavor, one might "do something for people," "help people," "do work that is useful for the community." The image of the sociologist involved here could be described as a secularized version of the liberal Protestant ministry, with the YMCA secretary perhaps furnishing the connecting link between sacred and profane benevolence. Sociology is seen as an up-to-date variation on the classic American theme of "uplift." The sociologist is understood as someone professionally concerned with edifying activities on behalf of individuals and of the community at large....

It is, of course, true that some Boy Scout types have become sociologists. It is also true that a benevolent interest in people could be the biographical starting point for sociological studies. But it is important to point out that a malevolent and misanthropic outlook could serve just as well. Sociological insights are valuable to anyone concerned with action in society. But this action need not be particularly humanitarian. Some American sociologists today are employed by governmental agencies seeking to plan more livable communities for the nation. Other American sociologists are employed by governmental agencies concerned with wiping communities of hostile nations off the map, if and when the necessity should arise. Whatever the moral implications of these respective activities may be, there is no reason why interesting sociological studies could not be carried on in both. Similarly, criminology, as a special field within sociology, has uncovered valuable information about processes of crime in modern society. This information is as valuable for those seeking to fight crime as it would be for those interested in promoting it. The fact that more criminologists have been employed by the police than by gangsters can be ascribed to the ethical bias of the criminologists themselves, the public relations of the police, and perhaps the lack of scientific sophistication of the gangsters. It has nothing to do with the character of the information itself. In sum, "working with people" can mean getting them out of slums or getting them into jail, selling them propaganda or robbing them of their money (be it legally or illegally), making them produce better automobiles or making them better bomber pilots. As an image of the sociologist, then, the phrase leaves something to be desired, even though it may serve to describe at least the initial impulse as a result of which some people turn to the study of sociology....

Social work, whatever its theoretical rationalization, is a certain *practice* in society. Sociology is not a practice, but an *attempt to understand*. Certainly, this understanding may have use for the practitioner. For that matter, we would contend that a more profound grasp of sociology would be of great use to the social worker, and that such a grasp would obviate the necessity of his descending into the mythological depths of the "subconscious" to explain matters that are typically quite conscious, much more simple, and indeed social in nature. But there is nothing inherent in the sociological enterprise of trying to understand society that necessarily leads to this practice or to any other. Sociological understanding can be recommended to social workers, but also to salesmen, nurses, evangelists, and politicians — in fact, to anyone whose goals involve the manipulation of men, for whatever purpose and with whatever moral justification.

This conception of the sociological enterprise is implied in the classic statement by Max Weber, one of the most important figures in the development of the field, to the effect that sociology is "value-free." Since it will be necessary to return to this a number of times later, it may be well to explicate it a little further at this point. Certainly the statement does not mean that the sociologist has or should have no values. In any case, it is just about impossible for a human being to exist without any values at all, although, of course, there can be tremendous variation in the values one may hold. The sociologist will normally have many values as a citizen, a private person, a member of a religious group, or as an adherent of some other association of people. But within the limits of his activities as a sociologist, there is one fundamental value only — that of scientific integrity. Even there, of course, the sociologist, being human, will have to reckon with his convictions, emotions, and prejudices. But it is part of his intellectual training that he tries to understand and control these as *biases* that ought to be eliminated, as far as possible, from his work. It goes without saying that this is not always easy to do, but it is not impossible. The sociologist tries to see what is there. He may have hopes or fears concerning what he may find. But he will try to see, regardless of his hopes or fears. It is thus an act of pure perception, as pure as humanly limited means allow, toward which sociology strives....

We would stress strongly that saying this does not imply that the sociologist has no responsibility to ask about the goals of his employers or the use to which they will put his work. But this asking is not sociological asking. It is asking the same questions that any man ought to ask himself about his actions in society. Again, in the same way, biological knowledge can be employed to heal or to kill. This does not mean that the biologist is free of responsibility as to which use he serves. But when he asks himself about this responsibility, he is not asking a biological question.

Another image of the sociologist, related to the two already discussed, is that of social reformer....

It is gratifying from certain value positions (including some of this writer's) that sociological insights have served in a number of instances to improve the lot of groups of human beings by uncovering morally shocking conditions, or by clearing away collective illusions, or by showing that socially desired results could be obtained in a more humane fashion. One might point, for example, to some applications of sociological knowledge in the penological practice of Western countries. Or one might cite the use made of sociological studies in the Supreme Court decision of 1954 on racial segregation in the public schools. Or one could look at the applications of other sociological studies to the humane planning of urban redevelopment. Certainly, the sociologist who is morally and politically sensitive will derive gratification from such instances. But, once more, it will be well to keep in mind that what is at issue here is not sociological understanding as such but certain applications of this understanding. It is not difficult to see how the same understanding could be applied with opposite intentions. Thus the sociological understanding of the dynamics of racial prejudice can be applied effectively by those promoting intragroup hatred as well as by those wanting to spread tolerance. And the sociological understanding of the nature of human solidarity can be employed in the service of both totalitarian and democratic regimes. It is sobering to realize that the same processes that generate consensus can be manipulated by a social group worker in a summer camp in the Adirondacks and by a communist brainwasher in a prisoner camp in China. One may readily grant that the sociologist can sometimes be called upon to give advice when it comes to changing certain social conditions deemed undesirable. But the image of the sociol-

ogist as social reformer suffers from the same confusion as the image of him as social worker.

If these images of the sociologist all have an element of "cultural lag" about them, we can now turn to some other images that are of more recent date and that refer themselves to more recent developments in the discipline. One such image is that of the sociologist as a gatherer of statistics about human behavior. The sociologist is here seen essentially as an aide-de-camp to an IBM machine. He goes out with a questionnaire, interviews people selected at random, then goes home, enters his tabulations onto innumerable punch cards, which are then fed into a machine. In all of this, of course, he is supported by a large staff and a very large budget. Included in this image is the implication that the results of all this effort are picayune, a pedantic restatement of what everybody knows anyway. As one observer remarked pithily, a sociologist is a fellow who spends $100,000 to find his way to a house of ill repute.

This image of the sociologist has been strengthened in the public mind by the activities of many agencies that might well be called parasociological — mainly agencies concerned with public opinion and market trends. The pollster has become a well-known figure in American life, importuning people about their views from foreign policy to toilet paper. Because the methods used in the pollster business bear close resemblance to sociological research, the growth of this image of the sociologist is understandable. The Kinsey studies of American sexual behavior have probably greatly augmented the impact of this image. The fundamental sociological question, whether concerned with premarital petting or with Republican votes or with the incidence of gang knifings, is always presumed to be "how often?" or "how many?" (Incidentally, the very few jokes current about sociologists usually relate to this statistical image... which jokes had better be left to the imagination of the reader.)

Statistical data by themselves do not make sociology. They become sociology only when they are sociologically interpreted, put within a theoretical frame of reference that is sociological. Simple counting, or even correlating different items that one counts, is not sociology. There is almost no sociology in the Kinsey reports. This does not mean that the data in these studies are not true or that they cannot be relevant to sociological understanding. They are, taken by themselves, raw materials that can be used in sociological interpretation. The interpretation, however, must be broader than the data themselves. So the sociologist cannot arrest himself at the frequency tables of premarital petting or extramarital pederasty. These enumerations are meaningful to him only in terms of their much broader implications for an understanding of institutions and values in our society. To arrive at such understanding, the sociologist will often have to apply statistical techniques, especially when he is dealing with the mass phenomena of modern social life. But sociology consists of statistics as little as philology consists of conjugating irregular verbs or chemistry of making nasty smells in test tubes....

How, then, are we to conceive of the sociologist? In discussing the various images of him that abound in the popular mind, we have already brought out certain elements that would have to go into our conception. We can now put them together. In doing so, we shall construct what sociologists themselves call an "ideal type." This means that what we delineate will not be found in reality in its pure form. Instead, one will find approximations to it and deviations from it, in varying degrees. Nor is it to be understood as an empirical average. We would not even claim that all individuals who now call themselves sociologists will recognize themselves without reservations in our conception, nor would we dispute the right of those who do not so recognize themselves to use the appellation. Our business is not excommunication. We would, however, contend that our "ideal type" corresponds to the self-conception of most sociologists in the mainstream of the discipline, both historically (at least in this century) and today.

The sociologist, then, is someone concerned with understanding society in a disciplined way. The nature of this discipline is scientific. This means that what the sociologist finds and says about the social phenomena he studies occurs with a certain rather strictly defined frame of reference. One of the main characteristics of this scientific frame of reference is that operations are bound by certain rules of evidence. As a scientist, the sociologist tries to be objective, to control his personal preferences and prejudices, to perceive clearly rather than to judge normatively. This restraint, of course, does not embrace the totality of the sociologist's existence as a human being but is limited to his operations as sociologist. Nor does the sociologist claim that his frame of reference is the only one within which society can be looked at. For that matter, very few scientists in any field would claim today that one should look at the world only scientifically. The botanist looking at a daffodil has no reason to dispute the right of the poet to look at the same object in a very different manner. There are many ways of playing....

The game of the sociologist, then, uses scientific rules. As a result, the sociologist must be clear in his own mind as to the meaning of these rules.

... [T]he interest of the sociologist is primarily theoretical. That is, he is interested in understanding for its own sake. He may be aware of or even concerned with the practical applicability and consequences of his findings—but at that point, he leaves the sociological frame of reference as such and moves into realms of values, beliefs, and ideas that he shares with other men who are not sociologists....

The sociologist... is a person intensively, endlessly, shamelessly interested in the doings of men. His natural habitat is all the human gathering places of the world, wherever men come together. The sociologist may be interested in many other things. But his consuming interest remains in the world of men, their institutions, their history, their passions. And because he is interested in men, nothing that men do can be altogether tedious for him. He will naturally be interested in the events that engage men's ultimate beliefs, their moments of tragedy and grandeur and ecstasy. But he will also be fascinated by the commonplace, the everyday. He will know reverence, but this reverence will not prevent him from wanting to see and to understand. He may sometimes feel revulsion or contempt, but this also will not deter him from wanting to have his questions answered. The sociologist, in his quest for understanding, moves through the world of men without respect for the usual lines of demarcation. Nobility and degradation, power and obscurity, intelligence and folly—these are equally interesting to him, however unequal they may be in his personal values or tastes. Thus his questions may lead him to all possible levels of society, the best and least known places, the most respected and the most despised. And, if he is a good sociologist, he will find himself in all these places because his own questions have so taken possession of him that he has little choice but to seek for answers.

It would be possible to say the same things in a lower key. We could say that the sociologist, but for the grace of his academic title, is the man who must listen to gossip despite himself, who is tempted to look through keyholes, to read other people's mail, to open closed cabinets. Before some otherwise unoccupied psychologist sets out now to construct an aptitude test for sociologists on the basis of sublimated voyeurism, let us quickly say that we are speaking merely by way of analogy. Perhaps some little boys consumed with curiosity to watch their maiden aunts in the bathroom later become inveterate sociologists. This is quite uninteresting. What interests us is the curiosity that grips any sociologist in front of a closed door behind which there are human voices. If he is a good sociologist, he will want to open that door, to understand these voices. Behind each closed door he will anticipate some new facet of human life not yet perceived and understood.

The sociologist will occupy himself with matters that others regard as too sacred or as too distasteful for dispassionate investigation. He will find rewarding the company of priests or of prostitutes, depending not on his personal preferences but on the questions he happens to be asking at the moment. He will also concern himself with matters that others may find much too boring. He will be interested in the human interaction that goes with warfare or with great intellectual discoveries, but also be interested in the relations between people employed in a restaurant or between a group of little girls playing with their dolls. His main focus of attention is not the ultimate significance of what men do, but the action in itself, as another example of the infinite richness of human conduct. So much for the image of our playmate.

In these journeys through the world of men, the sociologist will inevitably encounter other professional Peeping Toms. Sometimes, these will resent his presence, feeling that he is poaching on their preserves. In some places, the sociologist will meet up with the economist; in others, with the political scientist; in yet others, with the psychologist or the ethnologist. Yet chances are that the questions that have brought him to these same places are different from the ones that propelled his fellow trespassers. The sociologist's questions always remain essentially the same: "What are people doing with each other here?" "What are their relationships to each other?" "How are these relationships organized in institutions?" "What are the collective ideas that move men and institutions?" In trying to answer these questions in specific instances, the sociologist will, of course, have to deal with economic or political matters, but he will do so in a way rather different from that of the economist or the political scientist....

The fascination of sociology lies in the fact that its perspective makes us see in a new light the very world in which we have lived all our lives. This also constitutes a transformation of consciousness. Moreover, this transformation is more relevant existentially than that of many other intellectual disciplines because it is more difficult to segregate in some special compartment of the mind. The astronomer does not live in the remote galaxies, and the nuclear physicist can, outside his laboratory, eat and laugh and marry and vote without thinking about the insides of the atom. The geologist looks at rocks only at appropriate times, and the linguist speaks English with his wife. The sociologist lives in society, on the job and off it. His own life, inevitably, is part of his subject matter. Men being what they are, sociologists manage to segregate their professional insights from their everyday affairs. But it is a rather difficult feat to perform in good faith.

The sociologist moves in the common world of men, close to what most of them would call *real*. The categories he employs in his analyses are only refinements of the categories by which other men live: power, class, status, race, ethnicity. As a result, there is a deceptive simplicity and obviousness about some sociological investigations. One reads them, nods at the familiar scene, remarks that one has heard all this before and don't people have better things to do than to waste their time on truisms — until one is suddenly brought up against an insight that radically questions everything one had previously assumed about this familiar scene. This is the point at which one begins to sense the excitement of sociology.

Let us take a specific example. Imagine a sociology class in a southern college at which almost all the students are white southerners. Imagine a lecture on the subject of the racial system of the South. The lecturer is talking here of matters that have been familiar to his students from the time of their infancy. Indeed, it may be that they are much more familiar with the minutiae of this system than he is. They are quite bored as a result. It seems to them that he is only using more pretentious words to describe what they already know. Thus he may use the term "caste," one commonly used now by American sociologists to describe the southern racial system. But in explaining the term, he shifts to traditional Hindu society, to make it clearer. He then goes on to analyze the magical beliefs inherent in caste taboos, the social dynamics of commensalism and connubium, the economic interests concealed within the system, the way in which religious beliefs relate to the taboos, the effects of the caste system on the industrial development of the society and vice versa — all in India. Suddenly, India is not very far away at all. The lecture then goes back to its southern theme. The familiar now seems not quite so familiar any more. Questions are raised that are new, perhaps raised angrily, but raised all the same. And at least some of the students have begun to understand that there are functions involved in this business of race that they have not read about in the newspapers (at least not those in their hometowns) and that their parents have not told them — partly, at least, because neither the newspapers nor the parents knew about them.

It can be said that the first wisdom of sociology is this: Things are not what they seem. This, too, is a deceptively simple statement. It ceases to be simple after a while. Social reality turns out to have many layers of meaning. The discovery of each new layer changes the perception of the whole....

People who like to avoid shocking discoveries, who prefer to believe that society is just what they were taught in Sunday School, who like the safety of the rules and the maxims of what Alfred Schuetz has called the "world-taken-for-granted," should stay away from sociology. People who feel no temptation before closed doors, who have no curiosity about human beings, who are content to admire scenery without wondering about the people who live in those houses on the other side of that river, should probably also stay away from sociology. They will find it unpleasant or, at any rate, unrewarding. People who are interested in human beings only if they can change, convert, or reform them should also be warned, for they will find sociology much less useful than they hoped. And people whose interest is mainly in their own conceptual constructions will do just as well to turn to the study of little white mice. Sociology will be satisfying, in the long run, only to those who can think of nothing more entrancing than to watch men and to understand things human.

It may now be clear that we have, albeit deliberately, understated the case in the title of this chapter. To be sure, sociology is an individual pastime in the sense that it interests some men and bores others. Some like to observe human beings, others like to experiment with mice. The world is big enough to hold all kinds, and there is no logical priority for one interest as against another. But the word *pastime* is weak in describing what we mean. Sociology is more like a passion. The sociological perspective is more like a demon that possesses one, that drives one compellingly, again and again, to the questions that are its own. An introduction to sociology is, therefore, an invitation to a very special kind of passion....

# 2. THE SOCIOLOGICAL IMAGINATION

C. WRIGHT MILLS

*"The individual can… know his own chances in life only by becoming aware of those of all individuals in his circumstances."*

C. Wright Mills, who died in 1962 at the age of 46, published two classic sociological works: **The Power Elite** and **The Sociological Imagination**. The first of these proved to be extremely important for studying the power structure in the United States. It inspired many sociologists to do research on power and inequality. It is also to Mills's credit that he saw that sociology, in its attempt to be scientific, was losing a spirit that had to be recovered. He called this spirit the "sociological imagination." In his book by that name, he criticized those of us who have lost that imagination, and he called for a renewed effort to help people deal with human problems through sharing the sociological perspective. The section that follows is most of Chapter I from **The Sociological Imagination**, entitled "The Promise." Here Mills, like Berger, shows us the possibilities that sociology holds for those who come to understand it. What people need, Mills contends, "is a quality of mind that will help them use information and to develop reason" to better understand the world and "what may be happening within themselves." This quality is "the sociological imagination."

Here is Mills's organization. It might help you to keep it in mind as you read:

1. "Ordinary men" have problems looking beyond their immediate situation at history and society.
2. The sociological imagination includes three questions that can be applied to a number of human situations.
3. The sociological imagination is the linking of personal problems to public issues.

(Mills, too, used the language of his time; again, you might notice the use of **he, him,** and **his.** Mills gives one the impression that only men can have the sociological imagination, but I am positive that he did not intend this.)

Nowadays, men often feel that their private lives are a series of traps. They sense that within their everyday worlds, they cannot overcome their troubles, and in this feeling, they are often quite correct: What ordinary men are directly aware of and what they try to do are bounded by the private orbits in which they live. Their visions and their powers are limited to the close-up scenes of job, family, neighborhood. In other milieux, they move vicariously and remain spectators. And the more aware they become, however vaguely, of ambitions and of threats that transcend their immediate locales, the more trapped they seem to feel.

Underlying this sense of being trapped are seemingly impersonal changes in the very structure of continent-wide societies. The facts of contemporary history are also facts about the success and the failure of individual men and women. When a society is industrialized, a peasant becomes a worker; a feudal lord is liquidated or becomes a businessman. When classes rise or fall, a man is employed or unemployed; when the rate of investment goes up or down, a man takes new heart or goes broke. When wars happen, an insurance salesman becomes a rocket launcher; a store clerk, a radar man; a wife lives alone; a child grows up without a father. Neither the life of an individual nor the history of a society can be understood without understanding both.

Yet men do not usually define the troubles they endure in terms of historical change and institutional contradiction. The well-being they enjoy, they do not usually impute to the big ups and downs of the societies in which they live. Seldom aware of the intricate connection between the patterns of their own lives and the course of world history, ordinary men do not usually know what this connection means for the kinds of men they are becoming and for the kinds of history-making in which they might take part. They do not possess the quality of mind essential to grasp the interplay of man and society, of biography and history, of self and world. They cannot cope with their personal troubles in such ways as to control the structural transformations that usually lie behind them.

Surely it is no wonder. In what period have so many men been so totally exposed at so fast a pace to such earthquakes of change? That Americans have not known such catastrophic changes as have the men and women of other societies is caused by historical facts that are now quickly becoming "merely history." The history that now affects every man is world history. Within this scene and this period, in the course of a single generation, one-sixth of mankind is transformed from all that is feudal and backward into all that is modern, advanced, and fearful. Political colonies are freed, new and less visible forms of imperialism are installed. Revolutions occur; men feel the intimate grip of new kinds of authority. Totalitarian societies rise and are smashed to bits — or succeed fabulously. After two centuries of ascendancy, capitalism is shown up as only one way to make

society into an industrial apparatus. After two centuries of hope, even formal democracy is restricted to a quite small portion of mankind. Everywhere in the underdeveloped world, ancient ways of life are broken up and vague expectations become urgent demands. Everywhere in the overdeveloped world, the means of authority and of violence become total in scope and bureaucratic in form. Humanity itself now lies before us, the supernation at either pole concentrating its most coordinated and massive efforts on the preparation of World War III.

The very shaping of history now outpaces the ability of men to orient themselves in accordance with cherished values. And which values? Even when they do not panic, men often sense that older ways of feeling and thinking have collapsed and that newer beginnings are ambiguous to the point of moral stasis. Is it any wonder that ordinary men feel they cannot cope with the larger worlds with which they are so suddenly confronted? That they cannot understand the meaning of their epoch for their own lives? That — in defense of selfhood — they become morally insensible, trying to remain altogether private men? Is it any wonder that they come to be possessed by a sense of the trap?

It is not only information that they need. In this Age of Fact, information often dominates their attention and overwhelms their capacities to assimilate it. It is not only the skills of reason that they need — although their struggles to acquire these often exhaust their limited moral energy.

What they need, and what they feel they need, is a quality of mind that will help them to use information and to develop reason in order to achieve lucid summations of what is going on in the world and of what may be happening within themselves. It is this quality, I am going to contend, that journalists and scholars, artists and publics, scientists and editors are coming to expect of what may be called the *sociological imagination*.

The sociological imagination enables its possessor to understand the larger historical scene in terms of its meaning for the inner life and the external career of a variety of individuals. It enables him to take into account how individuals, in the welter of their daily experience, often become falsely conscious of their social positions. Within that welter, the framework of modern society is sought; within that framework, the psychologies of a variety of men and women are formulated. By such means the personal uneasiness of individuals is focused on explicit troubles, and the indifference of publics is transformed into involvement with public issues.

The first fruit of this imagination — and the first lesson of the social science that embodies it — is the idea that the individual can understand his own experience and gauge his own fate only by locating himself within his period, that he can know his own chances in life only by becoming aware of those of all individuals in his circumstances. In many ways, it is a terrible lesson; in many ways, a magnificent one. We do not know the limits of man's capacities for supreme effort or willing degradation, for agony or glee, for pleasurable brutality or the sweetness of reason. But in our time, we have come to know that the limits of "human nature" are frighteningly broad. We have come to know that every individual lives, from one generation to the next, in some society; that he lives out a biography, and that he lives it out within some historical sequence. By the fact of his living, he contributes — however minutely — to the shaping of this society and to the course of its history, even as he is made by society and by its historical push and shove.

The sociological imagination enables us to grasp history and biography and the relations between the two within society. That is its task and its promise. To recognize this task and this promise is the mark of the classic social analyst. It is characteristic of Herbert Spencer — turgid, polysyllabic, comprehensive; of E. A. Ross — graceful, muckraking, upright; of Auguste Comte and Emile Durkheim; of the intricate and subtle Karl Mannheim. It is the quality of all that is intellectually excellent in Karl Marx; it is the clue to Thorstein Veblen's brilliant and ironic insight, to Joseph Schumpeter's many-sided constructions of reality; it is the basis of the psychological sweep of W. E. H. Lecky no less than of the profundity and clarity of Max Weber. And it is the signal of what is best in contemporary studies of man and society.

No social study that does not come back to the problems of biography, of history, and of their intersections within a society has completed its intellectual journey. Whatever the specific problems of the classic social analysts, however limited or however broad the features of social reality they have examined, those who have been imaginatively aware of the promise of their work have consistently asked three sorts of questions:

1. What is the structure of this particular society as a whole? What are its essential components, and how are they related to one another? How does it differ from other varieties of social order? Within it, what is the meaning of any particular feature for its continuance and for its change?
2. Where does this society stand in human history? What are the mechanics by which it is changing? What is its place within and its meaning for the development of humanity as a whole? How does any particular feature we are examining affect — and how is it affected by — the historical period in which it moves? And this period — what are its essential features? How does it differ from other periods? What are its characteristic ways of history making?
3. What varieties of men and women now prevail in this society and in this period? And what varieties are coming to prevail? In what ways are they selected and formed, liberated and repressed, made sensitive and blunted? What kinds of "human nature" are revealed in the conduct and character we observe in this society in this period? And what is the meaning for "human nature" of each and every feature of the society we are examining?

Whether the point of interest is a great power state or a minor literary mood, a family, a prison, a creed — these are the kinds of questions the best social analysts have asked. They are the intellectual pivots of classic studies of man in society — and they are the questions inevitably raised by any mind possessing the sociological imagination. For that imagination is the capacity to shift from one perspective to another — from the political to the psychological; from the examination of a single family to the comparative assessment of the national budgets of the world; from the theological school to the military establishment; from considerations of an oil industry to studies of contemporary poetry. It is the capacity to range from the most impersonal and remote transformations to the most intimate features of the human self — and to see the relations between the two. Back of its use there is always the urge to know the social and historical meaning of the individual in the society and in the period in which he has his quality and his being.

That, in brief, is why it is by means of the sociological imagination that men now hope to grasp what is going on in the world, and to understand what is happening in themselves as minute points of the intersections of biography and history within society. In large part, contemporary man's self-conscious view of himself as at least an outsider, if not a permanent stranger, rests on an absorbed realization of social relativity and of the transformative power of history. The sociological imagination is the most fruitful form of this self-consciousness. By its use, men whose mentalities have swept only a series of limited orbits often come to feel as if suddenly awakened in a house with which they had only supposed themselves to be familiar. Correctly or incorrectly, they often come to feel that they can now provide themselves with adequate summations, cohesive assessments, comprehensive orientations. Older decisions that once appeared sound now seem to them products of a mind unaccountably dense. Their capacity for astonishment is made lively again. They acquire a new way of thinking, they experience a transvaluation of values. In a word, by their reflection and by their sensibility, they realize the cultural meaning of the social sciences.

Perhaps the most fruitful distinction with which the sociological imagination works is between "the personal troubles of milieu" and "the public issues of social structure." This distinction is an essential tool of the sociological imagination and a feature of all classic work in social science.

*Troubles* occur within the character of the individual and within the range of his immediate relations with others; they have to do with his self and with those limited areas of social life of which he is directly and personally aware. Accordingly, the statement and the resolution of troubles properly lie within the individual as a biographical entity and within the scope of his immediate milieu — the social setting that is directly open to his personal experience and, to some extent, his willful activity. A trouble is a private matter: values cherished by an individual are felt by him to be threatened.

*Issues* have to do with matters that transcend these local environments of the individual and the range of his inner life. They have to do with the organization of many such milieux into the institutions of an historical society as a whole, with the ways in which various milieux overlap and interpenetrate to form the larger structure of social and historical life. An issue is a public matter: some value cherished by publics is felt to be threatened.

Often, there is a debate about what that value really is and about what it is that really threatens it. This debate is often without focus if only because it is the very nature of an issue, unlike even widespread trouble, that it cannot be very well defined in terms of the immediate and everyday environments of ordinary men. An issue, in fact, often involves a crisis in institutional arrangements; often, it also involves what Marxists call "contradictions" or "antagonisms."

In these terms, consider unemployment. When, in a city of 100,000, only one man is unemployed, that is his personal trouble. For its relief, we properly look to the character of the man, his skills, and his immediate opportunities. But when in a nation of 50 million employees, 15 million are unemployed, that is an issue, and we may not hope to find its solution within the range of opportunities open to any one individual. The very structure of opportunities has collapsed. Both the correct statement of the problem and the range of possible solutions require us to consider the economic and political institutions of the society, not merely the personal situation and character of a scatter of individuals.

Consider war. The personal problem of war, when it occurs, may be how to survive it or how to die in it with honor; how to make money out of it; how to climb into the higher safety of the military apparatus; or how to contribute to the war's termination. In short, according to one's values, to find a set of milieux and within it to survive the war or make one's death in it meaningful. But the structural issues of war have to do with its causes; with what types of men it throws up into command; with its effects on economic, political, family, and religious institutions; with the unorganized irresponsibility of a world of nation-states.

Consider marriage. Inside a marriage, a man and a woman may experience personal troubles, but when the divorce rate during the first four years of marriage is 250 out of every 1,000 attempts, this is an indication of a structural issue having to do with the institutions of marriage and family and other institutions that bear upon them.

Or consider the metropolis — the horrible, beautiful, ugly, magnificent sprawl of the great city. For many upper-class people, the personal solution to "the problem of the city" is to have an apartment with a private garage under it in the heart of the city, and forty miles out, a house by Henry Hill, garden by Garrett Eckbo, on a hundred acres of private land. In these two controlled environments — with a small staff at each end and a private helicopter connection — most people could solve many of the problems of personal milieux caused by the facts of the city. But all this, however splendid, does not solve the public issues that the structural fact of the city poses. What should be done with this wonderful monstrosity? Break it all up into scattered units, combining residence and work? Refurbish it as it stands? Or, after evacuation, dynamite it and build new cities according to new plans in new places? What should those plans be? And who is to decide and to accomplish whatever choice is made? These are structural issues; to confront them and to solve them requires us to consider political and economic issues that affect innumerable milieux.

Insofar as an economy is so arranged that slumps occur, the problem of unemployment becomes incapable of personal solution. Insofar as war is inherent in the nation-state system and in the uneven industrialization of the world, the ordinary individual in his restricted milieu will be powerless — with or without psychiatric aid — to solve the troubles this system (or lack of system) imposes on him. Insofar as the family as an institution turns women into darling little slaves and men into their chief providers and unweaned dependents, the problem of a satisfactory marriage remains incapable of purely private solution. Insofar as the overdeveloped megalopolis and the overdeveloped automobile are built-in features of the overdeveloped society, the issues of urban living will not be solved by personal ingenuity and private wealth.

What we experience in various and specific milieux, I have noted, is often caused by structural changes. Accordingly, to understand the changes of many personal milieux, we are required to look beyond them. And the number and variety of such structural changes increase as the institutions within which we live become more embracing and more intricately connected with one another. To be aware of the idea of social structure and to use it with sensibility is to be capable of tracing such linkages among a great variety of milieux. To be able to do that is to possess the sociological imagination....

# 3. SOCIOLOGY: THE STUDY OF HUMAN SOCIETY

ALAN WOLFE

*"Sociology's fragility... is not the result of controversies over method or theory. The challenge is far more serious than those, for it involves the question of whether the subjects of this new science — human beings themselves — have any distinctive features that require a distinctive science to be understood."*

To some people, sociology is not necessary because the study of human beings can be found in the realms of biology and psychology, history, political science, and economics. Wolfe looks at this question and argues that sociology arose— and is still necessary—because it focuses on human society, a very unique subject matter. He reminds us that sociology is anthropocentric (that is, it focuses on the human as its subject matter) and that we must not lose sight of how important society, culture, and mind are in creating our essence.

Sociology, one of the youngest of the social sciences, may also prove to be one of the most short lived. The product of a progressive intellectual milieu, sociology announced a faith in the ability of people to control the world they had created. Just as the forces of civilization and culture were beating back the irrationality and wildness of nature, so the forces of reason and science would create order out of what was once a Hobbesian war of all against all. Sociology's optimism stood in sharp contrast to the debunking realism that had prevailed in political thought since Machiavelli and the playful cynicism that Mandeville contributed to the science of economics. To its earlier practitioners, sociology was the queen of the sciences because it was at one and the same time noble, caring, and somewhat imperious.

Begun at a time when the problems of industrialization, urbanization, and bureaucratization raised in compelling form the question of what it means for humans to live together in groups... sociology's two greatest discoveries were the self and society—and neither of them had much in common with the individual and the state. Unlike the individual, who in liberal theory was governed by an unvarying human nature, the *self* was embedded in culture and was plastic enough to develop and learn. Unlike the state, which in theory exercised a monopoly of violence, *society* was the product of consensus openly arrived at, ruled by the norms created out of the behavior of real people in real life. Sociology was the product of a particular intellectual opening, a period—no one now knows how brief—in which it seemed possible to maintain order without sacrificing liberty.

This precariousness of sociology gives its subject matter a temporality, in contrast with the more timeless concerns of economics and political science. No one doubts that there will always be money, that some will try to get more of it than others, and thus that scarcities of valuable things will always constitute the human condition. Similarly, despite the shock effect he thought he would have on polite opinion, Gaetano Mosca's discovery that there will always be some who rule and

others who will be ruled no longer seems especially noteworthy. But that society can continue to exist, that ties of solidarity will continue to link people together as partners in a common project—this is a riskier proposition. The rise of totalitarian states in this century showed that organic unity can destroy the social self as well as the atomistic individual. The popularity of laissez-faire conservatism in the late twentieth century, two hundred years after its significant flaws were exposed, shows that untrammeled individualism can weaken society as well as the state. Late in arriving, sociology could be early in leaving.

Its departure would be a tragedy. For the very fragility and temporality of the social make it worth preserving. If the social ties that link people together in groups are unappreciated, there is little need for a discipline emphasizing their continued importance. And if such ties are universal and permanent, we need hardly concern ourselves with the ways in which changes in social and intellectual fashion threaten them. Sociology, unlike the other social sciences, requires constant rediscovery, taking us by surprise at precisely those moments in which we forget about its existence. Always vulnerable, it is always changing, critically reexamining itself to account for rapid social transformation. The more we take society for granted, the more we need to rethink its importance.

And, it seems, we *do* take the social very much for granted. Modern societies are composed of dense cities, complex bureaucracies, huge industries—all of which depend on fragile social ties to function at all. We rarely understand the importance of these ties until their breakdown results in crime, chaos, or lowered productivity; and we all too often rely on models of human behavior that pay little attention to them. The concerns of sociology—especially ties of trust, caring, and personal knowledge—are in one sense trivial and obvious and in another sense vital and irreplaceable. They are so crucial to our existence as human beings that we can, for long periods of time, forget about them completely.

The classical social theorists of the nineteenth century understood better than we do the potential fragility of the social. For them, the social world was an essential aspect of the human world, and the human world was understood to be a very recent discovery. Indeed, compared to the natural world, which has been with us since the beginning of time, the social world seemed not only miraculous but also improbable. Nineteenth-century sociologists could not take society for granted because it was all so new to them. Today, surrounded by societies that seem overdeveloped in their density and complexity, we would rather ignore the social than argue for its special role in our existence.

No other aspect of nineteenth-century social theory better captured this sense of society's fragility than the almost automatic anthropocentric assumptions it contained. Sociology was a product of the notion that humans were, and ought to be, at the center of our attention. Its founding thinkers agreed that the line between humans and the worlds surrounding them was dangerously thin and that, therefore, humans and their accomplishments required a special defense. This sense that the social could at any moment be taken back by other worlds recently conquered gave nineteenth-century social theory its predisposition to view our own species as superior to everything else.

From the perspective of nineteenth-century sociology, two worlds surrounded human creations: the supernatural world above them and the animal world below them. At one level, sociology's anthropocentrism represented a long struggle on the part of secular thinkers to turn attention away from superhuman entities to human ones. Asserting the centrality of the human was a way of insisting that the products of people's activity, including religion itself, grew out of the capacity of individuals to make the world in which they lived.

The milieu that led sociology to its anthropocentrism was shaped by sociology's relationship not only to the superhuman but also to the "subhuman," the world of other animal species. Sociology separated itself from the world of nature just as vigorously as it separated itself from the world of God. Nearly all thinkers in the sociological tradition regarded humans as a special and distinct species capable of taking control over its destiny. No one doubted that humans were driven by biology, or that some aspects of their behavior were similar to the behavior of other animal species. Obviously, humans lived in nature and therefore were, to some degree, subject to the laws of natural science. But because humans built culture out of nature, their affairs could not be understood on the basis of laws borrowed directly from the study of the nonhuman world. Different from religion,

sociology would also be different from science — at least the biological sciences. It would certainly borrow much from science, as indeed it would from religion, but its ultimate calling would be neither prophecy nor taxonomy.

Sociology and religion have settled into a relationship of tolerable coexistence. Because the intellectual turf of both is similar, sociologists soon developed respect for religion, and religious thinkers made their peace with sociology. But if a war ended between the human-centeredness of sociology and the God-centeredness of religion, no peace exists between the human-centeredness of sociology and the challenge to anthropocentrism coming from those who respect nature and other animal species. The contemporary intellectual milieu, which finds little to question in the secularism of sociology, challenges at every turn the sociological separation of culture from nature. It is precisely the commitment to humans and their accomplishments — an outgrowth of the Enlightenment and its faith in powers of mind and reason — that marks the difference between the late-nineteenth-century intellectual environment and the late-twentieth-century milieu. Sociology's fragility, in its latest manifestation, is not the result of controversies over method or theory. The challenge is far more serious than those, for it involves the question of whether the subjects of this new science — human beings themselves — have any distinctive features that require a distinctive science to be understood....

Although reflections on the distinctiveness of the human species are a constant in the history of sociological (and anthropological) thought, the features believed to constitute the human difference have varied. Some theorists — including not only Marx but also eighteenth-century political economists and the early Durkheim, in his analysis of the division of labor — regarded the human difference as a producing difference: We are what we make, and what we usually make is culture. Yet these notions of *homo faber* no longer seem to provide the best way to understand the potential, as opposed to the actuality, of the human condition. Other animal species make tools. They also, depending on how the term is defined, possess culture. A recent revolution in ethnology — which provides far more closely grained accounts of how animals actually live in the world — renders a good deal of nineteenth-century philosophical anthropology obsolete. We share more with the world of nature than we were once prepared to admit.

Even Marx recognized that an emphasis on *homo faber* was not enough. "A spider conducts operations that resemble those of a weaver, and a bee puts to shame many an architect in the construction of her cells," he wrote in *Capital*. "But what distinguishes the worst architect from the best of the bees is this: that the architect raises his structure in imagination before he erects it in reality."[1] Nineteenth-century social theory, in seeking the feature of human distinctiveness, added culture to nature. The twentieth-century version of the same quest will have to add mind to culture. For human thought processes are different not only from those of other animal species, which lack powers of interpretation and imagination, but also from the minds (if minds they be) of computers, which, for all their powers of calculation, also cannot imagine worlds other than the ones for which they have been programmed. Contemporary theories of human distinctiveness, in short, ought to stress interpretation rather than production: We are what we imagine ourselves capable of being. As Charles Taylor's work in particular demonstrates, any contemporary theory of the human difference is much more likely to emphasize our narrative capacities, our abilities to tell stories that make sense out of the situations in which we find ourselves.[2] We are, in Taylor's phrase, "self-interpreting animals," in the sense that what we are is indistinguishable from how we understand ourselves.[3] From the interpretative point of view, human beings are different from other species not just because their culture is more complex but because their development is not preprogrammed by their genetic structures. They can bend the instructions given to them in ways that the giver of instructions could not have anticipated; therefore, the rules they follow and the programs that guide their actions are their own. They can alter and shape the rules that govern them because they add mind to culture, in addition to adding culture to nature. Self-understanding makes self-governance possible....

Despite an emerging cosmology that questions any account that privileges human beings and their affairs, this is no time to give up the quest for a special and unique social science. It is not because we have liberated ourselves completely from biology that we need special tools to understand and realize our potential; we remain biological beings, we live in nature, and some aspects of what we do (although increasingly fewer and fewer) can be understood on the basis of biological laws. Nor is it because — as nineteenth-century social theorists believed — we have added the realm of culture to the realm of nature that a distinct social science is justified. To be sure, we *have* added a realm of culture, one that has dynamics that are different from biological imperatives and that consequently demand a different science. The classic thinkers in the tradition of social theory were trying to develop that science, proposing theories — often highly structural theories — that sought laws of the cultural realm to supplement the laws of the biological realm.

The more modern people become, the more their affairs are governed by something other than both biology and culture. That something else is *mind*. Unlike our biological destiny, mind enables us to have a say in the rules that govern how we reproduce ourselves. Unlike our cultural destiny, mind confronts the way we usually have done things with an imagined capacity to do things in other ways. We cannot, nor should we ever, rule out the biological and cultural sciences as ways of understanding some of what we do. But if we want to understand some of the most interesting things about us, we need to add the interpretative sciences to them. Most animal species are governed only by their genes. Some, at least according to contemporary ethologists, have the rudiments of culture. But only one species is subject to the dynamics of three different imperatives — nature, culture, and mind. And that species requires a specific social science that can elevate mind to the status of nature and culture.

## ENDNOTES

1. Cited in Hannah Arendt, *The Human Condition* (Chicago: University of Chicago Press, 1958), 99.
2. Charles Taylor, *Sources of the Self: The Making of Modern Identity* (Cambridge, MA: Harvard University Press, 1989).
3. Charles Taylor, *Philosophical Papers*, vol. 1: *Human. Agency and Language* (Cambridge, MA: Cambridge University Press, 1985), 45-76.

# 4. A SOCIOLOGIST'S JOURNEY

JESSIE BERNARD

*"What passion I came to invest in feminism was aimed at its relevance for the sociology of knowledge. I could understand how it had happened that practically all human knowledge had been achieved by men, that it dealt with problems they were interested in, that it was from their perspective. I had to accept that. But the male bias did not have to be perpetuated. I wanted the discipline of sociology to be as good as it could be by any standard."*

Jessie Bernard's journey as a sociologist and feminist is described in this brief autobiography. Professor Bernard tries to capture here why she eventually became a sociologist and how her sociology affected her feminism—and vice versa. It is a very interesting autobiography because there are elements of conflict and issues of concern that she identifies that so many people who are in the profession still must contend with: the use of science to understand and benefit human beings, the conflict we face trying to both understand society and to create a just society, and the relevance of sociology for understanding the human condition.

… At the University of Minnesota, I majored in English and wrote stories, essays, and novels on assignment. It was not until I was a junior, though, that I discovered my true genre. One of my English professors suggested that I take a course or two with Professor Bernard in the sociology department. I did. I didn't realize until later that I was going to get hooked, that sociology was to be my genre. In fact, I was still writing novels a decade later in a seminar at Washington University. But my fate was sealed. There was no way I could escape it. I was doomed to a life at the typewriter—even worse, a compulsory life at the typewriter. And the words were to be not literature but sociology. I am not discounting the part played in this switch by an engaging teacher. But neither can I deny the fascination of the subject matter itself.…

I entered college at age sixteen in January 1920. By that time, World War I had been over a little more than a year, and the twentieth century was well on its way. Women had already been making themselves felt by doing important work like establishing government agencies, running the Children's Bureau and the Women's Bureau, transforming the Poor Laws, exploring new kinds of services for new urbanites, and designing a modern welfare state for the New Deal a decade later. They were to achieve suffrage that year. Now young women were demanding even more—the right to smoke, drink, wear short skirts, dance sexy dances, even appropriate Freud, and in general thumb their noses at the now-jettisoned nineteenth-century standards of ladylike behavior.

Women's clothes had changed—not only outer garments but underclothes as well. The year before I came to campus, there had been a "corsetless coed" movement, and women were now wearing garter belts to keep their stockings up or just rolling them below the knee. Brassieres had already replaced beribboned camisoles or corset covers. Women were freer in their behavior. They walked differently.

The men returning from the war did not know what to make of all this. They did not understand

From *Authors of Their Own Lives: Intellectual Autobiographies by Twenty American Sociologists*, pp. 323–348 by Bennett Berger, Copyright © 1990 The Regents of the University of California and the University of California Press.

this postwar generation. They misread our bobbed hair, rolled stockings, short skirts, and uncorseted bodies. They had gone to war at the tail end of the nineteenth century and returned in the twentieth. They had never known twentieth-century women before the war. They were not ready for them after the war.

My generation is remembered as a Charleston-dancing, Prohibition-defying, sex-indulging young people roaring through the twenties in reaction to the end of the trauma of war. I do not remember the 1920s that way. True, we did go to private rooms at hotel parties for wine. But we were quiet, well behaved, low key. The men wanted us to be safe, and they protected us. If anyone had annoyed us by unwelcome advances, he would have been stopped. When I had to be on campus especially early for a college event, I sometimes spent the night in my date Mark's bed in an apartment he shared with a classmate and his wife. Mark never once so much as hinted at the possibility of sharing the bed with me. I never went to a "blind pig." I did not dance the Charleston, although I did dance cheek to cheek, but so innocently that my brother and I were once asked to leave the floor of a dance hall for such impropriety.

Sociology had just barely achieved academic respectability and legitimacy as a member of the community of science when I was introduced to it in the early 1920s. At Yale, W. G. Sumner, ostensibly an economist, was teaching Republican doctrine to undergraduates but also assembling a great store of historical and anthropological materials for his course on the science of society, published in a book, *Folkways*, still fascinating almost eighty years later. Race was attracting a lot of attention. It was all that Franz Boas at Columbia could do to defuse the racism that tainted immigration policy. At the University of Chicago, Robert Park was turning the city of Chicago into a laboratory for the study of urban life. Theories of progress were still being taught at my alma mater, Minnesota. There was a lot for this discipline to tend to, and I soon wanted to be part of it.

Professor Bernard always had a lot of groupies around him—as well as radicals. Incredible as it seems in the 1980s, communist groups were not forbidden or negatively sanctioned on that midwestern campus in the 1920s. When the Seekers asked Professor Bernard to be their faculty adviser,

he accepted. It seemed a matter of course. He took social criticism seriously, holding it to be an important part of his function as a sociologist.

Mate selection was once a major research interest among family sociologists, and they produced a sizable store of data. But there remain a lot of subtleties that might well fall between the cracks of all the variables. I was courted by the most eligible man in the social circles I moved in. It was precisely his social eligibility that made it ultimately impossible for me to marry him. When I heard about his family's lifestyle, their comings and goings, I drooped. I was intimidated by the homes his family and relatives lived in, by the kind of social life they engaged in, by the clothes they wore and how they wore them, by the style they entertained in. His wife would have a kind of life I could never successfully, or at least happily, live. She would have to run a certain kind of household, with elegance, dress a certain kind of way, with flair, entertain in a certain mode, with sophistication. I had no stomach for that way of living, no talents or skills for it. Just as Jo in *Little Women* knew that she could not marry Laurie, I knew I could not marry him. I ended up by marrying my professor, L. L. Bernard.

I was twenty-two years old. I had my second degree and was working toward my third. I had been elected to Phi Beta Kappa and Sigma Xi. I had presented my master's thesis, which had already won a local prize, to the American Sociological Society. I had lived in a warm, safe world, free to roam but protected on all sides. I had read a lot of books and taken a lot of courses. I was massively ignorant. I was vulnerable. What I had seen ahead of me was a pleasant career as Professor Bernard's research assistant. He was an enchanting man to work with and for. As my mentor, he had shaped my mentality. I saw the world through his eyes. But I had not seen marriage to him in the cards. I had not been looking closely enough.

The marriage lasted till death did us part, just over twenty-four years—if it could be called the same marriage over all that time. It was at first an apprentice-master relationship. It was to end as a collegial one....

I entered academia professionally in 1940, fairly well along in my career. Family had not been a major sociological interest of mine; the department at Minnesota had not played it up. Broken families, homeless men, and illegitimacy were dealt with in courses in the social work curriculum under Mrs. Mudgett at one end of the corridor; "the" family, on a quite different wavelength, came under sociology at the other. Robert Merton said in 1972 that "the handful of women sociologists were expected to study problems of women, principally as these related to marriage and the family". I was a little late in recognizing this expectation. But, sure enough, just as Merton had said, when I became a college teacher—at Lindenwood College—the family became my beat. It was taken for granted that it would....

Although a dedicated sociologist, I proved to be an undisciplined one. I did not take easily to the restriction of discipline boundaries. I enjoyed excursions into outside territory. I have been the prototypical marginal man. Although I became identified with the sociology of marriage and family, I have been equally concerned with the sociology of knowledge, especially of science, and of course with its history. Outside of my discipline, I have enjoyed community with psychologists, historians, anthropologists, home economists, even —at some remove—mathematicians.

As a Comtean positivist, I believed, as the positive philosophy taught, that mathematics was the queen of all the sciences, including sociology. True, the only practicable way of using it was in the form of statistics, a subject not yet wholly at home in sociology departments when I was a graduate student. F. S. Chapin had been reduced to assigning a textbook in biostatistics in his graduate course on social trends.

World War I had enormously stimulated growth in measuring instruments. I was in the audience when L. L. Thurstone told us that even attitudes could be measured (1929). Years later, there were instruments for measuring anything one could think of. In the early 1930s at Washington University, I came in contact with a "measurement freak" in the psychology department. He was a compulsive measurer, and I caught the fever. I wanted to measure everything. It became a mania. Just point me to it and I was off and running to measure it, at least to count until measuring instruments became available.

At mid-century, I was enormously attracted to the game theorists. They seemed to be the wittiest among all the social science communities. They wrote with a sense of humor. The games they concocted for their players were fascinating. They were mean people. They were always trying to do one another in. And sometimes, as among those notorious prisoners, they were deadlocked, even with their fate depending on trust in one another. I was, nevertheless, attracted to the theory and tried to apply it to marriage and family....

I have experienced a number of epiphanies in my life. Only two are relevant to my career as a sociologist. Both had to do with the sociology of knowledge, one related to the Nazi degradation of science and the other to the feminist augmentation of it.

In the 1940s, half a dozen articles—on power, science, conflict—issued from my typewriter. They did not add up to an integrated treatise, but they did cohere; they elaborated a consistent theme. From one perspective or another they portrayed a mind if not in anguish at least in a state of serious malaise. If I had waited to write them all together, they might have constituted a book on the nature of science and of scientists and on the uses to which science is put—or, rather, on the loss of my nineteenth-century heritage of faith in science. It was a troubled time in which, almost day by day, I was learning about the underside of science and the vulnerability of scientists. It was a decade of growing disillusionment with science, scientists, and the uses to which science can be put.

In my part of *Origins of American Sociology* (1942), I had traced the burgeoning belief in science as the means, in effect, of social salvation, as exhibited in the American Social Science Movement, which was characterized by a worship of science. I had paid tribute to the "monumental dream" of a society based on science. I had been dazzled by the idea of a science in the service of human betterment. I "believed" in it. I had organized my intellectual life around it. It served as a sort of religion, an integrating force, in my life. I had a great deal invested in it.

In the first decades of this century, it had been easy, as part of the nineteenth-century optimism, to accept that century's idea of scientists as ethical men, as, in fact, the heroes they were depicted as being in biographies and fiction. True, there did surface, from time to time, examples of the fragility of the ideals of science. There were researchers who violated its canons, who manipulated their data, falsified results. But the sanctions imposed by peers were so severe in such cases that at least in one, that of Paul Kammerer, exposure precipitated suicide.

The first world-class example of the contamination of science by ideology that I knew about was the notorious case in the USSR in which Lysenko had to design his research to prove the ascendancy of environment over genes in plant and animal experiments. The disastrous results in time supplied a corrective.

A decade after I had paid tribute to the nineteenth-century's "monumental dream" of science in the service of humankind, disillusioned, I was writing: "The scientist is the key man in control of the greatest power in the world today, the power of science. Men who want to control that power are not going to permit the scientist to remain aloof. Nor are scientists in a position to withstand them." What happened in those ten years? It is hard to trace one's intellectual tracks. But, for one thing, we had by then begun, little by little, to learn the story of science in Germany in the 1930s and of the behavior of scientists. In my parochial naiveté, I had not known that my nineteenth-century image of the scientist was, in effect, a parody—or rather a burlesque—of what had actually been going on there. I hadn't noticed the scientists' feet of clay.

It was to take us a long time to learn what had been going on in the scientific community in Germany in the 1930s. There, even the cynosure of all the sciences, the science in the most strategic position to protect its mores—physics itself—was being politicized. Some, including two Nobel laureates, had—horrible dicta—propounded proper "Aryan" physics, which was based on observation and experimentation, and fought "Jewish" physics, which was too mathematical and theoretical. The Nazi "dismissal policy" in the universities was soon to correct the overrepresentation of such non-Aryan "deviationism." Why had their fellow Aryan scientists permitted this drain on their talent resources? Why had they not resisted the dismissal of these "non-Aryan" scientists? Why had so many of them chosen "prudential acquiescence," "inner emigration"? "The foremost concern of the physics community during the Nazi years was the protection of their autonomy against political encroachment." Why did they not see that acceptance of the dismissal policy was, actually, acceptance of such political encroachment? Why did "the ethically correct course of action… [seem to be to] learn to be silent without exploding?" (Beyerchen 1981, 207). Beyerchen comments that it was "not that scientists were political cowards, but that they did not know how to be political heroes."

There may have been extenuating circumstances. The dismissal policy was implemented by way of what conflict theorists have called "salami tactics," small incremental steps. There seemed to be no point big enough to take a stand on. There seemed to be no moment to say, no more. If we accepted the dismissal last week, why fight this new one now?…

It was not, of course, these "Aryan" physicists themselves who were to perpetrate the Holocaust of the 1940s. That could not be laid at their door. But the mentality that could accept the dismissal policy—as drastic for their scientific colleagues as the expropriation of more material treasures was among less distinguished "non-Aryans"—thus stamping it with an anti-Jewish ideology, cannot be held wholly innocent of complicity either.

The violation of the canons of science, the imposition of the Star of David on Jews, the discriminatory laws—these we were just beginning to learn about in the 1930s. We began to hear also about the Nazi use of human subjects in medical and pharmaceutical research, of race tests based on skin and hair and eye color in an effort to "Germanize" their population. There were also reports of breeding retreats where unmarried Nordic women were invited to come to have their Nordic babies. The old nineteenth-century chimera of eugenics was once more becoming visible. There were stories of euthanasia of the old and unfit. But not yet about the Final Solution.

Our ignorance was not fortuitous. It was, in fact, performing well the intended function of ignorance. The Nazis had been understandably secretive about their policy of extermination. They had gone to great lengths to keep it as hidden as possible (or at least as inconspicuous as possible), even to the prospective victims themselves. If the function of ignorance was so well performed, it is understandable that the rest of the world knew so little.

Information about the crematoria percolated only slowly by way of the mass media. It came in bits and pieces, an item here, an item there, often in formal reports not easy to understand without context. My own writing had not been influenced by it at all. Until now, it had been only the intellectual significance of Nazism for science that had had an impact on me. But subliminally, it all must have been adding up in my mind. For, suddenly, it began to fall into place. I remember the very moment when it happened. I was in the university library reading an article on the psychology of the extermination camp. I had, in my own professional training, read countless books on prisons, prisoners, war. But nothing prepared me for this. Was it scientific? real? accurate? I was completely at sea. I could not handle it. There was nothing in my experience or reading that gave me an intellectual preparation for it.

There have been other holocausts in human history. The destruction of whole cities was not uncommon in Old Testament times. The Armenians still remember the massacre more than half a century ago, as do the Ukrainians the starvation visited on them by Stalin's agricultural policies. But there has never been, as here, a demonstration, coldly and scientifically carried out by civilian bureaucrats, that reduced the human being to less than zero.

By the end of the decade, the intrinsic ethics in science had become indisputably clear to me. The argument of its value-free nature was untenable. It was still strongly urged by some, including George Lundberg, an outstanding representative of the positivist position in sociology. He had been a fellow graduate student at Minnesota. He retained his firm belief in the value-free position. In 1949, I published a letter to the *American Sociological Review* in which I noted my misgivings that he was overselling science in his book *Can Science Save Us?* (1947). It seemed to me he had oversimplified many of the ethical implications inherent in the application of science to social life. He hoped for the time when science would be used for what the "masses of men" wanted as determined by polling. These "masses" were to articulate the ends to the achievement of which science would be applied....

As I have sat here reviewing the intellectual trauma of that difficult time, I am struck with its relevance some forty years later. In the 1940s, the great scientific ogre was the atomic bomb. And as some of the scientists who had thought it through and solved the theoretical problems came to be filled with guilt, they organized to prevent its ever

being used again. And later, with the discovery of the double helix and the burgeoning advances in medical knowledge and technologies, all the old ethical problems vis-à-vis the uses of science multiplied almost endlessly....

Not the least of the traumas I experienced regarding my own disillusionment with science and scientists was having to recognize the painful traumas LLB was also experiencing. There was no way, as he himself had recognized, that science could be prevented from being used perversely. I never discussed the matter with him. And by the end of the 1940s, he was already a spent man, too ill to care. This brilliant man, this galvanizing teacher, this idealist, was dying.

After the dark night of the 1940s and 1950s, the renaissance of feminism in the 1960s was like a burst of beautiful lights that illuminated the scene and brought with it a spreading warmth. The turbulent 1960s reached me first through my daughter—a freshman at Sarah Lawrence—who, along with her peers across the country, was becoming angry at the anticommunist activities of the House Un-American Activities Committee (HUAC) while researching it for a college term paper. For all intents and purposes, she might herself have been one of those protesting Berkeley students. To me, it seemed quite far away. And anyway California students seemed always to be involved in something or other avant garde. But this time, I had to catch up. The movement was spreading beyond civil rights. There was all this talk about drop-outs, hippies, and, most ominously, drugs. Presently, it was necessary for me to face the issues in my own household.

Thus at the same time that I was tangling with the military to prove the authenticity of my son's conscientious-objector status, my living room floor was sometimes lined wall to wall with youngsters from school he had brought to Washington for antiwar demonstrations. The issues of peace and civil rights were bringing conflict and challenge to our very doorsteps. Nor was I exempted. I was myself participating in the early activities of the Women-Strike-for-Peace movement. It seemed little enough.

Toward the end of that tumultuous decade, I became aware of an amazing underground network press, of articles and papers mimeographed, stenciled, sometimes printed—from Boston, New York, Washington, Chicago, Memphis, Berkeley—which were circulating among women and carrying astounding contents: reports of feminist meetings, of feminist ideologies, of feminist arguments. This was obviously something that, as a sociologist, I had to know more about. It wasn't going to be easy. The women I approached were not hospitable. I finally managed to get an invitation to a meeting. This is how I later reported on my first lesson:

Early in 1968, I became exposed to the Women's Liberation Movement in the underground press. My first reaction was purely academic; I saw it primarily as something interesting to study, as something I had a professional obligation to observe. When, after considerable effort on my part, I received an invitation to a consciousness-raising session, one of the young women there said that I "threatened" her. Sitting quietly on the floor in their midst, showing, so far as I knew, no disapproval at all, my academic objectivity, my lack of involvement, my impersonality, was giving off bad vibrations. This incident gave me something to think about, including my stance vis-à-vis research and also my discipline.

A few years later, all the excitement generated by this movement began to surface in the established press, and the cauldron of ideas, theories, and insights bubbled throughout our society. The power of sisterhood was beginning to emerge.

Although I had intended originally to watch the new movement primarily as a research concern, like so many others who came to scoff, I remained—if not to pray, at least to ponder. It proved to be the first rumbling of a resurgence of feminism. It gave us the concept of sexism that rendered a whole sociological universe visible. Like the term "racism," which we had not felt a need for until the 1960s, when it first got into the dictionaries—because until then such concepts as prejudice and race hatred had seemed adequate for the analytic job—so also with sexism: We now needed it to help us first to see and then to analyze sociological phenomena we had not bothered to analyze before.

The feminism I had been reared in had subsided after 1920 and been all but wiped out by the feminine mystique in the 1950s. I was myself among the mothers of the baby-boom babies associated with that mystique. My initial response to this renaissance of feminism was not, however, as a member of that cohort, but as a sociologist.

"Your feminism is too cerebral," I was once told. I could see what my accuser meant. For although I was, to borrow from the Friends' vocabulary, a "convinced" sociologist, I was also, to use the conservative Christian terminology, a "born-again" feminist. Not, that is, a knee-jerk or gut feminist. I was—I believe—convinced by its logic and persuaded by its ethos. It made sense to me even on the basis of male criteria. That it conformed to the values I believed in was icing on the cake. I had been so far from being a born feminist that I had to be alerted to sexism. I had to be told when I had been insulted. I learned even to laugh about it.

What passion I came to invest in feminism was aimed at its relevance for the sociology of knowledge. I could understand how it had happened that practically all human knowledge had been achieved by men, that it dealt with problems they were interested in, that it was from their perspective. I had to accept that. But the male bias did not have to be perpetuated. I wanted the discipline of sociology to be as good as it could be by *any* standard. Ignorance or rejection of the growing corpus of feminist research relevant for sociological analyses was detrimental to the discipline. I became dedicated to the incorporation into the corpus of human knowledge of the insights and data contributed by this scholarship.

Not that I eschewed activism to achieve a wide gamut of specific, practical, immediate changes that justice called for (from potable water, to occupational training, to simple industrial technologies, to health care in the third world, to affirmative action, to equal pay for work of equivalent value, and to women's control over their own bodies in the developed countries) but that I thought the most useful form of activism for me was investment in the spreading of the feminist message—in writing.

My feminist activist writing has taken the form not only of sociological writing but also of letters on behalf of women in academic jeopardy, on behalf of promotion and tenure. And, of course, in writing checks. There have also been marches, demonstrations, meetings, and fundraising events....

Whatever form feminist activism takes, it seeks structural changes in the institutions of a society—laws, court decisions, contracts, guidelines, regulations, administrative orders, and the like. Some forms seek change in the "minds and hearts" as expressed in the manners and morals of a society, in the sexist humor that puts women down, in the insulting expressions, in the ignorance of female sexuality, in the refusal to take the ideas of women seriously, in the implication of male superiority, and the like. Blatant discrimination, exploitation, and oppression can be dealt with by formal political means. Subtler forms call for additional and different remedies.

I am finding, in brief, that although my professional feminism tends to be cerebral as charged—dedicated to the improvement of my discipline—my personal feminism is more than merely an intellectual preoccupation. Like a great and increasing number of men, I believe that the con-

tribution of the female world to the making of policy everywhere is long overdue. I find myself "believing" in feminism as I once did in the nature of science—and hoping that it will not suffer the same fate. I find myself hurt when the female world falls short of what I conceive of as its potential. I find I have a vested interest that it find its own way and not become merely a reflection of the male world.

In the last few years, my interests have turned in the direction of the female world seen from a global perspective. As a participant in an increasing number of international meetings of women from all over the world and as a member of international feminist networks and as an eager acolyte in a burgeoning cadre of women researchers learning and teaching about the lives of women everywhere, I continue to find myself—at eighty-six—doing sociology with sustained excitement and verve. Everyone should be so lucky.

# 5. THE FOUNDATIONS OF SOCIAL SCIENCE

HAROLD KINCAID

*"Based on what we know about the social sciences now, we have no reason to think that the social sciences can proceed without meeting the basic standards of the natural sciences. However unique the methods of good social science are, they still embody the basic virtues driving the natural sciences."*

In this brief introduction to his book, Harold Kincaid defends the importance of and possibility for good science in the study of human society.

After finishing the first volume of *Capital*, Karl Marx sent a copy of the book along with an admiring note to Charles Darwin. Apparently, Darwin found little of interest in Marx's work, for

the pages in his copy of *Capital* went uncut. Although Darwin was obviously open to revolutionary ideas in science, he was politically and socially moderate, adhering to the Victorian mores of his upper-class upbringing. Darwin had no desire to be associated with a radical like Marx. Nonetheless, Darwin and Marx did have something very deep in common: a belief that the human species is part of

Kincaid, Harold. *Philosophical Foundations of the Social Sciences.* Cambridge, England: Cambridge University Press, 1996, pp. 1-6.

the natural order and thus amenable to scientific understanding. Darwin revolutionized biology and our self-understanding by identifying the process-es governing the evolution of species. Marx thought he had done the same for human society. Human society, like any other natural object, was subject to scientific investigation; Marx's task was to "lay bare its laws of motion." He, like Darwin, thought that we could understand the human species, in all its forms, with scientific rigor....

The debate over naturalism did not begin or end with Marx. Marx's commitment to a science of society simply extended an Enlightenment tenet. Just as reason could penetrate a complex natural world, so too could it analyze and evaluate human affairs. Human behavior and culture, care-fully investigated, reveal patterns and laws. What Newton did for the natural world, Montesquieu, Stewart, and Smith thought could be done for the social world. Durkheim, Weber, Radcliffe-Brown, and others carried on the tradition after Marx.

What exactly does this naturalist tradition hold about the social sciences? The naturalism I defend asserts *roughly* that:

1. The social sciences can be good science by the stan-dards of the natural sciences.
2. The social sciences can only be good science by meeting the standards of the natural sciences.

My main concern shall be with the first thesis. It argues that the canons of scientific rationality can guide our study of the social realm. Of course, actual social research does and will continue to employ methods found nowhere in the natural sci-ences and vice-versa. But in concrete research, the different natural sciences employ diverse methods as well. Behind those different practices lies a com-mitment to certain basic scientific virtues. Natu-ralists believe those virtues can also undergird the methods of social research.

The idea that the social sciences *can* be good .science has several interpretations, depending on how we understand "can." Many philosophers and social scientists think that no social science is pos-sible; there are, in their view, conceptual consid-erations ruling out naturalism. Others allow that science in the social sciences is possible in princi-ple but doubt that it is in practice. My aim is to argue with both. Social science can, in principle

and in practice, achieve the basic virtues of the natural sciences. I shall argue for this claim quite directly. No conceptual arguments show social sci-ence in principle impossible; some social research shows that the social sciences sometimes achieve full scientific rigor.

Thus the naturalism I advocate holds that some social science is good science. Note, however, that naturalism does not imply that all is well in social re-search. It would be easy enough to defend natural-ism simply by defining good science very broadly — as, for example, "a concern for the facts," something the worst social science shares with our best physics. Yet that defense would both be trivial and make us mere cheerleaders for whatever social scientists hap-pen to produce. The naturalism presented here has no such implications. Large parts of the social sci-ences do fail to produce good science. Still, that sit-uation can be and sometimes is overcome.

The second naturalist thesis I shall defend as-serts that good social science must follow the stan-dards of the natural sciences. This claim is apparently the more controversial of the two be-cause it tells us not just what *can* happen but what *must* happen. However, how we understand this "must" will determine how radical this claim really is. Legislating what science must be like is risky business — and a business with a long history of failure. One important theme of this book is that we cannot decide the fate of the social sciences on *a priori* conceptual grounds. Thus I shall not argue that good social sciences could never result from methods entirely unknown to the natural sciences. We cannot rule out the possibility that the social sciences might teach us something about funda-mental scientific virtues. Indeed, the natural sci-ences have often learned specific investigative techniques from the social sciences.

How then can we say that the social sciences *must* proceed by the standards of the natural sci-ences? We can only make a guarded claim based on what we know about social scientific practice as it exists now and its likely permutations. Noth-ing about current social research shows that good social science proceeds by standards and methods not found in the natural sciences. Social scientists sometimes claim that social phenomena call for entirely unique routes to confirmation and expla-nation. Their claims, I argue, are unfounded. Nei-ther the meaningful nature of social phenomena nor their explanation by appeal to functions nor anything else shows that current social science has its own, entirely special route to knowledge. So, based on what we know about the social sciences now, we have no reason to think that the social sciences can proceed without meeting the basic standards of the natural sciences. However unique the methods of good social science are, they still embody the basic virtues driving the natural sciences....

Furthermore, if a science of human social behavior is impossible, that leaves us with an intellectual puzzle and an existential problem. The puzzle is why our most successful intellectual enterprise should be of no use when it comes to what we care most about, namely, ourselves. The existential problem is that if naturalism is false, we apparently have little hope of understanding ourselves. Human life is permeated with social processes. If we cannot find reasonable evidence about the causes of social events, we have little chance of fully understanding who we are, where we have been, or where we are going.

Our attitude toward a naturalistic social science also has serious implications for what social scientists should be doing. If social science is impossible, then the search for well-confirmed causal generalizations and the like are a waste of time.

The debate over naturalism is thus also a debate over how social research should proceed....

The practical consequences run equally deep. If no social science is possible, if the best that social scientists can do is give us many different kinds of literary "thick" descriptions of social reality, then social policy is groundless. Imagine that we could have no real knowledge about social processes. Government intervention in social and economic affairs would be inane. How could we evaluate educational programs, prison reform, economic policy and so on without having well-confirmed generalizations about the causes of the social phenomena? We could not. Without knowledge of causes, we have no idea what factors should be manipulated or in which direction. Policy making would be guessing in the dark. Likewise, social movements to eliminate racism and sexism would be misguided, for they would have no rational basis for acting. Although many critics of naturalistic social science come from the left, rejecting naturalism really has quite conservative implications. Of course, even a real social science might not give us a basis for action: We might learn that some social problems are practically ineliminable. But, obviously, even that information would also make important differences to policy....

# 6. MEN AND WOMEN OF THE CORPORATION: A STUDY IN SOCIOLOGY

ROSABETH KANTER

*"A combination of methods such as used in the classical sociological field studies emerges as the most valid and reliable way to develop understanding of such a complex social reality as the corporation. I used each source of data, and each informant, as a check against the others."*

Science is difficult. It is meant to be. Scientists are people, and because people make value judgments and are biased, procedures are developed to control the *individual scientist so that evidence gathered is as good as possible. Each science —physics, biology, and psychology, for example—develops its own techniques. Sociology uses several—it is a science characterized by diversity rather than commitment to one way.*

*Rosabeth Kanter's study of **Men and Women of the Corporation** is an excellent example of how science is sometimes done in sociology. Kanter studied one case, one corporation; although this is an important limitation, her particular approach allowed her to understand one organization in real depth. As a responsible scientist, Kanter tells the reader why she did the study and exactly how she did the study. It is imperative that this be done so that other scientists have the opportunity to judge her work—both her thinking and her research.*

This study represents primarily a search for explanation and theory rather than just a report of empirical research. I was interested in understanding a complex social reality and its impact on the people who experienced it. I wanted to develop concepts that would make sense out of the actions of people located in different parts of organizational worlds. With Michel Crozier, I wanted to demonstrate that everyone is rational[1], that everyone within an organization, no matter how silly or irrational their behavior seemed, was reacting to what their situation made available, in such a way as to preserve dignity, control, and recognition from others. Throughout the hierarchy, people had in common the fact of being limited by their organizational circumstance. Finally, I wanted to develop concepts with a dynamic flavor: how processes and cycles that bounded and limited people's options were set in motion.

I also had a series of normative interests. I wanted to further the cause of equality for women in organizations, but I wanted to see the nature of organizations, not men or women as individuals, as the villain of the piece, for I was convinced that men were just as much bound and limited by organizational systems that existed in the present time as were women. I hoped to provide further evidence of the inevitability of binds and dilemmas in which organizations find themselves as long as they are structured the way they typically are: too large, too hierarchical, not democratic enough, not justifying either the number or power of man-

agers, inequitable in their distribution of rewards and opportunities, fostering one view of success as vertical mobility, and not conscious enough or taking responsibility enough for their impact on the family. The current division of labor in organizations has seemed to me, as it has seemed to a large number of others, neither functional nor inevitable. I wanted to explain dysfunctional behavior in organizations—common organizational problems—in such a way that decision-makers could see the benefits to them of developing what I considered more humane, more equitable, and smaller-scale solutions to problems. I was interested in offering practical insight and suggestions that would both be useful to individuals in making sense out of their situations, especially in helping women understand the traps that organizations held out for them, as presently structured, and that would help decision-makers and program planners think more innovatively about new policies and procedures in organizations. Thus, I felt that the merit of this study would stand or fall not on specific details of findings but on the whole it presents: a comprehensive ordering of the experiences and reactions of men and women in organizations, seen as a function of properties of their situations.

However, I am a firm believer in the necessary interplay between theory and empirical observation. This case study is thus empirically grounded in a case study of a single organization, composed of multiple projects. The case provided material out of which to generate the concepts and flesh for giving meaning to the abstract propositions I was developing. Periodically, over a five-year period, I was a consultant, participant-observer, and researcher at Industrial Supply Corporation, primarily within one division. Changes that took place in Indsco or its people during the five-year period that affect material I report are mentioned in the text.

I have disguised Indsco's identity as best I could, and I have occasionally changed details of numbers and stories, for a variety of ethical and legal reasons. I promised confidentiality and anonymity to everyone with whom I came into contact; this was an important part of the surveys, and I also felt that I would not want to violate the confidences of many people who gave me information that could potentially have negative impact on their own jobs. I also felt that the validity of the observations reported here would not be affected by disguising the identity of Indsco. After my initial formulations were developed, I held conversations with informants in three other large corporations where I also had consulting relationships in order to satisfy myself that Indsco, although containing its own culture, was not particularly unique in the relationships I observed. I learned that Indsco, indeed, was typical, and its story could be that of many large organizations. Furthermore, I was often a "guest" at Indsco and a confidante to many of its people, and I owed something to my hosts. Some of the research I conducted was initiated or invited by people at Indsco who wanted more insight into their own functions.

On other occasions, however, I was on my own and followed only my own agenda; many people were aware that I was writing a book but were not aware of what specific use I would be making of the information I gathered. I spent most of my time at headquarters, supplemented by trips to a number of field locations; I visited foreign offices, and I saw a number of informants in their homes.

The following sources of information were utilized in developing concepts and drawing conclusions; they provided the basis for both quantitative and qualitative analysis:

1. A mail survey I designed, taking two to three hours to complete, of 205 sales workers and sales managers out of a population of 350. The sample was all men, for there were no women in the sales force when the survey was conducted. The sample size reflected the number of those to whom questionnaires were sent who chose to return them. It was slightly underrepresentative of the oldest age group in sales. The survey was preceded by open-ended interviewing of 30 people in sales and related functions, including officers, staff people, and new hires. The purpose of these interviews was to elicit from the respondents the kinds of questions they thought ought to be included in the survey. Then there was a pretest group of 8. The core of the survey was a 34-item measure of commitment derived from questions about attitude toward the company based on a theory of commitment I had developed in my previous research on utopian communities.[2] The measure consisted of one general question about overall loyalty and eleven questions on each of three dimensions of commitment: sense of long-term investment in the organization, willingness to put in extra effort and continue to participate (instrumental or continuance commitment); sense of belonging, sense of membership in a collectivity, ties with other people (affective or cohesion commitment); belief in the goals and purposes of the organization, in its worth and moral virtue (moral or control commitment). There were also a series of questions about the immediate work setting, decision-making, and reward systems; personal priorities and perceived skills; and training opportunities within the company....

2. Interviews with the first 20 women to enter the sales force, both individually and in groups. These women were questioned about their personal background; route to the company; experiences with orientation and training; experiences with peers, managers, and customers; sources of support or discomfort; and attitudes about the company. Eight left the Indsco sales force subsequently.

3. Access to a survey of 111 nonexempt employees on attitudes toward promotion. This was not a sample because it depended on volunteers who chose to attend a meeting at which they were asked to fill out the survey. Respondents were roughly representative of the total population in sex, although women at the lower end of the nonexempt scale were somewhat overrepresented....

4. A content analysis I conducted of 100 performance appraisal forms turned in on nonexempt clerical personnel, largely secretaries, as part of a consulting project to help personnel staff develop a satisfactory program. Interviews with secretaries and bosses were held in conjunction with this project.

5. Group discussions, recorded verbatim. Such meetings were explicitly defined as data collection. One consisted of 22 men and women in a number of different jobs, from managers through secretaries, together for four days, discussing career concerns and relations between men and women in the company. Another consisted of three sets of discussions among 20 executives and 5 personnel specialists on

topics such as managerial skills, career pathways and preparation for their present job, and sources of frustration; these discussions were held in conjunction with task force meetings and professional conventions. Twelve husbands and wives met for two days to discuss work/family issues as they occurred in the large corporation.

6. Participant-observation in meetings. Sometimes these were set up to provide people in Indsco with feedback from earlier projects or data collection efforts…. Sometimes they were meetings discussing new programs or the application of research findings that I was allowed to attend because my experience might be relevant. In one or two cases, I was invited to meetings by Indsco managers who were interested in having an outsider present with whom they could later discuss the events of the meeting. Often beforehand, an informant or the person who invited me would describe the participants to me: their career stage, their present position, and their characteristic style. Such descriptions and accompanying anecdotes were often a very valuable source of concepts, ideas, and material.

7. Personal participant-observation in training programs or interviews with staff. I paid attention both to official events and to informal interaction that took place before and after sessions and at social events.

8. A large set of documents. The bulk of these were public documents such as company newsletters (corporate, divisional, field locations), newspapers, booklets for new hires, annual reports, and blank forms used in a variety of personnel programs. I also had occasional access to statistical reports, internal memoranda, and reports, but I do not cite or draw from anything confidential in this case study.

9. Individual conversations. These were generally on specific topics with anyone I had reason to visit. They occurred in offices, at social gatherings, at lunch, or at people's homes. Usually, these were of mutual benefit because the respondent would know of my interest in organizational behavior and ask me many questions. The "interviews" I could conduct in this fashion broadened my territory and my view of the organization considerably. (Melville Dalton called this the technique of "conversational interviewing.")

10. A small group of people with whom I built close working relationships over the years. These people were largely in functions where they were well placed to see a large number of people in a large number of levels at Indsco. They could tell me about the history of the company and a variety of experiences in the organization as well as provide information about the issues in their own careers. I could also use them to check out stories I gathered elsewhere. These people were especially valuable

because they were interested in similar questions, and they wanted to encourage social science attention to the new human problems of the corporation. Some of them were very wise and very insightful. Although occasionally they would seem embarrassed at not being "experts" in social science, I always found that they knew much more than they thought, and my discussions with them were very enjoyable. In some sense, they participated with me as "co-researchers," and our conversations always tended to be characterized by open exchange. I promised them complete confidentiality; otherwise I would thank them publicly for their help here.

Generally, I tried to follow up on people I had seen earlier, and for some people I had career information extending over the entire five-year period, from personal knowledge. I tended to record everything I could that occurred in my presence. I did this almost automatically, even though I had not yet defined the situation as "research," because, as all good consultants know, it is wise to keep complete notes and collect as much system information as possible in order to be maximally helpful to clients. I found even time waiting outside of people's offices valuable. Time designated as "social" in which I engaged in informal discussions with people was perhaps the most valuable of all. When I could, I asked people to describe other people and their situation to me. This is because I found that people were often unable to tell me what I needed to know about their own behavior and attitudes, but other people in their offices served as useful informants.

Much of what I gathered informally was in the form of stories and retrospective accounts of events. I think that the reasons for this were embedded in the nature of large, complex organizations themselves. First, there is not much to observe directly because I was interested in administration and in what takes place in offices. Unlike studies of plants or clerical workers in large offices, much of what "occurred" at Indsco happened in small, private offices behind closed doors, over the telephone, or at meetings to which outsiders were definitely not invited. Short of taking an inside job, I would not have had access. Yet with a job at Indsco, I would have been much more limited and confined. My roamings as a consultant and outside researcher brought me in touch with many more people, and I could ask questions that insiders would probably not have been able to ask of people in other functions without arousing undue suspicion. Second, many events other than routine daily activities take place over a long time frame, and daily observation would be a very slow way to gather material about such occurrences. Finally, the system was so large as to be almost boundaryless. Because my interest extended to the system as a whole rather than to small units within it, I often found that the best way to wander over such a large territory was to ask people to tell me all that they knew rather than try to discover it for myself by personal observation.

On the whole, I would estimate the number of my personal on-site contact days to be over 120, and the number of people with whom I held more than momentary conversations at well over 120. An additional 500 people participated in the written surveys or performance appraisals which were the primary source of the quantitative data I report.

Crozier framed the methodological problems inherent in studies of large-scale organizations well: "Comprehensive studies of human relations problems at the management level are usually hampered by two sets of difficulties. First, the complexity of the role structure in modern organizations causes much ambiguity and overlapping, making it impossible to match really comparable cases and to use rigorous methods meaningfully. Second, the general emphasis on status and promotions gives a crucial importance to the human relations game, thus preventing the researcher from obtaining reliable data on the central problem of power relationships."[4] Thus, a combination of methods such as used in the classical sociological field studies emerges as the most valid and reliable

way to develop understanding of such a complex social reality as the corporation. I used each source of data, and each informant, as a check against the others. In this way, consistent tendencies could be noted. Nothing that I report was totally unique or true of only one person. I chose illustrative examples and quotations that were more widely supported (indeed, it was often frustrating not to be able to use all my material), and important exceptions are also mentioned in the text.

The other important base for this study should not be neglected. This was, of course, an extensive review of the sociological, social psychological, psychological, and organizational behavior literatures. I considered this a part of the study critical to its success. I worked back and forth between the literature and the field. I formulated hypotheses and questions from the literature, and I could test the generalizability of my field observations through literature review. With C. Wright Mills, I believe that reading can also be a valid form of research.[5]

## ENDNOTES

1. Michel Crozier, *The Bureaucratic Phenomenon* (Chicago: University of Chicago Press, 1964), p. 150.
2. Rosabeth Moss Kanter, *Commitment and Community* (Cambridge, MA: Harvard University Press, 1972).
3. Melville Dalton, *Men Who Manage* (New York: Wiley, 1959), p. 280.
4. Crozier, *The Bureaucratic Phenomenon*, p. 112.
5. C. Wright Mills, *The Sociological Imagination* (New York: Oxford University Press, 1959). See especially his essay "On Intellectual Craftsmanship."

# Part II
# SOCIAL INTERACTION AND SOCIALIZATION

What is the nature of the human being? That is, what are we, apart from what we learn?

To the sociologist, human nature cannot be understood apart from society. We are, by our very nature, social beings. It is inconceivable to have human beings in nature who are not also social beings.

Part II begins with an examination of the social nature of the human being by reminding us that we regularly act in a world populated by other people, and that their presence makes a big difference to who we are and what we do. We interact with them. In interaction, we are socialized by them; and through them, we are shaped by the society and groups that are represented by them.

The selections by Charles Cooley and Kingsley Davis focus on a central question that most people have asked in one way or another: What would we be like without some social life? Both focus on the importance of "socialization," the process by which society forms each individual and by which each of us comes to take on qualities characteristic of the human species.

Berger and Luckmann introduce us to the power of socialization. Not only does society and its representatives socialize what we become, but this socialization is one of the principal ways we are controlled by it. The individual "internalizes" society.

Erving Goffman introduces us to the importance of "social interaction," the action that people take toward one another in everyday situations. As we act back and forth, we influence others, and we are influenced by them.

The two final selections in Part II give us two interesting and insightful examples of socialization as it comes to shape the individual. The selection by Richard Jenkins describes what identity is and why it is so intimately tied to social interaction; the selection by Timothy Curry explains how important socialization is to athletes, who even come to learn how to define something so personal as pain.

# 7. HUMAN NATURE

CHARLES COOLEY

*"Human functions are so numerous and intricate that no fixed mechanism could provide for them. They are also subject to radical change, not only in the life of the individual but from one generation to another."*

Human beings are characterized by flexibility, plasticity, and teachability. Our nature is not commanded by what we inherit in our genes, but by our social life. Charles Cooley's description still represents well the sociological view of human nature.

...Thus the plastic, indeterminate character of human heredity involves a long and helpless infancy; and this, in turn, is the basis of the human family, because the primary and essential function of the family is the care of children. Those species of animals in which the young are adequately prepared for life by definite heredity have no family at all, while those which more or less resemble man as regards plastic heredity, resemble him also in having some rudiments, at least, of a family. Kittens, for instance, are cared for by the mother for several months and profit in some measure by her example and instruction.

More generally, this difference as regards plasticity means that the life-activities of the animal are comparatively uniform and fixed, while those of man are varied and changing. Human functions are so numerous and intricate that no fixed mechanism could provide for them. They are also subject to radical change, not only in the life of the individual but from one generation to another. The only possible hereditary basis for them is an outfit of indeterminate capacities that can be developed and guided by experience as the needs of life require.

I see a flycatcher sitting on a dead branch, where there are no leaves to interrupt his view. Presently, he darts toward a passing insect, hovers about him

From *Human Nature and Social Order*, by Charles Horton Cooley, 1922, pp. 20-22, 31-34, Schocken Books, Inc. Originally published by Scribner and Sons.

a few seconds, catches him, or fails to do so, and returns to his perch. That is his way of getting a living: He has done it all his life and will go on doing it to the end. Millions of other flycatchers on millions of other dead branches are doing precisely the same thing. And this has been the life of the species for unknown thousands of years. They have, through the germ-plasm, a definite capacity for this — the keen eye, the swift, fluttering movement to follow the insect, the quick, sure action of the neck and bill to seize him — all effective with no instruction and very little practice.

Man has a natural hunger, like the flycatcher, and a natural mechanism of tasting, chewing, swallowing, and digestion; but his way of getting the food varies widely at different times of his life, is not the same with different individuals, and often changes completely from one generation to another. The great majority of us gain our food, after we have left the parental nest, through what we call a job, and a job is any activity whatever that a complex and shifting society esteems sufficiently to pay us for. It is very likely, nowadays, to last only part of our lives and to be something our ancestors never heard of. Thus whatever is most distinctively human — our adaptability, our power of growth, our arts and sciences, our social institutions and progress — is bound up with the indeterminate character of human heredity.

Of course, there is no sharp line, in this matter of teachability, between man and the other animals. The activities of the latter are not wholly predetermined, and in so far as they are not, there is a learn-ing process based on plastic heredity. The higher animals — horses, dogs, and elephants, for example — are notably teachable, and may even participate in the changes of human society, as when dogs learn to draw carts, trail fugitives, guide the lost, or

perform in a circus. And, on the other side, those activities of man that do not require much adapta-tion, such as the breathing, sucking, and crying of infants, and even walking (which is learned without instruction when the legs become strong enough), are provided for by definite heredity....

# 8. A CASE OF EXTREME ISOLATION

KINGSLEY DAVIS

*"Clearly, the history of Isabelle's development is different from that of Anna's. In both cases, there was an exceedingly low, rather blank, intellectual level to begin with. In both cases, it seemed that the girl might be congenitally feeble-minded. In both, a consider-ably higher level was reached later on. But the Ohio girl achieved a normal mentality within two years, whereas Anna was still marked inadequate at the end of four and a half years."*

Kingsley Davis compares two cases of human isolation. The potential of both chil-dren was clearly retarded because of social isolation. However, nothing human is fixed: Isabelle got close attention, learned language, and was able to overcome early isolation. Anna did not get close attention, and her mental development did not progress very far. Interaction and the early acquisition of language seem to be central to human growth.

Early in 1940, there appeared in the *American Journal of Sociology* an account of a girl called Anna.[1] She had been deprived of normal contact and had received a minimum of human care for almost the whole of her first six years of life....

When finally found and removed from the room in the grandfather's house at the age of near-ly six years, the child could not talk, walk, or do anything that showed intelligence. She was in an extremely emaciated and undernourished condi-tion, with skeleton-like legs and a bloated ab-domen. She had been fed on virtually nothing except cow's milk during the years under her mother's care.

Reprinted from "Final Note on a Case of Extreme Isolation," by Kingsley Davis, in *American Journal of Sociology* 52 (1947), pp. 432–437. Used with permission.

Anna's condition when found, and her subse-quent improvement, have been described in the previous report. It now remains to say what hap-pened to her after that.

## LATER HISTORY

In 1939, nearly two years after being discovered, Anna had progressed, as previously reported, to the point where she could walk, understand simple commands, feed herself, achieve some neatness, remember people, and so on. But she still did not speak, and, although she was much more like a normal infant of something over one year of age in mentality, she was far from normal for her age....

On August 30, 1939, she was taken to a private home for retarded children.... A final report from the school, made on June 22, 1942, and evidently the last report before the girl's death, pictured only a slight advance over that given above. It said that Anna could follow directions, string beads, identify a few colors, build with blocks, and differentiate between attractive and unattractive pictures. She had a good sense of rhythm and loved a doll. She talked mainly in phrases but would repeat words and try to carry on a conversation. She was clean about clothing. She habitually washed her hands and brushed her teeth. She would try to help other children. She walked well and could run fairly well, although clumsily. Although easily excited, she had a pleasant disposition.

## INTERPRETATION

Such was Anna's condition just before her death. It may seem as if she had not made much progress, but one must remember the condition in which she had been found. One must recall that she had no glimmering of speech, absolutely no ability to walk, no sense of gesture, not the least capacity to feed herself even when the food was put in front of her, and no comprehension of cleanliness. She was so apathetic that it was hard to tell whether or not she could hear. And all this at the age of nearly ten years. Compared with this condition, her capacities at the time of her death seem striking indeed, although they do not amount to much more than a two-and-a-half-year mental level. One conclusion therefore seems safe, namely, that her isolation prevented a considerable amount of mental development that was undoubtedly part of her capacity. Just what her original capacity was, of course, is hard to say; but her development after her period of confinement (including the ability to walk and run, to play, dress, fit into a social situation, and, above all, to speak) shows that she had at least this much capacity — capacity that never could have been realized in her original condition of isolation.

A further question is this: What would she have been like if she had received a normal upbringing from the moment of birth? A definitive answer would have been impossible in any case, but even an approximate answer is made difficult by her early death. If one assumes, as was tentatively surmised in the previous report, that it is "almost im-

possible for any child to learn to speak, think, and act like a normal person after a long period of early isolation," it seems likely that Anna might have had a normal or near-normal capacity, genetically speaking. On the other hand, it was pointed out that Anna represented "a marginal case, [because] she was discovered before she had reached six years of age," an age "young enough to allow for some plasticity."[2] While admitting, then, that Anna's isolation may have been the major cause (and was certainly a minor cause) of her lack of rapid mental progress during the four and a half years following her rescue from neglect, it is necessary to entertain the hypothesis that she was congenitally deficient....

## COMPARISON WITH ANOTHER CASE

If a child could be discovered who had been isolated about the same length of time as Anna but had achieved a much quicker recovery and a greater mental development, it would be a stronger indication that Anna was deficient to start with.

Such a case does exist. It is the case of a girl found at about the same time as Anna and under strikingly similar circumstances....

Born apparently one month later than Anna, the girl in question, who has been given the pseudonym Isabelle, was discovered in November 1938, nine months after the discovery of Anna. At the time she was found, she was approximately six and a half years of age. Like Anna, she was an illegitimate child and had been kept in seclusion for that reason. Her mother was a deaf-mute, having become so at the age of two, and it appears that she and Isabelle had spent most of their time together in a dark room shut off from the rest of the mother's family. As a result, Isabelle had no chance to develop speech; when she communicated with her mother, it was by means of gestures. Lack of sunshine and inadequacy of diet had caused Isabelle to become rachitic. Her legs in particular were affected; they "were so bowed that as she stood erect, the soles of her shoes came nearly flat together, and she got about with a skittering gait."[3] Her behavior toward strangers, especially men, was almost that of a wild animal, manifesting much fear and hostility. In lieu of speech, she made only a strange croaking sound. In many ways, she acted like an infant. "She was apparently utterly unaware of relationships of any kind. When presented with a ball for the first time, she held it in the palm of her hand, then reached out and stroked my face with it. Such behavior is comparable to that of a child of six months."[4] At first, it was even hard to tell whether or not she could hear, so unused were her senses. Many of her actions resembled those of deaf children.

It is small wonder that, once it was established that she could hear, specialists working with her believed her to be feeble-minded. Even on non-verbal tests, her performance was so low as to promise little for the future. Her first score on the Stanford-Binet was 19 months, practically at the zero point of the scale. On the Vineland social maturity scale, her first score was 39, representing an age level of two and a half years.[5] "The general impression was that she was wholly uneducable and that any attempt to teach her to speak, after so long a period of silence, would meet with failure."[6]

In spite of this interpretation, the individuals in charge of Isabelle launched a systematic and skillful program of training. It seemed hopeless at first. The approach had to be through pantomime and dramatization, suitable to an infant. It required one week of intensive effort before she even made her first attempt at vocalization. Gradually she began to respond, however, and, after the first hurdles had at last been overcome, a curious thing happened. She went through the usual stages of learning characteristic of the years from one to six, not only in proper succession but far more rapidly than normal. In a little over two months after her first vocalization, she was putting sentences together. Nine months after that, she could identify words and sentences on the printed page, could write well, could add to ten, and could retell a story after hearing it. Seven months beyond this point, she had a vocabulary of 1,500 to 2,000 words and was asking complicated questions. Starting from an educational level of between one and three years (depending on what aspect one considers), she had reached a normal level by the time she was eight and a half years old. In short, she covered in two years the stages of learning that ordinarily require six.[7] Or, to put it another way, her IQ trebled in a year and a half.[8] The speed with which she reached the normal level of mental development seems analogous to the recovery of

body weight in a growing child after an illness, the recovery being achieved by an extra fast rate of growth for a period after the illness until normal weight for the given age is again attained.

When the writer saw Isabelle a year and a half after her discovery, she gave him the impression of being a very bright, cheerful, energetic little girl. She spoke well, walked and ran without trouble, and sang with gusto and accuracy. Today, she is over fourteen years old and has passed the sixth grade in a public school. Her teachers say that she participates in all school activities as normally as other children. Although older than her classmates, she has fortunately not physically matured too far beyond their level.[9]

Clearly, the history of Isabelle's development is different from that of Anna's. In both cases, there was an exceedingly low, rather blank, intellectual level to begin with. In both cases, it seemed that the girl might be congenitally feeble-minded. In both, a considerably higher level was reached later on. But the Ohio girl achieved a normal mentality within two years, whereas Anna was still marked inadequate at the end of four and a half years. This difference in achievement may suggest that Anna had less initial capacity. But an alternate hypothesis is possible.

One should remember that Anna never received the prolonged and expert attention that Isabelle received. The result of such attention, in the case of the Ohio girl, was to give her speech at an early stage, and her subsequent rapid development seems to have been a consequence of that. "Until Isabelle's speech and language development, she had all the characteristics of a feeble-minded child." Had Anna—who, from the standpoint of psychometric tests and early history, closely resembled this girl at the start—been given a mastery of speech at an earlier point by intensive training, her subsequent development might have been much more rapid.[10]

The hypothesis that Anna began with a sharply inferior mental capacity is therefore not established. Even if she were deficient to start with, we have no way of knowing how much so. Under ordinary conditions, she might have been a dull normal or, like her mother, a moron. Even after the blight of her isolation, if she had lived to maturity, she might have finally reached virtually the full level of her capacity, whatever it may have been.

That her isolation did have a profound effect on her mentality, there can be no doubt. This is proved by the substantial degree of change during the four and a half years following her rescue.

Consideration of Isabelle's case serves to show, as Anna's case does not clearly show, that isolation up to the age of six, with failure to acquire any form of speech and hence failure to grasp nearly the whole world of cultural meaning, does not preclude the subsequent acquisition of these. Indeed, there seems to be a process of accelerated recovery in which the child goes through the mental stages at a more rapid rate than would be the case in normal development. Just what would be the maximum age at which a person could remain isolated and still retain the capacity for full cultural acquisition is hard to say. Almost certainly it would not be as high as age fifteen; it might possibly be as low as age ten. Undoubtedly, various individuals would differ considerably as to the exact age.

Anna's is not an ideal case for showing the effects of extreme isolation, partly because she was possibly deficient to begin with, partly because she did not receive the best training available, and partly because she did not live long enough. Nevertheless, her case is instructive when placed in the record with numerous other cases of extreme isolation. This and the previous article about her are meant to place her in the record. It is to be hoped that other cases will be described in the scientific literature as they are discovered (as unfortunately they will be), for only in these rare cases of extreme isolation is it possible "to observe concretely separated two factors in the development of human personality which are always otherwise only analytically separated: the biogenic and the sociogenic factors."[11]

## ENDNOTES

1. Kingsley Davis, "Extreme Social Isolation of a Child." *American Journal of Sociology*, XLV (January 1940), pp. 554–65.
2. Ibid.
3. Francis N. Maxfield, "What Happens When the Social Environment of a Child Approaches Zero." The writer is greatly indebted to Mrs. Maxfield and to Professor Horace B. English, a colleague of Professor Maxfield, for the privilege of seeing this manuscript and other materials collected on isolated and feral individuals.
4. Marie K. Mason, "Learning To Speak after Six and One-Half Years of Silence." *Journal of Speech Disorders*, VII (1942), pp. 295–304.
5. Maxfield, unpublished manuscript.
6. Mason, *op. cit.*, p. 299.
7. Ibid., *pp.* 300–304.
8. Maxfield, unpublished manuscript.
9. Based on a personal letter from Dr. Mason to the writer, May 13, 1946.
10. This point is suggested in a personal letter from Dr. Mason to the writer, October 22, 1946.
11. J. A. L. Singh and Robert M. Zingg, *Wolf-Children and Feral Man* (New York: Harper & Bros., 1941), pp. 248–51.

# 9.  SOCIALIZATION: THE INTERNALIZATION OF SOCIETY

PETER L. BERGER AND THOMAS LUCKMANN

*"Primary socialization accomplishes what (in hindsight, of course) may be seen as the most important confidence trick that society plays on the individual — to make appear as necessity what is in fact a bundle of contingencies, and thus to make meaningful the accident of his birth."*

*From beginning to end, the human being is socialized. Socialization brings the external world inside the individual. Both "primary socialization" and "secondary socialization" cooperate to do this, but, as Peter Berger and Thomas Luckmann emphasize, "primary socialization is really the most important one for the individual." This selection examines primary socialization, and it is organized as follows:*

1. *Significant others are representatives of society and social class.*
2. *Significant others form the individual's identity.*
3. *Eventually, a generalized other is created that represents a coherent society.*

...Only when he has achieved this degree of internalization is an individual a member of society. The ontogenetic process by which this is brought about is socialization, which may thus be defined as the comprehensive and consistent induction of an individual into the objective world of a society or a sector of it. Primary socialization is the first socialization an individual undergoes in childhood through which he becomes a member of society. Secondary socialization is any subsequent process that inducts an already socialized individual into new sectors of the objective world of his society.... 

It is at once evident that primary socialization is usually the most important one for an individual, and that the basic structure of all secondary socialization has to resemble that of primary socialization. Every individual is born into an objective social structure within which he encounters the significant others who are in charge of his socialization.[1] These significant others are imposed on him. Their definitions of his situation are posited for him as objective reality. He is thus born into not only an objective social structure but also an objective social world. The significant others who mediate this world to him modify it in the course of mediating it. They select aspects of it in accordance with their own location in the social structure, and also by virtue of their individual, biographically rooted idiosyncrasies. The social world is "filtered" to the individual through this double selectivity. Thus the lower-class child not only absorbs a lower-class perspective on the social world, he absorbs it in the idiosyncratic col-

oration given it by his parents (or whatever other individuals are in charge of his primary socialization). The same lower-class perspective may induce a mood of contentment, resignation, bitter resentment, or seething rebelliousness. Consequently, the lower-class child will not only come to inhabit a world greatly different from that of an upper-class child, but may do so in a manner quite different from the lower-class child next door.[2]

It should hardly be necessary to add that primary socialization involves more than purely cognitive learning. It takes place under circumstances that are highly charged emotionally. Indeed, there is good reason to believe that without such emotional attachment to significant others, the learning process would be difficult if not impossible.[3] The child identifies with the significant others in a variety of emotional ways. Whatever they may be, internalization occurs only as identification occurs. The child takes on the significant others' roles and attitudes, that is, internalizes them and makes them his own. And by this identification with significant others, the child becomes capable of identifying himself, of acquiring a subjectively coherent and plausible identity. In other words, the self is a reflected entity, reflecting the attitudes first taken by significant others toward it;[4] the individual becomes what he is addressed as by his significant others. This is not a one-sided, mechanistic process. It entails a dialectic between identification by others and self-identification, between objectively assigned and subjectively appropriated identity....

What is most important for our considerations here is the fact that the individual not only takes on the roles and attitudes of others, but in the same process takes on their world. Indeed, identity is objectively defined as location in a certain world and can be subjectively appropriated only *along with* that world. Put differently, all identifications take place within horizons that imply a specific social world. The child learns that he is what he is called. Every name implies a nomenclature, which in turn implies a designated social location.[5] To be given an identity involves being assigned a specific place in the world. Because this identity is subjectively appropriated by the child ("I *am* John Smith"), so is the world to which this identity points. Subjective appropriation of identity and subjective appropriation of the social world are merely different aspects of the *same* process of internalization, mediated by the *same* significant others.

Primary socialization creates in the child's consciousness a progressive abstraction from the roles and attitudes of specific others to roles and attitudes *in general*. For example, in the internalization of norms, there is a progression from "Mummy is angry with me now" to "Mummy is angry with me *whenever* I spill the soup." As additional significant others (father, grandmother, older sister, and so on) support the mother's negative attitude toward soup-spilling, the generality of the norm is subjectively extended. The decisive step comes when the child recognizes that *everybody* is against soup-spilling, and the norm is generalized to "one does not spill soup" – "one" being himself as part of a generality that includes, in principle, *all* of society insofar as it is significant to the child. This abstraction from the roles and attitudes of concrete significant others is called the *generalized other*.[6] Its formation within consciousness means that the individual now identifies not only with concrete others but with a generality of others, that is, with a society. Only by virtue of this generalized identification does his own self-identification attain stability and continuity. He now has not only an identity vis-à-vis this or that significant other, but an identity *in general*, which is subjectively apprehended as remaining the same no matter what others, significant or not, are encountered. This newly coherent identity incorporates within itself all the various internalized roles and attitudes – including, among many other things, the self-identification as a non-spiller of soups.

The formation within consciousness of the generalized other marks a decisive phase in socialization. It implies the internalization of soci-

ety as such and of the objective reality established therein, and, at the same time, the subjective establishment of a coherent and continuous identity. Society, identity, *and* reality are subjectively crystallized in the same process of internalization. This crystallization is concurrent with the internalization of language. Indeed, for reasons evident from the foregoing observations on language, language constitutes both the most important content and the most important instrument of socialization.

When the generalized other has been crystallized in consciousness, a symmetrical relationship is established between objective and subjective reality. What is real "outside" corresponds to what is real "within." Objective reality can readily be "translated" into subjective reality, and vice versa. Language, of course, is the principal vehicle of this ongoing translating process in both directions. It should, however, be stressed that the symmetry between objective and subjective reality cannot be complete. The two realities correspond to each other, but they are not coextensive. There is always more objective reality "available" than is actually internalized in any individual consciousness, simply because the contents of socialization are determined by the social distribution of knowledge. No individual internalizes the totality of what is objectivated as reality in his society, not even if the society and its world are relatively simple ones. On the other hand, there are always elements of subjective reality that have not originated in socialization, such as the awareness of one's own body prior to and apart from any socially learned apprehension of it. Subjective biography is not fully social. The individual apprehends himself as being both inside *and* outside society.[7] This implies that the symmetry between objective and subjective reality is never a static, once-for-all state of affairs. It must always be produced and reproduced *in actu*. In other words, the relationship between the individual and the objective social world is like an ongoing balancing act....

In primary socialization, there is no *problem* of identification. There is no choice of significant others. Society presents the candidate for socialization with a predefined set of significant others, whom he must accept as such with no possibility of opting for another arrangement. *Hic Rhodus, hic salta*. One must make do with the parents fate has regaled one with. This unfair disadvantage inherent in the situation of being a child has the obvious consequence that, although the child is not simply passive in the process of his socialization, it is the adults who set the rules of the game. The child can play the game with enthusiasm or with sullen resistance. But, alas, there is no other game around. This has an important corollary. Because the child has no choice in the selection of his significant others, his identification with them is quasi-automatic. For the same reason, his internalization of their particular reality is quasi-inevitable. The child does not internalize the world of his significant others as one of many possible worlds. He internalizes it as *the* world, the only existent and only conceivable world, the world *tout court*. It is for this reason that the world internalized in primary socialization is so much more firmly entrenched in consciousness than worlds internalized in secondary socializations. However much the original sense of inevitability may be weakened in subsequent disenchantments, the recollection of a never-to-be-repeated certainty — the certainty of the first dawn of reality — still adheres to the first world of childhood. Primary socialization thus accomplishes what (in hindsight, of course) may be seen as the most important confidence trick that society plays on the individual — to make appear as necessity what is in fact a bundle of contingencies, and thus to make meaningful the accident of his birth.

The specific contents that are internalized in primary socialization vary, of course, from society to society. Some are found everywhere. It is language that must be internalized above all. With language, and by means of it, various motivational and interpretative schemes are internalized as institutionally defined — wanting to act like a brave little boy, for instance, and assuming that little boys are naturally divided into the brave and the cowardly. These schemes provide the child with institutionalized programs for everyday life, some immediately applicable to him, others anticipating conduct socially defined for later biographical stages — the bravery that will allow him to get through a day beset with tests of will from one's peers and from all sorts of others, and also the bravery that will be required of one later — when one is initiated as a warrior, say, or when one might be called by the god. These programs, both the immediately applicable and the anticipatory, differentiate one's identity from that of others — such as girls, slave boys, or boys from another clan. Finally, there is internalization of at least the rudiments of the legitimating apparatus; the child learns "why" the programs are what they are. One must be brave because one wants to become a real man; one must perform the rituals because otherwise the gods will be angry; one must be loyal to the chief because only if one does will the gods support one in times of danger; and so on.

In primary socialization, then, the individual's first world is constructed. Its peculiar quality of firmness is to be accounted for, at least in part, by the inevitability of the individual's relationship to his very first significant others....

Primary socialization ends when the concept of the generalized other (and all that goes with it) has been established in the consciousness of the individual. At this point, he is an effective member of society and in subjective possession of a self and a world. But this internalization of society, identity, and reality is not a matter of once and for all. Socialization is never total and never finished.

## ENDNOTES

1. Our description here, of course, leans heavily on the Meadian theory of socialization.
2. The concept of "mediation" is derived from Sartre, who lacks, however, an adequate theory of socialization.
3. The affective dimension of early learning has been especially emphasized by Freudian child psychology, although there are various findings of behavioristic learning theory that would tend to confirm this. We do not imply acceptance of the theoretical presuppositions of either psychological school in our argument here.
4. Our conception of the reflected character of the self is derived from both Cooley and Mead. Its roots may be found in the analysis of the "social self" by William James (*Principles of Psychology*).
5. On nomenclature, *cf.* Claude Lévi-Strauss, *La pensée sauvage*, pp. 253 ff.
6. The concept of the "generalized other" is used here in a fully Meadian sense.
7. Compare Georg Simmel on the self-apprehension of man as both inside and outside society. Plessner's concept of "eccentricity" is again relevant here.

# 10. PRESENTATION OF SELF IN EVERYDAY LIFE

ERVING GOFFMAN

*"When an individual appears in the presence of others, there will usually be some reason for him to mobilize his activity so that it will convey an impression to others that is in his interests to convey."*

Erving Goffman approaches the human being as an actor performing on a stage. His descriptions of interaction are classic. This insightful selection is one of his most famous.

What happens when we enter the presence of others? Use this as a guide to your reading:

1. Others seek to know who we are. We control our actions to give off the picture we want to give off.
2. Others will also seek to act to control the definition of the situation.
3. A working consensus is created.
4. Ongoing interaction may question the initial picture.
5. Preventive tactics help preserve the interaction and keep actors from embarrassment.

Here, Goffman brilliantly describes something that occurs in all of our lives, every day. He gives us insight into something familiar.

When an individual enters the presence of others, they commonly seek to acquire information about him or to bring into play information about him already possessed. They will be interested in his general socio-economic status, his conception of self, his attitude toward them, his competence, his trustworthiness, and so on. Although some of this information seems to be sought almost as an end in itself, there are usually quite practical reasons for acquiring it. Information about the individual helps to define the situation, enabling others to know in advance what he will expect of them and what they may expect of him. Informed in these ways, the others will know how best to act in order to call forth a desired response from him.

For those present, many sources of information become accessible and many carriers (or "sign-vehicles") become available for conveying this information. If unacquainted with the individual, observers can glean clues from his conduct and appearance that allow them to apply their previous experience with individuals roughly similar to the one in front of them or, more important, to apply untested stereotypes to him. They can also assume from past experience that only individuals of a particular kind are likely to be found in a given social setting. They can rely on what the individual says about himself or on documentary evidence he provides as to who and what he is. If

From *The Presentation of Self in Everyday Life*, by Erving Goffman. Copyright © 1959 by Erving Goffman. Used with permission of Doubleday, a division of Bantam Doubleday Dell Publishing Group, Inc.

they know, or know of, the individual by virtue of experience prior to the interaction, they can rely on assumptions as to the persistence and generality of psychological traits as a way of predicting his present and future behavior.

However, during the period in which the individual is in the immediate presence of the others, few events may occur that directly provide the others with the conclusive information they will need if they are to direct wisely their own activity. Many crucial facts lie beyond the time and place of interaction or lie concealed within it. For example, the "true" or "real" attitudes, beliefs, and emotions of the individual can be ascertained only indirectly, through his avowals or through what appears to be involuntary expressive behavior. Similarly, if the individual offers the others a product or service, they will often find that, during the interaction, there will be no time and place immediately available for eating the pudding that the proof can be found in. They will be forced to accept some events as conventional or natural signs of something not directly available to the senses. In Ichheiser's terms,[1] the individual will have to act so that he intentionally or unintentionally *expresses* himself, and the others will in turn have to be *impressed* in some way by him.

The expressiveness of the individual (and therefore his capacity to give impressions) appears to involve two radically different kinds of sign activity: the expression that he *gives*, and the expression that he *gives off*. The first involves verbal symbols or their substitutes that he uses admittedly and solely to convey the information he and the others are known to attach to these symbols. This is communication in the traditional and narrow sense. The second involves a wide range of action that others can treat as symptomatic of the actor, the expectation being that the action was performed for reasons other than the information conveyed in this way. As we shall have to see, this distinction has an only initial validity. The individual does, of course, intentionally convey misinformation by means of both of these types of communication, the first involving deceit, the second feigning....

He may wish [others] to think highly of him, or to think that he thinks highly of them, or to perceive how in fact he feels toward them, or to obtain no clear-cut impression; he may wish to ensure sufficient harmony so that the interaction can be sustained, or to defraud, get rid of, confuse, mislead, antagonize, or insult them. Regardless of the particular objective the individual has in mind and of his motive for having this objective, it will be in his interest to control the conduct of the others, especially their responsive treatment of him.[2] This control is achieved largely by influencing the definition of the situation the others come to formulate, and he can influence this definition by expressing himself in such a way as to give them the kind of impression that will lead them to act voluntarily in accordance with his own plan. Thus, when an individual appears in the presence of others, there will usually be some reason for him to mobilize his activity so that it will convey an impression to others that is in his interest to convey. Because a girl's dormitory mates will glean evidence of her popularity from the calls she receives on the phone, we can suspect that some girls will arrange for calls to be made, and Willard Waller's finding can be anticipated:

It has been reported by many observers that a girl who is called to the telephone in the dormitories will often allow herself to be called several times, in order to give all the other girls ample opportunity to hear her paged....[3]

I have said that when an individual appears before others, his actions will influence the definition of the situation they come to have. Sometimes, the individual will act in a thoroughly calculating manner, expressing himself in a given way solely to give the kind of impression to others that is likely to evoke from them a specific response he is concerned to obtain. Sometimes, the individual will be calculating in his activity but be relatively unaware that this is the case. Sometimes, he will intentionally and consciously express himself in a particular way, but chiefly because the tradition of his group or social status require this kind of expression and not because of any particular response (other than vague acceptance or approval) that is likely to be evoked from those impressed by the expression. Sometimes, the traditions of an individual's role will lead him to give a well-designed impression of a particular kind, and yet he may be neither consciously nor unconsciously disposed to create such an impression. The others, in their turn, may be suitably impressed by the individual's efforts to convey something, or may misunderstand the situation and come to conclusions that are warranted neither by the individual's intent nor by the facts. In any case, in so far as the others act *as if* the individual had conveyed a particular impression, we may take a functional or pragmatic view and say that the individual has "effectively" projected a given definition of the situation and "effectively" fostered the understanding that a given state of affairs obtains....

When we allow that the individual projects a definition of the situation when he appears before others, we must also see that the others, however passive their role may seem to be, will themselves effectively project a definition of the situation by virtue of their response to the individual and by virtue of any lines of action they initiate to him. Ordinarily, the definitions of the situation projected by the several different participants are sufficiently attuned to one another so that open contradiction will not occur. I do not mean that there will be the kind of consensus that arises when each individual present candidly expresses what he really feels and honestly agrees with the expressed feelings of the others present. This kind of harmony is an optimistic ideal, and in any case is not necessary for the smooth working of society. Rather, each participant is expected to suppress his immediate heartfelt feelings, conveying a view of the situation he feels the others will be able to find at least temporarily acceptable. The maintenance of this surface of agreement, this veneer of consensus, is facilitated by each participant concealing his own wants behind statements that assert values to which everyone present feels obliged to give lip service. Further, there is usually a kind of division of definitional labor. Each participant is allowed to establish the tentative official ruling regarding matters that are vital to him but not immediately important to others, for example, the rationalizations and justifications by which he accounts for his past activity. In exchange for this courtesy, he remains silent or noncommittal on matters important to others but not immediately important to him. We have then a kind of interactional *modus vivendi.* Together, the participants contribute to a single overall definition of the situation that involves not so much a real agreement as to what exists but rather a real agreement as to whose claims concerning what issues will be tem-

porarily honored. Real agreement will also exist concerning the desirability of avoiding an open conflict of definitions of the situation.[4] I will refer to this level of agreement as a "working consensus." It is to be understood that the working consensus established in one interaction setting will be quite different in content from the working consensus established in a different type of setting. Thus, between two friends at lunch, a reciprocal show of affection, respect, and concern for the other is maintained. In service occupations, on the other hand, the specialist often maintains an image of disinterested involvement in the problem of the client, while the client responds with a show of respect for the competence and integrity of the specialist. Regardless of such differences in content, however, the general form of these working arrangements is the same.

In noting the tendency for a participant to accept the definitional claims made by the others present, we can appreciate the crucial importance of the information the individual *initially* possesses or acquires concerning his fellow participants, for it is on the basis of this initial information that the individual starts to define the situation and starts to build up lines of responsive action. The individual's initial projection commits him to what he is proposing to be and requires him to drop all pretenses of being other things. As the interaction among the participants progresses, additions and modifications in this initial informational state will of course occur, but it is essential that these later developments be related without contradiction to, and even built up from, the initial positions taken by the several participants. It would seem that an individual can more easily make a choice as to what line of treatment to demand from and extend to the others present at the beginning of an encounter than he can alter the line of treatment being pursued once the interaction is underway....

Given the fact that the individual effectively projects a definition of the situation when he enters the presence of others, we can assume that events may occur within the interaction that contradict, discredit, or otherwise throw doubt on this projection. When these disruptive events occur, the interaction itself may come to a confused and embarrassed halt. Some of the assumptions on which the responses of the participants had been predicated become untenable, and the participants find themselves lodged in an interaction for which the situation has been wrongly defined and is now no longer defined. At such moments, the individual whose presentation has been discredited may feel ashamed while the others present may feel hostile, and all the participants may come to feel ill at ease, nonplussed, out of countenance, embarrassed, experiencing the kind of anomie generated when the minute social system of face-to-face interaction breaks down.

In stressing the fact that the initial definition of the situation projected by an individual tends to provide a plan for the cooperative activity that follows — in stressing this action point of view — we must not overlook the crucial fact that any projected definition of the situation also has a distinctive moral character. It is this moral character of projections that will chiefly concern us in this report. Society is organized on the principle that any individual who possesses certain social characteristics has a moral right to expect that others will value and treat him in an appropriate way. Connected with this principle is a second, namely that an individual who implicitly or explicitly signifies that he has certain social characteristics ought, in fact, to be what he claims he is. In consequence, when an individual projects a definition of the situation and thereby makes an implicit or explicit claim to be a person of a particular kind, he automatically exerts a moral demand on the others, obliging them to value and treat him in the manner that persons of his kind have a right to expect. He also implicitly forgoes all claims to be things he does not appear to be[5] and hence forgoes the treatment that would be appropriate for such individuals. The others find, then, that the individual has informed them as to what *is*, and as to what they *ought* to see as the "is."

One cannot judge the importance of definitional disruptions by the frequency with which they occur, for apparently they would occur more frequently were not constant precautions taken. We find that preventive practices are constantly employed to avoid these embarrassments, and that corrective practices are constantly employed to compensate for discrediting occurrences that have not been successfully avoided. When the individual employs these strategies and tactics to protect his own projections, we may refer to them as "defensive practices"; when a participant employs them to save the definition of the situation projected by another, we speak of "protective practices" or "tact." Together, defensive and protective practices comprise the techniques employed to safeguard the impression fostered by an individual during his presence before others. It should be added that although we may be ready to see that no fostered impression would survive if defensive practices were not employed, we are less ready perhaps to see that few impressions could survive if those who received the impression did not exert tact in their reception of it.

In addition to the fact that precautions are taken to prevent disruption of projected definitions, we may also note that an intense interest in these disruptions comes to play a significant role in the social life of the group. Practical jokes and social games are played in which embarrassments that are to be taken unseriously are purposely engineered.[6] Fantasies are created in which devastating exposures occur. Anecdotes from the past — real, embroidered, or fictitious — are told and retold, detailing disruptions that occurred, almost occurred, or occurred and were admirably resolved. There seems to be no grouping that does not have a ready supply of these games, reveries, and cautionary tales to be used as a source of humor, a catharsis for anxieties, and a sanction for inducing individuals to be modest in their claims and reasonable in their projected expectations. The individual may tell himself through dreams of getting into impossible positions. Families tell of the time a guest got his dates mixed and arrived when neither the house nor anyone in it was ready for him. Journalists tell of times when an all-too-meaningful misprint occurred, and the paper's assumption of objectivity or decorum was humorously discredited. Public servants tell of times a client ridiculously misunderstood form instructions, giving answers that implied an unanticipated and bizarre definition of the situation.[7] Seamen, whose home away from home is rigorously he-man, tell stories of coming back home and inadvertently asking mother to "pass the fucking butter."[8] Diplomats tell of the time a near-sighted queen asked a republican ambassador about the health of his king.[9]

To summarize, then, I assume that when an individual appears before others, he will have many motives for trying to control the impression they receive of the situation. This report is concerned with some of the common techniques that persons employ to sustain such impressions and with some of the common contingencies associated with the employment of these techniques. The specific content of any activity presented by the individual participant, or the role it plays in the interdependent activities of an on-going social system, will not be at issue; I shall be concerned only with the participant's dramaturgical problems of presenting the activity before others. The issues dealt with by stagecraft and stage management are sometimes trivial, but they are quite general; they seem to occur everywhere in social life, providing a clear-cut dimension for formal sociological analysis.

## ENDNOTES

1. Gustav Ichheiser, "Misunderstandings in Human Relations," Supplement to *The American Journal of Sociology*, LV (September, 1949), pp. 6-7.
2. Here I owe much to an unpublished paper by Tom Burns of the University of Edinburgh. He presents the argument that in all interaction a basic underlying theme is the desire of each participant to guide and control the responses made by the others present. A similar argument has been advanced by Jay Haley in a recent unpublished

paper, but in regard to a special kind of control, that having to do with defining the nature of the relationship of those involved in the interaction.
3. Willard Waller, "The Rating and Date Complex," *American Sociological Review*, II, p. 730.
4. An interaction can be purposely set up as a time and place for voicing differences in opinion, but in such cases, participants must be careful to agree not to disagree on the proper tone of voice, vocabulary, and degree of seriousness in which all arguments are to be phrased, and on the mutual respect that disagreeing participants must carefully continue to express toward one another. The debaters' or an academic definition of the situation may also be invoked suddenly and judiciously as a way of translating a serious conflict of views into one that can be handled within a framework acceptable to all present.
5. This role of the witness in limiting what it is the individual can be has been stressed by Existentialists, who see it as a basic threat to individual freedom. See Jean Paul Sartre, *Being and Nothingness*, trans. by Hazel E. Barnes (New York: Philosophical Library, 1956), pp. 365 *ff.*
6. E. Goffman, "Communication Conduct in an Island Community," (unpublished Ph.D. dissertation, Department of Sociology, University of Chicago, 1953).
7. Peter Blau, "Dynamics of Bureaucracy" (Ph.D. dissertation, Department of Sociology, Columbia University, forthcoming, University of Chicago Press), pp. 127-129.
8. Walter M. Beattie, Jr., "The Merchant Seaman" (unpublished M.A. report, Department of Sociology, University of Chicago, 1950), p. 35.
9. Sir Frederick Ponsonby, *Recollections of Three Reigns* (New York: Dutton, 1952), p. 46.

# 11. SOCIAL IDENTITY

RICHARD JENKINS

*"All human identities are in some sense — and usually a stronger rather than a weaker sense — social identities. It cannot be otherwise...."*

The title Jenkins gives this chapter in his book is "Knowing Who We Are." How do we know who we are? How do we know who other people are? Why is it important? It all relates to our everyday social interaction, the negotiation of who we are as we relate to one another in our social life.

It is a cold Friday night, and windy. You are dressed for dancing, not the weather. Finally, you reach the head of the queue outside the night club. The bouncer — although nowadays they prefer to be called doormen — raises his arm and lets your friend in. He takes one look at you and demands proof of your age. All you have in your pockets is money. That isn't enough.

You telephone the order line of a clothing catalog to buy a new jacket. The young man who answers asks for your name, address, credit card number and expiration date, your customer reference number if you have one; all in order to establish your status as someone to whom, in the absence of a face-to-face encounter, goods can be dispatched in confidence. And also, of course, to make sure that you're on the mailing list.

The immigration official asks you for your passport. She looks at your nationality, at where you were born. Your name. She checks your visa. These indicate your legitimacy as a traveler, your desirability as an entrant. She looks at the photograph, she looks at you. She asks you the purpose of your visit. She stamps the passport and wishes you a pleasant stay. Already she is looking over your shoulder at the person behind you.

On a train, the stranger in the opposite seat excuses herself. She has noticed you reading last week's newspaper from a small town several hundred miles to the east. You explain that your mother posts it to you so that you can keep up with the news from home. She recognized the newspaper because her husband is from your home town. You, it turns out, were at school with her brother-in-law. Before leaving the train she gives you her telephone number.

In everyday situations such as these, one's identity is called into question and established (or not). But the presentation or negotiation of identity is not always so ordinary or trivial: It can shake the foundations of our lives. Imagine, for example, the morning of your sixty-fifth birthday. With it, as well as birthday cards, will come retirement, a pension, a concessionary public transport pass, special rates every Tuesday at the hairdresser. Beyond that again, in the promise of free medical prescriptions and the beckoning Day Centre, hover the shades

of infirmity, of dependence, of disability. Although it will be the same face you see in the bathroom mirror, you will no longer be quite the person you were yesterday. Nor can you ever be again.

Sometimes, a changed or strange situation makes the difference. An unfamiliar neighborhood, an ethnically divided city: a casual encounter can transform one's taken-for-granted identity into a dangerous liability. Something as simple as the "wrong" accent or an "ethnic" surname on your driving license can become a warrant for violence, even murder. Whether the ethnic identification is "correct" or not — in your eyes — may make no difference. Identity is often in the eye of the beholder.

Or take a different time scale, and another kind of transformation. What changes and negotiations are required by "coming out," to assume a public identification as a gay man or a lesbian? What kind of response from others is the "right" response? Which others matter? And what does such a process represent? The construction of a new identity, or the revelation of an authentic and primordial self?

Social identity is also important on a wider stage than the encounters or thresholds of individual lives. Imagine a contested border region. It might be anywhere in the world. There are different ways to settle the issue: warfare, a referendum, international arbitration. Whatever the means adopted, the outcome has implications for the identities of people on both sides. And it may not be accepted by those who find their new national identity uncongenial. Similarly, the referenda about the European Union in the early 1990s in Scandinavia were as much about the preservation and transformation of identity as anything else.

To return to gay and lesbian identity, mass public occasions such as Gay Pride in London or the Sydney Mardi Gras are affirmations that being gay or being lesbian are collective identifications. For individual participants, these occasions may (or, indeed, may not) affirm their own particular sexual identities, but these gatherings are collective rituals of identification and political mobilization before they are anything else.

These scenarios, different as they are, exemplify social identity in everyday life. It is the most mundane of things, and it can be the most extraordinary. But what does it mean to say that these

From Chapter 1 of *Social Identity*, by Richard Jenkins. London: Routledge, 1996.

situations all involve social identity? What do they have in common? How do we know who we are, and how do others identify us? How does our sense of ourselves as unique individuals square with the realization that, always and everywhere, we share aspects of our identity with many others? To what extent is it possible to become someone, or something, other than what we now are? Is it possible to "just be myself?"…

What is identity, and what is social identity? Social identity is a characteristic or property of humans as social beings. The word *identity*, however, embraces a universe of creatures, things, and substances that is wider than the limited category of humanity. As such, its general meanings are worthy of brief attention, to provide a base line from which to begin our consideration of specifically social identity.

Consulting the Oxford English Dictionary yields a Latin root (*identitas*, from *idem*, "the same") and two basic meanings. The first is a concept of absolute sameness: "this is identical to that." The second is a concept of distinctiveness that presumes consistency or continuity over time. Approaching the idea of sameness from two different angles, the notion of identity simultaneously establishes two possible relations of comparison between persons or things: *similarity* on the one hand, and *difference* on the other.

Exploring the matter further, the verb *to identify* is a necessary accompaniment of identity: There is something active about the word that cannot be ignored. Identity is not "just there," it must always be established. This adds two further meanings to our catalog: to classify things or persons, and to associate oneself *with* something or someone else (for example, a friend, a hero, a party, or a philosophy). Each locates identity within the ebb and flow of practice and process; they are both things people do. The latter, in the context of social relations, also implies a degree of reflexivity.

We are now firmly in the realm of social identity… All human identities are in some sense — and usually a stronger rather than a weaker sense — *social* identities. It cannot be otherwise, if only because identity is about meaning, and meaning is not an essential property of words and things. Meanings are always the outcome of agreement or disagreement, always a matter of convention

and innovation, always to some extent shared, always to some extent negotiable.

Some contemporary writers about identity treat it as a basic datum that simply "is." This pays insufficient attention to how identity "works" or "is worked," to process and reflexivity, to the social construction of identity in interaction and institutionally. Understanding these processes is central to understanding what social identity is. Identity can in fact only be understood *as* process. As "being" or "becoming." One's social identity — indeed, one's social identities, for who we are is always singular and plural — is never a final or settled matter. Not even death can freeze the picture: There is always the possibility of a *post mortem* revision of identity (and some identities, that of a martyr, for example, can only be achieved beyond the grave).

So, how to define "social identity?" Minimally, the expression refers to the ways in which individuals and collectivities are distinguished in their social relations with other individuals and collectivities. It is the systematic establishment and signification, between individuals, between collectivities, and between individuals and collectivities, of relationships of similarity and difference. Taken — as they can only be — together, similarity and difference are the dynamic principles of identity, the heart of social life:

…The practical significance of men for one another…is determined by both similarities and differences among them. Similarity as fact or tendency is no less important than difference. In the most varied forms, both are the great principles of all internal and external development. In fact, the cultural history of mankind can be conceived as the history of the struggles and conciliatory attempts between the two.

(Simmel 1950: 30)

Social identity is a game of "playing the *vis-à-vis*" (Boon 1982: 26). Social identity is our understanding of who we are and of who other people are, and, reciprocally, other people's understanding of themselves and of others (which includes us). Social identity, is, therefore, no more essential than meaning; it too is the product of agreement and disagreement, it too is negotiable.

Human social life is unimaginable without some means of knowing who others are and some sense of who we are. Because we cannot rely on our sense of smell or our animal non-verbals (although these are not insignificant in the negotiation of identity during encounters), one of the first things we do on meeting a stranger is attempt to locate them on our social maps, to identify them. And not always successfully: "Mistaken identity" is a common motif of interaction. Someone we thought was Ms. A in fact turns out to be Mrs. Q, or we take someone for French when they are Belgian.

All kinds of people other than social scientists have cause to reflect on social identity during their everyday lives. A common theme in everyday discourse, for example, is lost or confused identity, about people not knowing "who they are," about a "crisis of identity." Sometimes people talk about "social identity"; sometimes they simply talk about "identity." More often than not, however, men and women going about the business of their daily lives are concerned with *specific* social identities. We talk, for example, about whether people are born gay or become gay as a result of the way in which they were brought up. About what it means to be "grown up." About what the difference is between Canadians and Americans. We observe the family who has just moved in around the corner and shake our heads: What can you expect? They come from the wrong part of town. We watch the television news and jump to all kinds of conclusions about current events on the basis of identifications such as "Muslim," "fundamentalist Christian," or whatever.

Social change is often accompanied by rhetoric about "identity under threat." Take, for example, the public debate in the United Kingdom about the European Union. While the regulations governing sausage manufacture are presented as a threat to the "British way of life," the prospect of monetary union in Europe conjures up centuries of strife with our continental neighbors and is interpreted as another attempt to undermine British national identity. Recent debates within the Scandinavian countries about the European Union have thrown a similar barrage of concerns, albeit triggered by different issues.

Whether in the abstract or the concrete, with reference to ourselves or to others, in personal depth or during superficial casual chat, with reference to individuality, nationality, social class, gender or age (etcetera…), it seems that we cannot do without some concepts with which to think about social identity, with which to query and confirm who we are and who others are. This is probably true no matter the language or culture; it has probably always been true. Without frameworks for delineating social identity and identities, I would be the same as you and neither of us could relate to the other meaningfully or consistently. Without social identity, there is, in fact, no society.

---

# 12.  SOCIALIZATION, PAIN, AND THE NORMALIZATION OF SPORTS INJURY

TIMOTHY JON CURRY

*"By the time Sam had reached the elite level in sports, he had already been thoroughly socialized into the informal expectations regarding pain and injury; they had become part of his personal orientation to the sport. Athletes like Sam who pin their chances of material success on a career in sports are aware that the confirmation of their status as*

*an athlete is both crucial and dependent on the opinions of those in the sport who adhere to the norms themselves."*


This is a description of how one individual—Sam—took on the identity of "wrestler." Timothy Curry interviewed Sam extensively and tried to learn the key turning points—"epiphanies"—in his wrestling career and developing identity. We are all socialized into various identities through social interaction, and this is one example. Note that a large part of Sam's socialization into wrestling influenced Sam's definition of things within himself—pain and injury. Even such personal matters result from socialization and are part of our developing social identities.


This study describes how Sam, an elite amateur wrestler competing in a "big-time" college wrestling program, came to accept pain and injury as a normal part of his sports role-identity. Although this is a single career history, the social processes involved in the normalization of sports injury affect thousands of athletes and sports enthusiasts....

[T]he normalization of sports injury needs to be examined in a broader context than the social construction of masculinity. Furthermore, it needs to be examined over an athlete's life course, because both primary and secondary socialization is likely to contribute to the normalization of injury. By the time the elite athlete appears on the scene in college or high school, he or she may already have developed an attitude that regards even serious injury as routine.

This research takes a role-identity approach that focuses on Sam's imaginative view of himself as an occupant of a social position (McCall and Simmons, 1978). Compatible with the notion of role-identity is the concept of career, defined in classic symbolic interactionist terms as having two components: an objective side, which involves moving through a sequence of social positions; and a subjective side, which involves the changes in self-conception that accompany these positional relocations (Goffman 1961; Lindesmith, Strauss, and Denzin 1991).

From "A Little Pain Never Hurt Anyone: Athletic Career Socialization and the Normalization of Sports Injury," by Timothy Jon Curry. Excerpted from pp. 273–290, *Symbolic Interaction*, 16(3), 1993.

As a career becomes established, it serves as a "moving perspective in which the person sees his life as a whole and interprets the meaning of his various attributes, actions, and the things that happen to him" (Hughes 1958, p. 63). A career history is similar to a life history in that certain decisive moments or experiences in the respondent's life are regarded as more important than others for interpretive analysis. These turning points or experiences that the respondent recollects are termed *epiphanies*. Denzin (1989, p. 17) suggests that the types of epiphanies employed by writers such as James Joyce may be useful in constructing life histories. He identifies four: minor or illustrative, major, cumulative, and relived. Minor or illustrative epiphanies reveal underlying tensions in a situation or relationship; major epiphanies concern important turning points or moments of truth when character is revealed. The cumulative epiphany occurs as a result of a series of events, and the relived epiphany refers to the process of reliving any of the other types of epiphanies or going through them again.

## PROCEDURES

This telling of Sam's career history involves one cumulative, three major, and two minor epiphanies. I gathered this history during three tape-recorded interviews, each lasting between one to two hours. The interviews were spread over several weeks....

The idea of using epiphanies to organize this material developed after the interviews themselves. There were simply too many injuries to report in detail, and a mere listing of these injuries would fail to communicate their relative significance to Sam or to his career. Several injuries — some quite severe — that Sam or I did not view as turning points have been omitted or are discussed very briefly....

## ATHLETIC CAREER SOCIALIZATION

Sam's family history was such that being an athlete was virtually an ascribed identity; the only question was what type of athlete he would become and how far he would go in his career. Sam's parents assumed that Sam would participate in sports as the natural order of things, and thus an athletic identity was "bestowed" on him before he was born (Weigert, Teitge, and Teitge 1986). Sam's father was still quite active in sports when his son was born, both as a player and as an owner of a local semiprofessional football team. He had been a good athlete in high school, participating in football, basketball, track, and baseball (but not wrestling). Sam's mother was also a good high school athlete — a runner. She was favorably disposed to having her son and his sisters participate in neighborhood sports at an early age. Her father also had been an accomplished athlete in high school; his sports including wrestling. Two of Sam's uncles on his mother's side had wrestled successfully in high school and participated in other sports. Sam's mother's youngest brother, his favorite uncle, was also very athletic, although he did not try out for high school sports. This uncle, at age sixteen, taught Sam his first wrestling moves: "When I was three, he'd come over and start tickling me. I'd run around and he'd grab my leg and take me down. He still follows my career."

Sam feels that his family's competitive spirit has influenced both him and his sisters. His elder sister, who is two years older than he, was already participating in T-ball when he was five. She and Sam continued to participate in sports together over the next six years. Sam's mother encouraged his sports participation, and his father helped organize the teams, eventually becoming a coach.

The earliest sports injury that Sam recollects occurred during his first year of T-ball:

I was at second base when a ball was hit to the outfield, but I wasn't paying attention. I turned around, and "Whap!" the ball hit me in the eye, and my eye swelled up real big. I got a big black eye, about the size of half a softball. I think I cried right when it happened, but after that it was all right. I sat back on the bench, and then I said, "Dad, let me go back out." I was really competitive, and I liked to play. He let me go back out, but I couldn't see very well, so I had to come out and sit on the bench anyway. After the game, I had to go to the doctor. The swelling was so bad they had me sit out in the sun for a few days to make it go down.

His parents' reaction to his first sports injury established a pattern that has not varied much over the course of his sports career. His mother reacted negatively to the injury; Sam remembers that she said, "'Oh, my poor baby,' and stuff like that." She "went nuts" over his father's decision to return him to the game, and refused to talk to her husband for a week after the game. Sam comments: "Now it's a constant battle between my mom and dad when I get hurt."

Upon reflecting on his parents' behavior, Sam realized that his mother reacted in much the same way as his grandmother had reacted when her sons were injured: "My grandmother never went to watch my uncles wrestle or play football. She'd watch them play baseball and basketball, but she couldn't handle the contact sports. To this day, she hasn't seen me wrestle." His mother acts the same, especially when he wrestles tough opponents. She leaves, pretending to go to the rest room.

His father, on the other hand, shows no emotional reaction to his injuries and claims that they are not significant. His father's lack of concern about Sam's injuries are identical to his lack of concern about his own injuries:

My dad played a lot of ball, and when he'd get hurt, he'd still play. I got to see my dad playing football and baseball and getting his nose broken and stuff like that. He broke his nose ten times, even had surgery done on it...he also had five knee surgeries, and one involved major reconstruction. I'm sure he's going to have arthritis some day. He had many broken fingers and other minor injuries. Thus, he knows what he is saying when he says I have only a slight injury, and he says, "Hey, let's get up; let's get going." He believes in the rough and tough idea. I'm seeing my dad playing ball with his broken nose and all kinds of busted fingers, and I think, "I want to be like Dad and be tough like that." In wrestling, we get all kinds of minor injuries, and we "shake it out" and still compete with them, so we're doing the same thing.

Thus, Sam's attitudes toward sports injury are linked to his earliest memories of his father's sports career, and to his father's definition of sports injury as normal and to be expected. Sam's routine acceptance of injury is challenged, however, by both his mother and his grandmother. The issue of the struggle, as Sam sees it, is being "rough and tough" versus "being treated like a baby." Not surprisingly, Sam has chosen the more masculine characterization of himself as tough; in this and the following accounts, he stresses repeatedly that his behavior is similar to his father's. In this regard, Sam's career history is similar to those alluded to by researchers who have studied the development of masculinity and the male identity. Sam used "toughness" in sports to separate himself from femininity and to develop masculinity; many other boys have used sports similarly (Connell 1990; Messner 1989).

At age seven, Sam began his socialization into what became his main career in sports. With his parents' encouragement, he became an active participant in the wrestling program at the neighborhood community center. There, he could wrestle with the older boys, and occasionally was coached by volunteers. His father orchestrated Sam's career by organizing trips and driving him to meets and tournaments: "I was in a national competition by the time I was seven, and right away my dad [was] worried about my season."

By the time Sam was eight-and-a-half or nine, he was participating in competitions sponsored by the Amateur Athletic Union (AAU); by the time he was ten, his father had organized a wrestling club. Thirty-five people joined, and they traveled to meets in Ohio and other states. Although Sam had no brothers to practice wrestling with at home, his elder sister was a good partner, and he wrestled with her. His cousin on his father's side also started wrestling when Sam was nine. Sam's sports circle, then, included family, friends, and neighbors, and, for the most part, was still considered recreational fun.

Sam views his family's involvement in sports as a special way to maintain closeness, especially with his father. To Sam, sports participation has been a means of expressing love: "We're not the kind of

people who are real mushy. I don't think I've told my dad I love him, but he knows that through all the stuff we do."

The meaning of sports and sports injury is thus deeply embedded in Sam's affection towards his father. An injury not only threatens his immediate participation in sports but also threatens the relationship he and his dad have established, a relationship that apparently cannot be reestablished as easily in other domains. As a means of expressing love, however, sports become problematic at higher levels of competition, because ever greater skill demands are placed on the participants. When an athlete can no longer achieve success, he may experience difficulty in maintaining bonds with teammates, coaches, and even his father (Curry 1991).

## Becoming Supermotivated

Sam's socialization into sports as a career accelerated when he began going to summer and weekend camps. His skills continued to improve, and he believed that he could excel with more training. At the national AAU tournaments, held in Lincoln, Nebraska, he learned about a wrestling camp that taught young athletes how to be "supermotivated." He and his father felt that attending this camp might give him an edge over the other boys, and this experience proved to be a major epiphany in Sam's career.

The coach of the camp had been a wrestler himself, and was well connected in the world of amateur wrestling. The camp gave Sam the idea that earning a college scholarship through wrestling was a real possibility: "There were a lot of kids from really poor families. He let them come, but he made them work for it. He'd let them know that just because they were poor they didn't have to go and be idiots."

The coach had been injured in a trampoline accident and was paralyzed from the waist down. Nonetheless, occasionally he left his wheelchair and crawled on to the mat to wrestle with the boys. Sam recollects that once he lectured the boys about being a quitter. He said, "Look at me, I didn't quit. I could have easily given up; instead I just got a million-dollar grant from the state to run this project." Sam feels that this camp taught him that hard work and discipline pay off, and that injury need not prevent success, even if it confines you to a wheelchair.

The coach stressed adherence to strict training rules and very vigorous exercise, even for his youngest students. Sam described a few of the techniques the coach used to instill discipline and motivation. On one occasion, Sam maintained the wrestler's crouch position for several hours, normally an impossible task for a preadolescent. The coach had rigged up a table top so that it could be lowered until it was a few feet from the floor, and Sam crouched underneath until the coach said it was time to quit. On another occasion, Sam was forced to run five miles with bags of sand in a knapsack on his back; the coach followed in his car to make sure that he kept moving. Such techniques were not used with all the boys, but mostly with those the coach believed had special talent. Sam was honored by receiving such attention, and was further gratified when he was given the privilege of sleeping in the coach's house during camp. At this young age, then, the experience of pain became associated with motivation to achieve excellence in sports and with special treatment as a favored athlete. Like bodybuilders, who learn to appreciate pain because it means that muscle tissue is being torn down and rebuilt (Ewald and Jiobu 1985), Sam learned to appreciate pain because it meant that he was becoming "supermotivated."

Sam's participation in sports camps and adult-supervised competition at an early age was not unusual; many parents seek to gain an edge for their children through such practices. Abusive treatment of children is not uncommon in these camps, in part because some parents and coaches are convinced that harsh discipline will make their children more competitive (Curry and Jiobu 1984, p. 56). As athletes such as Sam come to define situations in roughly the same manner as their coaches, they acquire the key values shared by elite athletes, including "what is prized and what is disdained" (Shibutani 1986, p. 156). What is disdained is not injury or pain themselves, but allowing pain or injury to stand in the way of accomplishing a goal.

## An End to Recreational Sports

From Sam's perspective, his first significant sports injury occurred when he was twelve years old. Be-side the black eye described earlier, he had jammed and broken several fingers, but because those injuries healed quickly and did not incapacitate him, they did not count as real injuries. He suffered a more serious injury when he was playing basketball with his sister's friends, who were fourteen or fifteen years old. One of the players, "a guy 6920 and 190 pounds," crashed into him and stepped heavily on his foot while trying to rebound the ball. No one believed that Sam was hurt, but he felt intense pain in his ankle and had to hop the half-mile home on one leg:

By the time I got to the edge of the grass, I could not stand on one leg anymore, so I crawled the rest of the way. My mom saw me and came running out and got me into the house. We took my shoe and sock off, and you could see the "c-o-n-v-e-r-s-e" on the heel mark on my ankle. You could still see it six weeks later. She rushed me to the hospital and got it X-rayed. Then they called my dad. His first comments are "What are you breaking your ankle for? We had to go to the tournament!" I'm thinking, "This guy must be crazy."

After reflecting further about what his father had said, however, Sam decided not to take risks in other sports and to focus on wrestling. Reluctantly, he gave up basketball, football, and other recreational sports he loved. This injury thus helped Sam define his sports career, but it also turned him away from what had been a routine and enjoyable part of his everyday life.

Sam's father was eager to narrow his choices in the hopes of creating greater opportunities for him. Coakley (1991) describes such a process as an "identity tunnel" in which young athletes are channeled into increasingly fewer activities, all of them sports related. By the time they are in their late teens, such youngsters will have few identities other than that of being a star athlete, and little experience with other roles. Now, Sam had entered the "identity tunnel."

### Rendezvous with Sports Medicine

Although Sam has been encouraged constantly by his father to consider injury simply as a normal part of his sports career, he has relied on his mother to attend to his actual medical needs and take him to the doctor or the hospital. As a result, he has been subjected to her fear of sports injury and her perspective of sports as recreation — views that undercut and challenged those of his father. His next wrestling injury marked a minor epiphany; it was the first time he received care from a specialist in sports medicine whose views supported those of his father.

When Sam broke his thumb at school during wrestling practice, his father sought care from his own sports medicine physician, who was both more knowledgeable and more tolerant about sports injuries:

My dad had this sports medicine guy way back then, who always looked at his stuff and fixed him up so he could play. Thereafter, when I would break a middle finger, I would get it taped and keep on wrestling. My mom hated my dad for this. This went on for three weeks. She hated him for taking me to this sports medicine guy. I wanted to wrestle too, but my mom couldn't understand why I would have to do this in the seventh grade. Never did make up with him over this. She finally just accepted my getting hurt all the time. When my mom got me started in sports, she said we could play, but if we got hurt we had to quit. That wasn't the way it turned out.

With a sports physician now on hand to smooth the way, the next four years involved no more than one week off at a time to treat four different broken fingers, including "a thumb and a pinky." The absence of any incapacitating injury was important because it allowed Sam to prove himself as an elite wrestler in statewide high school competition.

Success in high school is seen as crucial by ambitious athletes such as Sam because they must demonstrate superior performance if they hope to win a scholarship to college. To illustrate, fewer than 5 percent of high school football, basketball, and baseball players are accepted into college sports programs (Coakley 1990).

***Becoming a Champion***  When asked "at what point [he] knew [he] had it all together as a wrestler," Sam replied that as a freshman in high school, he had begun to achieve everything he wanted. At one large tournament for high school wrestlers, he set a new record for the number of persons defeated in a single weight class (128). From that moment, Sam knew that he had begun

to make a reputation for himself and that he would be recognized by others as an elite wrestler. He still identifies strongly with those who have won: "All the big names, the guys that have gotten to the Olympics, they have won that tournament. I've still got things I want to achieve, but right there I knew I would be a good college wrestler."

By the time Sam was a senior in high school, he had won the state tournament three times. He had failed, however, to win the Catholic Invitational Tournament (CIT). This prestigious tournament was especially important to his teammates and coaches at the Catholic high school he attended. Although he had finished second and third in previous CITs, Sam was worried that "everybody would say I was a fluke" if he failed to finish first in his senior year. Other well-known wrestlers had won this tournament as well as the state championship in their senior year. Shortly before the tournament, however, he came home from practice with a sore knee. He thought nothing of it, but by next morning the knee was stiff.

By practice time, the knee had swollen to the size of a baseball and was very sore. ("When I banged it on the wrestling pad, it would be so painful that I just wanted to drop on my butt and hold it.") At first, Sam assumed he would have to miss the tournament, but an assistant coach persuaded him to go ahead and wrestle, even with the pain. A shot of cortisone from the local hospital reduced the pain and swelling. Both his father and a physical therapist were doubtful about the wisdom of competing and feared that he was taking things too far by risking further injury to his knee. His high school coach was also fearful, and insisted that Sam demonstrate his ability to wrestle during practice with teammates. Sam himself felt that he had a 50–50 chance of making the knee worse, but nonetheless decided it was worth the risk to win the tournament for himself and the school. Even so, he confesses now that he was "kind of scared." To make matters even more difficult, because Sam had not initially planned on entering the tournament, he had gained a few pounds and was over the weight limit. On the way to the tournament, he rode an exercise bike for several hours in the back of a recreational vehicle to lose those pounds. He arrived both dehydrated and with a swollen, sore knee. During the tournament, he wore two knee pads and continuously asked himself, "Why am I doing this?" The answer was that he believed he "was going someplace, and the college recruiters will be at the meet." As it turned out, Sam faced a freshman in the final round of the competition, and won the match easily. He felt he had lived up to other people's expectations and had proved that he was not "a fluke."

Overall, this experience with the CIT was a major epiphany in Sam's career and his developing sense of self. It was the first time he had wrestled in real pain, and against the wishes of a medical specialist and his father. In this way, he demonstrated that he was prepared to take risks and to "pay the price for success." In mastering his fear of the knee injury, Sam also became more aware of his body's vulnerabilities. In the past, he had never worn knee pads, but now, he said, "I started to take care of my knees." The implication is that Sam's identity transformation from an amateur athlete to an expert was nearly complete; he now realized that he should attempt to protect himself more adequately if he hoped to continue on this career path.

At this point in his sports career, it appears that Sam's masculinity needs and interpersonal relations with his father were becoming leitmotifs rather than dominant themes. Sam had internalized a sports role-identity sufficiently to be concerned about his reputation and was seeking athletic immortality by establishing a record that would live on in his high school after he was gone. In other words, he was concerned with his post-self — how he would be remembered by the members of the wrestling subculture in the future (Schmitt and Leonard 1986). The use of pain killers (and steroids) is a serious problem in high school athletics partly because of such pressures induced by self and others (Goldman 1992; Guttmann 1988).

### Routinization of Injury at the University
Because Sam had had a stellar career in high school, he was offered scholarships to several universities. Having traveled to a number of the major wrestling schools in AAU competition, he thought he already knew what they were like. He made his selection on the basis of his personal knowledge of the coach and the assistant coach who had been hired recently to upgrade the program. Sam believed that the assistant coach would be a good

wrestling partner for him, and that the head coach would provide valuable career advice. (These expectations have been met.)

Less expected, however, was the sudden increase in exposure to injuries. If Sam had thought about it, he might have wondered why the letter his parents received from the athletic director welcoming their son to the sports program stressed that all athletes were fully covered for their medical expenses during practices and competition but that the university's coverage ended at graduation. Sam soon discovered that his opponents were stronger and more experienced, and his teammates were more determined and competitive.

Moreover, the situational clues for normalizing injury were highly visible in the wrestling room. Medical trainers were present during all practices, and a sports physician was usually on call in the building. Practice seldom stopped for long when a wrestler was injured; the wrestler moved or was moved out of the way, and the coaches showed little concern or sympathy. The norm was to ignore injuries and to continue practicing. According to Sam:

When our heavyweight got hurt and he was screaming, coach said: "Be quiet, you'll be okay. Take the pain." Some people heard it and didn't understand…he just wanted him to take it like a man.

The ambulatory injured, or "walking wounded," were still expected to come to practice; if possible, they worked out on the rowing machines or exercise bikes. These machines were positioned in plain view at the front of the room, and someone was always riding them. Experienced wrestlers hated to be seen on machines during practice because it meant that they had lost their status temporarily as team members.

The coach's philosophy was that wrestling is primarily a matter of having a winning attitude and that worrying about injury would interfere with that attitude. If a wrestler sustained what appeared to be a serious injury, it had to be documented and certified by the medical staff to be accepted by the coach. One dramatic case showed what could happen if a wrestler claimed an injury that could not be documented. In this incident, a "walk-on" wrestler suddenly began writhing and moaning on the floor during practice, covering his face with his hands. Apparently, he had received a blow to his neck or head. Because all head or spinal injuries were taken very seriously by the medical staff, he was rushed to the hospital for observation and tests. Tests, however, did not reveal any evidence of injury, and the wrestler refused to remain in the hospital for extended observation. (He had midterm examinations to take). He never regained a position on the team because the coach suspected he was malingering, and the team physician would not clear him for practice because he refused further observation. He spent the rest of the season as an onlooker.

At the elite level, those who do not share the norms that normalize pain and injury risk being dropped from the team or placed in secondary positions, as demonstrated by the case of the unfortunate walk-on. By the time Sam had reached the elite level in sports, he had already been thoroughly socialized into the informal expectations regarding pain and injury; they had become part of his personal orientation to the sport. Athletes like Sam who pin their chances of material success on a career in sports are aware that the confirmation of their status as an athlete is both crucial and dependent on the opinions of those in the sport who adhere to the norms themselves (Donnelly and Young 1988; Hughes and Coakley 1991; McCall and Simmons 1978).

### Completing the Cycle: Becoming a Role Model

We end Sam's career history at the conclusion of his junior year. When asked how the season had gone, he reported that he was 31-9-2 for the year. Still, he added, "[During the regular season] it's not like I got beat by nine guys; one guy beat me three times, one guy twice, and the other two were by two different guys. So I only got beat by four guys, and I ended up beating them during the season too…I only lost in two dual meets all season long." In an important boost to his self-esteem and career plans, he qualified for the national championships and was one of four members of the team to be designated All-American, even though his fifth-place finish was personally disappointing.

Sam has spent 14 of his 21 years working on wrestling, and his hopes that it will "pay off for [him]" depend greatly on what happens in the next few years. He wants to be a wrestling coach, perhaps combining this position with a career as a sports commentator and public speaker. In order to achieve this ambition, he believes he must become a conference and national champion, earn a spot on the Olympic team, and win a medal. Although these high aspirations may seem farfetched to others, Sam regards them as possibilities because he associates daily with people who have achieved such goals in their own careers. If these plans do not materialize, Sam has contingent career plans that he will pursue….

Because Sam's involvement in wrestling has become an important part of who he is and what he wants to become, he accepts pain and injury as part of his role-identity, rather than as a sign of bravery or macho masculinity: "I knew they [injuries] were going to happen. So yeah, I accept it. It doesn't scare me—I knew that eventually I'd hurt my knee or break my ankle. You start getting competitive, and you can be injured pretty easy."

Injury is an unavoidable part of Sam's sport. Sam's coach has been injured severely, as have all the assistant coaches. Moreover, we should not forget that Sam routinely injures others: he broke the hand of an assistant coach in practice, and he has cut his training partner's face many times ("fifty stitches' worth so far").

Moreover, as Sam's injuries have accumulated, so has his experience in dealing with them; they have given him a unique fund of professional knowledge and information. His ability to draw on these experiences provides him with considerable independence in assessing the possible risks an injury poses for his career. Thus, while Sam's attitude toward injury may seem cavalier to others, it is anything but. He has experienced and recovered from many injuries, and he realizes fully the pain and anguish they cause.

## CONCLUSION

Sam's career history reveals some important insights regarding the cumulative effects of primary and secondary socialization for the normalization of the pain of injury. I conclude by reviewing key steps in the socialization process that highlight how masculinity and male identity issues became intertwined with professionalization. First, Sam's prenatal sports identity was shaped by the expectations of his immediate and extended family. By the time he was six years old, his sense of self was embedded thoroughly in sports. Second, early in childhood, Sam accepted his father's definition of sports injuries as routine and insignificant. Sam used "toughness" in sports to separate himself from femininity and to develop masculine identity; simultaneously, he also learned that athletes had to be tough if they were to be good in sports. Third, as a youth, Sam associated pain with excellence in sports and with special treatment as an athlete. He also learned that sports activity and achievement could serve as a means of expressing love between himself and his father. By the time he was twelve, Sam had entered an "identity tunnel," which focused his activities around wrestling. At this point, career concerns became as important as masculinity issues.

Fourth, as he matured, Sam developed considerable experience with pain and injury. His sense of mastery and competency was strengthened by overcoming progressively more serious injuries. As part of this secondary socialization into the normalization of pain and injury, he encountered physicians and medical trainers who kept him functional, if not healthy. Fifth, his most serious injuries came late in his career as his teammates and opponents became stronger and more skilled at dangerous techniques. Finally, as Sam's athletic career neared conclusion, he had less time to accomplish the career goals he had envisioned, and the pressure to ignore injury intensified accordingly. In sum, then, Sam's case indicates that masculinity needs or issues were of greatest importance during primary socialization, while professionalization became an increasing important factor during secondary socialization.

Sam's case offered some important insights for understanding apparent contradictions concerning masculinity, professionalization, and the meaning of injury. For example, Sam did not feel especially proud of his injuries, was initially reluctant to discuss them, and seldom referred to them as signs of masculinity. While outsiders might believe that honor and esteem were bestowed on wrestlers for withstanding pain and injury, among the athletes themselves, the occurrence of injury brought no special respect. In fact, too much attention to pain and injury lost respect because it implied a lack of focus on the primary task: competition and winning. Sam's reluctance to discuss his injuries thus reflected the

status concerns of an elite athlete. On the other hand, Sam felt obligated to maintain the appearance of toughness on several occasions during his career — in the wrestling room, at the hospital, and in sports camp. Thus, while it can be said that on such occasions Sam assumed a macho identity, his most consistent concern was with maintaining or regaining peak performance.

In addition, Sam's perspective of sports injuries as normal continued after his masculinity needs were met. The persistence of such a belief, however, requires a more complex explanation than either masculinity needs or professionalization alone. Such an explanation begins by recognizing that contradictory definitions of the meaning of sports injury are gradually eliminated once an athlete has entered the identity tunnel. To illustrate, Sam's father, coaches, and physicians normalized injury to such an extent that routine occurrences such as broken fingers were not considered significant. Moreover, once Sam had internalized this orientation to injury, it was not likely to be modified. Change would require a major conversion of the self, similar in some regards to a religious conversion (Hewitt and Hewitt 1986). Indeed, such a change would threaten the social relations built up over a lifetime within an entire sports community; many sports, such as wrestling, cannot be engaged in without injury. Thus, maturity and loss of skills will not automatically bring about a change in attitude towards sports injury by former athletes. Sam, like his father, is likely to persist in believing that a little pain never hurt anybody.

## REFERENCES

Coakley, Jay J. 1990. *Sport in Society*. St. Louis: Times Mirror/ Mosby.
——. 1991. "Reconceptualizing 'Burnout' Among Adolescent Athletes: From a Personal Trouble to a Social Issue." Presidential address at the annual conference of the North American Society for the Sociology of Sport, Milwaukee, WI.
Connell, R. W. 1990. "An Iron Man: The Body and Some Contradictions of Hegemonic Masculinity." Pp. 83–95 in *Sport, Men, and the Gender Order*, edited by Michael A. Messner and Donald F. Sabo. Champaign, IL: Human Kinetics Books.
Curry, Timothy Jon. 1991. "Fraternal Bonding in the Locker Room: A Profeminist Analysis of Talk About Competition and Women." *Sociology of Sport Journal* 8: 119–135.

Curry, Timothy Jon and Robert M. Jiobu. 1984. *Sports: A Social Perspective*. Englewood Cliffs, NJ: Prentice-Hall.

Denzin, Norman K. 1989. *Interpretive Interactionism*. Newbury Park, CA: Sage.

Donnelly, Peter and Kevin Young. 1988. "The Construction and Confirmation of Identity in Sport Subcultures." *Sociology of Sport Journal* 5: 223–240.

Ewald, Keith and Robert M. Jiobu. 1985. "Explaining Positive Deviance: Becker's Model and the Case of Runners and Body Builders." *Sociology of Sport Journal* 2: 144–156.

Goffman, Erving. 1961. "The Moral Career of the Mental Patient." Pp. 128–169 in *Asylums: Essays on the Social Situation of Mental Patients and Other Inmates*. Garden City, NY: Doubleday.

Goldman, Bob. 1992. "Retooling Your Body." *Fitness Plus* 3: 21–24.

Guttmann, Allen. 1988. *A Whole New Ball Game*. Chapel Hill: University of North Carolina Press.

Hewitt, John P. and Myrna Livingston Hewitt. 1986. *Introducing Sociology*. Englewood Cliffs, NJ: Prentice-Hall.

Hughes, Everett C. 1958. *Men and Their Work*. New York: Free Press.

Hughes, Robert and Jay Coakley. 1991. "Positive Deviance Among Athletes: The Implications of Overconformity to the Sport Ethic." *Sociology of Sport Journal* 8: 307–325.

Lindesmith, Alfred R., Anselm L. Strauss, and Norman K. Denzin. 1991. *Social Psychology*, 7th ed. Englewood Cliffs, NJ: Prentice-Hall.

McCall, George J. and J. L. Simmons. 1978. *Identities and Interactions*, rev. ed. New York: Free Press.

Messner, Michael A. 1989. "Masculinities and Athletic Careers." *Gender and Society* 3: 71–88.

Schmitt, Raymond L. and Wilbert M. Leonard, II. 1986. "Immortalizing the Self through Sport." *American Journal of Sociology* 91: 1088–1111.

Shibutani, Tamotsu. 1986. *Social Processes*. Berkeley: University of California Press.

Weigert, Andrew J., J. Smith Teitge, and Dennis W. Teitge. 1986. *Society and Identity*. Cambridge: Cambridge University Press.

# Part III
# SOCIAL ORGANIZATION

Out of social interaction develops social organization. Groups, formal organizations, communities, and societies are all examples of organization. Part III tries to show the diversity and importance of social organization in all our lives.

There is a commonality among all types of organization: Social interaction and a set of agreements—rules, ideas, and structure—that hold organization together. Susan Wheelan introduces us to two views of the group in social science. Dexter Dunphy describes the importance of primary groups, and Ruth Horowitz describes the importance of one primary group from the perspective of those who are part of it. Horowitz also introduces us to the meaning of a community. Kai Erikson underlines the importance of community by showing us what happens when communities are destroyed. Finally, Marvin Olsen introduces us to the most all-encompassing social organization of them all: society.

# 13.  WHAT IS A GROUP? TWO VIEWS

SUSAN A. WHEELAN

*"From this author's perspective, groups are very real…. Groups influence our thoughts and behavior even when we are alone…. Groups expand or limit our personal choices and even the contents of our minds…. Forces that are so powerful cannot be ignored or denied."*

For sociology to be a discipline in the academic community, it must cut out an area of study and show its relevance to understanding something. Because it arrived late to the university scene, it has had to fight hard in relation to other disciplines—especially psychology and biology—in its claim that the "social world" must be understood on its own terms, and that other disciplines, by focusing on individuals, do not capture this world. Wheelan's selection makes this argument and offers some possible reasons as to why it is so difficult for people to see organizations of people—what she calls "groups" — as worthy of study.

*Webster's* Ninth New Collegiate Dictionary (1989) defines a *group* as "a number of individuals assembled together or having some unifying relationship" (p. 539). In contrast, Luft (1984) defines a group as follows:

…a living system, self-regulating through shared perception and interaction, sensing, and feedback, and through interchange with the environment. Each group has unique wholeness qualities that become patterned by way of members' thinking, feeling, and communicating, into structured subsystems. The group finds some way to maintain balance while moving through progressive changes, creating its own guidelines and rules, and seeking its own goals through recurring cycles of interdependent behavior. (p. 2)

These two definitions could not be more different. The first suggests that the term *group* is merely a convenient way to classify individuals who have, at least at the time, some common characteristic. The second asserts that a group is a living entity that transcends and cannot be explained by individual experience. In fact, Luft's definition suggests that a group may be as real as an individual, because an individual could readily be defined in a similar way. An individual is also a living system, self-regulating through shared perception and interaction, sensing, and feedback. An individual has unique wholeness qualities, or personality, that become patterned by way of thinking, feeling, and communicating. Individuals also seek to maintain balance while moving through progressive developmental changes, creating their own guidelines and rules, and seeking their own goals through recurring cycles of interaction with others.

For nearly a century, there has been debate among social scientists about the reality of groups. In 1895, Gustav Le Bon warned that groups are very real and potentially dangerous. He proposed that a group can take over the minds of its members and, in some cases, cause individuals to behave savagely (Le Bon 1960).

From Susan A. Wheelan, *Group Processes: A Developmental Perspective.* Copyright © 1994 by Allyn and Bacon. Reprinted/ Adapted by permission.

In recent times, the reemergence of youthful street gangs who attack innocent strangers has renewed scientific and public interest in this phenomenon originally described by Le Bon. The term *wilding* has been applied to such incidents and discussion, concern, and public outcry have ensued.

On the other hand, F. H. Allport (1924) maintained that groups are not real. They exist only in the behavior of individuals. A group is simply the shared thoughts, feelings, and behavior patterns that exist among group members. Other theories, however, disagreed with Allport's and stressed that a group is an entity that cannot be explained by understanding the total individual psychologies of its members (Agazarian & Peters 1981; Durkheim 1897; Lewin 1951; Trotter 1916; Warriner 1956). Still others, while not using Le Bon's term *group mind*, used similar concepts to describe group-level phenomena. Cartwright and Zander (1968), for example, maintained that a group can be emotionally healthy or pathological. Cattell (1951) described groups as possessing different personalities....

The debate over the reality of groups continues.... Many writers and researchers have described the U.S. ideological focus on individualism (Bellah, Madsen, Sullivan, Swidler & Tipton 1985; Mills 1959; Slater 1966). There tends to be a bias in U.S. theories and research toward the study of the individual as opposed to the group. Zander (1979) spoke of this bias when he said that "the theories that do exist...seldom aid in understanding groups as such, or even the behavior of members in behalf of their groups, because the theories often are based on ideas taken from individual psychology, and these are primarily concerned with the actions of individuals for the good of those individuals" (p. 423).

...Americans have been described as materialistic. That is, things that can be seen are worthy of study, whereas things that cannot be seen are relegated to the realm of myth and superstition. Groups cannot be seen *per se*. When we look at a group, we see a collection of individuals. Individuals have a clear physical reality. The physical reality of groups is not as apparent. Therefore, we tend to study the individual members much more than the group-as-a-whole (Agazarian & Peters 1981).

D. T. Campbell (1958) stated that differences in the reality of an object or person as compared to a group are a matter of perception. Physical objects or beings have boundaries and are solid. We can use all our senses to confirm their reality. We can touch, see, hear, and use other senses to test the reality of an object or human being. Fewer sources of data can confirm the reality of a group. However, some of the factors that organize our perceptions of physical objects can be applied to groups as well. In determining whether a number of objects or persons are an entity, we take proximity and boundaries into account. Similarity and sharing a common fate are also principles that organize our perceptions. Thus, a number of individuals, who are perceived as similar in some ways, are found in close proximity, and seem to share a common fate, can be as much an entity as physical objects meeting the same criteria. For example, we recognize an ecosystem composed of animals, plants, bacteria, and their environment as an entity. In our daily experience, we also recognize groups as entities. We speak of the team's loss, the workgroup's success, the government's policy, and the class's behavior. In our minds, an ecosystem or a group is an entity composed of interdependent elements....

Cassirer (1957), a philosopher, believed that human behavior could only be understood by looking at the context in which it occurred and at how societal institutions mutually influence each other and the individual. Mead (1934) said that even the contents of our minds and our self-concepts are learned in interaction with others. Lewin (1951) agreed. What motivates individual behavior is the influences and tensions affecting the individual at a particular point in time and in a particular social situation. The social situation, or group, is not merely a collection of people but a set of relationships and roles. Thus, we must learn more about these social situations and the laws that govern them in order to understand individuals.

Much of the research conducted by students of Lewin and other social scientists reinforces the validity of groups. Our perception of such an obvious thing as length, for example, can be altered by social pressure (Asch 1951). If others say that the shortest rod is the longest, we may agree. Perception is altered by the conventions and pressures of the group (Sherif 1936). The role one holds in a group alters individual behavior as well. Thus, when assigned the role of prison guard, we become more punitive (Zimbardo, Haney, Banks, & Jaffe 1973). Even conscience has not been found to be a stable personality characteristic. Rather, our moral choices are influenced by the groups we belong to and the norms and structures of those groups (Latane & Darley 1968; Milgram 1974).

Other evidence for the reality of groups includes research on the consistency of group development, regardless of individual member characteristics (for examples, see Bennis & Shepard 1956; Caple 1978; Schutz 1966; Tuckman 1965). Also, group goals exert considerable influence on individual behavior (Zander & Newcomb 1967). The physical environment in which a group is operating affects group structure and productivity (Carr & Dabbs 1974; Glass, Singer, & Friedman 1969). The amount of cohesion in a group differentially affects morale, communication, and productivity (Schutz 1958; Shaw & Shaw 1962). Group rules or norms also influence individual behavior and group outcomes (Farrell 1979, 1982; Geller, Goodstein, Silver, & Sternberg 1974).

Finally, common sense tells us that we are profoundly influenced by our group memberships. How we understand facts, events, and even ourselves depends on our memberships. How we behave and how we judge the correctness of our behavior are strongly influenced by our membership and reference groups as well….

From this author's perspective, groups are very real. Groups vary in size from two people to millions of people, and one cannot understand a small group without reference to many larger groups and systems that influence the smaller group. Further, the study of group development and dynamics is presented as potentially critical to human survival. Groups influence our thoughts and behavior even when we are alone. There are many groups that we do not choose to belong to. We are born into a number of groups, and these groups profoundly shape who we are and what we can become. Groups expand or limit our personal choices and even the contents of our minds. At the macro level, the actions of groups expand or limit our chances for physical and psychological survival (Moscovici 1990). Forces that are so powerful cannot be ignored or denied.

## REFERENCES

Agazarian, Y. & R. P. Peters (1981). *The Visible and Invisible Group*. London: Routledge and Kegan Paul.

Allport, F. H. (1924). *Social Psychology*. Boston: Houghton Mifflin.

Asch, S. E. (1951). "Effects of Group Pressure upon the Modification and Distortion of Judgments." In H. Guetzkow (Ed.), *Groups, Leadership and Men* (pp. 177–190). Pittsburgh: Carnegie Press.

Bass, B. M. (1960). *Leadership, Psychology, and Organizational Behavior*. New York: Harper and Row.

Bellah, R., R. Madsen, W. M. Sullivan, A. Swidler, & S. M. Tipton (1985). *Habits of the Heart: Individualism and Commitment in American Life*. New York: Harper and Row.

Bennis, W. G., & H. A. Shepard (1956). "A Theory of Group Development." *Human Relations*, 9, pp. 415–437.

Campbell, D. T. (1958). "Common Fate, Similarity, and Other Indices of the Status of Aggregates of Persons as Social Entities." *Behavioral Science*, 3, pp. 14–25.

Caple, R. B. (1978). "The Sequential Stages of Group Development." *Small Group Behavior*, 9, pp. 470–476.

Carr, S. J., & J. M. Dabbs (1974). "The Effects of Lighting, Distance, and Intimacy of Topic on Verbal and Visual Behavior." *Sociometry*, 37, pp. 592–600.

Cartwright, D., & A. Zander (Eds.). (1968). *Group Dynamics: Research and Theory*. (3d ed.). New York: Harper and Row.

Cassirer, E. (1953–1957). *The Philosophy of Symbolic Forms* (Vols. 1–3). New Haven, CT: Yale University Press.

Cattell, R. B. (1951). "New Concepts for Measuring Leadership in Terms of Group Syntality." *Human Relations*, 4, pp. 161–184.

Comte, A. (1855). *The Positive Philosophy of Auguste Comte*. Trans. Harriet Martineau. New York: Calvin Blanchard.

Durkheim, E. (1897). *Le Suicide*. Paris: F. Alcan. Translation (1951), Glencoe, IL: The Free Press.

Farrell, M. P. (1979). "Collective Projection and Group Structure: The Relationship Between Deviance and Projection in Groups." *Small Group Behavior*, 10, pp. 81–100.

Farrell, M. P. (1982). "Artists' Circles and the Development of Artists." *Small Group Behavior*, 13 (4), pp. 451–474.

Geller, G. M., L. Goodstein, M. Silver, & W. C. Sternberg (1974). "On Being Ignored: The Effects of the Violation of Implicit Rules of Social Interaction." *Sociometry*, 37, pp. 541–556.

Glass, D. C., J. E. Singer, & L. N. Friedman (1969). "Psychic Cost of Adaptation to an Environmental Stressor." *Journal of Personality and Social Psychology*, 12, pp. 200–210.

Hogan, R. (1975). "Theoretical Egocentrism and the Problem of Compliance." *American Psychologist*, 30, pp. 533–539.

Latane, B., & J. M. Darley (1968). "Group Inhibition of Bystander Intervention in Emergencies." *Journal of Personality and Social Psychology*, 10, pp. 215–221.

Le Bon, G. (1895). *The Crowd*. New York: Viking. Reprint 1960.

Lewin, K., R. Lippitt, & R. K. White (1939). "Patterns of Aggressive Behavior in Experimentally Created 'Social Climates.'" *Journal of Social Psychology*, 10, pp. 217–299.

Lewin, K. (1951). *Field Theory in Social Science* (D. Cartwright, Ed.). New York: Harper.

Mead, G. H. (1934). *Mind, Self and Society*. Chicago: University of Chicago Press.

Milgram, S. (1974). *Obedience to Authority*. New York: Harper and Row.

Mills, C. W. (1959). *The Sociological Imagination*. London: Oxford University Press.

Moscovici, S. (1990). "The Generalized Self and Mass Society." In H. T. Himmelweit & G. Gaskell (Eds.), *Societal Psychology* (pp. 66–91). Newbury Park, CA: Sage.

Pepitone, A. (1981). "Lessons from the History of Social Psychology." *American Psychologist*, 36, pp. 972–985.

Schutz, W. C. (1958). *FIRO: A Three Dimensional Theory of Interpersonal Behavior*. New York: Rinehart.

Schutz, W. C. (1966). *The Interpersonal Underworld*. Palo Alto, CA: Science and Behavior Books.

Shaw, M. E., & L. M. Shaw (1962). "Some Effects of Socio-metric Grouping upon Learning in a Second Grade Classroom. *Journal of Social Psychology*, 57, 453–458.

Shaw, M. E. (1981). *Group Dynamics: The Psychology of Small Group Behavior* (3d ed.). New York: McGraw-Hill.

Sherif, M. (1936). *The Psychology of Social Norms*. New York: Harper.

Slater, P. (1966). *Microcosm*. New York: Wiley.

Trotter, W. (1916). *Instincts of the Herd in Peace and War*. London: Hogarth Press.

Tuckman, B. W. (1965). *Developmental Sequences and Systems Theory*. Barre, MA: Clark University Press.

Warriner, C. H. (1956). "Groups are Real: A Reaffirmation." *American Sociological Review*, 21, pp. 549–554.

*Webster's Ninth New Collegiate Dictionary* (1989). Springfield, MA: Merriam-Webster.

Zander, A. (1979). "The Psychology of Group Processes." *Annual Review of Psychology*, 30, pp. 417–452.

Zander, A., & T. Newcomb (1967). "Group Levels of Aspiration in United Fund Campaigns." *Journal of Personality and Social Psychology*, 6, pp. 157–162.

Zimbardo, P. G., C. Haney, W. Banks, & D. Jaffe (April 8, 1973). "A Pirandeloian Prison: The Mind Is a Formidable Jailer." *New York Times Magazine*, pp. 38–60.

# 14. THE IMPORTANCE OF PRIMARY GROUPS

## DEXTER C. DUNPHY

*"Ideology had only an indirect effect on fighting effectiveness in both the U.S. and the German armies. The crucial variable was the degree of preservation of the cohesive primary unit."*

Humans exist in a host of groups. One type of group is called the **primary group**, originally described by Charles Cooley. This article describes the meaning and importance of primary groups. It examines one example: the military unit.

Over our lifetime, we spend much of our time in small groups. We are born into a family. As we grow older, we venture out from our family into the play groups of childhood and later into the cliques and crowds of adolescence. We marry and establish a new family group of our own and participate in the work groups and leisure groups of

From *The Primary Group: A Handbook for Analysis and Field Research*, by Dexter C. Dunphy, pp. 3–5, 24–27, 31–34, 38. Copyright © 1972 by Dexter C. Dunphy. Reprinted by permission of Prentice-Hall, Inc., Englewood Cliffs, NJ.

adulthood. Out of the associations formed in these groups, we fashion and have fashioned in us a changing and developing conception of self; we learn ways of behaving appropriate to varied social situations, and we acquire a set of social values and attitudes that allow us to respond to the structure and pressures of the larger society about us....

For reasons that we will examine here, social scientists have devoted relatively little effort to a close and detailed study of such groups, even though these groups play a vital part in creating human personality and maintaining the integration of the secondary structures of society. We use the term *primary group* to describe groups of this kind. The term was first introduced into social science by Charles Horton Cooley in 1909. At that time, Cooley wrote in his book *Social Organization*:

By primary groups, I mean those characterized by intimate face-to-face association and cooperation. They are primary in several senses, but chiefly in that they are fundamental in forming the social nature and ideas of the individual. The result of intimate association, psychologically, is a certain fusion of individualities in a common whole, so that one's very self, for many purposes at least, is the common life and purpose of the group. Perhaps the simplest way of describing this wholeness is by saying that it is a "we," it involves the sort of sympathy and mutual identification for which "we" is the natural expression.[1]

In Cooley's definition, the word *primary* is used mainly in reference to the fundamental effect such groups have on the formation of the individual personalities of their members. Cooley makes this even clearer when he goes on to state: "The view here maintained is that human nature is not something existing separately in the individual, but a *group-nature* or *primary phase of society*, a relatively simple and general condition of the social mind."[2] Thus the term *primary* refers to the fact that such groups are the earliest kind of human association experienced by the maturing individual and also that the primary, or basic, human qualities are learned in them. Cooley's definition also makes it clear that the effect of such groups on the personalities of members derives from the internalization by them of a psychological representation or image of the group, and that such an identification is indicated by a strong emotional involvement with the group and its members.

In *Introductory Sociology*, written with Angell and Carr, Cooley specified five basic characteristics of primary groups:

- Face-to-face association
- The unspecialized character of the association
- Relative permanence
- The small number of persons involved
- The relative intimacy prevailing among the participants[3]

Cooley himself did not designate larger, more formally organized groups as *secondary groups* but the latter term is now widely used and the two kinds of groups are frequently contrasted.

Later writers dealing specifically with the concept have attempted to modify it in various ways. For instance, Shils gave explicit and thoughtful attention to Cooley's criteria in his important work on the effects of primary group membership in the army in World War II[4] and in his more recent review of primary group research.[5] Shils argues that the existence of an implicit set of group norms is another necessary aspect of the primary group:

By "primary group" we mean a group characterized by a high degree of solidarity, informality in the code of rules that regulate the behavior of its members, and autonomy in the creation of these rules.[6]

## THE STUDY OF PRIMARY GROUPS

Thus, although the primary group is a "small group" in the sense in which that term is used in the social sciences, it is a particular kind of small group. Small groups vary all the way from *ad hoc* collections of students assembled for a single experimental hour to long-term emotionally involving, highly institutionalized groups such as families. It is the latter rather than the former kind of small group to which the term *primary group* refers.

However, the concept of a primary group is better thought of as a variable than as categorical. A group is primary insofar as it is based on and sustains spontaneous participation, particularly emotional involvement and expression. It also provides intrinsic personal satisfaction, that is, personal relationships in the primary group are considered valuable in themselves and not only as means to other ends. This element of intrinsic value is often lacking in formal secondary relations that are explicitly designed to be instrumental.

We define a primary group therefore as *a small group that persists long enough to develop strong emotional attachments between members, at least a set of rudimentary, functionally differentiated roles, and a subculture of its own that includes both an image of the group as an entity and an informal normative system that controls group-relevant action of members*. For Cooley, the important general categories of such groups in our society were "groups of the family, the playground, and the neighborhood."[7] We feel it is necessary to include other kinds of groups that meet our definition but that Cooley did not recognize. As we see it, the following general classes of groups are properly referred to as primary groups:

- Families.
- Free association peer groups of childhood, adolescence, and adulthood. This category would include delinquent gangs and some small, cohesive political elites ("cabals").
- Informal groups existing in organizational settings such as classroom groups, factory work groups, small military units, and "house churches."
- Resocialization groups such as therapy groups, rehabilitation groups, and self-analytic groups....

## AN EXAMPLE: PRIMARY GROUPS IN MILITARY ORGANIZATION

There is a...tradition of organizational analysis that has centered about the problem of maintaining the morale and combat effectiveness of military personnel in armies. Morale has always been a central issue in military organizations, and military organizations have often been organized in small units. However, it was not until World War II that the crucial role of primary groups in maintaining military morale and effectiveness was seriously studied.

A number of excellent studies,[8] appearing since World War II, present information on the role of primary groups in military organizations in both the allied and German armies. However, we shall focus on Shils and Janowitz's study[9] of the Wehrmacht because their conclusions are most succinctly stated and are representative of those found in other studies.

Shils and Janowitz set out to explain the reasons why German army units continued fighting even after central command disintegrated, supplies ceased, and it was obvious that German capitulation was inevitable. During this time, there was remarkably little desertion or active surrender by individuals or groups. It had been suggested that the morale and resistance of the German forces could be attributed to the effectiveness of the Nazi propaganda machine. Shils and Janowitz reviewed the extensive studies made by the Intelligence Section of the Psychological Warfare Di-

vision of SHAEF and came to conclusions that challenge this assumption. They stated their basic hypotheses, which are confirmed by their analysis, as follows:

1. It appears that a soldier's ability to resist is a function of the capacity of his immediate primary group (his squad or section) to avoid social disintegration. When the individual's immediate group, and its supporting formations, met his basic organic needs, offered him affection and esteem from both officers and comrades, supplied him with a sense of power, and adequately regulated his relations with authority, the element of self-concern in battle, which would lead to disruption of the effective functioning of his primary group, was minimized.
2. The capacity of the primary group to resist disintegration was dependent on the acceptance of political, ideological, and cultural symbols (all secondary symbols) only to the extent that these secondary symbols became directly associated with primary gratifications.
3. Once disruption of primary group life resulted through separation, breaks in communications, loss of leadership, depletion of personnel, or major and prolonged breaks in the supply of food and medical care, such an ascendancy of preoccupation with physical survival developed that there was very little "last ditch" resistance.
4. Finally, as long as the primary group structure of the component units of the Wehrmacht persisted, attempts by the Allies to cause disaffection by the invocation of secondary and political symbols (e.g., about the ethical wrongness of the Nationalist Socialist system) were mainly unsuccessful. By contrast, where Allied propaganda dealt with primary and personal values, particularly physical survival, it was more likely to be effective.[10]

From the point of view of the conscripted soldier, this had the following meaning:

For the ordinary German soldier, the decisive fact was that he was a member of a squad or section that maintained its structural integrity and that coincided roughly with the *social* unit that satisfied some of his major primary needs. He was likely to go on fighting, provided he had the necessary weapons, as long as the group possessed leadership with which he could identify himself, and as long as he gave affection to and received affection from the other members of his squad and platoon. In other words, as long as he felt himself to be a member of his primary group and therefore bound by the expectations and demands of its other members, his soldierly achievement was likely to be good.[11]

The authors pointed out that the German general staff instituted a replacement system that maintained the integrity of the primary groups in the army. Units that had undergone a victory were maintained as units as far as possible and when replacements were necessary, the entire personnel of a division would be withdrawn from the front as a unit. Replacements were made while the unit was out of the front line so that a unit was given time to assimilate new members before going into battle again.

Janowitz and Little also suggest[12] that the existence of cohesive primary groups does not necessarily contribute to the goals of the military organization. If this is to happen, the primary group must actively espouse the goals of the larger organization of which it is a part. Essentially the same conclusion was reached by Speien. He noted that studies of U.S. soldiers during World War II showed that they had little knowledge of and little verbalized commitment to the war.[13] He then raised the question: Why, if this were true, did they fight so well? He concluded, on reviewing the evidence available, that this was because primary group relations sustained morale and supported a generalized commitment to the military and its goals. Janowitz and Little illustrate this with the case of segregated Negro units in World War II, which were very cohesive but developed "defensive norms" that broke with the general commitment because these groups interpreted military authority as depreciating their personal dignity. Shils has also argued along the same lines, stating that "primary group solidarity functions in the corporate body to strengthen the motivation for the fulfillment of substantive prescriptions or sense of obligation.... It cannot be said that goals are set by membership in the primary group but only that efforts to achieve the legitimate, formally prescribed goals may be strengthened by such membership."[14]

A key position in terms of the integration of primary group goals and organizational goals is that of the formal leader of the unit, for example, the platoon leader. The leader occupies the classical position of middle man similar to the role of foreman of a work team in industry. He must be close enough to the men for them to identify with him and yet, at the same time, he must also represent the demands of higher authority. Shils has stressed the enlisted man's desire for a protective personal relationship with an authority figure in this kind of position, and emphasized the effectiveness of "an exemplary and protective leader" in raising morale in U.S. military units.[15]

Shils and Janowitz give evidence that indicates that the primary group in the army acts as a family surrogate, and that a man's real family loyalties were one of the most substantial threats to the solidarity of the army unit.[16] The captured German soldiers themselves identified with the family-like nature of their units with statements like: "We were a big happy family." In addition, it became clear that soldiers were most likely to desert while on furlough, or after receiving distressing news from their families. Similarly, the members of units were most likely to discuss surrendering among themselves after concretely recalling family experiences. Because of these factors, families of soldiers were instructed to avoid mentioning family deprivations in letters to the front and, as Allied bombing of the civilian population became more severe, personal messages to the front were censored to prevent distressing family news reaching the men. Thus the soldier was able to transfer his primary loyalties to his unit while physically with the unit, providing that he felt secure about his family. While actually with his family, his loyalties to them tended to be reactivated at the expense of those to his military unit. Interestingly enough, it was those men who had the most normal identification pattern in the family who were able to identify most firmly with the military unit. This same point is also supported by evidence presented by Grinker and Spiegal.[17] It is the person with a faulty family identification pattern who is most likely to be a deviant member of a military unit and a deserter to the other side in a stress situation.

A limiting variable influencing the cohesiveness in military organizations, as in factories, is the technology with which the military unit is working. Different weapons systems require different kinds of team relationships. A submarine, for example, demands continued close contact among the crew over lengthy periods of time and virtually cuts off outside social contact. An airplane is similar but returns more quickly to base and so allows more frequent contact with non-crew members. By contrast, the members of a rifle squad in battle may readily lose contact with one another and so experience a sense of isolation from the expectations and support of other group members.

Evidence to clinch the importance of primary group cohesion as a basis for morale and effectiveness comes from those German units whose integrity was not established or adequately maintained. As the war progressed, it became increasingly difficult to maintain the integrity of primary groups. The survivors of groups suffering severe casualties were regrouped and new units of recruits were thrust directly into battle without the opportunity of solidifying primary group ties. It was in units of these kinds that desertions and active surrender occurred. In these situations, the individual seemed to readily remove his emotional ties and identifications from the group and refocus them on himself. The individual regressed to a narcissistic state and became concerned with saving his own skin — marked contrast to situations in which men in intact primary groups would fight to the bitter end.

Shils has argued that the primary group reduces a soldier's fear of death and injury by counterposing against such fear a need for approval by his comrades.[18] As evidence, he quoted the fact that replacements to U.S. combat units were more likely to say "prayer helps a lot" whereas veterans looked to concrete support from their comrades.

Thus ideology had only an indirect effect on fighting effectiveness in both the U.S. and the German armies. The crucial variable was the degree of preservation of the cohesive primary unit. The soldier fights to protect the primary group and to live up to the expectations of his fellow group members. The army in battle is the prototype of the organization under stress, and military studies illustrate most vividly the crucial role of the primary group in preserving organizational cohesiveness and goal directedness....

## ENDNOTES

1. Cooley, Charles H. 1909. *Social Organization: A Study of the Larger Mind*. New York: Scribners, p. 23.
2. Ibid., p. 29.
3. Cooley, Charles H., Robert C. Angell, and Lowell J. Carr. 1933. *Introductory Sociology*. New York: Scribners, p. 53.
4. Shils, Edward. 1950. "Primary Groups in the American Army" in Robert K. Merton and Paul F. Lazarsfeld, Eds., *Continuities in Social Research*. Glencoe, IL: Free Press, pp. 16–25.
5. Shils, Edward. 1952. "The Study of the Primary Group" in Daniel Lerner and Harold Lasswell, *The Policy Sciences*. Stanford, CA: Stanford University Press, pp. 44–69.
6. Ibid., p. 44.
7. Cooley, Charles H. *Introductory Sociology*, p. 32.
8. Shils, Edward S. and Morris Janowitz, "Cohesion and Disintegration in the Wehrmacht in World War II," *Public Opinion Quarterly*, Vol. 12 (Summer 1948), (reprinted by permission of Elsevier Science Publishing Co., Inc. Copyright © 1948 by the Trustees of Columbia University). Samuel A. Stouffer. et al., eds., *The American Soldier*, vols. 1 and 2 (Princeton, NJ: Princeton University Press, 1949); Morris Janowitz and Roger Little, Sociology and the Military Establishment, rev. ed. (New York: Russell Sage Foundation, 1965), particularly Chap. 4, "Primary Groups and Military Effectiveness," pp. 77–99; Robert K. Merton and Paul L. Lazarsfeld, eds., *Continuities in Social Research: Studies in the Scope and Method of the American Soldier* (Glencoe, IL: Free Press, 1950); Roy R. Grinker and John P. Spiegal, *Men Under Stress* (Philadelphia: Blakiston, 1945).
9. Shils and Janowitz. "Cohesion and Disintegration in the Wehrmacht," pp. 280–315.
10. Ibid., pp. 281–2.
11. Ibid., p. 284.
12. Janowitz and Little, *Sociology and the Military Establishment*, p. 78.
13. Speien in *Continuities in Social Research*.
14. Shils in *Continuities in Social Research*, op. cit., p. 22.
15. Ibid.
16. Shils and Janowitz, "Cohesion and Disintegration in the Wehrmacht."
17. Grinker and Spiegal, *Men Under Stress*, Chap. 2.
18. Shils in *Continuities in Social Research*.

# 15. HONOR AND REPUTATION IN THE CHICANO GANG

RUTH HOROWITZ

*"The gang provides a culturally acceptable peer group in which an individual can act as a member of a collectivity in the otherwise individualistic, competitive world of the streets."*

This is an insightful description of life in a Chicano gang. It comes from a book-length study of the Chicago Chicano community. It underlines the fact that it is difficult for those of us outside the community to fully understand why events happen as they do in the community. Instead of explaining gang activities as examples of chaos, disorder, deviance, and lawlessness, Horowitz shows us the importance of honor and reputation in the gang, and links many of the activities of gang members to these values. The gang is a **group**, and groups have rules and values to which members must conform. The gang, like all groups, establishes ways to make members **feel** important.

## YOUNG MEN IN THE STREETS: HONOR AND REPUTATION

...When they were not in school, most of the male youths spent most of their time outdoors, whatever the time of the year or the weather. Even when the temperature dropped below freezing, many could be found huddled in one of the parks until eight or nine in the evening. There were few places to go indoors: their homes were too crowded, the drinking age was twenty-one, and one settlement house prohibited anyone over fourteen from entering. The only public indoor facilities were the community-run social service center; the park building (from which the Lions were often expelled); and the second settlement house, which had been taken over by local activists and sometimes stayed open late. With the limited park space and the densely populated neighborhood, there

Horowitz, Ruth, *Honor and the American Dream.* Copyright © 1983 by Rutgers, The State University of New Jersey. Reprinted by permission of Rutgers University Press.

was insufficient territory for any one group to "own" much except for a bench or a single corner. Several gangs congregated at each park, and many unaffiliated youths associated with the gangs. There was little way for different groups to segregate themselves spatially and not constantly be crossing borders.

Gangs play a major role in the lives of many area males. Approximately 70 percent join one for at least a short period between the ages of twelve and seventeen, though not all tough young men join gangs. There are eight major gangs in the area, each of which is segmented by age: miniatures (ages eleven to twelve), midgets (thirteen to fourteen), littles (fifteen to seventeen), juniors (eighteen to twenty-one), and seniors (twenty-one and over). Each section has between fifteen and forty members. Not every gang has members in each category throughout its history. In addition, many short-lived gangs developed rapidly and disappeared just as fast. Although different age groups may bear the same gang name, they are not necessarily allied on all occasions. For example, in one situation, the Senior Greeks helped the Little and Junior Lions against the Junior Greeks.

It is usually possible to identify an individual as a member of a particular gang by his hangout and his official jacket sweater with the gang's emblem and its color on a stripe on the shoulder, the collar, and the belt. Sometimes they wear shoes or shirts in their colors. Neither method of identification is infallible. Many nonmembers associate with members, and members do not necessarily wear their colors all the time. Most young men in gangs wear similar clothing styles, but many other youths dress like them. Most take great care with their clothes. Len of the Lions told several other members of the gang, "I wouldn't ever wear jeans, they don't keep a crease and bag at the knees." Only those outside the street scene appear to be largely unconcerned with style and the latest fashions.

Although many youths join gangs for approximately a year, the majority of males (aged eleven to eighteen) are not in gangs at any one time. This does not mean that they can avoid interpersonal violence or even try to. In this chapter, I examine the context in which violence occurs among male youths on 32nd Street both as individuals and as members of gangs, and the different meanings of violence and its relationship to identity....

On 32nd Street, a violent response to threats to self-esteem is embedded in a code of personal honor. Honor is a normative code that stresses the inviolability of one's manhood and defines breaches of etiquette, violations of a female relative's sexual purity, and accusations of dependency on others, in an adversarial idiom. Honor sensitizes people to violations that are interpreted as derogations of fundamental properties of the self. Within a more conventional normative framework, these same actions might be appraised and evaluated as mere violations of etiquette that would be ignored or excused, or as violations of the law that would require the police. Young men tend to fluctuate between commitments to conventional and to honor-bound responses. Normative ambiguity exists when it is unclear which norms should govern interpersonal relations. The lack of commitment to either code links interaction to the marginal position of the community in the wider society, to the tension between aspiring to succeed and the limited possibility of doing so.

All male youths experience the structural position of the community, although reactions to the tensions between the excitement of street life and conventional pursuits vary. Some drift toward gangs that expressly pursue excitement and develop a strong street identity, while others prefer to pursue more conventional careers. Yet no one avoids the tension between street life and convention on 32nd Street. The meaning of violence in the construction of identity and reputation among male youths and youth groups varies from one identity orientation to another, but it is always rooted in a concern for personal honor.

## INSULT, HONOR, AND VIOLENCE

Honor revolves around a person's ability to command deference in interpersonal relations. A person doubts his own efficacy or suspects that he is viewed as weak when he believes he has been publicly humiliated. This situation is particularly critical to men who do not have a history of personal accomplishments or who cannot draw on valued social roles to protect their self-esteem when they are confronted by an insulting action. In an honor-bound subculture that emphasizes manhood and defines violations of interpersonal etiquette in an adversarial manner, any action that challenges a person's right to deferential treatment in *public* — whether derogating a person, offering a favor that may be difficult to return, or demonstrating lack of respect for a female relative's sexual purity — can be interpreted as an insult and a potential threat to manhood. Honor demands that a man be able physically to back his claim to dominance and independence.

### Sensitivity to Insult

A situation is defined as insulting when an actor believes another person intends to place him in a demeaning light. When he is placed in a position where he may be viewed as weak, an individual experiences a lack of self-esteem. Sensitivity to a perceived insult is particularly keen in public situations, where judgments can be made readily by others and the actor perceives himself unable to neutralize or negate the intentions of the insulter.

In a context where men believe it is important that an honorable man be in control of all situations, infringement of any rules of interpersonal etiquette may be perceived as insulting, casting doubt on a man's ability to control. How a person responds to perceived insult reflects directly on the kind of person he is and determines whether others will perceive him as admirable or contemptible. An insult is a challenge to his right to deferential treatment. His interpretation of others' intentions and his reactions to them have real consequences for his standing among his peers. Honor is not something that one has permanently; it can always be challenged and must therefore continually be reaffirmed before one's peers.

## Responding to Perceived Insult

How should one respond to insult within the context of the code of honor? When actions are interpreted as insulting, honor compels an individual to take an unequivocal stand, to immediately enforce his claim to precedence no matter how small the incident may seem. Because honor concerns actions that reflect personal decisions and judgments, disputes over honor must be settled personally, not through the legal system. Direct action takes priority over legal judgments of right and wrong. One young man spent two years in jail for shooting and severely wounding the man who raped his sister. He did not even consider going to the police at the time. It was his duty, he said, to repair the affront. Some things cannot be left to the law. Dishonor is experienced as a loss of one's manhood, which is culturally defined as the ability to enforce claims to a dominant position in interpersonal relations and to resist similar claims by others. The response must be physical: violence is triggered by the norms of the code of personal honor.

The physical response must follow certain rules if this act is to contribute to an identity as an honorable man. Violence must be used only when an insult is appraised as intentional. Shooting someone in the back for fun is not following the rules, nor is beating someone while robbing him, unless the victim has failed to demonstrate sufficient deference to his captors.

Moreover, as in cowboy movies, the style violence takes is critical if others are to approve its use. Ronny, a member of the Lions gang, was chastised by another member for breaking a bottle over his opponent's head instead of beating him with his fists to win a fight. Winning a fight

with an obviously weaker person is not evaluated as honorable. The bigger youth should not need to react because of his obvious superiority in strength. In certain situations, however, the inequality of sides may be justified. When a new member is being initiated into a gang, he may be jumped by three members. He will lose, and by losing, he does not change the status rankings of old members within the gang. All the new member must do is put up a good fight. Paulie's arm was broken but that was because he fought so well that the Lions "had to break it."

The importance of the style and the situational legitimacy of violence is exemplified by the reactions to movies in which personal dominance is gained through violence. Gang discussions of these movies merged directly into discussions of gang fights. Gang members saw the violence as realistic, little different in style from violence in their own lives. Young men expressed their pleasure when personal dominance was expressed through violence. In one movie, a married woman overtly flirted with another man. Her husband did nothing about it and continued to ignore his wife. The man with whom the wife had been flirting raped her, which the Lions thought was a legitimate action to maintain his honor because she was tempting him and acting as though she dominated his life. Raping her was domination of her by dishonoring her husband. Even youths who do not generally subscribe to a code of personal dominance through violence saw the rape as virtuous and honorable. The only way her husband could regain his honor was to kill the rapist; the Lions cheered when he did so....

## The Use of Guns

For the youths of 32nd Street, as for the cowboy, guns are an important symbol of a lifestyle. During the late 1960s, the number of guns obtained illegally by young people, particularly gangs on 32nd Street, increased rapidly. Using guns to gain personal domination raises several problems. First, guns change the possibilities of gaining personal dominance through violence. Unlike a good fight with physical contact, using a gun does not test real skills—a twelve-year-old or a woman can shoot a grown man. Shooting someone does little to prove real superiority. Second, using a gun increases the possibility of getting into trouble with the law. Getting caught with an unregistered gun, particularly if the person is over sixteen, is a considerably more serious offense than beating up someone in a fist fight or getting caught with a bat or chain. Third, fighting with guns increases the possibility of a life-or-death encounter. Confronted by an armed person, the other may not even get a chance to react. One slight tug at the trigger may result in death.

The ready availability of .22s, .38s, .45s, and sawed-off shotguns has changed the form of gaining dominance, particularly among the gangs. No longer are there prearranged fights, as in the 1950s, when large numbers of youths gathered to fight with bats, chains, and switchblades. Although it was possible to kill with a knife, it took much more skill, and an opponent had a much greater chance of protecting himself. Most conflicts now involve either a few armed youths who go out looking for the gang with whom they are warring or two individuals in a spur-of-the-moment fight. One young man was shot and killed by someone in a moving car. His companions could not identify the killer. Several other youths who were nearby did identify the killer, who received little approbation.

Although most youths are aware of the legal ramifications of being caught with a gun, they feel that carrying a gun is necessary because they assume (often mistakenly) that everyone else has one. Enrique was dismissed from a job that he really enjoyed when his employers learned he had been arrested on a weapons charge. Although the other Lions thought his dismissal unfair, they were well aware that the charge was serious, and that Enrique was lucky to receive probation at age nineteen. If a youth is challenged by someone with a gun and if he does not have one, he is at a disadvantage. Sam of the Lions claimed, "I never go anywhere without my heat [gun]; you aren't anyone without one. It's dangerous." The feeling of being helpless without a gun is exacerbated by the knowledge that anyone could have one. Elaborate preparations are made to carry guns secretly. Portable radios are often fitted to carry the weapons. "We saw them carry guns in dictionaries on TV but it would look funny — us carrying dictionaries," Amos, another gang member, explained as he showed me the radio.

A number of older gang members say that it is better to have the younger members kill. One Se-

nior Greek was quick to point out that a juvenile would be much less severely punished for the offense. When a twelve- or fourteen-year-old kills someone in a gang fight, he is likely to receive a sentence of two years or less, whereas an adult might receive a life sentence.

Ambivalent feelings about the use of guns and those who use them is indicated by the fact that although gang sweaters are rarely lost, guns seem to be lost frequently. "The pigs were after me, so when I came around the alley, I threw it in the garbage. I really looked for it after the pigs cut out, but it wasn't there. Now what am I going to do without a piece [gun]? I got two dudes after my ass," Len told the Lions when they chastised him for losing another gun. Amos explained, "Like one dude has one, then when we need heats cause we expect trouble, we can't find half of them. I guess we got six heats between all of us [about thirty-five youths]."

Further indications of ambivalence toward those who use guns to defend their honor are the stories told by older gang members of "good clean" fights between gangs, by which they mean there were no guns — only chains, bats, and knives. Face-to-face combat really indicated how strong a man and his gang were, they claimed. Now, one of the Senior Greeks told a young member of the Lions, a twelve-year-old "punk" can shoot and kill a strong and tough man. That does not change others' evaluations of the "punk." The young Lion nodded his agreement.

Yet these older men also carry and use guns. Alberto, who at twenty-five drove a public bus, was still a Senior Greek. He had responsibilities (a wife and two kids) and wanted the good things in life (a nice place to live, a stereo, a good time). He did not want to get killed; he said guns scared him. But he did fight and he did carry a gun sometimes. His sister said he punched a man who had been looking at his wife. The fight was broken up but Alberto chipped his tooth. Three weeks later, he shot at someone who kept staring at him at a bar, but no one was hit.

## ETIQUETTE AND CONVENTION

There is no reason why a conventional response cannot be given in a situation that may be interpreted either as insulting or as inoffensive. Most young men have conventional social skills.... Most gang members have attended formal affairs in tuxedos and have behaved appropriately. Although they do not go to downtown restaurants frequently because of the expense, they have all been there. With their knowledge of "polite" social skills and ability to use them, most youths can respond to situations as improprieties rather than as insults.

A conventional response in this situation can best be conceived as *impression management* (Goffman 1959). Impression management implies that the actor maintains enough distance from the action to deflect any imputations of unworthiness away from himself and onto the properties of the situation. The necessary responses, then, are not violent. For example, if someone's foot is in my path and I trip, I can blame the crowded space and say "excuse me." This places the onus on the situation or the setting that happens to bring the two people together, rather than on an intention to violate another's personal space. Alternatively, I could believe the person purposely stuck out his foot so that I would fall and make a fool of myself, which would call for an honor-bound response....

"Coolness," which is much admired, may switch the onus onto the situation rather than the person. Coolness is the ability to stand back from certain situations and rationally evaluate others' actions. If, however, the offender is seen as *purposely* ignoring the other's feelings, then the victim's honor is being tampered with and the incident requires an immediate response.

## NORMATIVE AMBIGUITY AND IDENTITY

Attributing meaning to others' intentions resolves a situation of normative ambiguity. Evaluating another's actions as intentionally insulting will tip this situation toward the code of honor, while evaluating the actions as unintentional will tip the situation toward convention. Both forms are considered proper modes of conduct, and young males may choose between the two responses. An ambiguous situation becomes a critical triggering event for a male youth because the manner in which he appraises and resolves the situation publicly reveals the type of person he perceives himself to be. Others' evaluations of the resolution then become part of his identity. On one extreme

are those who rarely appraise situations as offenses to their honor. On the other extreme are those who frequently question others' claims to precedence in order to start a fight. Because most youths refuse to commit themselves wholeheartedly to conventional or honor-bound responses, the individual may invoke either set of norms to interpret the actions of others and to justify conduct. An individual may say on one occasion that killing is morally wrong and fighting over an infraction of the rules of etiquette is silly, and on another occasion the same person may say that it is necessary to defend one's honor, even by murder. There is a real tension between the rough-and-tumble excitement of street life and conventional behavior, and not all youths resolve it in a similar manner. Each decision made, however, can be critical to others' evaluations of a man's identity as an honorable person....

## COLLECTIVE IDENTITY AS IMAGE PROMOTERS: THE LIONS

...As a member of a gang, the basic parameters of an identity are laid out by membership. Although some individual reputations extend beyond an identity as a gang member ("That's Gilberto, he's a Lion" rather than "That dude's a Lion"), many are known largely by their affiliations. As a member, one *is* a Lion, and that group has a certain reputation as a gang. It becomes each member's responsibility to uphold that reputation. The collective reputation of the gang is potentially at stake in situations of normative ambiguity if the following three conditions are satisfied:

First, at least one party to a face-to-face encounter must feel that the presence of the other party in this setting or his behavior on this occasion endangers his safety and impugns his dignity. In light of the actor's definition of the situation as threatening and provocative, he must make a decision on the spot. If he does not assume the role of an aggressor, he may play the part of a victim. Second, the actor must respond to this emotionally charged situation in a way that visibly reveals his resolve (i.e., he feels his words, gestures or actions express a definite intention) to inflict physical injury on his antagonist or by actually doing so. Third, the actor must account for his conduct on this occasion in terms of his status as a member of a gang (Horowitz and Schwartz 1974, pp. 238-239).

...Responsibility for defending the name of the gang against collective insults becomes a criterion for continued membership.

## The Construction of Gang Reputations

In seeking to protect and promote their reputations, gangs often engage in prolonged "wars," which are kept alive between larger fights by many small incidents and threats of violence. Following each incident, one gang claims precedence, which means that the other group must challenge them if they want to retain their honor and reassert their reputation. On-the-spot insults are not always necessary to provoke a fight, and claims to precedence are carried over from one incident to the next. If a group's desire to be treated with deference is not honored, the group must claim precedence. Members must also go out to claim deferential treatment and superiority by demonstrating lack of respect for their enemies. For example, the war between the Lions and Aces continued over three years with intermittent claims to precedence by each side. Expectations of affronts and small skirmishes kept up the momentum of the conflict. If either side had failed to respond publicly to the other's challenge, the challenging gang's reputation would have become increasingly formidable.

In one incident, when Rat Man thought he saw some Aces riding in a car, he shot at them but the .38 did not go off. "We are at war," he said, and that is what a gang member is supposed to do when he sees an enemy. After more incidents, several Lions borrowed a car, took two guns, and went looking for the Aces. When they returned, they claimed they had gotten off three shots but no one was hit. During this period, an Angel shot and killed an Ace, and the Lions expressed regret they had not done it. They criticized the Angel's method to avoid loss of respect in their own eyes. Later, Amos and two other Lions ran into the Ace who had thrown a brick through Amos's mother's window. Amos beat the Ace unconscious with the butt of his gun, but the Ace regained consciousness a few days later and identified Amos as his as-

sailant. Amos claimed he would have killed him but he had no ammunition.

Several incidents in which no actual meeting occurred helped to perpetuate the war. Sometimes, some of the Senior Greeks who congregated at El Pueblo Park joined the Lions. On one occasion, I counted thirty Lions, six guns, numerous baseball bats, several chains, and many broken bottles ready for use. One of the Greeks was frightened enough to demand that another Greek leave his gun at the park when he had to leave for a few minutes. Everyone raced back and forth across the park and a lookout was posted at each corner. The darker it got, the louder and more violent the talk about the Aces became. By 9:30, people began to announce, "I've got to go home now." By 10:30 the park was almost empty. These no-show events help to maintain the fervor and momentum of the conflict. They allowed the waiting group to assert that the others were too frightened to show up and thereby to claim precedence over them.

These were only a few of the events that occurred between the Lions and the Aces over a two-year period of their war. The Lions also took several trips into the Ace's territory and the two gangs had a big fight over a sweater. There was roughly one major incident—which may or may not have ended in conflict—each month. After each incident, someone loses and someone gains a claim to precedence over the other. The general feeling of the community in the year that most of these events occurred was that the Lions were the most violent and the least polished of any of the gangs.

When an incident is defined as a collective insult, all members must participate to ensure the continued reputation of the group or to better it. Participation also promotes group loyalty and solidarity. Members must participate even if they do not agree with a particular incident or the group is drawn into a situation by the irresponsible behavior of a member. If a person weakens the gang's right to claim deference from others by losing his sweater to another gang, someone has to get it back or the entire group suffers....

Having an identity as a Lion does not preclude membership in another type of group; however, to remain a Lion, loyalty must be demonstrated continually. Protecting the gang's claim to precedence from other gangs takes priority over any other affiliation. At one dance a Lion, Enrique, wearing a gang sweater, spoke for the Brown Berets during intermission. During the speech, Enrique talked about peace among all Latinos, but as a Lion he was arming himself against the rumored invasion of the Aces. Several of the other Lions also started associating with the Brown Berets. Nico and Ronny were the first to join. Ronny said he joined because they had helped his retarded brother over Christmas. Several of the Brown Berets started to come to the park, and several Lions drifted into the Brown Berets. They attended several meetings, and Enrique and Jim started wearing the jacket of the Berets. The Lions who did not join called the ones who did "copouts" for their dual loyalty. Several of the new Brown Berets were assigned to be armed guards, which impressed them very much. But there was too much talk and too little action, and the Lions were demanding a demonstration of loyalty. Within three months, they all dropped the Berets. The two identities were too difficult to retain. Their identities as Lions were too important to become secondary to that of the Brown Berets....

Group solidarity through commitment to the Lions' collective identity and reputation is reinforced by some sanctioned rules and regulations. These rules, however, are usually flexible, as is the organization of the group. Techniques of choosing leaders, their powers, and decision-making processes vary between groups; moreover, rules for joining and quitting and for the collection of dues are flexible. There are also differences in the way a group moves from one age segment to the next. Some groups move as a collectivity and must fight with an older group to move up. In other groups, an individual moves up when he becomes of age and the older group thinks he is good enough. In 1971, the Lions were all one group. Later they decided to divide into the Littles and the Juniors and held separate official meetings. "It just happened, we didn't hassle it, the older dudes became the Juniors and the rest, Littles. We [Juniors] don't have any real officers, we're friends, and we can have meetings when we want," explained Enrique. Most members of both groups hung out at the park, although a few did not. Only on two occasions did the Littles become involved in an incident in which the Juniors did not. Age segments of other gangs are not necessarily this close....

## Friends and Partners: Gang Cohesion

Friendship, although sometimes strained, and mutual support are important factors in group solidarity. Although some studies claim that gangs have few internal cohesive mechanisms such as group goals, membership stability, and role differentiation (Klein 1971), on 32nd Street, members bolster each other and individual friendships are solidified into partners that frequently entail significant mutual sacrifices.

Examples of the social support given members can be drawn from the excuses made when a member loses a fight for his personal reputation: the enemy did not fight fairly, he was much bigger, or he had a weapon. It is not the fault of the gang member if he seemed to end up at the bottom or sustained a larger wound. His reputation is not lowered as much by his loss as his opponent's win is deflated. There is no zero-sum game in terms of winning or losing a fight: No one loses completely. It was obvious to everyone that Sam had lost a fight. (It was not defined as a gang fight.) He had a black eye and looked terrible, but everyone had an explanation for the situation: The other man had a bottle, Sam was jumped from behind, the other man was bigger. Privately, several observers, including Lions, told me that the reason the other had a bottle was that Sam had a knife. Everyone thought Sam had fought hard and no one wanted him to feel that his esteem was lowered. His reputation was weakened outside the gang, but no one would admit this within the gang.

Most important, there is always someone around to hang out with. Meeting day after day in the same location provides a sense of continuity and social support. Even when the temperature drops below freezing, several of the Lions can be found at the park. Even the members who are going out steadily with a particular young woman usually bring her to the park for a part of the evening. She usually talks with the other women and he with the Lions. When several of the Lions joined the Brown Berets and began to spend less time at the park, the others continually bemoaned their absence.

Being a partner connotes very close ties with another man, and these relationships are generally long-standing and public. In fact, in extreme cases, a man will go to jail for his partner. Partners always stand up for each other and can say almost anything to each other. One of the Lions went to jail for a murder but never revealed the name of his accomplice (his partner).

There are, however, characteristics of this system of obtaining a reputation and maintaining honor that make trust and close ties among gang members difficult. A member's status within the gang is important in judging whether or not an incident is a collective insult and in legitimizing the absence of a member from gang action. Status within the gang is based on the evaluation of a member's reputation in the street, and that reputation is precarious. It may shift with each new attempt to assert and defend a claim to precedence. With the sensitivity of gang members to insult and the precarious nature of reputation, there is always a possibility that one gang member will judge another's behavior as not properly deferential. Although both Jim and Ham were regular members of the gang, neither was in the small inner circle. Jim was smaller than Ham but probably faster. Ham almost killed Jim one summer evening in the park. Jim called Ham, who is very dark, a "nigger" to his face. Ham interpreted this as an intended insult and started to fight. Several good punches were thrown before Ham's sister was able to separate them and drag her brother home. Because everyone is so sensitive to insult, it is possible for anyone to be perceived as an insulter, with the exception of one's partner.

This type of situation accounts for much of the fighting within the gang. Over an eighteen-month period, however, there were only three fights among the Lions that progressed further than a few teasing shoves or some verbal insults. Each time it looked as though there might be a fight, it was stopped by other members. If a fight had continued, a reordering of status relationships might have been necessary and someone might really have lost. Instead, the hierarchy remained fairly loose with attempts to build a strong reputation focused on challenges outside the gang. A successful challenger can improve his reputation without a fellow member actually losing status. Moreover, the extensive and intensive mutual obligation system links members both existentially and symbolically and minimizes internal competition....

The gang provides a culturally acceptable peer group in which an individual can act as a member of a collectivity in the otherwise individualistic, competitive world of the streets. A youth can be a "tough warrior" and experience the solidarity of a collectivity. Membership is one way of mediating the tension between the basically competitive experience of getting a reputation and succeeding in school and the solidarity experienced within the family unit. There the collectivity is considered more important than the individual member.

## ENDNOTES

Goffman, Erving. 1959. *Presentation of Self in Everyday Life.* New York: Doubleday Anchor.

Horowitz, R., and G. Schwartz. 1974. "Honor, Normative Ambiguity, and Gang Violence." *American Sociological Review* 39:238–251.

Klein, Malcolm W. 1971. *Street Gangs and Street Workers.* Englewood Cliffs, NJ: Prentice-Hall.

Toch, Hans. 1969. *Violent Men.* Chicago: Aldine.

# 16. COLLECTIVE TRAUMA AT BUFFALO CREEK

KAI ERIKSON

*"Most of the traumatic symptoms experienced by the Buffalo Creek survivors are a reaction to the loss of communality as well as a reaction to the disaster itself; the fear, apathy, and demoralization one encounters along the entire length of the hollow are*

*derived from the shock of being ripped out of a meaningful community setting as well as the shock of meeting that cruel black water. The line between the two phenomena is difficult to draw. But is seems clear that much of the agony experienced on Buffalo Creek is related to the fact that the hollow is quiet, devastated, without much in the way of a nourishing community life."*

Humans are social beings. Their lives are embedded in social organization. They live their lives in groups, communities, and societies. Organization is something we take for granted. Really, how important is it? Sometimes it is easiest to understand something when it is no longer there for us. Here is a tragic episode in the history of West Virginia, in which several communities were wiped out by a disastrous flood. Kai Erickson studied the people along Buffalo Creek, and his book described the effects of this tragedy on their lives. In the process, Erickson tried to understand what the end to community meant to these people, creating a loss that nothing could correct. How important was their community? Read this and imagine yourself in their place.

---

*History stopped on the day of the flood.*

[*Editor's Note:* The disastrous Buffalo Creek, West Virginia, flood occurred on February 26, 1972. The sudden collapse of the Pittston Company's (the local coal company and absentee landlord's) massive refuse pile dam unleashed 132 million gallons of water and coal waste materials on the unsuspecting residents of Buffalo Creek. The rampaging wave of water and sludge traveled down the creek in waves of between twenty and thirty feet and at speeds sometimes approaching thirty miles per hour. Buffalo Creek's sixteen small towns were devastated by the deluge, over 125 people were killed, and over four thousand survivors were left homeless.]

Some 615 survivors of the Buffalo Creek flood were examined by psychiatrists one and one-half years after the event, and 570 of them, a grim 93 percent, were found to be suffering from an identifiable emotional disturbance. A skeptical neighbor from another of the behavioral sciences may want to make allowance for the fact that psychiatrists looking for mental disorder are more than apt to find it; but even so, the sheer volume of pathology is horrifying. The medical names for the conditions observed are depression, anxiety, phobia, emotional liability,

hypochondria, apathy; and the broader syndrome into which these various symptoms naturally fall is post-traumatic neurosis, or, in a few cases, post-traumatic psychosis. But the nearest expressions in everyday English would be something like confusion, despair, and hopelessness.

Most of the survivors responded to the disaster with a deep sense of loss — a nameless feeling that something had gone grotesquely awry in the order of things, that their minds and spirits had been bruised beyond repair, that they would never again be able to find coherence, that the world as they knew it had come to an end. Now these feelings, of course, were experienced as a generalized, pervading sense of gloom, and the men and women of the hollow did not try to catalog the various strains that contributed to it. But there are recognizable themes in the stories they tell that give us some idea of what the sources of their pain might be.

## ON BEING NUMBED

Almost everybody who survived the disaster did so by the thinnest of margins; and the closeness of their escapes, combined with the relentless savagery of the water, left them feeling numbed and depleted — almost as if the mad rush to safety had consumed most of their energy and the ferocity of the waves passing below them had somehow drawn off what reserves were left.

No sooner had they escaped, however, then people began to feel that they were unable to move, caught in a sluggish bank of fog, held back — as in a dream — by forces that slackened the muscles and paralyzed the will. A number of people remember having gone limp or having lost control of their limbs. Quite a few others compared their reactions to a dream state. And some simply went blank in mind as well as limp in body, as if yielding to the enormity of what was happening.

This process of retreating into a limp slump has been noted again and again in disaster research. But on Buffalo Creek, the process appears to have been somewhat exaggerated by the extraordinary power of the flood and by the helpless state in which it left its victims. To be drained of energy, to be emptied of motive and self, is to be on the verge of death itself — and that is how many of the survivors viewed their own condition later.

## FACES OF DEATH

Virtually everyone on Buffalo Creek had a very close encounter with death, either because they felt doomed themselves or because they lost relatives and friends or because they came into contact with dead bodies. The upper half of the valley, where most of the serious destruction took place, was strewn with the signs of a terrible tragedy. But people who lived downstream were not spared the agony of this scene either, for the current carried it to them. So death seemed to be everywhere, overhead, underfoot, crouched in every pile of wreckage, waiting to be recognized....

## SURVIVAL AND GUILT

Where one finds death on so large a scale, one also finds guilt. It is one of the ironies of human life that individuals are likely to regret their own survival when others around them are killed in what seems like a meaningless and capricious way, in part because they cannot understand by what logic they came to be spared. People who sense the hand of God in it have many hard questions to ponder, and none of them are very comforting....

## THE FURNITURE OF SELF

...It is important to remember that the people of the creek had invested a great deal of time and money and pride in the process of converting the old company shacks into comfortable new dwellings. The flood cleaned out some ragged housing as it made its way down the hollow — more than the residents like to remember — but the average home had been renovated in a hundred ways. A refurbished house on Buffalo Creek served as the emblem of one's rise out of poverty. It was a measure of security, an extension of self, a source of identity. It was not only the outer shell in which one lived out one's life, but a major feature of that life.

Moreover, people lost possessions of considerable meaning to them — not only trucks and cars and appliances with an established trade-in value but mementos of no measurable worth that were highly cherished. Objects such as family Bibles or photographs, a father's favorite gun or a mother's proudest embroidery, had a place in the household almost like holy relics, and their loss was deeply mourned. They were a link with the past, and they were a link with the future.

## LOSS OF FAITH IN ORDER

The disaster on Buffalo Creek had the effect of reducing people's already brittle confidence in the natural and especially in the social order....

The Buffalo Creek survivors, without saying so directly, have quite clearly lost much of their confidence in the workings of nature. They are troubled about the condition of the mountains, now scraped out inside and slashed with strip mine benches; they are troubled about the water poised over their heads in other dams both real and imaginary; they are troubled about tornadoes and avalanches, floods and rock slides, earthquakes and explosions; and they are troubled about the natural capacity of their bodies and spirits to handle all the emergencies of life.

Moreover, the people of Buffalo Creek have lost their confidence in the coal company responsible for the dam. This point may be difficult to explain, because most readers will have no difficulty at all understanding why they might resent the company. But it was part of the life of the creek. It employed hundreds of people and was represented locally by officials who lived in the area, were known by first names, and were merged into the community as individual persons. The residents knew that the company was a giant corporation with headquarters in New York, but they continued to visualize it as a kind of manorial presence at the head of the hollow that was implicated somehow in the affairs of the community. It was a proprietor, a patron – and it had obligations to fulfill.

The company violated those obligations, first by building an unworthy dam, and second by reacting to the disaster in the manner of a remote bureaucracy with holdings to protect rather than in the manner of a concerned patron with constituents to care for. The heart of the company turned out to be located a thousand miles away, and its first reflex was to treat the survivors – many of them employees with decades of loyal service – as potential adversaries in a court action.

The people who speak for the company would not come out into the light, would not take the risk of establishing eye contact, would not expose themselves even for the purposes of finding out how the residents of the hollow were faring; and if this situation provoked a gentle annoyance in some survivors, it provoked a deep indignation in others. So the prevailing feeling is one of bitterness, a bitterness so sharp that it seems to speak of betrayal as well as of personal injury.

## UNIQUENESS OF BUFFALO CREEK

So these were some of the effects of the individual trauma – that first numbing moment of pain and shock and helplessness. A few paragraphs of description can scarcely begin to convey what the tragedy must have felt like to the survivors or how it has influenced their lives, but the themes noted here correspond closely to ones noted in reports of other disasters; to that extent at least, what happened on Buffalo Creek is similar to all those other floods

and bombings and hurricanes and earthquakes that interrupt the flow of human life so often.

But there are differences, too. Two years after the flood, Buffalo Creek was almost as desolate as it had been the day following – the grief as intense, the fear as strong, the anxiety as sharp, the despair as dark. People still looked out at the world with vacant eyes and drifted from one place to another with dulled and tentative movements. They rarely smiled and rarely played. They were not sure how to relate to one another. They were unsettled and deeply hurt.

Under normal circumstances, one would expect the survivors of such a disaster to convalesce gradually as the passage of time acted to dim old memories and generate new hopes. It is a standard article of psychiatric wisdom that the symptoms of trauma ought to disappear over time, and when they do not – as was generally the case on Buffalo Creek – a peculiar strain of logic is likely to follow. If one has not recovered from the effects of trauma within a reasonable span of time, or so the theory goes, it follows that the symptoms themselves must have been the result of a mental disorder predating the event itself.

Unless we are ready to entertain the possibility that virtually all the people on Buffalo Creek suffered from a palpable emotional disorder on the morning of February 26, 1972, we will have to look elsewhere for a way to explain their distress; and my argument is that a second trauma, a *collective trauma*, followed closely on the first, immobilizing recovery efforts and bringing a number of other problems into focus.

## LOSS OF COMMUNALITY

The people of Buffalo Creek were wrenched out of their communities and torn away from the very human surround in which they had been so deeply enmeshed. Much of the drama is drained away when we begin to talk of such things, partly because the loss of communality seems a step removed from the vivid terror of the disaster itself and partly because the people of the hollow, so richly articulate when describing the flood and their reaction to it, do not really know how to express what their separation from the familiar tissues of home has meant to them. The closeness of communal ties is experienced on Buffalo Creek as a part of the natural order of things, and residents are no more aware of that presence than fish are aware of the water they swim in. It is simply there, the envelope in which they live, and it is taken entirely for granted.

Communality on Buffalo Creek can best be described as a state of mind shared among a particular gathering of people; and this state of mind, by definition, does not lend itself to sociological abstraction. It does not have a name or a cluster of distinguishing properties. It is a quiet set of understandings that become absorbed into the atmosphere and are thus a part of the natural order. And the key to that network of understanding is a constant readiness to look after one's neighbors—or rather, to know without being asked what needs to be done.

The difficulty is that people invest so much of themselves in that kind of social arrangement that they become absorbed by it, almost captive to it, and the larger collectivity around you becomes an extension of your own personality, an extension of your own flesh. This pattern not only means that you are diminished as a person when that surrounding tissue is stripped away, but that you are no longer able to reclaim as your own the emotional resources invested in it. To "be neighborly" is not a quality you can carry with you into a new situation like negotiable emotional currency: The old community was your niche in the classical ecological sense, and your ability to relate to that niche meaningfully is not a skill easily transferred to another setting. This situation is true whether you move into another community, or whether a new set of neighbors moves in around your old home....

In places like Buffalo Creek, the community in general can be described as the locus for activities that are normally regarded as the exclusive property of individuals. It is the *community* that cushions pain, the *community* that provides a context for intimacy, the *community* that represents morality and serves as the repository for old traditions.

Most of the traumatic symptoms experienced by the Buffalo Creek survivors are a reaction to the loss of communality as well as a reaction to the disaster itself: The fear, apathy, and demoralization one encounters along the entire length of the hollow are derived from the shock of being ripped out of a meaningful community setting as well as the shock of meeting that cruel black water.

The line between the two phenomena is difficult to draw. But it seems clear that much of the agony experienced on Buffalo Creek is related to the fact that the hollow is quiet, devastated, without much in the way of a nourishing community life.

## MORALE AND MORALITY

The Buffalo Creek survivors must face the post-disaster world in a state of severe demoralization, both in the sense that they have lost much of their individual morale and in the sense that they have lost (or fear they have lost) many of their moral anchors. The lack of morale is reflected in a weary apathy, a feeling that the world has more or less come to an end and that there are no longer any compelling reasons for doing anything. People are drained of energy and conviction in part because the activities that once sustained them on an everyday basis—working, caring, playing—seem to have lost their direction and purpose in the absence of a larger communal setting. They feel that the ground has gone out from under them.

The clinical name for this state of mind, of course, is *depression*; and one can hardly escape the impression that it is, at least in part, a reaction to the ambiguities of post-disaster life in the hollow. Most of the survivors never realized the extent to which they relied on the rest of the community to reflect back a sense of meaning to them, never understood the extent to which they depended on others to supply them with a point of reference. When survivors say they feel "adrift," "displaced," "uprooted," "lost," they mean that they do not seem to belong to anything and that there are no longer any familiar social landmarks to help them fix their position in time and space. They are depressed, yes, but it is a depression born of the feeling that they are suspended pointlessly in the middle of nowhere.

This failure of personal morale is accompanied by a deep suspicion that moral standards are beginning to collapse all over the hollow; and in some ways, at least, it would appear that they are. As so frequently happens in human life, the forms of misbehavior people find cropping up in their midst are exactly those about which they are most sensitive. The use of alcohol, always problematic in mountain society, has evidently increased, and there are rumors spreading throughout the trailer camps that drugs have found their way to the creek. The theft rate has risen too, and this rise has always been viewed in Appalachia as a sure index of social disorganization.

The cruelest cut of all, however, is that once close and devoted families are having trouble staying within the pale they formerly observed so carefully. Adolescent boys and girls appear to be slipping away from parental control and are becoming involved in nameless delinquencies, and there are reports from several of the trailer camps that younger wives and husbands are meeting one another in circumstances that violate all the local codes. A home is a moral sphere as well as a physical dwelling, of course, and it would seem that the boundaries of moral space began to splinter as the walls of physical space were washed down the creek.

Yet the seeming collapse of morality on Buffalo Creek differs in several important respects from the kinds of anomie sociologists think they see elsewhere in modern America. For one thing, those persons who seem to be deviating most emphatically from prevailing community norms are usually the first to judge their own behavior as unacceptable and even obnoxious. Adolescents are eager to admit that they sometimes get into trouble, and those of their elders who drink more than the rules of the hollow normally permit are likely to call themselves "alcoholics" under circumstances that seem remarkably premature to jaded strangers from the urban North. To that extent, the consensus has held: local standards as to what qualifies as deviation remain largely intact, even though a number of people see themselves as drifting away from that norm.

Moreover, there is an interesting incongruity in the reports of immorality one hears throughout the hollow. It would seem that virtually everyone in the trailer camps is now living next to persons of lower moral stature than was the case formerly, and this situation, of and by itself, is a logistical marvel. Where did all those sordid people come from? How could a community of decent souls suddenly generate so much iniquity?

It probably makes sense to suppose that quite a few of the survivors are acting more coarsely now than they did before the disaster. But something else may be going on here, too. The relative strangers who move next door and bring their old life-styles with them may be acting improperly by some objective measure or they may not, but they are always acting in an unfamiliar way—and the fact of the matter may very well be that strangers, even if they come from the same general community, are almost by definition less "moral" than neighbors. They do not fall within the pale of local clemency and so do not qualify for the allowances neighbors make for one another on the grounds that they know the motives involved.

The old community had niches for some forms of deviation, like the role of the town drunk, and ways to absorb others into the larger tissue of communal life. But the disaster washed away the packing around those niches, leaving the occupants exposed to the frowning glances of new neighbors. So the problem has two dimensions. On the one hand, people who had not engaged in any kind of misbehavior before are now, by their own admission, doing so. On the other hand, the unfamiliar manners of a stranger seem to hint darkly of sin all by themselves, and personal habits that once passed as mild eccentricities in the old neighborhood now begin to look like brazen vices in the harsher light of the new....

## LOSS OF CONNECTION

It would be stretching a point to imply that the communities strung out along Buffalo Creek were secure nests in which people had found a full measure of satisfaction and warmth, but it is wholly reasonable to insist that they were like the air people breathed—sometimes harsh, sometimes chilly, but always a basic fact of life. For better or worse, the people of the hollow were deeply enmeshed in the fabric of their community; they drew their very being from it. And when the fabric was torn away by the disaster, people found themselves exposed and alone, suddenly dependent on their own personal resources.

And the cruel fact of the matter is that many survivors, when left on their own mettle, proved to have but few resources—not because they lacked the heart or the competence, certainly, but because they had always put their abilities in the service of the larger society and did not know how to recall them for their own purposes. A good part of their personal strength turned out to be the reflected strength of the collectivity—on loan, as it were, from the communal store—and they discovered to their great discomfort that they were not good at making decisions, not good at getting along with others, not good at maintaining themselves as separate persons in the absence of a supportive surround.

Many survivors fear that they are beginning to suffer the kind of stunned disorientation and even madness that can result from prolonged stretches of isolation. One result of this fear is that people tend to draw further and further into themselves and to become even more isolated. This behavior is that of wounded animals who crawl off somewhere to nurse their hurts. It is also the behavior of people who string rough coils of barbed wire around their lonely outposts because they feel they have nothing to offer those who draw near.

So the lonesomeness increases and is reinforced. People have heavy loads of grief to deal with, strong feelings of inadequacy to overcome, blighted lives to restore—and they must do all these things without much in the way of personal resources or self-confidence. Solving problems and making decisions—those are the hard part.

The inability of people to come to terms with their own isolated selves is counterpointed by an inability to relate to others on an interpersonal, one-to-one basis. Human relations along Buffalo Creek took their shape from the expectations pressing in on them from all sides like a firm but invisible mold: They were governed by the customs of the neighborhood, the traditions of the family, the ways of the community. And when the mold was stripped away by the disaster, something began to happen to those relationships. This situation was true of everyday acquaintances, but it was doubly true of marriages....

In places like Buffalo Creek, where attachments between people are seen as a part of the natural scheme of things—inherited by birth or acquired by proximity—the idea of "forming" friendships or "building" relationships seems a little odd. These attachments are not engineered; they simply happen when the communal tone is right. So people are not sure what to do.

One result of these problems is that what remains of the community seems to have lost its most significant quality—the power it generated in people to care for each other in times of need, to console each other in times of distress, to protect each other in times of danger. Looking back, then, it does seem that the general community was stronger than the sum of its parts. When the people of the hollow were sheltered together in the embrace of a secure community, they were capable of extraordinary acts of generosity; but when they tried to relate to one another as individuals, as separate entities, they found that they could no longer mobilize whatever resources are required for caring and nurturing.

Behind this inability to care is a wholly new emotional tone on the creek—a deep distrust even of old neighbors, a fear, in fact, of those very persons on whom one once staked one's life. A disaster like the one that hammered Buffalo Creek makes everything in the world seem unreliable, even other survivors, and that base is a very fragile one on which to build a new community.

## ENDNOTES

*Kai T Erikson is professor of sociology and chairman of the American Studies Program at Yale University. Formerly, he taught at the University of Pittsburgh and Emory University. He is a former president of the Society for the Study of Social Problems (1970-71).*

*The conclusions expressed in this article are based on personal interviews with the flood's survivors, legal depositions, psychiatric evaluations, letters from survivors to their attorneys, and answers to mail questionnaires developed and administered by the author. The excerpts have been presented without supporting documentation in the interests of space.*

*[Current affiliation: Yale University]*

# 17. SOCIETY

MARVIN E. OLSEN

*"Societies are the most inclusive and complex type of social organization in today's world."*

Marvin E. Olsen here describes **society** simply as the largest and most complex social organization within which all other social organization is located. Olsen's definition is a good place to begin understanding society, although it does not reflect the many differences and controversies that exist among sociologists over the meaning of society.

Societies are the most inclusive and complex type of social organization in today's world. Most other organizations exist within the confines of a society, all aspects of human social life are encompassed by a society, and to a large extent, the way in which a society functions will influence all the patterns of social ordering and subcultures that comprise it. In recent years, the term *society* has come into wide popular usage, but for social-scientific purposes, it can be defined in this manner: A *society is a broadly inclusive social organization that possesses both functional and cultural autonomy and that dominates all other types of organization.*[1]

The ideas of societal functional and cultural autonomy require some elaboration. Functional autonomy can be demonstrated in several different ways. First, most social relationships occur within the boundaries of a society, with only a small minority of all relationships involving actors from different societies—and in these later cases, the society retains control over their continuation. Second, a society is relatively self-sufficient, or independent of other societies. Self-sufficiency does not mean that a society provides all its necessary resources or satisfies all the needs of its members, but rather that it establishes the social procedures and mechanisms by which all resources are pro-

cured and all needs are satisfied. Third, a society possesses functional autonomy in decision making. It is the ultimate decision-making unit for all its members, and hence has sovereignty over all decisions concerning them. Fourth, a society is the supreme organization to which its members give loyalty and which they defend against disruptive external and internal forces.

A society possesses cultural autonomy to the extent that its members share a common, distinctive, and unique culture. Any number of specific traits of this culture may be shared with other societies, including technical and scientific knowledge, customs and traditions, language, norms, and values. At the same time, many subparts of a society may hold numerous cultural ideas of their own that are not shared throughout the whole society. Nevertheless, the common culture of the total society—and especially its dominant social values and norms—form a distinctive and unified set of ideas that is unique to that society.

Like communities, societies have historically been located within a defined territorial area; some theorists include the requirement of spatial unity in their definition of a society. As long as communication and transportation facilities were severely limited, spatial unity was a requisite for functional and cultural autonomy. Given the technological developments of the twentieth century, however, this necessity no longer exists. We have already discarded the idea that a society must be territorially contiguous, and in the not too distant future, space travel and space stations may permanently obliterate the spatial unity of many societies.

The terms *state* and *nation* are frequently used interchangeably with *society*, but technically each has a different meaning. A state is a specifically defined political entity, centering around a government. It is, in effect, a political network, or polity. In many instances, the boundaries of a state are conterminous with those of its total society; the state is then the whole society as viewed from a purely political perspective. In Africa, though, many political states still contain several relatively anonymous native societies, while the separate states of the United States are clearly not societies (although the United States as a whole is simultaneously a state and a society). In short, a state is a political unit, while a society is a considerably more inclusive social organization, of which its government is only one aspect. A nation, in the contemporary sense of the word, exists when a political state coincides with a total society and when the polity is the dominant social network within the society. In other words, a nation is the particular kind of society that happens to be prevalent in today's world. Indeed, because all major contemporary societies are also nations, it is difficult for us to realize that this is not a theoretical imperative. Historically, however, societies have not always been nations — as demonstrated by military and early colonial empires, in which a single political unit spanned many separate societies. Conceivably, too, a society might exist in which the religious, educational, or some other major network was the dominant sphere of power.

## ENDNOTES

1. This definition is adapted from Ronald Freedman et al., *Principles of Sociology*, revised edition. (New York: Holt, Rinehart, and Winston, 1956), p. 78.

# Part IV
## SOCIAL STRUCTURE

Social organization inevitably develops the pattern called **social structure**, the network of statuses or positions that people come to occupy in relation to one another. Students and professor are positions in a classroom; husband, wife, and children are positions in a family; upper class, middle class, and lower class are positions in society. Our position in each social structure influences much of what we **do**, what we **think**, and who we **are**. Sociologists examine human action within the context of social structure. The selections in Part IV are all attempts to understand social structure and the impact it has on the individual actor.

The first selection by William Foote Whyte examines the social structure of a friendship group. The next two selections focus on the importance of **role** in social structure. A role can most easily be understood as the set of expectations that others have for the individual in his or her position within the social structure. The idea is that role (other people's expectations) shapes what the actor does. Philip E. Zimbardo's article is an excellent example of how "mature, emotionally stable, normal, intelligent college students" are transformed when placed into dehumanizing positions. Philip Meyer describes a set of experiments by Stanley Milgram where people agree to inflict pain simply because their role demands it.

Almost all social structures are unequal. All the selections in Part IV contain elements of social power. Where positions are formal, they become "authority," and people who fill these positions claim the "legitimate right to command" some and the "obligation to obey" others. In the last selection, Herbert Kelman and V. Lee Hamilton remind us of the atrocities carried out in times of war because people claim they were ordered to do so by others who had legitimate authority within social structure.

# 18. CORNER BOYS: A STUDY OF CLIQUE BEHAVIOR

WILLIAM FOOTE WHYTE

*"The members have clearly defined relations of subordination and superordination, and each group has a leader."*

Even informal groups have social structures, and almost always the positions are unequal in power. This article discusses the relationships between leaders and followers in informal groups. As Whyte declares, "The existence of a hierarchy of personal relations in these cliques is seldom explicitly recognized by the other corner boys." Yet Whyte's analysis clearly describes such a hierarchy of positions. Group action depends on approval by the "top man." The leader in turn takes the structure into account when he or she acts. This analysis is a classic study that has influenced the study of groups in natural settings.

Here is a brief outline of topics in the article:

1. The nature of "Cornerville"
2. Inequality in groups
3. Position means the power to influence
4. The Social and Athletic Club: an analysis of structure
5. The Millers: an analysis of the leader position
6. The system of mutual obligation
7. The role of the leader

This paper presents some of the results of a study of leadership in informal groupings or gangs of corner boys in "Cornerville," a slum area of a large eastern city. The aim of the research was to develop methods whereby the position (rank or status) of the individual in his clique might be empirically determined; to study the bases of group cohesion and of the subordination and superordination of its members; and, finally, to work out means for determining the position of corner gangs in the social structure of the community....

From "Corner Boys," by William Foote Whyte, in *American Journal of Sociology*, Vol. 46. Copyright © 1941 by the University of Chicago. Reprinted by permission of the University of Chicago Press.

The population of the district is almost entirely of Italian extraction. Most of the corner boys belong to the second generation of immigrants. In general, they are men who have had little education beyond grammar school and who are unemployed, irregularly employed, or working steadily for small wages.

Their name arises from the nature of their social life. For them, "the corner" is not necessarily at a street intersection. It is any part of the sidewalk that they take for their social headquarters, and it often includes a poolroom, barroom, funeral parlor, barber shop, or clubroom. Here they may be found almost any afternoon or evening, talking and joking about sex, sports, personal relations, or politics in season. Other social activities either take place "on the corner" or are planned there.

The existence of a hierarchy of personal relations in these cliques is seldom explicitly recognized by the corner boys. Asked if they have a leader or boss, they invariably reply, "no, we're all equal." It is only through the observation of actions that the group structure becomes apparent. My problem was to apply methods that would produce an objective and reasonably exact picture of such structures.

In any group containing more than two people, there are subdivisions to be observed. No member is equally friendly with all other members. In order to understand the behavior of the individual member, it is necessary to place him not only in his group but also in his particular position in the subgroup.

My most complete study of groupings was made from observations in the rooms of the Cornerville Social and Athletic [S. and A.] Club. This was a club of corner boys, which had a membership of about 50 and was divided primarily into two cliques, which had been relatively independent of each other before the formation of the club. There were, of course, subdivisions in each clique….

As I conceive it, position in the informal group means power to influence the actions of the group. I concentrated my attention on the origination of action, to observe who proposed an action, to whom he made the proposal, and the steps that followed up to the completion of the action. I was dealing with "pair events" and "set events," to use the terminology of Arensberg and Chapple. A *pair event* is an event between two people. A *set event* is an event in which one person originates action for two or more others at the same time….

It is observation of set events that reveals the hierarchical basis of informal group organization….

At the top of the Cornerville S. and A. Club, we have Tony, Carlo, and Dom. They were the only ones who could originate action for the entire club. At the bottom were Dodo, Gus, Pop, Babe, Marco, and Bob, who never originated action in a set event involving anyone above their positions. Most of the members fell into the intermediate class. They terminated action on the part of the top men and originated action for the bottom men. Observations of the actions of the men of the intermediate class when neither top nor bottom men were present revealed that there were subdivisions or rankings within that class. This does not mean

that the intermediate or bottom men never have any ideas as to what the club should do. It means that their ideas must go through the proper channels if they are to go into effect.

In one meeting of the Cornerville S. and A. Club, Dodo proposed that he be allowed to handle the sale of beer in the clubrooms in return for 75 percent of the profits. Tony spoke in favor of Dodo's suggestion but proposed giving him a somewhat smaller percentage. Dodo agreed. Then Carlo proposed to have Dodo handle the beer in quite a different way, and Tony agreed. Tony made the motion, and it was carried unanimously. In this case, Dodo's proposal was carried through, after substantial modifications, on the actions of Tony and Carlo.

In another meeting, Dodo said he had two motions to make: that the club's funds be deposited in a bank and that no officer be allowed to serve two consecutive terms. Tony was not present at this time. Dom, the president, said that only one motion should be made at a time and that, furthermore, Dodo should not make any motions until there had been opportunity for discussion. Dodo agreed. Dom then commented that it would be foolish to deposit the funds when the club had so little to deposit. Carlo expressed his agreement. The meeting passed on to other things without action on the first motion and without even a word of discussion on the second one. In the same meeting, Chris moved that a member must be in the club for a year before being allowed to hold office. Carlo said that it was a good idea, he seconded the motion, and it carried unanimously.

All my observations indicate that the idea for group action that is carried out must originate with the top man or be accepted by him so that he acts on the group. A follower may originate action for a leader in a pair event, but he does not originate action for the leader and other followers at the same time—that is, he does not originate action in a set event that includes the leader.

One may also observe that, when the leader originates action for the group, he does not act as if his followers were all of equal rank. Implicitly, he takes the structure of the group into account. An example taken from the corner gang known as the "Millers" will illustrate this point. The Millers were a group of 20 corner boys who were divided into two subgroups. Members of both subgroups frequently acted together; but, when two activities occupied the men at the same time, the division generally fell between the subgroups. Sam was the leader of the Millers. Joe was directly below him in one subgroup. Chichi led the other subgroup. Joe as well as Sam were in positions to originate action for Chichi and his subgroup.

It was customary for the Millers to go bowling every Saturday night. On this particular Saturday night, Sam had no money, so he set out to persuade the boys to do something else. They followed his suggestion. Later, Sam explained to me how he had been able to change the established social routine of the group. He said:

I had to show the boys that it would be in their own interests to come with me — that each one of them would benefit. But I knew I only had to convince two of the fellows. If they start to do something, the other boys will say to themselves, "If Joe does it — or if Chichi does it — it must be a good thing for us too." I told Joe and Chichi what the idea was, and I got them to come with me. I didn't pay no attention to the others. When Joe and Chichi came, all the other boys came along too.

Another example from the Millers indicates what happens when the leader and the man next to him in rank disagree on group policy. This is Sam talking again:

One time we had a raffle to raise money to build a camp on Lake _____ [on property lent them by a local business man]. We had collected $54, and Joe and I were holding the money…. That week I knew Joe was playing pool, and he lost three or four dollars gambling. When Saturday came, I says to the boys, "Come on, we go out to Lake _____. We're gonna build that camp on the hill…." Right away Joe said "If yuz are gonna build the camp on the hill, I don't come. I want it on the other side…." All the time I knew he had lost the money, and he was only making up excuses so he wouldn't have to let anybody know…. Now the hill was really the place to build that camp. On the other side, the ground was swampy. That would have been a stupid place…. But I knew that if I tried to make them go through with it now, the group would split up into two cliques. Some would come with me, and some would go with Joe…. So I let the whole thing drop for a while…. After, I got Joe alone, and I says to him, "Joe, I know you lost some of that money, but that's all right. You can pay up when you have it and nobody will say nothin'. But Joe, you know we shouldn't have the camp

on the other side of the hill because the land is no good there. We should build it on the hill…." So he said, "All right," and we got all the boys together, and we went out to build the camp.

Under ordinary circumstances, the leader implicitly recognizes and helps to maintain the position of the man or men immediately below him, and the group functions smoothly. In this respect, the informal organization is similar to the formal organization. If the executive in a factory attempts to pass over his immediate subordinates and gives orders directly to the men on the assembly line, he creates confusion. The customary channels must be used.

The social structures vary from group to group, but each one may be represented in some form of hierarchy. The members have clearly defined relations of subordination and superordination, and each group has a leader….

Out of these interactions arises a system of mutual obligations that is fundamental to group cohesion. If the men are to carry on their activities as a unit, there are many occasions when they must do favors for one another. Frequently, one member must spend money to help another who does not have the money to participate in some of the group activities. This creates an obligation. If the situation is later reversed, the recipient is expected to help the man who gave him aid. The code of the corner boy requires him to help his friends when he can and to refrain from doing anything to harm them. When life in the group runs smoothly, the mutual obligations binding members to one another are not explicitly recognized. A corner boy, asked if he helped a fellow member because of a sense of obligation, will reply, "No, I didn't have to do it. He's my friend. That's all." It is only when the relationship breaks down that the underlying obligations are brought to light. When two members of the group have a falling-out, their actions form a familiar pattern. One tells a story something like this: "What a heel Blank turned out to be. After all I've done for him, the first time I ask him to do something for me, he won't do it." The other may say: "What does he want from me? I've done plenty for him, but he wants you to do everything." In other words, the actions that were performed explicitly for the sake of friendship are now revealed as being part of a system of mutual obligations.

Not all the corner boys live up to their obligations equally well, and this factor partly accounts for the differentiation in status among the men. The man with a low status may violate his obligations without much change in his position. His fellows know that he has failed to discharge certain obligations in the past, and his position reflects his past performances. On the other hand, the leader is depended on by all the members to meet his personal obligations. He cannot often fail to do so without causing confusion and losing his position. The relationship of status to the system of mutual obligations is most clearly revealed when we consider the use of money. Although all the men are expected to be generous, the flow of money between members can be explained only in terms of the group structure.

The Millers provide an illustration of this point. During the time I knew them, Sam, the leader, was out of work except for an occasional odd job; yet, whenever he had a little money, he spent it on Joe and Chichi, his closest friends, who were next to him in the structure of the group. When Joe or Chichi had money, which was less frequent, they reciprocated. Sam frequently paid for two members who stood close to the bottom of the structure and occasionally for others. The two men who held positions immediately below Joe and Chichi in the subgroups were considered very well off according to Cornerville standards. Sam said that he occasionally borrowed money from them, but never more than 50 cents at a time. Such loans he tried to repay at the earliest possible moment. There were four other members, with positions ranging from intermediate to the bottom, who nearly always had more money than Sam. He did not recall ever having borrowed from them. He said that the only time he had obtained a substantial sum from anyone around his corner was when he borrowed 11 dollars from a friend who was the *leader* of another corner-boy group.

The system is substantially the same for all the groups on which I have information. The leader spends more money on his followers than they on him. The farther down in the structure one looks, the fewer are the financial relations which tend to obligate the leader to a follower. This does not mean that the leader has more money than others or even that he necessarily spends more — although he must always be a free spender. It means that the financial relations must be explained in social terms. Unconsciously, and in some cases consciously, the leader refrains from putting himself under obligation to those with low status in the group....

The leader is the man who knows what to do. He is more resourceful than his followers. Past events have shown that his ideas were right. In this sense, "right" simply means satisfactory to the members. He is the most independent in judgment. Although his followers are undecided about a course of action or the character of a newcomer, the leader makes up his mind. When he gives his word to one of "his boys," he keeps it. The followers look to him for advice and encouragement, and he receives more of the confidences of the members than any other man. Consequently, he knows more about what is going on in the group than anyone else. Whenever there is a quarrel among the boys, he will hear of it almost as soon as it happens. Each party to the quarrel may appeal to him to work out a solution; and, even when the men do not want to compose their differences, each one will take his side of the story to the leader at the first opportunity. A man's standing depends partly on the leader's belief that he has been conducting himself as he should.

The leader is respected for his fairmindedness. Whereas there may be hard feelings among some of the followers, the leader cannot bear a grudge against any man in the group. He has close friends (men who stand next to him in position), and he is indifferent to some of the members; but if he is to retain his reputation for impartiality, he cannot allow personal animus to override his judgment.

The leader need not be the best baseball player, bowler, or fighter, but he must have some skill in whatever pursuits are of particular interest to the group. It is natural for him to promote activities in which he excels and to discourage those in which he is not skillful; and, insofar as he is thus able to influence the group, his competent performance is a natural consequence of his position. At the same time, his performance supports his position.

It is significant to note that the leader is better known and more respected outside of his group than is any of his followers. His social mobility is greater. One of the most important functions he performs is that of relating his group to other groups in the district. His reputation outside the group tends to support his standing within the group, and his position in the group supports his reputation among outsiders.

It should not be assumed from this discussion that the corner boys compete with one another for the purpose of gaining leadership. Leadership is a product of social interaction. The men who reach the top in informal groups are those who can perform skillfully the actions required by the situation. Most such skills are performed without long premeditation....

# 19. PATHOLOGY OF IMPRISONMENT

PHILIP E. ZIMBARDO

*"At the end of only six days, we had to close down our mock prison because what we saw was frightening."*

This article needs little introduction because it truly speaks for itself. It represents the very best example of the power of social structure; how situations place people in roles, and how people subsequently become transformed, doing things they would never think of doing outside those roles.

In an attempt to understand just what it means psychologically to be a prisoner or prison guard, Craig Haney, Curt Banks, Dave Jaffe, and I created our own prison. We carefully screened over 70 volunteers who answered an ad in a Palo Alto city newspaper and ended up with about two dozen young men who were selected to be part of this study. They were mature, emotionally stable, normal, intelligent college students from middle-class homes throughout the United States and Canada. They appeared to represent the cream of the crop of this generation. None had any criminal record and all were relatively homogeneous on many dimensions initially.

Half were arbitrarily designated as prisoners by a flip of a coin, the others as guards. These were the roles they were to play in our simulated prison. The guards were made aware of the potential seriousness and danger of the situation and their own vulnerability. They made up their own formal rules for maintaining law, order, and respect, and were generally free to improvise new ones during their eight-hour, three-man shifts. The prisoners were unexpectedly picked up at their homes by a city policeman in a squad car, searched, handcuffed, fingerprinted, booked at the Palo Alto station house, and taken blindfolded to our jail. There they were stripped, deloused, put into a uniform, given a number, and put into a cell with two other prisoners where they expected to live for the next two weeks. The pay was good ($15 a day) and their motivation was to make money.

We observed and recorded on videotape the events that occurred in the prison, and we interviewed and tested the prisoners and guards at various points throughout the study. Some of the videotapes of the actual encounters between the prisoners and guards were seen on the NBC News feature "Chronolog" on November 26, 1971.

At the end of only six days, we had to close down our mock prison because what we saw was frightening. It was no longer apparent to most of the subjects (or to us) where reality ended and their roles began. The majority had indeed become prisoners or guards, no longer able to

From "Pathology of Imprisonment," by Philip Zimbardo, in *Society*, Vol. 9, No. 6. Copyright © 1972 by Transaction Publishers; all rights reserved. Reprinted by permission of Transaction Publishers.

clearly differentiate between role playing and self. There were dramatic changes in virtually every aspect of their behavior, thinking, and feeling. In less than a week, the experience of imprisonment undid (temporarily) a life-time of learning; human values were suspended, self-concepts were challenged, and the ugliest, most base, pathological side of human nature surfaced. We were horrified because we saw some boys (guards) treat others as if they were despicable animals, taking pleasure in cruelty, while other boys (prisoners) became servile, dehumanized robots who thought only of escape, of their own individual survival, and of their mounting hatred for the guards.

We had to release three prisoners in the first four days because they had such acute situational traumatic reactions as hysterical crying, confusion in thinking, and severe depression. Others begged to be paroled, and all but three were willing to forfeit all the money they had earned if they could be paroled. By then (the fifth day), they had been so programmed to think of themselves as prisoners that when their request for parole was denied, they returned docilely to their cells. Now, had they been thinking as college students acting in an oppressive experiment, they would have quit once they no longer wanted the $15 a day we used as our only incentive. However, the reality was not quitting an experiment but "being paroled by the parole board from the Stanford County Jail." By the last days, the earlier solidarity among the prisoners (systematically broken by the guards) dissolved into "each man for himself." Finally, when one of their fellows was put in solitary confinement (a small closet) for refusing to eat, the prisoners were given a choice by one of the guards: give up their blankets and the incorrigible prisoner would be let out, or keep their blankets and he would be kept in all night. They voted to keep their blankets and to abandon their brother.

About a third of the guards became tyrannical in their arbitrary use of power, in enjoying their control over other people. They were corrupted by the power of their roles and became quite inventive in their techniques of breaking the spirit of the prisoners and making them feel they were worthless. Some of the guards merely did their jobs as tough but fair correctional officers, and several were good guards from the prisoners' point of view because they did them small favors and were

friendly. However, no good guard ever interfered with a command by any of the bad guards; they never intervened on the side of the prisoners, they never told the others to ease off because it was only an experiment, and they never even came to me as prison superintendent or experimenter in charge to complain. In part, they were good because the others were bad; they needed the others to help establish their own egos in a positive light. In a sense, the good guards perpetuated the prison more than the other guards because their own needs to be liked prevented them from disobeying or violating the implicit guards' code. At the same time, the act of befriending the prisoners created a social reality that made the prisoners less likely to rebel.

By the end of the week, the experiment had become a reality, as if it were a Pirandello play directed by Kafka that just keeps going after the audience has left. The consultant for our prison, Carlo Prescott, an exconvict with 16 years of imprisonment in California's jails, would get so depressed and furious each time he visited our prison, because of its psychological similarity to his experiences, that he would have to leave. A Catholic priest who was a former prison chaplain in Washington, D.C., talked to our prisoners after four days and said they were just like the other first-timers he had seen.

But in the end, I called off the experiment, not because of the horror I saw out there in the prison yard, but because of the horror of realizing that *I* could have easily traded places with the most brutal guard or become the weakest prisoner full of hatred at being so powerless that I could not eat, sleep, or go to the toilet without permission of the authorities. *I* could have become Calley at My Lai, George Jackson at San Quentin, one of the men at Attica.

Individual behavior is largely under the control of social forces and environmental contingencies rather than personality traits, character, will power, or other empirically unvalidated constructs. Thus we create an illusion of freedom by attributing more internal control to ourselves, to the individual, than actually exists. We thus underestimate the power and pervasiveness of situational controls over behavior because (a) they are often nonobvious and subtle, (b) we can often avoid entering situations in which we might be so controlled, and

(c) we label as "weak" or "deviant" people in those situations who do behave differently from how we believe we would.

Each of us carries around in our heads a favorable self-image in which we are essentially just, fair, humane, and understanding. For example, we could not imagine inflicting pain on others without much provocation or hurting people who had done nothing to us, who in fact were even liked by us. However, there is a growing body of social psychological research which underscores the conclusion derived from this prison study. Many people, perhaps the majority, can be made to do almost anything when put into psychologically compelling situations — regardless of their morals, ethics, values, attitudes, beliefs, or personal convictions. My colleague, Stanley Milgram, has shown that more than 60 percent of the population will deliver what they think is a series of painful electric shocks to another person even after the victim cries for mercy, begs them to stop, and then apparently passes out. The subjects complained that they did not want to inflict more pain but blindly obeyed the command of the authority figure (the experimenter) who said that they must go on. In my own research on violence, I have seen mild-mannered coeds repeatedly give shocks (which they thought were causing pain) to another girl, a stranger whom they had rated very favorably, simply by being made to feel anonymous and put in a situation in which they were expected to engage in this activity.

Observers of these and similar experimental situations never predict their outcomes and estimate that it is unlikely that they themselves would behave similarly. They can be so confident only when they are outside the situation. However, because the majority of people in these studies do act in nonrational, nonobvious ways, it follows that the majority of observers would also succumb to the social psychological forces in the situation.

With regard to prisons, we can state that the mere act of assigning labels to people and putting them into a situation in which those labels acquire validity and meaning is sufficient to elicit pathological behavior. This pathology is not predictable from any available diagnostic indicators we have in the social sciences, and it is extreme enough to modify in very significant ways fundamental attitudes and behavior. The prison situation, as presently arranged, is guaranteed to generate severe enough pathological reactions in both guards and prisoners as to debase their humanity, lower their feelings of self-worth, and make it difficult for them to be part of a society outside their prison.

# 20.  IF HITLER ASKED YOU TO ELECTROCUTE A STRANGER, WOULD YOU? PROBABLY

PHILIP MEYER

*"They are somehow engaged in something from which they cannot liberate themselves. They are locked into a structure, and they do not have the skills or inner resources to disengage themselves."*

No systematic study of positions and power is as clearly to the point as the Milgram experiments done at Yale University in the 1960s. Here is an article written about Milgram's findings. The importance of social structure is made clear: In the **position** of experimental subject, the individual is transformed, willing to take orders from the scientist, an authority seen as having a legitimate right to command. It is easy to react to this by claiming "I would never do it," but maybe a more objective response would be "Why do people do things like this? Why might I do something like this?" What forces are at work in social situations that lead the individual to do things he or she might not normally do?

In the beginning, Stanley Milgram was worried about the Nazi problem. He doesn't worry much about the Nazis anymore. He worries about you and me, and, perhaps, himself a little bit, too.

Stanley Milgram is a social psychologist, and when he began his career at Yale University in 1960, he had a plan to prove, scientifically, that Germans are different. The Germans-are-different hypothesis had been used by historians, such as William L. Shirer, to explain the systematic destruction of the Jews by the Third Reich. One madman could decide to destroy the Jews and even create a master plan for getting it done. But to implement it on the scale that Hitler did meant that thousands of other people had to go along with the scheme and help to do the work. The Shirer thesis, which Milgram set out to test, is that Germans have a basic character flaw that explains the whole thing, and this flaw is a readiness to obey authority without question, no matter what outrageous acts the authority commands.

The appealing thing about this theory is that it makes those of us who are not Germans feel better about the whole business. Obviously, you and I are not Hitler, and it seems equally obvious that we would never do Hitler's dirty work for him. But now, because of Stanley Milgram, we are compelled to wonder. Milgram developed a laboratory experiment that provided a systematic way to measure obedience. His plan was to try it out in New Haven on Americans and then go to Germany and try it out on Germans. He was strongly motivated by scientific curiosity, but there was also some moral content in his decision to pursue this line of research, which was in turn colored by his own Jewish background. If he could show that Germans are more obedient than Americans, he

From "If Hitler Asked You to Electrocute a Stranger, Would You? Probably," by Philip Meyer, in *Esquire* Magazine. Copyright © 1970 by Hearst Corp.

could then vary the conditions of the experiment and try to find out just what it is that makes some people more obedient than others. With this understanding, the world might, conceivably, be just a little bit better.

But he never took his experiment to Germany. He never took it any farther than Bridgeport. The first finding, also the most unexpected and disturbing finding, was that we Americans are an obedient people: not blindly obedient, and not blissfully obedient, just obedient. "I found so much obedience," says Milgram softly, a little sadly, "I hardly saw the need for taking the experiment to Germany."

There is something of the theater director in Milgram, and his technique, which he learned from one of the old masters in experimental psychology, Solomon Asch, is to stage a play with every line rehearsed, every prop carefully selected, and everybody an actor except one person. That one person is the subject of the experiment. The subject, of course, does not know he is in a play. He thinks he is in real life. The value of this technique is that the experimenter, as though he were God, can change a prop here, vary a line there, and see how the subject responds. Milgram eventually had to change a lot of the script just to get people to stop obeying. They were obeying so much that the experiment wasn't working — it was like trying to measure oven temperature with a freezer thermometer.

The experiment worked like this: If you were an innocent subject in Milgram's melodrama, you read an ad in the newspaper or received one in the mail asking for volunteers for an educational experiment. The job would take about an hour and pay $4.50. So you make an appointment and go to an old Romanesque stone structure on High Street with the imposing name of The Yale Interaction Laboratory. It looks something like a broadcasting studio. Inside, you meet a young, crew-cut man in a laboratory coat who says he is Jack Williams, the experimenter. There is another citizen, fiftyish, Irish face, an accountant, a little overweight, and very mild and harmless looking. This other citizen seems nervous and plays with his hat while the two of you sit in chairs side by side and are told that the $4.50 checks are yours no matter what happens. Then you listen to Jack Williams explain the experiment.

It is about learning, says Jack Williams in a quiet, knowledgeable way. Science does not know much about the conditions under which people learn, and this experiment is to find out about negative reinforcement. Negative reinforcement is getting punished when you do something wrong, as opposed to positive reinforcement, which is getting rewarded when you do something right. The negative reinforcement in this case is electric shock. You notice a book on the table, titled, *The Teaching-Learning Process*, and you assume that this has something to do with the experiment.

Then Jack Williams takes two pieces of paper, puts them in a hat, and shakes them up. One piece of paper is supposed to say, "Teacher" and the other, "Learner." Draw one and you will see which you will be. The mild-looking accountant draws one, holds it close to his vest like a poker player, looks at it, and says, "Learner." You look at yours. It says, "Teacher." You do not know that the drawing is rigged, and both slips say "Teacher." The experimenter beckons to the mild-mannered "learner."

"Want to step right in here and have a seat, please?" he says. "You can leave your coat on the back of that chair…roll up your right sleeve, please. Now, what I want to do is strap down your arms to avoid excessive movement on your part during the experiment. This electrode is connected to the shock generator in the next room.

"And this electrode paste," he says, squeezing some stuff out of a plastic bottle and putting it on the man's arm, "is to provide a good contact and to avoid a blister or burn. Are there any questions now before we go into the next room?"

You don't have any, but the strapped-in "learner" does.

"I do think I should say this," says the learner. "About two years ago, I was in the veterans' hospital…they detected a heart condition. Nothing serious, but as long as I'm having these shocks, how strong are they—how dangerous are they?"

Williams, the experimenter, shakes his head casually. "Oh, no," he says. "Although they may be painful, they're not dangerous. Anything else?"

Nothing else. And so you play the game. The game is for you to read a series of word pairs: for example, *blue-girl, nice-day, fat-neck*. When you finish the list, you read just the first word in each pair and then a multiple-choice list of four other words, including the second word of the pair. The learner, from his remote, strapped-in position, pushes one of four switches to indicate which of the four answers he thinks is the right one. If he gets it right, nothing happens and you go on to the next one. If he gets it wrong, you push a switch that buzzes and gives him an electric shock. And then you go on to the next word. You start with 15 volts and increase the number of volts by 15 for each wrong answer. The control board goes from 15 volts on one end to 450 volts on the other. So that you know what you are doing, you get a test shock yourself, at 45 volts. It hurts. To further keep you aware of what you are doing to that man in there, the board has verbal descriptions of the shock levels, ranging from "Slight Shock" at the left-hand side, through "Intense Shock" in the middle, to "Danger: Severe Shock" toward the far right. Finally, at the very end, under the 435-volt and 450-volt switches, there are three ambiguous Xs. If, at any point, you hesitate, Mr. Williams calmly tells you to go on. If you still hesitate, he tells you again.

Except for some terrifying details, which will be explained in a moment, this is the experiment. The object is to find the shock level at which you disobey the experimenter and refuse to pull the switch.

When Stanley Milgram first wrote this script, he took it to 14 Yale psychology majors and asked them what they thought would happen. He put it this way: Out of one hundred persons in the teacher's predicament, how would their break-off points be distributed along the 15-volt to 450-volt scale? They thought a few would break off very early, most would quit someplace in the middle, and a few would go all the way to the end. The highest estimate of the number out of 100 who would go all the way to the end was three. Milgram then informally polled some of his fellow scholars in the psychology department. They agreed that very few would go to the end. Milgram thought so, too.

"I'll tell you quite frankly," he says, "before I began this experiment, before any shock generator was built, I thought that most people would break off at 'Strong Shock' or 'Very Strong Shock.' You would get only a very, very small proportion of people going out to the end of the shock generator, and they would constitute a pathological fringe."

In his pilot experiments, Milgram used Yale students as subjects. Each of them pushed the shock switches, one by one, all the way to the end of the board.

So he rewrote the script to include some protests from the learner. At first, they were mild, gentlemanly, Yalie protests, but "it didn't seem to have as much effect as I thought it would or should," Milgram recalls. "So we had more violent protestation on the part of the person getting the shock. All the time, of course, what we were trying to do was not to create a macabre situation, but simply to generate disobedience. And that was one of the first findings. This was not only a technical deficiency of the experiment, that we didn't get disobedience. It really was the first finding: that obedience would be much greater than we had assumed it would be and that disobedience would be much more difficult than we had assumed."

As it turned out, the situation did become rather macabre. The only meaningful way to generate disobedience was to have the victim protest with great anguish, noise, and vehemence. The protests were tape-recorded so that all the teachers ordinarily would hear the same sounds and nuances, and they started with a grunt at 75 volts, proceeded through a "Hey, that really hurts," at 125 volts, got desperate with, "I can't stand the pain, don't do that," at 180 volts, reached complaints of heart trouble at 195, an agonized scream at 285, a refusal to answer at 315, and only heart-rending, ominous silence after that.

Still, 65 percent of the subjects, 20-to-50-year-old American males, everyday, ordinary people, like you and me, obediently kept pushing those levers in the belief that they were shocking the mild-mannered learner, whose name was Mr. Wallace, and who was chosen for the role because of his innocent appearance, all the way up to 450 volts.

Milgram was now getting enough disobedience so that he had something he could measure. The next step was to vary the circumstances to see what would encourage or discourage obedience. There

seemed very little left in the way of discouragement. The victim was already screaming at the top of his lungs and feigning a heart attack. So whatever new impediment to obedience reached the brain of the subject had to travel by some route other than the ear. Milgram thought of one.

He put the learner in the same room with the teacher. He stopped strapping the learner's hand down. He rewrote the script so that, at 150 volts, the learner took his hand off the shock plate and declared that he wanted out of the experiment. He rewrote the script some more so that the experimenter then told the teacher to grasp the learner's hand and physically force it down on the plate to give Mr. Wallace his unwanted electric shock.

"I had the feeling that very few people would go on at that point, if any," Milgram says. "I thought that would be the limit of obedience that you would find in the laboratory."

It wasn't.

Although seven years have now gone by, Milgram still remembers the first person to walk into the laboratory in the newly rewritten script. He was a construction worker, a very short man. "He was so small," says Milgram, "that when he sat on the chair in front of the shock generator, his feet didn't reach the floor. When the experimenter told him to push the victim's hand down and give the shock, he turned to the experimenter, and he turned to the victim, his elbow went up, he fell down on the hand of the victim, his feet kind of tugged to one side, and he said, 'Like this, boss?' Zzumph!"

The experiment was played out to its bitter end. Milgram tried it with 40 different subjects. And 30 percent of them obeyed the experimenter and kept on obeying.

"The protests of the victim were strong and vehement, he was screaming his guts out, he refused to participate, and you had to physically struggle with him in order to get his hand down on the shock generator," Milgram remembers. But 12 out of 40 did it.

Milgram took his experiment out of New Haven. Not to Germany, just 20 miles down the road to Bridgeport. Maybe, he reasoned, the people obeyed because of the prestigious setting of Yale University. If they couldn't trust a learning center that had been there for two centuries, who could they trust? So he moved the experiment to an untrustworthy setting.

The new setting was a suite of three rooms in a run-down office building in Bridgeport. The only identification was a sign with a fictitious name: "Research Associates of Bridgeport." Questions about professional connections got only vague answers about "research for industry."

Obedience was less in Bridgeport. Forty-eight percent of the subjects stayed for the maximum shock, compared to 65 percent at Yale. But this was enough to prove that far more than Yale's prestige was behind the obedient behavior.

For more than seven years now, Stanley Milgram has been trying to figure out what makes ordinary American citizens so obedient. The most obvious answer — that people are mean, nasty, brutish, and sadistic — won't do. The subjects who gave the shocks to Mr. Wallace to the end of the board did not enjoy it. They groaned, protested, fidgeted, argued, and in some cases, were seized by fits of nervous, agitated giggling.

"They even try to get out of it," says Milgram, "but they are somehow engaged in something from which they cannot liberate themselves. They are locked into a structure, and they do not have the skills or inner resources to disengage themselves...."

"The results, as seen and felt in the laboratory," he has written, "are disturbing. They raise the possibility that human nature, or more specifically the kind of character produced in American democratic society, cannot be counted on to insulate its citizens from brutality and inhumane treatment at the direction of malevolent authority. A substantial proportion of people do what they are told to do, irrespective of the content of the act and without limitation of conscience, so long as they perceive that the command comes from a legitimate authority. If, in this study, an anonymous experimenter can successfully command adults to subdue a 50-year-old man and force on him painful electric shocks against his protest, one can only wonder what government, with its vastly greater authority and prestige, can command of its subjects...."

Stanley Milgram has his problems, too. He believes that in the laboratory situation, he would not have shocked Mr. Wallace. His professional critics reply that in his real-life situation, he has done the equivalent. He has placed innocent and naive subjects under great emotional strain and pressure in selfish obedience to his quest for knowledge. When you raise this issue with Milgram, he has an answer ready. There is, he explains patiently, a critical difference between his naive subjects and the man in the electric chair. The man in the electric chair (in the mind of the naive subject) is helpless, strapped in. But the naive subject is free to go at any time.

Immediately after he offers this distinction, Milgram anticipates the objection.

"It's quite true," he says, "that this is almost a philosophic position, because we have learned that some people are psychologically incapable of disengaging themselves. But that doesn't relieve them of the moral responsibility."

The parallel is exquisite. "The tension problem was unexpected," says Milgram in his defense. But he went on anyway. The naive subjects didn't expect the screaming protests from the strapped-in learner. But they went on.

"I had to make a judgment," says Milgram. "I had to ask myself, was this harming the person or not? My judgment is that it was not. Even in the extreme cases, I wouldn't say that permanent damage results."

Sound familiar? "The shocks may be painful," the experimenter kept saying, "but they're not dangerous."

After the series of experiments was completed, Milgram sent a report of the results to his subjects and a questionnaire, asking whether they were glad or sorry to have been in the experiment. Eighty-three and seven-tenths percent said they were glad and only 1.3 percent were sorry; 15 percent were neither sorry nor glad. However, Milgram could not be sure at the time of the experiment that only 1.3 percent would be sorry.

Kurt Vonnegut, Jr., put one paragraph in the preface to *Mother Night*, in 1966, which pretty much says it for the people with their fingers on the shock-generator switches, for you and me, and maybe even for Milgram. "If I'd been born in Germany," Vonnegut said, "I suppose I would have *been* a Nazi, bopping Jews and gypsies and Poles around, leaving boots sticking out of snowbanks, warming myself with my sweetly virtuous insides. So it goes."

Just so. One thing that happened to Milgram back in New Haven during the days of the experiment was that he kept running into people he'd watched from behind the one-way glass. It gave him a funny feeling, seeing those people going about their everyday business in New Haven and knowing what they would do to Mr. Wallace if or-dered to. Now that his research results are in and you've thought about it, you can get this funny feeling too. You don't need one-way glass. A glance in your own mirror may serve just as well.

# 21. THE MY LAI MASSACRE: A MILITARY CRIME OF OBEDIENCE

## HERBERT KELMAN AND V. LEE HAMILTON

*"The slaughter at My Lai is an instance of a class of violent acts that can be described as sanctioned massacres.... The occurrence of sanctioned massacres cannot be adequately explained by the existence of psychological forces.... Instead, the major instigators for this class of violence derive from the policy process.... Thus it is more instructive to look not at the motives for violence but at the conditions under which the usual moral inhibitions against violence become weakened."*

This selection is part of Chapter 1 in the book, **Crimes of Obedience**. The My Lai massacre is one example of a crime in which individuals claimed that they were simply following the orders of someone who had a right to command them.

The My Lai massacre took place in the midst of war. The soldier is supposed to obey —yet obedience is supposed to be tempered by "ordinary sense and understanding," by moral convictions that make disobedience an obligation and obedience a crime. How is one supposed to know? Crimes committed in the midst of authority structures are all too common, not because people are simply mean or violent, but because the nature of the structure itself makes obedience seem morally acceptable.

In their conclusion to the chapter, the authors identify three processes that encourage people to surrender moral standards to commit sanctioned massacres: authorization, routinization, and dehumanization. There is a warning here: Each of us may be moral in most situations, but we may sometimes find ourselves in positions within social structures in which we are told to do something we know is wrong. What will we do?

March 16, 1968, was a busy day in U.S. history. Stateside, Robert F. Kennedy announced his presidential candidacy, challenging a sitting president from his own party — in part out of opposition to an undeclared and disastrous war. In Vietnam, the war continued. In many ways, March 16 may have been a typical day in that war. We will probably never know. But we do know that on that day, a typical company went on a mission — which may or may not have been typical — to a village called Son (or Song) My. Most of what is remembered from that mission occurred in the subhamlet known to Americans as My Lai 4.

The My Lai massacre was investigated, and charges were brought in 1969 and 1970. Trials and disciplinary actions lasted into 1971. Entire books have been written about the army's year-long cover-up of the massacre (for example, Hersh 1972), and the cover-up was a major focus of the army's own investigation of the incident. Our central concern here is the massacre itself — a crime of obedience — and public reactions to such crimes, rather than the lengths to which many went to deny the event. Therefore this account concentrates on one day: March 16, 1968.[1]

Many verbal testimonials to the horrors that occurred at My Lai were available. More unusual was the fact that an army photographer, Ronald Haeberle, was assigned the task of documenting the anticipated military engagement at My Lai — he documented a massacre instead. Later, as the story of the massacre emerged, his photographs were widely distributed and seared the public conscience. What might have been dismissed as unreal or exaggerated was depicted in photographs of demonstrable authenticity. The dominant image appeared on the cover of *Life*: Piles of bodies jumbled together in a ditch along a trail — the dead all apparently unarmed. All were Oriental, and all appeared to be children, women, or old men. Clearly there had been a mass execution, one whose image would not quickly fade.

So many bodies (over twenty in the cover photo alone) are hard to imagine as the handiwork of one killer. These were not. They were the product of what we call a *crime of obedience*. Crimes of obedience begin with orders. But orders are often vague and rarely survive with any clarity the transition from one authority down a chain of subordinates to the ultimate actors. The operation at Son My was no exception.

"Charlie" Company, Company C, under Lt. Col. Frank Barker's command, arrived in Vietnam in December 1967. As the army's investigative unit, directed by Lt. Gen. William R. Peers, characterized the personnel, they "contained no significant deviation from the average" for the time. Seymour S. Hersh (1970) described the "average" more explicitly: "Most of the men in Charlie Company had volunteered for the draft, only a few had gone to college for even one year. Nearly half were black, with a few Mexican-Americans. Most were eighteen to twenty-two years old. The favorite reading matter of Charlie Company, like that of other line infantry units in Vietnam, was comic books" (p. 18). The action at My Lai, like that throughout Vietnam, was fought by a cross-section of those Americans who either believed in the war or lacked the social resources to avoid participating in it. Charlie Company was indeed average for that time, that place, and that war.

Two key figures in Charlie Company were more unusual. The company's commander, Capt. Ernest Medina, was an upwardly mobile Mexican-American who wanted to make the army his career, although he feared that he might never advance beyond captain because of his lack of formal education. His eagerness had earned him a nickname among his men: "Mad Dog Medina." One of his admirers was the platoon leader, Second Lt. William L. Calley, Jr., an undistinguished, five-foot-three-inch junior-college dropout who had failed four of the seven courses in which he had enrolled his first year. Many viewed him as one of those "instant officers" made possible only by the army's then-desperate need for manpower. Whatever the cause, he was an insecure leader whose frequent claim was "I'm the boss." His nickname among some of the troops was "Surfside 5 1/2," a reference to the swashbuckling heroes of a popular television show, "Surfside 6."

The Son My operation was planned by Lieutenant Colonel Barker and his staff as a search-and-destroy mission with the objective of rooting out the Forty-Eighth Viet Cong Battalion from their base area of Son My village. Apparently, no written orders were ever issued. Barker's superior, Col. Oran Henderson, arrived at the staging point the day before. Among the issues he reviewed with the assembled officers were some of the weaknesses of prior operations by their units, including their failure to be appropriately aggressive in pursuit of the enemy. Later briefings by Lieutenant Colonel Barker and his staff asserted that no one except Viet Cong was expected to be in the village after 7 A.M. on the following day. The "innocent" would all be at the market. Those present at the briefings gave conflicting accounts of Barker's exact orders, but he conveyed at least a strong suggestion that the Son My area was to be obliterated. As the army's inquiry reported: "While there is some conflict in the testimony as to whether LTC Barker ordered the destruction of houses, dwellings, livestock, and other foodstuffs in the Song My area, the preponderance of the evidence indicates that such destruction was implied, if not specifically directed, by his orders of 15 March" (Peers Report, in Goldstein et al. 1976, p. 94).

Evidence that Barker ordered the killing of civilians is even more murky. What does seem clear, however, is that — having asserted that civilians would be away at the market — he did not specify what was to be done with any who might nevertheless be found on the scene. The Peers Report therefore considered it "reasonable to conclude that LTC Barker's minimal or nonexistent instructions concerning the handling of noncombatants created the potential for grave misunderstandings as to his intentions and for interpretation of his orders as authority to fire, without restriction, on all persons found in target area" (Goldstein et al. 1976, p. 95). Because Barker was killed in action in June 1968, his own formal version of the truth was never available.

Charlie Company's Captain Medina was briefed for the operation by Barker and his staff. He then transmitted the already vague orders to his own men. Charlie Company was spoiling for a fight, having been totally frustrated during its months in Vietnam — first by waiting for battles that never came, then by incompetent forays led by inexperienced commanders, and finally by mines and booby traps. In fact, the emotion-laden funeral of a sergeant killed by a booby trap was held on March 15, the day before My Lai. Captain Medina gave the orders for the next day's action at the close of that funeral. Many were in a mood for revenge.

It is again unclear what was ordered. Although all participants were still alive by the time of the trials for the massacre, they were either on trial or probably felt under threat of trial. Memories are often flawed and self-serving at such times. It is apparent that Medina relayed to the men at least some of Barker's general message — to expect Viet Cong resistance, to burn, and to kill livestock. It is not clear that he ordered the slaughter of the inhabitants, but some of the men who heard him thought he had. One of those who claimed to have heard such orders was Lt. William Calley.

As March 16 dawned, much was expected of the operation by those who had set it into motion. Therefore a full complement of "brass" was present in helicopters overhead, including Barker, Colonel Henderson, and their superior, Major General Koster (who went on to become commandant of West Point before the story of My Lai broke). On the ground, the troops were to carry with them one reporter and one photographer to immortalize the anticipated battle.

The action for Company C began at 7:30 as their first wave of helicopters touched down near the subhamlet of My Lai 4. By 7:47, all of Company C was present and set to fight. But instead of the Viet Cong Forty-Eighth Battalion, My Lai was filled with the old men, women, and children who were supposed to have gone to market. By this time, in their version of the war, and with whatever orders they thought they had heard, the men from Company C were nevertheless ready to find Viet Cong everywhere. By nightfall, the official tally was 128 VC killed and three weapons captured, although later unofficial body counts ran as high as 500. The operation at Son My was over. And by nightfall, as Hersh reported: "the Viet Cong were back in My Lai 4, helping the survivors bury the dead. It took five days. Most of the funeral speeches were made by the Communist guerrillas. Nguyen Bat was not a Communist at the time of the massacre, but the incident changed his mind. 'After the shooting,' he said, 'all the villagers became Communists'" (1970, p. 74). To this day, the memory of the massacre is kept alive by markers and plaques designating the spots where groups of villagers were killed, by a large statue, and by the My Lai Museum, established in 1975 (Williams 1985).

But what could have happened to leave American troops reporting a victory over Viet Cong when in fact they had killed hundreds of noncombatants? It is not hard to explain the report of victory; that is the essence of a cover-up. It is harder to understand how the killings came to be committed in the first place, making a cover-up necessary.

## MASS EXECUTIONS AND THE DEFENSE OF SUPERIOR ORDERS

Some of the atrocities on March 16, 1968, were evidently unofficial, spontaneous acts: rapes, tortures, killings. For example, Hersh (1970) describes Charlie Company's Second Platoon as entering "My Lai 4 with guns blazing" (p. 50); more graphically, Lieutenant "Brooks and his men in the second platoon to the north had begun to systematically ransack the hamlet and slaughter the people, kill the livestock, and destroy the crops. Men poured rifle and machine-gun fire into huts without knowing—or seemingly caring—who was inside" (pp. 49–50).

Some atrocities toward the end of the action were part of an almost casual "mopping-up," much of which was the responsibility of Lieutenant LaCross's Third Platoon of Charlie Company. The Peers Report states: "The entire 3rd Platoon then began moving into the western edge of My Lai (4), for the mop-up operation.... The squad...began to burn the houses in the southwestern portion of the hamlet" (Goldstein et al. 1976, p. 133). They became mingled with other platoons during a series of rapes and killings of survivors for which it was impossible to fix responsibility. Certainly, to a Vietnamese, all GIs would by this point look alike: "Nineteen year-old Nguyen Thi Ngoc Tuyet watched a baby trying to open her slain mother's blouse to nurse. A soldier shot the infant while it was struggling with the blouse, and then slashed it with his bayonet." Tuyet also said she saw another baby hacked to death by GIs wielding their bayonets. "Le Tong, a twenty-eight-year-old rice farmer, reported seeing one woman raped after GIs killed her children. Nguyen Khoa, a thirty-seven-year-old peasant, told of a thirteen-year-old girl who was raped before being killed. GIs then attacked Khoa's wife, tearing off her clothes. Before they could rape her, however, Khoa said, their six-year-old son, riddled with bullets, fell and saturated her with blood. The GIs left her alone" (Hersh 1970, p. 72). All of Company C was implicated in a pattern of death and destruction throughout the hamlet, much of which seemingly lacked rhyme or reason.

But a substantial amount of the killing was *organized* and traceable to one authority: the First Platoon's Lt. William Calley. Calley was originally charged with 109 killings, almost all of them mass executions at the trail and other locations. He stood trial for 102 of these killings, was convicted of 22 in 1971, and at first received a life sentence. Although others—both superior and subordinate to Calley—were brought to trial, he was the only one convicted for the My Lai crimes.

Thus, the only actions of My Lai for which *anyone* was ever convicted were mass executions, ordered and committed. We suspect that there are commonsense reasons why this one type of killing was singled out. In the midst of rapidly moving events with people running about, an execution of stationary targets is literally a still life that stands out and whose participants are clearly visible. It can be proven that specific people committed specific deeds. An execution, in contrast to the shooting of someone on the run, is also more likely to meet the legal definition of an act resulting from intent—with malice aforethought. Moreover, American military law specifically forbids the killing of unarmed civilians or military prisoners, as does the Geneva Convention between nations. Thus common sense, legal standards, and explicit doctrine all made such actions the likeliest target for prosecution....

The day's quiet beginning has already been noted. Troops landed and swept unopposed into the village. The three weapons eventually reported as the haul from the operation were picked up from three apparent Viet Cong who fled the village when the troops arrived and were pursued and killed by helicopter gunships. Obviously, the Viet Cong did frequent the area. But it appears that by about 8:00 A.M., no one who met the troops was aggressive, and no one was armed. By the laws of war, Charlie Company had no argument with such people.

As they moved into the village, the soldiers began to gather its inhabitants together. Shortly after 8:00 A.M., Lieutenant Calley told Pfc. Paul Meadlo that "you know what to do with" a group of villagers Meadlo was guarding. Estimates of the numbers in the group ranged as high as eighty women, children, and old men, and Meadlo's own estimate under oath was thirty to fifty people. As Meadlo later testified, Calley returned after ten or fifteen minutes: "He [Calley] said, 'How come they're not dead?' I said, 'I didn't know we were supposed to kill them.' He said, 'I want them dead.' He backed off twenty or thirty feet and started shooting into the people—the Viet Cong—shooting automatic. He was beside me. He burned four or five magazines. I burned off a few, about three. I helped shoot 'em" (Hammer 1971, p. 155). Meadlo himself and others testified that Meadlo cried as he fired; others reported him later to be sobbing and "all broke up." It would appear that to Lieutenant Calley's subordinates, something was unusual and stressful in these orders.

At the trial, the first specification in the murder charge against Calley was for this incident; he was accused of the premeditated murder of "an unknown number, not less than thirty, Oriental human beings, males and females of various ages, whose names are unknown, occupants of the village of My Lai 4, by means of shooting them with a rifle" (Goldstein et al. 1976, p. 497).

Among the helicopters flying reconnaissance above Son My was that of CWO Hugh Thompson. By 9:00 or soon after, Thompson had noticed some horrifying events from his perch. As he spotted wounded civilians, he sent down smoke markers so that soldiers on the ground could treat them. They killed them instead. He reported to headquarters, trying to persuade someone to stop what was going on. Barker, hearing the message, called down to Captain Medina. Medina, in turn, later claimed to have told Calley that it was "enough for today." But it was not yet enough.

At Calley's orders, his men began gathering the remaining villagers—roughly seventy-five individuals, mostly women and children—and herding them toward a drainage ditch. Accompanied by three or four enlisted men, Lieutenant Calley executed several batches of civilians who had been gathered into ditches. Some of the details of the process were entered into testimony in such accounts as Pfc. Dennis Conti's: "A lot of them, the people, were trying to get up and mostly they was just screaming and pretty bad shot up.... I seen a woman tried to get up. I seen Lieutenant Calley fire. He hit the side of her head and blew it off" (Hammer 1971, p. 125).

Testimony by other soldiers presented the shooting's aftermath. Specialist Four Charles Hall, asked by Prosecutor Aubrey Daniel how he knew the people in the ditch were dead, said: "There was blood coming from them. They were just scattered all over the ground in the ditch, some in piles and some scattered out 20, 25 meters perhaps up the ditch.... They were very old people, very young children, and mothers.... There was blood all over them" (Goldstein et al. 1976, pp. 501–02). And Pfc. Gregory Olsen corroborated the general picture of the victims: "They were—the majority were women and children, some babies. I distinctly remember one middle-aged Vietnamese male dressed in white right at my feet as I crossed. None of the bodies were mangled in any way. There was blood. Some appeared to be dead, others followed me with their eyes as I walked across the ditch" (Goldstein et al. 1976, p. 502).

The second specification in the murder charge stated that Calley did "with premeditation, murder an unknown number of Oriental human beings, not less than seventy, males and females of various ages, whose names were unknown, occupants of the village of My Lai 4, by means of shooting them with a rifle" (Goldstein et al. 1976, p. 497). Calley was also charged with and tried for shootings of individuals (an old man and a child); these charges were clearly supplemental to the main issue at trial—the mass killings and how they came about.

It is noteworthy that, during these executions, more than one enlisted man avoided carrying out Calley's orders, and more than one, by sworn oath, directly refused to obey them. For example, Pfc. James Joseph Dursi testified, when asked if he fired when Lieutenant Calley ordered him to: "No. I just stood there. Meadlo turned to me after a couple of minutes and said 'Shoot! Why don't you shoot! Why don't you fire!' He was crying and yelling. I said, 'I can't! I won't!' And the people were screaming and crying and yelling. They kept firing for a couple of minutes, mostly automatic and semi-automatic" (Hammer 1971, p. 143)....

Disobedience of Lieutenant Calley's own orders to kill represented a serious legal and moral threat to a defense *based* on superior orders, such as Calley was attempting. This defense had to assert that the orders seemed reasonable enough to carry out, that they appeared to be legal orders. Even if the orders in question were not legal, the defense had to assert that an ordinary individual could not and should not be expected to see the distinction. In short, if what happened was "business as usual," even though it might be bad business, then the defendant stood a chance of acquittal. But under direct command from "Surfside 5 1/2," some ordinary enlisted men managed to refuse, to avoid, or at least to stop doing what they were ordered to do. As "reasonable men" of "ordinary sense and understanding," they had apparently found something awry that morning; and it would have been hard for an officer to plead successfully that he was more ordinary than his men in his capacity to evaluate the reasonableness of orders.

Even those who obeyed Calley's orders showed great stress. For example, Meadlo eventually began to argue and cry directly in front of Calley. Pfc. Herbert Carter shot himself in the foot, possibly because he could no longer take what he was doing. We were not destined to hear a sworn version of the incident because neither side at the Calley trial called him to testify.

The most unusual instance of resistance to authority came from the skies. CWO Hugh Thompson, who had protested the apparent carnage of civilians, was Calley's inferior in rank but was not in his line of command. He was also watching the ditch from his helicopter and noticed some people moving after the first round of slaughter — chiefly children who had been shielded by their mothers' bodies. Landing to rescue the wounded, he also found some villagers hiding in a nearby bunker. Protecting the Vietnamese with his own body, Thompson ordered his men to train their guns on the Americans and to open fire if the Americans fired on the Vietnamese. He then radioed for additional rescue helicopters and stood between the Vietnamese and the Americans under Calley's command until the Vietnamese could be evacuated. He later returned to the ditch to unearth a child buried, unharmed, beneath layers of bodies. In October 1969, Thompson was awarded the Distinguished Flying Cross for heroism at My Lai, specifically (albeit inaccurately) for the rescue of children hiding in a bunker "between Viet Cong forces and advancing friendly forces" and for the rescue of a wounded child "caught in the intense crossfire" (Hersh 1970, p. 119). Four months earlier, at the Pentagon, Thompson had identified Calley as having been at the ditch.

By about 10:00 A.M., the massacre was winding down. The remaining actions consisted largely of isolated rapes and killings, "clean-up" shootings of the wounded, and the destruction of the village by fire. We have already seen some examples of these more indiscriminate and possibly less premeditated acts. By the 11:00 A.M. lunch break, when the exhausted men of Company C were relaxing, two young girls wandered back from a hiding place only to be invited to share lunch. This surrealist touch illustrates the extent to which the soldiers' action had become dissociated from its meaning. An hour earlier, some of these men were making sure that not even a child would escape the executioner's bullet. But now, the job was done and it was time for lunch — and in this new context, it seemed only natural to ask the children who had managed to escape execution to join them. The massacre had ended. It remained only for the Viet Cong to reap the political rewards among the survivors in hiding.

The army command in the area knew that something had gone wrong. Direct commanders, including Lieutenant Colonel Barker, had first-hand reports, such as Thompson's plaints. Others had such odd bits of evidence as the claim of 128 Viet Cong dead with a booty of only three weapons. But the cover-up of My Lai began at once. The operation was reported as a victory over a stronghold of the Viet Cong Forty-Eighth....

William Calley was not the only man tried for the events at My Lai. The actions of over thirty soldiers and civilians were scrutinized by investigators; over half of these had to face charges or disciplinary action of some sort. Targets of investigation included Captain Medina, who was tried, and various higher-ups, including General Koster. But Lieutenant Calley was the only person convicted, the only person to serve time.

The core of Lieutenant Calley's defense was superior orders. What this meant to him — in contrast to what it meant to the judge and jury — can be gleaned from his responses to a series of questions from his defense attorney, George Latimer, in which Calley sketched out his understanding of the laws of war and the actions that constitute doing one's duty within those laws:

*Latimer*: Did you receive any training...which had to do with the obedience to orders?

*Calley*: Yes, sir.

*Latimer*: ...what were you informed [were] the principles involved in that field?

*Calley*: That all orders were to be assumed legal, that the soldier's job was to carry out any order given him to the best of his ability.

*Latimer*: …what might occur if you disobeyed an order by a senior officer?

*Calley*: You could be court-martialed for refusing an order and refusing an order in the face of the enemy, you could be sent to death, sir.

*Latimer*: [I am asking] whether you were required in any way, shape, or form to make a determination of the legality or illegality of an order?

*Calley*: No, sir. I was never told that I had the choice, sir.

*Latimer*: If you had a doubt about the order, what were you supposed to do?

*Calley*: …I was supposed to carry the order out and then come back and make my complaint (Hammer 1971, pp. 240–41).

Lieutenant Calley steadfastly maintained that his actions within My Lai had constituted, in his mind, carrying out orders from Captain Medina. Both his own actions and the orders he gave to others (such as the instruction to Meadlo to "waste 'em") were entirely in response to superior orders. He denied any intent to kill individuals and any but the most passing awareness of distinctions among the individuals: "I was ordered to go in there and destroy the enemy. That was my job on that day. That was the mission I was given. I did not sit down and think in terms of men, women, and children. They were all classified the same, and that was the classification that we dealt with, just as enemy soldiers." When Latimer asked if in his own opinion Calley had acted "rightly and according to your understanding of your directions and orders," Calley replied, "I felt then and I still do that I acted as I was directed, and I carried out the orders that I was given, and I do not feel wrong in doing so, sir" (Hammer 1971, p. 257).

His court-martial did not accept Calley's defense of superior orders and clearly did not share his interpretation of his duty. The jury evidently reasoned that, even if there had been orders to destroy everything in sight and to "waste the Vietnamese," any reasonable person would have realized that such orders were illegal and should have refused to carry them out. The defense of superior orders under such conditions is inadmissible under international and military law. The U.S. Army's *Law of Land Warfare* (Dept. of the Army, 1956), for example, states that "the fact that the law of war has been violated pursuant to an order of a superior authority, whether military or civil, does not deprive the act in question of its character of a war crime, nor does it constitute a defense in the trial of an accused individual, unless he did not know and could not reasonably have been expected to know that that act was unlawful" and that "members of the armed forces are bound to obey only lawful orders" (Falk et al. 1971, pp. 71–72).

The disagreement between Calley and the court-martial seems to have revolved around the definition of the responsibilities of a subordinate to obey, on the one hand, and to evaluate, on the other…. For now, it can best be captured via the charge to the jury in the Calley court-martial, made by the trial judge, Col. Reid Kennedy. The forty-one pages of the charge include the following:

Both combatants captured by and noncombatants detained by the opposing force…have the right to be treated as prisoners…. Summary execution of detainees or prisoners is forbidden by law…. I therefore instruct you…that if unresisting human beings were killed at My Lai (4) while within the effective custody and control of our military forces, their deaths cannot be considered justified…. Thus if you find that Lieutenant Calley received an order directing him to kill unresisting Vietnamese within his control or within the control of his troops, *that order would be an illegal order.*

A determination that an order is illegal does not, of itself, assign criminal responsibility to the person following the order for acts done in compliance with it. Soldiers are taught to follow orders, and special attention is given to obedience of orders on the battlefield. Military effectiveness depends on obedience of orders. On the other hand, the obedience of a soldier is not the obedience of an automaton. A soldier is a reasoning agent, obliged to respond, not as a machine, but as a person. The law takes these factors into account in assessing criminal responsibility for acts done in compliance with illegal orders.

The acts of a subordinate done in compliance with an unlawful order given him by his superior are excused and impose no criminal liability upon him unless the superior's order is one which a man of *ordinary sense and understanding* would, under the circumstances, know to be unlawful, or if the order in question is actually known to the accused to be unlawful (Goldstein et al. 1976, pp. 525–526; emphasis added).

By this definition, subordinates take part in a balancing act, one tipped toward obedience but tempered by "ordinary sense and understanding."

A jury of combat veterans proceeded to convict William Calley of the premeditated murder of no less than twenty-two human beings. (The army, realizing some unfortunate connotations in referring to the victims as "Oriental human beings," eventually referred to them as "human beings.") Regarding the first specification in the murder charge, the bodies on the trail, he was convicted of premeditated murder of not less than one person. (Medical testimony had been able to pinpoint only one person whose wounds as revealed in Haeberle's photos were sure to be immediately fatal.) Regarding the second specification, the bodies in the ditch, Calley was convicted of the premeditated murder of not less than twenty human beings. Regarding additional specifications that he had killed an old man and a child, Calley was convicted of premeditated murder in the first case and of assault with intent to commit murder in the second.

Lieutenant Calley was initially sentenced to life imprisonment. That sentence was reduced: first to twenty years, eventually to ten (the latter by Secretary of Defense Callaway in 1974). Calley served three years before being released on bond. The time was spent under house arrest in his apartment, where he was able to receive visits from his girlfriend. He was granted parole on September 10, 1975.

## SANCTIONED MASSACRES

The slaughter at My Lai is an instance of a class of violent acts that can be described as sanctioned massacres (Kelman 1973): acts of indiscriminate, ruthless, and often systematic mass violence, carried out by military or paramilitary personnel while engaged in officially sanctioned campaigns, the victims of which are defenseless and unresisting civilians, including old men, women, and children. Sanctioned massacres have occurred throughout history. Within American history, My Lai had its precursors in the Philippine war around the turn of the century (Schirmer 1971) and in

the massacres of American Indians. Elsewhere in the world, one recalls the Nazis' "final solution" for European Jews, the massacres and deportations of Armenians by Turks, the liquidation of the kulaks and the great purges in the Soviet Union, and more recently the massacres in Indonesia and Bangladesh, in Biafra and Burundi, in South Africa and Mozambique, in Cambodia and Afghanistan, in Syria and Lebanon....

The occurrence of sanctioned massacres cannot be adequately explained by the existence of psychological forces—whether these be characterological dispositions to engage in murderous violence, or profound hostility against the target—so powerful that they must find expression in violent acts unhampered by moral restraints. Instead, the major instigators for this class of violence derive from the policy process. The question that really calls for psychological analysis is why so many people are willing to formulate, participate in, and condone policies that call for the mass killings of defenseless civilians. Thus it is more instructive to look not at the motives for violence but at the conditions under which the usual moral inhibitions against violence become weakened. Three social processes that tend to create such conditions can be identified: authorization, routinization, and dehumanization. Through *authorization*, the situation becomes so defined that the individual is absolved of the responsibility to make personal moral choices. Through *routinization*, the action becomes so organized that there is no opportunity for raising moral questions. Through *dehumanization*, the actors' attitudes toward the target and toward themselves become so structured that it is neither necessary nor possible for them to view the relationship in moral terms.

### Authorization

Sanctioned massacres by definition occur in the context of an authority situation, a situation in which, at least for many of the participants, the moral principles that generally govern human relationships do not apply. Thus, when acts of violence are explicitly ordered, implicitly encouraged, tacitly approved, or at least permitted by legitimate authorities, people's readiness to commit or condone them is enhanced. That such acts are authorized seems to carry automatic justification for them. Behaviorally, authorization obviates the necessity of making judgments or choices. Not only do normal moral principles become inoperative, but — particularly when the actions are explicitly ordered — a different kind of morality, linked to the duty to obey superior orders, tends to take over.

In an authority situation, individuals characteristically feel obligated to obey the orders of the authorities, whether or not these orders correspond with their personal preferences. They see themselves as having no choice as long as they accept the legitimacy of the orders and of the authorities who give them. Individuals differ considerably in the degree to which — and the conditions under which — they are prepared to challenge the legitimacy of an order on the grounds that the order itself is illegal, or that those giving it have overstepped their authority, or that it stems from a policy that violates fundamental societal values. Regardless of such individual differences, however, the basic structure of a situation of legitimate authority requires subordinates to respond in terms of their role obligations rather than their personal preferences; they can openly disobey only by challenging the legitimacy of the authority. Often, people obey without question even though the behavior they engage in may entail great personal sacrifice or great harm to others.

An important corollary of the basic structure of the authority situation is that actors often do not see themselves as personally responsible for the consequences of their actions. Again, there are individual differences, depending on actors' capacity and readiness to evaluate the legitimacy of orders received. Insofar as they see themselves as having had no choice in their actions, however, they do not feel personally responsible for them. They were not personal agents, but merely extensions of the authority. Thus, when their actions cause harm to others, they can feel relatively free of guilt. A similar mechanism operates when a person engages in antisocial behavior that was not ordered by the authorities but was tacitly encouraged and approved by them — even if only by making it clear that such behavior will not be punished. In this situation, behavior that was formerly illegitimate is legitimized by the authorities' acquiescence.

In the My Lai massacre, it is likely that the structure of the authority situation contributed to the massive violence in both ways — that is, by conveying the message that acts of violence against Vietnamese villagers were *required*, as well as the message that such acts, even if not ordered, were *permitted* by the authorities in charge. The actions at My Lai represented, at least in some respects, responses to explicit or implicit orders. Lieutenant Calley indicated, by orders and by example, that he wanted large numbers of villagers killed. Whether Calley himself had been ordered by his superiors to "waste" the whole area, as he claimed, remains a matter of controversy. Even if we assume, however, that he was not explicitly ordered to wipe out the village, he had reason to believe that such actions were expected by his superior officers. Indeed, the very nature of the war conveyed this expectation. The principal measure of military success was the "body count" — the number of enemy soldiers killed — and any Vietnamese killed by the U.S. military was commonly defined as a "Viet Cong." Thus, it was not totally bizarre for Calley to believe that what he was doing at My Lai was to increase his body count, as any good officer was expected to do.

Even to the extent that the actions at My Lai occurred spontaneously, without reference to superior orders, those committing them had reason to assume that such actions might be tacitly approved of by the military authorities. Not only had they failed to punish such acts in most cases, but the very strategies and tactics that the authorities consistently devised were based on the proposition that the civilian population of South Vietnam — whether "hostile" or "friendly" — was expendable. Such policies as search-and-destroy missions, the establishment of free-shooting zones, the use of antipersonnel weapons, the bombing of entire villages if they were suspected of harboring guerrillas, the forced migration of masses of the rural population, and the defoliation of vast forest areas helped legitimize acts of massive violence of the kind occurring at My Lai.

Some of the actions at My Lai suggest an orientation to authority based on unquestioning obedience to superior orders, no matter how destructive the actions these orders call for. Such obedience is specifically fostered in the course of military training and reinforced by the structure of the military authority situation. It also reflects, however, an ideological orientation that may be more widespread in the general population, as some of the data presented in this volume will demonstrate.

## Routinization

Authorization processes create a situation in which people become involved in an action without considering its implications and without really making a decision. Once they have taken the initial step, they are in a new psychological and social situation in which the pressures to continue are powerful. As Lewin (1947) has pointed out, many forces that might originally have kept people out of a situation reverse direction once they have made a commitment (once they have gone through the "gate region") and now serve to keep them in the situation. For example, concern about the criminal nature of an action, which might originally have inhibited a person from becoming involved, may now lead to deeper involvement in efforts to justify the action and to avoid negative consequences.

Despite these forces, however, given the nature of the actions involved in sanctioned massacres, one might still expect moral scruples to intervene; but the likelihood of moral resistance is greatly reduced by transforming the action into routine, mechanical, highly programmed operations. Routinization fulfills two functions. First, it reduces the necessity of making decisions, thus minimizing the occasions in which moral questions may arise. Second, it makes it easier to avoid the implications of the action because the actor focuses on the details of the job rather than on its meaning. The latter effect is more readily achieved among those who participate in sanctioned massacres from a distance—from their desks or even from the cockpits of their bombers.

Routinization operates both at the level of the individual actor and at the organizational level. Individual job performance is broken down into a series of discrete steps, most of them carried out in automatic, regularized fashion. It becomes easy to forget the nature of the product that emerges from this process. When Lieutenant Calley said of My Lai that it was "no great deal," he probably implied that it was all in a day's work. Organizationally, the task is divided among different offices, each of which has responsibility for a small portion of it. This arrangement diffuses responsibility and limits the amount and scope of decision making that is necessary. There is no expectation that the moral implications will be considered at any of these points, nor is there any opportunity to do so. The organizational processes also help further legitimize the actions of each participant. By proceeding in routine fashion—processing papers, exchanging memos, diligently carrying out their assigned tasks—the different units mutually reinforce each other in the view that what is going on must be perfectly normal, correct, and legitimate. The shared illusion that they are engaged in a legitimate enterprise helps the participants assimilate their activities to other purposes, such as the efficiency of their performance, the productivity of their unit, or the cohesiveness of their group (Janis 1972).

Normalization of atrocities is more difficult to the extent that there are constant reminders of the true meaning of the enterprise. Bureaucratic inventiveness in the use of language helps to cover up such meaning. For example, the SS had a set of *Sprachregelungen*, or "language rules," to govern descriptions of their extermination program. As Arendt (1964) points out, the term *language rule* in itself was "a code name; it meant what in ordinary language would be called a *lie*" (p. 85). The code names for killing and liquidation were "final solution," "evacuation," and "special treatment." The war in Indochina produced its own set of euphemisms, such as "protective reaction," "pacification," and "forced-draft urbanization and modernization." The use of euphemisms allows participants in sanctioned massacres to differentiate their actions from ordinary killing and destruction and thus to avoid confronting their true meaning.

## Dehumanization

Authorization processes override standard moral considerations; routinization processes reduce the likelihood that such considerations will arise. Still, the inhibitions against murdering one's fellow human beings are generally so strong that the victims must also be stripped of their human status if they are to be subjected to systematic killing. Insofar as they are dehumanized, the usual principles of morality no longer apply to them.

Sanctioned massacres become possible to the extent that the victims are deprived in the perpetrators' eyes of the two qualities essential to being perceived as fully human and included in the moral compact that governs human relationships: *identity* (standing as independent, distinctive individuals, capable of making choices and entitled to live their own lives) and *community* (fellow membership in an interconnected network of individuals who care for each other and respect each other's individuality and rights) (Kelman 1973; see also Bakan 1966 for a related distinction between "agency" and "communion"). Thus, when a group of people is defined entirely in terms of a category to which they belong, and when this category is excluded from the human family, moral restraints against killing them are more readily overcome.

Dehumanization of the enemy is a common phenomenon in any war situation. Sanctioned massacres, however, presuppose a more extreme degree of dehumanization, insofar as the killing is not in direct response to the target's threats or provocations. It is not what they have done that marks such victims for death but who they are — the category to which they happen to belong. They are the victims of policies that regard their systematic destruction as a desirable end or an acceptable means. Such extreme dehumanization becomes possible when the target group can readily be identified as a separate category of people who have historically been stigmatized and excluded by the victimizers. Often, the victims belong to a distinct racial, religious, ethnic, or political group regarded as inferior or sinister. The traditions, the habits, the images, and the vocabularies for dehumanizing such groups are already well established and can be drawn on when the groups are selected for massacre. Labels help deprive the victims of identity and community, as in the epithet "gooks" that was commonly used to refer to Vietnamese and other Indochinese peoples.

The dynamics of the massacre process itself further increase the participants' tendency to dehumanize their victims. Those who participate as part of the bureaucratic apparatus increasingly come to see their victims as bodies to be counted and entered into their reports, as faceless figures that will determine their productivity rates and promotions. Those who participate in the massacre directly — in the field, as it were — are reinforced in their perception of the victims as less than human by observing their very victimization. The only way they can justify what is being done to these people — both by others and by themselves — and the only way they can extract some degree of meaning out of the absurd events in which they find themselves participating (see Lifton 1971, 1973) is by coming to believe that the victims are subhuman and deserve to be rooted out. And thus the process of dehumanization feeds on itself.

## ENDNOTES

1. In reconstructing the events of that day, we consulted Hammer (1970), in addition to the sources cited in the text. Schell (1968) provided information on the region around My Lai. Concerning Vietnam and peasant rebellions, we consulted FitzGerald (1972), Paige (1975), Popkin (1979), and Wolf (1969).

## REFERENCES

Arendt, H. (1964). *Eichmann in Jerusalem: A Report on the Banality of Evil*. New York: Viking Press.

Bakan, D. (1966). *The Duality of Human Existence*. Chicago: Rand McNally.

Department of the Army. (1956). *The Law of Land Warfare* (Field Manual, No. 27–10). Washington, D.C.: U.S. Government Printing Office.

Falk, R. A., G. Kolko, & R. J. Lifton (Eds.). (1971). *Crimes of War*. New York: Vintage Books.

FitzGerald, F. (1972). *Fire in the Lake: The Vietnamese and the Americans in Vietnam*. Boston: Atlantic-Little, Brown.

Goldstein, J., B. Marshall, & J. Schwartz (Eds.). (1976). *The My Lai Massacre and Its Cover-Up: Beyond the Reach of Law?* (The Peers report with a supplement and introductory essay on the limits of law). New York: Free Press.

Hammer, R. (1970). *One Morning in the War*. New York: Coward-McCann.

———. (1971). *The Court-Martial of Lt. Calley*. New York: Coward, McCann, & Geoghegan.

Hersh, S. (1970). *My Lai 4: A Report on the Massacre and Its Aftermath.* New York: Vintage Books.

———. (1972). *Cover-Up.* New York: Random House.

Janis, I. L. (1972). *Victims of Groupthink: A Psychological Study of Foreign-Policy Decisions and Fiascoes.* Boston: Houghton Mifflin.

Kelman, H. C. (1973). "Violence without Moral Restraint: Reflections on the Dehumanization of Victims and Victimizers." *Journal of Social Issues*, 29(4), 25–61.

Lewin, K. (1947). "Group Decision and Social Change." In T. M. Newcomb & E. L. Hartley (Eds.), *Readings in Social Psychology.* New York: Holt.

Lifton, R. J. (1971). "Existential Evil." In N. Sanford, C. Comstock, & Associates, *Sanctions for Evil: Sources of Social Destructiveness.* San Francisco: Jossey-Bass.

———. (1973). *Home from the War—Vietnam Veterans: Neither Victims nor Executioners.* New York: Simon & Schuster.

Paige, J. (1975). *Agrarian Revolution: Social Movements and Export Agriculture in the Underdeveloped World.* New York: Free Press.

Popkin, S. L. (1979). *The Rational Peasant: The Political Economy of Rural Society in Vietnam.* Berkeley: University of California Press.

Schell, J. (1968). *The Military Half.* New York: Vintage Books.

Schirmer, D. B. (1971, April 24). *My Lai Was Not the First Time.* New Republic, pp. 18–21.

Williams, B. (1985, April 14–15). "'I Will Never Forgive,' Says My Lai Survivor." *Jordan Times* (Amman), p. 4.

Wolf, E. (1969). *Peasant Wars of the Twentieth Century.* New York: Harper & Row.

# Part V
# SOCIAL CLASS

Social class is probably the most obvious way people are structured in society. Before the 1960s, most Americans believed that the United States was indeed a land of opportunity where each individual had an equal chance to make it to the top. Since then, most of us have come to realize that some people are born into poverty and find it very difficult to escape, while others are born into luxury with almost no chance to become poor. Many people do change their class to some extent, but the amount of change is usually small. No matter how we might try to deny its importance, class remains an important part of people's lives. It affects their "life chances" (their opportunities in life), and their "life style" (how they live their lives) in very direct and indirect ways.

What is the meaning of democracy in a society characterized by a class system that excludes large numbers of people from participating, and which seems to be getting more extreme and less mobile? Is there any way to limit the riches of the few and the poverty of so many? What is the future of our society if present trends continue?

Sociologists tend to see class as an economic rank in society that makes a big difference in everyone's life. Almost always, class is considered in studies that sociologists perform and in theories they develop.

Five selections discuss class in Part V of this book. Gilbert and Kahl give an excellent overview of the class structure in the United States. Stephen Higley focuses on the upper class, and Robert Coles on the children of affluence in America. S. M. Miller asks us to examine what difference great inequalities make in society, and finally, Herbert Gans examines why it is so difficult to rid society of poverty. These selections are not the last word on class, but they represent some of the ways sociologists examine the meaning and importance of this very important structure in society.

# 22. THE AMERICAN CLASS STRUCTURE

## DENNIS GILBERT AND JOSEPH A. KAHL

"*Our general conclusion, then, is that the American class structure is moving in the direction of greater inequality. The occupational structure is changing in a way that puts the people at the bottom at a distinct disadvantage. Wealth and income are being more concentrated. The poverty rate is rising. The pace of upward mobility is slowing. The balance of political power is shifting toward the privileged.*"

This selection is the final chapter from a very fine book whose purpose is to describe the classes in the United States. It is very difficult to draw class lines, but here Gilbert and Kahl identify six classes, recognizing that their division is not the only way classes can be described. By carefully defining their classes, they are able to outline the basic economic divisions in our society and identify the significant social trends concerning inequality.

## HOW MANY CLASSES ARE THERE?

...We start with the recognition that there are three basic sources of income available to households in this country: capitalist property, labor force participation, and government transfers. Labor force participation (which accounts for most of the income of most of the people) is shaped by the fact that our economy depends on an occupational division of labor organized into bureaucratic units. Occupational placement is linked, in turn, to educational preparation. Sources of income, along with experiences on the job and in consumption communities, are verbalized as symbols of the system and the niches people occupy within it. One of the key aspects of a person's perception of place in the system is anticipation of change in the near future: Is one stuck, or is there a chance to advance? Another involves the degree of independence in carrying out one's work activities.

Combining the criteria of source of income, occupation, and educational credentials, plus the related processes of symbolization, we can create an

From Dennis Gilbert and Joseph A. Kahl, *The American Class Structure: A New Synthesis*, 4th ed. © 199, by Joseph A. Kahl. Reprinted by permission of Wadsworth Publishing Co.

"ideal type" picture of the class structure. The several criteria tend to cluster in a pattern that identifies six classes in the contemporary United States:

- A capitalist class, subdivided into nationals and locals, whose income is derived largely from return on assets.
- An upper-middle class of university-trained professionals and managers (a few of whom ascend to such heights of bureaucratic dominance that they become part of the capitalist class).
- A middle class of people who follow orders on the job from those with upper-middle-class credentials, yet have sufficient vocational skills to make good livings and enjoy a comfortable, mainstream style of life. They usually feel secure in their situation and may look forward to some movement up the hierarchy. Most wear white collars, but some wear blue.
- A working class of people who are less skilled than members of the middle class and work at highly routinized, closely supervised manual and clerical jobs. Their work provides them with a relatively stable income sufficient to maintain a living standard just below the mainstream, but they have little prospect of advancing in the hierarchy because they typically lack the necessary educational credentials. Thus, they concentrate on achieving security through seniority rather than promotion.
- A working-poor class, consisting of people employed in low-skill jobs, often in marginal firms. The members of this class are typically laborers, service work-

ers, or low-paid operators. Their incomes leave them well below mainstream living standards. Moreover, they cannot depend on steady employment, and far from anticipating advancement, they are at risk of dropping into the class below them.

- An underclass, whose members have little or no participation in the labor force. They may work erratically or at part-time jobs, but their lack of skills, incomplete education, and spotty employment records make it difficult for them to find regular, full-time positions. Some receive income from illegal activities. Many depend on government transfers for their support. Symbolically, their loose relationship to the labor market and dependence on government handouts anchor them at the bottom of the prestige order.

There are two cutting points that are the least obvious: that between the middle and working classes and that between the working poor and the underclass. Let us examine these divisions in some detail.

The distinction between working poor and underclass becomes difficult when we consider the tendency of some individuals to move repeatedly back and forth across this boundary. Yet the distinction seems worth maintaining. As we move up or down in the hierarchy, away from the boundary, the problem of oscillating mobility is less serious. Moreover, the symbolic difference between having a job, even a marginal one, and welfare dependence is clear....

The line between middle class and working class has been blurred by trends that have reduced the traditional differences between blue-collar and white-collar employment. A declining income differential, the increasing routinization of clerical tasks, and the corresponding drop in the prestige value of a white collar *per se*, have all served to close the gap between shop and office. Viewed in terms of major occupational groupings, the problem centers on the sales, clerical, and craft categories. Our way of dividing these groupings between middle and working class is based on a distinction between workers whose jobs are highly routinized, closely supervised, low in prerequisite training or education, and low in pay, and those who are in the opposite situation. On this basis, we had no trouble placing semiprofessional jobs and the lowest-paid managerial jobs in the middle class, or operatives in the working class. The assembly-line character of modern office work and the low salaries associated with most clerical jobs led us to place clerical workers in the working class. We split sales workers into two groups: those engaged in retail work and "others." The latter group includes insurance salesmen, real estate agents, manufacturers' representatives, and other people who work quite independently and have much higher incomes than the retail workers. Our decision to place most craft workers and foremen in the middle class is based on similar considerations. They are well paid, skilled, and relatively independent in their work. Moreover, the prestige attached to such occupations places them well above other blue-collar workers.

In summary, we are suggesting a model of the class structure based primarily on a series of qualitative economic distinctions. From top to bottom, they are ownership of income-producing assets, possession of sophisticated educational credentials, a combination of independence and freedom from routinization at work, entrapment in the marginal sector of the labor market, and limited labor force participation.

Our scheme is shown in Table 22.1. If we round off the numbers from the distributions of each variable treated separately and do a little guessing, we can estimate that the capitalist class includes about 1 percent of the population; the upper-middle class, about 14 percent; the middle and working classes, 60 percent; and the working poor and underclass, 25 percent. We can exemplify this model by going into a little more detail about each of the six classes....

## CAPITALIST CLASS

The very small class of super-rich capitalists at the top of the hierarchy has an influence on economy and society far beyond their numbers. They make investment decisions that open or close employment opportunities for millions of others. They contribute money to political parties, and they often own newspapers or television companies, thereby gaining impact on the shaping of the consciousness of all classes in the nation. The capitalist class tends to perpetuate itself: It passes on assets and styles of life (including networks of contacts with other influential people) to its children. This creation of lineage is of sufficient importance to them that they are active in creating and supporting preparatory schools and universities for their children and for carefully selected newcomers who can be socialized into their world view.

TABLE 22.1.    Model of the American Class Structure: Classes by Typical Situations

| Proportion of Households | Class | Education | Occupation of Family Head | Family Income, 1990 |
|---|---|---|---|---|
| 1% | Capitalist | Prestige university | Investors, heirs, executives | Over $750,000, mostly from assets |
| 14% | Upper middle | College, often with postgraduate study | Upper managers and professionals; medium business owners | $70,000 + |
| 60% | Middle | At least high school; often some college or apprenticeship | Lower managers; semiprofessionals; nonretail sales; craftspeople; foremen | About $40,000 |
| | Working | High school | Operatives; low-paid craftspeople; clerical workers; retail sales workers | About $25,000 |
| 25% | Working poor | Some high school | Service workers; laborers; low-paid operatives and clericals | Below $20,000 |
| | Underclass | Some high school | Unemployed or part-time; many welfare recipients | Below $13,000 |

The super-rich operate on the national and international scene. They have less prominent counterparts in local communities—the people who own the local banks, department stores, car dealerships, real estate empires, and newspapers. They, too, are capitalists and belong in this class, albeit at the margins.

Our definition produces a very small top class: Those who own substantial income-producing assets. After a generation or two, those holdings are often distributed among so many heirs that a larger group of less rich and less powerful people results. If one studies local communities and counts all those who have a prominent name and live in big houses and belong to the best country club, one will emerge with a larger group (perhaps double or triple our 1 percent). But if one focuses on assets of sufficient size to grant the economic power that we consider crucial, the group shrinks in size....

## UPPER-MIDDLE CLASS

...The upper-middle class is the group in our society most shaped by formal education. A college degree is usually the minimum requirement, and postgraduate study in business management, law, engineering, or medicine is increasingly required. Currently, close to 25 percent of young people get college degrees, and at least half of them pursue

some additional training; about 20 percent of all adults have a degree.

...About 17 percent of the current labor force is classified as professionals and technicians and another 13 percent as managers, officials, and proprietors. But we noted that many of the workers in these categories are semiprofessionals, technicians, or low-level managers with modest salaries, limited training, and circumscribed authority. We estimate that only about 14 percent of the total work force has the combination of university degrees, authority and independence on the job, and high income to qualify for the upper-middle class.

The extent to which adolescents in high school (urged on by their parents and teachers) so often strive to prepare themselves for upper-middle class jobs is a clear indication that these positions have become the symbols of success that motivate many Americans. They may not grant prestige equivalent to a title of nobility in the Germany of Max Weber, but they certainly represent the sign of having "made it" in contemporary America. The incomes of households in this group range upwards of $70,000 a year (about twice the mean in 1990) and tend to increase with age. They are sufficient to purchase houses and cars and travel that become public symbols for all to see and for advertisers to portray with words and pictures that connote success, glamour, and high style. Those who have reached this level of success are likely to convince themselves that they deserve what they receive, that they have earned morally just rewards from the diligent use of superior talent. Sometimes they may grow anxious from the strains of competition, but in general they are satisfied that they have achieved a proper share of the American dream.

## MIDDLE CLASS

We have remarked before that a stratification hierarchy is clearest (and incidentally, mobility is the weakest) at the extremes. When we move toward the center, distinctions become blurred, people move more often during their lives from one slot to another, and symbolizations become ambiguous. This is particularly true at the point where the middle class and the working class intersect— or better, overlap—so the reader should not expect precision of classification.

It takes at least a high school diploma to get most middle-class jobs, but the diploma is a prerequisite more than a guarantee of such employment. About 80 percent of the total adult population has a high school diploma, and many have received some training beyond it short of a four-year college degree. Those with the best schooling have the most chance to become the semiprofessionals, technicians, and lower-level managerial people we mentioned earlier—about 15 percent of the work force. They are joined in the loose grouping we call the middle class with the upper two thirds of those classified as salespeople and craftspeople—another 12 percent of the work force. Typical household incomes for this level are around $40,000 a year, but there is considerable variation, based particularly on the number of people in the household who are employed. Middle-class positions usually provide greater job security and wider opportunities for advancement than working-class positions, and younger members of the class are likely to be working in situations where some opportunities to advance in the hierarchy are available.

Symbolization of the middle class tends to get confused by an ideological tradition that says that most Americans are *middle class*. It is a "good," mainstream sort of phrase that a lot of people adopt — including those who are both higher and lower in the hierarchy than the ones we are trying to discuss at this point. Thus, most surveys show 35 to almost 50 percent of our population identifying with the term and only about 2 percent willing to call themselves *upper class*. If we subtract about 15 percent for the upper and upper-middle classes as we have defined them, the size of the remaining middle class according to self-identification is from 20 to 35 percent of the population. Using a composite of various symbols that people use to classify not only themselves but their neighbors, Coleman and Rainwater decided that one third were middle class. Our own estimate is on this order.

## WORKING CLASS

The core of the working class is easy to identify: semiskilled machine operatives, in factories and elsewhere, who make up 15 percent of the work force. But they are joined by lots of others whose work lives and incomes are not markedly different, such as clerks and salespeople whose tasks are routine and mechanized and require little skill beyond literacy and a short period of on-the-job training (some 14 percent of the work force), and the better-paid persons in the service jobs (another 3 percent). Individuals move easily among these classifications. Often, one member of a family wears a blue and another a white collar, and nobody much notices the difference. Households typically earn $25,000 or less.

In opinion surveys, at least half the population usually chooses the label *working class* for themselves, but evidence indicates that some do so because they particularly dislike certain alternative terms, such as *lower class....* Our estimate for the working class comes to around 30 percent of households.

In general, working-class families earn less than middle-class families, and more particularly, they are less secure in their incomes. The working class is more susceptible to layoffs in time of recession because employers have less invested in their training and experience. Insecurity of work is often combined with a subjective feeling of vulnerability because of lower levels of education. Relatively few members of the group have training beyond a high school diploma, and over a third (especially the older ones) did not graduate. Yet by contrast with those below them in the hierarchy, working-class people generally anticipate that layoffs will be temporary and that they can support their families in a simple but decent manner most of the time.

## WORKING POOR

In 1990, the government called 13.5 percent of the population *poor*, and studies that follow families over time show that in a nine-year period, some 25 percent of them fell below the poverty line at least once. Of the total work force (and many of the poorest and most discouraged people have withdrawn from it), between 6 and 8 percent are likely to be unemployed at any one moment, and about 20 percent are likely to be unemployed at least once during any given year.

Thus, it appears that about one fifth of our working families live under duress: They oscillate in income from just above to below the poverty line, they are threatened with periodic unemployment, or they have no chance to work at all. Those among them — probably a little more than half — who are often working but not earning enough money on a steady basis to bring them close to the mainstream style of consumption, we label the *working poor*.

The working poor include the unskilled laborers, most people in service jobs, and some of the lower-paid factory workers (especially in marginal firms). Many employed single mothers find themselves in this class. Their incomes depend on the number of weeks a year they are employed and on the number of workers in the family. Most families would feel fortunate in a year that brought in $15,000. Some adults have finished high school; a great many have not. They are unable to save money to cover contingencies, so insecurity is a normal part of their lives. The one part of the welfare system that was beneficial to them, the food stamp program, was slashed in the budgets of the Reagan administration, which eliminated participation by most of the working poor. Once retired, members of this class are entirely dependent on their social security pensions, for it is unlikely that they have been enrolled in a private retirement plan that could supplement the government payments.

## UNDERCLASS

Those who are seldom employed and are poor most of the time form the underclass in our society. Many suffer long-term deprivation from low education, low employability, low income, and eventually low self-esteem. Some are kept out of the labor force by age or disability. For a great many, their problems are magnified because they belong to minority groups who are stigmatized and suffer discrimination in the labor market. Or they are single mothers, who must make their way in a job world that pays women less than men. Many who cannot get and keep jobs that pay enough to live on are dependent on the welfare system.

The conditions of life in the underclass are sufficiently difficult and demeaning that it is hard — although not impossible — for children to get enough education and enough hope to climb up to higher levels. The future chances for avoiding a life of poverty for these children are about fifty-fifty.

The descriptions of the six classes just given are summarized in Table 22.1. It is clear that no single variable can be used to delineate these classes, so our synthesis is based on a combination of variables. We believe that they tend to form patterns that are caught by our scheme in a way that is meaningful in two senses. (1) It is congruent with much of the research literature that goes into detail on one or two variables at a time, as well as with the more qualitative community studies that tend to combine many variables into symbolic groupings. (2) It is congruent with the way most Americans tend to see the system and their place within it. Of course, we are thinking here in terms of averages, of typical situations; many individuals and families are hard to place in the scheme, either because they are higher in position on one variable than on another, or because they are mobile, or because two or more members of a family work and have disparate jobs....

## IS THE AMERICAN CLASS STRUCTURE CHANGING?

The evidence...leaves little doubt that the answer to this question is *yes*. Let's take a look at the details.... If we examine the classes one by one, we can find evidence of gradual change in the course of recent decades, a process that appears to have accelerated in recent years.

The national capitalist class has been undergoing a steady consolidation since the 1930s. The family-controlled firm is giving way to a system of corporations directed by professional managers. As this happens, wealthy families are diversifying their holdings, and top corporate managers are being drawn into the capitalist class they serve by financial rewards and social ties. Local capitalist classes...have been affected by the tendency of national corporations to move into local markets, often absorbing the banks and department stores through which small-town fortunes were built. The younger generation of this class is moving into professional and managerial careers. Many will enjoy additional income derived from inherited wealth.

These changes are creating the basis for a more cohesive capitalist class, whose members are free from parochial identification with a particular firm, economic sector, or locality. In politics, this tendency is reinforced by the growing influence of business-dominated PACs and policy planning and research organizations that defend the interests of the capitalist class as a whole rather than those of individual capitalists.

Our upper-middle class [is growing in size as]...the growing organizational and technological complexity of our society increases the demand for specialists with sophisticated training. Salaried managers and professionals replace individual entrepreneurs and independent professionals as the mainstays of the upper-middle class. The gap in income, politics, and lifestyle between this class and the rest of the population has replaced the traditional blue-collar/white-collar division as the most important cleavage in the American class structure.

The middle class is changing in ways that parallel the transformation of the upper-middle class. The petty businessmen...are being supplanted by lower-level managers. Teachers, a significant sector of this class...are being joined by large numbers of semiprofessionals from other fields. As the number of routinized, low-skilled jobs has grown, the shop-office distinction, which once divided the middle class from the working class, has been replaced by a more subtle distinction based on preparation for the job and independence at work.

"The disappearing middle class" has become a recurrent theme for political observers, marketing analysts, and pop sociologists. We are convinced, to the contrary, that the middle class is growing. Of course, the middle class can be made to disappear and reappear by manipulating the way it is defined. From our perspective, it is not the middle class but rather the middle-income group that is shrinking. The facts are these: The distribution of income is becoming less egalitarian, with more people finding themselves at the (relative) extremes and fewer in the middle. In the period from 1973 to 1988, the median family income remained stable at about $32,000 (in 1988 dollars), but the proportion of families near this amount declined. Suppose that we define *middle income* as $25,000 to $50,000 (still using 1988 dollars). The proportion of families in this range declined from 43 to 37 percent, while the proportions both above and below increased. Clearly, the middle-income group has been thinning out (U.S. Census 1990b:14).

Behind this redistribution lie the postindustrial changes in the economy and corresponding shifts in the occupational structure.... High-paying blue-collar jobs in manufacturing and other goods-producing sectors are being replaced by low-wage jobs in the service industries; real wages in manufacturing are shrinking; high unemployment rates have become a permanent feature of the economy. These trends, together with the growing number of female-headed households created by divorce, are sharply reducing the incomes of many working-class families. At the other end of the occupational scale, there are ample opportunities for qualified managers, professionals, and technicians. Many of these new jobs fall into the middle class by our criteria, but they frequently pay enough, especially when combined with a second income, to place a family over the $50,000 benchmark. Thus, the middle class is thriving, while the working class is languishing. Both tendencies push people out of the middle-income range....

The economic developments just described, together with persistent high rates of unemployment, are forcing many members of the working class into our working poor category or even the underclass. Some members of the working class, or their offspring, will qualify for middle-class jobs. All these tendencies in the class system are contributing to the erosion of the working class.

As the working class has declined, so has the size and political weight of the labor movement. The growing political efficacy of business and the shrinking influence of labor have destroyed the class balance of power that ruled American politics for a generation after World War II. Like job opportunities and income, political power is shifting upward in the class system.

## TOWARD GREATER INEQUALITY

The trends we have been describing point to growing social inequality in the United States. In fact, the evidence we examined in our major stratification variables pointed in the same direction.

Income data give us the clearest picture of change. As we have seen, from the late 1940s, when the government started regular income surveys, until the early 1970s, incomes were usually rising and gradually becoming more equal. Since then, most households have seen their incomes stagnate or even decline, and income has become more concentrated. Many families have been able to stay even only by increasing the number of household members in the labor force. Young families have experienced an absolute decline in the purchasing power of their incomes — an especially bad sign for the future.

The 1980s was a period of stark contrasts in income trends. From 1977 until 1990, while the poverty rate was rising, the average income of the top 1 percent of households jumped from $300,000 to $550,000. In 1979, the average corporate chief executive officer earned twenty-nine times more than the average factory worker; by 1988, CEOs were earning ninety-three times as much. Regressive changes in the federal tax system have exacerbated these growing income disparities.

These developments in income distribution and tax policy have contributed to an abrupt increase in the concentration of wealth. Like the rise in income inequality, this represents a reversal of long-term trends. The greatest gains have been made by the super-rich. We noted that the real net worth of *Forbes'* 400 richest Americans doubled in the course of the 1980s. By the end of the decade, the top 1 percent of households held a greater share of aggregate net worth than the bottom 90 percent.

The shifts in the occupational structure described earlier are contributing to a lessening of upward mobility in recent years. We found that upward mobility still exceeds downward mobility, and succession of sons to their fathers' status is close to what it was in the 1960s. But especially among younger workers, opportunities appear to be stagnating. The rate of downward mobility has increased, there is less movement up from blue-collar to white-collar positions, and it is becoming harder to move into the better white-collar positions. When we compared the occupations of sons with the occupations of fathers in successive periods, we concluded that the structural sources of upward mobility were shrinking.

Our study of mobility demonstrated that a college degree gives a powerful boost to the probability of career success. We learned that in the 1970s, minorities moved closer to whites, women moved closer to men, and low-income households moved closer to high-income households in their chances of obtaining a college degree. But in the 1980s, progress halted for minorities, and young people from low-income families were slipping backward in their access to higher education.

Our general conclusion, then, is that the American class structure is moving in the direction of greater inequality. The occupational structure is changing in a way that puts the people at the bottom at a distinct disadvantage. Wealth and income are being more concentrated. The poverty rate is rising. The pace of upward mobility is slowing. The balance of political power is shifting toward the privileged.

The floundering U.S. economy is certainly chief among the forces responsible for these regressive trends. But there are others, including the troubles of our families, the nation's unresolved dilemmas of race and gender, and the deterioration of our political institutions. If we do not find a way to address these deep-seated problems, class inequalities will continue to grow.

## ENDNOTES

1. U.S. Bureau of the Census. 1990 *Trends in Income, by Selected Characteristics: 1947 to 1988.* Current Population Reports. Series p-60, no.167.

# 23. THE INSTITUTIONS OF THE AMERICAN UPPER CLASS

STEPHEN HIGLEY

*"The upper class has a distinct set of institutions that provide social and physical separation from the rest of society, and these institutions inculcate an intricate set of values and beliefs in both young and old. They affirm cultural and group solidarity within the upper class and clearly delineate class boundaries."*

Class should not simply be defined as economic. Some researchers emphasize class as a more or less united group, a prestige and economic grouping of people who share common interests, who regularly interact and share a way of life, who identify themselves and are identified by others as constituting a ranked group in society. When class is defined this way, the researcher will attempt to examine closely the extent to which one class is separated from all the others. Here is an excellent summary of the American upper class, probably the most separated and united class in the United States.

Modern conceptions of social class are rooted in the writings of Karl Marx and the great German sociologist, Max Weber. Gilbert and Kahl credit Weber with introducing "a conceptual clarity which was often lacking in Marx's reference to social class" (Gilbert and Kahl 1987, 8). Whereas the Marxian conception of social class is fundamentally determined by one's relationship to the means of production, Weber refined the Marxist definition to include the concept of status as well as class.... Weber viewed class solidarity as dependent on a group awareness of a common fate, a consideration of one another as equals, and the development of joint action to pursue common interests. Weber's definition of class and status is best put in his own words:

Status groups are normally communities. They are, however, often of an amorphous kind. In contrast to the pure-

From Chap. 2 inStephen Richard Higley, *Privilege, Power, and Place*. Rowman & Littlefield, 1995.

ly economically determined "class situation," we wish to designate as "status situation" every typical component of the life fate of men that is determined by a specific, positive or negative social estimation of honor....

In content, status honor is normally expressed in the fact that above all else, a specific style of life can be expected from all those that wish to belong to the circle. Linked with this expectation are restrictions on "social intercourse" (that is, intercourse that is not subservient to economic or any other of business's "functional" purposes). These restrictions may confine normal marriage to within the status circle and may lead to complete endogomous enclosure....

Of course, material monopolies provide the most effective motives for the exclusiveness of a status group.... With an increased enclosure of the status group, the conventional preferential opportunities for special employment grow into a legal monopoly of special offices for the members....

With some over-simplification, one might thus say that "classes" are stratified according to their relations to the production and acquisition of goods; where "status groups" are stratified according to the principles of their consumption of goods as represented by special "styles of life." (Weber 1946, 186–193)

Weber defines the group of families that are at the apex of society's social order as members of both the American upper class and the uppermost American status group. For the purposes of this paper, the term *upper class* will be used as a descriptive term that denotes both class and status.

Using the *Social Register* to define the American upper class fits neatly within the Weberian definitions of class and status groups. From a class perspective, the American upper class exhibits a class solidarity derived from the group awareness that they share a common fate. They consider one another equals, and their voting behavior in support of the Republican Party and their charitable efforts are the most obvious manifestations of their ability for joint action in the pursuit of common interests.

The uppermost American status group also corresponds closely to the Weberian definition of a status group. Those who are listed in the *Social Register* are chosen primarily for the style of life (and, implicitly, the system of values) they exhibit. The main purpose of the *Social Register* is to restrict social intercourse for the members by acting as a ready reference as to who is "in" and who is "out" of proper society. Although it is hard to confirm (because of the *Social Register's* policy of not responding to inquiries), the *Social Register* strives to "confine normal marriage to within the status circle" by requiring members who marry outside the *Register* to resubmit themselves and their bride or groom for membership. And the *Social Register* is but one element of the upper class's complete system of socialization. The American upper class has attempted to separate itself socially from the *hoi polloi* literally from birth to death. From favored maternity hospitals and attending physicians to specific retirement homes such as Dunwoody Village in Newtown Square, Pennsylvania, and Cathedral Village in Washington, D.C., the *Social Register* succinctly fulfills the Weberian definition of a status group. Between birth and retirement are a full array of socializing institutions: prep schools, Ivy League schools, debutante balls, and metropolitan clubs, to name a few.

According to Weber, social class is determined by an individual's relation to the production and acquisition of goods. The upper-class families listed in the *Social Register* are direct descendants of the men who made great fortunes during the Gilded Age (1870–1910). Baltzell's research on

Philadelphia clearly shows the links between the original fortune makers and the *Social Register* listees of 1940 (Baltzell 1958, 17-24). Because the vast majority of new listings are born into the *Social Register* (rather than inducted as new members), undoubtedly the 1988 listees are overwhelmingly descended from the same families. If social class is determined by one's relation to the production and acquisition of goods, the American upper class as defined by the *Social Register* is truly a social class as well as a status group.

Weber wrote extensively on the relationship of class and status, viewing status as ultimately dependent on class (Gilbert and Kahn 1987, 10). The short-term and long-term economic success of the upper class is fundamentally important to maintaining the style of life that differentiates the upper class from the other classes in society. Once a family no longer has the economic resources to give its members the advantages that money can buy in the United States, the fall from social grace is swift and sure. The family that is reduced to "shabby gentility" is an often-used literary device that underlines the importance of liquid assets to continued good standing in American society.

The men and women who defined late-nineteenth- and early-twentieth-century American upper-class society were overwhelmingly white, Anglo-Saxon, and Protestant. As the personal, ethnic, and religious characteristics were unofficially codified, social and generational seasoning became equally important for acceptance into upper-class society. No amount of improperly socialized new money could buy its way into "proper" upper-class society....

If one subscribes to the Weberian theory that status is ultimately dependent on economic control and wealth, there are clear implications that the influence of white, Anglo-Saxon Protestants will inevitably decline in the twenty-first century. Although "WASP" and "upper class" have been synonymous in the past, it is apparent that the ethnic definition of upper class will be transformed and redefined in the future.

The transformation, or de-WASPing, of the upper class that is now taking place in the United States is not easily evident to the casual observer. The status order will eventually reflect the economic order, although there are a multitude of cultural bulwarks that make the change slower and more subtle than [some] anticipate. There is a powerful WASP cultural inertia in the United States, and it will take decades to effect changes in the way Americans define themselves culturally. WASP culture is essentially derivative of the English nobility, and to this day, Anglophilia continues to pervade the American upper class. Because the upper class provides a value and consumptive role model for the American upper-middle class, upper-class values are in turn transmitted to the rest of American society — the upper-middle class being relatively large and visible to the rest of society….

## THE ELEMENTS OF UPPER-CLASS COHESION

Weber (1946) stated, "status honor is normally expressed by the fact that above all else a specific style of life can be expected from all those who wish to belong to the circle." The American upper class has a large number of institutions and associational arrangements that have made it possible for members to pass through life with very little significant contact with other social classes. This section reviews the most important of these institutions: private boarding schools (prep schools), colleges, metropolitan and country clubs, and the Episcopal and Presbyterian churches. The role of debutante balls, service organizations, and charitable organizations as contributing factors in maintaining upper-class cohesion will also be explored. Finally, an in-depth look at the *Social Register* will examine the role of neighborhood and community in upper-class cohesiveness.

### Private Preparatory Schools

Of all of the institutions that inculcate upper-class values, private preparatory schools may have the greatest role (Cookson and Persell 1985, 13–30). The role of private education begins with upper-class day schools. Baltzell, in his examination of the role of education, termed the local institutions *provincial family surrogates* in that their outlooks were local in nature (Baltzell 1958, 292–300). Baltzell chronicles the changing role and fortunes of the Protestant Episcopal Academy, the first educator of large numbers of Philadelphia's young

male upper class. The Episcopal Academy was founded in 1785 and began catering consciously to the upper class in 1846. The institution's move in 1921 to the suburban Main Line in pursuit of its clientele maintained its primacy in Philadelphia. The Episcopal Academy was not without competitors, however; other day schools were Haverford, Penn Charter, and Chestnut Hill. There were also day schools (such as Springside, Shipley, and Agnes Irwin) for upper-class girls in Philadelphia that served the same socializing functions as the boys' schools (Baltzell 1958, 300–301).

The day schools' popularity began to wane in the second half of the nineteenth century as boarding schools became the preferred method of educating young upper-class men and women. Boarding schools made it possible to completely control the social and educational environment of the students (Cookson and Persell 1985, 31–48). Parents could be assured that their child would be raised away from the distractions of the large cities and their hordes of newly arrived aliens. The prep schools were staffed with teachers who could be relied on to transmit the values of the upper class. The WASP ethic of civility, honesty, principle, and service was imparted within a totally structured environment. The schools, particularly the Episcopalian schools, were modeled after the public schools of England, complete with "forms" for grades and "headmasters" for principals.

The day schools increasingly turned to the nouveau riche to fill the slots left by the defections of some of their constituency. In his 1980 article, "The Rise of American Boarding Schools and the Development of a National Upper Class," Levine writes that the original purpose of the schools was to protect the "old guard" of the upper class from the arrivistes with their newly minted family fortunes created during the last quarter of the nineteenth century. He theorizes that New England led the way in the creation of boarding schools as the Boston Brahmins reacted to their imminent social eclipse by the much larger fortunes the Gilded Age was producing. The elites of cities such as New York and Philadelphia were able to participate in the industrialization of America, whereas the Boston Brahmins, whose fortunes were grounded largely in the trade from the Far East, were not as effective in gaining a share of the new wealth. The boarding schools were but one of a series of institutions founded during this era to create social distance between old money and new money. Country clubs and metropolitan clubs were other examples. It was also during this time that books such as the *Social Register* and various blue books were published to provide a scorecard as to who was in and who was out of proper society.

More important than the social distancing function prep schools provide is the common socializing force they exert on young men and women of the upper class. C. Wright Mills felt that prep schools were an essential element in the calculus of preserving privilege. He wrote:

As a selection and training place of the upper classes, both old and new, the private school is a unifying influence, a force for the nationalization of the upper classes. The less important the pedigreed family becomes in the careful transmission of moral and cultural traits, the more important the private school — rather than the upper-class family — as the most important agency for transmitting the traditions of the upper social classes and regulating the new admission of wealth and talent. It is the characterizing point in the upper-class experience. (Mills 1956, 64–65)

Although upper-class schools were originally conceived to buffer the old guard from the nouveau riche, the need to infuse the upper class with new talent and money and the need to socialize the parvenus into the minutiae of upper-class culture led to the acceptance of some newly moneyed families. As sociologist Randall Collins notes, "Schools primarily teach vocabulary and inflection, styles of dress, aesthetic tastes, values and manners" (Collins 1971, 101). Levine's 1980 study found that, in general, it took one generation to socialize upper-class fortunes. The sons of fathers who acquired large fortunes in the early twentieth century often placed their children in the most prestigious boarding schools. The fathers were not above building a new library or classroom building to ensure their son's entrance. In most cases, the sons went on to Ivy League schools and became members of the upper-class secret societies and eating clubs. They were also likely to be listed in the *Social Register.* Gaining membership in upper-class secret societies and eating clubs would not present a problem because sponsorship would come easily from former schoolmates who were already members of the clubs.

Although there were literally hundreds of schools founded in the Gilded Age, a hierarchy of preferred schools quickly developed. At the top of the list in terms of prestige are the five Episcopalian boarding schools known collectively as St. Grottlesex (St. Paul's, St. Mark's, St. George's, Groton, and Middlesex). St. Paul's is often held up as the quintessential upper-class school (Domhoff 1983). Located in Concord, New Hampshire, it has a campus of eighty buildings (for six hundred students) and is situated on two thousand acres of woods and open land. In 1981, the student-faculty ratio was 6.3 to 1 and the average class size was twelve.

The second group of prestigious prep schools is represented by Choate, Hotchkiss, and Kent — nondenominational schools that were founded specifically to cater to the burgeoning market for private, exclusive education at the turn of the century.

The two oldest schools are usually put in a class by themselves. The Phillips Academy (commonly called Andover) and the Phillips Exeter Academy were founded originally to provide secondary education for a large array of students before the advent of the public school system. With the growth of the public school systems, Andover and Exeter became oriented strictly to preparing students for college. Both schools are larger and less aristocratic and have higher academic standards than the other boarding schools mentioned (Cookson and Persell 1985, 38).

In summary, boarding schools offered a place where the upper class could rest assured that class-supportive values would be instilled in their young. Their children would be exposed to only those nouveau riche children who were "acceptable" and to none of the perceived evils of the city. They would make valuable social and business friendships that would be nourished in college and in the world of private clubs during their adult lives.

## An Upper-Class College Education

Just as there are preferred upper-class boarding schools to attend, there are preferred universities for young men and women of the upper class. The three universities that are considered most desirable by upper class parents are Harvard, Yale, and Princeton. These three are followed by any other school in the Ivy League (Brown University has become increasingly popular among students) or any number of small prestigious schools located primarily in New England (for example, Williams, Amherst, or Trinity). If an upper-class family lives in a state with an academically prestigious public university, such as Wisconsin, Michigan, or California, it is increasingly considered appropriate to attend those universities. In addition, there are selected private regional universities that are considered acceptable if one is not accepted at one's first choice. Examples of these schools are Duke, Stanford, and Northwestern.

Baltzell was able to discern a major trend in upper-class college attendance in his study of the 1940 Philadelphia *Social Register*. The oldest generation (those over 65 years old) were much more likely to have attended a local institution (the University of Pennsylvania, Haverford College, or Swarthmore College) than to have attended any of the other Ivy League schools (42 percent to 22 percent). The younger generation were more likely to have attended Ivy League schools (other than Penn) than local schools (36 percent to 31 percent) (Baltzell 1958, 319–328). These findings support Baltzell's contention that the twentieth century has witnessed the nationalization of the American upper class. The Ivy League schools, especially Harvard, Princeton, and Yale, have become the most desired universities for Philadelphia's upper class, in spite of the presence of an Ivy League school and two prestigious smaller schools in the Philadelphia metropolitan area.

The Ivy League schools have had a long and fruitful relationship with the sixteen most prestigious boarding schools. The relationship has evolved over time as the entrance requirements to the Ivy League schools have changed and become infinitely more rigorous. Harvard started the change in 1926 when it began a policy of pursuing superior students with or without the proper social credentials. To be sure, attendance at an elite prep school is still the most assured route to the Ivy League, but it is no longer the only one. The boarding schools have remade themselves in Harvard's image—demanding more from their students with the realization that a gentleman's "C" would no longer ensure entrance to Harvard, Princeton, or Yale. Those prep schools that did not upgrade their curriculums to meet Harvard's demands fell swiftly from upper-class favor (St.

Mark's School in Southborough, Massachusetts, fell and returned to grace in this manner). The percentage of students at the sixteen most prestigious boarding schools that attended Harvard, Princeton, or Yale dropped precipitously from 67 percent in the 1930s to 21 percent in 1973. An analysis of admissions to all the Ivy League schools done by Cookson and Persell showed that in the 1982 school year, 42 percent of the graduates of the sixteen most prestigious prep schools were accepted at Ivy League Schools. This compares with 27 percent accepted from other leading prep schools and 26 percent accepted from the entire applicant pool.

In 1982, students who attended private schools made up approximately 10 percent of all students applying for college, yet at Harvard, Princeton, and Yale, they made up 34, 40, and 40 percent, respectively, of the entering freshman class (Cookson and Persell 1985, 167–189). It is clear, then, that there is a real connection between the socially prominent boarding schools and the Ivy League schools.

## Fraternities and Eating Clubs

Once a young man has been accepted at Harvard, Princeton, or Yale, he is confronted with a large university that is dominated in numbers, if not tone, by members of other social classes. The solution to the problem of having to mix with the upper-middle class (or worse) is a system of private clubs similar to the fraternities and sororities found on many American campuses. The system of private clubs is best described in the words of Baltzell:

An intricate system of exclusive clubs, like the fraternities on less rarefied American campuses, serve to insulate the members of the upper class from the rest of the students at Harvard, Princeton, and Yale. There are virtually "two nations" at Harvard. The private-school boys, with their accents, final clubs, and Boston debutante parties—about one-fifth of the student body—stand aloof and apart from the ambitious, talented, and less polished boys who come to Cambridge each year from public schools over the nation. (Baltzell 1958, 329–330)

The private eating clubs of Princeton were formed in the years following Woodrow Wilson's 1906 ban on fraternities. Juniors and Seniors joined eating clubs that had a "pecking order" based on social status. Upper-class young men usually joined the Ivy Club or the Cottage Club. The exclusivity of the eating clubs ended in the 1960s when the university compelled the clubs to accept all who had applied but had not been accepted.

At Harvard, Porcellian is the club of the most prestigious boarding schools such as St. Paul's and Groton. Other social clubs that are notable but of slightly less status are A.D., Fly, Spee, Delphic, and Owl. Porcellian's counterpart at Yale is the Fence Club. As at Harvard, there are a host of slightly less prestigious clubs to join. Perhaps the senior societies are even more important than the social clubs at Yale. The two most important are the elite and meritorious Skull and Bones Club (of which former President George Bush is a member) and the more socially exclusive Scroll and Key Club. The purpose of these clubs is to build class solidarity and personal alliances that will be translated into lifetime friendships and business relationships at graduation (Baltzell 1958, 330–334).

At each critical juncture of a young person's life, the upper class has developed a series of supporting institutions to link individuals with a shared outlook and value system. By carefully molding young upper-class people into the established value system, the upper class assures its own continuity.

## The Upper-Class World of Private Clubs

On graduation, young men and women begin their careers with yet another array of private clubs that will act as an extended class-oriented family. One can differentiate between two types of private clubs, the metropolitan dining clubs and the more familiar suburban country clubs. Baltzell maintains that the metropolitan clubs are much more important than country clubs in terms of the social ascription of status.

Unlike the American middle classes, and resembling the lower classes, in fact, the Philadelphia upper class is largely male dominated and patriarchal. The social standing of the male family head, the best index of which is his metropolitan club affiliation, usually determines the social position of the family as a whole (Baltzell 1958, 336).

The first American metropolitan club, following the British experience with such clubs, grew out of an informal gathering of the leading citizens to discuss daily affairs over coffee. In the days before reliable newspapers, it was a way to pass on news and keep informed of current events. The first club formed in the United States was the Philadelphia Club in 1835. It was closely followed by the Union Club of New York City, which was founded in 1836 (Baltzell 1958, 335–363). The metropolitan club subculture, with its distinctive mores and value rituals, was perceptively outlined by Wecter:

The social club in America has done a great deal to keep alive the gentleman in the courtly sense. Here is a peculiar asylum from the Pandemonium of commerce, the bumptiousness of democracy, and the feminism of his own household. Here he is technically invisible from the critical female eye—a state of bliss reflected in the convention that a gentleman never bows to a lady from a club window and does not, according to best form, discuss ladies there. The club is the Great Good Place with its comfortable and slightly shabby leather chairs, the pleasant malt-like effluvium of its bar, the newspaper room with a club servant to repair quickly the symptoms of disarray, the catholicity of magazines from highbrows to *La Vie Parisienne* which in less stately company would seem a trifle sophomoric, the abundant newspaper, the good cigars and hearty carnivorous menus....

With what Henry James called "a certain light of fine old gentlemanly prejudice to guide it," the preeminently social club welcomes the serious frivolity of horses, hounds, foxes, and boats, but not the effeminate frivolity of aestheticism. Pedantry is also frowned upon; except for the *Social Register*, the *World Almanac*, and *Lloyd's Register of American Yachts*, not a volume in the club library has been taken down since the cross-word puzzle craze. It is comforting to think that one's sons and grandsons will sit in these same chairs, and firelight will flicker on the same steel engravings and oil portraits of past presidents—and though the stars may wheel in their courses and crowned heads totter to the guillotine, this little world will remain, so long as first mortgages and government bonds endure. (Wecter 1937, 253–255)

This evocative description of metropolitan clubs was written in 1937 and is dated in some details but still accurate in its main thrust.

There have been several recent legal challenges to the all-male membership policies of metropolitan clubs. The Supreme Court has ruled against the males-only policies of the clubs. The main argument made by female complainants was that women are excluded from important business transactions that are discussed in the clubs. Aldrich maintains that the women's victory will be mainly Pyrrhic because it is considered extremely bad form to discuss business in metropolitan clubs (Aldrich 1988, 122–123). However, Aldrich does not address the valuable alliances made in leisure that lead to business deals later, outside the confines of the club.

The suburban country club is less important than the metropolitan club, but it is significant in that the entire family are members and there are facilities and activities for all. The first American country club was established in 1882 in Brookline, Massachusetts; it is simply called The Country Club. These clubs are most frequently associated with golf, but they may include facilities for swimming, tennis, and, in some cases, polo. Americans are familiar with suburban country clubs, which have been enthusiastically established by the upper-middle class throughout the country.

As in the case of the metropolitan clubs, there is a status hierarchy among the country clubs. Because of the relatively small number of upper-class families, upper-class country clubs make up only a small portion of the private equity country clubs in the United States.

Yacht clubs are also an integral part of upper-class social life. Again, only a select few of the yacht clubs in America are favored by the American upper class. Similarly, there are a large number of historically oriented clubs, such as the well-known Daughters of the American Revolution and more obscure clubs such as the American Association of the Sovereign Military Order of Malta.

The *Social Register* lists those clubs most frequented by the upper class; there are 194 listed in the 1988 edition.

## Religion and the Upper Class

"However much details differ, stratification is found in all American communities, and religion is always one of its salient features" (Pope 1948, 89). Observers of the American scene have long commented on the status differentiation of Protestant denominations. The upper class has had a long association with the Protestant Episcopal Church and to a lesser degree with the Presbyterian Church. The Episcopalian connection is a logical extension of the Anglophilia of the American

upper class because the church has a number of characteristics that make it attractive to upper-class men and women. The richness of the church's ritual, the classic traditionalism of most Episcopalian architecture, and the sophisticated, urbane, and intellectual nature of its leaders have great appeal to the upper class (Cookson and Persell 1985, 44–48). The Episcopalian Church was very close to an established church for some parts of colonial America and was, in fact, the established church of the state of Virginia until 1786. Although the church suffered during and immediately following the Revolutionary War because of its close association with England and her Loyalists, it quickly recovered its status as a church of the educated elite in the postwar period.

The appeal of the Episcopalian Church to the upper class overrode the appeal of other denominations. Quakerism in Philadelphia and Congregationalism and Unitarianism in Boston had long and deeply rooted favor among the upper classes. Yet, following the Civil War, most upper-class Philadelphians and Bostonians gravitated to the Episcopalian Church. In fact, there was a huge upsurge in Episcopalian membership in the post-Civil War period — the membership grew from 160,000 communicants in 1866 to 720,000 in 1900 (Baltzell 1958, 223–261).

Baltzell confirmed the alliance statistically by analyzing the church membership of those people in the upper class who were in both the 1940 edition of *Who's Who in America* and the 1940 Philadelphia *Social Register*. *Who's Who's* listing of church membership enabled Baltzell to determine religious affiliation for 226 upper-class heads of households. Although 35 percent did not acknowledge a church membership, 42 percent were affiliated with the Episcopalian Church (compared with 1.0 percent of the total U.S. population). An additional 13 percent of those in *Who's Who* listed the Presbyterian Church as their place of worship (compared to 1.2 percent of the general population). Because of the general privacy of religious information, it is difficult to verify Baltzell's findings. However, it is fair to say that the subjective information on the relationship is indeed overwhelming. Of course, not all Episcopalians are upper class. The actual number of upper-class families within the church is small compared to the total membership of Episcopalian churches; however, the church carries the distinctive imprint of upper-class support, philanthropy, and values.

## Debutante Balls

The debutante season consists of a series of parties, teas, and dances held by upper-class families to formally announce the arrival and availability of their daughters for suitable matrimonial partners. Each major city holds a grand ball that is the highlight of the season. Debutante "coming-out" parties are yet another means of reinforcing class solidarity because the young women and men who participate are carefully screened to ensure upper-class exclusivity. Because upper-class endogamy is highly valued, the debutante season is a formal process, the sole purpose of which is to encourage and create upper-class familial unions. Although there is often a philanthropic cause behind the tens of thousands of dollars spent for each coming out, none of the participants are under any illusion as to the real purpose behind the festivities. The debutante season strengthens the bonds of intrametropolitan upper-class social relationships just as shared summer resort holidays strengthen intermetropolitan alliances.

During the activism of the 1960s and 1970s, interest in the debutante experience declined among young upper-class women. However, the disinclination to participate has all but disappeared in the 1980s and 1990s, and the debutante season continues to be an important upper-class ritual.

## Service Clubs and Charitable Philanthropies of the Upper Class

Participating in service clubs or being on the board of major cultural, medical, or educational institutions is a time-honored role for both upper-class men and women. The favored institutions realize that upper-class interest results in large donations and a certain social cachet that has tangentially beneficial fund-raising appeal to the other target of charitable fund-raising: the upper-middle class. The involvement of the upper class provides a real benefit for the institution and allows individuals to derive a sense of contribution to society. The chosen charitable organizations invariably reinforce traditional areas of upper-class interests. In Chicago, for example, the favored organizations

and institutions include the Chicago Symphony, the Lyric Opera, Northwestern Hospital, the Art Institute, and the Field Museum.

## The **Social Register**

Before the Civil War, "society" in most large American cities, including New York City, was small enough that members of the upper class knew each other informally. Invitations to balls and other "serious" social events were handled either by personal secretaries or by the hostess herself. There were also self-appointed social arbiters whose dictates could help the unsure hostess in determining who was "in" and who was "out" of society.

The role of individual society kingmakers would soon be eclipsed with the appearance of the first *Social Register* in 1886. Hundreds of new fortunes were being made (and lost) during the last two decades of the nineteenth century, and a book was needed to take the place of personal knowledge as to a family's acceptability in polite society.

The first edition of the *Social Register* was a listing of society in Newport, Rhode Island. The next year, 1887, saw the first appearance of the New York City edition. It has been published continuously ever since that date. The *Social Register* was not the first of its kind; there were many books that purported to list society in the 1880s. The secret of success for the founder, Louis Keller, was the quality of his list and his refusal to clutter the book with advertisements for wine merchants, dressmakers, and the like.

Keller was from the fringe of society, yet he was able to parlay the *Social Register* into the definitive guide to society's upper class. Another component of Keller's success was a strict code of secrecy that has been conscientiously maintained to the present. The all-enveloping veil of secrecy has given the book a mystique that has made it all the more alluring to those who aspire to join. The aura of exclusivity is enhanced by the *Social Register's* policy of rarely speaking to the press or publicly commenting on itself in any way.

Keller incorporated his idea as the Social Register Association; new editions quickly followed the New York City volume in Philadelphia and Boston (1890), Baltimore (1892), Chicago (1893), Washington, D.C. (1903), St. Louis and Buffalo (1903), Pittsburgh (1904), San Francisco (1906), and Cleveland and Cincinnati-Dayton (1910). At its height in the 1920s, there were 24 volumes. Many of these editions failed during the Great Depression because of the lack of a large and sophisticated industrial elite and/or insufficient interest on the part of the local population. This would explain the absence of a large number of *Social Register* families from Detroit, a city that made its fortune in the 1920s, and the three post-World War II growth centers of Dallas, Houston, and Los Angeles. The families that dominate the *Social Register* were created during the Gilded Age, and the sunbelt families would have to wait for their generational acculturation into upper-class mores.

Originally, there was a combined Atlanta-Savannah-Charleston-Richmond edition for the South, but it also failed. As one southern matron was heard to say, "In Richmond, we don't need a book to tell us who is in society." This sentiment reflects the small size of most southern aristocracies and the fact that most aristocratic southern families knew their peers intimately (Amory 1960, 123–132).

The *Social Register* has remained the only social listing for the thirteen cities listed above since 1939. In 1977, the twelve editions were combined into one large book—a reflection of the national solidarity of the upper class and also of cost considerations (Birmingham 1978). The *Social Register* has subsequently become an address and telephone book for the American upper class. Along with this basic information, the *Register* also lists which boarding school and which university members attended, the year in which he or she graduated, and their club memberships. Members may also list their children and the schools they are attending or their current addresses. It has several useful appendices: "Married Maidens," a listing of the maiden names of the wives (very helpful in a divorce-prone culture), and "Dilatory Domiciles," for those who are late in returning their annual questionnaires. There is also a separate volume published each summer called the *Summer Social Register*. The summer edition lists summer homes and also has a yacht registry that lists the home port, tonnage, and year built for each yacht. As the upper class has added winter homes in the post-World War II period, they have tended to list those addresses in the main *Social Register* (*Social Register* 1988).

The 1988 edition of the *Social Register* has 32,398 conjugal family listings. This is down from approximately 38,000 families in the 1984 edition. About 3,500 families were dropped in the 1985 edition and there have apparently been additional deletions since that date. As usual, there was no public comment from the Social Register Association as to why individuals were dropped.

Getting into the *Social Register* and being dropped from the book have been subjects of endless speculation among the upper class and among gossip columnists. The best term to describe the process is *idiosyncratic*. There are three methods for obtaining membership. The most likely way to get in is to be born into it. The second is to marry into a listed family. However, a new bride or groom who is not in the *Register* must submit a new application to be accepted or rejected (without comment) by the "advisory committee." (The makeup of the committee has been the subject of much speculation, and some have questioned if there really is one.) The third way to gain a listing in the *Social Register* is to apply for membership. The prospective member fills out an application and if it passes initial review, he or she must then supply the committee with four or five recommendations from current listees. The application then goes to the advisory committee and the applicant is either accepted or rejected without comment. It is believed that the number that gain membership through this process is extremely limited (Winfrey 1980).

Even the ownership of the *Social Register* is veiled in mystery. When Keller died in 1924, he left the Association to several heirs. It was purchased by Malcolm Forbes in 1977 and remained in his family after his death in 1989, but who actually owns it is not known.

The reasons why members are dropped from the *Social Register* has also been the subject of much musing. Perhaps the surest way to guarantee elimination is to publicly disparage the *Social Register* or to be publicly disgraced. As long as one's personal foibles do not become public knowledge, one seems to be immune from being dropped. Another way to be banished is to marry an entertainer—one of the many groups of people who are *personae non gratae* in the *Social Register*.

The largest groups that are systematically excluded from the *Social Register* are Jews, African Americans, and Asian Americans. Although there are one known Black and several Jewish members, the *Social Register* remains a compendium that is overwhelmingly white, Anglo-Saxon, and Protestant American (*Newsday*, December 12, 1984, 10–11). A small percentage of the listees have French and Dutch surnames, but it is a challenge to find German, Scandinavian, or southern European surnames anywhere in the *Social Register*.

There are members of the upper class who have asked to have their names removed from the *Social Register* because of the *Register's* discriminatory practices. Alfred Gwynne Vanderbilt and "Jock" Whitney were among the notable society people who asked to be deleted. It is politically astute for politicians to request that their names be deleted. George Bush had his name deleted before he received his complimentary listings as vice president and president. Former presidents and the chief justice of the Supreme Court are also given complimentary listings. There are many retired senators who are listed once it is "safe" to be associated with an organization that is so blatant in its discrimination.

The credibility of the *Social Register* as a listing of the American upper class is unassailable. Although it is by no means a complete listing, it is a large and excellent sampling. It is true that the core thirteen cities are overrepresented, but every writer who has examined the book has agreed with its value as an indicator of upper-class status. It has been used repeatedly as the authoritative designator of the American upper class (Firey 1947; Baltzell 1958; Ingham 1978; Cookson and Persell 1985; Levine 1980).

The upper class has a distinct set of institutions that provide social and physical separation from the rest of society, and these institutions inculcate an intricate set of values and beliefs in both young and old. They affirm cultural and group solidarity within the upper class and clearly delineate class boundaries.

## REFERENCES

Aldrich, N. W., Jr. 1988. *Old Money: The Mythology of America's Upper Class*. New York: Knopf.

Baltzell, E. D. 1958. *Philadelphia Gentlemen: The Making of a National Upper Class*. New York: Free Press.

Birmingham, N. 1978. "Ask Me No Secrets." *Town and Country* vol. 132, October, 181.

Collins, R. 1971. "Functional and Conflict Theories of Educational Stratification." *American Sociological Review* 36: no.6, December 1,002–1,019.

Cookson, P. W., 3r. and C. H. Persell, 1985. *Preparing for Power*. New York: Basic.

Domhoff, G. W. 1983. *Who Rules America Now?* New York: Touchstone.

Firey, W. 1947. *Land Use in Central Boston*. Cambridge, MA: Harvard University Press.

Gilbert, D., and I A. Kahl. 1987. *The American Class Structure*. Chicago: Dorsey.

Ingham, J. N. 1978. *The Iron Barons*. Westport, CT: Greenwood.

Levine, S. B. 1980. "The Rise of American Boarding Schools and the Development of a National Upper Class." *Social Problems* 28, no.1: 63–94.

Mills, C. W. 1956. *The Power Elite*. London: Oxford University Press.

Pope, L. 1948. "Religion and the Class Structure." *The Annals of the American Academy of Political and Social Science* 256: 84–91.

Social Register Association. 1986. *Social Register 1887, Facsimile Edition*. New York: Social Register Association.

Social Register Association. 1987. *Social Register 1988*, Vol. CII. New York: Social Register Association.

Social Register Association. 1987. *Social Register, Summer 1988*, Vol. CII. New York: Social Register Association.

Wecter, D. 1937. *The Saga of American Society*. New York: Charles Scribner's Sons.

Winfrey, C. 1980. "Society's 'In' Book: Does it Still Matter?," *New York Times*, 2 February.

# 24. CLASS, HEALTHCARE, AND DEMOCRACY

## S. M. MILLER

*"What are today's strong moral claims for greater economic equality? Two are offered here: The improvement of health and the realization of political democracy. The argument is that inequalities in health and political influence related to economic circumstances are incompatible with cherished ideals about this nation and therefore should be rectified."*

Here is a selection that takes a slightly different approach to class. It focuses on the question of justice. It maintains that political pressure to create a more equal society is not great, so that people must somehow develop a "moral case." Miller develops such a case, focusing on two issues: health care and political democracy. By doing this, he highlights many of the problems that challenge our society. He makes an appeal to the reader: "We need to face up to the never-ending challenge of inequalities and the damages they inflict."

This chapter emphasizes the importance of values in the development of a politics that would seek to reduce inequalities. Although it is important to show that the American distribution of income, wealth, and services has become more unequal, this alone is not enough. Unfortunately, expanded disparities in the command over resources do not lead automatically to efforts to reduce them. The political will to counter poverties and inequalities grows when unrest, policies to promote economic growth, and moral values converge. The first two pressures for reduced inequalities are not strong at this time. Consequently, it is particularly important to offer a normative case for the reduction of inequalities, demonstrating that their effects violate core American values. Two such key normative concerns are health and democracy, and this chapter sketches the evidence that inequalities undermine both.

From "Equality, Morality, and the Health of Democracy," by S. M. Miller, in *Myths about the Powerless*, ed. M. Brinton Lykes, Temple Press, 1996.

## MORAL CLAIMS

### The Need for a Moral Case

...Economically, the country is looking to increases in foreign demand for products, not to increases in domestic consumption, as the key economic stimulant. Thus, it is more difficult today to convince many that increasing the incomes of those at the lower levels of the income distribution profile will have a great effect on improving general economic functioning. This is particularly true as tax aversiveness limits the possibility of raising government revenues in order to spend more on social programs, and as widespread fears about the future of the American economy lead to the acceptance of declining real wages and employment quality. Thus, an economic argument for greater economic equality is not likely to be compelling under current circumstances.

Social turbulence might lead to efforts to reduce economic inequalities, but it seems to have lost much of its effectiveness. The 1992 outbreak in Watts, perhaps the most destructive one in this century, has not led to sizable improvements in the economic situation for the area. Minor adjustments, at best, seem to be the typical response to local uprisings. If there were many Watts, would the demand for reducing inequalities overcome the pressure for suppressing uprisings? A guess: The response to upheaval is more likely to be military might rather than economic change.

The inescapable conclusion is that a convincing moral case for lessening inequalities is especially important today. Even if economic pressures and social unrest were positive factors in inducing concern for reducing inequalities, normative concerns would still be important. Certainly, this is the case when disruption occurs: people can simply be angry at the unrest when they feel it has little justification. In the economic situation, it is important that those who are to benefit have what is generally regarded as a creditable claim for their gain. The tarnishing of the poor as welfare cheats and an undeserving underclass undermines their claims to improving their economic conditions (Ryan 1981). (Reducing the taxes on the rich was not based on their moral claim but on the assertion that their greater income would lead to savings and thus to investment, with a gain in economic growth that presumably would benefit almost all. The pressure to increase the taxes on the rich occurred at the beginning of the Clinton administration not only because of the need for more tax revenues to reduce budget deficits but also from the feeling that the enormous gains of this small group may have harmed the economy over the long run.)

Many public intellectuals and media pundits resist ideas of and measures for greater equality as not only drags on the economy, but as downplaying the personal responsibilities and obligations of those at the bottom (Kaus 1992; Mead 1986; Murray 1984). They see the antisocial behavior of an "undeserving poor" rewarded and unfair burdens imposed on others, as exemplified in the cry against "reverse discrimination." Arguments over moral claims cannot be avoided.

With the likely prospect of high levels of unemployment and slow if not declining rates of growth in household incomes of those who are not well-to-do, inequality is likely to increase. Only strong moral

claims can offset fears about the future of the economy, for the political pressure will be for any kind of economic growth even if inequalities expand.

What are today's strong moral claims for greater economic equality? Two are offered here: the improvement of health and the realization of political democracy. The argument is that inequalities in health and political influence related to economic circumstances are incompatible with cherished ideals about this nation and therefore should be rectified.

## The Moral Claim to Health

Not long ago, many politicians and physicians debated whether access to medical care was a right or a privilege. (In the early 1960s, a leader of the American Medical Association still contended that it was a privilege.) The enactment of Medicare and Medicaid in the mid-sixties ended that controversy, even if it did not provide care for all, by establishing the principle (if not always the practice) that all people deserved medical attention.

Today, a deeper national commitment goes beyond the right to access medical care to the right to equal chances of good health and long life. Neither class nor race should affect our health prospects. It is no longer morally acceptable that economic or social differences should privilege some and disadvantage others in vital matters of life and death. Even if one believes that individual differences in merit and desert alone produce economic differences, they are repugnant if they result in disparities in longevity or infant mortality.

Although the link between class and race on one side and good health on the other is not well known, it should be. Understanding that inequalities are associated persistently with shorter and less healthy lives creates a strong claim that they should be reduced.

Overwhelming international and U.S. evidence shows that economic inequalities affect health. Raising average incomes in nations with high per-capita income does not reduce disparities in health conditions and mortality (Kawachi, Levine, Miller, Lasch, & Amick 1994). Although health indicators such as longevity or infant mortality manifest distinctive improvement over time, differences among socioeconomic classes have continued

(Wilkinson 1992, 1083). For some health conditions, they have even widened. Clearly, the distribution of income (or education or occupational standing) has health consequences: Individuals higher in the social hierarchy typically enjoy better health than do those below; SES [socioeconomic] differences are found for rates of mortality and morbidity for almost every disease and condition." Clearly, "social class is among the strongest known predictors of illness and health" (Adler, Boyce, Chesney, Cohen, Folkman, Kahn, & Syme 1994, 15, 22).

Do narrowed inequalities improve health prospects? Japan's rapid improvement in life expectancy is instructive, for it has been "accompanied by a narrowing in the differences in income between the richest and poorest." A comparison of Japan with Britain concludes that it is not cultural differences but widening inequalities that explain the slower improvement of life expectancy in Britain since 1965 (Marmot & Smith 1989, 1551). A crossnational comparison concludes that "there is a significant tendency for mortality to be lower in countries with a more egalitarian distribution of income" (Wilkinson 1992, 165). This conclusion applies to the United States: It has the lowest percentage of income received by the lowest 70 percent of households, and the second lowest life expectancy of advanced industrial nations (Wilkinson 1992, 166).

Health researchers emphasize "the gradient," pointing to the variety of findings that show that "the association of SES and health occurs at every level of the SES hierarchy, not simply below the threshold of poverty" (Adler et al. 1994, 15). As one goes down the socioeconomic ladder in the United States, rates of poor health and high mortality typically increase. Inequality differences are displayed in health outcomes.

An important study of differences in mortality rates of American socioeconomic groups was replicated in 1986. (The age range was from 25 to 65.) The findings are deeply disturbing. Although mortality declined overall during the twenty-six-year period, class differences did not wither. Not only did "the inverse relation between mortality and socioeconomic status (persist) in 1986 and was stronger than in 1960," but "the disparity in mortality rates according to income and education increased for men and women, whites and blacks,

and family members and unrelated persons…. Despite an overall decline in death rates in the United States since 1960, poor and poorly educated people still die at higher rates than those with higher incomes or educations, and this disparity increased between 1960 and 1986" (Pappas, Queen, Hadden, & Fisher 1993, 103). A survey of developed countries concluded that "social class differences in health have not narrowed despite growing affluence and the fall of absolute poverty" (Wilkinson 1992, 168).

Black-white differences in mortality rates also increased (Pappas et al. 1993, 103, 107; Miller 1989, 505–506). Another study estimated that family income differences explain 38 percent of the excess mortality among blacks compared to whites (Otten, Teutsch, Williamson, & Marks 1990, 845–850). A third study found that when environmental and economic variables are controlled, black-white differences are reduced by 75 percent: "racial differences in mortality are therefore in large part a consequence of poverty, not racial genotype" (Mencik 1991, 1).

In a series of charts, the important Kaiser Foundation report *Pathways to Health* depicted social class (income) differences for males in mortality from all causes, heart disease, and cancer as well as similar differences for all Americans in selected chronic diseases, lung cancer, and osteoarthritis (Bunker, Gomby & Kehrer 1989, 118–135). The results showed that economic differences make a difference in longevity.

An intensive study of Alameda County, California, over a nine-year period compared the mortality experience of Oakland residents, thirty-five years of age or older, who lived in a poverty area, with the situation of those residing in nonpoverty sections of the city. Even after a variety of adjustments for health status, race, income, access to medical care, and other influences, those in the poverty area had "higher age-, race-, and sex-adjusted mortality" (Haan, Kaplan, & Camacho 1987, 989).

In a study of a self-assessed quality of health, a U.S. Public Health survey found that "excellent health" was associated with class position. (Self-reported health is a widely used indicator of actual health.) Among those classified as upper-middle and upper class, 53 percent reported themselves as in excellent health; of those in the middle classes, 37 percent gave themselves this rating; and of those in the lower classes, only 28 percent regarded themselves as in excellent health. In an analysis of data from the 1991 National Opinion Research Center survey, Karen Ferroggiaro and I found similar differences by income in self-reported conditions of health.

Many other studies point in the same direction: Where you stand in the American socioeconomic profile affects your mortality and health prospects. Dutton and Levine's (1989) authoritative review concludes that "one of the most striking features of the relationship between SES and health is its pervasiveness and persistence over time. This relationship is found in virtually every measure of health status: age-adjusted mortality for all causes of death as well as specific causes, the severity of acute disease and the incidence of severe infectious conditions, the prevalence and severity of nearly every chronic disease, and measures of disability and restricted activity." (p. 31; see also Levine 1993).

Perhaps the most disturbing finding is that the United States is not only high in U.S. infant mortality rates compared to other developed nations but that socioeconomic differences in infant mortality rates are substantial. Although the general level of infant mortality has decreased in the United States, disparities in income and race remain (Gortmaker & Wise 1994, 6).

Such findings are disturbing because the United States spends more per capita on health and medical care than other nations. As a consequence, Gortmaker and Wise (1994) argue that "the first priority [in dealing with infant mortality] is not more obstetricians and pediatricians or hospitals, not even more prenatal clinics or well-baby clinics, but rather to provide more social, financial, and educational support to families with pregnant women and infants" (p. 2).

It is now deeply accepted in U.S. society that differences in mortality by class and race are not acceptable, and that good health and longevity should not be restricted to those who are better off. Americans suffer health-wise because of their position in the social hierarchy. In the health-conscious USA, showing that inequalities are associated with shorter and less healthy lives strengthens the political impact of the moral claims for greater equality.

## ECONOMIC EQUALITY AND POLITICAL DEMOCRACY

The United States has had two great assertions for supporting the contention that it is the greatest nation on earth: (1) its streets may not be paved with gold, but here many people can earn decent incomes and (2) this is a land of democracy. Political democracy is widely cherished, at least in general sentiment if not in everyday practice. It is not only instrumental to other goals, but it "is important in its own right—it is a goal in itself, not merely a means to an end" (Verba et al. 1987, 157). Central to democracy is political equality, which means that each person has equal influence on the political process through elections and other means.

With the lowering, although certainly not the elimination, of many of the barriers to voting that were imposed on African Americans, the deepest blemishes on American democracy now are the great disparities in voting rates and the enormous influence on legislation and its implementation of the lobbying and money of business and other organizations.

Elections are key components of democracy. They shape both political cultures and governmental policies (Dunham 1991, 226). "The ideal of equality...in relation to political influence is more firmly entrenched than is that of equality...in economic matters.... If using differential economic resources in politics subverts desirable political equality, then that ideal becomes an argument for decreased income inequality" (Verba et al. 1987, 4–5). "Not only is income more unequally distributed [than in Japan and Sweden], but the economically advantaged are somewhat more likely to convert economic into political advantage" in the United States (Verba et al. 1987, 14).

This nation, as is now widely known, has much lower levels of voting in national elections than comparable countries (Teixeira 1987, 7). Americans are taught to pride themselves on free elections. Yet, in reality, only half of the voting population has a direct effect on the presidential election process. Participation in state and local levels is even lower.

Even more significant is that "the relationship between socioeconomic status and political participation is strongest in the United States among the Western democracies" (Chen 1992, 175, 183). Another study, concentrating on the United States, concludes that "relative income, or the voter's position on the income distribution, is a very important determinant of voter turnout" (Filer, Kenny, & Morton 1993, 81). Although turnout in presidential elections declined overall from 1960 to 1988, the decline was much greater for the lowest income quintile — from 65.2 percent to 47.4 percent — than for the highest quintile, which ebbed slightly from 96.2 percent to 95.6 percent (Leighley & Nagler 1992, 731).

The pattern is clear: Voting levels are related to income (and/or other socioeconomic variables, such as education). Those with lower incomes vote less than those with higher incomes. Filer, Kenny, and Morton (1993) report that the differences in voting rates of the top and bottom income quartiles of whites increased from 18.2 percent in 1960 to 28.7 percent in 1976 (p. 72). Race disparities in voting are also significant: African Americans vote less than do whites. To be of low income or marginalized in the United States impairs one's participation in the political process.

This pattern has been termed _selective demobilization_ by Walter Dean Burnham, a leading analyst of trends in voting rates. This "class-based skew to political participation" was probably not the case a century ago, but after 1900, class differences in political participation expanded. New Deal programs "temporarily relieved the [socioeconomic] bias in turnout." After World War II, the differences increased, and it is likely that "the gap in turnout between upper- and lower-level people may have increased after 1960" (Bennett & Bennett 1986, 184–85). Although experts argue about whether the differences between the top and bottom socioeconomic groups have widened or stabilized in recent years, the differences between SES groups remain significant. As Leighley and Nagler (1992) conclude, "stability is not necessarily good news" (p. 734).

A somewhat different way of looking at voting turnout and socioeconomic position is in terms of

the impact of economic adversity. In contrast to theoretical outlooks about democracy, the fact is that the poor, the unemployed, and the financially troubled are likely to vote even less than they once had as they suffer economic reverses and are preoccupied with coping with them. Consequently, their voices and concerns are little represented and have little impact. The paradox is that as their concerns grow and their need for political response mounts, "the very problem that is foremost in their minds impedes their participation in the political process" (Rosenstone 1982, 44). The disparities in voting rates by socioeconomic groups form one of the most biting indictments of the practice of American democracy.

A second infraction of democracy is the influence of the moneyed on political actions and inactions. As Greider (1992) and many others have stressed, "the political inequality generated by inequalities of wealth" is most disturbing. "Money is power in American politics" (Greider 1992, 50, 28). The Democratic Party, which many regard as the representative of those who suffer, is beholden to large funders, as a number of analyses show (Edsall & Edsall 1992; Kuttner 1987).

The importance of money in elections and policy is an affront to the ideal of democracy in which each person is regarded as having equal weight. "The decayed condition of American democracy" (Greider 1992, 11) supports the moral claim for reducing inequalities. Taking money out of politics is not only an important factor in the reduction of inequalities but also a moral call to pay attention to the impact of inequalities on democracy.

Increasing the voter participation of lower socioeconomic groups might affect issues and the political responses to them in addition to overcoming the impact of big money. As Piven and Cloward (1988) conclude, "A 'New Politics'...requires new constituencies" that can develop from the ranks of the low voting socioeconomic groups. "[A] substantial influx of new voters can be expected, over time, to exert pressures for new leaders and progressive appeals that reflect their interests" (p. 253). Extending this analysis, new constituencies can reduce the power of money by forcing politicians to be concerned about the emergence of new voting blocs. Candidates and elected officials might then have a different stance on economic and equality issues if more people of lower socioeconomic levels were organized and voted. The data above strongly suggest that as people move up the income ladder and inequalities are reduced, they are more likely to vote.

Thus, easing the barriers to voting, as was done with the Motor Voter Law of 1993, is a big step. Nonetheless, reducing inequalities in the socioeconomic sphere will also be important in promoting the emergence of new constituencies and in realizing democracy.

## BEYOND EQUALITY

When the issues of poverty and inequality gain attention, the usual response is that economic growth and enhanced productivity will eliminate or reduce them. "A rising tide lifts all ships" is the reassuring metaphor. The recurrent but surprising recognition of the persistence or reappearance of poverty and inequality overwhelms the metaphor. As Jencks (1992) argued, doubling or tripling everyone's income would not eliminate poverty, let alone inequality. Needs change. To be included in American society, one now requires a telephone, a television set, and often a car. What is happening to those who are better off in society affects what happens to those in lower socioeconomic situations. If the omnipresence of automobiles has curtailed public transportation and if the dispersion of jobs requires long travel, then a car is now a necessary part of one's economic (as well as social) life (Jencks 1992, 7-8; Sen 1992)....

Even if concerns about the quality of democracy and the distribution of health are not sufficiently compelling to lead to lessened inequalities, they and similar issues merit open discussion, for they question what kind of society we seek and what changes and costs would result from realizing it. Most discussions of economic reasons for equality are narrowly phrased in terms of economic growth, implying that we only want more of the same. But the issue of equality should lead to questions of value: What is the worth of what is to be better distributed? Although economic equality tends to be measured in terms of dollars and cents, it should be framed in terms of what is to

be achieved in daily life[1] — socially and politically as well as economically. After long neglect, philosophical discourse, stimulated particularly by the writings of Rawls (1971) and Dworkin (1977), debates moral claims to justice. We similarly need to face up to the never-ending challenge of inequalities and the damages they inflict.

## ENDNOTES

1. Sen's (1992) emphasis on "equality of what?" and "capabilities" comes close to this question but fails to deal directly with the issue of competing values, except to point to the likelihood that seeking one goal blocks the achievement of others.

## REFERENCES

Adler, N. E., T. Boyce, M. A. Chesney, S. Cohen, S. Folkman, R. L. Kahn, & S. L. Syme (1994). "Socioeconomic Status and Health: The Challenge of the Gradient." *American Psychologist*, 49(1), 15-24.

Bennett, S. E., & L. L. M Bennett (1986). "Political Participation." In S. Long (Ed.), *Annual Review of Political Science* (Vol. 1, pp. 157-197). Norwood, NJ: Ablex.

Bunker, J. P., D. S. Gomby, & B. H. Kehrer (Eds.) (1989). *Pathways to Health: The Role of Social Factors*. Menlo Park, CA: The Henry J. Kaiser Family Foundation.

Chen, K. (1992). *Political Alienation and Voting Turnout in the United States, 1960-1988*. San Francisco: Mellon Research University Press.

Dunham, P. (1991). *Electoral Behavior in the United States*. Englewood Cliffs, NJ: Prentice Hall.

Dutton, D. B., & S. Levine (1989). "Socioeconomic Status and Health: Overview, Methodological Critique, and Reformulation." In J. P. Bunker, D. S. Gomby, & B.H. Kehrer (Eds.), *Pathways to Health: The Role of Social Factors* (pp. 29-69). Menlo Park, CA: The Henry J. Kaiser Family Foundation.

Dworkin, R. (1977). *Taking Rights Seriously*. Cambridge, MA: Harvard University Press.

Edsall, T. B., & M. D. Edsall (1992). *Chain Reaction: The Impact of Race, Rights, and Taxes on American Politics*. New York: W. W. Norton.

Filer, J., L. W. Kenny, & R. B. Morton (1993). "Redistribution, Income, and Voting."

Gortmaker, S. L., & P. H. Wise (1994). *The First Injustice: Socioeconomic Disparities in Infant Mortality in the United States: Theoretical and Policy Perspectives* [draft]. Harvard School of Public Health and The Health Institute. Boston: New England Medical Center, Society and Health Program.

Greider, W. (1992). *Who Will Tell the People: The Betrayal of American Democracy*. New York: Simon & Schuster.

Haan, M., G. A. Kaplan, & T. Camacho (1987). "Poverty and Health: Prospective Evidence from the Alameda County Study." *American Journal of Epidemiology,* 125(6).

Jencks, C. (1992). *Rethinking Social Policy: Race, Poverty, and the Underclass.* Cambridge, MA: Harvard University Press.

Kaus, M. (1992). *The End of Equality.* New York: Basic Books.

Kawachi, I., S. Levine, S. M. Miller, K. Lasch, & B. Amick III (1994). *Income Inequality and Life Expectancy: Theory, Research, and Policy.* Working Paper Series. Harvard School of Public Health and The Heath Institute, Boston: New England Medical Center, Society and Health Program.

Kuttner, R. (1987). *The Life of the Party.* New York: Elizabeth Sifton Books-Viking.

Leighley, J. E., & J. Nagler (1992). "Socioeconomic Class Bias in Turnout, 1964-1988: The Voters Remain the Same." *American Political Science Review,* 86(3), 725-736.

Levine, S. (1993). *Inequality and Health* [draft]. Harvard School of Public Health and The Health Institute. Boston: New England Medical Center, Society and Health Program.

Marmot, M. G., & G. D. Smith (1989). "Why Are the Japanese Living Longer?" *British Medical Journal,* 299; 1547–1551.

Mead, L. (1986). *Beyond Entitlement: The Social Obligations of Citizenship.* New York: Free Press.

Menchik, P. L. (1991, January). "Poverty and Mortality Rates." *Insights.*

Miller, S. M. (1989). "Race in the Health of America." In D. P. Willis (Ed.), *Health Policies and Black Americans* (pp. 500-531). New Brunswick, NJ: Transaction.

Miller, S. M., & P. A. Roby (1970). *The Future of Inequality.* New York: Basic Books.

Murray, C. (1984). *Losing Ground: American Social Policy 1950-1989.* New York: Basic Books.

Oliver, M., & T. Shapiro (1990, April). "Wealth of a Nation: A Reassessment of Asset Inequality in America Shows at Least One-Third of Households Are Asset-Poor." *American Journal of Economics and Sociology,* pp. 129–150.

Otten, M. W., Jr., S. M. Teutsch, D. F. Williamson, & J. S. Marks (1990). "The Effects of Known Risk Factors on the Excess Mortality of Black Adults in the United States." *Journal of the American Medical Association,* 263, 845–850.

Pappas, G., S. Queen, W. Hadden, & G. Fisher (1993). "The Increasing Disparity in Mortality Between Socioeconomic Groups in the United States, 1960 and 1986." *New England Journal of Medicine,* 329(2), 103–109.

Piven, F. F., & R. Cloward (1988). *Why Americans Don't Vote.* New York: Pantheon.

Rawls, J. (1971). *A Theory of Justice.* Cambridge, MA: Harvard University Press.

Rosenstone, S. J. (1982). "Economic Adversity and Voter Turnout." *American Journal of Political Science,* 26(1), 25-6.

Ryan, W. (1981). *Equality.* New York: Pantheon.

Sen, A. (1992). *Inequality Reexamined.* Cambridge, MA: Harvard University Press.

Teixeira, R. A. (1987). *Why Americans Don't Vote.* Westport, CT: Greenwood.

Verba, S., S. Kelman, G. R. Orren, I. Miyake, J. Watanuki, I. Kabashima, & G. D. Ferree, Jr. (1987). *Elites and the Idea of Equality.* Cambridge, MA: Harvard University Press.

Wilkinson, R. G. (1992). "National Mortality Rates: The Impact of Inequality?" *American Journal of Public Health,* 82(8), 1082–1084.

---

# 25. THE CHILDREN OF AFFLUENCE

ROBERT COLES

*"There is, I think, a message that virtually all quite well-off American families transmit to their children — an emotional expression of those familiar, classbound prerogatives, money, and power. I use the word entitlement to describe that message."*

Robert Coles has done a number of studies concerning class in the United States, focusing especially on the ideas and lives of children of poverty. This article is about the children of the affluent—those whom Coles describes as possessing a state of mind called **entitlement**, which claims as rights that which others regard as luxuries. This analysis goes far in showing how one's class influences what one expects from life, how those expectations are claimed as a matter of right, and how they influence what the child actually "chooses" to do in life.

Dramatic and secluded; old, historic, and architecturally interesting; large and with good grounds; private and palatial; beautifully restored; big, interesting, high up, and with an uninterrupted view; so the real-estate descriptions go. In the cities, it is a town house or luxury apartment on Nob Hill, Beacon Hill, the Near North Side, the Garden District. Outside the major cities, the house is in a town, township, village, station, even crossing. Anything to make it clear that one does not live simply "in the suburbs," that one is outside or away—well outside or well away, as it is so often put. The houses vary: imitation English castles; French provincial; nineteenth-century American; contemporary one-levels in the tradition of Gropius or Neutra. Sometimes the setting is formal, sometimes it is a farm—animals, rail fences, pastureland, a barn, maybe a shed or two, a flower garden, and more recently, a few rows of vegetables. Sometimes there is a swimming pool, a tennis court, a greenhouse. Sometimes the house stands on a hill, affords a view for miles around. Sometimes trees stand close guard; and beyond them, thick brush and more trees, a jumble of them: no view, but complete privacy. Sometimes there is a paved road leading from a street up to the house's entrance. Sometimes the road is a dusty path or a trail—the casual countrified scene, prized and jealously guarded.

The trees matter; so do the grass and the shrubbery. These are not houses in a row, with patches of new grass, fledgling trees, and a bush or two. These are homes surrounded by spacious lawns and announced by tall, sturdy trees. Hedges are common, carefully arranged. And often there is a brook running through the land.

In Texas or in New Mexico, the architecture of the houses changes, as do to a degree the flora and fauna. Now the homes are ranches, big sprawling ones, many rooms in many wings. Acres and acres of land are given over to horse trails, gardens, large swimming pools, even airplane strips for private planes. In New Mexico, the large adobe houses boast nearby cacti, corrals, and so often, stunning views: across a valley, over toward mountains miles and miles away.

From *The Atlantic Monthly*, September 1977. By permission of Robert Coles.

In such settings are a small group of America's children raised. I have for years visited the homes of boys and girls whose parents are well-to-do indeed, and sometimes quite wealthy. They are parents whose decisions have affected, in one way or another, the working-class and poor families I have worked with—growers, mine owners, other prominent businessmen, lawyers, and bankers, or real estate operators. I have wanted to know how their children grew up, how their children see themselves—and how they see their much more humble age-mates, with whom they share American citizenship, if nothing else. Put differently, I have wanted to know how the extremes of class, poverty, and wealth variously affect the psychological and moral development of a particular nation's particular century's children.

"Comfortable, comfortable places" was the way one girl described her three homes: an enormous duplex apartment in Chicago, a ski lodge in Aspen, and a lovely old New England clapboard home by the ocean toward the end of Cape Cod. She was not bragging; she knew a pleasurable, cozy, even luxurious life when she saw one (had one), and was at ease describing its many, consistent comforts. She happened to be sitting on a large sofa as she offered her observation. She touched a nearby pillow, also rather large, then moved it a bit closer to herself. In a rather uncharacteristic burst of proprietary assertiveness, the girl said: "I'd like to keep this pillow for my own house, when I'm grown up."

Children like her have a lot to look after and, sometimes, feel attached to. At the same time, they may often be overwhelmed with toys, gadgets, presents. These are children who have to contend with, as well as to enjoy, enormous couches, pillows virtually as big as chairs, rugs that were meant to be in the palaces of the Middle East, dining room tables bigger than the rooms many American children share with brothers or sisters. Always they are aware of the importance and fragility of objects: a vase, a dish, a tray, a painting or lithograph or pencil sketch, a lamp. How much of that world can the child even comprehend? Sometimes, in a brave attempt to bring everything under control, a young child will enumerate (for the benefit of a teacher or a friend) all that is his or hers, the background against which a life is carried on.

Finally, the child may grow weary, abandon the spoken catalog and think of one part of his or her life that means *everything*: a snake that can reliably be seen in a certain stretch of mixed grass and shrubbery along the driveway; a pair of pheasants who come every morning to the lawn and appear remarkably relaxed as they find food; a dog or a cat or a pony or a pet bird; a friend who lives near a summer home, or the son or daughter of a Caribbean cook or maid; a visit to an amusement park—a visit which, for the child, meant more than dozens of toys, some virtually untouched since they arrived; or a country remembered above all others —Ireland or England, France or Switzerland.

These are children who learn to live with *choices*: more clothes, a wider range of food, a greater number of games, toys, hobbies, than other boys and girls may ever be able to imagine for themselves. They learn also to assume instruction—not only at school, but at home—for tennis, swimming, dancing, horseback riding. And they learn, often enough, to feel competent at those sports, in control of themselves while playing them, and not least, able to move smoothly from one to the other rather than driven to excel. It is as if the various outdoor sports are like suits of clothing, to be put on, enjoyed, then casually slipped off.

Something else many of these children learn: The newspapers, the radio, the television offer news not merely about "others" but about neighbors, friends, acquaintances of one's parents—or about issues one's parents take seriously, talk about, sometimes get quite involved in. These are children who have discovered that the "news" may well be affected, if not crucially molded, by their parents as individuals or as members of a particular segment of society. Similarly, parental authority wielded in the world is matched by parental authority exerted at home. Servants are called in, are given instructions or, indeed, even replaced summarily. In a way, those servants—by whatever name or names they are called—are for these American children a microcosm of the larger world, as they will experience it. They are the people who provide convenience and comfort. They are the people who, by and large, aim to please. Not all of them "live in"; there are cleaning women, delivery people, caretakers, town inspectors, plumbers and carpenters and electricians, carriers of telegrams, of flowers, of special delivery letters. Far more than their parents, the children observe the coming and going, the back-door bustle, the front-door activity of the "staff."

It is a complicated world, a world that others watch with envy and with curiosity, with awe, anger, bitterness, resentment. It is a world, rather often, of action, of talk believed by the talkers to have meaning and importance, of schedules or timetables. It is a world in motion—yet, at times, one utterly still: a child in a garden, surrounded by the silence that acres of lawn or woods can provide. It is a world of excitement and achievement. It is an intensely private world that can suddenly become vulnerable to the notice of others. It is, obviously, a world of money and power—a twentieth-century American version of both. It is also a world in which children grow up, come to terms with their ample surroundings, take to them gladly, deal with them anxiously, and show themselves boys and girls who have their own special circumstances to master—a particular way of life to understand and become a part of.

## ENTITLED

It won't do to talk of *the* affluent in America. It won't do to say that in our upper-middle-class suburbs, or among our wealthy, one observes clear-cut, consistent psychological or cultural characteristics. Even in relatively homogeneous places, there are substantial differences in home-life, in values taught, hobbies encouraged, beliefs advocated or sometimes virtually instilled.

But it is the obligation of a psychological observer like me, who wants to know how children make sense of a certain kind of life, to document as faithfully as possible the way a common heritage of money and power affects the assumptions of particular boys and girls. Each child, of course, is also influenced by certain social, racial, cultural, or religious traditions, or thoroughly idiosyncratic ones—a given family's tastes, sentiments, ideals. And yet, the sheer fact of class affiliation has enormous power over a child's inner life....

Wealth does not corrupt nor does it ennoble. But wealth does govern the minds of privileged children, gives them a peculiar kind of identity that they never lose, whether they grow up to be stockbrokers or communards, and whether they lead healthy or unstable lives. There is, I think, a message that virtually all quite well-off American families transmit to their children—an emotional expression of those familiar, classbound prerogatives, money and power. I use the word *entitlement* to describe that message.

The word was given to me by the rather rich parents of a child I began to talk with almost two decades ago, in 1959. I have watched those parents become grandparents, and have seen what they described as "the responsibilities of entitlement" handed down to a new generation. When the father, a lawyer and stockbroker from a prominent and quietly influential family, referred to the "entitlement" his children were growing up to know, he had in mind a social rather than a psychological phenomenon: the various juries or committees that select the Mardi Gras participants in New Orleans's annual parade and celebration. He knew that his daughter was "entitled" to be invited.

He wanted, however, to go beyond that social fact. He talked about what he had received from his parents and what he would give to his children, "automatically, without any thought," and what they too would pass on. The father was careful to distinguish between the social entitlement and "something else," a "something else" he couldn't quite define but knew he had to try to evoke if he was to be psychologically candid:

Our children have a good life ahead of them; and I think they know it now. I think they did when they were three or four, too. It's *entitlement*, that's what I call it. My wife didn't know what I was talking about when I first used the word. She thought it had something to do with our ancestry. Maybe it does. I don't mean to be snide. I just think our children grow up taking a lot for granted, and it can be good that they do, and it can be bad. It's like anything else; it all depends. I mean, you can have spoiled brats for children, or you can have kids who want to share what they have. I don't mean give away all their money. I mean be responsible, and try to live up to their ideals, and not just sit around wondering which island in the Caribbean to visit this year, and where to go next summer to get away from the heat and humidity here in New Orleans.

At the time, he said no more; at the time, I wasn't especially interested in pursuing the sub-

ject. But as months became years, I came back to that word *entitlement*. There is, as it happens, a psychiatric term that closely connects with it. *Narcissistic entitlement* is the phrase, when referring to a particular kind of "disturbed" child. The term could be used in place of the more conventional, blunter ones: a smug, self-satisfied child; or a child who thinks he owns the world, or will one day. It is an affliction that strikes particularly the wealthy child....

If narcissism is something a migrant child or a ghetto child has to contend with, it will take on one flavor (narcissistic despair, for instance), whereas for a child of wealth, narcissistic entitlement is the likely possibility. The child has much, but wants and expects more, all assumed to be his or hers by right—at once a psychological and material inheritance that the world will provide. One's parents will oblige, will be intermediaries, will go back and forth—bringing from stores or banks or wherever those various offerings that serve to gratify the mind's sense of its own importance, its own *due*.

This syndrome is one that wealthy parents recognize instinctively, often wordlessly—and fear. When their children are four, five, and six, parents able to offer them virtually anything sometimes begin to pull back, in concern if not in outright horror. Not only has a son become increasingly demanding or petulant; even when he is quiet, he seems to be sitting on a throne of sorts—expecting things to happen, wondering with annoyance why they don't, reassuring himself and others that they will or, if they don't, shrugging his shoulders and waiting for the next splendid moment.

It was just such an impasse—not dramatic, but quite definite and worrisome—that prompted the New Orleans father quoted earlier to use the word *entitlement*. He had himself been born to wealth, as will be the case for generations of his family to come, unless the American economic system changes drastically in the future. But he was worried about what a lot of money can do to a personality. When his young daughter, during a Mardi Gras season, kept *assuming* she would one day receive this honor and that honor—indeed, become a Mardi Gras queen—he realized that his notion of "entitlement" was not quite hers. *Noblesse oblige* requires a gesture toward others.

He was not the only parent to express such a concern to me in the course of my work. In homes where mothers and fathers profess no explicit reformist persuasions, they nevertheless worry about what happens to children who grow up surrounded by just about everything they want, virtually on demand. "When they're like that, they've gone from spoiled to spoiled rotten — and beyond, to some state I don't know how to describe."

Obviously, it is possible for parents to have a lot of money yet avoid bringing up their children in such a way that they feel like members of a royal family. But even parents determined not to spoil their children often recognize what might be called the existential (as opposed to strictly psychological) aspects of their situation. A father may begin rather early on lecturing his children about the meaning of money; a mother may do her share by saying *no*, even when *yes* is so easy to say. Such a child, by the age of five or six, has very definite notions of what is possible, even if it is not always

permitted. That child, in conversation, and without embarrassment or the kind of reticence and secretiveness that come later, may reveal a substantial knowledge of economic affairs. A six-year-old girl I spoke to knew that she would, at twenty-one, inherit half a million dollars. She also knew that her father "only" gave her twenty-five cents a week, whereas some friends of hers received as much as a dollar. She was vexed; she asked her parents why they were so "strict." One friend had even used the word "stingy" for the parents. The father, in a matter-of-fact way, pointed out to the daughter that she did, after all, get "anything she really wants." Why, then, the need for an extravagant allowance? The girl was won over. But admonitions don't always modify the quite realistic appraisal children make of what they are heir to; and they don't diminish their sense of entitlement — a state of mind that pervades their view of the world....

# 26.  THE USES OF POVERTY: THE POOR PAY ALL

HERBERT J. GANS

*"Many of the functions served by the poor could be replaced if poverty were eliminated, but almost always at higher costs to others, particularly more affluent others."*

This article examines the poor in America and shows how they are used in society and how they function for the rest of us. Herbert J. Gans is saying: Let's face it, you and I benefit from having the poor. Do not think that Gans is saying there must be a class of poor; instead he is arguing that, in capitalism, the poor are exploited in a number of ways. Eliminating the poor will be costly to the affluent. Poverty is then tied to the structure of society: People are kept in low positions in large part for the benefit of those in high positions. Those in high positions, because they benefit, refuse to make real changes that deal with ending poverty.

Associating poverty with positive functions seems at first glance to be unimaginable. Of course, the slumlord and the loan shark are commonly known to profit from the existence of poverty, but they are viewed as evil men, so their activities are classified among the dysfunctions of poverty. However, what is less often recognized, at least by the conventional wisdom, is that poverty also makes possible the existence or expansion of respectable professions and occupations, for example, penology, criminology, social work, and public health. More recently, the poor have provided jobs for professional and paraprofessional "poverty warriors," and for journalists and social scientists, this author included, who have supplied the information demanded by the revival of public interest in poverty.

Clearly, then, poverty and the poor may well satisfy a number of positive functions for many nonpoor groups in American society. I shall describe thirteen such functions — economic, social, and political — that seem to me most significant.

## THE FUNCTIONS OF POVERTY

*First*, the existence of poverty ensures that society's "dirty work" will be done. Every society has such work: physically dirty or dangerous, temporary, dead-end and underpaid, undignified and menial jobs. Society can fill these jobs by paying higher wages than for "clean" work, or it can force people who have no other choice to do the dirty work — and at low wages. For America, poverty functions to provide a low-wage labor pool that is willing — or, rather, unable to be unwilling — to perform dirty work at low cost. Indeed, this function of the poor is so important that in some southern states, welfare payments have been cut off during the summer months when the poor are needed to work in the fields. Moreover, much of the debate about the negative income tax and the family assistance plan has concerned their impact on the work incentive, by which is actually meant the incentive of the poor to do the needed dirty work if the wages therefrom are no larger than the income grant. Many economic activities that involve dirty work depend on the poor for their existence:

restaurants, hospitals, parts of the garment industry, and "truck farming," among others, could not persist in their present form without the poor.

*Second*, because the poor are required to work at low wages, they subsidize a variety of economic activities that benefit the affluent. For example, domestics subsidize the upper-middle and upper classes, making life easier for their employers and freeing affluent women for a variety of professional, cultural, civic, and partying activities. Similarly, because the poor pay a higher proportion of their income in property and sales taxes, among others, they subsidize many state and local governmental services that benefit more affluent groups. In addition, the poor support innovation in medical practice as patients in teaching and research hospitals and as guinea pigs in medical experiments.

*Third*, poverty creates jobs for a number of occupations and professions that serve or "service" the poor, or protect the rest of society from them. As already noted, penology would be minuscule without the poor, as would the need for police. Other activities and groups that flourish because of the existence of poverty are the numbers game, the sale of heroin and cheap wines and liquors, Pentecostal ministers, faith healers, prostitutes, pawn shops, and the peacetime army, which recruits its enlisted men mainly from among the poor.

*Fourth*, the poor buy goods others do not want and thus prolong the economic usefulness of such goods — day-old bread, fruit and vegetables that would otherwise have to be thrown out, secondhand clothes, and deteriorating automobiles and buildings. They also provide incomes for doctors, lawyers, teachers, and others who are too old, poorly trained, or incompetent to attract more affluent clients.

In addition to economic functions, the poor perform a number of social functions.

*Fifth*, the poor can be identified and punished as alleged or real deviants in order to uphold the legitimacy of conventional norms. To justify the desirability of hard work, thrift, honesty, and monogamy, for example, the defenders of these norms must be able to find people who can be accused of being lazy, spendthrift, dishonest, and promiscuous. Although there is some evidence that the poor are about as moral and law-abiding as anyone else, they are more likely than middle-class transgressors to be caught and punished when they participate in deviant acts. Moreover, they lack the political and cultural power to correct the stereotypes that other people hold of them and thus continue to be thought of as lazy, spendthrift, and so on, by those who need living proof that moral deviance does not pay.

*Sixth*, and conversely, the poor offer vicarious participation to the rest of the population in the uninhibited sexual, alcoholic, and narcotic behavior in which they are alleged to participate and which, being freed from the constraints of affluence, they are often thought to enjoy more than the middle classes. Thus many people, some social scientists included, believe that the poor not only are more given to uninhibited behavior (which may be true, although it is often motivated by despair more than by lack of inhibition) but derive more pleasure from it than affluent people (a finding that research by Lee Rainwater, Walter Miller, and others shows to be patently untrue). However, whether the poor actually have more sex and enjoy it more is irrelevant; as long as middle-class people believe this to be true, they can participate in it vicariously when instances are reported in factual or fictional form.

*Seventh*, the poor also serve a direct cultural function when culture created by or for them is adopted by the more affluent. The rich often collect artifacts from extinct folk cultures of poor people; and almost all Americans listen to the blues, Negro spirituals, and country music, which originated among the southern poor. Recently, they have enjoyed the rock styles that were born, like the Beatles, in the slums, and in the last year, poetry written by ghetto children has become popular in literary circles. The poor also serve as culture heroes, particularly, of course, to the left; but the hobo, the cowboy, the hipster, and the mythical prostitute with a heart of gold have performed this function for a variety of groups.

*Eighth*, poverty helps guarantee the status of those who are not poor. In every hierarchical society, someone has to be at the bottom; but in American society, in which social mobility is an important goal for many and people need to know where they stand, the poor function as a reliable and relatively permanent measuring rod for status comparisons. This is particularly true for the working class, whose politics is influenced by the need to maintain status distinctions between themselves and the poor, much as the aristocracy must find ways of distinguishing itself from the *nouveaux riches*.

*Ninth*, the poor also aid the upward mobility of groups just above them in the class hierarchy. Thus a goodly number of Americans have entered the middle class through the profits earned from the provision of goods and services in the slums, including illegal or nonrespectable ones that upper-class and upper-middle-class businessmen shun because of their low prestige. As a result, members of almost every immigrant group have financed their upward mobility by providing slum housing, entertainment, gambling, narcotics, and the like to later arrivals—most recently to blacks and Puerto Ricans.

*Tenth*, the poor help to keep the aristocracy busy, thus justifying its continued existence. "Society" uses the poor as clients of settlement houses and beneficiaries of charity affairs; indeed, the aristocracy must have the poor to demonstrate its superiority over other elites who devote themselves to earning money.

*Eleventh*, the poor, being powerless, can be made to absorb the costs of change and growth in American society. During the nineteenth century, they did the backbreaking work that built the cities; today, they are pushed out of their neighborhoods to make room for "progress." Urban renewal projects to hold middle-class taxpayers in the city and expressways to enable suburbanites to commute downtown have typically been located in poor neighborhoods because no other group will allow itself to be displaced. For the same reason, universities, hospitals, and civic centers also expand into land occupied by the poor. The major costs of the industrialization of agriculture have been borne by the poor, who are pushed off the land without recompense; and they have paid a large share of the human cost of the growth of American power overseas, for they have provided many of the foot soldiers for Vietnam and other wars.

*Twelfth*, the poor facilitate and stabilize the American political process. Because they vote and participate in politics less than other groups, the political system is often free to ignore them. Moreover, because they can rarely support Republicans, they often provide the Democrats with a captive constituency that has no other place to go. As a result, the Democrats can count on their votes, and be more responsive to voters — for example, the white working class — who might otherwise switch to the Republicans.

*Thirteenth*, the role of the poor in upholding conventional norms (see the fifth point, earlier) also has a significant political function. An economy based on the ideology of *laissez faire* requires a deprived population that is allegedly unwilling to work or that can be considered inferior because it must accept charity or welfare in order to survive. Not only does the alleged moral deviancy of the poor reduce the moral pressure on the present political economy to eliminate poverty, but socialist alternatives can be made to look quite unattractive if those who will benefit most from them can be described as lazy, spendthrift, dishonest, and promiscuous.

## THE ALTERNATIVES

I have described thirteen of the more important functions poverty and the poor satisfy in American society, enough to support the functionalist thesis that poverty, like any other social phenomenon, survives in part because it is useful to society or some of its parts. This analysis is not intended to suggest that because it is often functional, poverty *should* exist, or that it *must* exist. For one thing, poverty has many more dysfunctions than functions; for another, it is possible to suggest functional alternatives.

For example, society's dirty work could be done without poverty, either by automation or by paying "dirty workers" decent wages. Nor is it necessary for the poor to subsidize the many activities they support through their low-wage jobs. This would, however, drive up the costs of these activities, which would result in higher prices to their customers and clients. Similarly, many of the professionals who flourish because of the poor could be given other roles. Social workers could provide counseling to the affluent, as they prefer to do anyway; and the police could devote themselves to traffic and organized crime. Other roles would have to be found for badly trained or incompetent professionals now relegated to serving the poor, and someone else would have to pay their salaries. Fewer penologists would be employable, however. And

Pentecostal religion could probably not survive without the poor — nor would parts of the second-hand and third-hand goods market. And in many cities, "used" housing that no one else wants would have to be torn down at public expense.

Alternatives for the cultural functions of the poor could be found more easily and cheaply. Indeed, entertainers, hippies, and adolescents are already serving as the deviants needed to uphold traditional morality and as devotees of orgies to "staff" the fantasies of vicarious participation.

The status functions of the poor are another matter. In a hierarchical society, some people must be defined as inferior to everyone else with respect to a variety of attributes, but they need not be poor in the absolute sense. One could conceive of a society in which the "lower class," though last in the pecking order, received 75 percent of the median income, rather than 15 to 40 percent, as is now the case. Needless to say, this would require considerable income redistribution.

The contribution the poor make to the upward mobility of the groups that provide them with goods and services could also be maintained without the poor's having such low incomes. However, it is true that if the poor were more affluent, they would have access to enough capital to take over the provider role, thus competing with, and perhaps rejecting, the "outsiders." (Indeed, owing in part to antipoverty programs, this is already happening in a number of ghettos, where white storeowners are being replaced by blacks.) Similarly, if the poor were more affluent, they would make less willing clients for upper-class philanthropy, although some would still use settlement houses to achieve upward mobility, as they do now. Thus "society" could continue to run its philanthropic activities.

The political functions of the poor would be more difficult to replace. With increased affluence, the poor would probably obtain more political power and be more active politically. With higher incomes and more political power, the poor would be likely to resist paying the costs of growth and change. Of course, it is possible to imagine urban renewal and highway projects that properly reimbursed the displaced people, but such projects would then become considerably more expensive, and many might never be built. This, in turn, would reduce the comfort and convenience of those who now benefit from urban renewal and expressways. Finally, hippies could serve also as more deviants to justify the existing political economy — as they already do. Presumably, however, if poverty were eliminated, there would be fewer attacks on that economy.

In sum, then, many of the functions served by the poor could be replaced if poverty were eliminated, but almost always at higher costs to others, particularly more affluent others. Consequently, a functional analysis must conclude that poverty persists not only because it fulfills a number of positive functions but also because many of the functional alternatives to poverty would be quite dysfunctional for the affluent members of society. A functional analysis thus ultimately arrives at much the same conclusion as radical sociology, except that radical thinkers treat as manifest what I describe as latent: That social phenomena that are functional for affluent or powerful groups and dysfunctional for poor or powerless ones persist; that when the elimination of such phenomena through functional alternatives would generate dysfunctions for the affluent or powerful, they will continue to persist; and that phenomena like poverty can be eliminated only when they become dysfunctional for the affluent or powerful, or when the powerless can obtain enough power to change society.

# Part VI

# ETHNIC AND RACIAL INEQUALITY

Society is not only structured by class, but also by race and ethnic-group membership.

To many Americans, diversity is a quality that makes us a unique and great society. To others, diversity is regarded as a basic cause for many of our problems. In either case, diversity has been and remains a way that power, privilege, and prestige is distributed in society. Nonwhites and Hispanics are systematically placed in low positions in relation to whites and Anglos. Hence, sociologists often will label such groups "minorities."

The selection by Ronald Takaki places the study of nonwhite minorities in a broad historical context to show the role of power and conflict in the formation and perpetuation of this structure. John Farley, in the second selection, follows this theme as he describes the origin of structure between Anglos and Mexicans in American society. Stephen Steinberg focuses on one aspect of that structure, occupational opportunities for African-Americans, and tries to show that this inequality did not have to be—except for the fact that our exclusion of African-Americans has never been faced and often encouraged by our actions as a society. Andrew Hacker's insightful description of the world in which African-Americans exist is both troubling and real. Clarence Page describes to us the identity problems he faces as a middle-class African-American.

Finally, "Beyond the Melting Pot," written by William A. Henry III for **Time**, examines the issues we must face in the next century as our society becomes even more ethnically diverse.

# 27. REFLECTIONS ON RACIAL PATTERNS IN AMERICA

RONALD TAKAKI

*"To diminish the significance of racial oppression in America's past and to define racial inequality as a problem of prejudice and limit the solution as the outlawing of individual acts of discrimination, as does Glazer, is effectively to leave intact the very structures of racial inequality."*

Ronald Takaki describes a history in American society of systematic oppression and exploitation of minorities. Takaki is reacting to the book written by Nathan Glazer that tried to make a case for the American heritage of acceptance and tolerance of minorities. There has been a "consensus" in our society, Glazer writes, to correct our inequalities through outlawing discrimination. We have, he continues, been a society that decided long ago that "the whole world would be allowed to enter," that each ethnic group would not be treated as a group but as individuals, and that each group would be able to maintain its own "character and distinctiveness." To Glazer, affirmative action has betrayed that consensus, but to Takaki, Glazer's book misses the essence of our past, exaggerates the consensus, and argues that correcting individual acts will not change the social structure that has developed for centuries.

When Allan Bakke filed his suit against the University of California Medical School at Davis in 1974, he surely did not expect his grievance to be elevated into circles of scholarship. Yet scholarly efforts to provide a theoretical justification for Bakke's claim that affirmative action policy discriminated against whites were already well underway. Consequently, four years later, racial minorities found themselves facing a scholarly theory of "reverse discrimination" as well as the Supreme Court's *Bakke* decision itself. During this time, Nathan Glazer of Harvard University has emerged as the leading architect of this new anti-affirmative action scholarship, and his book, *Affirmative Discrimination: Ethnic Inequality and Public Policy*, spearheaded the intellectual assault on affirmative action.... At the heart of Glazer's theory is a hope, a vision of a good society in which "men and women are judged on the basis of their abilities rather than their color, race, or ethnic origin." The "first principle of a liberal society," he insists, is the assertion that "the individual and the individual's interests and good and welfare are the test of a good society." Thus for Glazer, there is only one proper solution to the problem of racial inequality: the heritage of discrimination can and should be overcome by "simply attacking discrimination."[1]

A theoretician of the anti-affirmative action backlash, Glazer gives articulation to an angry pop-

This article appeared in its full and original form in Ronald Takaki, "Reflections on Racial Patterns in America," *Ethnicity and Public Policy*, Winston A. Van Horne and Thomas V. Tonnesen, eds., Milwaukee: UW System American Ethnic Studies Coordinating Committee, 1982, pp. 1–23. Reprinted by permission of The Board of Regents, University of Wisconsin System.

ular mood, a widespread resentment against the demands of racial minorities, and a moral outrage felt by the Allan Bakkes of America. He both describes and supports the point of view of the white ethnics: "They entered a society in which they were scorned; they nevertheless worked hard, they received little or no support from government or public agencies, their children received no special attention in school or special opportunity to attend college…. They contrast their situation with that of blacks and other minority groups today and see substantial differences in treatment. They consider themselves patriotic and appreciative of the United States even though they received no special benefit." Although Glazer admits the comparison may be "crude and unfair," he essentially agrees with its main contention, that blacks and other racial minorities should not receive "special" opportunities, "special" treatment, or "special" benefits. Instead, they should emulate the example of the white ethnics.[2]

In his opening chapter, "The Emergence of an American Ethnic Pattern," Glazer develops the historical and theoretical underpinnings of his critique of affirmative action policies. He uses this to provide the conceptual framework for the entire book and refers to its main points throughout the study. Viewing affirmative action policies from his historical perspective, Glazer asks at the end of the book: "How have policies which so sharply reverse the consensus developed over two hundred years of American history established themselves so powerfully in a scant ten years?"[3]

But what was that "consensus" which had developed over two hundred years? According to Glazer, the mid-1960s witnessed the emergence of a "national consensus" on solutions to the problems of racial and ethnic prejudice. This consensus was reflected in three laws: the Civil Rights Act of 1964, the Voting Rights Act of 1965, and the Immigration Act of 1965. Essentially, these laws prohibited discrimination based on race, color, religion, or national origin. But "paradoxically," Glazer argues, a new policy of affirmative action or "discrimination" was then instituted, and the consensus was "broken." Thus was shattered the "culmination" of the development of a "distinctive American orientation of ethnic difference and diversity with a history of almost 200 years."[4]

Glazer bases his theory of an American ethnic pattern on three historical developments or "decisions":

First, the entire world would be allowed to enter the United States. The claim that some nations or races were to be favored in entry over others was, for a while, accepted, but it was eventually rejected. And once having entered into the United States—and whether that entry was by means of forced enslavement, free immigration, or conquest—all citizens would have equal rights. No group would be considered subordinate to another.

Second, no separate ethnic group was to be allowed to establish an independent polity in the United States. This was to be a union of states and a nation of free individuals, not a nation of politically defined ethnic groups.

Third, no group, however, would be required to give up its group character and distinctiveness as the price of full entry into the American society and polity.

All three decisions were inclusionist rather than exclusionist. Although a notion favoring the entry of particular immigrants or races was accepted "for a while," American society eventually allowed the inclusion of all racial and ethnic groups. The decisions were also egalitarian: All citizens, regardless of race, ethnicity, or religion, would have equal rights. These decisions also promoted tolerance and acceptance of cultural and ethnic diversity: A group would be allowed to maintain its cultural values and identity. Finally, all three decisions minimized, even denied, differences between the experiences of "racial" and white "ethnic" groups in American history.[5]

Although Glazer describes the three decisions as integral parts of the "central" American pattern, he does acknowledge the existence of contrary "actions"—black slavery, anti-immigrant nativism, the "near extermination" of the American Indian, the lynching of Chinese, the relocation of Japanese Americans during World War II, and so forth. He even notes that, "for fifty years, between the 1890s and the 1930s, exclusivism was dominant." Nevertheless, for Glazer, all these contrary developments do not represent the "large direction," the "major tendency to a greater inclusiveness," in American history.[6] Thus the three decisions are claimed to be major components of historical reality in America; as a historian, I had to ask whether the claim could stand the test of a rigorous and critical examination of the historical evidence.

More specifically, I had to ask whether Glazer's theory of an American "ethnic" pattern could explain the history of racial minorities in America.

The first is the most important of all three decisions, for it permitted the "entire" world to enter the United States and extended "equal" rights to all citizens regardless of their means of entry. For us to determine whether this decision actually existed historically and whether it represented a major pattern, we need to review the history of citizenship and the right of suffrage in the United States. We also need to develop a more precise chronological measurement of how long "for a while" really was.[7]

The phrase "for a while" could refer to the early national period, when Congress made its first effort to define American citizenship in the Naturalization Law of 1790. This law specified that only free "white" immigrants would be eligible for naturalized citizenship. Clearly, this law did not allow the "entire" world to enter the United States as potential citizens or members of the body politic. Non-"white" immigrants were not permitted to be naturalized until the Walter-McCarran Act of 1952, which stated that "the right of a person to become a naturalized citizen of the United States shall not be denied or abridged because of race...." What is important to note here about the first naturalization law is the fact that it remained in effect for 162 years, or for a very long time.[8]

One of the first laws to be passed by Congress, the Naturalization Law of 1790 acquired special significance in the nineteenth century because of westward expansionism and the entry of Chinese laborers into America. The two developments were closely linked. Shortly after the end of the war against Mexico, which enabled the United States to annex California, Aaron H. Palmer, a "Counsellor of the Supreme Court of the United States," submitted to Congress a plan for the extension of American markets into Asia and the importation of Chinese workers to develop American industries. "The commodious port of San Francisco," he declared, "is destined to become the great emporium of our commerce on the Pacific; and so soon as it is connected by railroad with the Atlantic States, will become the most eligible point of departure for steamers to...China." To build the transcontinental railroad as well as to bring the

"fertile lands of California" under cultivation, Palmer recommended the immigration of Chinese. Here, in this remarkable report, was a public policy blueprint that explicitly integrated American expansion into Asia with Asiatic immigration to America.[9]

During the next three decades, tens of thousands of Chinese were recruited to work in this country. Between 1850 and 1880, the Chinese population in the United States increased from 7,520 to 105,465, a fifteen-fold increase; in 1870 the Chinese constituted 8.6 percent of the total population of California and an impressive 25 percent of the wage-earning force. But the inclusion of the Chinese in the economic structure was accompanied by their political exclusion. Not "white," they were ineligible for naturalized citizenship. They were, in effect, migrant laborers, forced to be foreigners forever. Unlike white "ethnic" immigrants such as Italians, Poles, and Irish, the Chinese were a politically proscribed labor force. They were a part of America's production process but not her body politic. American businessmen expected them to be here only on a temporary basis and located them in a racially segmented labor market. Central Pacific Railroad employer Charles Crocker, for example, told a legislative committee: "I do not believe they are going to remain here long enough to become good citizens, and I would not admit them to citizenship." Crocker also explained how the presence of Chinese workers could elevate white workers in a stratified racial/occupational structure: "I believe that the effect of Chinese labor upon white labor has an elevating instead of a degrading tendency. I think that every white man who is intelligent and able to work, who is more than a digger in a ditch...who has the capacity of being something else, can get to be something else by the presence of Chinese labor easier than he could without it.... There is proof of that in the fact that after we got the Chinamen to work, we took the more intelligent of the white laborers and made foremen of them." Businessmen "availed" themselves of this "unlimited" supply of "cheap" Chinese labor to build their railroads and operate their factories. After the Chinese migrant workers had completed their service, they were urged to return to their homeland, while others came to replace them. The employers of Chinese labor did not want these workers to remain in this country and become "thick" (to use Crocker's term) in American society.[10]

Enacted long before the entry of Asians into America, the Naturalization Law also had another consequence for immigrants from the east. Where white "ethnic" immigrants were legally entitled to own land in this country, Asian immigrants were subjected to a special form of discrimination. Defined as "aliens ineligible for citizenship," Chinese and other Asian immigrants were also denied, by state legislation, the right to own property in California, Washington, Arizona, Oregon, Idaho, Nebraska, Texas, Kansas, Louisiana, Montana, New Mexico, Minnesota, and Missouri. Thus Asian immigrants were excluded from the very process of land ownership, social mobility, and transformation of immigrants into Americans that Frederick Jackson Turner celebrated in his famous essay on the significance of the frontier in American history.[11]

Ironically, the Naturalization Law also excluded Native Americans from citizenship. Although they were born in the United States, they were regarded as members of tribes, or as domestic subjects or nationals; their status was considered analogous to children of foreign diplomats born here. As "foreigners," they could not seek naturalized citizenship, for they were not "white." Even the Fourteenth Amendment, which defined federal citizenship, did not apply to Native Americans. Although Native Americans could become United States citizens through treaties with specific tribes or through allotment programs such as the Dawes Act of 1887, general citizenship for the original American was not granted until 1924.[12]

But what happened to nonwhite citizens? Did they have "equal" rights, particularly the right of suffrage? Citizenship did not necessarily carry this right, for states determined the requirements for voting. A review of this history reveals a basic political inequality between white citizens and nonwhite citizens.

The 1965 Voting Rights Act did not actually culminate a history of political inclusion for blacks. In the North, during the most important period of political inclusion — the era of Jacksonian Democracy — the establishment of universal manhood suffrage was for white men only. In re-

ality, the inclusion of greater numbers of white men, including recent Irish immigrants, was usually accompanied by the exclusion of black citizens from the suffrage. The New York Constitution of 1821, for example, granted the vote to all free "white" male citizens who possessed a freehold, paid taxes, had served in the state militia, or had worked on the highways; it also retained the property requirement for black citizens, increasing it from $100 to $250. The Pennsylvania Constitution of 1838 went even further: It provided for universal "white" manhood suffrage and thus disenfranchised black citizens completely. In the South, except for a brief period during Reconstruction, black citizens were systematically excluded from participation in the political process. Thus the 1965 law, enacted in response to massive black pressure and protest under the leadership of Martin Luther King, was a break from a long history of denial of voting rights to racial as opposed to "ethnic" minority citizens.[13]

This difference between race and ethnicity in terms of suffrage may also be seen in the experiences of Native Americans. Although the Treaty of Guadalupe Hidalgo had offered United States citizenship to Mexicans living within the acquired territories, the 1849 Constitution of California granted the right of suffrage only to every "white" male citizen of the United States and only to every "white" male citizen of Mexico who had elected to become a United States citizen. A color line, in short, had been drawn for the granting of suffrage to American citizens in California. Native Americans were also proscribed politically in other states. The Fifteenth Amendment, which provided that the right to vote shall not be denied or abridged because of race or color, did not apply to noncitizen Indians. Even after Indians were granted citizenship under the 1924 law, however, many of them were designated "Indians not taxed" or "persons under guardianship" and disenfranchised in states like Arizona, New Mexico, Idaho, and Washington.[14]

Study of the history of citizenship and suffrage disclosed a racial and exclusionist pattern. For 162 years, the Naturalization Law, while allowing various European or "white" ethnic groups to enter the United States and acquire citizenship, specifically denied citizenship to other groups on a racial basis. Although suffrage was extended to white men, it was withheld from men of color. Thus what actually developed historically in American society was a pattern of citizenship and suffrage that drew a very sharp distinction between "ethnicity" and "race."

Like the first one, the second and third decisions also require our critical examination. According to Glazer, all Americans would be viewed and treated as "free individuals," not members of "politically defined ethnic groups" or "polities." Still, Americans could, if they wished, maintain an ethnic group identity on a voluntary basis. They would be allowed to have their distinctive religion, their own language, their own schools, and even to maintain their "loyalty" to their "old country."[15]

Although decisions two and three may have been true for white "ethnic" groups like the Irish and Germans, they certainly do not accurately describe the historical experiences of "racial" groups. This difference was particularly evident during World War II when Japanese Americans, unlike German Americans and Italian Americans, were forcefully interned in relocation camps. They were, in effect, defined and treated as a "polity" by the federal government. Of the 120,000 internees, 70,000 were United States citizens by right of birth. Japanese in America were not regarded as "free individuals" but as members of a polity simply because of their Japanese ancestry. In the camps, draft-age Nisei men were required to fill out and sign a loyalty questionnaire entitled "Statement of United States Citizenship of Japanese Ancestry." At the end of the long list of questions, they were asked:

No. 27. Are you willing to serve in the armed forces of the United States on combat duty wherever ordered?

No. 28. Will you swear unqualified allegiance to the United States of America and faithfully defend the United States from any or all attack by foreign or domestic forces, and forswear any form of allegiance or obedience to the Japanese emperor, to any other foreign government, power or organization?

Young men of Italian or German ancestry were not subjected to such a "loyalty" test.[16]

The Native American experience also does not fit well into decisions two and three. Indians have historically been formally treated as members of polities, not as "free individuals." The Constitution of the United States recognized Indian tribes as polities: Article I, Section 2, excluded from state representation in Congress "Indians not taxed"; and Article I, Section 4, granted Congress the power to "regulate Commerce with foreign Nations…and with Indian Tribes." The Indian Trade and Intercourse Act of 1802 provided that no land cessions in Indian territory could be made except by "treaty" between Congress and the Indian tribe. The view of Indian tribes as polities was explicitly expressed in the 1871 case of *McKay* v. *Campbell*. Denying that the Fourteenth Amendment had extended citizenship to Indians, the court ruled:

To be a citizen of the United States by reason of his birth, a person must not only be born within its territorial limits, but he must also be born subject to its jurisdiction…. But the Indian tribes within the limits of the United States have always been held to be distinct and independent political communities, retaining the right of self-government, though subject to the protecting power of the United States.

The removal of Choctaws, Creeks, and Cherokees in the 1830s and the relocation of Sioux and Cheyennes on reservations in the 1870s were also based on the conception of Indian tribes as polities.[17]

This policy of defining Indians as members of tribes and as members of culturally distinct groups was used as a way to control them. The strategy can be seen in the actions of two important policy makers on Indian affairs. President Andrew Jackson, claiming that Indians were culturally distinct and could not survive in white civilization, proposed their removal beyond the Mississippi River. By regarding Indian tribes as polities, Jackson was able to negotiate removal treaties with them and to transfer Indian lands into the "markett," to use the president's spelling. As Commissioner of Indian Affairs in 1872, Francis Amasa Walker saw that he could not continue Jackson's policy of removing Indians beyond the Mississippi River. By then, the "markett" had already reached the Pacific Ocean, and a new future for the Indian in the West had to be defined. Walker's proposal was to "consolidate" Indian tribes onto one or two "grand reservations." According to his plan, warlike tribes would be relocated on extensive tracts in the West, and all Indian "bands" outside of the reservation would be "liable to be struck by the military at any time, without warning, and without any implied hostility to those members of the tribe" living within the reservation. For Walker, it was a policy of military convenience to treat Indian tribes as polities.[18]

Yet, it must be noted, federal Indian policies were not entirely consistent. At times, they also reflected an inclusionist pattern. Even Walker's reservation system was designed to "civilize" Indians and prepare them for entry into American white society. His proposal would enable the federal government to extend over Indians what Walker called "a rigid reformatory discipline." The crucial term is *reformatory*. On the reservations, Indians would be trained, "required" to learn the arts of industry, and placed on a course of "self-improvement." Not allowed to "escape work," Indians would be helped over the rough places on "the white man's road." Furthermore, some federal policies prohibited the recognition of Indian tribes as independent polities in the United States. The Indian Appropriation Act of 1871, for example, provided that "hereafter no Indian nation or tribe within the territory of the United States shall be acknowledged or recognized as an independent nation, tribe, or power, with whom the United States may contract by treaty." But the aim of this law was not to recognize Indians as "free individuals" but to reduce tribal power and give railroad corporations access to Indian lands and right-of-way through Indian territory.[19]

Federal inclusionist policies also required the Indian to give up his group character and distinctiveness as the "price" of full entry into American society and polity. Nowhere can this be seen more clearly than in the Dawes Act of 1887, also known as the Indian Allotment Act. This law, which white reformers hailed as the "Indian Emancipation Act," promised to bring to a close a "century of dishonor." What it actually did was to grant the president power, at his discretion and without the Indians' consent, to break up reservations and allot

lands to individual Indians. The Dawes Act also permitted the federal government to secure tribal consent to sell "surplus" reservation lands — lands that remained after allotment had taken place — to white settlers. The effect of this policy on the Indian land base was predictable. Between 1887 and 1934, when the allotment policy was terminated, 60 percent of the Indian land base had been transferred to whites: 60 million acres had been sold as "surplus" lands to whites by the federal government, and 27 million acres — or two-thirds of the land allotted to individual Indians — had been transferred to whites through private transactions. This tremendous reduction of the Indian land base has had a very destructive impact on Native American cultures — their distinctive religions, languages, and ethnic group identities. The law also conferred citizenship on the allottees and any other Indians who would abandon their tribes and adopt the "habits of civilized life." Thus the Dawes Act, offering Indians entry, exacted a "price...."[20]

America, despite its racial pattern of domination and exclusion, contained a counterpointing perspective. In his resonant musings, a lonely poet — Walt Whitman — celebrated a vision of democratic tolerance and indiscriminate inclusionism. In Whitman's "America," peoples of all colors could come together, mixing in a great democracy yet respecting the rich cultural diversity of a multiracial society. Thus the poet sang:

*Of every hue and caste am I, of every rank and religion,*
*A farmer, mechanic, artist, gentleman, sailor, quaker,*
*Prisoner, fancy-man, rowdy, lawyer, physician, priest,*
*I resist any thing better than my own diversity.*

Whitman saluted "all the inhabitants of the earth." For the American poet, "all races and cultures" were to be "accepted, to be saluted, not to be controlled or placed in hierarchy." And in America, all were to be welcomed: "Chinese, Irish, German, pauper or not, criminal or not — all, all, without exceptions." Ours was not to be a society for "special types" but for the "great mass of people — the vast, surging, hopeful army of workers."[21]

But Whitman's was not the vision of America's public policy makers. Where the poet offered a democratic alternative, the representatives to Congress enacted the 1790 Naturalization Law and the 1882 Chinese Exclusion Act. Where the poet joyfully perceived the promise of a culturally diverse America, federal officials removed Indians and relocated Japanese Americans. Where the poet embraced an egalitarianism for all, regardless of race, men in power like Jefferson, Rush, and Walker worked to build a homogeneous society for special types. Where the poet welcomed all immigrants into the "hopeful army of workers," corporate leaders like Crocker constructed racially divided, segmented labor markets that reflected an American racial pattern.

This pattern was discerned long ago by Herman Melville and emblematized in his description of the crew of the *Pequod* and the whaling industry's labor force. "Not one in two of the many thousand men before the mast employed in the American whale fishery are American born, though pretty nearly all the officers are," reported Melville's Ishmael. "Herein it is the same with the American whale fishery as with the American army and military and merchant navies, and the engineering forces employed in the construction of the American Canals and Railroads. The same, I say, because in all these cases the native American liberally provides the brains, the rest of the world as generally supplying the muscles." A significant supply of the "muscles" on board the *Pequod* had been drawn from workers of color — blacks, Indians, Pacific Islanders, and Asians. The social divisions within the ship's crew represented the occupational/racial structure in American labor and society. Although not all whites were officers, all officers or men on deck were white, and all workers of color were below deck.[22]

The American racial pattern that Melville depicted in 1851 still largely exists today in its basic form and will continue long after the enactment of legislation prohibiting discrimination based on color, race, or ethnic origin, unless public policies act affirmatively to overcome racial inequality. Because of racially exclusionist forces and developments in American history, racial inequality and occupational stratification have come to coexist in a mutually reinforcing and dynamic structural relationship that continues to operate

more powerfully than direct forms of racial prejudice and discrimination. To diminish the significance of racial oppression in America's past and to define racial inequality as a problem of prejudice and limit the solution as the outlawing of individual acts of discrimination, as does Glazer, is effectively to leave intact the very structures of racial inequality.

## ENDNOTES

1. Nathan Glazer, *Affirmative Discrimination: Ethnic Inequality and Public Policy* (New York: 1978, originally published in 1975), pp. 220, 197, xi.
2. Ibid., p. 194.
3. Ibid., p. 204.
4. Ibid., pp. 3–5.
5. Ibid., p. 5.
6. Ibid., pp. 5–7, 15, 17.
7. Ibid., p. 5.
8. *Debates and Proceedings in the Congress of the United States,* 1789–1791, 2 vols. (Washington, D.C.: 1834), vol. 1: 998, 1284, vol. 2: 1148–56, 1162, 2264. For the Walter-McCarran Act, see Frank Chuman, *The Bamboo People: The Law and Japanese-Americans* (Del Mar, Calf.: 1976) p. 312.
9. Aaron H. Palmer, *Memoir, Geographical, Political, and Commercial, on the Present State, Productive Resources, and Capabilities for Commerce, of Siberia, Manchuria, and the Asiatic Islands of the Northern Pacific Ocean; and on the Importance of Opening Commercial Intercourse with Those Countries,* March 8, 1848. U.S. Cong., Senate, 30th Cong., 1st sess., Senate misc. no. 80, pp. 1, 52, 60, 61.
10. Charles Crocker, testimony, in *Report of the Joint Special Committee to Investigate Chinese Immigration,* Senate Report No. 689, 44th Cong., 2nd sess., 1876–77, pp. 667, 679, 680.
11. Chuman, *Bamboo People,* pp. 217, 218.
12. Felix S. Cohen, *Handbook of Federal Indian Law* (Albuquerque: 1958, originally published in 1942), pp. 153–59.
13. See Takaki, *Iron Cages: Race and Culture in 19th-Century America* (New York: 1979), p. 111.
14. Francis Newton Thorpe (ed.), *The Federal and State Constitutions, Colonial Charters, and Other Organic Laws of the States, Territories, and Colonies Now or Heretofore Forming the United States of America* (Washington: 1909), vol. 1. *Treaty of Guadalupe Hidalgo,* p. 381, *Constitution of California,* 1849, p. 393; Cohen, *Handbook of Federal Indian Law,* pp. 155–59.
15. Glazer, *Affirmative Discrimination,* pp. 5, 22–29.
16. "Statement of United States Citizenship of Japanese Ancestry," quoted in Michi Weglyn, *Years of Infamy: The Untold Story of America's Concentration Camps* (New York: 1976), p. 155.
17. Cohen, *Handbook of Federal Indian Law,* p. 155.

18. Andrew Jackson, "First Annual Message to Congress," in James D. Richardson (ed.), *A Compilation of the Messages and Papers of the Presidents, 1789-1897* (Washington: 1897), 2: 456–58; Jackson to General John Coffee, April 7, 1832, in John Spencer Bassett, ed., *Correspondence of Andrew Jackson*, 6 vols. (Washington: 1926), 4: 430; Francis Amasa Walker, *The Indian Question* (Boston: 1874), pp. 10, 62–67.

19. Francis Amasa Walker, *Annual Report of the Commissioner of Indian Affairs to the Secretary of the Interior for the Year 1872* (Washington: 1872), pp. 11, 63, 64, 77–79, 94, 95; *In-dian Appropriation Act*, quoted in Walker, *Indian Question*, p. 5.

20. For a discussion of the Dawes Act, see Takaki, *Iron Cages*, pp. 188–93.

21. Walt Whitman, *Leaves of Grass and Selected Prose* (New York: 1958), pp. 38, 1, 25, 18, 78, 83, 89, 399–400, 340, 121, 343; Walt Whitman, in Horace Traubel, *With Walt Whitman in Canada*, 2 vols. (New York: 1915), 2: 34–35.

22. Herman Melville, *Moby Dick, or the Whale* (Boston: 1956, originally published in 1851), pp. 108.

# 28. MEXICAN AMERICANS

## JOHN FARLEY

*"By 1900, even the largest and wealthiest Mexican landowners had generally been deprived of their land.... The Chicano agricultural laborer was in a position only marginally better than slavery.... [Most] found themselves in a caste system with little chance of advancement."*

To understand dominant-minority relations, it is important to know the historical background. Here, John Farley concisely describes the relationships between Anglos and Mexican-Americans in Texas and the Southwest. The themes in this history are similar to those of other minorities: conflict, power, economic exploitation, and the emergence of a relatively permanent social structure. Chicanos differ from other minorities, however, in one important way: Economic exploitation involved first their land, then their labor.

## EARLY CONTACTS

The first contact between Mexicans and Americans came about in what is now the southwestern United States. This contact increased to a sizable scale in the early 1800s, as the Mexican population expanded northward and the American population expanded westward. This Mexican population was mostly mestizo, a mixture of Spanish and Indian, which was by that time the overwhelming majority of the Mexican population. There were

From *Majority-Minority Relations*, pp. 116–123, by John E. Farley. Copyright © 1982. Reprinted by permission of Prentice-Hall, Inc., Englewood Cliffs, NJ.

also, however, some recent white immigrants from Spain, who preferred to think of themselves as Spanish rather than Mexican and were generally so recognized. At this time, the present-day states of Texas, California, New Mexico, Arizona, and Utah were all part of Mexico, as were most of Colorado and small parts of three other states. The relationship between white Americans, or Anglos, and Mexicans during this period might best be described as having elements of both cooperation and competition. There was a certain amount of competition, but there was little ethnic stratification between Mexicans and Anglos. Both groups were landowners, farmers, and ranchers; Mexicans were operating ranches on a large scale in Texas by the late eighteenth century, and later in California, especially after Mexico became independent from Spain in 1822 (Meier and Rivera 1972, Chapter 3). In addition to the general absence of ethnic inequality, the competition between Anglos and Mexicans was limited and — as we have indicated — was counterbalanced by significant elements of cooperation....

To summarize, then, Mexican and Anglo residents in the early stages of southwestern settlement lived side by side in relatively equal status, with relatively cooperative relationships. In each of the three major areas (Texas, California, and Nuevo Mexico, which largely comprised present-day Arizona and New Mexico), the life style and mode of production was somewhat different, but in all three, the pattern was one of relative equality with substantial elements of cooperation. Of course, both groups in different ways oppressed the southwestern Indian people, but they treated and regarded one another as relative equals.

## ORIGINS OF ETHNIC STRATIFICATION

### Texas

During the 1830s, a chain of events began that was to prove disastrous for Mexicans living in Aztlan, as the region of Mexico that became part of the United States is sometimes called. By the early 1830s, conflict had arisen in Mexico over the role of that country's national government. Some Mexicans, the centralists, wanted a strong national government that would exercise close administrative control over all of Mexico. Others, the federalists, wanted a looser confederation with greater local autonomy, not unlike the system of the United States. Most Texans — both Mexican and Anglo — favored the latter approach and sided with the federalists. Ultimately, centralists came to control Mexico's national government. The army came to Texas to control the dissident federalists, but in the process spilled so much blood that a revolution was started and Texas ended up — for a short time — as an independent nation (Alvarez 1973). This chain of events upset the power balance, creating new demands for land among whites in Texas in a way that resulted almost overnight in gross social

inequality between Anglos and Mexicans. Why did this happen? First, Texas's independence from Mexico accelerated the influx of white immigrants, mostly from the United States South. Before long, Anglos outnumbered Mexicans in Texas by a ratio of five to one (Grebler et al. 1970, 40). These immigrants brought with them the prejudices of the South as well as a tremendous demand for land. Many sought to set up a plantation system for raising cotton, similar to the pattern in the South. Outnumbering the Mexicans as they did, they soon appealed for admission to the United States, and in 1845, Texas was annexed. The situation now was totally changed, and the past cooperation of the Mexicans with the Anglos was forgotten. Most Mexicans were quickly deprived of their land, either by force or by American law (backed by force), which consistently served Anglo, not Mexican, interests. By 1900, even the largest and wealthiest Mexican landowners had generally been deprived of their land (Alvarez 1973).

During this period, there was also a great upsurge in anti-Mexican prejudice, which further contributed to the subordination of the now Mexican-American people in Texas. Alvarez (1973) cites three major reasons for this upsurge in prejudice. First, the warfare with Mexico had led most Anglos to view *all* Mexicans as former enemies, even though most of them had also opposed Mexico's centralist government and many had fought for Texas's independence from Mexico. Second, as noted, many had learned intense race prejudice in the United States South and readily applied notions of racial inferiority to Mexicans. Finally, racist ideology served an economic purpose in supporting and rationalizing the Anglos' actions of taking land from the Mexicans.

### California and Nuevo Mexico

Most of the rest of the Southwest — California and Nuevo Mexico — became part of the United States in 1848 as a result of the Treaty of Guadelupe Hidalgo, which ended the Mexican War. This war was the result of a number of factors, particularly Mexican objections to the annexation of Texas by the United States, American desire to expand westward into Nuevo Mexico and California, and border disputes all along the U.S.-Mexican border

(Meier and Rivera 1972, Chapter 4). During this war, Nuevo Mexico surrendered itself to the United States without a fight, in part because of opposition to the centralist government of Mexico. In California, the situation was somewhat different. The cooperation between Anglos and *Californios* (Mexican settlers in California) during the 1820s and 1830s increasingly turned to conflict during the 1840s as more and more Anglo settlers came to northern California over the Oregon trail. Here, too, opposition to the centralists among both Anglos and Mexicans was strong enough that California declared its independence from Mexico in 1836. In 1840, however, California returned to Mexican control. But increasingly, the influx of white settlers caused Anglo-*Californio* conflicts which ended any cooperation between the two, even though both had opposed the centralists in Mexico. In 1846, a new independence movement known as the Bear Flag Revolt took place. This movement came to be pretty much controlled by Anglos, who soon antagonized *Californios* in Los Angeles so strongly that they rebelled against the Anglos, who by now were openly proclaiming California to be United States territory. This led to the only serious fighting in the part of the Mexican War that occurred in what is now the United States, and led to effective American control of California by 1847. Meanwhile, the major fighting of the war was taking place in Mexico, which had been invaded by U.S. troops. In 1847, Mexico City was captured; a year later, the Treaty of Guadelupe Hidalgo was signed and ratified. This treaty ceded most of California and Nuevo Mexico to the United States, formally recognized American sovereignty over Texas, and resolved the border disputes along the Texas-Mexico boundary in favor of the United States. In protocol accompanying the treaty, the United States agreed in writing to recognize the land ownership of Mexicans in the ceded territories. The 80,000 Mexicans living in the ceded territories also were given U.S. citizenship rights, and most became citizens.[1] A few years later, the present United States-Mexican border was established when the Gadsden Purchase (1853) ceded the southern parts of present-day Arizona and New Mexico to the United States.

As was the case a few years earlier in Texas, the annexation of Nuevo Mexico and California caused a critical change in the power structure, which sooner or later proved disastrous for the Mexican people living in these two territories. The familiar pattern was repeated: Once there was a sizable influx of Anglos into an area, the Anglos and Mexican-Americans came into competition over land. Once this happened, the Mexican-Americans were nearly always deprived of their land, despite the international agreement (and numerous verbal promises) that this would not happen. Sometimes the land was simply taken by force. At other times, the legal system accomplished the same result. This was possible because the Mexican and American concepts of land ownership were different, as were the methods for legally proving a land claim (Meier and Rivera 1972). Thus, many Mexicans who could easily have proven their claims in Mexican courts could not do so in American courts. It is also true, of course, that judges and magistrates were usually Anglo and protected Anglo interests, and that Anglo landowners were often better able to afford quality lawyers. Furthermore, even when Mexican-Americans did eventually win their claims, they were so deeply in debt from the cost of the legal battle — some dragged on for as long as seventeen years — that they often lost part or all of their land because of the debt (Meier and Rivera 1972, 80). Put simply, the balance of power was totally on the side of the Anglo-Americans....

## CAUSE OF ANGLO-CHICANO INEQUALITY

This brief discussion of the early history of Anglo-Chicano relations is sufficient to confirm that Noel's (1968) theory about the origins of ethnic stratification can be applied to Mexican-Americans as well as to other U.S. minorities.[2] Only in the presence of all three elements cited by Noel — ethnocentrism, competition, and unequal power — did patterns of near-total domination of Chicanos by Anglos emerge. Early competition for land and the whites' superior power and numbers brought this about first in Texas. The Treaty of Guadelupe Hidalgo gave political and legal power to whites throughout the Southwest, but this did not immediately cause great ethnic inequality except in northern California, where the Gold Rush began almost immediately after the treaty. In other areas, subordination of the Mexican-American population tended to come when there was a sizable influx of whites—in the 1870s and 1880s in southern California, and later in New Mexico. This influx added the element of competition as whites wanting land deprived Mexican-Americans of their land claims. It also increased both white ethnocentrism and the inequality of the power balance.

As with blacks and Indians, racist stereotypes developed and were used to justify mistreatment of Chicanos. Another form of ethnocentrism was the concept of "manifest destiny," which was used to justify annexation of Mexican territory and to displace both Mexican-Americans and Indians from their lands. This view was that the white man's supernaturally willed destiny was to rule and "civilize" all of North America, from coast to coast. Thus, the conquest of indigenous Indian and Mexican-American populations and the taking of their lands could be justified—it was God's will. The other factor, unequal power, was also increased with a large influx of whites. Whites became a numerical majority, which augmented the legal and political power they already held. For all these reasons, there was a close association between the numerical balance of Anglos and Chicanos and the amount of inequality between the two groups in various times and places throughout the Southwest.

In some regards, the history of Chicanos is very different from that of blacks and Native Americans. Only Chicano history involves the conquest by force of a sovereign, internationally recognized nation-state and the abrogation of rights accorded to its citizens by that nation. In spite of this and other differences, however, the origin of Anglo-Chicano inequality seems to involve the same three elements as [with]...Afro-Americans and Native Americans.

## EXPLOITATION OF CHICANOS FOR LABOR

Another way in which Mexican-Americans are unique among the three groups...is that only they were exploited on a large scale for *both* their land and their labor in this country. Blacks had no land here because they were not indigenous: They were brought here under a system of forced migration to be exploited for their labor. Indians...were never enslaved on a large scale, and their resistance to forced assimilation, as well as their forced isolation on the reservation, generally kept white employers from seeing them as an easy source of cheap labor. Mexican-Americans, however, soon came to be exploited for their labor as well as their land. We have already discussed at length the exploitation of Chicanos for their land and the reasons behind it. In the remainder of this section, we shall examine the ways in which Anglos took advantage of Mexican-Americans as a source of cheap labor.

As Mexican-Americans were being displaced from their land by whites during the 1850–1900 period, whites in the Southwest were developing an economic system largely built around mining, large-scale agriculture, and railroad transportation. These types of economic activity, especially mining and large-scale agriculture, are highly labor-intensive and are most profitable when there is a large labor supply. The owners of the ranches and mines accordingly sought a supply of laborers willing to do hard, dirty work for low wages (Grebler et al. 1970, 51). Although bonded laborers from Asia were brought to the west to do some of this work, Mexican-Americans became the most important source of such labor....

By the early twentieth century, the Chicano agricultural laborer was in a position only marginally better than slavery, in a system that in some ways resembled the paternalistic pattern of race relations. To a large degree, Mexican-Americans were restricted to certain low-paying, low-status jobs, so that ethnicity largely determined one's status and economic position. Frequently, the total control over minority group life associated with paternalistic systems was present for farm and mine workers, who were required to buy their goods at inflated prices at the company or ranch store and were closely supervised by labor contractors. Frequently, too, the system of labor was more unfree than free, because workers were often bound to their employers to work off the debts incurred at these company stores. Finally, there was the paternalism — the constant assertion by ranch, farm, and mine owners that their Mexican-American workers were happy, that the owners had their best interests at heart, and that the workers needed "close supervision" because they were incapable of functioning on their own. And, of course, there was the oft-repeated claim that Mexican-Americans were incapable of work other than unskilled farm or labor work and that they were especially suited to this type of work....

The situation was highly exploitative. Hours were long, pay exceedingly low, food and housing were poor, and education was practically nonexistent. Especially in the rural areas, few Chicanos were permitted to rise above this status so that the system of stratification closely fit the caste model: One's status was pretty well determined by one's ethnic group.... Most Mexican-Americans in the latter nineteenth and early twentieth centuries found themselves in a caste system with little chance of advancement....

## ENDNOTES

1. Although Indians in the ceded territories previously had the right of Mexican citizenship, they did not receive the right of U.S. citizenship (Meier and Rivera 1972, 70).
2. For more complete discussions of Chicano history, see the previously cited publications as well as McWilliams, 1949, which is considered by some to be the best general work on Mexican-American history in the southwest.

## REFERENCES

Alvarez, Rodolfo. 1973. "The Psycho-Historical and Socioeconomic Development of the Chicano Community in the United States." *Social Science Quarterly* 53:920–942. Reprinted in Norman R. Yetman and C. Hoy Steele (eds.), *Majority and Minority: The Dynamics of Racial and Ethnic Relations*. Boston: Allyn and Bacon, 1975.

Grebler, Leo, Joan W. Moore, and Ralph C. Guzman. 1970. *The Mexican-American People*. New York: The Free Press.

Meier, Matt S., and Felicano Rivera. 1972. *The Chicanos: A History of Mexican Americans*. New York: Hill and Wang.

Noel, Donald L. 1968. "A Theory of the Origin of Ethnic Stratification." *Social Problems* 16: 157–172.

# 29. OCCUPATIONAL OPPORTUNITIES AND RACE

STEPHEN STEINBERG

*"This job crisis is the single-most important factor behind the familiar tangle of problems that beset black communities. Without jobs, nuclear families become unglued or are never formed. Without jobs, or husbands with jobs, women with young children are forced onto the welfare rolls. Without jobs, many ghetto youth resort to the drug trade or other illicit ways of making money.... In short, there is no exit from the racial quagmire unless there is a national commitment to address the job crisis in black America."*

The real source of the oppression of African-Americans in the United States lies in our occupational structure. In the world of work, we are segregated and we always have been. Where opportunities to correct this have arisen, we have not committed ourselves to correcting this. Stephen Steinberg looks at the history of

slavery and immigration and how both have produced and maintained this segregation. Then he examines the "myth of the black middle class" and points out
that instead of bringing about true integration of the work force, middle-class
occupations have continued to perpetuate a society of occupational segregation.
Finally, he examines job discrimination in relation to the black working class and
poor. Without solving the problem of work, according to Steinberg, "the legacy
of slavery," American racism in all areas of life, will continue.

The essence of racial oppression is not the distorted and malicious stereotypes that whites have of
blacks. These constitute the *culture* of oppression,
not to be confused with the thing itself. Nor is the
essence of racism epitomized by sitting in the back
of a bus. In South Africa, this was called "petty
apartheid" as opposed to "grand apartheid," the latter referring to political disfranchisement and the
banishment of millions of blacks to isolated and
impoverished "homelands." In the United States,
the essence of racial oppression — *our* grand
apartheid — is a racial division of labor, a system of
occupational segregation that relegates most blacks
to work in the least desirable job sectors or that excludes them from job markets altogether.[1]

The racial division of labor had its origins in
slavery when some 650,000 Africans were import-
ed to provide cheap labor for the South's evolving
plantation economy. During the century after the
abolition of slavery, the nation had the perfect opportunity to integrate blacks into the North's burgeoning industries. It was not Southern racism but
its Northern variant that prevented this outcome.
This is worth emphasizing because it has become
customary — part of America's liberal mythology
on race — to place the blame for the nation's racist
past wholly on the South. But it was not Southern
segregationists and lynch mobs who excluded
blacks from participating in the critical early phas-
es of industrialization. Rather, it was an invisible
color line across *Northern* industry that barred
blacks categorically from employment in the vast
manufacturing sector, except for a few menial and
low-paying jobs that white workers spurned. Nor
can the blame be placed solely on the doorstep of
greedy capitalists, those other villains of liberal
iconography. Workers themselves and their unions

were equally implicated in maintaining a system
of occupational apartheid that reserved industrial
jobs for whites and that relegated blacks to the
preindustrial sector of the national economy. The
long-term effects were incalculable because this
closed off the only major channel of escape from
racial oppression in the South. Indeed, had the industrial revolution not been "for whites only," it
might have obviated the need for a civil rights revolution a century later.

The exclusion of blacks from the industrial sector was possible only because the North had access to an inexhaustible supply of immigrant labor.
Some 24 million immigrants arrived between 1880
and 1930. A 1910 survey of twenty principal mining and manufacturing industries conducted by
the United States Immigration Commission found
that 58 percent of workers were foreign born.
When the Commission asked whether the new immigration resulted in "racial displacement," it did
not have blacks in mind, but rather whites who
were native born or from old immigrant stock. Except for a cursory examination of the competition
between Italian and black agricultural workers in
Louisiana, nothing in the forty-volume report so
much as hints at the possibility that mass immigration might have deleterious consequences for
blacks, even though black leaders had long complained that immigrants were taking jobs that, they
insisted, rightfully belonged to blacks.[2]

If blacks were superfluous so far as Northern industry was concerned, the opposite was true in the
South, where black labor was indispensable to the
entire regional economy. Furthermore, given the
interdependence between the regional economies
of the South and the North, occupational
apartheid had indirect advantages for the North as
well. Remember that the cotton fiber that Irish,
Italian, and Jewish immigrants worked with in
mills and sweatshops throughout the North was

From *Turning Back*, by Stephen Steinberg. Beacon Press, 1995.

supplied by black workers in the South. In effect, a system of labor deployment had evolved whereby blacks provided the necessary labor for Southern agriculture, and European immigrants provided the necessary labor for Northern industry.

This regional and racial division of labor cast the mold for generations more of racial inequality and conflict. Not until the First World War were blacks given significant access to Northern labor markets. In a single year — 1914 — the volume of immigration plummeted from 1.2 million immigrant arrivals to only 327,000. The cutoff of immigration in the midst of an economic expansion triggered the Great Migration, as it was called, of Southern blacks to the urban North. Industries not only employed blacks in large numbers but even sent labor agents to the South to recruit black workers. Between 1910 and 1920, there was a net migration of 454,000 Southern blacks to the North, a figure that exceeded the volume of the previous forty years combined. Here is historical proof that blacks were just as willing as Europe's peasants to uproot themselves and migrate to cities that offered the opportunity for industrial employment. To suggest that blacks "were not ready to compete with immigrants," as the author of a recent volume on immigration does, is a flagrant distortion of history.[3] The simple truth is that Northern industry was open to immigrants and closed to blacks. Whatever opprobrium was heaped on these immigrants for their cultural and religious difference, they were still beneficiaries of racial preference.

It is generally assumed that the Second World War provided a similar demand for black labor, but initially this was not the case. Because the war came on the heels of the Depression, there was a surfeit of white labor and no compelling need to hire blacks.[4] Indeed, it was blacks' frustration with their exclusion from wartime industries that prompted A. Philip Randolph and his followers to threaten a march on Washington in 1941 until Roosevelt issued his executive order banning discrimination in federal employment and defense contracts. The opening up of Northern labor markets triggered another mass migration of Southern blacks — 1.6 million migrated between 1940 and 1950; by the end of the war, 1.5 million black workers were part of the war-production work force. This represented an unprecedented breach in the nation's system of occupational apartheid — one that set the stage for future change as well.

Still, as recently as 1950, two-thirds of the nation's blacks lived in the South, half of them in rural areas. It was not the Civil War, but the mechanization of agriculture a century later that finally liberated blacks from their historic role as agricultural laborers in the South's feudal economy. By the mid-fifties, even the harvest of cotton became mechanized with the mass production of International Harvester's automatic cotton picking machine. The number of man-hours required to produce a bale of cotton was reduced from 438 in 1940, to 26 in 1960, to only 6 in 1980.[5] Agricultural technology had effectively rendered black labor obsolete, and with it the caste system whose underlying function had been to regulate and exploit black labor.[6] Thus it was that in one century, white planters went all the way to Africa to import black laborers; in the next century, the descendants of Southern planters gave the descendants of African slaves one-way bus tickets to Chicago and New York.

When blacks finally arrived in Northern cities, they encountered a far less favorable structure of opportunity than had existed for immigrants decades earlier.[7] For one thing, these labor markets had been captured by immigrant groups who engaged in a combination of ethnic nepotism and unabashed racism. For another, the occupational structures were themselves changing. Not only were droves of manufacturing jobs being automated out of existence, but a reorganization of the global economy resulted in the export of millions of manufacturing jobs to less developed parts of the world.

Thus the fact that the technological revolution in agriculture lagged nearly a half-century behind the technological revolution in industry had fateful consequences for blacks at both junctures. First, blacks were restricted to the agricultural sector during the most expansive periods of the industrial revolution. Then, they were evicted from rural America and arrived in Northern cities at a time when manufacturing was beginning a steep and irreversible decline. Yet…the fact that more blacks were not integrated into Northern labor markets cannot be explained only in terms of the operation of color-blind economic forces. At least as important was the pervasive racism that restricted the access of black workers not only to jobs in declining industries, but also to new jobs in the expanding service sector....

## THE IMMIGRATION DILEMMA

The economic fortunes of African-Americans have always been linked to immigration. Suppose that Europe's "huddled masses" had been flocking to the New World in the seventeenth century. Then Southern planters would not have been impelled to go all the way to Africa to find laborers, and the nation would have been spared the ignominy of slavery. Suppose, on the other hand, that the huddled masses of Europe had *not* flocked to America's cities during the century after slavery. Then Northern industrialists would have had to put aside their racist predilections and tapped the pool of black laborers in the South who were desperate to escape the yoke of Southern oppression. Indeed, this is precisely what happened during both World Wars when the cutoff of immigration led to the absorption of blacks into Northern labor markets. The two brief intervals in the twentieth century when immigration was at low ebb marked the two major periods of economic and social advancement for African-Americans.

The post-civil rights era presented yet another opportunity to integrate blacks into the occupational mainstream, especially given the sharp decline of the white birth rate and the improved climate of tolerance toward blacks. But once again, African-Americans have had to cope with an enormous influx of immigrants, this time from Asia, Latin America, and the Caribbean. Ironically, it was the civil rights movement that led to the passage of the 1965 Hart-Celler Act, which abolished the national origins quotas that had restricted immigration outside of Europe. In the two ensuing decades, there have been some 15 million immigrant arrivals, not to mention millions more who are undocumented.[8]

This massive volume of immigration amounts to a double whammy as far as African-Americans are concerned: Not only has there been an erosion of job structures in cities with high concen-

trations of blacks, but black workers must compete with increasing numbers of immigrants for scarce jobs. William Julius Wilson's whole emphasis is that the United States has been exporting millions of jobs to the Third World. However, the nation is also importing workers from these same countries at an even faster rate. The availability of large numbers of foreign workers allows employers to exercise their racial preferences when it comes to hiring new workers. As the last hired, blacks often find themselves in the hiring queue even behind recent immigrants....

To be sure, immigration may on balance be beneficial for the economy as a whole, as the apostles of immigration contend. There is obvious validity in the claim that immigrants do not just take jobs, they create them as well. This is especially evident when one examines the thriving ethnic economies in "gateway cities" like Los Angeles, New York, San Francisco, and Miami. On the other hand, as Jacqueline Jackson has pointed out, "too often the jobs created are not for domestic minorities but for the next wave of immigrants recruited through ethnic networks."[9] Besides, what is at issue here is not whether immigration is generally beneficial to the American economy, but whether it is specifically detrimental to the interests of African-Americans and other marginal workers....

While demographers, economists, and sociologists debate the effects of immigration, a groundswell of resentment has built up within the black community itself. Public opinion polls indicate that a solid majority of blacks see immigrants as competitors for jobs and would favor lowering the ceiling on immigration.[10] Yet most black leaders have been reluctant to speak out against immigration policy. For one thing, many blacks sympathize with these struggling minorities, some of whom are also of African descent. For another, black leaders do not want to feed the forces of xenophobia and reaction that are behind the recent upsurge of nativism. Finally, black leaders have been wary about jeopardizing their coalition with Hispanics in Congress and elsewhere, even though public opinion polls indicate that most rank-and-file Hispanics also would support a lower ceiling on immigration[11]....

Here we arrive at the critical question. If the rationale behind immigration has to do with declining fertility rates and an anticipated decline in new labor force entrants, why is policy not directed at addressing the scandalously high rates of black unemployment? Why is there no crash program to provide job training for minority youth whose detachment from the job market has so many deleterious consequences for themselves as well as the rest of the society? Why is there no serious effort to enforce antidiscrimination laws and to tear down racist barriers in major occupational structures, including the so-called "ethnic economy" in which racial discrimination is virtually endemic? Why are there no incentives or mandates to induce employers to hire and train unemployed youths?

It is difficult to escape the conclusion that political and economic leaders have given up on black youth and opted to rely on immigrants to make up for any labor deficits....

The immigration of some 15 million documented immigrants over the past several decades represents another missed opportunity in American history. The nation could have taken advantage of a secular decline in its working-age population to integrate blacks and other marginal groups into the occupational mainstream. More is involved here than achieving parity and justice for blacks. This was the nation's chance to attack the structures of inequality that rend the society, undermining the stability of political institutions and compromising the quality of life.

Why was the opportunity missed? To have acted otherwise would have required a level of commitment to racial equality that was lacking. It would also have required programs and expenditures for which there was no political will. In the final analysis, the nation succumbed once again to its endemic racism and to its collective indifference to the plight of its black citizens. Although immigration has produced a more racially diverse population, paradoxically, this new diversity has reinforced the preexisting structure of occupational apartheid.[12]

## THE MYTH OF THE BLACK MIDDLE CLASS

At first blush, the existence of a large black middle class would suggest that racist barriers in occupations are no longer insurmountable—in other words, that occupational apartheid is not the problem it was in times past. To be sure, the existence of this middle class signifies a historic breakthrough. Never before have so many blacks been represented at the higher echelons of the occupational world—in the professions and in corporate management. Never before have so many blacks found employment in core industries, in both the white-collar and blue-collar sectors. Nor can this new black middle class, given its size, be dismissed as "window dressing" or "tokenism." Yet there are other grounds for doubting that the existence of this large black middle class signifies the demise of occupational apartheid.

In the first place, insofar as this black middle class is an artifact of affirmative action policy, it cannot be said to be the result of the autonomous workings of market forces. In other words, the black middle class does not reflect a lowering of racist barriers in occupations so much as the opposite: Racism is so entrenched that without government intervention there would be little "progress" to boast about.

Second, although a substantial segment of the new black middle class is found in corporate management, there is a pattern of racial segregation *within* these structures (similar to what happens in many "integrated" schools). Studies have found that many black managers work in personnel functions, often administering affirmative action programs. Others function as intermediaries between white corporations and the black community or the black consumer.[13] Cut off from the corporate mainstream, these black executives often find themselves in dead-end jobs with little job security. By outward appearances, they have "made it" in the white corporate world, but their positions and roles are still defined and circumscribed by race.

Much the same thing can be said about the black business sector. In an incisive analysis of "The Making of the Black Middle Class," Sharon Collins provides the following account:

Black entrepreneurs are concentrated in segregated rather than generalized services. In 1979, 68 percent of black-owned businesses were in retail and selected services that marketed their wares almost exclusively to black consumers. In 1979, 99 percent of all minority business was based on federal procurement or sales to the minority consumers.[14]

In her analysis of data on Chicago-based minority professional service firms, Collins found a similar pattern of racial segmentation, even with firms doing business with the government:

Personnel service firms provided workers for units with racial concerns, such as the Office of Manpower. Black law firms were hired for contact compliance and labor-management issues in segregated services such as Housing and Urban Development. Certified public accountant firms performed pre-grant and general audits for segregated sites such as Cook County Hospital. Management consulting firms provided technical assistance primarily to agencies such as Chicago's Department of Human Services or the Federal Office of Minority Business Development. Engineers provided professional services to predominantly black sites such as Chicago's Northshore Sanitary District.[15]

In short, the much ballyhooed growth of black-owned business has generally occurred within the framework of a racially segregated economy.[16]

Finally, there is the double-edged sword associated with public sector employment. On the one hand, the fact that government employment has opened up to blacks marks another change of historic dimensions. For two decades after the Second World War, black representation in government was largely restricted to the Postal Service and to low-level clerical and service positions. As noted earlier, today some 1.6 million blacks, constituting one-fourth of the entire black labor force, are employed by government. Indeed, this is the source of much of the "progress" we celebrate.

On the other hand, it shows once again that racial progress has depended on the intervention of government, in this instance as a direct employer. Furthermore, within the ranks of government, there is a great deal of internal segregation. For the most part, blacks employed in government are social welfare providers in such areas as education, welfare, health, employment security, and public housing. Essentially, they function as intermediaries and as a buffer between white America and the black underclass. As Michael Brown and Steven Erie have argued, "the principal economic legacy of the Great Society for the black community has been the creation of a large-scale social welfare economy of publicly funded middle-income service providers and low-income service and cash transfer recipients."[17]

To conclude, as Collins does, that "the growth of a black middle class is *not* evidence of a decline in racial inequality in the United States" is perhaps an overstatement.[18] After all, the sheer existence of a large black middle class means that blacks are no longer a uniformly downtrodden people. On the other hand, it may signify not the *dissolution* so much as an *artful reconfiguration* of caste boundaries in the occupational world. To control the disorder emanating from the ghettos of America, a new class of "Negro jobs" has been created. They are not the dirty, menial, and backbreaking jobs of the past. On the contrary, they are coveted jobs that offer decent wages and job security. Nevertheless, they are jobs that are pegged for blacks and that function within the context of racial hierarchy and division.

Precisely because the new black middle class is largely a product of government policy, its future is subject to the vagaries of politics. Already it is apparent, as two economists have concluded, that "the epoch of rapid black relative economic advance ended sometime in the late 1970s and early 1980s and...some of the earlier gains eroded in the 1980s."[19] Court decisions restricting minority set-asides have already had a severe impact on black businesses.[20] The current attack on affirmative action will inevitably lead to a further erosion of black socioeconomic gains. Finally, just as blacks benefited disproportionately from the growth of government, they will certainly be severely affected by the current movement to cut the size of the government and the scope of government services. Black public-sector workers are especially vulnerable to layoffs because they are disproportionately found in positions that are heavily dependent on federal subsidies.[21]

## THE JOB CRISIS IN BLACK AMERICA

If the new black middle class does not signify a fundamental decline in racial inequality, then what are we to conclude about the persistence and growth of the black underclass? In *Poor People's Movements*, written in 1979, Piven and Cloward provided an apt description of the current situation when they wrote: "In effect, the black poor progressed from slave labor to cheap labor to (for many) no labor at all."[22] Indeed, a job crisis of the magnitude that existed in the society at large during the Great Depression afflicts black America today. In the Depression, the crisis was defined as such, and extraordinary programs were developed to overhaul basic economic institutions and to create jobs for the unemployed. In the case of the black job crisis, however, social policy has been predicated on the assumption that black unemployment stems from the deficiencies of black workers, and social policy has rarely advanced beyond some meager job training programs.[23]

A few statistics will suffice to convey the dimensions of this job crisis. In 1994, the unemployment rate was 11.5 percent for blacks and 5.3 percent for whites.[24] According to one estimate, blacks would need 1.6 million jobs to achieve parity with whites. The job deficit for black men over 20 is 736,000 jobs; for black women over 20, it is 150,000 jobs; and for black teenagers it is 500,000 jobs.[25]

As is often pointed out, the government's measure of unemployment is only the tip of the iceberg because it leaves out "discouraged workers" who have given up looking for work, as well as "involuntary part-time workers" who want full-time employment. The National Urban League has developed its own measure of "hidden unemployment" that includes these two groups. In 1992, the League's hidden unemployment rate was 13.3 percent for whites and 25.5 percent for blacks. Thus, one-quarter of the black population, involving roughly 3 million workers, are effectively jobless.[26] Even this figure does not sufficiently reflect the depth of the problem because it leaves out the working poor — those who are employed full time, but whose wages leave them below the poverty line.

This job crisis is the single-most important factor behind the familiar tangle of problems that beset black communities. Without jobs, nuclear families become unglued or are never formed. Without jobs, or husbands with jobs, women with young children are forced onto the welfare rolls. Without jobs, many ghetto youth resort to the drug trade or other illicit ways of making money. Ironically, those who end up in prison do find work — in prison shops that typically pay fifty cents or less

an hour — only to find themselves jobless on the outside. Given this fact, the high rate of recidivism should come as no surprise. For different reasons, schools are generally ineffective in teaching children whose parents lack stable jobs and incomes. In short, there is no exit from the racial quagmire unless there is a national commitment to address the job crisis in black America.

Tragically, this nation does not have the political will to confront its legacy of slavery, even if this means nothing more than providing jobs at decent wages for blacks who continue to be relegated to the fringes of the job market. Instead, a mythology has been constructed that, in ways reminiscent of slavery itself, alleges that blacks are inefficient and unproductive workers, deficient in the work habits and moral qualities that delivered other groups from poverty....

What would be involved in restoring racial justice to the national agenda? We must begin where the civil rights revolution ended — by attacking the deep-seated institutionalized inequalities that exist between the white and black citizens of this nation. The historic achievement of the civil rights revolution was to tear down the walls of segregation. The challenge today is to erect the structures of racial equality. If occupational apartheid is the essence of American racism, as has been argued here, then the keystone of remedial social policy must be a concerted attack on occupational apartheid....

Any serious effort to resume the unfinished racial agenda must begin with the detailed policy agenda laid out by the Kerner Commission in 1968. At the top of this agenda was a series of proposals dealing with employment, consistent with the promise of the Employment Act of 1946 to provide "a useful job at a reasonable wage for all who wish to work." Specific proposals included beefing up the enforcement powers of the Equal Employment Opportunities Commission, creating new jobs in both the public and private sectors, providing subsidies to employers to hire and train the hard-core unemployed, and launching programs of economic development and social reconstruction targeted for poverty areas and racial ghettos.

Another policy initiative follows from the analysis in this chapter:

Immigration policy must take into account the legitimate interests of native workers, especially those on the economic margin. After all, the meaning of citizenship is diminished if it does not include the right to a job at decent wages.[27] For African-Americans who have toiled on American soil for centuries, and whose sons and daughters have died in the nation's wars, the case for national action is especially urgent. Today we are confronted with the spectacle of these oldest of Americans again being passed over by new waves of immigrants. It is difficult to escape the conclusion that present immigration policy not only subverts the cause of racial justice, but, given the immense human and social costs of the racial status quo, is also antithetical to the national interest.

To be sure, other principles weigh on the formulation of immigrant policy. Many immigrants — especially Mexicans who are migrating to territory once possessed by Mexico — have historical and moral claim for access to American labor markets. Also to be considered is the proud liberal tradition of America as an asylum for the dispossessed. Like the immigrants of yore, the new immigrants contribute immeasurably to "the building of America," its culture as well as its economy. These factors, however, must be balanced against the deleterious effects that the continuing volume of immigration has on groups on the economic margin — not only African-Americans but on the immigrants themselves and their children....

We need a renewed national commitment to dealing with the job crisis that afflicts black America. This would begin with vigorous enforcement of antidiscrimination laws. However, the lesson of the post-civil-rights era is that antidiscrimination laws are minimally effective unless they are backed up with compliance checks and other enforcement mechanisms — in short, affirmative action. The significance of affirmative action is that it amounts to a frontal assault on the racial division of labor. Whatever its limitations, affirmative action has produced the most significant departure from the occupational caste system that has existed since slavery. If racial progress is to continue, affirmative action must be extended to wider segments of the work force.

Again, it may seem gratuitous to say this at a time when racism and reaction are feeding on one another, and there is a tidal wave of opposition against affirmative action. However, there is a maddening illogic to the current crusade against welfare, crime, out-of-wedlock births, and the other "pathologies" associated in the popular mind with the ghetto population. Unless jobs and opportunities are targeted for black youth and young adults, punitive legislation and the withdrawal of public assistance will only produce more desperation and even greater disorder....

The job crisis in black America is allowed to fester for one basic reason: Because the power elites of this nation regard these black communities as politically and economically expendable. They can afford to do so as long as they are not under great countervailing pressure, either from a mobilized black protest movement or from spontaneous ghetto uprisings. This is a situation of politics-as-usual so long as poverty and joblessness manifest themselves as "quiet riots" — that is, as crime and violence that can be contained through a criminal justice system that currently has a prison population exceeding one million people.

On the other hand, when these communities do finally erupt in full-scale riots, as South Central Los Angeles did in the aftermath of the Rodney King episode, suddenly race is back on the national agenda. Even the mainstream media resisted the temptation merely to resort to moral platitudes. *Newsweek* proclaimed that "This Was No Riot, It Was a Revolt," and described "the siege of LA" as a "bloody wake-up call" to reverse the neglect of America's inner cities.[28]

## ENDNOTES

1. For an excellent analysis of the historical relationship between race and occupational structures, see Harold M. Baron, "The Demand for Black Labor," *Radical America* 5 (March-April 1971); and idem, "The Web of Urban Racism," in *Institutional Racism in America*, ed. Louis L. Knowles and Kenneth Prewitt (Englewood Cliffs, N.J.: Prentice-Hall, 1969), pp. 134-76.
2. See Lawrence H. Fuchs, "The Reactions of Black Americans to Immigration," in *Immigration Reconsidered*, ed. Virginia Yans-McLaughlm (New York: Oxford University Press, 1990), especially pp. 295-97, and David J. Hellwig, "Patterns of Black Nativism," *American Studies* 23 (Spring 1982).
3. Muller, Thomas. 1993. *Immigrants and the American City.* New York: New York University Press, p. 91.
4. Myrdal, Gunnar. 1994. *An American Dilemma: The Negro Problem and Modern Democracy.* New York: Harper & Row, p. 1005.
5. Government Printing Office. 1975. *Historical Statistics of the United States.* Washington, D.C.: Government Printing Office, p. 500. Jaynes, Gerald David and Robin M.

Williams, Jr. 1989. A *Common Destiny*. Washington, D.C.: National Academy Press, p. 273.

6. Piven, Frances Fox and Richard A. Cloward. 1979. *Poor People's Movements*. New York: Vintage Books, Chapter 4.

7. In a paper written for the National Advisory Commission on Civil Disorders in 1968, Herbert Gans debunked the notion that blacks arriving in Northern cities were following in the footsteps of earlier immigrants and could therefore anticipate the same beneficial outcomes. "Escaping from Poverty: A Comparison of the Immigrant and Black Experience," in *People, Plans, and Policies* (New York: Columbia University Press, 1991), Chapter 18.

8. For a recent demographic analysis of the new immigration, see Reuben C. Rumbaut, "Origins and Destinies: Immigration to the United States Since World War II," *Sociological Forum* 9 (December 1994), pp. 583–621.

9. Jackson, "Seeking Common Ground for Blacks and Immigrants," p. 95.

10. For example, a 1983 national poll found that 69 percent of black respondents agreed that "illegal immigrants are a major harm to U.S. jobless," and 73 percent said that "the U.S. should admit fewer or a lot fewer legal immigrants." Jackson, "Seeking Common Ground for Blacks and Immigrants," p. 96. For a comprehensive review of poll findings on the immigration issue, see Muller, *Immigrants and the American City*, pp. 161–66.

    A recent New York Times/CBS News Poll found that the percentage of Americans who favored a decrease in immigration had risen to 61 percent, up from 49 percent when the question was last asked in 1986. Compared to whites, black Americans were nine percentage points more likely to see immigrants taking jobs away, but nine percentage points less likely to prefer a decrease in immigration. Seth Mydans, "Poll Finds Tide of Immigration Brings Hostility," *New York Times*, June 27, 1993.

11. For an informative discussion of the role that black organizations and the Congressional Black Caucus played in the debate over the Simpson-Mazzoli bill in 1983 and 1984, see Muller, *Immigrants and the American City*, pp. 52–67.

12. A note on the politics of immigration. As Otis L. Graham, Jr., suggests, it is a mistake to equate immigration restriction with xenophobia or reaction; "Illegal Immigration and the Left," *Dissent* 29 (Summer 1980). Historically, elements of organized labor, including unions made up largely of immigrants, have favored restrictive immigration policies because they feared that unlimited immigration depressed wages and standards, created a bottom tier of immigrant workers, and prevented changes in the structure of the secondary labor market. For Graham's more recent statements on this issue, see "Immigration and the National Interest," in *U.S. Immigration in the 1980s: Reappraisal and Reform*, ed. David Simcox, pp. 124–36; and "Uses and Misuses of History in the Debate Over Immigration Reform," *The Public Historian*, 8, no. 2 (Spring 1986), pp. 41–64.

    Although working-class opposition to immigration often stemmed from xenophobia and racism, other legitimate interests were also involved. This has been acknowledged by John Higham, author of *Strangers in the Land* — the classic history of nativism — in the preface to the book's second edition. In the revised edition of *Send These to Me: Immigrants in Urban America* (Baltimore: Johns Hopkins University Press, 1984), Higham writes sympathetically of the Simpson-Mazzoli bill, which included sanctions on employers who hired undocumented workers. The commission that led to the passage of this legislation was headed by a prominent liberal, Father Theodore Hesburgh.

    On the other hand, free-market economists and business interests have championed the cause of expanded immigration. See, for example, M. S. Forbes, Jr., "We Need More People," *Forbes* (February 9, 1987); "The Rekindled Flame," Editorial, *Wall Street Journal*, July 3, 1989; Michael J. Mandel and Christopher Farrell, "The Immigrant: How They're Helping to Revitalize the U.S. Economy," *Business Week* (July 13, 1992); Wattenberg and Zinsmeister, "The Case for More Immigration," pp. 19–25; and Simon, "The Case for Greatly Increased Immigration," pp. 89–103.

13. Heidrick and Stuggles, Inc., "Chief Personnel Executives Look at Blacks in Business," cited in Sharon M. Collins, "The Making of the Black Middle Class," *Social Problems* 30 (April 1983), p. 379. See also Sharon M. Collins, "The Marginalization of Black Executives," *Social Problems* 36 (October 1989), pp. 317–29; and idem, "Blacks on the Bubble: The Vulnerability of Black Executives in White Corporations," *Sociological Quarterly* 34 (August 1993), pp. 429–47.

14. Collins, "The Making of the Black Middle Class," p. 377.

15. Ibid. p. 379.

16. Also to be considered are the many and subtle ways in which old-fashioned racism afflicts even the black middle class. For two recent works, see Joe E. Feagin and Melvin P Sikes, *Living with Racism* (Boston: Beacon Press, 1994); and David Wellman, *Portraits of White Racism* (Cambridge: Cambridge University Press, 1993).

17. Brown, Michael K. and Steven P. Erie. "Blacks and the Legacy of the Great Society: The Economic and Political Impact of Federal Social Policy," *Public Policy* 29 (Summer 1981), p. 301.

18. Collins, "The Making of the Black Middle Class," p. 379.

19. Bound, John and Richard B. Freeman. "Black Economic Progress: Erosion of the Post-1965 Gains in the 1980s," in *The Question of Discrimination*, Shulman and Darity (eds.), p. 47.

20. de Courcy Hinds, Michael. "Minority Business Set Back Sharply by Courts' Rulings," *New York Times*, December 23, 1991.

21. For example, when the Reagan administration reduced social spending between 1980 and 1981, 76 percent of the 400 employees laid off in Chicago's Department of Human Services were black, as were 40 percent of the 186 workers laid off in the Department of Health. In contrast, the federal cutbacks barely affected the predominantly white work force in Chicago's Streets and Sanitation Department, which is funded with local revenues. Collins, "The Making of the Black Middle Class," p. 377.

22. Piven and Cloward, *Poor People's Movements*, p. 184.

23. As Margaret Weir points out with respect to the 1960s: "This decade of intellectual ferment and policy experimentation left a surprisingly meager legacy for employment policy. Labor market policy became subsumed into the poverty program, offering job preparation to those on the fringes on the labor market, and to the black poor in

particular." *Politics and Jobs* (Princeton, NJ: Princeton University Press, 1992). For an incisive analysis of the political functions of job training programs, see Gordon Lafer, "Minority Unemployment, Labor Market Segmentation, and the Failure of Job Training Policy in New York City," *Urban Affairs Quarterly* 28 (December 1992).

24. U.S. Department of Labor, Bureau of Labor Statistics. *Employment and Earnings, January 1995*. Washington, D.C.: Government Printing Office.

25. Swinton, David H. "The Economic Status of African-Americans: 'Permanent' Poverty and Inequality," in *The State of Black America* (Washington, D.C.: National Urban League, 1991), p. 53. Swinton states that the remainder of the overall shortage is caused by demographic factors.

26. "Quarterly Economic Report on the African-American Worker," National Urban League, Report No. 32 (September 1992). Jim Sleeper writes: "...what kinds of hard work and moral discipline may people who envision a democratic and just society demand even of the poorest and most oppressed; what, indeed, would it be condescending and worse not to demand of 'the least among us'?" *The*

*Closest of Strangers* (New York: W. W. Norton, 1990), p. 37. Regarding the scarcity of jobs, see George James, "The Job Is Picking Up Garbage; 100,000 Want It," *New York Times*, September 21, 1990.

27. At least in principle, this has been government policy over the past half-century. With the passage of the Employment Act of 1946, a large bipartisan majority in Congress endorsed the principle that "it is the continuing policy and responsibility of the Federal Government" to bring about "conditions under which there will be afforded useful employment opportunities...for those able, willing, and seeking work." This principle was affirmed in the 1978 Humphrey-Hawkins Act. Except for a few sporadic attempts at government job creation programs, however, the mechanisms to achieve full employment have never been put into place. On the contrary, government fiscal policy is commonly used to engineer unemployment in order to contain inflation. For an astute analysis of "the political collapse of full employment," see Weir, *Politics and Jobs*, Chapter 5.

28. Hackworth, David H. "This Was No Riot, It Was a Revolt." *Newsweek* (May 11, 1992), p. 30; and ibid., (May 25, 1992), p. 33.

# 30.  BLACKS IN AMERICA

ANDREW HACKER

*"In the eyes of white Americans, being black encapsulates your identity. No other racial or national origin is seen as having so pervasive a personality or character. Even if you write a book on Euclidean algorithms or Renaissance sculpture, you will still be described as a 'black author.'" Although you are a native American, with a longer lineage than most, you will never be accorded full membership in the nation or society. More than that, you early learn that this nation feels no need or desire for your physical presence."*

This is a powerful chapter from a very enlightening book, **Two Nations**. The purpose of this book is to show that the unique position of African-Americans makes it difficult to create a society of equal opportunity.

Andrew Hacker claims that race matters—and it matters a lot. It matters because our society has always regarded race as a basis for oppression and discrimination. Hacker is especially sensitive to the position of the African-American, and this chapter captures their situation like no other selection I have ever read.

Hacker makes a single point in this chapter: Being black in America has consequences—in the areas of wealth, identity, raising children, occupational opportunities, place of residence, and treatment in the criminal justice system. Being black influences how one is viewed, how one discusses one's life and achievements, and how one sees society, whites, and police. Being black influences what one says to people, what they say, and what happens in day-to-day interactions with whites. And, finally, being black has consequences for the strain and rage one feels toward one's own position in society.

Hacker is beckoning us to understand all this by trying to place ourselves in the position of blacks in American society.

Most white Americans will say that, all things considered, things aren't so bad for black people in the United States. Of course, they will grant that many problems remain. Still, whites feel there has been steady improvement, bringing blacks closer to parity, especially when compared with conditions in the past. Some have even been heard to muse that it's better to be black because affirmative action policies make it a disadvantage to be white.

What white people seldom stop to ask is how they may benefit from belonging to their race. Nor is this surprising. People who can see do not regard their vision as a gift for which they should offer thanks. It may also be replied that having a white skin does not immunize a person from misfortune or failure. Yet even for those who fall to the bottom, being white has a worth. What could that value be?

Let us try to find out by means of a parable: Suspend disbelief for a moment, and assume that what follows might actually happen:

You will be visited tonight by an official you have never met. He begins by telling you that he is extremely embarrassed. The organization he represents has made a mistake, something that hardly ever happens.

According to their records, he goes on, you were to have been born black: to another set of parents, far from where you were raised.

However, the rules being what they are, this error must be rectified, and as soon as possible. So at midnight tonight, you will become black. And this will mean not simply a darker skin, but the bodily and facial features associated with African ancestry. However, inside you will be the person you always were. Your knowledge and ideas will remain intact. But outwardly you will not be recognizable to anyone you now know.

Reprinted with permission of Scribner, A Division of Simon & Schuster from *Two Nations: Black and White, Separate, Hostile, Unequal*, by Andrew Hacker. Copyright © 1992 by Andrew Hacker.

Your visitor emphasizes that being born to the wrong parents was in no way your fault. Consequently, his organization is prepared to offer you some reasonable recompense. Would you, he asks, care to name a sum of money you might consider appropriate? He adds that his group is by no means poor. It can be quite generous when the circumstances warrant, as they seem to in your case. He finishes by saying that their records show you are scheduled to live another fifty years—as a black man or woman in America.

How much financial recompense would you request?

When this parable has been put to white students, most seemed to feel that it would not be out of place to ask for $50 million, or $1 million for each coming black year. And this calculation conveys, as well as anything, the value that white people place on their own skins. Indeed, to be white is to possess a gift whose value can be appreciated only after it has been taken away. And why ask so large a sum? Surely this needs no detailing. The money would be used, as best it could, to buy protection from the discriminations and dangers white people know they would face once they were perceived to be black.

Of course, no one who is white can understand what it is like to be black in America. Still, were they to spend time in a black body, here are some of the things they would learn.

In the eyes of white Americans, being black encapsulates your identity. No other racial or national origin is seen as having so pervasive a personality or character. Even if you write a book on Euclidean algorithms or Renaissance sculpture, you will still be described as a "black author." Although you are a native American, with a longer lineage than most, you will never be accorded full membership in the nation of society. More than that, you early learn that this nation feels no need or desire for your physical presence. (Indeed, your people are no longer in demand as cheap labor.)

You sense that most white citizens would heave a sigh of relief were you simply to disappear. While few openly propose that you return to Africa, they would be greatly pleased were you to make that decision for yourself.

Your people originated in Africa, and you want to feel pride in your homeland. After all, it was where humanity began. Hence your desire to know more of its peoples and their history, their culture and achievements, and how they endure within yourself. W. E. B. Du Bois said it best: "two thoughts, two unrecognizable stirrings, two warring ideals in one black body."

Yet there is also your awareness that not only America, but also much of the rest of the world, regards Africa as the primal continent— the most backward, the least developed—by almost every modern measure. Equally unsettling, Africa is regarded as barely worth the world's attention, a region no longer expected to improve in condition or status. During its periodic misfortunes—usually famine or slaughter—Africa may evoke compassion and pity. Yet the message persists that it must receive outside help because there is little likelihood that it will set things right by itself.

Then there are the personal choices you must make about your identity. Unless you want to stress a Caribbean connection, you are an American and it is the only citizenship you have. At the same time, you realize that this is a white country, which expects its inhabitants to think and act in white ways. How far do you wish to adapt, adjust, assimilate, to a civilization so at variance with your people's past? For example, there is the not-so-simple matter of deciding on your diction. You know how white people talk and what they like to hear. Should you conform to those expectations, even if it demands denying or concealing much of your self? After all, white America gives out most of the rewards and prizes associated with success. Your decisions are rendered all the more painful by the hypocrisy of it all because you are aware that, even if you make every effort to conform, whites will still not accept you as one of their own.

So to a far greater degree than for immigrants from other lands, it rests on you to create your own identity. But it is still not easy to follow the counsel of Zora Neale Hurston: "Be as black as you want to be." For one thing, that choice is not always left to you. By citizenship and birth, you may count as an American, yet you find yourself agreeing with August Wilson when he says, "we're a different people." Why else can you refer to your people as "folks" and "family," to one another as "sisters" and "brothers," in ways whites never can?

There are moments when you understand Toni Morrison's riposte, "At no moment in my life have I ever felt as though I were an American." This in turn gives rise to feelings of sympathy with figures like Cassius Clay, H. Rap Brown, Lew Alcindor, and Stokely Carmichael, who decided to repatriate themselves as Muhammad Ali, Jamil Abdullah al-Amin, Kareem Abdul-Jabbar, and Kwame Touré.

Those choices are not just for yourself. There will be the perplexing—and equally painful—task of having to explain to your children why they will not be treated as other Americans: that they will never be altogether accepted, that they will always be regarded warily, if not with suspicion or hostility. When they ask whether this happens because of anything they have done, you must find ways of conveying that, no, it is not because of any fault of their own. Further, for reasons you can barely explain yourself, you must tell them that much of the world has decided that you are not and cannot be their equals; that this world wishes to keep you apart, a caste it will neither absorb nor assimilate.

You will tell your children this world is wrong. But, because that world is there, they will have to struggle to survive, with scales weighted against them. They will have to work harder and do better, yet the result may be less recognition and reward. We all know life can be unfair. For black people, this knowledge is not an academic theory but a fact of daily life.

You find yourself granting that there are more black faces in places where they were never seen before. Within living memory, your people were barred from major league teams; now they command the highest salaries in most professional sports. In the movies, your people had to settle for roles as servants or buffoons. Now at least some of them are cast as physicians, business executives, and police officials. But are things truly different? When everything is added up, white America still prefers its black people to be performers who divert them as athletes and musicians and comedians.

Yet where you yourself are concerned, you sense that in mainstream occupations, your prospects are quite limited. In most areas of employment, even after playing by the rules, you find yourself hitting a not-so-invisible ceiling. You wonder if you are simply corporate wallpaper, a protective coloration they find it prudent to display. You begin to suspect that a "qualification" you will always lack is white pigmentation.

In theory, all Americans with financial means and a respectable demeanor can choose where they want to live. For over a generation, courts across the country have decreed that a person's race cannot be a reason for refusing to rent or sell a residence. However, the law seems to have had little impact on practice because almost all residential areas are entirely black or white. Most whites prefer it that way. Some will say they would like a black family nearby, if only to be able to report that their area is integrated. But not many do. Most white Americans do not move in circles where racial integration wins social or moral credit.

This does not mean it is absolutely impossible for a black family to find a home in a white area. Some have, and others undoubtedly will. Even so, black Americans have no illusions about the hurdles they will face. If you look outside your designated areas, you can expect chilly receptions, evasive responses, and outright lies: a humiliating experience, rendered all the more enraging because it is so repeated and prolonged. After a while, it becomes too draining to continue the search. Still, if you have the income, you will find an area to your liking; but it will probably be all black. In various suburbs and at the outer edges of cities, one can see well-kept homes, outwardly like other such settings. But a closer view shows all the householders to be black.

This is the place to consider residential apartheid—and that is what it is—in its full perspective. Black segregation differs markedly from that imposed on any other group. Even newly arrived immigrants are more readily accepted in white neighborhoods.

Nor should it be assumed that most black householders prefer the racial ratios in areas where they currently reside. Successive surveys have shown that, on average, only about one in eight say they prefer a neighborhood that is all or mostly black, which is the condition most presently confront. The vast majority—some 85 percent—state they would like an equal mixture of black and white neighbors. Unfortunately, this degree of racial balance has virtually no chance of being realized. The reason, very simply, is that hardly any whites will live in a neighborhood or community where half the residents are black. So directly or indirectly, white Americans have the power to decide the racial composition of communities and neighborhoods. Most egregious have been instances in which acts of arson or vandalism force black families to leave. But such methods are exceptional. There are other, less blatant, ways to prevent residential integration from passing a certain "tipping" point.

Here we have no shortage of studies. By and large, this research agrees that white residents will stay—and some new ones may move in—if black arrivals do not exceed 8 percent. But once the black proportion passes that point, whites begin to leave the neighborhood and no new ones will move in. The vacated houses or apartments will be bought or rented by blacks, and the area will be on its way to becoming all black….

Americans have extraordinarily sensitive antennae for the colorations of neighborhoods. In virtually every metropolitan area, white householders can rank each enclave by the racial make-up of the residents. Given this knowledge, where a family lives becomes an index of its social standing. Although this is largely an economic matter, proximity to blacks compounds this assessment. For a white family to be seen as living in a mixed —or changing—neighborhood can be construed as a symptom of surrender, indeed as evidence that they are on a downward spiral.

If you are black, these white reactions brand you as a carrier of contamination. No matter what your talents or attainments, you are seen as infecting a neighborhood simply because of your race. This is the ultimate insult of segregation. It opens wounds that never really heal and leaves scars to remind you how far you stand from full citizenship.

• • •

Except when you are in your own neighborhood, you feel always on display. On many occasions, you find you are the only person of your race present. You may be the only black student in a college classroom, the only black on a jury, the sole

black at a corporate meeting, the only one at a social gathering. With luck, there may be one or two
others. You feel every eye is on you, and you are
not clear what posture to present. You realize that
your presence makes whites uncomfortable; most
of them probably wish you were not there at all.
But because you are, they want to see you smile so
that they can believe you are being treated well.
Not only is an upbeat air expected, but you must
never show exasperation or anger, let alone anything that could look like a chip on your shoulder. Not everyone can keep such tight control. You
don't find it surprising that so many black athletes
and entertainers seek relief from those tensions.

Even when not in white company, you know
that you are forever in their conversations. Ralph
Ellison once said that, to whites, you are an "invisible man." You know what he meant. Yet for all
that, you and your people have been studied and
scrutinized and dissected, caricatured, and pitied
or deplored, as no other group ever has. You see
yourself reduced to data in research, statistics in reports. Each year, the nation asks how many of your
teenagers have become pregnant, how many of
your young men are in prison. Not only are you
continually on view, you are always on trial.

What we have come to call "the media" looms
large in the lives of almost all Americans. Television and films, newspapers and magazines, books
and advertising, all serve as windows on a wider
world, providing real and fantasized images of the
human experience. The media also help us to fill
out our own identities, telling us about ourselves,
or the selves we might like to be.

If you are black, most of what is available for
you to read and watch and hear depicts the activities of white people, with only rare and incidental
allusions to persons like yourself. Black topics and
authors and performers appear even less than your
share of the population, not least because the rest
of America doesn't care to know about you. Whites
will be quick to point out that there have been successful "black" programs on radio and television, as
well as popular black entertainers and best-selling
authors. Yet in these and other instances, it is
whites who decide which people and productions
will be underwritten, which almost always means
that "black" projects have to appeal to whites as
well. You sometimes sense that much that is
"black" is missing in artists like Jessye Norman and

Toni Morrison, Paul Robeson, and Bill Cosby, who
you sense must tailor their talents to white audiences. You often find yourself wishing they could
just be themselves, among their own people.

At the same time, you feel frustration and dis-
gust when white America appropriates your music,
your styles, indeed your speech and sexuality. At
times, white audiences will laud the originality of
black artists and performers and athletes. But in
the end, they feel more comfortable when white
musicians and designers and writers and athletic
coaches adapt black talents to white sensibilities.

Add to this your bemusement when movies and
television series cast more blacks as physicians and
attorneys and executives than one will ever find in
actual hospitals or law firms or corporations. True,
these depictions can serve as role models for your
children, encouraging their aspirations. At the
same time, you do not want white audiences to
conclude that since so many of your people seem
to be doing well, little more needs to be done.

Then there are those advertisements showing
groups of people. Yes, one of them may be black,
although not too black, and always looking happy
to be in white company. Still, these blacks are seldom in the front row, or close to the center. Even
worse, you think you have detected a recent trend:
In advertisements that include a person of color,
you see Asians being used instead of blacks....

Well, what about assimilation? Here you receive the same message given immigrants: If you
wish to succeed, or simply survive, adapt to the
diction and demeanor of the Anglo-American
model. But even if you opt for that path, you will
never receive the acceptance accorded to other
groups, including newcomers arriving from as far
away as Asia and the Middle East. In the view of
those who set the rules, if you are of African origin,
you will never fully fit the image of a true American. Notice how even blacks who espouse conservative opinions are regarded more as curiosities
than as serious citizens.

Whether you would like to know more white
people is not an easy question to answer. So many
of the contacts you have with them are stiff and
uneasy, hardly worth the effort. If you are a
woman, you may have developed some cordial acquaintances among white women at your place of
work because women tend to be more relaxed
when among themselves. Still, very few black men

and women can say that they have white "friends," if by that is meant people they confide in or entertain in their homes.

Of course, friendships often grow out of shared experiences. People with similar backgrounds can take certain things for granted when with one another. In this respect, you and white people may not have very much in common. At the same time, by no means all your outlooks and interests relate to your race. There probably are at least a few white people you would like to know better. It just might be that some of them would like to know you. But as matters now stand, the chances that these barriers will be broken do not appear to be very great.

Societies create vocabularies, devising new terms when they are needed, and retaining old ones when they serve a purpose. Dictionaries list words as obsolete or archaic, denoting that they are no longer used or heard. But one epithet survives, because people want it to. Your vulnerability to humiliation can be summed up in a single word. That word, of course, is *nigger.*

When a white person voices it, it becomes a knife with a whetted edge. No black person can hear it with equanimity or ignore it as "simply a word." This word has the force to pierce, to wound, to penetrate, as no other has. There have, of course, been terms like *kike* and *spic* and *chink.* But these are less frequently heard today, and they lack the same emotional impact. Some nonethnic terms come closer, such as *slut* and *fag* and *cripple.* Yet, *nigger* stands alone with its power to tear at one's insides. It is revealing that whites have never created so wrenching an epithet for even the most benighted members of their own race.

Black people may use *nigger* among themselves, but with a tone and intention that is known and understood. Even so, if you are black, you know that white society devised this word and keeps it available for use. (Not officially, of course, or even in print; but you know it continues to be uttered behind closed doors.) Its persistence reminds you that you are still perceived as a degraded species of humanity, a level to which whites can never descend.

You and your people have problems, far more than your share. And it is not as if you are ignorant of them, or wish to sweep them under a rug. But how to frame your opinions is not an easy matter. For example, what should you say about black crime or addiction or out-of-wedlock pregnancies? Of course, you have much to say on these and other topics, and you certainly express your ideas when you are among your own people. And you can be critical — very critical — of a lot of behavior you agree has become common among blacks.

However, the white world also asks that black people conduct these discussions in public. In particular, they want to hear you condemn black figures they regard as outrageous or irresponsible. This cannot help but annoy you. For one thing, you have never asked for white advice. Yet whites seem to feel that you stand in need of their tutelage, as if you lack the insight to understand your own interests. Moreover, it makes sense for members of a minority to stand together, especially because so many whites delight in magnifying differences among blacks. Your people have had a long history of being divided and conquered. At the same time, you have no desire to be held responsible for what every person of your color thinks or does. You cannot count how many times you have been asked to atone for some utterances of Louis Farrakhan, or simply to assert that he does not speak for you. You want to retort that you will choose your own causes and laments. Like other Americans, you have no obligation to follow agendas set by others....

You may, by a combination of brains and luck and perseverance, make it into the middle class. And like all middle-class Americans, you will want to enjoy the comforts and pleasures that come with that status. One downside is that you will find many white people asking why you aren't doing more to help members of your race whom you have supposedly left behind. There is even the suggestion that, by moving to a safer or more spacious area, you have callously deserted your own people.

Yet hardly ever do middle-class whites reflect on the fact that they, too, have moved to better neighborhoods, usually far from poorer and less equable persons of their own race or ethnic origins. There is little evidence that middle-class whites are prepared to give much of themselves in aid of fellow whites who have fallen on misfortune. Indeed, the majority of white Americans have chosen to live in sequestered suburbs, where they are insulated from the nation's losers and failures.

Compounding these expectations, you find yourself continually subjected to comparisons with other minorities or even members of your own race. For example, you are informed that blacks who have emigrated from the Caribbean earn higher incomes than those born in the United States. Here the message seems to be that color by itself is not an insurmountable barrier. Most stinging of all are contrasts with recent immigrants. You hear people just off the boat (or, nowadays, a plane) extolled for building businesses and becoming productive citizens. Which is another way of asking why you haven't matched their achievements, considering how long your people have been here.

Moreover, immigrants are praised for being willing to start at the bottom. The fact that so many of them manage to find jobs is taken as evidence that the economy still has ample opportunities for employment. You want to reply that you are not an immigrant, but as much a citizen as any white person born here. Perhaps you can't match the mathematical skills of a teenager from Korea, but then neither can most white kids at suburban high schools. You feel much like a child being chided because she has not done as well as a precocious sister. However, you are an adult, and do not find such scolding helpful or welcome.

No law of humanity or nature posits a precise format for the family. Throughout history and even in our day, households have had many shapes and structures. The same strictures apply to marriage and parental relationships. All this requires some emphasis, given concerns expressed about "the black family" and its presumed disintegration. In fact, the last several decades have seen a weakening of domestic ties in all classes and races.

Black Americans are fully aware of what is happening in this sphere. They know that most black children are being born out of wedlock and that these youngsters will spend most of their growing years with a single parent. They understand that a majority of their marriages will dissolve in separation or divorce, and that many black men and women will never marry at all. Black Americans also realize that tensions between men and women sometimes bear a violence and bitterness that can take an awful toll.

If you are black, you soon learn it is safest to make peace with reality: to acknowledge that the conditions of your time can undercut dreams of enduring romance and "happily ever after." This is especially true if you are a black woman because you may find yourself spending many of your years without a man in your life. Of course, you will survive and adapt, as your people always have. Central in this effort will be joining and sustaining a community of women — another form of a family — on whom you can rely for love and strength and support.

If you are a black woman, you can expect to live five fewer years than your white counterpart. Among men, the gap is seven years. Indeed, a man living in New York's Harlem is less likely to reach sixty-five than is a resident of Bangladesh. Black men have a three-times-greater chance of dying of AIDS, and outnumber whites as murder victims by a factor of seven. According to studies, you get less sleep, are more likely to be overweight and to develop hypertension. This is not simply caused by poverty. Your shorter and more painful life results, in considerable measure, from the anxieties that come with being black in America.

If you are a black young man, life can be an interlude with an early demise. Black youths do what they must to survive in a hostile world, with the prospect of violence and death on its battlefields. Attitudes can turn fatalistic, even suicidal: gladiators without even the cheers of an audience.

When white people hear the cry, "the police are coming!" it almost always means, "help is on the way." Black citizens cannot make the same assumption. If you have been the victim of a crime, you cannot presume that the police will actually show up; or, if they do, that they will take much note of your losses or suffering. You sense police officials feel that blacks should accept being robbed or raped as one of life's everyday risks. It seems to you obvious that more detectives are assigned to a case when a white person is murdered.

If you are black and young and a man, the arrival of the police does not usually signify help but something very different. If you are a teenager simply socializing with some friends, the police may order you to disperse and get off the streets. They may turn on a searchlight, order you against a wall. Then comes the command to spread your legs and empty out your pockets, and stand splayed there while they call in your identity over their radio. You may be a college student and sing in a church choir, but that will not overcome the police presumption that you have probably done something they can arrest you for.

If you find yourself caught up in the system, it will seem like alien terrain. Usually your judge and prosecutor will be white, as will most members of the jury as well as your attorney. In short, your fate will be decided by a white world.

This may help to explain why you have so many harsh words for the police, even though you want and need their protection more than white people do. After all, there tends to be more crime in areas where you live, not to mention drug dealing and all that comes in its wake. Black citizens are at least twice as likely as whites to become victims of violent crimes. Moreover, in almost all these cases, the person who attacks you will be black. Because this is so, whites want to know, why don't black people speak out against the members of their race who are causing so much grief? The reason is partly that you do not want to attack other blacks while whites are listening. At least equally important is that, although you obviously have no taste for violence, you are also wary of measures that might come with a campaign to stamp out "black crime…." At this point, you might simply say that you are not sure that you want a more vigorous police presence if those enforcers are unable to distinguish between law-abiding citizens and local predators. Of course, you want to be protected. But not if it means that you and your friends and relatives end up included among those the police harass or arrest….

As you look back on the way this nation has treated your people, you wonder how so many have managed to persevere amid so much adversity. About slavery, of course, too much cannot be said. Yet even within living memory, there were beaches and parks – in the North as well as in the South – where black Americans simply could not set foot. Segregation meant separation without even a pretense of equal facilities. In Southern communities that had only a single public library or swimming pool, black residents and taxpayers could never borrow a book or go for a swim. Indeed, black youths were even forbidden to stroll past the pool, lest they catch a glimpse of white girls in their bathing costumes.

How did they endure the endless insults and humiliations? Grown people being called by their first names, having to avert their eyes when ad-dressed by white people, even being expected to step off a sidewalk when whites walked by. Overarching it all was the terror, with white police and prosecutors and judges possessing all but total power over black lives. Not to mention the lynchings by white mobs, with victims even chosen at random, to remind all blacks of what could happen to them if they did not remain compliant and submissive.

You wonder how much that has changed. Suppose that you find yourself having to drive across the country, stopping at gasoline stations and restaurants and motels. As you travel across the heart of white America, you can never be sure how you will be received. Although the odds are that you will reach your destination alive, you cannot be so sure that you will not be stopped by the police or spend a night in a cell. So you would be well advised to keep to the speed limit and not exceed it by a single mile. Of course, white people are pulled over by state troopers; but how often are their cars searched? Or if a motel clerk cannot "find" your reservation, is it because she has now seen you in person? And are all the toilet facilities at this service station really out of order?

The day-to-day aggravations and humiliations add up bit by bitter bit. To take a depressingly familiar example, you stroll into a shop to look at the merchandise, and it soon becomes clear that the clerks are keeping a watchful eye on you. Too quickly, one of them comes over to inquire what it is you might want, and then remains conspicuously close as you continue your search. It also seems that they take an unusually long time verifying your credit card. And then you and a black friend enter a restaurant and find yourselves greeted warily, with what is obviously a more anxious reception than that given to white guests. Yes, you will be served, and your table will not necessarily be next to the kitchen. Still, you sense that they would rather you had chosen some other eating place. Or has this sort of thing happened so often that you are growing paranoid?

So there is the sheer strain of living in a white world, the rage you must suppress almost every day. No wonder black Americans, especially black men, suffer so much from hypertension. (If ever an illness had social causes, this is certainly one.) To be black in America means reining in your opinions and emotions as no whites ever have to do.

Not to mention the forced and false smiles you are expected to contrive to assure white Americans that you harbor no grievances against them.

Along with the tension and the strain and the rage, there come those moments of despair. At times, the conclusion seems all but self-evident that white America has no desire for your presence or any need for your people. Can this nation have an unstated strategy for annihilating your people? How else, you ask yourself, can one explain the incidence of death and debilitation from drugs and disease; the incarceration of a whole generation of your men; the consignment of millions of women and children to half-lives of poverty and dependency?[1] Each of these debilities has its causes; indeed, analyzing them has become a minor industry. Yet with so much about these conditions that is so closely related to race, they say something about the larger society that has allowed them to happen.

This is not to say that white officials sit in secret rooms, plotting the genocide of black America. You understand as well as anyone that politics and history seldom operate that way. Nor do you think of yourself as unduly suspicious. Still, you cannot rid yourself of some lingering mistrust. Just as your people were once made to serve silently as slaves, could it be that if white America begins to conclude that you are becoming too much trouble, it will find itself contemplating more lasting solutions?

## ENDNOTES

1. In 1990, when a sample of black Americans were asked if they thought that the government was deliberately encouraging drug use among black people, 64 percent felt that this might be true. When asked if they suspected that AIDS had been purposely created by scientists to infect black people, 32 percent believed there might be some truth in this view.

# 31.  RACE AND MIDDLE CLASS IDENTITY IN AMERICA

CLARENCE PAGE

*"Today I live a well-integrated life in the suburbs. Black folks still tell me how to be 'black' when I stray from the racial party lines, while white folks tell me how to be 'color-blind.' I still feel as frustrated in my attempts to transcend race as a reluctant lemming must feel while being rushed over the brink by its herd. But I find I have plenty of company in my frustration. Integration has not been a simple task for upwardly mobile African-Americans, especially for those of us who happen also to be parents."*

Here is the perspective of a commentator, essayist, journalist, African American, who has become middle class and "integrated." Yet he expresses uneasiness about his identity in American society. Color always was and continues to be an important part of American society, he writes. Although choices abound for black people ("if they can afford them"), we are not a colorblind society, and we need to be honest about that. Change is taking place, but serious questions remain about "who I am" and what kind of society we should become. Page describes the importance of living in a diverse society, but a diverse society should not allow race to matter for purposes of discrimination and oppression of people.

The message in this essay is not an easy one to understand because it shows the complexities of racial and ethnic differences: the desire to claim an identity for oneself, yet the discrimination that others use to exclude those who claim it; the opportunities that exist for many African Americans, yet the continued denial of opportunity for large numbers; the integration that is at the surface, the sharp division underneath.

Race has long had a rude presence in my life. While visiting relatives in Alabama as a child in the 1950s, I first saw water fountains marked "white" and "colored." I vaguely recall being excited. I rushed over to the one marked "colored" and turned it on, only to find, to my deep disappointment, that the water came out clear, just like the water back home in Ohio.

"Segregation," my dad said. I'd never heard the word before. My southern-born parents explained that it was something the white folks "down home" practiced. Some "home." Yet unpleasant experiences in the North already had taught me a more genteel, yet no less limiting, version.

"There are places white people don't want colored to go," my elders told me in their soft southern accents, "and white people make the rules."

We had plenty of segregation like that in the North. We just didn't have the signs, which made it cheaper and easier to deny. We could look out of my schoolhouse window to see a public swimming pool closed to nonwhites. We had to go across town to the separate-but-equal "pool for colored." The steel mill that was our town's biggest employer held separate picnics for colored and white employees, which seemed to be just fine with the employees. Everyone had a good time, separately and unequally. I think the colored folks, who today would be called the "black community," were just happy to have something to call their own.

When I was about six years old, I saw a television commercial for an amusement park near the southern Ohio factory town where I grew up.

I chose to go. I told my parents. They looked at each other sadly and informed me that "little colored kids can't go there." I was crushed.

"I wish I was white," I told my parents.

"No, you don't!" Mom snapped. She gave me a look terrible enough to persuade me instantly that no, I didn't.

"Well, maybe for a few minutes, anyway?" I asked. "Just long enough for me to get past the front gate?" Then I could show them, I thought. I remember I wanted to show them what a terrific kid I was. I felt sorry for the little white children who would be deprived of getting to know me.

Throughout our childhood years, my friendships with white schoolchildren (and with Pancho from the only Latino family in the neighborhood) proceeded without interruption. Except for the occasional tiff over some injudicious use of the N-word or some other slur we had picked up from our elders, we played in each other's backyards as congenially as Spanky, Buckwheat, and the rest of the gang on the old Hal Roach *Our Gang* comedies we used to watch on television.

Yet it quickly became apparent to me that my white friends were growing up in a different reality from the one to which I was accustomed. I could tell from the way one white friend happily discussed his weekend at LeSourdesville Lake that he did not have a clue of my reality.

"Have you been?" he asked.

"Colored can't go there," I said, somewhat astonished that he had not noticed.

"Oh, that can't be," he said.

For a moment, I perked up, wondering if the park's policy had changed. "Have you seen any colored people there?" I asked.

My white friend thought for a moment, then realized that he had not. He expressed surprise. I was surprised that he was surprised.

By the time I reached high school in the early 1960s, LeSourdesville Lake would relax its racial prohibitions. But the lessons of it stuck with me. It taught me how easily white people could ignore the segregation problem because, from their vantage point, it was not necessarily a problem. It was not necessarily an advantage to them, either, although some undoubtedly thought so. White people of low income, high insecurity, or fragile ego could always say that, no matter how badly off they felt, at least they were not black. Segregation helped them uphold and maintain this illusion of superiority. Even those white people who considered themselves to have a well-developed sense of social conscience could easily rationalize segregation as something that was good for both races. We played unwittingly into this illusion, I thought, when my friends and I began junior high school and, suddenly thrust into the edgy, high hormonal world of adolescence, quickly gravitated into social cliques according to tastes and race.

It became even more apparent to me that my white friends and I were growing up in *parallel realities*, not unlike the parallel universes described in the science fiction novels and comic books I adored—or the "parallel realities" experienced by Serbs, Bosnians, and Croatians as described years later by feminist writer Slavenka Drakulic in *The Balkan Express*. Even as the evil walls of legal segregation were tumbling down, thanks to the hard-fought struggles of the civil rights movement, it occurred to me that my reality might never be quite the same as that experienced by my white friends. We were doomed, I felt, to dwell in our parallel realities. Separated by thick walls of prejudice, we would view each other through windows of stained-glass perceptions, colored by our personal experiences. My parents had taught me well.

"Don't be showin' yo' color," my parents would admonish me in my youth, before we would go out in public, especially among white folks. The phrase had special meaning in Negro conversations. Imbued with many subtle meanings and nuances, the showing of one's "color" could be an expression of chastisement or warning, admonishment or adulation, satire or self-hatred, anger or celebration. It could mean acting out or showing anger in a loud and uncivilized way.

Its cultural origins could be traced to the Africa-rooted tradition of "signifying," a form of witty, deliberately provocative, occasionally combative word play. The thrill of the game comes from taking one's opponent close to the edge of tolerable insult. Few

subjects—except perhaps sex itself—could be a more sensitive matter between black people than talk about someone else's "color." The showing of one's "color," then, connoted the display of the very worst stereotypes anyone ever dreamed up about how black people behaved. "White people are not really white," James Baldwin wrote in 1961, "but colored people can sometimes be extremely colored."

Sometimes you can still hear black people say, in the heat of frustration, "I almost showed my color today," which is a way of saying they almost lost their "cool," "dropped the mask," or "went off." Losing one's cool can be a capital offense by black standards, for it shows weakness in a world in which spiritual rigor is one of the few things we can call our own. Those who keep their cool repress their "color." It is cool, in other words, to be colorless.

The title of [the volume from which this chapter is taken], *Showing My Color*, emerged from my fuming discontent with the current fashions of *racial denial*, steadfast repudiations of the difference race continues to make in American life. Old liberals, particularly white liberals who have become new conservatives, charge that racial pride and color consciousness threaten to "Balkanize" American life, as if it ever was a model of unity. Many demand that we "get past race." But denials of a cancer, no matter how vigorous they may be, will not make the malignancy go away.

No less august a voice than the Supreme Court's conservative majority has taken to arguing in the 1990s for a "colorblind" approach to civil rights law, the area of American society in which color and gender consciousness have made the most dramatic improvement in equalizing opportunities.

The words of the Reverend Martin Luther King, Jr., have been perverted to support this view. Most frequently quoted is his oft-stated dream of the day when everyone would "not be judged by the color of their skin but by the content of their character." I would argue that King never intended for us to forget *all* about color. Even in his historic "I Have a Dream" speech, from which this line most often is lifted, he also pressed the less-often quoted but piquantly salient point about "the promissory note" America gave freed slaves, which, when they presented it, was returned to them marked "insufficient funds."

• • •

I would argue that too much has been made of the virtue of "color-blindness." I don't want Americans to be blind to my color as long as color continues to make a profound difference in determining life chances and opportunities. Nor do I wish to see so significant a part of my identity denied. "Ethnic differences are the very essence of cultural diversity and national creativity," black social critic Albert Murray wrote in *The Omni-Americans* (1970). "The problem is not the existence of ethnic differences, as is so often assumed, but the intrusion of such differences into areas where they do not belong."

Where, then, *do* they belong? Diversity is enriching, but race intrudes rudely on the individual's attempts to define his or her own identity. I used to be "colored." Then I was "Negro." Then I became "black." Then I became "African-American." Today I am a "person of color." In three decades, I have been transformed from a "colored person" to a "person of color." Are you keeping up with me?

Changes in what we black people call ourselves are quite annoying to some white people, which is its own reward to some black people. But if white people are confused, so are quite a few black people. There is no one way to be black. We are a diverse people amid a nation of diverse people. Some black people are nationalists who don't want anything to do with white people. Some black people are assimilationists who don't want anything to do with other black people. Some black people are integrationists who move in and out of various groups with remarkable ease. Some of us can be any of the three at any given time, depending on when you happen to run into us.

Growing up as part of a minority can expose the individual to horrible bouts of identity confusion. I used to think of myself as something of a *transracial man*, a figure no less frustrated than a transsexual who feels trapped in the body of something unfamiliar and inappropriate to his or her inner self.

These bouts were most torturous during adolescence, the period of life when, trembling with the shock of nascent independence from the ways of one's elders, the budding individual stitches together the fragile garments of an identity to be worn into adulthood. Stuttering and uncooperative motor skills left me severely challenged in dancing, basket shooting, and various social ap-

plications; I felt woefully inadequate to the task of being "popular" in the hot centers of black social activity at my integrated high school and college. "Are you black?" an arbiter of campus militancy demanded one day, when he "caught" me dining too many times with white friends. I had the skin pass, sure enough, but my inclinations fell well short of his standards. But I was not satisfied with the standards of his counterparts in the white world, either. If I was not "black" enough to please some blacks, I would never be "white" enough to please all whites.

Times have changed. Choices abound for black people, if we can afford them. Black people can now go anywhere they choose, as long as they can pay the bill when they get there. If anyone tries to stop them or any other minorities just because of their color, the full weight of the federal government will step in on the side of the minorities. I thank God and the hard-won gains of the civil rights revolution for my ability to have more choices. But the old rules of race have been replaced in many ways by new ones.

• • •

Today, I live a well-integrated life in the suburbs. Black folks still tell me how to be "black" when I stray from the racial party lines, while white folks tell me how to be "color-blind." I still feel as frustrated in my attempts to transcend race as a reluctant lemming must feel while being rushed over the brink by its herd. But I find I have plenty of company in my frustration. Integration has not been a simple task for upwardly mobile African-Americans, especially for those of us who happen also to be parents.

A few years ago, after talking to black friends who were raising teenage boys, I realized that I was about to face dilemmas not unlike those my parents faced. My son was turning three years old. Everyone was telling me that he was quite cute, and because he was the spitting image of his dad, I was the last to argue.

But it occurred to me that in another decade he would be not three but thirteen. If all goes well, somewhere along the way he is going to turn almost overnight from someone who is perceived as cute and innocent into someone who is perceived as a menace, the most feared creature on America's urban streets today, a *young black male*. Before he, like me when I was barred from a childhood amusement park, would have a chance to let others get to know him, he would be judged not by the content of his character, but by the color of his skin....

• • •

My mom is gone now, after helping set me up with the sort of education that has freed me to make choices. I have chosen to move my father to a nice, predominantly white, antiseptically tidy retirement village near me in Maryland with large golf courses and swimming pools. It is the sort of place he might have scrubbed floors in but certainly not have lived in back in the old days. It has taken him a while to get used to having so many well-off white people behaving so nicely and neighborly to him, but he has made the adjustment well.

Still the ugly specter of racism does not easily vanish. He and the other hundred or so African-American residents decided to form a social club like the other ethnically or religiously based social clubs in the village. One night during their meeting in the main social room, someone scrawled *KKK* on little sheets of paper and slipped them under the windshields of some of their cars in the parking lot. "We think maybe some of the white people wanted the blacks to socialize with the whites, not in a separate group," one lady of the club told me. If so, they showed an unusual method for extending the arms of brotherhood.

I live in a community that worships diversity like a state religion, although individuals sometimes get tripped up by it. The excellent Spanish "immersion" program that one of the county's "magnet" schools installed to encourage middle-class parents to stay put has itself become a cover for "white flight" by disgruntled white parents. Many of them, despite a lack of empirical evidence, perceive the school's regular English program as inferior, simply because it is 90 percent minority and mostly composed of children who come from a less-fortunate socioeconomic background. So the Spanish immersion classes designed to encourage diversity have become almost exclusively white and Asian America, while the English classes have become almost exclusively — irony of ironies — black and Latino, with many of the children learning English as a second language. Statistically, the school is "diverse" and "integrated." In reality, its student body is divided by an indelible wall, separate but supposedly equal....

Despite all these color-conscious efforts to educate the county's children in a color-blind ideal of racial equality, many of our children seem to be catching on to race codes anyway, although with a twist suitable to the hip-hop generation. One local junior high school teacher, when he heard his black students referring to themselves as "bad," had the facts of racial life explained to him like this: They were not talking about the "bad means good" slang popularized by Michael Jackson's *Bad* album. They meant "bad" in the sense of misbehaving and poorly motivated. The black kids are "bad," the students explained, and the white kids are "good." The Asian kids are "like white," and the Latino kids "try to be bad, like the blacks." Anyone who tried to break out of those stereotypes was trying to break the code, meaning that a black or Latino who tried to make good grades was "trying to be white."

It is enough, as Marvin Gaye famously sang, to make you want to holler and throw up both your hands. Yet my neighbors and I hate to complain too loudly because, unlike other critics you may read or hear about, we happen to be a liberal community that not only believes in the dream of integration and true diversity, but actually is trying to live it.

We reside in Montgomery County, Maryland, the most prosperous suburban county per capita in the Washington, D.C., area. Each of the above-mentioned controversies has been reported in the pages of the *Washington Post* and other local media, right under the noses and, in some cases, within the families of some of the nation's top policy makers....

We see icons of black success — Colin Powell, Douglas Wilder, Bill Cosby, Oprah Winfrey, Bryant Gumbel, the two Michaels: Jordan and Jackson — not only accepted but adored by whites in ways far removed from the arm's-length way white America regarded Jackie Robinson, Willie Mays, Lena Horne, and Marian Anderson.

Yet, although the media show happy images of blacks, whites, Asians, and Hispanics getting along, amicably consuming the good life, a fog of false contentment conceals menacing fissures cracking the national racial landscape.

Despite the growth of the black middle class, most blacks and whites live largely separate lives. School integration actually peaked in 1967, according to a Harvard study, and has declined ever since. Economic segregation has proceeded without interruption, distancing poor blacks not only from whites but also from upwardly mobile blacks, making the isolation and misery of poor blacks worse. One out of every two black children lives below the poverty line, compared to one out of every seven white children. Black infants in America die at twice the rate of white infants. A record-setting million inmates crowd the nation's prisons, half of them black. The black out-of-wedlock birth rate has grown from about 25 percent in 1965 to more than 60 percent (more than 90 percent in the South Bronx and other areas of concentrated black poverty) in 1990.

The good news is very good, but the bad news has become steadily worse. Economically, we are still playing catch-up. In 1865, newly freed from slavery, African Americans controlled 3 percent of the wealth in America, United States Civil Rights Commissioner Arthur Fletcher tells me. Today, we still control just 3 percent of the wealth. After all this time, we have become free, more often than not, to make other people wealthier. The decline of industrial America, along with low-skill, high-pay jobs, has left much of black America split in two along lines of class, culture, opportunity and hope. The "prepared" join the new black middle class, which grew rapidly in the 1970s and early 1980s. The unprepared populate a new culture, directly opposed not only to the predominantly white mainstream, but also to any blacks who aspire to practice the values of hard work, good English, and family loyalty that would help them to join the white mainstream. The results of this spiritual decline, along with economic decline, have been devastating. Although more black women go to college than ever before, it has become a commonplace to refer to young black males as an endangered species. New anti-black stereotypes replace the old. Prosperous, well-dressed African Americans still complain of suf-

fering indignities when they try to hail a taxicab. The fact that the taxi that just passed them by was driven by a black cabby, native born or immigrant, makes no difference....

Behind our questions of race lurk larger questions of identity, our sense of who we are, where we belong, and where we are going. Our sense of place and peoplehood within groups is a perpetual challenge in some lives, particularly lives in America, a land where identity bubbles quite often out of nothing more than a weird alchemy of history and choice. "When I discover who I am, I'll be free," Ralph Ellison once wrote.

I reject the melting pot metaphor. People don't melt. Americans prove it on their ethnic holidays, in the ways they dance, in the ways they sing, in the culturally connected ways they worship. Displaced peoples long to celebrate their ethnic roots many generations and intermarriages after their ancestors arrived in their new land. Irish-American celebrations of St. Patrick's Day in Boston, Chicago, and New York City are far more lavish than anything seen on that day in Dublin or Belfast. Mexican-American celebrations of Cinco de Mayo, the Fifth of May, are far more lavish in Los Angeles and San Antonio than anything seen that day in Mexico City. It is as if holidays give us permission to expose our former selves as we imagine them to be. Americans of European descent love to show their ethnic cultural backgrounds. Why do they get nervous only when black people show their love for theirs? Is it that black people on such occasions suddenly remind white people of vulnerabilities black people feel quite routinely as a minority in a majority white society? Is it that white people, by and large, do not like this feeling, that they want nothing more than to cleanse themselves of it and make sure that it does not come bubbling up again? Attempts by Americans to claim some ephemeral, all-inclusive "all-American" identity reminds me of Samuel Johnson's observation: "Sir, a man may be so much of everything, that he is nothing of anything."

Instead of the melting pot metaphor, I prefer the mulligan stew, a concoction my parents tell me they used to fix during the Great Depression, when there was not a lot of food around the house and they "made do" with whatever meats, vegetables, and spices they had on hand. Everything went into the pot and was stirred. up, but the pieces didn't melt. Peas were easily distinguished from carrots or potatoes. Each maintained its distinctive character. Yet each loaned its special flavor to the whole, and each absorbed some of the flavor from the others. That flavor, always unique, always changing, is the beauty of America to me, even when the pot occasionally boils over….

African Americans are as diverse as other Americans. Some become nationalistic and ethnocentric. Others become pluralistic or multicultural, fitting their black identity into a comfortable niche among other aspects of themselves and their daily lives. Whichever they choose, a comfortable identity serves to provide not only a sense of belonging and protection for the individual against the abuses of racism, but also, ultimately, a sturdy foundation from which the individual can interact effectively with other people, cultures, and situations beyond the world of blackness.

"Identity would seem to be the garment with which one covers the nakedness of the self," James Baldwin wrote in *The Devil Finds Work* (1976), "in which case, it is best that the garment be loose, a little like the robes of the desert, through which one's nakedness can always be felt, and, sometimes, discerned. This trust in one's nakedness is all that gives one the power to change one's robes."

The cloak of proud black identity has provided a therapeutical warmth for my naked self after the chilly cocoon of inferiority imposed early in my life by a white-exalting society. But it is best worn loosely, lest it become as constricting and isolating for the famished individual soul as the garment it replaced.

The ancestral desire of my ethnic people to be "just American" resonates in me. But I cannot forget how persistently the rudeness of race continues to intrude between me and that dream. I can defy it, but I cannot deny it….

# 32. BEYOND THE MELTING POT

WILLIAM A. HENRY III

*"The 'browning of America' offers tremendous opportunity for capitalizing anew on the merits of many peoples from many lands. Yet this fundamental change in the ethnic makeup of the U.S. also poses risks. The American character is resilient and thrives on change. But past periods of rapid evolution have also, alas, brought out deeper, more fearful aspects of the national soul."*

In the twenty-first century, white Americans will become a **numerical** minority group. Already, we are experiencing a tremendous change in the ethnic make-up of society. Henry describes many of the difficulties we will face as a result. Government will be made more difficult, racial and ethnic conflict will undoubtedly increase, and schools will be tested like never before. We are one society, but what will this mean in the twenty-first century?

Someday soon, surely much sooner than most people who filled out their Census forms last week realize, white Americans will become a minority group. Long before that day arrives, the presumption that the "typical" U.S. citizen is someone who traces his or her descent in a direct line to Europe will be part of the past. By the time these elementary students at Brentwood Science Magnet School in Brentwood, CA, reach mid-life, their diverse ethnic experience in the classroom will be echoed in neighborhoods and workplaces throughout the U.S.

Already, one American in four defines himself or herself as Hispanic or nonwhite. If current trends in immigration and birth rates persist, the Hispanic population will have further increased by an estimated 21 percent, the Asian presence by about 22 percent, blacks by almost 12 percent and whites by a little more than 2 percent when the 20th century ends. By 2020, a date no further into the future than John F. Kennedy's election is in the past, the number of U.S. residents who are Hispanic or nonwhite will have more than doubled, to nearly 115 million, while the white population will not be increasing at all. By 2056, when someone born today will be 66 years old, the "average" U.S. resident, as defined by Census statistics, will trace his or her descent to Africa, Asia, the Hispanic world, the Pacific Islands, Arabia — almost anywhere but white Europe.

Although there may remain towns or outposts where even a black family will be something of an oddity, where English and Irish and German surnames will predominate, where a traditional (some will wistfully say "real") America will still be seen on almost every street corner, they will be only the vestiges of an earlier nation. The former majority will learn, as a normal part of everyday life, the meaning of the Latin slogan engraved on U.S. coins — *E Pluribus Unum*, one formed from many.

Among the younger populations that go to school and provide new entrants to the work force,

Reported by Naushad S. Mehta, New York; Sylvester Monroe, Los Angeles; and Dan Winbush, Atlanta.

the change will happen sooner. In some places, an America beyond the melting pot has already arrived. In New York State, some 40 percent of elementary and secondary school children belong to an ethnic minority. Within a decade, the proportion is expected to approach 50 percent. In California, white pupils are already a minority. Hispanics (who, regardless of their complexion, generally distinguish themselves from both blacks and whites) account for 31.4 percent of public school enrollment, blacks add 8.9 percent, and Asians and others amount to 11 percent — for a nonwhite total of 51.3 percent. This finding is not only a reflection of white flight from desegregated public schools. Whites of all ages account for just 58 percent of California's population. In San Jose, bearers of the Vietnamese surname *Nguyen* outnumber the *Jones*es in the telephone directory fourteen columns to eight.

Nor is the change confined to the coasts. Some 12,000 Hmong refugees from Laos have settled in St. Paul. At some Atlanta low-rent apartment complexes that used to be virtually all black, social workers today need to speak Spanish. At the Sesame Hut restaurant in Houston, a Korean immigrant owner trains Hispanic immigrant workers to prepare Chinese-style food for a largely black clientele. The Detroit area has 200,000 people of Middle Eastern descent; some 1,500 small grocery and convenience stores in the vicinity are owned by a whole subculture of Chaldean Christians with roots in Iraq. "Once America was a microcosm of European nationalities," says Molefi Asante, chairman of the department of African-American studies at Temple University in Philadelphia. "Today, America is a microcosm of the world."

History suggests that sustaining a truly multiracial society is difficult, or at least unusual. Only a handful of great powers of the distant past — Pharaonic Egypt and Imperial Rome, most notably — managed to maintain a distinct national identity while embracing, and being ruled by, an ethnic mélange. The most ethnically diverse contemporary power, the Soviet Union, is beset with secessionist demands and near-tribal conflicts. But such comparisons are flawed because those empires were launched by conquest and maintained through an aggressive military presence. The U.S.

was created, and continues to be redefined, primarily by voluntary immigration. This process has been one of the country's great strengths, infusing it with talent and energy. The "browning of America" offers tremendous opportunity for capitalizing anew on the merits of many peoples from many lands. Yet this fundamental change in the ethnic makeup of the U.S. also poses risks. The American character is resilient and thrives on change. But past periods of rapid evolution have also, alas, brought out deeper, more fearful aspects of the national soul.

## POLITICS: NEW AND SHIFTING ALLIANCES

A truly multiracial society will undoubtedly prove much harder to govern. Even seemingly race-free conflicts will be increasingly complicated by an overlay of ethnic tension. For example, the expected showdown in the early 21st century between the rising number of retirees and the dwindling number of workers who must be taxed to pay for the elders' Social Security benefits will probably be compounded by the fact that a large majority of recipients will be white, whereas a majority of workers paying for them will be nonwhite.

Although previous generations of immigrants believed they had to learn English quickly to survive, many Hispanics now maintain that the Spanish language is inseparable from their ethnic and cultural identity and seek to remain bilingual, if not primarily Spanish-speaking, for life. They see legislative drives to make English the sole official language—which have prevailed in some fashion in at least 16 states—as a political backlash. Says Arturo Vargas of the Mexican American Legal Defense and Educational Fund: "That's what English-only has been all about—a reaction to the growing population and influence of Hispanics. It's human nature to be uncomfortable with change. That's what the Census is all about, documenting changes and making sure the country keeps up."

Racial and ethnic conflict remains an ugly fact of American life everywhere, from working-class ghettos to college campuses, and those who do not raise their fists often raise their voices over affirmative action and other power sharing. When Florida Atlantic University, a state-funded insti-

tution under pressure to increase its low black enrollment, offered last month to give free tuition to every qualified black freshman who enrolled, the school was flooded with calls of complaint, some protesting that nothing was being done for "real" Americans. As the numbers of minorities increase, their demands for a share of the national bounty are bound to intensify, while whites are certain to feel ever more embattled. Businesses often feel whipsawed between immigration laws that punish them for hiring illegal aliens and antidiscrimination laws that penalize them for demanding excessive documentation from foreign-seeming job applicants. Even companies that consistently seek to do the right thing may be overwhelmed by the problems of diversifying a primarily white managerial corps fast enough to direct a work force that will be increasingly nonwhite and, potentially, resentful.

Nor will tensions be limited to the polar simplicity of white versus nonwhite. For all Jesse Jackson's rallying cries about shared goals, minority groups often feel keenly competitive. Chicago's Hispanic leaders have leapfrogged between white and black factions, offering support wherever there seemed to be the most to gain for their own community. Says Dan Soils of the Hispanic-oriented United Neighborhood Organization: "If you're thinking power, you don't put your eggs in one basket."

Blacks, who feel they waited longest and endured most in the fight for equal opportunity, are uneasy about being supplanted by Hispanics or, in some areas, by Asians as the numerically largest and most influential minority—and even more, about being outstripped in wealth and status by these newer groups. Because Hispanics are so numerous and Asians are such a fast-growing group, they have become the "hot" minorities, and blacks feel their needs are getting lower priority. As affirmative action has broadened to include other groups—and to benefit white women perhaps most of all—blacks perceive it as having waned in value for them.

## THE CLASSROOM: WHOSE HISTORY COUNTS?

Political pressure has already brought about sweeping change in public school textbooks over the past couple decades and has begun to affect the core humanities curriculum at such elite universities as Stanford. At stake at the college level is whether the traditional "canon" of Greek, Latin, and West European humanities study should be expanded to reflect the cultures of Africa, Asia, and other parts of the world. Many books treasured as classics by earlier generations are now seen as tools of cultural imperialism. In the extreme form, this thinking rises to a value-deprived neutralism that views all cultures, regardless of the grandeur or paucity of their attainments, as essentially equal.

Even more troubling is a revisionist approach to history in which groups that have gained power in the present turn to remaking the past in the image of their desires. If 18th, 19th, and earlier 20th century society should not have been so dominated by white Christian men of West European ancestry, they reason, then that past society should be reinvented as pluralist and democratic. Alternatively, the racism and sexism of the past are treated as inextricable from — and therefore irremediably tainting — traditional learning and values.

Although debates over college curriculum get the most attention, professors generally can resist or subvert the most wrong-headed changes and students generally have mature-enough judgment to sort out the arguments. Elementary and secondary school curriculums reach a far broader segment at a far more impressionable age, and political expediency more often wins over intellectual honesty. Exchanges have been vituperative in New York, where a state task force concluded that "African-Americans, Asian-Americans, Puerto Ricans, and Native Americans have all been victims of an intellectual and educational oppression.... Negative characterizations, or the absence of positive references, have had a terribly damaging effect on the psyche of young people." In urging a revised syllabus, the task force argued, "Children from European culture will have a less arrogant perspective of being part of a group that has 'done it all.'" Many intellectuals are outraged. Political scientist Andrew Hacker of Queens College lambastes a task-force suggestion that children be taught how "Native Americans were here to welcome new settlers from Holland, Senegal, England, Indonesia, France, the Congo, Italy, China, Iberia." Asks Hacker: "Did the Indians re-

ally welcome all those groups? Were they at Ellis Island when the Italians started to arrive? This is not history but a myth intended to bolster the self-esteem of certain children and, just possibly, a platform for advocates of various ethnic interests."

## VALUES: SOMETHING IN COMMON

Economic and political issues, however much emotion they arouse, are fundamentally open to practical solution. The deeper significance of America's becoming a majority nonwhite society is what it means to the national psyche, to individuals' sense of themselves and their nation — their idea of what it is to be American. People of color have often felt that whites treated equality as a benevolence granted to minorities rather than as an inherent natural right. Surely that condescension will wither.

Rather than accepting U.S. history and its meaning as settled, citizens will feel ever more free to debate where the nation's successes sprang from and what its unalterable beliefs are. They will clash over which myths and icons to invoke in education, in popular culture, in ceremonial speechmaking from political campaigns to the State of the Union address. Which is the more admirable heroism: the courageous holdout by a few conquest-minded whites over Hispanics at the Alamo, or the anonymous expression of hope by millions who filed through Ellis Island? Was the subduing of the West a daring feat of bravery and ingenuity, or a wretched example of white imperialism? Symbols deeply meaningful to one group can be a matter of indifference to another. Says University of Wisconsin chancellor Donna Shalala: "My grandparents came from Lebanon. I don't identify with the Pilgrims on a personal level." Christopher Jencks, professor of sociology at Northwestern, asks, "Is anything more basic about turkeys and Pilgrims than about Martin Luther King and Selma? To me, it's six of one and half a dozen of the other, if children understand what it's like to be a dissident minority. Because the civil rights struggle is closer chronologically, it's likelier to be taught by someone who really cares."

Traditionalists increasingly distinguish between a "multiracial" society, which they say would be fine, and a "multicultural" society, which they deplore. They argue that every society needs a universally accepted set of values and that new arrivals should therefore be pressured to conform to the mentality on which U.S. prosperity and freedom were built. Says Allan Bloom, author of the best-selling *The Closing of the American Mind*: "Obviously, the future of America can't be sustained if people keep only to their own ways and remain perpetual outsiders. The society has got to turn them into Americans. There are natural fears that today's immigrants may be too much of a cultural stretch for a nation based on Western values."

The counterargument, made by such scholars as historian Thomas Bender of New York University, is that if the center cannot hold, then one must redefine the center. It should be, he says, "the ever changing outcome of a continuing contest among social groups and ideas for the power to define public culture." Besides, he adds, many immigrants arrive committed to U.S. values; that is part of what attracted them. Says Julian Simon, professor of business administration at the University of Maryland: "The life and institutions here shape immigrants and not vice versa. This business about immigrants changing our institutions and our basic ways of life is hogwash. It's nativist scare talk."

## CITIZENSHIP: FORGING A NEW IDENTITY

Historians note that Americans have felt before that their historical culture was being overwhelmed by immigrants, but conflicts between earlier-arriving English, Germans, and Irish and later-arriving Italians and Jews did not have the obvious and enduring element of racial skin color. And there was never a time when the nonmainstream elements could claim, through sheer numbers, the potential to unite and exert political dominance. Says Bender: "The real question is whether or not our notion of diversity can successfully negotiate the color line."

For whites, especially those who trace their ancestry back to the early years of the Republic, the American heritage is a source of pride. For people of color, it is more likely to evoke anger and sometimes shame. The place where hope is shared is in the future. Demographer Ben Wattenberg, formerly perceived as a resister to social change, says, "There's a nice chance that the American myth in the 1990s and beyond is going to ratchet another step toward this idea that we are the universal nation. That rings the bell of manifest destiny. We're a people with a mission and a sense of purpose, and we believe we have something to offer the world."

Not every erstwhile alarmist can bring himself to such optimism. Says Norman Podhoretz, editor of *Commentary*: "A lot of people are trying to undermine the foundations of the American experience and are pushing toward a more Balkanized society. I think that would be a disaster, not only because it would destroy a precious social inheritance but also because it would lead to enormous unrest, even violence."

Although know-nothingism is generally confined to the more dismal corners of the American psyche, it seems all too predictable that during the next decades many more mainstream white Americans will begin to speak openly about the nation they feel they are losing. There are not, after all, many nonwhite faces depicted in Norman Rockwell's paintings. White Americans are accustomed to thinking of themselves as the very picture of their nation. Inspiring as it may be to the rest of the world, significant as it may be to the U.S. role in global politics, world trade, and the pursuit of peace, becoming a conspicuously multiracial society is bound to be a somewhat bumpy experience for many ordinary citizens. For older Americans, raised in a world where the numbers of whites were greater and the visibility of nonwhites was carefully restrained, the new world will seem ever stranger. But as the children at Brentwood Science Magnet School, and their counterparts in classrooms across the nation, are coming to realize, the new world is here. It is now. And it is irreversibly the America to come.

# Part VII
# GENDER INEQUALITY

Probably all societies are structured by gender. Men and women are differentiated, categorized, and assigned roles, identities, and differing levels of power, prestige, and privilege. Although numerically a majority in society, women still constitute a minority in American society in terms of position in relation to men.

Cynthia Fuchs Epstein is interested in the important differences between men and women and their causes. Her selection questions the research and thinking that many of us are tempted to accept (that real differences are biological), and tries to make a case for the social basis for our differences. That selection is followed by one by Andrew Hacker, who examines the economic inequality that exists between men and women in the United States. Finally, Patricia Yancey Martin and Robert A. Hummer ask important questions about our views of women in society as they play themselves out in one social institution, the fraternity. The question remains: To what extent does violence against women, including rape, exist because of how we define what it means to be a man and a woman in society?

# 33. SAMENESS AND DIFFERENCE BETWEEN MEN AND WOMEN

CYNTHIA FUCHS EPSTEIN

*"Gender boundaries are maintained by feminists and antifeminists, scholars and lay people alike. None of us is free from them; it is no wonder that our scholarship is oriented toward finding them. The means of boundary maintenance may be mechanical and physical, but they are always conceptual and symbolic. They are difficult to work out because they are reinforced in the unnoticed habits and language of everyday life, vigilantly attended to by an individual's family and friends, business associates and colleagues."*

What are the important distinctions between men and women? How important are they? What is the reason they exist? Why is it so easy for many of us—including scientists—to think of their being a real essence that distinguishes men from women? Professor Epstein examines these issues in a logical and critical manner. She makes a strong case for why we must seriously question the importance of biological differences between men and women. To follow her argument, it might be useful to divide her points as follows:

1. Real differences between men and women are not natural differences.
2. Many scientists and others are attracted to biological explanations of differences.
3. Research emphasizing biology tends to exaggerate differences.
4. Human beings change; men and women change; individuals change. Characteristics change because of social interaction. Assumptions about male/female differences tend to ignore change.
5. Differences between men and women found in the research are not very significant. Research does not pay enough attention to fashion, gender roles, importance of the supposed attributes to people's lives, complexity of attributes, and social controls on behavior.
6. We need to use a more social control approach to understanding male and female differences, one that looks at the pressures operating on men and women.
7. To understand differences between men and women, we should turn to a theoretical model called the "protean self," the view of human beings as contradictory, complex, and adaptable.

(Editor's Note: An earlier version of this paper was presented at a conference. "Beyond Difference as a Model for Studying Gender: In Search of New Stories to Tell," May 19-21, 1995. I would like to acknowledge the research assistance of Betsy Wissinger and Barry Davison.

The support of the Alfred Sloan Foundation for research assistance for part of this paper is also acknowledged with gratitude. Correspondence regarding this article should be addressed to Professor Cynthia Fuchs Epstein. Ph.D. Program in Sociology, CUNY Graduate Center, 33 West 42 Street, New York, NY 10036.)

From "Sameness and Difference Between Men and Women," by Cynthia Fuchs Epstein, in *Journal Of Social Issues*, Vol. 53, no. 2, 1997, pp. 259—278.

...Categorization, often leading to dichotomization, is an efficient tool in the creation of social order (Epstein, 1985). In society — in the home and in public institutions — it further functions to provide the basis for a hierarchic division of labor. In science and social thought, categorization is necessary for analytic thinking. But the choice of categories — and their use as tools of social differentiation, whether at work, home, or in science — is rife with pitfalls.

Categorizations about groups of people are usually based on a difference model and its conceptual ally, essentialism. *Essentialism* focuses on what are believed to be basic biological, cognitive, and emotional differences that differentiate groups. Essentialism justifies unequal treatment, and at an extreme, aggressive and subordinating behavior against groups regarded as "other." Kai Erikson (1996) calls the process whereby one people manages to neutralize the humanity of another as "social speciation." The belief in basic sex differences has, of course, justified men's dominance and women's subordination in most spheres of social life. Of course, men and women are distinctive with regard to their reproductive organs and secondary sex characteristics. But neither sex is distinctive with regard to ambitions, talents, interests, and intelligence. Yet, men and women are often forced to display the qualities of behavior, interest, or appearance that a person of that sex is supposed to possess naturally (Goffman 1977), which may situate them differently (or segregate them) in the family (Goode 1964) and at work (Reskin & Hartmann 1986)....

Women are certainly positioned differently than men in most societies, and may even exhibit patterned behavior associated with their gender, but it is questionable whether their nature accounts for such differences, or rather, as will be suggested here, the differences come from formal and informal social controls ranging from microinteractions to formal policies.

Women do act differently than men in certain ways, for example, in engaging in low-prestige and low-paying work (Epstein 1970; Acker 1990; Reskin & Hartmann 1986); in participating less in political decision-making roles (Epstein & Coser, eds. 1981); in assuming more responsibilities for the family (Rossi 1964; Hochschild 1989; Shelton 1996) and charitable work; and in gaining less recognition for their contributions to society,

whether they be in the paid or nonpaid sectors. However, these are not reasonable extensions of women's "nature...."

## PITFALLS OF RESEARCH ON DIFFERENCE AND SAMENESS

### Orientation of the Research and Bias

In the past, the assumption of basic differences between women and men with regard to cognitive functioning and emotional qualities was both a source of justification for women's subordinate position in many groups and a basis for their exclusion from professions, political decision-making, and business management (Epstein 1970, 1988). As with race (Gould 1981), even scientists sought to support claims to women's inferiority (Fausto-Sterling 1985) or "otherness" with regard to cognitive and emotional factors (Shennan & Beck 1979). For example, many social researchers have explained job segregation and the clustering of women in low-prestige occupations not by the impact of stereotyping and discrimination, but by the presumed compatibility of women for the work or other social roles, and the natural propensity of men for higher level work. In recent times, biological determinants of sex differences, particularly brain studies (Fausto-Sterling), have been referred to for the purpose of showing the source of reported differences in activities from test scores in math to "women's ways of leading." Rosener (personal communication) claims biology is part of the basis for the different leadership styles women demonstrate (1995). Yet, as Tavris (1992) points out, citing the work of Hyde and Linn and other scientists, there are virtually no differences in the attributes that brain differences are supposed to explain, and more important, the brain studies themselves have been criticized for their method (some are done on rats, all with a tiny sample size and evidence of overlaps between the sexes; see Fausto-Sterling).

The natural propensities argument does not hold up more generally. It has not met the test of time as women flock to jobs formerly regarded as inappropriate for them, such as law and medicine, and as they have assumed highly visible positions in government, as Attorney General, Supreme

Court Justice, and Secretary of State. Yet, in recent years, "difference" is accepted by some feminist scholars and used to justify elevating women above men on issues of morality or empathy (Gilligan 1982), or suggesting they have alternative modes of understanding (Tannen 1990; Belenky et al. 1986). Often, there is a hint that their way (that is, understanding or morality) is superior to that of men. In *Deceptive Distinctions* (1988), I detailed the evidence for overturning the view that women are basically different from men. This view is also supported by comprehensive reviews of Aries (1996), Feingold (1992), and Tavris (1992) who, on the basis of an overview of research, wisely concluded in the book *The Mismeasure of Woman"…* [that] women are not the better sex, the inferior sex, or the opposite sex." Yet there has been enormous spillover effect from the work of Gilligan (1982), who suggested that women had alternate modes of morality in many fields including legal studies and educational theory. The appeal of women having a "different way of knowing," also offered by social philosophers such as Harding (1996) or historians like Keller (1978), has increased the attractiveness of the idea of women's difference, although the research showing differences often does not hold up on re-analysis or replication (Epstein 1988). (*See also* Belenky, Clinchy, Goldberger & Tarule 1986.)

## Methodology

Because scholarship on difference is framed by researchers and theorists representing multiple fields and orientations, outcomes of their research are not consistent. However, "findings" are often cited across fields without attention to the methodology. Not only do some scholars use different standards of proof, many deny that proof is even obtainable, yet nevertheless make claims for basic differences. For example, many scholars from the humanities look for "evidence" in support of their theories, from personal experience or individual narratives, and some use psychoanalytic techniques using literature and myth as "evidence" for their judgments. Many psychologists use laboratory experiments and tests; other psychologists and sociologists use case studies, surveys, and field stud-

ies. Using personal experience or psychoanalytic technique tends to emphasize difference, while using objective techniques (however much they fall short of an objective ideal) reveals much more similarity between men and women. As noted earlier, the similarities with regard to cognitive and emotional qualities (that is, that the huge overlap in characteristics of men and women are far greater than the variation among each sex) have been shown by analyzing clusters of studies and assessing their relative merit. Most of these (but not all, *see* Eagly 1987), for example, show not only the overlap but that the differences once found at the ends of distributions have been decreasing with time, probably caused by changes in social factors affecting the differences seen in the past (Feingold 1992). In fact, it may be that claims of large-scale differences between females and males in the past have had the social consequences of contributing to whatever differences are still identified through tests, observations, and other indicators.

The problem of the method used to assess difference is great. Some of the most cited "difference" research is a phenomenon of the method. In studies of leadership, aggression, "caring," and so on, it is not unreasonable to assume that men and women will report behavior that is in conformity with a (positive) stereotyped view of a male and female model. For example, it is widely believed that women and men have different styles of leadership (Rosener 1995), although many observers (including subordinates of women leaders, *see* Aries 1996) indicate they exhibit the same range of behaviors as men. But women are less likely to report the dominant and competitive behavior that is reported by observers (Snodgrass & Rosenthal 1984). Even so, many women are convinced they have a different style (*see* Keller 1978; Gilligan 1982; Harding 1986; Belenky, Clinchy, Goldberger, & Tarule 1986; Tannen 1990; Smith 1990; and Rosener 1995), and supervisors often agree, offering them jobs in human resources and excluding them from staff jobs that would give them the experience to rise in a corporation (Kanter 1977). These beliefs, of course, result in a pattern that is interpreted as proof of preference and aptitude. In neither case does the observation provide support for an essentialist theory of gender differentiation based on biological, psychological, or sociological criteria....

## Static versus Dynamic and Uni-Dimensional versus Multidimensional Concepts

The paired terms *male* and *female*, and *masculine* and *feminine*, are conceptual models. They are static; they are uni-dimensioned. Over time, people in various cultural settings have chosen particular indicators to define them. As we know, cultures vary with regard to what characteristics they attribute to men and women (for example, women are regarded as emotional in American society, but men are regarded as emotional in Iranian society).

As I pointed out elsewhere (Epstein 1973), the 1970s (and as we later learned, the 1980s) provided situations that proved to be natural field experiments indicating how much people could change (Friedan 1976). Because of the Civil Rights and Women's Movements, thousands of people engaged in activities that were unusual for persons of their gender or race, acting assertively, taking advantage of opportunities to engage in upward mobility, and changing self images and behaviors. Although the "change" model has been supported in much research (including that of the MacArthur Foundation Research Network on Successful Midlife Development spearheaded by Gilbert Brim), many academic and popular theories remain static. In studies of telephone company workers, I have found that women change how they feel about themselves (secure) and how they act (with authority and confidence) when they are promoted into a management job (Epstein, forthcoming).

## Attributes as Interactional

Whatever the attribution, most male and female characteristics may be regarded in interactional settings (Deaux & Major 1987; Ridgeway 1997); thus, the status and rank of the other side matters. Power, age, and ethnic statuses all structure the playing out of gender-related behaviors, and they also vary in particular situations and historical periods.

These characteristics are also embedded in a life cycle and time framework. At any point at which maleness and femaleness are being assessed or evaluated, females and males of particular ages are being observed. Yet women and men often exhibit very different characteristics at young, middle, and older ages (women often gaining in authority, and men often demonstrating more nurturing qualities after retirement). Some men gain this during childrearing years when they take on child-care responsibility (*see* Brody).

The issue of the life course is of great interest because many studies that define male and female behavior are based on studies conducted in schools or laboratory settings (using school-aged children or young adults). Yet characteristics of youngsters often disappear through maturity, developmental changes, socialization, or acquisition of different social roles. One important example of this can be found in the literature on aggression. Because aggression is a defining characteristic of males and not females, it has been found that although significant differences are found among girls and boys, especially preschoolers, these differences may also vary by method of study; most important, differences in aggression in adulthood tend to be small (Hyde 1990). Norms regarding the appropriateness of women expressing aggression also change (Zuckerman et al. 1991).

## Meaningful Differences

The magnitude of difference in behavior and preferences of men and women is also important to consider from a scientific point of view. Usually large differences would be the measure of meaningful sex variation, even though studies might show *statistically* significant differences when the actual differences might be quite tiny, and thus *socially* insignificant. Thus, the purpose of the inquiry ought to determine social "significance." As an example, politicians are usually concerned with otherwise insignificant differences between groups because a tiny difference can determine the results of an election. From a social science point of view, it is the case that most women and men vote generally the same way. For example, in the 1996 congressional race, 55 percent of women voted for Democrats as opposed to 46 percent of men, according to a poll by *The New York Times* (November 7, 1996) — the notable "gender gap." But focus is on the nine percent who voted differently and not the 91 percent who voted the same. Who are these nine percent? Reviewing the polls, Teixeira (1997) found non-college educated women, nervous about maintaining middle-class status, were the source of the difference. It was not higher income women who voted the same as men. In the 1992 presidential race, the disparity between males and females was even less — six percent. But as Hout and his colleagues point out (Hout et al. 1995) class differences in voting patterns are twice as large as gender differences. In 1992, 55 percent of white women voted for Republican congressional candidates (*Wall Street Journal*, May 22, 1995). Thus there is a sector of the female constituency that votes differently from men because they have different interests (more depend on government aid and work for government agencies, for example), and not because as women they have a different nature or morality.

Most reporting that refers to women as a collectivity with regard to preferences or capacities is based on very small percentages, and may vary over time. The reporting indicates an ignorance of how to interpret a statistical distribution. It refers to categories as if they were mutually exclusive, such as "black" and "white," and ignores the many hues that differentiate skin color among people. In the case of sex, like defining a racial category, many of the same kinds of conceptualizations that are understood to be real representations are in fact not descriptive of individuals within a group. Consider that racial laws in some states classified a person as black when they had one-sixteenth black "blood." They could have as easily described such individuals as "white." Similarly, using small differences to distinguish "male" or "female" behavior (often not more than a two or three percent difference) in any observed characteristic among a sample of males and females is enough to convince people that a particular man or woman can be located at the end of the distribution where those small differences lie (Sherif 1979).

## Fashions in Gender Behavior

Tastes change in popular culture, and with them the practices associated with men and women and believed to be rooted in their natures. Some practices change because legal changes open women's options. Other practices change because social conditions permit or repress certain kinds of activity. This phenomenon is too extensive to document, but a few examples illustrate the social construction of sex-related behavior.

1. **Assertiveness:** Many feminist historians have documented women's assertiveness in labor union activity at certain points and places in history (Turbin 1995; Costello 1991; Vallas 1993), yet traditionally, public collective action has not been associated with women.

2. **Interest in and use of guns:** The use of firearms has been considered a natural prerogative of men, and people look to its sources in the play behavior of boys who often "turn" objects into guns and play "cops and robbers." This is used as an example of men's "natural" aggression and women's "natural" passivity. But girls and women now are more interested in guns than in the past. A significant number take target practice, and women comprise 15 to 20 percent of the National Rifle Association's membership (Epstein 1995). The NRA even elected their first woman president in 1995 (*Wall Street Journal*, May 22, 1995). In Israel, women, who are conscripted into the army, commonly train with guns and carry them unless they are religious and are not required to join the army.

3. **Interest and participation in traditionally "male professions":** In the United States, women and men choose to go to medical and law schools in almost equal numbers (Epstein 1993), a radical change from the time when it was believed that women did not enjoy the conflict of the courtroom (Epstein 1993) or the challenge of the operating room (Lorber 1984). In 1963, women constituted only 3.8 percent of entering classes in professional schools (Epstein 1993), and it was believed that women had no interest in medicine or the law. (Of course, in the case of applications to professional school before the 1960s, when there was such a small number of women applying, one could understand why it was believed that women did not have the same preference for attendance that men had.)

4. **Verbal behavior:** Studies of speech show that men's and women's voices are influenced by social expectations and social controls. For example, a recent article in the *Wall Street Journal* reported that "elevator girls" in Japan were once required to speak in a high-pitched voice deemed essentially feminine, but now are permitted to speak in a more natural, lower tone.

## Gender Attributes as a Function of Social Roles

Position in life and the subsequent social roles one takes on may be an important factor in determining the behavior of any man or woman, boy or girl. Most of the attributes affixed to a particular gender usually refer to attitudes and behavior that are normatively prescribed and controlled in the context of the social roles people acquire (or have thrust on them); they may become internalized, but even if they are, they may be activated or deactivated for a moment or forever. Arlie Hochschild (1983) and others have pointed to the "emotion work" that women are asked to do in certain occupational roles, such as showing nurturant behavior and friendliness in their jobs as flight attendants, nurses, and waitresses. These behaviors are clearly normative and reinforced by social controls, supervisors, or peers.

## Quantification of Attributes

In associating various qualities with men or women, little attention is given to how much of the attribute they display. Yet people may display normative attributes for their sex when situations demand it, and not in situations in which they are not subject to controls. Furthermore, they may internalize some of the characteristics in greater or lesser amounts. It is entirely possible for a person to feel or be a little nurturant or very nurturant; one can be aggressive occasionally or very often, and one can alternate such qualities in one's various social roles, or even within the same role. For example, some mothers may be loving toward their children, looking out for their interests, yet harsh and punitive using corporal punishment depending on the cultural practices of their group (as the research of Waters [1994] shows for Jamaican culture).

## Situational Attributes

As already noted, a person can manifest an attribute under particular conditions and not under other conditions. They may operate nurturantly or aggressively, depending on the situation in which they are located and depending on with whom the person is in interaction. For example, a person may be attentive to a nonfunctioning aged parent in the company of other family members but not when that person is alone.

## Inappropriate "Halo Effects" of Gender Practices

Noting differences (however measured) in one sphere is used to suggest comparable differences in another, even though they may be irrelevant. Here the logic of causality is seriously questionable. The following illustrations point out the illogical and contradictory nature of several widely held "common sense" assertions about gender differences in some kinds of behavior.

1. Many women and men explain women's low representation in the ranks of management through their lack of experience in team sports. This comes from a romantic notion about the ennobling nature of team sports and an ideal of cooperation that is associated with them. Yet other scholars claim women practice connection and are not as individualistic as men, claiming men become leaders because they are more individualistic (Chodorow 1978; Gilligan 1982).
2. Some explanations for why women become clerks is that they are able to endure monotony because of the repetitive tasks they perform at home. Yet their sewing ability is not regarded as useful in potential roles as surgeons as it might well be, if there were a more compelling logic to these associations.

## Social Control

An overview of research on gender distinctions indicates that there has been insufficient attention to the impact of social controls on behavior in the models explaining observed sex differences. As I pointed out in *Deceptive Distinctions* (1988), when controls are not implemented or differentially applied, individuals of either sex act out and feel *multiple* versions of the prescriptions related to their social roles and internalize them idiosyncratically. This reality leads to enormous variation within each sex or gender category. However, controls on behavior — punishments for deviation — may result in patterned behavior that is then regarded as "normal," which means that individuals are unaware of how superficial and variable many attributes associated with each sex are.

## Multiple Realities

Broad categories and loose boundaries (such as "man" or "American") make for multiple interpretations and thus multiple realities of those in the category. Cohen (1985) notes that because boundaries (that set groups apart) are conceptually set, they may be perceived in rather different terms, not only by people on opposite sides of them, but by those on the same side. All social categories are variable in meaning, according to his view, and often the contents of a category are so unclear that it exists largely in terms of its symbolic boundaries. Such terms as *just* and *unjust*, and perhaps, *masculine* and *feminine*, may be impossible to spell out with precision. However, the range of meanings that can be subsumed by these terms (which are, of course, symbols) can be glossed over precisely because they allow their adherents to attach their own meanings to them. Interpretations of any category also vary according to the circumstances of interaction and how the interaction is defined in the context in which it occurs. The same behavior may be interpreted differently in different settings. For example, in all-female groups, women may act in a bawdy manner without fear of being perceived as unfeminine, although bawdiness is usually regarded as male behavior. Westwood (1985) shows this type of behavior for a group of hosiery company workers in Great Britain, and Yarrow (1987) shows that in West Virginia, male coal miners are kept in line just by accusing them of being soft, asking for safety equipment, for example. However, in some all-male groups (for example, in sports and war), men often demonstrate tender and caring behavior that might be interpreted as unmanly in mixed groups. When such behavior becomes public, however, redefinition or reinterpretation about what is "normal" for a particular category of people may occur.

## Multiple Selves

Women are not only different within the category of women, they are also different within the category of "self." That is, aspects of the "self" may include differing and even contradictory components

(Haraway 1991; Nicholson 1990; Crosby 1987; Thoits 1983; Spence 1984 & 1985). Merton's (1968) work on the role-set specified structurally that there are dynamics of role relationships. The people specifying a single feminine self act as if women and men play out their roles with reliable consistency—as if they possessed monotone personalities. People prefer the idea of a person as a single being with a body and soul that match. They believe it to be an indicator of integrity. The notion of oneness fits neatly into scientific categories that one can run through a computer or code on a data sheet. That sense of consistency is good for a political agenda; we see that in times of conflict, people tend to focus on one aspect of their beliefs or the "self" to differentiate themselves from the opposition. Such clustering ends up by aligning people in a category with a name—such as communist, radical, liberal, conservative, Serb, Bosnian, man, or woman. Thus people suppress the ideas or traits that both they and their opposing counterpart hold. Here, the stereotyped name is *woman* or *man*, and the polarization of a multitude of characteristics is made across the board (Epstein 1988).

On the other hand, there are collective agreements about certain connotations that are culturally persistent, and no matter whether the definition of a category makes sense, gatekeepers of the traditional view will do all they can to make a boundary intractable, and they often do so with the compliance of those who may suffer from the distinction—or at most, derive only secondary benefits (Epstein 1988).

## Social Controls

Gender boundaries are maintained by feminists and antifeminists, scholars and lay people alike. None of us is free from them; it is no wonder that our scholarship is oriented toward finding them. The means of boundary maintenance may be mechanical and physical, but they are always conceptual and symbolic. They are difficult to work out because they are reinforced in the unnoticed habits and language of everyday life, vigilantly attended to by an individual's family and friends, business associates and colleagues. Control in the way we think, then, can be exercised at the micro level, at not always perceptible levels of notice, although it is also true that people often may be clearly aware that words, like rituals or ceremonies, are instruments, tools, and weapons that erect walls or bring them down. At base, language itself creates boundaries by providing the terms by which real or assumed behaviors and attributes are grouped....

## AN ALTERNATIVE MODEL

In the preceding discussion, I have suggested that some ways of viewing sex differences ought to be revised if not abandoned. As an illustration of what I believe to be a productive model, I propose a version of Lifton's notion of the "protean self" (1994). As pointed out elsewhere (Epstein 1996), this notion offers a theory that suggests a wide set of possibilities for individuals. Rooted in observation and the experience of a world that is rapidly changing personally and globally, Lifton's model reflects the seeming paradoxes of "odd combinations" of identity elements and subselves, even those "mutually irreconcilable." Experience suggests that real people are quite capable of vastly contradictory behaviors and transformations that stem from different elements of themselves. Lifton noted this phenomenon in his studies of Nazi doctors who were humane in their normal practices with Christian German patients but who tortured German Jewish concentration camp victims. Many other less dramatic but contradictory elements of people's selves are also documented by Lifton. In feminist history, the example of Emma Goldman stands out: an anarchist, an assassin and a fiery orator who had a number of lovers; and Rosa Luxemberg, similarly a political figure with a great gift for public speaking, an organizer, who from jail made doll clothes for my late colleague, the sociologist Rose Coser, who herself was a brilliant theorist, author, the designer of a class action suit in the university, and a master chef. But most contradictory selves are lodged in people whose lives are less dramatic. Quite ordinary men may be tender lovers and fathers but brutal in business, and unremarkable women may be both nurturant mothers and ruthless fighters in local political campaigns. Moreover, people may move from personalities characterized by shyness to self assertion, or from combative to affiliative, as the social spheres in which they move give them opportunity and en-

couragement. Although this variety is there for all to observe, countless scholars and other people are wedded to a model of a constant "self" so that confronting everyday paradoxes is troubling.

Individuals whose selves do not conform to social expectations or prescriptions, or whose personalities seem inconsistent, disorderly, or heterogeneous, face disapproval from others and from within themselves. Such people are often regarded as hypocritical or impaired psychologically; many therefore try to get their disparate selves in order or pressure others to do so. A search for consistency may be human even while inconsistency may be normal.

Of course, people differ with regard to their vulnerability to constraints on change. There are, after all, highly gifted adapters — "method actors" of self — self-motivators who can change themselves and create new selves; and there are leaden social actors who cling (or are forced to cling) to identities that are set early. But such adaptability is not necessarily random. Members of some social groups or categories are permitted more diversity and change in their selves than are others; men more than women; urban dwellers more than small-town inhabitants; artists more than ministers. Thus, social norms act on the self to enrich or diminish its potential; with the demand that individuals of certain backgrounds and origins "be" selves, and not merely act roles that are consistent with social expectations. Because new roles often (but not always) create "selves," individuals face social controls that permit or prohibit their acquisition. Men and women are subjected to these pressures on the basis of gender, race, social class, and family history. A person is instructed to "be" a woman or "be" a man — not merely to act like one. In the United States, a man continues to face pressures to be strong, aggressive, and ambitious; a woman is admonished to be loving, affiliative, nurturant, and altruistic. These traits are played out, of course, in the context of social roles in which they are the prescribed behaviors. But usually, the cultural view is that these women and men are only doing what comes naturally. What people "are," suggests Lifton, is complex; they are compelled to do things to which they are attracted. These may be consistent things, but they may be contradictory. They may enlarge or diminish the person in public evaluation. But the potential, he insists, is wide. American women today provide evidence for the model of proteanism in human nature. The last few decades have provided the perfect "field experiment" to indicate how variable people's selves—especially women's selves—may be, how changeable. More dramatically today than at any time in history, American women are recognized as publicly and personally complex creatures. The ambivalence that greets these changes also indicates the extent to which cultural and social controls determine the ability to change and to accept the notion of change in themselves.

Our studies should more directly relate to this experience, and we should derive our models from it—not from the armchair or the paradigmatic legacies of theorists who had a stake in the status quo. The more one goes into the field to do actual research on women's behavior, the more one finds that the concepts we call male and female—or gender—comprise multiple realities for the individual and for society. The concepts of male and female are a vehicle for making assignments to various instrumental and emotional tasks in society. They act as a control apparatus for keeping people in line; the concepts provide a justification system for hierarchy. Researchers should note that male and female gender are concepts, not things. What they are is always in question; they are not steady states. The theory and research methodology that labels gender characteristics and defines them according to custom without checking them against reality cheats women and men of their right to be evaluated as individuals, with an array of human characteristics.

## ENDNOTES

Acker, J. (1990). "Hierarchies, Jobs, Bodies: A Theory of Gendered Organizations." *Gender & Society*, 4: 139-158.

Aries, E. (1996). *Men and Women in Interaction: Reconsidering the Differences*. New York: Oxford University Press.

Belenky, M. F., B. M. Clinchy, N. R. Goldberger, & J. M. Tarule. (1986). *Women's Ways of Knowing: The Development of Self, Voice, and Mind*. New York: Basic Books.

Chodorow, N. (1978). *The Reproduction of Mothering: Psychoanalysis* and *the Sociology of Gender*. Berkeley, CA: University of California Press.

Cohen, A. (1985). *The Symbolic Construction of Communities*. London: Tavistock.

Costello, C. (1991). *We're Worth It! Women and Collective Action in the Insurance Workplace*. Chicago: University of Illinois Press.

Crosby, F. (1987). *Spouse, Parent, Worker: On Gender and Multiple Roles*. New Haven: Yale University Press.

Deaux, K., & B. Major. (1987). "Putting Gender into Context: An Interactive Model of Gender-Related Behavior." *Psychological Review*, 94(2), 369-389.

Eagly, A. H. (1987). *Sex Differences in Social Behavior: A Social Role Interpretation*. Hillsdale, NJ: Erl-

Epstein, C. F. (1996). "The Protean American Woman: Anxiety and Opportunity." In C. B. Strozier and M. Flynn (Eds.), *Trauma and Self* (pp. 159-174). Lanham, Maryland: Rowman and Littlefield.

Epstein, C. F. (1995). "Pistol-Packing Mamas." *Dissent*, Fall. 536-537.

Epstein, C. F. (1993). *Women in Law* (2nd ed.). Chicago: University of Illinois Press.

Epstein, C. F. (1988). *Deceptive Distinctions, Sex, Gender and the Social Order*. New Haven: Yale University Press.

Epstein, C. F (1985). "Ideal Roles and Real Roles: Or the Fallacy of the Misplaced Dichotomy." *Research in Social Stratification and Mobility*, 4, 29-51

Epstein, C. F. (1973). "Separate and Unequal: Notes on Women's Achievement." *Social Policy*. 6(5), 17-23.

Epstein, C. F. (1970). *Woman's Place: Options and Limits in Professional Careers*. Berkeley: University of California Press.

Epstein, C. F. & R. L. Coser. (Eds.). (1981). *Access to Power: Cross-National Studies of Women and Elites*. Boston: Allen & Unwin.

Erikson, K. (1996). "On Pseudospeciation and Social Speciation." In C. Strozier and M. Flynn (Eds.), *Genocide, War, and Human Survival* (pp. 51-57). Lanham, Maryland: Rowman and Littlefield.

Fausto-Sterling, A. (1985). *Myths of Gender: Biological Theories about Women and Men*. New York: Basic Books.

Feingold, A. (1992). "Sex Differences in Variability in Intellectual Abilities: A New Look at an Old Controversy." *Review of Educational Research*, 62(1). 61-84.

Foucault, M. (1977). *The Order of Things*. London: Tavistock.

Friedan, B. (1976). *It Changed My Life*. New York: Random House.

Friedan, B. (1963). *The Feminine Mystique*. New York: Simon and Schuster.

Gilligan, C. (1982). In a *Different Voice*. Cambridge, MA: Harvard University Press.

Goffman, E. (1977). "Arrangements Between the Sexes," *Theory and Society* 4, 301-331.

Goode, W. J. (1964). *The Family*, (2nd ed.). Englewood Cliffs. NJ: Prentice Hall.

Gould, S. J. (1981). *The Mismeasure of Man*. New York: Norton.

Hall, S. (1984). "Cultural Studies at the Center: Some Problematics and Problems." In S. Hall, D. Hobson, A. Lowe, & P. Willis (Eds.), *Culture, Media, Language*. London: Hutchison.

Haraway, D. (1991). *Simians, Cyborgs, and Women*. New York: Routledge.

Harding, S. (1986). *The Science Question in Feminism*, Ithaca, NY: Cornell University Press.

Hochschild, A. R. (1989). *The Second Shift: Working Parents and the Revolution at Home*. New York: Viking.

Hochschild, A. R. (1983). *The Managed Heart: Commercialization of Human Feeling*. Berkeley, CA: University of California Press.

Hout, M., C. Brooks, & J. Manza (1995, December). "The Democrative Class Struggle in the United States: 1948–1992," *American Sociological Review*, 60. 805–828.

Hyde, J. S. (1990). *Understanding Human Sexuality*. New York: McGraw Hill.

Irigary, L. (1981). "And the One Doesn't Stir Without the Other." *Signs*. 7(1). 60–67.

Johnson, D. (1996, November 28). "What Do Women Want?" *The New York Review of Books*, 22–28.

Kanter, R. M. (1977). *Men and Women of the Corporation*. New York: Basic Books.

Keller, E. F. (1978, September). "Gender and Science." *Psychoanalysis and Contemporary Thought*. 409–433.

Lifton, R. J. (1994), *The Protean Self*. New York: Basic Books.

Lorber. J. (1984). *Women Physicians: Careers, Status, and Power*. New York: Methuen.

Merton, R. K. (1968). *Social Theory and Social Structure*. Glencoe, IL: The Free Press.

Nicholson, L. (1990). *Feminism/Postmodernism*. New York: Routledge.

Reskin, B. and H. Hartmann. (1986). *Women's Work, Men's Work: Sex Segregation on the Job*. Washington, DC: National Academy Press.

Ridgeway, C. (1997). "Interaction and the Conservation of Gender Inequality." *American Sociological Review*, 62(2), 218–235.

Rosener, J. (1995). *America's Competitive Secret: Utilizing Women as a Management Strategy*. New York: Oxford University Press.

Rossi, A. (1964, Spring). "The Equality of Women: An Immodest Proposal." *Daedalus*, 93, 607–52.

Shelton, B. A. & J. Daphne. (1996). "The Division of Household Labor." *American Review of Sociology*, 22, 299–322.

Sherif, C. W. (1979). "Bias in Psychology." In J. A. Sherman & E. T. Beck (Eds.), *The Prism of Sex: Essays in the Sociology of Knowledge* (pp. 93–133). Madison, WI: The University of Wisconsin Press.

Sherman, J. A. & E. T. Beck (Eds.) (1979). *The Prism of Sex: Essays in the Sociology of Knowledge*. Madison, WI: University of Wisconsin Press.

Smith, D. E. (1990). *The Conceptual Practices of Power: A Feminist Sociology of Knowledge*. Boston, MA: Northeastern University Press.

Snodgrass, S. E. & R. Rosenthal. (1984). "Females in Charge: Effects of Sex of Subordinate and Romantic Attachment Status Upon Self Ratings of Dominance." *Journal of Personality*. 52 (4), 353–371.

Spence, J. T. (1985). "Gender Identity and Its Implications for Concepts of Masculinity and Femininity." In T. Sondregger (Ed.), *Nebraska Symposium on Motivation*, (pp. 59–95). Lincoln, NE: University of Nebraska Press.

Spence, J. T. (1984). "Masculinity, Femininity, and Gender-Related Traits: A Conceptual Analysis and Critique of Current Research." *Progress in Experimental Personality Research*, 13, 1–97.

Tannen, D. (1990). *You Just Don't Understand: Women and Men in Conversation*. New York: Morrow.

Tavris, C. (1992). *The Mismeasure of Woman*. New York: Simon and Schuster.

Teixeira, R. (1997, Spring). "Finding the Real Center: Lessons of the 1996 Elections." *Dissent*. 51–59.

Thoits, P. (1983). "Multiple Identities and Psychological Well-Being: A Reformulation and Test of the Social Isolation Hypothesis." *American Sociological Review*, 48. 74–87.

Turbin, C. (1992). *Working Women of Collar City: Gender, Class, and Community in Troy, 1864–86*. Chicago: University of Illinois Press.

Vallas, S. (1993), *Power in the Workplace: The Politics of Production at AT&T*. Albany: State University of New York Press.

Waters, M. (1994). "Ethnic and Racial Identities of Second-Generation Black Immigrants in New York City." *International Migration Review*, 28, 795–820.

Westwood, S. (1985). *All Day Every Day: Factory and Family in the Making of Women's Lives*. Champaign: University of Illinois Press.

Yarrow, M. (1987, April). "Class and Gender in the Developing Consciousness of Appalachian Coal Miners." Paper presented to the Fifth UMIST-ASTON Annual Conference on Organization and Control of the Labor Process. Manchester, England.

Zuckerman, H., J. Cole, & J. Bruer. (1991). *The Outer Circle: Women in the Scientific Community*. New York: Norton.

# 34. THE GENDER GAP: CONTOURS AND CAUSES

*ANDREW HACKER*

*"Although the typical woman's wallet is fuller than ever before, it is still measurably thinner than the typical American man's. And although it is now true that when men and women hold the same jobs, they tend to be paid the same wage, women still have less chance of reaching the highest earnings levels. What's more, even though more women*

*are entering occupations traditionally held by men, once they get there, the positions start to decline in prestige and pay."*

What is nice about this selection is its simplicity. It very carefully lays out the relative position of women and men in the economic world. It focuses on the income differences between them, and emphasizes that although there have been gains in equity, there are also some disturbing trends. Hacker also investigates segregation in the workplace and emphasizes the many ways in which women are excluded from top jobs in society, and ultimately, get less money and power.

American women are still far from economic parity. In some spheres, progress has been made, and those gains will be documented here. There can be no denying that these advances are long overdue and far from sufficient. Yet the story is not wholly one of improvement. An unhappy fact of our times is that in some ways women are worse off than they were in the past.

Although the typical woman's wallet is fuller than ever before, it is still measurably thinner than the typical American man's. And although it is now true that when men and women hold the same jobs, they tend to be paid the same wage, women still have less chance of reaching the highest earnings levels. What's more, even though more women are entering occupations traditionally held by men, once they get there, the positions start to decline in prestige and pay.

But the world of work offers only a partial view of the economic disparities between the sexes. So it makes sense to look at the population as a whole. In 1995, the median income for the 92.1 million adult men was $22,562, while the midpoint for the 96.0 million women was $12,130. This means women receive $538 for every $1,000 going to men. This is not an auspicious ratio. Indeed, it could be construed as society's verdict that women's needs and contributions amount to half of those of men. But even that figure can be viewed as evidence of progress: As recently as 1975, American women received a paltry $382 for each $1,000 received by men.

However, this aggregate comparison has limited meaning because most men hold full-time jobs,

whereas the majority of women have no earnings from employment or work only part-time. Indeed, almost 10 million women told the Census Bureau in 1995 that they had no incomes at all, or at least none that came to them in their own names. Most of these women are nonworking wives, ranging from blue-collar homemakers to the spouses of top executives. Their lack of a personal income pulls down the gender ratio. And when we examine marriages where both partners work, the typical wife emerges earning only $418 for each $1,000 made by her husband. (Few wives have investments of their own that yield them comfortable independent incomes.)

So marriage is the chief cause of the income gap and will remain so as long as it relegates more women than men to tending to the home and caring for the children. In fact, over 40 percent of at-home wives either have no children or all of their youngsters are grown...most of these women never developed careers, and few have shown much interest in entering the work force. There are still husbands who declare that they do not want their wives to work, and not all are affluent executives who want their mates available to pack their suitcases and entertain business clients. In the households where only the husband brings home a paycheck, his earnings are often quite modest. Over a third of these breadwinners make less than $30,000 a year. Thus many families still rank what they see as domestic values ahead of whatever material benefits additional earnings would produce....

...Although the fact that more women are working has increased their income relative to men, the fact that more are on their own has had a countervailing effect. Today, over one-fifth of all families are headed by single women. And in more than a third of these households, the mother has never been married. Some of the single women heading families receive public assistance, which is intended to keep them alive but below the poverty line. And although over half find work, their median income is only $17,170, and fewer than a third have incomes that exceed $25,000 a year.

## PROGRESS TOWARD PARITY?

Interestingly enough, the first signs of progress toward economic parity between men and women came during the still-traditional 1950s. This was supposed to be a period when women eschewed paid employment and instead opted for early marriage and a procession of children. Yet as Table 34.1 shows, the pay ratio of women who were working rose by 25 percent, from $486 to $607, the largest increase of any postwar decade. Several reasons for this stand out. To start, women were abandoning what had been one of their principal occupations, and an ill-paid one at that: domestic service. Back in 1940, 2.4 million women cleaned and cooked and cared for children in other people's homes; by 1970, only half that number were so employed. It appears that the women who chose to work were expecting more from their jobs, including better pay. Even if many women were still secretaries, the corporate world was remaking its own image. The sassy gum chewers of Hollywood such as Joan Blondell would not fit in with the new carpeted corridors. At this time, also, two other major occupations for women began to pay more, for the classic economic reasons. Nurses and school-teachers were in short supply because so many women were staying at home. In the suburbs, the future-oriented middle class was willing

to pay for quality education and health care. Starting in the world of "women's" work, a ripple effect caused women's expectations to rise even in the domesticated Eisenhower era.

But progress came to a halt. The pay ratio reached by 1960 remained essentially the same in 1970 and 1980. Hence, the slogan *59 Cents!* that was emblazoned on protest placards in the early days of the women's movement, often accompanied by a popular ballad of the time: "Fifty-nine cents for every man's dollar; fifty-nine cents, it's a low-down deal!" These laments were not unavailing; during the 1980s the ratio rose from $602 to $716. One stimulus was that lawyers and judges began applying the hitherto somnolent Equal Pay Act of 1963, which said that at jobs that called for "equal skill, effort, and responsibility," there could be no gap in "wages to employees of the opposite sex." Also significant was that fewer women were becoming secretaries and nurses or teachers, just as an earlier generation had abandoned domestic service. If we total up these traditionally "female" occupations, in 1970 they had absorbed 28 percent of all employed women, but by 1995, only 18 percent. Indeed, in 1995, the work force had 700,000 fewer secretaries than in 1980. An obvious reason is the advent of word-processing equipment, which facilitates copying and correcting. Also, in many organizations, the position has been retitled "assistant." And, as a further sign of our times, just as women were less willing to do routine typing, men were adapting to the keyboard because it was the only way to communicate with a computer. And in a reverse twist, the number of household workers began to rise in the 1980s, reflecting a demand for nannies in two-career families.

Statistics also indicate that women have been investing their time and effort in ways that augment their economic value. Postponing marriage and children is one route to a higher income; additional education is another. In 1994, the most recent figures at this writing, women accounted for well over half — 54 percent — of those awarded bachelor's degrees, compared to 43 percent in 1970 and 35 percent in 1960. Even more graphic has been their entry into professional programs. As Table 34.2 shows, in 1964 they were barely visible in engineering, dentistry, and business administration, and received well under 10 percent of degrees awarded in architecture, law, and medicine. Today, apart from engineering, women have

TABLE 34.1.    Cause for Applause?

| Year | Percent Working | Pay Ratio to Men |
|------|-----------------|------------------|
| 1950 | 31.4% | $486 |
| 1960 | 34.8% | $607 |
| 1970 | 42.6% | $594 |
| 1980 | 51.5% | $602 |
| 1990 | 57.5% | $716 |
| 1995 | 58.7% | $714 |

TABLE 34.2.   Proportion of Degrees Awarded to
Women

| Professional Programs | 1964 | 1994 |
|---|---|---|
| Architecture | 4.0% | 36.6% |
| Engineering | 0.4% | 16.4% |
| Business (MBA level) | 2.7% | 36.5% |
| Dentistry | 0.7% | 38.5% |
| Medicine | 6.5% | 37.9% |
| Law | 3.1% | 43.0% |
| Pharmacy | 13.9% | 66.8% |
| Academic doctorates | 10.6% | 44.1%* |

* American citizens only.

TABLE 34.3.   Women's Earnings (per $1,000
Received by Men)

| Occupation | 1983 | 1995 |
|---|---|---|
| *More Than 10 Percent Improvement* | | |
| Chefs and cooks | $711 | $885 |
| Realtors | $683 | $794 |
| Production inspectors | $563 | $649 |
| Waiters and waitresses | $721 | $822 |
| Public administrators | $701 | $786 |
| Computer analysts | $773 | $860 |
| *Less Than 10 Percent Improvement* | | |
| Journalists | $782 | $855 |
| Retail sales | $636 | $693 |
| Insurance adjusters | $651 | $691 |
| Financial managers | $638 | $674 |
| Education administrators | $671 | $708 |
| Janitors and cleaners | $810 | $844 |
| Engineers | $828 | $862 |
| Accountants | $706 | $734 |
| College faculty | $773 | $781 |
| *Deterioration* | | |
| High school teachers | $886 | $881 |
| Health technicians | $839 | $813 |
| Electronic assemblers | $857 | $808 |
| Lawyers | $890 | $818 |
| Physicians | $816 | $649 |

made substantial strides in most professional programs. In the 1995 entering classes at Yale, Stanford, and Johns Hopkins medical schools, they
outnumbered men.

But an increased presence in many occupations
and professions does not necessarily lead to greater
equity in earnings for women. Table 34.3 presents
a mixed picture. The Bureau of Labor Statistics
only began releasing pay differentials in 1983, but
that at least allows comparisons across a twelve-
year period. Although some occupations have witnessed modest progress, in none have women's
earnings breached the 90 percent mark, and in
many they are still below 70 percent. Even more
disturbing is the finding that, in some fields,
women's remuneration has actually dropped relative to men's. Among salaried lawyers and physicians and high-school teachers, women comprise
a large share of those recently entering those professions, which may account for their lower wages.
But among health technicians and electronic as-
semblers, the proportion of women has actually
been dropping, which means another explanation
is needed....

## SEXUAL SEGREGATION

By most measures, the last quarter century has
seen steady moves by women into positions traditionally reserved for men. As Table 34.4 shows, the
advances have been real in fields as varied as medicine and meat cutting and bartending. But in
some cases, progress may be less than it first appears. In 1970, insurance adjusters were mainly

men, and in their well-paid work they examined
burnt-out buildings and wrecked cars. Today, insurance adjusters are mainly women, who sit at
computer terminals entering insurance claims.
Many are part-time employees, with few or no benefits. And some...even do their jobs from their
homes. Or, to cite another example, in 1970, the
typical typesetter was a well-paid union worker
who set hot lead for a newspaper in a printing
plant. Today, type is generally keyed in electronically by women who are paid a fraction of what
their male forerunners received. Many of the new
women pharmacists count out pills for mail-order
services and never see a customer. Few of the incoming female physicians will have practices of
their own, but will be employed — or subject to
scrutiny — by health-maintenance organizations.

Indeed, it has been argued that occupations
start to admit women just when a field is beginning to decline in prestige and economic standing. That happened many years ago, when men
ceased being bank tellers. Sometimes, as with type-

TABLE 34.4.    Women's Shares Within Occupations

|  | 1970 | 1995 |
| --- | --- | --- |
| Total workforce | 38.0% | 46.1% |
| *Considerable Change* | | |
| Insurance adjustors | 29.6% | 73.9% |
| Typesetters | 16.8% | 67.3% |
| Educational administrators | 27.8% | 58.7% |
| Publicists | 26.6% | 57.9% |
| Bartenders | 21.0% | 53.5% |
| Government administrators | 21.7% | 49.8% |
| College faculty | 29.1% | 45.2% |
| Insurance agents | 12.9% | 37.1% |
| Pharmacists | 12.1% | 36.2% |
| Photographers | 14.8% | 27.1% |
| Lawyers | 4.9% | 26.4% |
| Physicians | 9.7% | 24.4% |
| Butchers and meatcutters | 11.4% | 21.6% |
| Architects | 4.0% | 19.8% |
| Telephone installers | 2.8% | 16.0% |
| Dentists | 3.5% | 13.4% |
| Police officers | 3.7% | 12.9% |
| Clergy | 2.9% | 11.1% |
| Engineers | 1.7% | 8.4% |
| Sheet-metalworkers | 1.9% | 7.5% |
| *Modest Change* | | |
| Hotel receptionists | 51.4% | 75.2% |
| Social workers | 63.3% | 67.9% |
| High-school teachers | 49.6% | 57.0% |
| Journalists | 41.6% | 53.2% |
| Realtors | 31.2% | 50.7% |
| Computer programmers | 24.2% | 29.5% |
| *Essentially No Change* | | |
| Dental hygienists | 94.0% | 99.4% |
| Secretaries | 97.8% | 98.5% |
| Registered nurses | 97.3% | 93.1% |
| Elementary-school teachers | 83.9% | 84.1% |
| Librarians | 82.1% | 83.2%. |
| *Men Replacing Women* | | |
| Telephone operators | 94.0% | 88.4% |
| Data entry keyers | 93.7% | 82.9% |
| Waiters and waitresses | 90.8% | 77.7% |
| Cooks and chefs | 67.2% | 44.5% |

leges, after years of being overstaffed in their top ranks, are tending to replace more of their retiring faculty members with discardable adjuncts. What may be added, although it hardly provides solace, is that young men who are also entering these and other professions will encounter the same barriers and rebuffs.

A smaller but still discernible pattern of change within the workforce has been the decision by some men to enter fields traditionally associated with women. The development began with flight attendants and then extended to nursing. By and large, these tend to be younger men who feel comfortable working with women. One has only to observe a plane's cabin crew to appreciate the symbiosis. And we are now accustomed to a male voice answering our requests for telephone numbers. The country has more restaurants with stylish pretensions than ever before, and one validation of that status is to have male waiters. Of course, many of these men view what they are doing as temporary or transitional. They may be deferring career decisions or waiting for openings in their chosen fields. Indeed, much of our service economy is predicated on the inclination of young people to remain single, to manage on modest pay, and to live and share expenses with other persons of their age.

Does the arrival of women really spell economic decline for an occupation or a profession? The task is to find whether gender is the operative factor or whether other forces are at work. Between 1970 and 1995, for example, women rose from being 4.9 percent of the country's lawyers to an impressive 26.4 percent. Yet what also happened was that the head count of lawyers more than tripled, rising from 288,000 to 894,000. So a growing glut of lawyers was the principal reason for the overall decline in pay for that profession. Moreover, of some 600,000 new lawyers, only about a third were women; so they should not be blamed for a falling wage scale.

Still, because so many of them are newcomers, relatively more women will be in an occupation's lower levels. In fact, earnings for younger people of both genders have become quite comparable. Among full-time workers under the age of twenty-five, women make $950 for every $1,000 paid to men. This approach to parity is even more revealing because she is still more likely to be starting out as a teacher while he is more apt to be a

setting, new technologies reconfigure the job. Moreover, women entering law and university teaching are finding that the ground rules have been changed. Until recently, most law partners and college professors enjoyed lifetime tenure. But now fewer attorneys can expect to become partners; and those who do can now be dismissed. Col-

better-paid engineer. And if they are both beginning engineers, today their pay will usually be identical. In fact, the *National Law Journal* found that among law school students graduating in 1994, for men the median starting salary was $48,000, while the typical woman graduate began at $50,000.

It is certainly true that more women take part-time jobs, frequently because they must be — or want to be — available for family obligations. Yet it is hard to find figures to support the presumption that women give less of themselves. We do have a few measures that fill in parts of the story. For example, it might be assumed that women will choose jobs that are closer to their homes so that they can attend to domestic duties or because they are less disposed to look farther afield for a better job. As it happens, the Census can provide an answer because it collates the "travel time to work" for all employed Americans. Its most recent published study showed that the one-way journey for men averaged 23.7 minutes, while the jobs that women chose called for a 20.3 minute trip. A difference of 3.4 minutes does not suggest that women are markedly less adventuresome.

One way to hold home-life factors constant is to confine the comparison to workers who have never been married. Of course, most of these workers are younger people. It is still assumed that some single women are marking time at their jobs and have no aspirations for lifetime careers. Yet we all know older women who never married, and almost all of them have made their jobs a major part of their lives. Indeed...the Census analysis of "never married" workers on full-time schedules found that women ended up earning $1,005 for every $1,000 made by men. So when it comes to dedication, the women are actually ahead. Moreover, current demographic data suggests that in the years ahead, more women will be foregoing marriage, which will expand the pool of women who will be able to compete with men on an equal footing.

Ascending an occupation's ladder generally requires years of experience, either within a single organization or in the field as a whole. No one will be surprised to learn that women as a group do not have as many years on their resumes. Lester Thurow stressed this point several years ago when he said that ages twenty-five to thirty-five are the takeoff years for careers, when one gets seasoned on the job and noticed for promotion. "But the decade between twenty-five and thirty-five," he said, "is precisely the decade when women are most apt to leave the labor force or become part-time workers." Thurow is about half right. In the time period he says is crucial, 73 percent of the men are fully employed, compared with only 51 percent of the women. But there is another way to look at work experience. By focusing on age distributions within the workforce, we find that women who are twenty-five to thirty-five account for 29 percent of all fully employed women, which turns out to be exactly the proportion for men in the same age range. As Thurow says, some men may be slated for success in this "takeoff" decade. The question is why so many fewer women are put on the promotion lists.

## EQUAL PAY FOR EQUAL WORK?

Of course, two people doing the same job should receive the same wage. But it isn't always easy to agree on whether identical work is being done. Nor is it easy to find statistics that assess the relative competence of men and women workers. But one way to start might be by limiting ourselves to all full-time workers who are in their early thirties, from thirty to thirty-four, a group that currently contains about 8 million men and 5 million women. The women in this cohort deserve to be taken seriously. Fully 20 percent have not yet been married, in most cases by their own decision, which suggests they have other aspirations. Another 17 percent are divorced or separated or widowed, which in most cases means they must now support themselves. And the remaining 63 percent who are married are combining full-time employment with domestic obligations. Also, at this age, about the same proportions of women and men have completed college, so the two genders look quite similar in their commitment to careers and their investments in education.

Of course, Table 34.5 cannot tell us whether the men and women are performing "equal" tasks. What we do see is that the women's median earnings stand at $825 per $1,000 for the men, a rela-

TABLE 34.5.  *Earnings of Full-Time Workers, Age 30 to 34*

| 7,905,000 Men | | 5,013,000 Women |
|---|---|---|
| 15.7% | Over $50,000 | 6.7% |
| 20.1% | $35,000 to $50,000 | 14.6% |
| 39.4% | $20,000 to $35,000 | 41.4% |
| 24.8% | Under $20,000 | 37.3% |
| $28,449 | Median Earnings | $23,479 |
| ($1,000) | (Ratio) | ($825) |

tively high ratio as current comparisons go, but still far from parity. This age group is important because it contains what should be the most promising echelon of women. Yet they are not even half as likely to have $50,000 jobs, and they are a third less apt to be in the $35,000 to $50,000 tier. In contrast, men are a third less likely to be found in the bottom bracket. The bottom line is that employers have shown much less inclination to promote accomplished women to $50,000 positions, while they seem to feel that as few men as possible should be made to take jobs paying less than $20,000. Another factor is that, thus far, women have been more likely than men to choose lower-paying professions: for example, in museums and galleries (average earnings: $18,928) or book publishing ($35,204), rather than, say, petroleum refining ($57,616) or as security and commodity brokers ($81,796).

A double standard for incomes persists not only on earth, but in the galaxies of stars. Over the years, the top moneymakers in the music industry have been all-male groups such as the Beatles, the Rolling Stones, the Eagles, Pink Floyd, and the Grateful Dead. Individual performers such as Michael Jackson, Garth Brooks, Billy Joel, and Elton John have made measurably more than the top female performers. Among authors, Stephen King, John Grisham, Tom Clancy, and Michael Crichton command larger advances than do such blockbusting novelists as Judith Krantz, Jackie Collins, and Patricia Cornwell. The men's books are then made into big-budget movies, while the women must settle for seeing theirs prepared as four-part specials for the small screen.

There is no shortage of theories to explain why this is the case. One certainly is that men have always put their stamp on art and entertainment, at the same time making sure that enough of what they produce will appeal to women. Many more women bought novels by Anthony Trollope and Charles Dickens compared with the number of men attracted to Jane Austen and the Brontés. True, women have contributed their movie dollars and television watching to Barbra Streisand and Roseanne and Oprah Winfrey. Yet, although these performers have become extremely rich, they still comprise a relatively short list. Of course, plays and movies and television series all have women stars, and most men do like seeing female faces and figures. But not always for their acting abilities. Indeed, men tend to shy away from entertainment in which women have too dominant a role. Recall how every episode of Mary Tyler Moore's long-running program had her surrounded by men with strongly written scripts. And with Roseanne, one suspects that insofar as men were watching her show, it was mainly because the women in their lives insisted having the program on.

It was not always this way. Table 34.6 shows two sets of rankings: on the left, Hollywood's best-paid stars in 1934, and on the right, the biggest moneymakers sixty years later in 1994. Most apparent, of course, is that a majority of the 1934 group were women.

It is interesting to ponder why female movie stars were popular and highly paid in the 1930s. There may be lessons worth resurrecting from that distant era of Janet Gaynor and Norma Shearer.

TABLE 34.6.  *The Top Ten: Hollywood's Best-Paid Stars Then and Now*

| 1934 | | 1994 |
|---|---|---|
| Will Rogers | #1 | Harrison Ford |
| Clark Gable | #2 | Sylvester Stallone |
| Janet Gaynor | #3 | Bruce Willis |
| Wallace Beery | #4 | Tom Hanks |
| Mae West | #5 | Kevin Costner |
| Joan Crawford | #6 | Clint Eastwood |
| Bing Crosby | #7 | Arnold Schwarzenegger |
| Shirley Temple | #8 | Michael Douglas |
| Marie Dressier | #9 | Jim Carrey |
| Norma Shearer | #10 | Robin Williams |

# 35. FRATERNITIES AND RAPE ON CAMPUS

PATRICIA YANCEY MARTIN AND ROBERT A. HUMMER

*"Our examination of men's social fraternities on college and university campuses as groups and organizations led us to conclude that fraternities are a physical and socio-cultural context that encourages the sexual coercion of women. We make no claims that all fraternities are 'bad' or that all fraternity men are rapists. Our observations indicated, however, that rape is especially probable in fraternities because of the kinds of organizations they are, the kinds of members they have, the practices their members engage in, and a virtual absence of university or community oversight."*

This article is about fraternities. Its aim is to show how the culture of the fraternity encourages values, ideas, and activities that lead to the sexual exploitation of women and even rape. Martin and Hummer began their investigation with a case of gang rape at Florida State University. They examined newspaper articles, interviewed students, administrators, alumni advisers to Greek organizations, judges, attorneys, rape-victim advocates, and state prosecutors. The research was supplemented by reports from other authors and agencies. Individuals embedded in fraternity life are influenced by a view of women that causes actions that would probably not occur outside that organization. The social patterns themselves encourage rape—"the fraternity as a group and organization is at issue."

Rapes are perpetrated on dates, at parties, in chance encounters, and in specially planned circumstances. That group structure and processes, rather than individual values or characteristics, are the impetus for many rape episodes was documented by Blanchard (1959) 30 years ago (also see Geis 1971), yet sociologists have failed to pursue this theme (for an exception, see Chancer 1987). A recent review of research (Muehlenhard and Linton 1987) on sexual violence, or rape, devotes only a few pages to the situational contexts of rape events, and these are conceptualized as potential risk factors for individuals rather than qualities of rape-prone social contexts.

Many rapes, far more than come to the public's attention, occur in fraternity houses on college and university campuses, yet little research has analyzed fraternities at American colleges and universities as rape-prone contexts (cf. Ehrhart and Sandler 1985). Most of the research on fraternities reports on samples of individual fraternity men. One group of studies compares the values, attitudes, perceptions, family socioeconomic status, psychological traits (aggressiveness, dependence), and so on, of fraternity and nonfraternity men (Bohrnstedt 1969; Fox, Hodge, and Ward 1987; Kanin 1967; Lemire 1979; Miller 1973). A second group attempts to identify the effects of fraternity membership over time on the values, attitudes, beliefs, or moral precepts of members (Hughes and Winston 1987; Marlowe and Auvenshine 1982; Miller 1973; Wilder, Hoyt, Doren, Hauck, and Zettle 1978; Wilder, Hoyt, Surbeck, Wilder, and

Carney 1986). With minor exceptions, little research addresses the group and organizational context of fraternities or the social construction of fraternity life (for exceptions, see Letchworth 1969; Longino and Kart 1973; Smith 1964).

Gary Tash, writing as an alumnus and trial attorney in his fraternity's magazine, claims that over 90 percent of all gang rapes on college campuses involve fraternity men (1988, p. 2). Tash provides no evidence to substantiate this claim, but students of violence against women have been concerned with fraternity men's frequently reported involvement in rape episodes (Adams and Abarbanel 1988). Ehrhart and Sandler (1985) identify over 50 cases of gang rapes on campus perpetrated by fraternity men, and their analysis points to many of the conditions that we discuss here. Their analysis is unique in focusing on conditions in fraternities that make gang rapes of women by fraternity men both feasible and probable. They identify excessive alcohol use, isolation from external monitoring, treatment of women as prey, use of pornography, approval of violence, and excessive concern with competition as precipitating conditions to gang rape (also see Merton 1985; Roark 1987).

The study reported here confirmed and complemented these findings by focusing on both conditions and processes. We examined dynamics associated with the social construction of fraternity life, with a focus on processes that foster the use of coercion, including rape, in fraternity men's relations with women. Our examination of men's social fraternities on college and university campuses as groups and organizations led us to conclude that fraternities are a physical and socio-cultural context that encourages the sexual coercion of women. We make no claims that all fraternities are "bad" or that all fraternity men are rapists. Our observations indicated, however, that rape is especially probable in fraternities because of the kinds of organizations they are, the kinds of members they have, the practices their members engage in, and a virtual absence of university or community oversight. Analyses that lay blame for rapes by fraternity men on "peer pressure" are, we feel, overly simplistic (cf. Burkhart 1989; Walsh 1989). We suggest, rather, that fraternities create a socio-cultural context in which the use of coercion in sexual relations with women is normative

and in which the mechanisms to keep this pattern of behavior in check are minimal at best and absent at worst. We conclude that unless fraternities change in fundamental ways, little improvement can be expected.

## METHODOLOGY

Our goal was to analyze the group and organizational practices and conditions that create in fraternities an abusive social context for women. We developed a conceptual framework from an initial case study of an alleged gang rape at Florida State University that involved four fraternity men and an 18–year-old coed. The group rape took place on the third floor of a fraternity house and ended with the "dumping" of the woman in the hallway of a neighboring fraternity house. According to newspaper accounts, the victim's blood-alcohol concentration, when she was discovered, was .349 percent, more than three times the legal limit for automobile driving and an almost lethal amount. One law enforcement officer reported that sexual intercourse occurred during the time the victim was unconscious: "She was in a life-threatening situation" (*Tallahassee Democrat*, 1988b). When the victim was found, she was comatose and had suffered multiple scratches and abrasions. Crude words and a fraternity symbol had been written on her thighs (*Tampa Tribune*, 1988). When law enforcement officials tried to investigate the case, fraternity members refused to cooperate. This led, eventually, to a five-year ban of the fraternity from campus by the university and by the fraternity's national organization.

In trying to understand how such an event could have occurred, and how a group of over 150 members (exact figures are unknown because the fraternity refused to provide a membership roster) could hold rank, deny knowledge of the event, and allegedly lie to a grand jury, we analyzed newspaper articles about the case and conducted open-ended interviews with a variety of respondents about the case and about fraternities, rapes, alcohol use, gender relations, and sexual activities on campus. Our data included over 100 newspaper articles on the initial gang rape case; open-ended interviews with Greek (social fraternity and sorority) and non-Greek (independent) students (N =

20); university administrators (N = 8, five men, three women); and alumni advisers to Greek organizations (N = 6). Open-ended interviews were held also with judges, public and private defense attorneys, victim advocates, and state prosecutors regarding the processing of sexual assault cases. Data were analyzed using the grounded theory method (Glaser 1978; Martin and Turner 1986). In the following analysis, concepts generated from the data analysis are integrated with the literature on men's social fraternities, sexual coercion, and related issues.

## FRATERNITIES AND THE SOCIAL CONSTRUCTION OF MEN AND MASCULINITY

Our research indicated that fraternities are vitally concerned—more than with anything else—with masculinity (cf. Kanin 1967). They work hard to create a macho image and context and try to avoid any suggestion of "wimpishness," effeminacy, and homosexuality. Valued members display, or are willing to go along with, a narrow conception of masculinity that stresses competition, athleticism, dominance, winning, conflict, wealth, material possessions, willingness to drink alcohol, and sexual prowess vis-a-vis women.

### Valued Qualities of Members

When fraternity members talked about the kind of pledges they prefer, a litany of stereotypical and narrowly masculine attributes and behaviors was recited, and feminine or woman-associated qualities and behaviors were expressly denounced (cf. Merton 1985). Fraternities seek men who are "athletic," "big guys," good in intramural competition, "who can talk college sports." Males "who are willing to drink alcohol," "who drink socially," or "who can hold their liquor" are sought. Alcohol and activities associated with the recreational use of alcohol are cornerstones of fraternity social life. Nondrinkers are viewed with skepticism and rarely selected for membership.[1]

Fraternities try to avoid "geeks," nerds, and men said to give the fraternity a "wimpy" or "gay" reputation. Art, music, and humanities majors, majors in traditional women's fields (nursing, home

economics, social work, education), men with long hair, and those whose appearance or dress violate current norms are rejected. Clean-cut, handsome men who dress well (are clean, neat, conforming, fashionable) are preferred. One sorority woman commented that "the top-ranking fraternities have the best-looking guys."

One fraternity man, a senior, said his fraternity recruited "some big guys, very athletic" over a two-year period to help overcome its image of wimpiness. His fraternity had won the interfraternity competition for highest grade-point average several years running but was looked down on as "wimpy, dancy, even gay." With their bigger, more athletic recruits, "our reputation improved; we're a much more recognized fraternity now." Thus a fraternity's reputation and status depends on members' possession of stereotypically masculine qualities. Good grades, campus leadership, and community service are "nice" but masculinity dominance—for example, in athletic events, physical size of members, athleticism of members—counts most.

Certain social skills are valued. Men are sought who "have good personalities," are friendly, and "have the ability to relate to girls" (cf. Longino and Kart 1973). One fraternity man, a junior, said: "We watch a guy [a potential pledge] talk to women.... [W]e want guys who can relate to girls." Assessing a pledge's ability to talk to women is, in part, a preoccupation with homosexuality and a conscious avoidance of men who seem to have effeminate manners or qualities. If a member is suspected of being gay, he is ostracized and informally drummed out of the fraternity. A fraternity with a reputation as wimpy or tolerant of gays is ridiculed and shunned by other fraternities. Militant heterosexuality is frequently used by men as a strategy to keep each other in line (Kimmel 1987).

Financial affluence or wealth, a male-associated value in American culture, is highly valued by fraternities. In accounting for why the fraternity involved in the gang rape that precipitated our research project had been recognized recently as "the best fraternity chapter in the United States," a university official said: "They were good-looking, a big fraternity, had lots of BMWs [expensive, German-made automobiles]." After the rape, newspaper stories described the fraternity members' affluence, noting the high number of members who owned expensive cars (*St. Petersburg Times*, 1988).

## The Status and Norms of Pledgeship

A *pledge* (sometimes called an *associate member*) is a new recruit who occupies a trial membership status for a specific period of time. The pledge period (typically ranging from 10 to 15 weeks) gives fraternity brothers an opportunity to assess and socialize new recruits. Pledges evaluate the fraternity also and decide whether they want to become brothers. The socialization experience is structured partly through assignment of a Big Brother to each pledge. Big Brothers are expected to teach pledges how to become a brother and to support them as they progress through the trial membership period. Some pledges are repelled by the pledging experience, which can entail physical abuse; harsh discipline; and demands to be subordinate, follow orders, and engage in demeaning routines and activities, similar to those used by the military to "make men out of boys" during boot camp.

Characteristics of the pledge experience are rationalized by fraternity members as necessary to help pledges unite into a group, rely on each other, and join together against outsiders. The process is highly masculinist in execution as well as conception. A willingness to submit to authority, follow orders, and do as one is told is viewed as a sign of loyalty, togetherness, and unity. Fraternity pledges who find the pledge process offensive often drop out. Some do this by openly quitting, which can subject them to ridicule by brothers and other pledges, or they may deliberately fail to make the grades necessary for initiation or transfer schools and decline to reaffiliate with the fraternity on the new campus. One fraternity pledge who quit the fraternity he had pledged described an experience during pledgeship as follows:

This one guy was always picking on me. No matter what I did, I was wrong. One night after dinner, he and two other guys called me and two other pledges into the chapter room. He said, "Here, X, hold this 25 pound bag of ice at arms' length 'til I tell you to stop." I did it even though my arms and hands were killing me. When I asked if I could stop, he grabbed me around the throat and lifted me off the floor. I thought he would choke me to death. He cussed me and called me all kinds of names. He took one of my fingers and twisted it until it nearly broke.... I stayed in the fraternity for a few more days, but then I decided to quit. I hated it. Those guys are sick. They like seeing you suffer.

Fraternities' emphasis on toughness, withstanding pain and humiliation, obedience to superiors, and using physical force to obtain compliance contributes to an interpersonal style that de-emphasizes caring and sensitivity but fosters intragroup trust and loyalty. If the least macho or most critical pledges drop out, those who remain may be more receptive to, and influenced by, masculinist values and practices that encourage the use of force in sexual relations with women and the covering up of such behavior (cf. Kanin 1967).

## Norms and Dynamics of Brotherhood

*Brother* is the status occupied by fraternity men to indicate their relations to each other and their membership in a particular fraternity organization or group. Brother is a male-specific status; only males can become brothers, although women can become "Little Sisters," a form of pseudomembership. "Becoming a brother" is a rite of passage that follows the consistent and often lengthy display by pledges of appropriately masculine qualities and behaviors. Brothers have a quasi-familial relationship with each other, are normatively said to share bonds of closeness and support, and are sharply set off from nonmembers. *Brotherhood* is a loosely defined term used to represent the bonds that develop among fraternity members and the obligations and expectations incumbent on them (cf. Marlowe and Auvenshine [1982] on fraternities' failure to encourage "moral development" in freshman pledges).

Some of our respondents talked about brotherhood in almost reverential terms, viewing it as the most valuable benefit of fraternity membership. One senior, a business-school major who had been affiliated with a fairly high-status fraternity throughout four years on campus, said:

Brotherhood spurs friendship for life, which I consider its best aspect, although I didn't see it that way when I joined. Brotherhood bonds and unites. It instills values of caring about one another, caring about community, caring about ourselves. The values and bonds [or broth-erhood] continually develop over the four years [in college] while normal friendships come and go.

Despite this idealization, most aspects of fraternity practice and conception are more mundane. Brotherhood often plays itself out as an overriding concern with masculinity and, by extension, femininity. As a consequence, fraternities comprise collectivities of highly masculinized men with attitudinal qualities and behavioral norms that predispose them to sexual coercion of women (cf. Kanin 1967; Merton 1985; Rapaport and Burkhart 1984). The norms of masculinity are complemented by conceptions of women and femininity that are equally distorted and stereotyped and that may enhance the probability of women's exploitation (cf. Ehrhart and Sandler 1985; Sanday 1981, 1986).

## Practices of Brotherhood

Practices associated with fraternity brotherhood that contribute to the sexual coercion of women include a preoccupation with loyalty, group protection and secrecy, use of alcohol as a weapon, involvement in violence and physical force, and an emphasis on competition and superiority.

*Loyalty, Group Protection, and Secrecy*   Loyalty is a fraternity preoccupation. Members are reminded constantly to be loyal to the fraternity and to their brothers. Among other ways, loyalty is played out in the practices of group protection and secrecy. The fraternity must be shielded from criticism. Members are admonished to avoid getting the fraternity in trouble and to bring all problems "to the chapter" (the local branch of a national social fraternity) rather than to outsiders. Fraternities try to protect themselves from close scrutiny and criticism by the Interfraternity Council (a quasi-governing body composed of representatives from all social fraternities on campus), their fraternity's national office, university officials, law enforcement, the media, and the public. Protection of the fraternity often takes precedence over what is procedurally, ethically, or legally correct. Numerous examples were related to us of fraternity brothers' lying to outsiders to "protect the fraternity."

Group protection was observed in the alleged gang rape case with which we began our study. Except for one brother, a rapist who turned state's evidence, the entire remaining fraternity membership was accused by university and criminal justice officials of lying to protect the fraternity. Members consistently failed to cooperate even though the alleged crimes were felonies, involved only four men (two of whom were not even members of the local chapter), and the victim of the crime nearly died. According to a grand jury's findings, fraternity officers repeatedly broke appointments with law enforcement officials, refused to provide police with a list of members, and refused to cooperate with police and prosecutors investigating the case (*Florida Flambeau*, 1988).

Secrecy is a priority value and practice in fraternities, partly because full-fledged membership is premised on it (for confirmation, see Ehrhart and Sandler 1985; Longino and Kart 1973; Roark 1987). Secrecy is also a boundary-maintaining mechanism, demarcating in-group from out-group, us from them. Secret rituals, handshakes, and mottoes are revealed to pledge brothers as they are initiated into full brotherhood. Because only brothers are supposed to know a fraternity's secrets, such knowledge affirms membership in the fraternity and separates a brother from others. Extending secrecy tactics from protection of private knowledge to protection of the fraternity from criticism is a predictable development. Our interviews indicated that individual members knew the difference between right and wrong, but fraternity norms that emphasize loyalty, group protection, and secrecy often overrode standards of ethical correctness.

*Alcohol as Weapon*   Alcohol use by fraternity men is normative. They use it on weekdays to relax after class and on weekends to "get drunk," "get crazy," and "get laid." The use of alcohol to obtain sex from women is pervasive — in other words, it is used as a weapon against sexual reluctance. According to several fraternity men whom we interviewed, alcohol is the major tool used to gain sexual mastery over women (cf. Adams and Abarbanel 1988; Ehrhart and Sandler 1985). One fraternity man, a 21-year-old senior, described alcohol use to gain sex as follows: "There are girls that you know will fuck, then some you have to put some effort into it…. You have to buy them drinks or find out if she's drunk enough…."

A similar strategy is used collectively. A fraternity man said that at parties with Little Sisters: "We provide them with 'hunch punch' and things get wild. We get them drunk and most of the guys end up with one." "'Hunch punch,'" he said, "is a girls' drink made up of overproof alcohol and powdered Kool-Aid, no water or anything, just ice. It's very strong. Two cups will do a number on a female." He had plans in the next academic term to surreptitiously give hunch punch to women in a "prim and proper" sorority because "having sex with prim and proper sorority girls is definitely a goal." These women are a challenge because they "won't openly consume alcohol and won't get openly drunk as hell." Their sororities have "standards committees" that forbid heavy drinking and easy sex.

In the gang rape case, our sources said that many fraternity men on campus believed the victim had a drinking problem and was thus an "easy make." According to newspaper accounts, she had been drinking alcohol on the evening she was raped; the lead assailant is alleged to have given her a bottle of wine after she arrived at his fraternity house. Portions of the rape occurred in a shower, and the victim was reportedly so drunk that her assailants had difficulty holding her in a standing position (*Tallahassee Democrat*, 1988a). While raping her, her assailants repeatedly told her they were members of another fraternity under the apparent belief that she was too drunk to know the difference. Of course, if she was too drunk to know who they were, she was too drunk to consent to sex (cf. Allgeier 1986; Tash 1988).

One respondent told us that gang rapes are wrong and can get one expelled, but he seemed to see nothing wrong in sexual coercion one-on-one. He seemed unaware that the use of alcohol to obtain sex from a woman is grounds for a claim that a rape occurred (cf. Tash 1988). Few women on campus (who also may not know these grounds) report date rapes, however; so the odds of detection and punishment are slim for fraternity men who use alcohol for "seduction" purposes (cf. Byington and Keeter 1988; Merton 1985).

***Violence and Physical Force*** Fraternity men have a history of violence (Ehrhart and Sandler 1985; Roark 1987). Their record of hazing, fighting, property destruction, and rape has caused them problems with insurance companies (Bradford 1986; Pressley 1987). Two university officials told us that fraternities "are the third riskiest property to insure behind toxic waste dumps and amusement parks." Fraternities are increasingly defendants in legal actions brought by pledges subjected to hazing (Meyer 1986; Pressley 1987) and by women who were raped by one or more members. In a recent alleged gang rape incident at another Florida university, prosecutors failed to file charges but the victim filed a civil suit against the fraternity nevertheless (*Tallahassee Democrat*, 1989).

***Competition and Superiority*** Interfraternity rivalry fosters in-group identification and out-group hostility. Fraternities stress pride of membership and superiority over other fraternities as major goals. Interfraternity rivalries take many forms, including competition for desirable pledges, size of pledge class, size of membership, size and appearance of fraternity house, superiority in intramural sports, highest grade-point averages, giving the best parties, gaining the best or most campus leadership roles, and, of great importance, attracting and displaying "good looking women." Rivalry is particularly intense over members, intramural sports, and women (cf. Messner 1989).

## FRATERNITIES' COMMODIFICATION OF WOMEN

In claiming that women are treated by fraternities as commodities, we mean that fraternities knowingly, and intentionally, *use* women for their benefit. Fraternities use women as bait for new members, as servers of brothers' needs, and as sexual prey.

### Women as Bait

Fashionably attractive women help a fraternity attract new members. As one fraternity man, a junior, said, "They are good bait." Beautiful, sociable women are believed to impress the right kind of pledges and give the impression that the fraternity can deliver this type of woman to its members. Photographs of shapely, attractive coeds are printed in fraternity brochures and videotapes that are distributed and shown to potential pledges. The women pictured are often dressed in bikinis, at the beach, and are pictured hugging the brothers of the fraternity. One university official says such recruitment materials give the message: "Hey, they're here for you, you can have whatever you want," and, "we have the best looking women. Join us and you can have them too." Another commented: "Something's wrong when males join an all-male organization as the best place to meet women. It's so illogical."

Fraternities compete in promising access to beautiful women. One fraternity man, a senior, commented that "the attraction of girls [i.e., a fraternity's success in attracting women] is a big status symbol for fraternities." One university official commented that the use of women as a recruiting tool is so well entrenched that fraternities that might be willing to forgo it say they cannot afford to unless other fraternities do so as well. One fraternity man said, "Look, if we don't have Little Sisters, the fraternities that do will get all the good pledges." Another said, "We won't have as good a rush [the period during which new members are assessed and selected] if we don't have these women around."

In displaying good-looking, attractive, skimpily dressed, nubile women to potential members, fraternities implicitly, and sometimes explicitly, promise sexual access to women. One fraternity man commented that "part of what being in a fraternity is all about is the sex" and explained how his fraternity uses Little Sisters to recruit new members:

We'll tell the sweetheart [the fraternity's term for Little Sister], "You're gorgeous; you can get him." We'll tell her to fake a scam and she'll go hang all over him during a rush party, kiss him, and he thinks he's done wonderful and wants to join. The girls think it's great too. It's flattering for them.

## Women as Servers

The use of women as servers is exemplified in the Little Sister program. Little Sisters are undergraduate women who are rushed and selected in a manner parallel to the recruitment of fraternity men. They are affiliated with the fraternity in a formal but unofficial way and are able, indeed required, to wear the fraternity's Greek letters. Little Sisters are not full-fledged fraternity members, however; and fraternity national offices and most universities do not register or regulate them. Each fraternity has an officer called Little Sister chairman who oversees their organization and activities. The Little Sisters elect officers among themselves, pay monthly dues to the fraternity, and have well-defined roles. Their dues are used to pay for the fraternity's social events, and Little Sisters are expected to attend and hostess fraternity parties and hang around the house to make it a "nice place to be." One fraternity man, a senior, described Little Sisters this way: "They are very social girls, willing to join in, be affiliated with the group, devoted to the fraternity." Another member, a sophomore, said: "Their sole purpose is social — attend parties, attract new members, and 'take care' of the guys."

Our observations and interviews suggested that women selected by fraternities as Little Sisters are physically attractive, possess good social skills, and are willing to devote time and energy to the fraternity and its members. One undergraduate woman gave the following job description for Little Sisters to a campus newspaper:

It's not just making appearances at all the parties but entails many more responsibilities. You're going to be expected to go to all the intramural games to cheer the brothers on, support and encourage the pledges, and just be around to bring some extra life to the house. [As a Little Sister] you have to agree to take on a new responsibility other than studying to maintain your grades and managing to keep your checkbook from bouncing. You have to make time to be a part of the fraternity and support the brothers in all they do. (*The Tomahawk*, 1988)

The title of *Little Sister* reflects women's subordinate status; fraternity men in a parallel role are called *Big Brothers*. Big Brothers assist a sorority primarily with the physical work of sorority rushes, which, compared to fraternity rushes, are more formal, structured, and intensive. Sorority rushes take place in the daytime and fraternity rushes at night, so fraternity men are free to help. According to one fraternity member, Little Sister status is a benefit to women because it gives them a social outlet and "the protection of the brothers." The gender-stereotypic conceptions and obligations of these Little Sister and Big Brother statuses indicate that fraternities and sororities promote a gender hierarchy on campus that fosters subordination and dependence in women, thus encouraging sexual exploitation and the belief that it is acceptable.

## Women as Sexual Prey

Little Sisters are a sexual utility. Many Little Sisters do not belong to sororities and lack peer support for refraining from unwanted sexual relations. One fraternity man (whose fraternity has 65 members and 85 Little Sisters) told us they had recruited "wholesale" in the prior year to "get lots of new women." The structural access to women that the Little Sister program provides and the absence of normative supports for refusing fraternity members' sexual advances may make women in this program particularly susceptible to coerced sexual encounters with fraternity men.

Access to women for sexual gratification is a presumed benefit of fraternity membership, promised in recruitment materials and strategies and through brothers' conversations with new recruits. One fraternity man said: "We always tell the guys that you get sex all the time, there's always new girls.... After I became a Greek, I found out I could be with females at will." A university official told us that, based on his observations, "no one [i.e., fraternity men] on this campus wants to have 'relationships.' They just want to have fun [i.e., sex]." Fraternity men plan and execute strategies aimed at obtaining sexual gratification, and this occurs at both individual and collective levels.

Individual strategies include getting a woman drunk and spending a great deal of money on her. As for collective strategies, most of our undergraduate interviewees agreed that fraternity parties often culminate in sex and that this outcome is planned. One fraternity man said fraternity parties often involve sex and nudity and can "turn into orgies." Orgies may be planned in advance, such as the Bowery Ball party held by one fraternity. A former fraternity member said of this party:

The entire idea behind this is sex. Both men and women come to the party wearing little or nothing. There are pornographic pinups on the walls and usually porno movies playing on the TV. The music carries sexual overtones.... They just get schnockered [drunk] and, in most cases, they also get laid.

When asked about the women who come to such a party, he said: "Some Little Sisters just won't go.... The girls who do are looking for a good time, girls who don't know what it is, things like that."

Other respondents denied that fraternity parties are orgies but said that sex is always talked about among the brothers and they all know "who each other is doing it with." One member said that most of the time, guys have sex with their girlfriends "but with socials, girlfriends aren't allowed to come and it's their [members'] big chance [to have sex with other women]." The use of alcohol to help them get women into bed is a routine strategy at fraternity parties.

## CONCLUSIONS

In general, our research indicated that the organization and membership of fraternities contribute heavily to coercive and often violent sex. Fraternity houses are occupied by same-sex (all men) and same-age (late teens, early twenties) peers whose maturity and judgment is often less than ideal. Yet fraternity houses are private dwellings that are mostly off-limits to, and away from the scrutiny of, university and community representatives, with the result that fraternity house events seldom come to the attention of outsiders. Practices associated with the social construction of fraternity brotherhood emphasize a macho conception of men and masculinity, a narrow, stereotyped conception of women and femininity, and the treatment of women as commodities. Other practices contributing to coercive sexual relations and the cover-up of rapes include excessive alcohol use, competitiveness, and normative support for deviance and secrecy (cf. Bogal-Allbritten and Allbritten 1985; Kanin 1967).

Some fraternity practices exacerbate others. Brotherhood norms require "sticking together" regardless of right or wrong; thus rape episodes are unlikely to be stopped or reported to outsiders, even when witnesses disapprove. The ability to use alcohol without scrutiny by authorities and alcohol's frequent association with violence, including sexual coercion, facilitates rape in fraternity houses. Fraternity norms that emphasize the value of maleness and masculinity over femaleness and femininity and that elevate the status of men and lower the status of women in members' eyes undermine perceptions and treatment of women as persons who deserve consideration and care (cf. Ehrhart and Sandler 1985; Merton 1985).

Androgynous men and men with a broad range of interests and attributes are lost to fraternities through their recruitment practices. Masculinity of a narrow and stereotypical type helps create attitudes, norms, and practices that predispose fraternity men to coerce women sexually, both individually and collectively (Allgeier 1986; Hood 1989; Sanday 1981, 1986). Male athletes on campus may be similarly disposed for the same reasons (Kirshenbaum 1989; Telander and Sullivan 1989).

Research into the social contexts in which rape crimes occur and the social constructions associated with these contexts illumine rape dynamics on campus. Blanchard (1959) found that group rapes almost always have a leader who pushes others into the crime. He also found that the leader's latent homosexuality, desire to show off to his peers, or fear of failing to prove himself a man are frequently an impetus. Fraternity norms and practices contribute to the approval and use of sexual coercion as an accepted tactic in relations with women. Alcohol-induced compliance is normative, whereas, presumably, use of a knife, gun, or threat of bodily harm would not be because the woman who "drinks too much" is viewed as "causing her own rape" (cf. Ehrhart and Sandler 1985).

Our research led us to conclude that fraternity norms and practices influence members to view the sexual coercion of women, which is a felony crime, as sport, a contest, or a game (cf. Sato 1988). This sport is played not between men and women but between men and men. Women are the pawns or prey in the interfraternity rivalry game; they prove that a fraternity is successful or prestigious. The use of women in this way encourages fraternity men to see women as objects and sexual coercion as sport. Today's societal norms support young women's right to engage in sex at their discretion, and coercion is unnecessary in a mutually desired encounter. However, nubile young women say they prefer to be "in a relationship" to have sex, while young men say they prefer to "get laid" without a commitment (Muehlenhard and Linton 1987). These differences may reflect, in part, American puritanism

and men's fears of sexual intimacy or perhaps intimacy of any kind. In a fraternity context, getting sex without giving emotionally demonstrates "cool" masculinity. More important, it poses no threat to the bonding and loyalty of the fraternity brotherhood (cf. Farr 1988). Drinking large quantities of alcohol before having sex suggests that "scoring" rather than intrinsic sexual pleasure is a primary concern of fraternity men.

Unless fraternities' composition, goals, structures, and practices change in fundamental ways, women on campus will continue to be sexual prey for fraternity men. As do all male enclaves dedicated to opposing faculty and administration and to cementing group ties, fraternity members eschew any hint of homosexuality. Their version of masculinity transforms women, and men with womanly characteristics, into the out-group. "Womanly men" are ostracized; feminine women are used to demonstrate members' masculinity. Encouraging renewed emphasis on their founding values (Longino and Kart 1973), service orientation and activities (Lemire 1979), or members' moral development (Marlowe and Auvenshine 1982) will have little effect on fraternities' treatment of women. A case for or against fraternities cannot be made by studying individual members. The fraternity as a group and organization is at issue. Located on campus along with many vulnerable women, embedded in a sexist society, and caught up in masculinist goals, practices, and values, fraternities' violation of women — including forcible rape — should come as no surprise.

## ENDNOTES

1. Recent bans by some universities on open-keg parties at fraternity houses have resulted in heavy drinking before coming to a party and an increase in drunkenness among those who attend. This may aggravate, rather than improve, the treatment of women by fraternity men at parties.

## REFERENCES

Allgeier, Elizabeth. 1986. "Coercive Versus Consensual Sexual Interactions." G. Stanley Hall Lecture to American Psychological Association Annual Meeting. Washington, DC, August.

Adams, Aileen and Gail Abarbanel. 1988. *Sexual Assault on Campus: What Colleges Can Do*. Santa Monica, CA: Rape Treatment Center.

Blanchard, W. H. 1959. "The Group Process in Gang Rape." *Journal of Social Psychology* 49:259-66.

Bogal-Allbritten, Rosemarie B. and William L. Allbritten. 1985. "The Hidden Victims: Courtship Violence Among College Students." *Journal of College Student Personnel* 43:201-4.

Bohrnstedt, George W. 1969 "Conservatism, Authoritarianism and Religiosity of Fraternity Pledges." *Journal of College Student Personnel* 27:36-43.

Bradford, Michael. 1986. "Tight Market Dries Up Night life at University." *Business Insurance* (March 2):2, 6.

Burkhart, Barry. 1989. Comments in Seminar on Acquaintance/Date Rape Prevention: A National Video Teleconference, February 2.

Burkhart, Barry R. and Annette L. Stanton. 1985. "Sexual Aggression in Acquaintance Relationships." Pp. 43-65 in *Violence in Intimate Relationships*, edited by G. Russell. Englewood Cliffs, NJ: Spectrum.

Byington, Diane B. and Karen W. Keeter. 1988. "Assessing Needs of Sexual Assault Victims on a University Campus." Pp. 23-31 in *Student Service: Responding to Issues and Challenges*. Chapel Hill: University of North Carolina Press.

Chancer, Lynn S. 1987. "New Bedford, Massachusetts, March 6, 1983-March 22, 1984: The 'Before and After' of a Group Rape." *Gender & Society* 1:239-60.

Ehrhart, Julie K. and Bernice R. Sandler. 1985. *Campus Gang Rape: Party Games?* Washington, DC: Association of American Colleges.

Farr, K. A. 1988. "Dominance Bonding Through the Good Old Boys Sociability Network." *Sex Roles* 18:259-77.

*Florida Flambeau*. 1988. "Pike Members Indicted in Rape." (May 19):1, 5.

Fox, Elaine, Charles Hodge, and Walter Ward. 1987. "A Comparison of Attitudes Held by Black and White Fraternity Members." *Journal of Negro Education* 56:521-34.

Geis, Gilbert. 1971. "Group Sexual Assaults." *Medical Aspects of Human Sexuality* 5:101-13.

Glaser, Barney G. 1978. *Theoretical Sensitivity: Advances in the Methodology of Grounded Theory*. Mill Valley, CA: Sociology Press.

Hood, Jane. 1989. "Why Our Society Is Rape-Prone." *New York Times*, May 16.

Hughes, Michael J. and Roger B. Winston, Jr. 1987. "Effects of Fraternity Membership on Interpersonal Values." *Journal of College Student Personnel* 45:405-11.

Kanin, Eugene J. 1967. "Reference Groups and Sex Conduct Norm Violations." *The Sociological Quarterly* 8:495-504.

Kimmel, Michael, ed. 1987. *Changing Men: New Directions in Research on Men and Masculinity*. Newbury Park, CA: Sage.

Kirshenbaum, Jerry. 1989. "Special Report, An American Disgrace: A Violent and Unprecedented Lawlessness Has Arisen Among College Athletes in All Parts of the Country." *Sports Illustrated* (February 27):16-19.

Lemire, David. 1979. "One Investigation of the Stereotypes Associated with Fraternities and Sororities." *Journal of College Student Personnel* 37:54-57.

Letchworth, G. E. 1969. "Fraternities Now and in the Future." *Journal of College Student Personnel* 10:118-22.

Longino, Charles F., Jr., and Gary S. Kart. 1973. "The College Fraternity: An Assessment of Theory and Research." *Journal of College Student Personnel* 31:118-25.

Marlowe, Anne F. and Dwight C. Auvenshine. 1982. "Greek Membership: Its Impact on the Moral Development of College Freshmen." *Journal of College Student Personnel* 40:53-57.

Martin, Patricia Yancey and Barry A. Turner. 1986. "Grounded Theory and Organizational Research." *Journal of Applied Behavioral Science* 22:141-57.

Merton, Andrew. 1985. "On Competition and Class: Return to Brotherhood." *Ms.* (September):60-65, 121-22.

Messner, Michael. 1989. "Masculinities and Athletic Careers," *Gender & Society* 3:71-88.

Meyer, T. J. 1986. "Fight Against Hazing Rituals Rages on Campuses." *Chronicle of Higher Education* (March 12):34-36.

Miller, Leonard D. 1973. "Distinctive Characteristics of Fraternity Members." *Journal of College Student Personnel* 31:126-28.

Muehlenhard, Charlene L. and Melaney A. Linton. 1987. "Date Rape and Sexual Aggression in Dating Situations: Incidence and Risk Factors." *Journal of Counselling Psychology* 34:186-96.

Pressley, Sue Anne. 1987. "Fraternity Hell Night Still Endures." *Washington Post* (August 11):B1.

Rapaport, Karen and Barry R. Burkhart. 1984. "Personality and Attitudinal Characteristics of Sexually Coercive College Males." *Journal of Abnormal Psychology* 93:216-21.

Roark, Mary L. 1987. "Preventing Violence on College Campuses." *Journal of Counselling and Development* 65:367-70.

Sanday, Peggy Reeves. 1981. "The Socio-Cultural Context of Rape: A Cross-Cultural Study." *Journal of Social Issues* 37:5-27.

——. 1986. "Rape and the Silencing of the Feminine." Pp. 84-101 in *Rape*, edited by S. Tomaselli and R. Porter. Oxford: Basil Blackwell.

*St. Petersburg Times*, 1988. "A Greek Tragedy." (May 19):1F, 6F.

Sato, Ikuya. 1988. "Play Theory of Delinquency: Toward a General Theory of 'Action.'" *Symbolic Interaction* 11:191-212.

Smith, T. 1964. "Emergence and Maintenance of Fraternal Solidarity." *Pacific Sociological Review* 7:29-37.

*Tallahassee Democrat*. 1988a. "FSU Fraternity Brothers Charged." (April 27):1A, 12A.

——. 1988b. "FSU Interviewing Students About Alleged Rape." (April 24):1D.

——. 1989. "Woman Sues Stetson in Alleged Rape." (March 19):3B.

*Tampa Tribune*. 1988. "Fraternity Brothers Charged in Sexual Assault of FSU Coed." (April 27):6B.

Tash, Gary B. 1988. "Date Rape." *The Emerald of Sigma Pi Fraternity* 75(4):1-2.

Telander, Rick and Robert Sullivan. 1989. "Special Report, You Reap What You Sow." *Sports Illustrated* (February 27):20-34.

*The Tomahawk.* 1988. "A Look Back at Rush, A Mixture of Hard Work and Fun." (April/May):3D.

Walsh, Claire. 1989. Comments in Seminar on Acquaintance/Date Rape Prevention: A National Video Teleconference, February 2.

Wilder, David H., Arlyne E. Hoyt, Dennis M. Doren, William E. Hauck, and Robert D. Zettle. 1978. "The Impact of Fraternity and Sorority Membership on Values and Attitudes," *Journal of College Student Personnel* 36:445–49.

Wilder, David H., Arlyne E. Hoyt, Beth Shuster Surbeck, Janet C. Wilder, and Patricia Imperatrice Carney. 1986. "Greek Affiliation and Attitude Change in College Students." *Journal of College Student Personnel* 44:510–19.

# Part VIII
## CULTURE

As people interact over time, they come to develop a shared reality; a perspective; a common definition of what is true, moral, and worthwhile. This, to most sociologists, is the meaning of culture. Americans share a culture. Most of us take that culture for granted, and we come to judge others (and one another) according to the qualities of that culture. Within the United States, there are many communities, formal organizations, and groups developing their own culture to an extent. Therefore, for example, Harvard University will have a different culture than Princeton University, General Motors, and Los Angeles County Hospital. Some organizations in the United States will not only develop a radically different culture than that shared by most Americans, but those organizations will sometimes challenge and eventually alter the general culture.

Four selections are included in Part VIII. Howard S. Becker introduces the meaning of culture in an excellent, interesting, and clear manner, drawing on his experience as a jazz musician. Derek Bok is interested in the questions many of us ask: Are we a better society than we were in the past, or are we worse? Before he tries to examine this question systematically, Bok puts forward five goals as constituting the basic goals of American culture. Gini and Sullivan's analysis of work shows us the importance of culture on people's view of work, as well as their willingness to do work. Finally, Arnold Goldstein challenges us to face the major role that violence plays in American culture, from its beginning to the present day.

Culture is a very valuable concept for understanding human action. Like structure, it arises in interaction and becomes a lasting social pattern for people who enter into the social organization to follow.

# 36. CULTURE: A SOCIOLOGICAL VIEW

*"On the one hand, culture persists and antedates the participation of particular peo-
ple in it. Indeed, culture can be said to shape the outlooks of people who participate
in it. But cultural understandings, on the other hand, have to be reviewed and remade
continually, and in the remaking, they change."*

This article is an attempt to describe the meaning of **culture** and to show its subtleties and importance. The following questions might be a good guide through
Becker's analysis:

1. What is culture?
2. How does culture aid collective action?
3. How does culture arise?
4. Why does culture stay the same and why does it change?
5. How does culture guide public behavior?
6. How does culture socialize the individual?
7. Why does culture make it easier for people to plan their lives?
8. What is the difference between culture and high culture?

I was for some years what is called a Saturday night musician, making myself available to whoever called and hired me to play for dances and parties in groups of varying sizes, playing everything from polkas through mambos, jazz, and imitations of Wayne King. Whoever called would tell me where the job was, what time it began, and usually would tell me to wear a dark suit and a bow tie, thus en-suring that the collection of strangers he was hir-ing would at least look like a band because they would all be dressed more or less alike. When we arrived at work, we would introduce ourselves — the chances were, in a city the size of Chicago (where I did much of my playing), that we were in fact strangers — and see who we knew in common and whether our paths had ever crossed before. The drummer would assemble his drums, the oth-ers would put together their instruments and tune up, and when it was time to start, the leader would announce the name of a song and a key — "Exact-ly Like You" in B flat, for instance — and we would begin to play. We not only began at the same time, but also played background figures that fit the melody someone else was playing and, perhaps most miraculously, ended together. No one in the audience ever guessed that we had never met until twenty minutes earlier. And we kept that up all night, as though we had rehearsed often and played together for years. In a place like Chicago, that scene might be repeated hundreds of times during a weekend.

What I have just described embodies the phe-nomenon that sociologists have made the core problem of their discipline. The social sciences are such a contentious bunch of disciplines that it makes trouble to say what I think is true, that they all in fact concern themselves with one or another version of this issue — the problem of col-lective action, of how people manage to act to-gether. I will not attempt a rigorous definition of collective action here, but the story of the Satur-day night musicians can serve as an example of

Becker, Howard, "Culture: A Sociological View," *Yale Review*,
September 2, 1982, 71:513–527. Copyright Yale University.

it. The example might have concerned a larger group—the employees of a factory who turn out several hundred automobiles in the course of a day, say. Or it might have been about so small a group as a family. It needn't have dealt with a casual collection of strangers, although the ability of strangers to perform together that way makes clear the nature of the problem. How do they do it? How do people act together so as to get anything done without a great deal of trouble, without missteps and conflict?

We can approach the meaning of a concept by seeing how it is used, what work it is called on to do. Sociologists use the concept of *culture* as one of a family of explanations for the phenomenon of concerted activity.... Robert Redfield defined culture as "conventional understandings made manifest in act and artifact." The notion is that the people involved have a similar idea of things, understand them in the same way, as having the same character and the same potential, capable of being dealt with in the same way; they also know that this idea is shared, that the people they are dealing with know, just as they do, what these things are and how they can be used. Because all of them have roughly the same idea, they can all act in ways that are roughly the same, and their activities will, as a result, mesh and be coordinated. Thus, because all those musicians understood what a Saturday night job at a country club consisted of and acted accordingly, because they all knew the melody and harmony of "Exactly Like You" and hundreds of similar songs, because they knew that the others knew this as they knew it, they could play that job successfully. The concept of culture, in short, has its use for sociologists as an explanation of those musicians and all the other forms of concerted action for which they stand....

Culture, however, explains how people act in concert when they *do* share understandings. It is thus a consequence (in this kind of sociological thinking) of the existence of a group of acting people. It has its meaning as one of the resources people draw on in order to coordinate their activities. In this it differs from most anthropological thinking in which the order of importance is reversed, culture leading a kind of independent existence as a system of patterns that make the existence of larger groups possible.

Most conceptions of culture include a great deal more than the spare definition I have just offered. But I think, for reasons made clear later, that it is better to begin with a minimal definition and then to add other conditions when that is helpful....

How does culture—shared understanding—help people to act collectively? People have ideas about how a certain kind of activity might be carried on. They believe others share these ideas and will act on them if they understand the situation in the same way. They believe further that the people they are interacting with believe that they share these ideas too, so that everyone thinks that everyone else has the same idea about how to do things. Given such circumstances, if everyone does what seems appropriate, action will be sufficiently coordinated for practical purposes. Whatever was under way will get done—the meal served, the child dealt with, the job finished—well enough that life can proceed.

The cultural process, then, consists of people doing something in line with their understanding of what one might best do under the given circumstances. Others, recognizing what was done as appropriate, will then consult their notions of what might be done and do something that seems right to them, to which others in return will respond similarly, and so on. If everyone has the same general ideas in mind, and does something congruent with that image or collection of ideas, then what people do will fit together. If we all know the melody and harmony of "Exactly Like You," and improvise accordingly, whatever comes out will sound reasonable to the players and listeners, and a group of perfect strangers will sound like they know what they are doing.

Consider another common situation. A man and woman meet and find each other interesting. At some stage of their relationship, they may consider any of a variety of ways of organizing their joint activities. Early on, one or the other might propose that they "have a date." Later, one or the other might subtly or forthrightly suggest that they spend the night together. Still later, they might try "living together." Finally, they might decide to "get married." They might skip some of these stages and they might not follow that progression, which in contemporary America is a progression of increasingly formal commitment. In other societies and at other times, of course, the stages and the

vould differ. But, whatever their va-
.r as there are names for those rela-
.nd stages, and insofar as most or all of
:n a society know those names and have
what they imply as far as continuing pat-
ter. ɔint activity are concerned, then the man
and v nan involved will be able to organize what
they ɔ by referring to those guideposts. When
one or the other suggests one of these possibilities,
the partner will know, more or less, what is being
suggested without requiring that every item be
spelled out in detail, and the pair can then organize their daily lives, more or less, around the patterns suggested by these cultural images.

What they do from day to day will of course not
be completely covered by the details of that imagery,
although they will be able to decide many details
by consulting it together and adapting what it suggests to the problem at hand. None of these images,
for example, really establishes who takes the garbage
out or what the details of their sexual activity may be,
but the images do, in general, suggest the kind of
commitments and obligations involved on both sides
in a wide range of practical matters.

That is not the end of the matter, however.
Consider a likely contemporary complication: The
woman, divorced, has small children who live with
her. In this case, the couple's freedom of action is
constrained, and no cultural model suggests what
they ought to do about the resulting difficulties.
The models for pairing and for rearing children
suggest incompatible solutions, and the partners
have to invent something. They have to improvise.

This raises a major problem in the theory of
culture I am propounding. Where does culture
come from? The typical cultural explanation of
behavior takes the culture as given, as preexisting
the particular encounter in which it comes into
play. That makes sense. Most of the cultural understandings we use to organize our daily behavior
are there before we get there and we do not propose to change them or negotiate their details with
the people we encounter. We do not propose a
new economic system every time we go to the grocery store. But those understandings and ways of
doing things have not always been there. Most of
us buy our food in supermarkets today, and that
requires a different way of shopping from the corner grocery stores of a generation ago. How did
the new culture of supermarkets arise?

One answer is that the new culture was imposed by the inventors of the concept, the owners
of the new stores that embodied it. They created
the conditions under which change was more or
less inevitable. People might have decided not to
shop in supermarkets and chain stores, but changing conditions of urban life caused so many of
them to use the new markets that the corner grocery, the butcher shop, the poultry and fish stores
disappeared in all but a few areas. Once that happened, supermarkets became the only practical
possibility left, and people had to invent new ways
of serving themselves.

So, given new conditions, people invent culture. The way they do it was suggested by William
Graham Sumner a century ago in *Folkways*. We
can paraphrase him in this way. A group finds itself
sharing a common situation and common problems. Various members of the group experiment
with possible solutions to those problems and report their experiences to their fellows. In the course
of their collective discussion, the members of the
group arrive at a definition of the situation, its problems and possibilities, and develop a consensus as
to the most appropriate and efficient ways of behaving. This consensus thenceforth constrains the
activities of individual members of the group, who
will probably act on it, given the opportunity. In
other words, new situations provoke new behavior.
But people generally find themselves in company
when dealing with these new situations, and because they arrive at their solutions collectively,
each assumes that the others share them. The beginnings of a new shared understanding thus come
into play quickly and easily.

The ease with which new cultural understandings arise and persist varies. It makes a difference, for one thing, how large a group is
involved in making the new understandings. At
one extreme, as I have noted, every mating couple,
every new family, has to devise its own culture to
cover the contingencies of daily interaction. At the
other, consider what happens during industrialization when hundreds of thousands — perhaps
millions — of people are brought from elsewhere
to work in the new factories. They have to come
from elsewhere because the area could not support that many people before industrialization. As
a result, the newcomers differ in culture from the
people already there, and they differ as well in the

role they play in the new industries, usually coming in at the bottom. When industrialization takes place on a large scale, not only does a new culture of the workplace have to be devised, but also a new culture of the cities in which they all end up living—a new experience for everyone involved.

The range of examples suggests, as I mean it to, that people create culture continuously. Because no two situations are alike, the cultural solutions available to them are only approximate. Even in the simplest societies, no two people learn quite the same cultural material; the chance encounters of daily life provide sufficient variation to ensure that. No set of cultural understandings, then, provides a perfectly applicable solution to any problem people have to solve in the course of their day, and they therefore must remake those solutions, adapt their understandings to the new situation in the light of what is different about it. Even the most conscious and determined effort to keep things as they are would necessarily involve strenuous efforts to remake and reinforce understandings so as to keep them intact in the face of what was changing.

There is an apparent paradox here. On the one hand, culture persists and antedates the participation of particular people in it. Indeed, culture can be said to shape the outlooks of people who participate in it. But cultural understandings, on the other hand, have to be reviewed and remade continually, and in the remaking, they change.

This is not a true paradox, however: The understandings last *because* they change to deal with new situations. People continually refine them, changing some here and some there but never changing all of them at once. The emphasis on basic values and coherence in the definition of culture arises because of this process. In making the new versions of the old understandings, people naturally rely on what they already have available, so that consciously planned innovations and revolutions seem, in historical perspective, only small variations on what came before.

To summarize, how culture works as a guide in organizing collective action and how it comes into being are really the same process. In both cases, people pay attention to what other people are doing and, in an attempt to mesh what they do with those others, refer to what they know (or think they know) in common. So culture is always being made, changing more or less, acting as a point of reference for people engaged in interaction.

What difference does it make that people continually make culture in the way I have described? The most important consequence is that they can, as a result, cooperate easily and efficiently in the daily business of life, without necessarily knowing each other very well.

Most occupations, for example, operate on the premise that the people who work in them all know certain procedures and certain ways of thinking about and responding to typical situations and problems, and that such knowledge will make it possible to assemble them to work on a common project without prior team training. Most professional schools operate on the theory that the education they offer provides a basis for work cooperation among people properly trained anywhere. In fact, people probably learn the culture that makes occupational cooperation possible in the workplace itself. It presents them with problems to solve that are common to people in their line of work, and provides a group of more experienced workers who can suggest solutions. In some occupations, workers change jobs often and move from workplace to workplace often (as do the weekend musicians), and they carry what they have learned elsewhere with them. That makes it easy for them to refine and update their solutions frequently, and thus to develop and maintain an occupational culture. Workers who do not move but spend their work lives in one place may develop a more idiosyncratic work culture, peculiar to that place and its local problems—a culture of IBM or Texas Instruments or (because the process is not limited to large firms) Joe's Diner.

At a different level of cooperative action, Goffman has described cultural understandings that characterize people's behavior in public. For instance, people obey a norm of "civil inattention," allowing each other a privacy that the material circumstances of, say, waiting for a bus, do not provide. Because this kind of privacy is what Americans and many others find necessary before they can feel comfortable and safe in public (Hall has shown how these rules differ in other cultures), these understandings make it possible for urban Americans to occupy crowded public spaces without making each other uneasy. The point is not trivial, because violations of these rules are at least in part responsible for the currently common fear that some public areas are "not safe," quite apart from whatever assaults have taken place in them. Most people have no personal knowledge of the alleged assaults, but they experience violation of what might be called the "Goffman rules" of public order as the prelude to danger and do not go to places that make them feel that way.

Cultural understandings, if they are to be effective in the organization of public behavior, must be very widely held. That means that people of otherwise varying class, ethnic, and regional cultures must learn them routinely and must learn them quite young, because even small children can disrupt public order very effectively. That requires, in turn, substantial agreement among people of all segments of the society on how children should be brought up. If no such agreement exists, or if some of the people who agree in principle do not manage to teach their children the necessary things, public order breaks down, as it often does.

In another direction, cultural understandings affect and "socialize" the internal experiences people have. By applying understandings they know to be widely accepted to their own perhaps inchoate private experiences, people learn to define those internal experiences in ways that allow them to mesh their activities relevant to those topics with those of others with whom they are involved. Consider the familiar example of falling in love. It is remarkable that one of the experiences we usually consider private and unique — falling in love — actually has the same character for most people who experience it. That is not to say that the experience is superficial, but rather that when people try to understand their emotional responses to others, one available explanation of what they feel is the idea, common in Western culture, of romantic love. They learn that idea from a variety of sources, ranging from the mass media to discussion with their peers, and they learn to see their own experiences as embodiments of it. Because most people within a given culture learn to experience love in the same way from the same sources, two people can become acquainted and successfully fall in love with each other — not an easy trick.

Because shared cultural understandings make it easy to do things in certain ways, moreover, their existence favors those ways of doing things and makes other ways of achieving the same end, which might be just as satisfactory to everyone involved, correspondingly less likely. Random events, which might produce innovations desirable to participants, occur infrequently. In fact, even when the familiar line of activity is not exactly to anyone's liking, people continue it simply because it is what everyone knows and knows that everyone else knows, and thus is what offers the greatest likelihood of successful collective action. Everyone knows, for instance, that it would be better to standardize the enormous variety of screw threads in this country, or to convert the United States to the metric system. But the old ways are the ones we know, and, of course, in this instance, they are built into tools and machines that would be difficult and costly to change. Many activities exhibit that inertia, and they pose a problem that sociologists have been interested in for many years: Which elements of a society or culture are most likely to change? William Fielding Ogburn, for instance, proposed sixty years ago that material culture (screw threads) changed more quickly than social organization, and that the resultant "lag" could be problematic for human society.

A final consequence: The existence of culture makes it possible for people to plan their own lives. We can plan most easily for a known future, in which the major organizational features of society turn out to be what we expected them to be and what we made allowances for in our planning. We need, most importantly, to predict the actions of other people and of the organizations that consist of their collective actions. Culture makes those actions, individual and collective, more predictable than they would otherwise be. People in traditional societies may not obey in every detail the complex marriage rules held out to them, but those rules supply a sufficiently clear guide for men and women to envision more or less accurately when they will marry, what resources will be available to them when they do, and how the course of their married life will proceed....

In modern industrial societies, workers can plan their careers better when they know what kinds of work situations they will find themselves in and what their rights and obligations at various ages and career stages will be. Few people can make those predictions successfully in this country any more, which indicates that cultural understandings do not always last the twenty or thirty years necessary for such predictability to be possible. When that happens, people do not know how to prepare themselves for their work lives and do not receive the benefits of their earlier investments in hard work. People who seemed to be goofing off or acting irrationally, for example, sometimes make windfall profits as the work world comes to need just those combinations of skills and experiences

that they acquired while not following a "sensible" career path. As technical and organizational innovations make new skills more desirable, new career lines open up that were not and could not have been predicted ten years earlier. The first generation of computer programmers benefited from that kind of good luck, as did the first generation of drug researchers, among others.

# 37.  GOALS IN AMERICAN LIFE

DEREK BOK

*"In order to evaluate the nation's progress, the surest way to proceed is not to argue endlessly over competing visions of the ideal society but to measure our record against the kind of society to which most Americans aspire. In a democracy, that is the most appropriate goal toward which a nation and its government should strive and the best yardstick for evaluating their performance."*

The author of this selection is interested in government and examines the view of government Americans tend to have. He tries to tackle whether or not we are better off as a society now than we have been in the past. Of course, he reminds us, it depends on what we want our society to be. In this introduction to his book, Derek Bok lays out five basic goals that seem to unite us. He asks: Have we been able to accomplish these goals? How well has government done? Simply put, he describes us as a people that seeks a good economy, a high quality of life, a chance for all people to achieve, personal security, and a mixture of freedom, sense of responsibility, and compassion toward those who are less fortunate. Are these really our goals? How well have we achieved them? In relation to accomplishing these goals, are we a better society or a worse one than we were?

...Although many people claim to know what ails the country, ascertaining the true state of affairs is actually more difficult than one might think from

Reprinted by permission of the publisher from *The State of the Nation*, by Derek Bok. Cambridge, Mass.: Harvard University Press. Copyright © 1966 by Derek Bok.

reading the current commentaries on America. There is sharp disagreement over the state of almost every institution and field of endeavor in the United States. To President Bill Clinton, Americans are "choking on a health care system that isn't working."[1] To Republican lawmakers (echoing President George Bush before them), Americans have the finest health care system in the world. According to

Jacques Attali, "Industry is the only lasting foundation of a nation's power, and it is in this sense that the signs of America's lasting decline are everywhere."[2] Yet the World Economic Forum, composed of leading business executives from many countries, recently pronounced American business the most competitive in the world. To Richard Goodwin, "It is no secret to most parents and concerned citizens that our public school system is a disaster."[3] According to a recent survey, however, 70 percent of American parents would give the school their children attend a grade of either A or B....[4]

There is a compelling reason for a careful, objective look at the full range of problems troubling Americans. Heated discussions are currently in progress all across the United States about the condition of our society. More than at any time in recent memory, familiar premises are being questioned, established ways of conducting the nation's affairs are under attack, policies that would have seemed unthinkable in earlier periods are being actively considered. At such a moment, it is especially important to agree, insofar as possible, on what the true condition of our society is and whether the nation is indeed "headed in the wrong direction." If it is, we need to know exactly where America is losing ground so that we can concentrate our efforts on the problems that need to be solved. If the country is not in a state of decline, we ought to know that, too – not merely to preserve our peace of mind but to keep from searching needlessly for scapegoats and conjuring up exaggerated and unnecessary remedies.

This study will reveal that although America has made progress in many important respects over the past forty years, the record of this country often compares quite poorly with that of most other leading industrial democracies. From a position of unequaled strength and prosperity, the United States has fallen behind other advanced nations in achieving many of the goals that large majorities of Americans care most about. The individualism, initiative, and independence that seemed to serve this country admirably during its first 150 years no longer appear to be working so well in the face of a new array of challenges. There are reasons, therefore, to justify the pessimism about America so starkly revealed by current opinion polls.

What accounts for this disappointing record? Government and the politicians who control it are the culprits most frequently singled out for blame. Over the past thirty years, confidence in public officials has eroded drastically.[5] A plurality of Americans now believe that Washington poses the greatest threat to the welfare of the nation. A majority has even concluded that the federal government generally makes matters worse when it decides to take hold of a problem.[6]

These sentiments leave Americans in an awkward spot. By large majorities, we aspire to a kind of society that no country has yet approximated without the aid of a strong and active government. By equally large margins, however, we harbor the gravest possible distrust of government and those charged with making it work. This is not a healthy state of affairs, nor does it seem viable in the long run. Something needs to be done to bring our views about ends and means into closer alignment.

At present, more and more people are concluding that the answer to this dilemma is to shrink the government drastically and rely much more on private initiative to build the kind of society most people want. This solution would at least reduce the role of the state to a level more in keeping with the public's low regard for its capacities. Yet comparing America's experience with that of several other leading industrial democracies yields a rather different conclusion. In many instances, it is true, poorly conceived and badly executed public policies have a lot to do with our disappointing record. But there are grave dangers in responding to our problems by constantly denigrating public officials and undermining their authority. Like it or not, a careful look at the record will reveal that the skill with which a government defines its role, constructs its policies, and carries out its programs has now become the chief factor that determines which modern democracies succeed best in building the kind of society their citizens desire. The challenge for America, then, is not to dismember the government but to learn how to help it function more effectively.

To meet this challenge successfully, it is best to begin by trying to grasp as clearly as possible just what part the government has played in this country and how it has both helped and hindered efforts to move society forward. Only then can Americans understand the record of their government sufficiently well that they will neither ask the State to assume responsibilities it is ill-equipped to perform nor insist on ill-considered remedies that weaken it in carrying out its essential tasks....

## ASSESSING THE NATION'S PROGRESS

How can one possibly hope to arrive at any firm conclusion about a question as amorphous as whether America is progressing or suffering a decline? With so much information to choose from, it is easy for advocates on either side to take almost any aspect of American life and argue that matters are either getting better or growing worse. Depending on one's conception of what an ideal society should be, different people can look at the same body of evidence and come away with radically different views of whether the nation has advanced or fallen back over the past thirty to forty years.

Fortunately, there is one firm rock on which to build. In order to evaluate the nation's progress, the surest way to proceed is not to argue endlessly over competing visions of the ideal society but to measure our record against the kind of society to which most Americans aspire. In a democracy, that is the most appropriate goal toward which a nation and its government should strive and the best yardstick for evaluating their performance.

Despite all the arguments that divide us, Americans remain surprisingly united on what the basic goals of the society ought to be. Five major aims enjoy especially broad support. They have consistently gained the approval of large majorities ever since polling organizations started to ask the public about its beliefs several decades ago. With these objectives as a guide, it is possible to determine how much progress the United States has made, not toward liberal goals or conservative goals but toward aims that Americans from every walk of life consider important.

The first of these objectives is a buoyant expanding economy. Economic growth, rising productivity, full employment, and stable prices are all vital to Americans because they make possible so much of what people want in order to live a satisfying life. When the economy ceases to expand, opportunities for advancement are fewer, and the struggle among interest groups for resources begins to intensify. Confidence erodes, America's influence in the world tends to diminish, and people are less inclined to sacrifice their interests for the common good. When unemployment rises, families suffer, breadwinners lose their sense of self-respect, and insecurity grows even for those who still have jobs. Year in and year out, therefore, voters judge politicians more heavily on the state of the economy than on any other factor.

The second important goal is a quality of life that includes elements transcending economic prosperity. For example, in addition to simply earning a good income, Americans want to preserve nature, breathe clean air, live in peaceful, pleasant neighborhoods, and enjoy a vibrant culture with art, music, literature and other forms of entertainment that appeal to every segment of a diverse population.

A third basic aim is a society that offers a chance for all people to achieve as much as they can in light of their talents, aspirations, and efforts. Americans may not care a great deal about equality of results; in fact, they have tolerated greater disparities in income and wealth than citizens of any other industrial democracy and have long been cool to proposals that would substantially redistribute income.[7] What they do believe in strongly, however, is equality of opportunity. Opportunity has been central to the American experience from the beginning. It has been nourished by successive waves of immigrants arriving here in search of a better life, and it continues to be a principle supported by more than 90 percent of the people.[8]

The fourth major goal for most Americans is to enjoy adequate personal security against the principal hazards of life — the risk of being victimized by crime, of being abandoned and destitute in old age, of being fired arbitrarily or injured on the job, of falling ill without being able to afford adequate health care. Left to their own devices, many people lack the resources to protect themselves against these dangers; they want some mechanism to give them the security they desire. That is why Social Security is among the most popular of all federal programs and why government outlays for crime prevention and health care enjoy more grass-roots support than almost any proposed public expenditures.

The fifth and last aspiration shared by large majorities of Americans is to preserve a set of fundamental values. One of these is individual freedom — the right to be safe from unjust or unnecessary interference, especially from the State, in the exercise of political and personal liberties. Every survey that asks people what they cherish most about being an American finds that personal freedom tops the list.[9] With individual freedom, however, comes a corresponding responsibility to respect the legitimate rights and interests of others. Polls that ask Americans what troubles them most about their country frequently show that one of their greatest concerns is that the sense of individual responsibility is eroding.[10] Beyond the desire for high ethical standards is a broader social concern — or compassion, if you will — toward the least fortunate members of society. Although there is much controversy over particular social welfare programs, most Americans want to help the poor, especially those who cannot help themselves. In fact, by the end of the 1980s, more than 60 percent of the public believed that the government was spending too *little* on the poor, whereas only 9 percent felt that it was spending too much.[11] Similar results have been recorded throughout the postwar period.[12]

The five basic goals just described are not unique to the United States; they are shared by all leading industrial democracies. What is distinctive about this country is the way in which Americans choose to go about achieving these objectives. At the core of this approach is an abiding faith in the power of self-reliant individuals — an optimism about what this country can achieve by giving people ample freedom and abundant opportunities to succeed to the limit of their abilities and ambitions. In comparison with the citizens of most other industrialized nations, Americans have tended to place much less stock in modifying the economy or changing the fruits of private enterprise to bring about greater equality of results. Instead, they have continued to believe that the entire society will move ahead faster if talented people are allowed to succeed and reap the rewards of their success. Conversely, Americans have always been suspicious of big government and skeptical about national efforts to achieve social goals through centralized planning and elaborate state programs.

The faith in self-reliant individualism plainly served this nation well for many generations. Natural resources helped the economy grow, and surrounding oceans kept it relatively safe from the destructive wars that ravaged most other leading countries. Favored by these advantages, competitive individualism seemed to produce all of the captains of industry and entrepreneurs, the risk takers and inventors, the institution builders and community leaders that the nation needed to grow and prosper. Starting with nothing but a barren wilderness, enterprising Americans made the United States the wealthiest country in the world by the end of the nineteenth century.

In the midst of this remarkable growth, of course, social problems of all kinds abounded. But conditions were hardly any better in other industrializing nations. Nor did these problems cause much anguish among the country's leaders. Although many people were aware of widespread suffering and want, few of them measured the progress of America or its place in the world by counting the number of poor people or comparing statistics on infant mortality.

With the Great Depression in the 1930s, followed immediately by the Second World War, conditions began to change. The goals of the United States grew more ambitious, as they did in all industrial democracies. Americans have long aspired to personal security, good health, individual freedom, and material comforts in their own lives. But only in the past sixty years has a broad consensus arisen that matters such as adequate housing, decent health care, proper nutrition, clean air and water, security in old age, and other benefits of life are conditions that all Americans should enjoy. Only in this period has the public begun to regard these conditions as objectives the country should try to reach and goals by which to measure our success as a nation.

At the very time when Americans were reformulating their aims, however, the circumstances of the country were beginning to change as well. No longer did the United States enjoy an abundance of open land. One by one, its natural resources ceased to be adequate for its needs. With its new industrial preeminence, America was no longer able to progress, as it did so often in the previous century, simply by copying innovations made in Europe. In addition, economic strength brought new and formidable global responsibilities. Increasingly, the United States felt compelled to assume a disproportionate share of the burden of maintaining international security, especially (until recently) against the threat of Communism.

In short, changing circumstances in the past half-century have presented America with a new challenge in trying to achieve the basic aspirations of the society. For more than 150 years, Americans demonstrated how well they could perform with abundant natural resources and limited national objectives. Since World War II, our task has been the more demanding one of trying to achieve much more ambitious goals under more constrained conditions. The question worth asking after a half-century of effort is how good a job the society has done of adapting its traditional style and institutions to a new and much more formidable set of challenges....

...Under the broad rubric of "economic prosperity," one would certainly wish to know how much the economy has grown, how rapidly productivity has increased, how much unemployment has occurred, and what the rate of inflation has been. In addition, one might want to know how much progress has occurred in fields that bear most directly on the long-term prospects for a healthy, growing economy-the amount of savings and investment, the progress in scientific discovery and technology, the quality of education, and the training given the work force to prepare for an increasingly sophisticated economy. A careful look at all these areas should give a reasonable sense of how well the economy has performed and how firm a foundation has been laid for continuing prosperity.

Improving the quality of life is a much more amorphous aim that can include many items such as personal safety and good health care; these items are discussed here under other national objectives. In the end, one can only hope to select a small, representative sample from the many activities that might in some way fit under this rubric. Three topics, however, seem important enough yet sufficiently diverse to capture something of the breadth and scope of this category. The first involves the physical surroundings in which Americans live — the dwellings in which they reside and the neighborhoods in which they live, raise families, and make friendships. The second topic has to do with the environment and the programs devised to protect the air, soil, and water from pollutants that jeopardize health, interfere with recreation, and endanger plant and animal life. The last of the three subjects is the arts, especially the efforts made in the past thirty years to expand the number of arts organizations and enlarge their audiences.

Opportunity is another goal with many facets. Three aspects of the subject, however, seem especially important for the purposes of this study. The first has to do with efforts to give every child a good start in life — a chance to be born healthy, to receive adequate nutrition in infancy, to be protected against illness, to have good child care if the parents work, and to have the help required to begin school in a state of readiness to learn. A second topic of great concern to America is the handicap of race, particularly for blacks, who have experienced such special problems throughout our history. A third important aspect of the subject has to do with the possibilities for a successful and satisfying career and whether all Americans, women as well as men, can achieve as much as their efforts, ambitions, and talents allow.

The quest for personal security is an easier goal to explore because there is wide agreement on the kinds of security that matter most to Americans. Everyone wants protection from being victimized by crime, especially from violent attacks. (Fear of crime was actually the chief cause of concern among Americans in 1994.) Another form of security that matters to almost everyone is the assurance of affordable, good quality health care in case of illness. Most people also want to be protected at work against the risks of accident and unfair treatment and the hardships of layoff and unemployment. The final need is for security in old age, chiefly protection against the risk of being forced into poverty because of a long-term illness or the death of a spouse at a time when one is often vulnerable and unable to help oneself.

The last great objective shared by most Americans — to have a society that respects basic values — may seem the most amorphous of all America's basic goals. Even so, it is possible to throw some light on the nation's progress in combining individual freedom with personal and social responsibility. A plausible way to chart the growth of personal freedom over the past few decades is to examine the work of the courts in defining the scope of individual liberty under the Constitution. Calculating the ebb and flow of personal responsibility is a much more complicated process, but one can search for clues by looking at trends in various types of behavior that reveal how much Americans obey the law and respect the legitimate interests of others. With enough indices of this kind, it may be possible to draw some rough conclusions about how well people are living up to their personal obligations and whether they are taking these responsibilities more or less seriously than in the past. Finally, the much-discussed subject of poverty should throw valuable light on how compassionate the society has been in responding to the plight of others and how seriously Americans take their collective responsibility to care for needy strangers.

The many fields of activity just described overlap, and some could plausibly be included under more than one of our national objectives. Together, however, they touch on each of America's basic social goals while being diverse enough to include all the most important segments of society — rich and poor, rural and urban, young and old, employed and unemployed, blacks and whites. Some of the topics lend themselves more readily than others to precise description and measurement. For each of these areas of endeavor, however, it is possible to establish in a general way what Americans are trying as a society to achieve. (The disputes that divide the country occur mainly over the methods to pursue and the amounts of money to spend on the task.) In housing, for example, federal legislation defines what most people would accept as a goal in any case — to provide "a decent home and a suitable living environment for every American." Similarly, in the field of crime, liberals and conservatives can agree that their common objective is to minimize the incidence of violent crime within the limits set by the Constitution and by widely accepted norms of justice and fair play in the society.

Using such general definitions of our aims, we should be able to describe — often quite precisely — how much progress the United States has made over the past few decades. In almost every case, we can also compare our record with that of other advanced industrial democracies. Such comparisons should provide a clearer sense of how much progress modern democratic societies are capable of making and thus throw additional light on how successful America has been in achieving the goals that matter most to us....

## ENDNOTES

1. Quoted in Michael Wines, "At the Capitol, Selling Health Plans Like Snake Oil," *New York Times*, A-24 (October 28, 1993).
2. Quoted in Richard N. Goodwin, *Promises to Keep*, 57 (1992).
3. Ibid., 146.
4. Stanley Elam, Lowell Rose, and Alec Gallup, "The 26th Annual *Phi Delta Kappan* Gallup Poll of the Public's Attitudes toward Public Schools," *Phi Delta Kappan*, 4 1. (September 1994).
5. William G. Mayer, *The Changing American Mind: How and Why American Public Opinion Changed between 1960 and 1988*, 343 (1992); Everett C. Ladd, "Generation Gap? What Generation Gap?" *Wall Street Journal*, A-16 (December 9, 1994); Times Mirror Center for the People and the Press, *The New Political Landscape*, 24 (1994).
6. ABC News poll, September 1994, Roper Center at the University of Connecticut, *Public Opinion Online*, Accession number 0232474.
7. According to Sidney Verba, the United States, both in de Tocqueville's era and today, is a society in which fundamental inequalities in economic status are tolerated, even encouraged, as long as they are based on achievement. *Elites and the Idea of Equality*, 43 (1987); see also Everett C. Ladd, *The American Ideology: An Explanation of the Origins, Meaning, and Role of American Values*, A22 (February 1992).
8. Times Mirror Center, *The New Political Landscape*, 152.
9. See "People for the American Way," *Democracy's Next Generation: A Study of Youth and Teachers*, 67(1989).
10. Times Mirror Center, *Voter Anxiety*, 180. For a discussion of these attitudes, see Everett Ladd, "The Myth of Moral Decline," *The Responsive Community*, 52 (Winter 1993-1994).
11. Everett C. Ladd, *The American Ideology: An Explanation of the Origins, Meaning, and Role of American Values*, 34 (February 1992).
12. See, generally, Fay Lomax Cook and Edith J. Barrett, *Support for the American Welfare State: The Views of Congress and the Public* (1992).

# 38. CULTURE AND THE DEFINITION OF WORK

A. R. GINI AND T. J. SULLIVAN

*"The work ethic in all its various formulations contains elements of both myth and reality.... [I]t helps perpetuate a certain perspective on reality that might not otherwise exist...."*

Gini and Sullivan introduce us to the idea of culture by focusing on the meaning of work. Western culture before the sixteenth century generally regarded work as a necessary but unattractive task. Protestantism eventually changed that view, and by the nineteenth century, the culture of America was one that regarded work as moral, as a good end in and of itself. Yet, not everyone accepted this view, and indeed there is evidence that this view was generally accepted only by the middle class, who, in turn, tried to control the laboring class through accepting its definition. The last part of this selection focuses on post–World War II America and our attempts to define work as noble despite its drudgery.

Folk wisdom has it that the main problem with work is that so few people are able to avoid it. For the vast majority, work is an inescapable and irreducible fact of existence. Work is a necessary evil, an activity that is required to sustain and justify the hours between sleeping, eating, and attempting to enjoy ourselves. It is, for most of us, like Larkin's toad: We cannot "drive the brute off." In its very worst light, work is seen as "something evil, a punishment, the great and grindingly inevitable burden of toil and mortality laid upon the human situation."[1] Studs Terkel's book *Working* has become the bible for those who feel that work is by definition degrading, debilitating, and dehumanizing. True believers need only open this text at random to find documented proof that work is one, if not the major, cause of "economic unfreedom," "physical debasement," "personal alienation," and "social ennui." At best, work looms so large and problematic in the lives of most of us that we tend to take it for granted and either calmly forget about it or actively suppress the full significance of its effect on our lives. It is simply *there*, as illness, death, taxes, and mortgage payments are there, something to be endured.[2] From this perspective, such statements as "Work is love made visible" (Kahlil Gibran) and "To work is to pray" (St. Benedict) are saccharine palliatives that in no way reflect the reality of the situation. The cynical response to such platitudes is, "If work has so many benefits, why is it that so many people spent so much of their lives trying to avoid it?" *Chicago Tribune* columnist Mike Royko accurately encapsulates the spirit of the "common man's" feelings about work when his alter ego in the column, Slats, says:

...[W]hy do you think the lottery is so popular? Do you think anybody would play if the super payoff was a job on the night shift in a meat packing plant? People play it so that if they win they can be rich and idle...like I told you years ago—if work is so good, how come they have to pay us to do it?[3]

From Chapter 1 of *It Comes with the Territory: An Inquiry Concerning Work and the Person*, by A. R. Gini and T. J. Sullivan. New York: Random House. Reprinted by permission.

The data being generated in academic circles support this commonsense portrait of work. Since the mid-1950s, a horde of sociologists and industrial psychologists have descended on the workplace in a frenetic attempt to probe, measure, and analyze how workers relate to work, what they feel about work, and how it affects personal values, private lives, and general world views. The reports from these investigations are not far removed from the "bar-room grumblings" most of us are familiar with. The surveys indicate that when asked the question, "Are Americans less motivated to work now?" employees answer both yes and no. The results indicate that some workers are satisfied with certain aspects of their work and others are not. The important point to keep in mind, however, is that for most people, the critical issue is not, "Do I still want to work?" as much as "Does my job turn me off?" Surveys show a consistently strong reaffirmation of the value of work for three-quarters of the population. Even more surprising, when asked if they would choose to continue to work even if they could live comfortably for the rest of their lives without doing so, most people say they would choose to work. A seeming contradiction appears when workers are asked: "If you were free to go into any type of job you wanted, what would your choice be?"

| | |
|---|---|
| The job he or she now has: | 38.1 |
| Retire and not work at all: | 1.9 |
| Prefer some other job to the job he or she has now: | 60.4[4] |

The paradox here is that, in general, people want to work but dislike their present jobs; they do not find the work fulfilling or expansive. Perhaps one of the characters in Studs Terkel's book most eloquently stated is the predicament in which many workers find themselves:

I think most are looking for a calling, not a job. Most of us, like the assembly line worker, have jobs that are not big enough for people.[5]

I believe that work is the means by which we become and complete ourselves as persons; we create ourselves in our work. To restate the old Italian proverb "You are what you eat," in regard to work "You are the work you do." We must be very careful, therefore, in the work we choose. Work is a necessary and defining activity in the development of the human personality. Work is the mark of man, and work molds man, or, as Gregory Baum has stated, "labor [work] is the axis of human self-making."[6] All of us need work, work that ennobles the product and ennobles the producer as well. This is what E. F. Schumacher has called "good work."

Although many people do not like their work, they need it to help them focus on reality, find a creative outlet, and define themselves as individuals. Finances aside, the main reason people don't like their work is that their jobs don't match their skills, interests, or talents. It isn't that all work is bad; it is rather that some work is bad for some people at some times. Ideally, the goal of work should be analogous to the Greek definition of happiness: "The use of all of one's powers to achieve excellence...."

For most of us, working is an entirely nondiscretionary activity. We must work in order to survive, certainly to survive with a modicum of security and comfort.[7] Historically, work has carried with it a certain coercive quality; one is forced to work, to do something in order to carry on. In primitive, subsistence societies, there was no distinction between working and not working. To be awake was to be working. A person was born, worked, and died....

I take it to be the case, however, that the common laments against work are not simply based on the fact that most of us are part of the captive work force and hence accept work as inevitable. In well over one hundred studies in the last twenty-five years, workers have regularly depicted their jobs as physically exhausting, boring, psychologically diminishing, or personally humiliating and unimportant.[8] In the opening lines of Working, Terkel compellingly exemplifies this point of view:

This book, being about work, is, by its very nature, about violence—to the spirit as well as to the body. It is about ulcers as well as accidents, about shouting matches as well as fist fights, about nervous breakdowns as well as kicking the dog around. It is above all (or beneath all) about daily humiliations. To survive the day is triumph enough for the walking wounded among the great many of us.[9]

The poor reputation that work currently enjoys has a long and convoluted history. The image of the "negative necessity" of work seems to have partial origins in the various etymologies of the word itself. The Greek word for "labor" (work), *ponos*, also means "sorrow."[10] In Latin, the word *labor* also means "extreme effort associated with pain." According to Hannah Arendt, "labor" has the same etymological root as *labare* ("to stumble under a burden"), signifying "trouble, distress, difficulty." The French word *travail* connotes "a heavy, burdensome task." It likewise is of Latin origin and originally denoted the *tripalium*, a three-pronged instrument of torture used by the Roman legionnaires, hence the suggestion of "sorrow and pain." In medieval German, the word *Arbeit* ("to labor") can also be translated to signify "tribulation, persecution, adversity, or bad times." Finally, the word "occupation" emerges from the Latin *occupare*, connoting the adversarial posture "of seizing hold of or grappling with a task." Clearly, these etymologies leave little doubt about antiquity's association of work with pain or irksomeness.[11]

The common perception of work as a "negative and ignoble" activity can also be traced to classical sources. The Bible tells us that originally there was no work to be done in the Garden of Eden; toil was described as a curse imposed by God to symbolize humankind's banishment. After the Fall, work became a necessary activity. For Milton, "man's first disobedience" resulted in the curse of work.[12] Genesis graphically expresses the curse that sin brought with it: "Cursed is the ground because of you; in toil you shall eat of it all the days of your life…. In the sweat of your face you shall eat bread till you return to the ground, for out of it you were taken."[13] One interpretation of the Jewish tradition perceives work as "painful drudgery" to which we are condemned by sin. It is accepted as an expiation through which one can atone for sin and prepare for the arrival of the Messiah. Work is a "heavy yoke" that is "hard to bear," and Ecclesiastes can be heard to sigh: "The labor of man does not satisfy the soul."[14] Primitive Christianity, like Judaism, regarded work as a punishment from God. But work was not only seen as a result of original sin, but also as a means to redemption by sharing the goods of one's labor with those who were in greater need. Thus work, as a means of charity, was a source of grace. Yet work is never exalted as anything in itself,

but only as an instrument of purification, charity, or expiation.

By the time of Thomas Aquinas in the thirteenth century, work was being considered a necessity of nature. According to Aquinas, each of us must use our God-given talents ("stewardship") in the service of both ourselves and others. In fulfilling the duty of work, we acquire skill, fulfill our obligations of charity, and pay homage to our creator. With the Scholastic synthesis, work became a natural right and duty, the sole legitimate basis for society, the foundation for property and profit, as well as the means for personal salvation.[15] Nonetheless, the work of this life was still thought to be of little consequence compared to the spiritual work of preparing to face God. By itself, work had no purpose, for only the contemplation of God could redeem life.[16]

To the ancient Greeks, whose physical labor was done by slaves, work brutalized the mind and made men unfit for the practice of the gentlemanly virtues. The Greeks regarded work as a curse, a drudgery, and a heavy-hearted activity. Plutarch in his chapter on Pericles remarks that no well-born man would want to be the craftsman Phidias. Because while a gentleman enjoys the contemplation of the sculptor's masterpieces, he himself would never consider using a hammer and chisel and being covered with dust, sweat, and grime.[17] The Greeks felt that work enslaved the worker, chained him to the will of others, and corrupted his soul. Work by its very nature inhibited the use of reason and thereby impeded the search for the ultimate ends of life. Work was accepted not as an end in itself but as a means by which some might be freed to pursue higher goals. Aristotle declared that just as the goal of war was peace, so the object of work was leisure. Leisure meant activity pursued free of compulsion or desire for gain, free for the contemplation of philosophical issues and truths. Aristotle saw work as a burden he had no duty to bear. He himself never worked, accepting the slavery of others because it freed him for leisure.[18]

Work both as a private activity and as a way of life began to take on a less onerous nature during the Renaissance and the Reformation. It was during this period that work, no matter how high or low the actual task, began to develop—at least at the theoretical level—a positive ethos of its own.

Most historians credit the origin of the work ethic to Martin Luther. According to Luther, one was summoned by God to a secular "calling" that today we would call a job.[19] Luther stressed that all callings were necessary to life; no one calling was to be recognized as more necessary or blessed than another, and, therefore, all callings had equal worth in the sight of God. For Luther, work was a form of serving God: "There is just one best way to serve God — to do most perfectly the work of one's profession." Thus the only way to live acceptably before God was through devotion to one's calling. However, God demanded more than occasional good works. He demanded a methodical life of good works in a unified pattern of work and worship.[20]

With John Calvin in the sixteenth century, we find Luther's ideas extended, systematized, and institutionalized. Work was divine, a way of serving God. Work was the will of God, and even ceaseless "dumb toil" sufficed to please Him. Calvin preached the "predestination of the elect." He believed that the elect could be recognized by certain outward signs, which included self-denial and devotion to duty, and that God caused the elect to prosper. "To prosper" or "to succeed" meant to enjoy not only wealth and happiness on earth, but eternal salvation. "Success" was the symbol of "selective salvation." Calvin managed, no matter how indirectly, to provide a rationale linking work and the Divine with material success and comfort.

In *The Protestant Ethic and the Spirit of Capitalism* (1905), Max Weber observed that the rise of Protestantism and the rise of capitalism generally coincided in England and throughout most European countries. Weber's explanation was that many basic Protestant ideas encouraged capitalistic activities. For example, the Reformation taught that each person would be individually judged by God, and that judgment would be based on one's whole life's work or "calling." The reformers also taught that the fruits of one's "calling" — money — should not be spent frivolously or unnecessarily. According to Weber, these ideas led to a life of hard work, self-discipline, asceticism, and concern with achievement. This ethic helped advance the rise of the private entrepreneur in that it led to the accumulation of money that could not be spent on luxuries, but that could and should be put into one's own business.[21]

Labor analyst Michael Cherrington maintains that the work ethic typically embraces one or more of the following beliefs:

1. People have a moral and religious obligation to fill their lives with heavy physical toil. For some, this means that hard work, effort, and drudgery are to be valued for their own sake; physical pleasures and enjoyments are to be shunned; and an ascetic existence of methodical rigor is the only acceptable way to live.
2. Men and women are expected to spend long hours at work, with little or no time for personal recreation and leisure.
3. A worker should have a dependable attendance record, with low absenteeism and tardiness.
4. Workers should take pride in their work and do their jobs well.
5. Workers should be highly productive and produce a large quantity of goods or services.
6. Employees should have feelings of commitment and loyalty to their profession, their company, and their work group.
7. Workers should be achievement oriented and constantly strive for promotions and advancement. High-status jobs with prestige and the respect of others are important indicators of a "good" person.
8. People should acquire wealth through honest labor and retain it through thrift and wise investments. Frugality is desirable; extravagance and waste should be avoided.[22]

For Weber, the work ethic seems to mean a commitment to work beyond its utility in providing a living. It is "a conviction that work is a worthwhile activity in its own right, not merely...the means to material comfort or wealth."[23]

The direct theological descendants of the Reformation, and of John Calvin in particular, were the dour Puritans who migrated to New England. Citing the parable of the talents (Matthew 25), Calvin urged the Puritans to prosper: "You may labor to be rich for God, though not for the flesh or sin."[24] The gospel of work in America was preached from many other pulpits: William Penn constantly reminded the Quakers of Philadelphia that "diligence is a virtue useful and laudable among men.... Frugality is a virtue too, and not of little use in life.... It is proverbial, 'A Penny sav'd is a Penny got.'"[25] Perhaps the real solidification of the work ethic in America occurred with its practical translation and secularization by Benjamin Franklin. In his various publications, Franklin taught that wealth was the result of virtue and the proper display of character. In his *Autobiography*, he defines the work ethic in his list of ideal traits: "Temperance, Silence, Order, Resolution, Frugality, Industry, Sincerity, Justice, Moderation, Cleanliness, Tranquillity, Chastity, Humility."[26] With Franklin, the work ethic shifted from a direct form of worshipping God to an indirect way of rendering service to God by developing one's character and doing good to others.[27] Unlike the Puritans, Franklin's craftsman no longer worked for God's glory, but for himself. He maintained that "God helps those who help themselves." Nevertheless, hard work remained the only standard for private success and social usefulness.

By the nineteenth century, the Protestant ethic in America had changed its name at least three times, but its essential focus had not changed at all. Whether it was called the *Protestant ethic*, the *Puritan ethic*, the *work ethic*, or the *immigrant ethic*, hard work was seen as good in and of itself, the only ticket to survival and the possibility of success. According to the noted labor historian Daniel T. Rogers, the central premise of the work ethic is that work is the core of the moral life. "Work made men useful in a world of economic scarcity. It staved off the doubts and temptations that preyed on idleness; it opened the way to deserved wealth and status; it allowed one to put the impress of mind and skill on the material world."[28] In many ways, the work ethic posited one's very right to existence; one achieved worth through work.

During the nineteenth century, we see the first stirrings of dissatisfaction with this ethic. These came not from churches, employers, or even workers themselves, but from artists. The popularity of Dickens's novels and of plays such as Gerhart Hauptmann's 1893 drama about cottage industries, *The Weavers*, were foreshadowings of a discontent that would manifest itself only in the mid-twentieth century. Until that time, the moral preeminence of work stood essentially unchallenged as an accepted social value. C. Wright Mills pointed out that "the gospel of work has been central to the historic tradition of America, to its image of itself, and to the images the rest of the world have of America."[29] There can be little question that this reverence for work, along with an abundance of natural resources and human capital, was an important determinant of America's

material success.[30] Moreover, because of this need for a pool of diligent laborers, every agent of authority and education proclaimed the merits of work. From Luther to Franklin to Horatio Alger, workers received a steady diet of exhortation and incantation from press, pulpit, and primer. All work was worthwhile and laudable; work well done would inevitably bring reward, and work avoided led to degradation and ruin.[31]

It is, however, important to keep in mind that tracing the idea of work through history is difficult, and the record is inconsistently one-sided. As Barbara Tuchman pointed out in *A Distant Mirror* (1978), the history of an ancient society is usually limited to the record keeping of the nobility and the intelligentsia. Few or no records are to be found depicting what the lower classes actually thought or felt about any momentous occurrence of their age. For example, we have no record of what a Greek slave, a medieval peasant, a Reformation craftsman, or a New England Puritan farmer had to say about the day-to-day experiences of work. We do however have the philosophical speculations of Aristotle, Aquinas, Calvin, and Jonathan Edwards.[32] We infer, therefore, that the proposition of the "nobility of work" is not a working-class concept but a middle-class one. We do not, however, embrace the cynical view that has labeled the Protestant work ethic as pure "ideological subterfuge" geared to maximizing the workers' efforts and thereby increasing the owners' pool of capital. Rather, we maintain that the Protestant work ethic has often been used as a means of masking the drudgery and necessity of work. We accept the notion that true believers were in fact theologically motivated in their actions and achieved a great deal of personal solace as well as material reward and comfort from their work. Moreover, we take it to be the case that those who subscribed to the more secularized version of the work ethic did so with the faithful expectation that their efforts would reap personal and social gain. Nonetheless, part of the overall effect of the work ethic was to acclimate the individual worker to the inevitable. We want to contend that the tradition of the work ethic glorified and legitimized work and gave it a teleological orientation—a sense of purpose or design—that helped to both sustain individual effort and ameliorate its temporal brutishness. Perhaps former President Richard Nixon's often quoted 1971 Labor Day speech best exemplifies our point. He said: "Scrubbing floors and emptying bedpans have just as much dignity as there is in any work done in this country — including my own...." We suggest that while both jobs must be done and done well, these jobs are too disparate in their impact and import to warrant serious comparison.

Daniel Yankelovich, in *New Rules: Searching for Self-Fulfillment in a World Turned Upside Down*, contends that the post-World War II formulation of the "work ethic myth" is the "giving/getting compact":

- Even though we no longer had anything in common, we stayed together. We didn't break up our marriage even when the children were grown.
- We lived on his salary even though I was making good money at the time. He said he would not feel right if we spent the money I earned for food and rent.
- I never felt I could do enough for my parents, especially my mother. She sacrificed a promising career as a singer to take care of us. I realize now that she must have been miserable most of the time. (Why?) Because she said so. She kept reminding us what she was giving up, but we didn't take her seriously.
- It never occurred to me not to have children. Now I realize I'd have felt less put upon if I had freely chosen that destiny and not had it chosen for me.
- I've worked hard all my life, and I've made a success out of it for myself and my family. We have a nice home. We have everything it takes to be comfortable. I've been able to send my kids to good schools, and my wife and I can afford to go anywhere we want. Yes, I have a real sense of accomplishment.
- Sure it was a rotten job. But what the hell. I made a good living, I took care of my wife and kids. What more do you expect?

The old giving/getting compact might be paraphrased this way:

I give hard work, loyalty, and steadfastness. I swallow my frustrations and suppress my impulse to do what I would enjoy, and do what is expected of me instead. I do not put myself first; I put the needs of others ahead of my own. I give a lot, but what I get in return is worth it. I receive an ever-growing standard of living and my family life with a devoted spouse and decent kids. Our children will take care of us in our old age if we really need it, which thank goodness we will not. I have a nice home, a good job, the respect of my friends and neighbors, a sense of accomplishment at having made something of my life. Last but not least, as an American, I am proud to be a citizen of the finest country in the world.[33]

For Yankelovich, no matter what the source or accuracy of this compact, it is difficult to exaggerate how important it has been in supporting the goals of American society in the postwar period. It lies at the very heart of what we mean by the "American dream." Right or wrong, the "giving/getting compact" has helped to sustain and direct the efforts of millions over the years.

The work ethic in all its various formulations contains elements of both myth and reality. In essence, it is a view of the world that promotes and helps to perpetuate a certain perspective on reality that might not otherwise exist. The work ethic is a myth in the sense that nineteenth-century philosopher Georges Sorel used the word; that is, that the truth of the myth is relatively unimportant as long as it furthers the end in view.[34] In general, it must be remembered that the work ethic is a product of an era of scarcity and deprivation, when one either worked or starved. It made the negative aspects of work bearable by giving work a moral quality. The conclusion remains that the work ethic was and is an ideology propagated by the middle classes for the working classes with just enough plausibility to make it credible....[35]

For all its glorification, and no matter how many honorifics we attach to it, work remains, in the eye of the common man, a task to be endured. As trade unionist Gus Tyler has stated, "There are at least two work ethics: that of the overseer and that of the overseen." He claims that workers are not opposed to the work ethic in any literal sense. "But work *per se* as an ethical imperative gets little, if any, attention because, to union people, work is such a necessity that it is almost unnecessary to construct a system of values, with theological overtones, to justify labor. If American unionists have an ethic, it is probably best summed up in the old slogan: 'a fair day's pay for a fair day's work.'"[36] From the unionist point of view, therefore, the proper and only response possible to Max Weber's question "Do we work to live or live to work?" is "We work to live." Most unionists are not so much guilty of working to live as they are guilty of being asked a question to which the answer is moot. If they are *compelled* to work in order to live, why bother asking? Recent appraisals of work and the worker by such scholars as Daniel Bell, Clark Kerr, Robert Strauss, and Daniel Yankelovich have confirmed the suspicion long held by most workers that dull, hard work is not necessarily ennobling and does not produce cultural heroes and role models. Working hard is a basic dimension of human existence; it is a duty. From this point of view, working is obligatory and, although it may at times well warrant a gray — if not red — badge of courage, it is basically a requirement of existence and only a means toward an end. As a character in a popular series of detective mysteries has put it: "If work was [such] a good thing, the rich would have it all and not let you do it."[37] Unquestionably, my favorite anecdote on this topic is the story of the rich man's response to his daughter's question "Is sex fun or work?" "Sex must be fun for women," he replied, "because if it were work, your mother would have the maid do it."

Nonetheless, the country's classic work ethic is by no means dead. The mythology lingers on and is perpetuated by diverse sources. The good word on work can now be heard from Jesse Jackson, Lee Iacocca, George Gilder, Ronald Reagan, and certain prime-time television beer commercials.

Jesse Jackson's interpretation of the work ethic stays, perhaps, closest to one of the original tenets of the doctrine; that is, "how to get more and do better." For Jackson, "black power" is economic success, as this is achieved by getting a piece of the action, working hard, saving, starting one's own business, being innovative, and/or constantly extending the scope and market of one's business. For Jackson, the black community will only achieve equality with the white community when it successfully emulates Benjamin Franklin's model. He has spent the last fifteen years exhorting blacks to take pride in who they are, to finish school, to work hard, to be, in short, Puritan. In many ways, his message and that of Operation PUSH is a restatement of immigrant work ethic exhortations to get a job, do well, work hard, and things will necessarily be better than they were before.

In recent years, Lee Iacocca has emerged not only as the chief spokesman for Chrysler but also, indirectly, as the spokesman for the entire American automobile industry and the sanctity of the American worker's ability. Iacocca's commercial presentations have the emotional punch of a Knute Rockne half-time pep talk. In general, the commercials deliver a message that can be paraphrased as follows: So the foreign cars have been made better! So they have given you better value! So they have on percentage outsold us in the last seven years! OK, we were wrong! We weren't listening to what you wanted! But we hear you now! We're sorry, we forgot what got us to where we are today! Americans can outbuild any car maker in the world! We can build cars that out-perform, outlast and out-distance all our competitors! American "know-how" created the auto industry! We've proven our abilities in the past, we'll prove them to you again! American ingenuity is based on the American worker! I believe in the American worker and so do you! Buy our cars, I personally guarantee them for five years and/or 50,000 miles! Buy American!

On a more academic level, George Gilder, former economist and Nixon White House speech writer, has put together a series of books and articles on the entrepreneurial ethic as the cornerstone of capitalistic prosperity.[38] For Gilder, it is the entrepreneur who creates the "trickle-down effect," which in turn stimulates the "invisible hard mechanism," thereby creating "the greatest possible good for the greatest possible number." For Gilder, the farsighted, risk-taking, hardworking, self-sacrificing businessman is the catalyst propelling the entire laissez-faire economic system.

Ronald Reagan consciously attempted to resuscitate the Jeffersonian model of the "rugged individual." This classic model is the individual who is able, by hard work, individual know-how, and personal ingenuity, to create and maintain most if not all the necessities of life. This is the model of the self-sufficient "agrarian atomist" who first conquered this country by farming the shores of the East Coast and then proceeded during the next 200 years to follow the challenge of our Western expansion. It is not altogether surprising that Reagan's image of the "rugged individual" closely resembles many of the main characters in novelist Louis L'Amour's Western sagas. L'Amour's heroes are self-directed individuals who came into a new region, pacified it, cultivated it, and made it a safe place to rear a family. For Reagan, this country's "manifest destiny" became a fact and not a slogan because of the vision, courage, and hard work of our pioneer ancestors. These are, he believes, the virtues that have made us strong and prosperous and that must be maintained and fostered if the dream of America is to be continued and fulfilled for those who come after us. And these are virtues strongly embodied in the traditional Protestant work ethic.

Prime-time beer commercials are mythic playlets, romanticizing and idealizing the Herculean efforts of men at work.[39] They depict men pouring molten ingots in factories, spanning huge chasms with cables of steel, cutting down tall trees in the mist of a rain forest, blasting tunnels through mountains of solid granite, sailing ancient square-riggers through tempestuous seas, skiing the Tetons to check for avalanche faults, and staging a multi-vehicle highway crash for the concluding scene of a Clint Eastwood film. And through all the grit of these various scenarios, the participants are, to a man, grinning from ear to ear at both their accomplishments and their camaraderie. After all of this, the worker-warriors retire to a local saloon where they consume large quantities of iced beer and debrief one another in a warm sundown glow of work well done and worth doing.

For all of the hoopla and popular promotion, we feel that the general work force remains unconvinced and unmoved. No matter what the gimmicks, slogans, and logos, too much of the work of life remains uninteresting, unenjoyable, and without obvious purpose and distinction. For too many of us, work is the "curse of Adam," and to be relieved of it would be counted a boon and a blessing. The term "Protestant work ethic," which began as an explanation for the economic behavior of an historical people, exists today almost solely as a pejorative phrase.[40] According to social critic Michael Harrington, whatever value it may have had, the Protestant work ethic has devolved to the notion that "a man establishes his worth in the eyes of his neighbor and his God…by doing drudgery and engaging in savings."[41]

## ENDNOTES

1. "What Is the Point Working?" *Time*, May 11, 1981. pp. 93–94.

2. Lee Braude, *Work and Workers: A Sociological Analysis* (New York: Praeger Publications, 1975), p. 3.

3. Mike Royko, "Silver Spoon Fits, Why Not Wear It?" *Chicago Tribune*, November 11, 1985, Sec. 1, p. 3.

4. Michael Maccoby and Katherine A. Terzi, "What Happened to the Work Ethic?" in W. Michael Hoffman and Thomas J. Wyly (eds.), *The Work Ethic in Business* (Cambridge, MA: Oelgeschlager, Gunn, and Hain, Publishers, 1981), pp. 31–34.

5. Studs Terkel, *Working* (New York: Pantheon Books, 1974), p. 521.

6. Gregory Baum, *The Priority of Labor* (New York: Paulist Press, 1982), p. 10.

7. Jay B. Rurlich, *Work and Love: The Crucial Balance* (New York: Summit Books, 1980), p. 29.

8. *Work in America: Report of a Special Task Force to the Secretary of Health, Education and Welfare* (Cambridge, MA: MIT Press, 1980), p. 13.

9. Terkel, *Working*, p. xi.

10. Hannah Arendt points out that the words *labor* and *work* are really two different words; for Arendt, they connote two different but not disparate meanings. The Latin work is *ponos*, the French *travail*, and the German *Arbeit*. The word *work* has different etymological roots. In Latin, "to work" is *facere* or *fabricari*; in Greek, it is *ergazesthai*; in French, it is *ouvrer*; and in German, *werken*. For Arendt, *labor* is the "toil of life," that "drudgery" that must be done to minister to the necessities of existence. To labor is to use one's body to achieve a task. *Work*, she feels, has a higher significance. It connotes "to make," "to do with intention," "to accomplish as task"; it refers to craftsmanship. Granting Professor Arendt these real and implied differences, we shall nevertheless use these terms as if they were synonymous.

11. Hannah Arendt, *The Human Condition* (Chicago: University of Chicago Press, 1958), pp. 48 n., 80 n., 110 n.

12. Braude, *Work and Workers*, p. 5.

13. *The New Oxford Annotated Bible* (New York: Oxford University Press), Gen. 3:17b–19.

14. Adriand Tilgher, *Homo Faber: Work Through the Ages*, trans. Dorothy Canfield Fisher (Chicago: Henry Regnery, 1965), pp. 11–12.

15. Ibid., pp. 29–40.

16. Sar A. Levitan and Wm. B. Johnston, *Work Is Here to Stay, Alas* (Salt Lake City: Olympian Publishing Co., 1973), p. 28.

17. *Plutarch's Lives* (New York: Modern Library, 1932), p. 183.

18. Levitan and Johnston, *Work Is Here to Stay, Alas*, p. 28.

19. Tilgher, *Homo Faber*, p. 49.

20. Michael Cherrington, *The Work Ethic: Working Values and Values that Work* (New York: AMACOM, 1980), pp. 20–33.

21. Michael Argyle, *The Social Psychology of Work* (New York: Taplinger Publishing, 1972), pp. 22–23.

22. Cherrington, *The Work Ethic*, p. 20.

23. Gerhard E. Lewski, *The Religious Factor: A Sociological Study of Religious Impact on Politics, Economics and Family Life* (New York: Doubleday, 1961), pp. 4–5.

24. Maccoby and Terzi, "What Happened to the Work Ethic?" p. 22.

25. Cherrington, *The Work Ethic*, p. 35.

26. Jesse L. Lemisch, *Benjamin Franklin: 'The Autobiography' and Other Writings* (New York: New American Library, 1961), p. 95.

27. Cherrington, *The Work Ethic*, p. 35.
28. Daniel T. Rodgers, *The Work Ethic in Industrial America, 1850–1920* (Chicago: University of Chicago Press, 1978), p. 14.
29. C. Wright Mills, "The Meaning of Work Throughout History," in Fred Best (ed.), *The Future of Work* (Englewood Cliffs, NJ: Prentice-Hall, 1973), p. 6.
30. Joseph F. Quinn, "The Work Ethic and Retirement," in *The Work Ethic—A Critical Analysis* (Madison, WI: Industrial Relations Research Association, 1983), p. 87.
31. Levitan and Johnston, *Work Is Here to Stay, Alas*, p. 31.
32. Ibid., p. 27.
33. Daniel Yankelovich, *New Rules: Searching for Self-Fulfillment in a World Turned Upside Down* (New York: Bantam Books, 1982), p. 7.
34. Jack Barbash, "Which Work Ethic?" in *The Work Ethic—A Critical Analysis*, p. 258.
35. Ibid., p. 232.
36. Gus Tyler, "The Work Ethic: A Union View," in *The Work Ethic—A Critical Analysis*, pp. 197–198.
37. Elmore Leonard, *Split Images* (New York: Avon, 1981), p. 13.
38. George Gilden, *Wealth and Poverty* (New York: Bantam Books, 1982); also *The Spirit of Enterprise* (New York: Simon and Schuster, 1984).
39. "What Is the Point of Working?" pp. 93–94.
40. Joseph Epstein, "Work and Its Contents," *The American Scholar*, Summer 1983, p. 307.
41. Eric Larrabee, "Time to Kill: Automation, Leisure, and Jobs," in Robert V. Guthrie (ed.), *Psychology in the World Today* (Reading, MA: Addison-Wesley, 1968), p. 312.

# 39. CULTURE AND VIOLENCE IN AMERICA

## ARNOLD GOLDSTEIN

*"So America's history is contradictory.... We are a free, democratic, progressive, creative country.... [We] have insulted, injured, assaulted, abused, raped, and murdered one another at levels that are dismayingly high...."*

This selection sketches our history by focusing on the theme of violence. How central is violence to our culture?

## HOW DID WE GET HERE?

The United States was born in a spirit of freedom and democracy, yet also with a strong belief in the use of individual and group violence. The Revolutionary War lasted seven years and succeeded in its goal of a new and independent nation. It also

began our two-century-long love affair with the gun, as four hundred thousand victorious citizen-soldiers helped proclaim the right to bear arms.

The new nation lay along the Eastern coast of a three-thousand-mile wide unexplored continent of buffalo and other game to kill, of Native Americans to displace, of a frontier to conquer. As our citizens began moving westward in the late 1700s, a frontier mentality went with them. Self-reliance, independence, and impatience with the poorly developed laws and law enforcement of the day were also part of this mentality. Justice often meant "frontier justice," in which groups of local citizenry took the law into their own hands: Hanging horse thieves or riding undesirables out of town were among the ways such early criminal sentencing was handled.

Although our mass media have long glamorized it, frontier living was rarely as easy and romantic as usually portrayed. Often, it was very difficult economically, which helped give rise to outlaw gangs, bank robbers, counterfeiters, and other criminal behavior. A tide of immigration to the United States commenced in earnest in the early 1800s, and grew to a flood of newcomers of diverse backgrounds to our shores as the twentieth century unfolded. The ingredients in this great, human melting pot often mixed poorly and often resulted in high levels of individual and group violence directed at these migrants, especially in the cities.

The Civil War, 1861 to 1865, pitted Northerner against Southerner and, at times, neighbor against neighbor, even cousin against cousin in bitter, lethal combat. Its price was high—well beyond the actual war casualties of 617,000 dead and 375,000 injured soldiers. Out of the war grew forces that yielded new and virulent forms of aggression throughout the country. Often stemming from war-related animosities, feuding, lynching, and high levels of vigilante activity erupted. The feud, primarily developing in Southern mountain states, was a kind of interfamily guerrilla warfare. Much more deadly in its effects was lynching, in which unorganized mobs captured and hung usually guiltless black persons. It is the shame of America that 3,209 recorded lynchings occurred during the years 1889 to 1918.

Vigilante aggression also became more organized during this post-Civil War period, with the Ku Klux Klan, the Bald Knobbers, the White Cappers, and many more such groups targeting not just blacks but several other minority groups as well. Also at this time, the much-romanticized cowboy gang became prominent. Their specialties—stagecoach, train, and bank robberies—to this day portrayed as exciting and heroic events, were plain and simple acts of criminal violence.

Much of the recorded violence in America in the late 1800s and early 1900s was group violence associated with the industrialization of our country. There were violent labor strikes in the mining, railroad, and auto industries as well as violent government response to the strikers. Although there are numerous accounts of violence by individuals during these years, actual numbers are largely un-

available because the FBI did not begin compiling crime statistics for murder, assault, rape, and similar violent crimes until 1933. Nevertheless, it is clear that during the years in which Prohibition was the law of the land (1920 to 1933), murder and mayhem between and among bootleggers and liquor hijackers in their rivalry for market control was at a level of often lethal intensity. During the two world wars and the economic depression in the 1930s, there was less violence here for individuals and groups. The same was true in other countries. Perhaps when citizens feel joined together against a common enemy, there is less motivation to attack each other.

As the twentieth century moved along, feuding, vigilante groups, lynching, and labor violence all receded, but aggression in seemingly new and more serious individual forms appeared. Spouse and child abuse has been with us all along, but was in a sense "discovered" as it became a matter for more public discussion and concern in the mid-1960s. It has since become recognized as widely practiced in our homes and severely damaging to many of our citizens. So too for the crime of rape, as the women's movement of this same period called our collective attention to its nature, its frequency, and its serious consequences. As is widely known, in this period, America's homicide rate far exceeded that of all other modern nations—and still does today.

Since the 1970s, the levels of murder, rape, abuse, and assault by adults are a continuing serious concern, but our main worry seems to be the flourishing of juvenile crime. Aided by the massive influx of drugs into our country, armed by our arsenal of weaponry, encouraged by its unremitting portrayal in the media, and in imitation of many of their heroes, our sons and daughters have reached new peaks of aggression in their lives, both as individuals and in growing numbers of gangs.

So America's history is contradictory. We are a free, democratic, progressive, creative country of protected citizen rights, rule by law, legal transfer of power, economic opportunity for at least most of our citizens, and much more that is good. We are also a country in which, for more than two hundred years, our people have insulted, injured, assaulted, abused, raped, and murdered one another at levels that are dismayingly high and seem to be growing. That is where we are and, briefly, how we got here.

# Part IX

# SOCIAL CONTROL AND SOCIAL DEVIANCE

**Social control** refers to all the various ways a society and its representatives attempt to ensure ongoing conformity and cooperation. The easiest way of exercising social control is to have people "willingly" obey the rules and accept both the structure and culture. This is attempted through socialization, the process by which various representatives of society form the human being by teaching him or her the social patterns of society.

Other than socialization, representatives of society attempt to ensure conformity by punishing nonconformity. In the first selection, Peter Berger shows us the wide range of methods used. Who ends up being punished? Those we define as "deviant." In fact, the labeling of people as deviant is one attempt to punish them for actions we dislike. Erich Goode's first selection is an excellent introduction to why certain acts and people are labeled deviant. Goode's second selection, "The Social Creation of Stigma," is a very thoughtful and challenging examination of how and why people stigmatize others, and what the implications are for those who are stigmatized. Stigmatization is a reflection of the values held by those of us who point fingers—and it is too easy for us to point fingers without carefully examining both society and our own motivations.

The selection by William J. Chambliss, "The Saints and the Roughnecks," has become a classic in sociology because it highlights how deviance is always subjective and very often class-biased. Charles E. Silberman discusses criminal violence and its harm to society, and, finally, John Irwin shows us how jail acts to isolate, label, control, and degrade people in society.

# 40. THE MEANING OF SOCIAL CONTROLS

PETER L. BERGER

*"No society can exist without social control. Even a small group of people meeting but occasionally will have to develop their mechanisms of control if the group is not to dissolve in a very short time."*

Social control is the "mechanism" used to "eliminate undesirable personnel and...'to encourage the others.'" It is the "means used by a society to bring its recalcitrant members back into line.... It is the negative sanctions or punishments that await those who attempt to stray from the fold." Peter Berger does two things in this article: (1) He describes the various kinds of controls, from violence to economic pressure to "ridicule, gossip, and opprobrium" (rejection). (2) He describes the many "systems" that exercise such controls, including the political system, employers, colleagues, various "social involvements," and finally "the circle of one's family and personal friends."

This is a fascinating description, but it is also a nightmare of sorts. 'The individual who, thinking consecutively of all the people he is in a position to have to please, from the collector of the Internal Revenue Service to his mother-in-law, gets the idea that all of society sits right on top of him." But Berger tells us only half of the social control story. There is also a whole host of **rewards** that operate to encourage conformity, from getting an "A" on an exam to a promotion on the job. These things also constitute social controls.

Social control is one of the most generally used concepts in sociology. It refers to the various means used by a society to bring its recalcitrant members back into line. No society can exist without social control. Even a small group of people meeting but occasionally will have to develop their mechanisms of control if the group is not to dissolve in a very short time. It goes without saying that the instrumentalities of social control vary greatly from one social situation to another. Opposition to the line in a business organization may mean what personnel directors call a *terminal interview* and

From *An Invitation to Sociology*, by Peter Berger. Copyright © 1963 by Peter L. Berger. Used by permission of Doubleday, a division of Bantam Doubleday Dell Publishing Group, Inc.

what those in a criminal syndicate call a *terminal automobile ride*. Methods of control vary with the purpose and character of the group in question. In either case, control mechanisms function to eliminate undesirable personnel and (as it was put classically by King Christopher of Haiti when he had every tenth man in his forced-labor battalion executed) "to encourage the others."

The ultimate and, no doubt, the oldest means of social control is physical violence. In the savage society of children, it is still the major one. But even in the politely operated societies of modern democracies, the ultimate argument is violence. No state can exist without a police force or its equivalent in armed might. This ultimate violence may not be used frequently. There may be innumerable steps before its application, in the way of warnings and reprimands. But if all the warnings are disregarded, even in so slight a matter as paying a traffic ticket, the last thing that will happen is that a couple of cops show up at the door with handcuffs and a Black Maria. Even the moderately courteous cop who hands out the initial traffic ticket is likely to wear a gun—just in case. And even in England, where he does not in the normal course of events, he will be issued one if the need arises....

In any functioning society, violence is used economically and as a last resort, with the mere threat of this ultimate violence sufficing for the day-to-day exercise of social control. For our purposes in this argument, the most important matter to underline is that nearly all men live in social situations in which, if all other means of coercion fail, violence may be officially and legally used against them....

Next in line after the political and legal controls, one should probably place economic pressure. Few means of coercion are as effective as those that threaten one's livelihood or profit. Both management and labor effectively use this threat as an instrument of control in our society. But economic means of control are just as effective outside the institutions properly called the economy. Universities or churches use economic sanctions just as effectively in restraining their personnel from engaging in deviant behavior deemed by the respective authorities to go beyond the limits of the acceptable. It may not be actually illegal for a minister to seduce his organist, but the threat of being barred forever from the exercise of his profession will be a much more effective control over this temptation than the possible threat of going to jail. It is undoubtedly not illegal for a minister to speak his mind on issues that the ecclesiastical bureaucracy would rather have buried in silence, but the chance of spending the rest of his life in minimally paid rural parishes is a very powerful argument indeed. Naturally such arguments are employed more openly in economic institutions proper, but the administration of economic sanctions in churches or universities is not very different in its end results from that used in the business world.

Where human beings live or work in compact groups, in which they are personally known and to which they are tied by feelings of personal loyalty (the kind that sociologists call *primary groups*), very potent and simultaneously very subtle mechanisms of control are constantly brought to bear on the actual or potential deviant. These are the mechanisms of persuasion, ridicule, gossip, and opprobrium. It has been discovered that in group discussions going on over a period of time, individuals modify their originally held opinions to conform to the group norm, which corresponds to a kind of arithmetic mean of all the opinions represented in the group. Where this norm lies obviously depends on the constituency of the group. For example, if you have a group of twenty cannibals arguing over cannibalism with one noncannibal, the chances are that in the end he will come to see their point and, with just a few face-saving reservations (concerning, say, the consumption of close relatives), will go over completely to the majority's point of view. But if you have a group discussion between ten cannibals who regard human flesh aged over sixty years as too tough for a cultivated palate and ten other cannibals who fastidiously draw the line at fifty, the chances are that the group will eventually agree on fifty-five as the age that divides the *déjeuner* from the *débris* when it comes to sorting out prisoners. Such are the wonders of group dynamics. What lies at the bottom of this apparently inevitable pressure toward consensus is probably a profound human desire to be accepted, presumably by whatever group is around to do the accepting. This desire can be manipulated most effectively—as is well known by group therapists, demagogues, and other specialists in the field of consensus engineering.

Ridicule and gossip are potent instruments of social control in primary groups of all sorts. Many societies use ridicule as one of the main controls over children—the child conforms not for fear of punishment but in order not to be laughed at. Within our own larger culture, "kidding" in this way has been an important disciplinary measure among southern Negroes. But most men have experienced the freezing fear of making oneself ridiculous in some social situation. Gossip, as hardly needs elaboration, is especially effective in small communities, where most people live their lives in a high degree of social visibility and inspectability by their neighbors. In such communities, gossip is one of the principal channels of communication, essential for the maintenance of the social fabric. Both ridicule and gossip can be manipulated deliberately by any intelligent person with access to their lines of transmission.

Finally, one of the most devastating means of punishment at the disposal of a human community is to subject one of its members to systematic opprobrium and ostracism. It is somewhat ironic to reflect that this is a favorite control mechanism with groups opposed on principle to the use of violence. An example of this would be "shunning" among the Amish and Mennonites. An individual who breaks one of the principal taboos of the group (for example, by getting sexually involved with an outsider) is "shunned." This means that, while permitted to continue to work and live in the community, not a single person will speak to him — ever. It is hard to imagine a more cruel punishment. But such are the wonders of pacifism....

It is possible, then, to perceive oneself as standing at the center (that is, at the point of maximum pressure) of a set of concentric circles, each representing a system of social control. The outer ring might well represent the legal and political system under which one is obligated to live. This is the system that, quite against one's will, will tax one, draft one into the military, make one obey its innumerable rules and regulations, if need be put one in prison, and in the last resort will kill one. One does not have to be a right-wing Republican to be perturbed by the ever-increasing expansion of this system's power into every conceivable aspect of one's life. A salutary exercise would be to note down for the span of a single week all the occasions, including fiscal ones, in which one came up against the demands of the politico-legal system. The exercise can be concluded by adding up the sum total of fines and/or terms of imprisonment that disobedience to the system might lead to. The consolation, incidentally, with which one might recover from this exercise would consist of the recollection that law-enforcement agencies are normally corrupt and of only limited efficiency.

Another system of social control that exerts its pressures towards the solitary figure in the center is that of morality, custom, and manners. Only the most urgent-seeming (to the authorities, that is) aspects of this system are endowed with legal sanctions. This does not mean, however, that one can safely be immoral, eccentric, or unmannered. At this point, all the other instrumentalities of social control go into action. Immorality is punished by loss of one's job, eccentricity by the loss of one's chances of finding a new one, bad manners by remaining uninvited and uninvitable in the groups that respect what they consider good manners. Unemployment and loneliness may be minor penalties compared to being dragged away by the cops, but they may not actually appear so to the individuals thus punished. Extreme defiance against the mores of our particular society, which is quite sophisticated in its control apparatus, may lead to yet another consequence — that of being defined, by common consent, as "sick."

Enlightened bureaucratic management (such as, for example, the ecclesiastical authorities of some Protestant denominations) no longer throws its deviant employees out on the street, but instead compels them to undergo treatment by its consulting psychiatrists. In this way, the deviant individual (that is, the one who does not meet the criteria of normality set up by management or by his bishop) is still threatened with unemployment and with the loss of his social ties, but in addition, he is also stigmatized as one who might very well fall outside the pale of responsible men altogether, unless he can give evidence of remorse ("insight") and resignation ("response to treatment"). Thus, the innumerable "counseling," "guidance," and "therapy" programs developed in many sectors of contemporary institutional life greatly strengthen the control apparatus of the society as a whole and especially those parts of it where the sanctions of the politico-legal system cannot be invoked.

But in addition to those broad coercive systems that every individual shares with vast numbers of fellow controllees, there are other and less extensive circles of control to which he is subjected. His choice of an occupation (or, often more accurately, the occupation in which he happens to end up) inevitably subordinates the individual to a variety of controls, often stringent ones. These are the formal controls of licensing boards, professional organizations, and trade unions — in addition, of course, to the formal requirements set by his particular employers. Equally important are the informal controls imposed by colleagues and coworkers. Again, it is hardly necessary to elaborate overly on this point. The reader can construct his own examples — the physician who participates in a prepaid comprehensive health insurance program, the undertaker who advertises inexpensive funerals, the engineer in industry who does not allow for planned obsolescence in his calculations, the minister who says that he is not interested in the size of the membership of his church (or rather, the one who acts accordingly — they nearly all say so), the government bureaucrat who consistently spends less than his allotted budget, the assembly-line worker who exceeds the norms regarded as acceptable by his colleagues, and so on. Economic sanctions are, of course, the most frequent and effective ones in these instances — the physician finds himself barred from all available hospitals, the undertaker may be expelled from his professional organization for "unethical conduct," the engineer may have to volunteer for the Peace Corps, as may the minister and the bureaucrat (in, say, New Guinea, where there is as yet no planned obsolescence, where Christians are few and far between, and where the governmental machinery is small enough to be relatively rational), and the assembly-line worker may find that all the defective parts of machinery in the entire plant have a way of congregating on his workbench. But the sanctions of social exclusion, contempt, and ridicule may be almost as hard to bear. Each occupational role in society, even in very humble jobs, carries with it a code of conduct that is very hard indeed to defy. Adherence to this code is normally just as essential for one's career in the occupation as technical competence or training.

The social control of one's occupational system is so important because the job decides what one may do in most of the rest of one's life — which voluntary associations one will be allowed to join, who will be one's friends, where one will be able to live. However, quite apart from the pressures of one's occupation, one's other social involvements also entail control systems, many of them less unbending than the occupational one, but some even more so. The codes governing admission to and continued membership in many clubs and fraternal organizations are just as stringent as those that decide who can become an executive at IBM (sometimes, luckily for the harassed candidate, the requirements may actually be the same). In less exclusive associations, the rules may be more lax and one may only rarely get thrown out, but life can be so thoroughly unpleasant for the persistent nonconformist to the local folkways that continued participation becomes humanly impossible. The items covered by such unwritten codes will, naturally, vary greatly. They may include ways of dressing, language, aesthetic taste, political or religious convictions, or simply table manners. In all these cases, however, they constitute control circles that effectively circumscribe the range of the individual's possible actions in the particular situation.

Finally, the human group in which one's so-called private life occurs, that is the circle of one's family and personal friends, also constitutes a control system. It would be a grave error to assume that this is necessarily the weakest of them all just because it does not possess the formal means of coercion of some of the other control systems. It is in this circle that an individual normally has his most important social ties. Disapproval, loss of prestige, ridicule, or contempt in this intimate group has far more serious psychological weight than the same reactions encountered elsewhere. It may be economically disastrous if one's boss finally concludes that one is a worthless nobody, but the psychological effect of such a judgment is incomparably more devastating if one discovers that one's wife has arrived at the same conclusion. What is more, the pressures of this most intimate control system can be applied at those times when one is least prepared for them. At one's job, one is usually in a better position to brace oneself, to be on one's guard, and to pretend than one is at home. Contemporary American "familism," a set of values that strongly emphasizes the home as a place of refuge from the tensions of the world and of personal fulfillment, contributes effectively to this control system. The man who is at least relatively prepared psychologically to give battle in his office is willing to do almost anything to preserve the precarious harmony of his family life. Last but not least, the social control of what German sociologists have called the "sphere of the intimate" is particularly powerful because of the very factors that have gone into its construction in the individual's biography. A man chooses a wife and a good friend in acts of essential self-definition. His most intimate relationships are those he must count on to sustain the most important elements of his self-image. To risk, therefore, the disintegration of these relationships means to risk losing himself in a total way. It is no wonder then that many an office despot promptly obeys his wife and cringes before the raised eyebrows of his friends.

If we return once more to the picture of an individual located at the center of a set of concentric circles, each one representing a system of social control, we can understand a little better that location in society means to locate oneself with regard to many forces that constrain and coerce one.

The individual who, thinking consecutively of all the people he is in a position to have to please, from the Collector of Internal Revenue to his mother-in-law, gets the idea that all of society sits right on top of him — and had better not dismiss that idea as a momentary neurotic derangement. The sociologist, at any rate, is likely to strengthen him in this conception, no matter [how much] other counselors may tell him to snap out of it....

# 41. AN INTRODUCTION TO DEVIANCE

ERICH GOODE

*"In all societies, large and small, industrialized or agrarian, some degree of individuality among members exists.... And in all societies, there is a point at which 'individuality' becomes deviance."*

Erich Goode's introduction to his textbook provides an understanding of the nature of deviance and how sociologists examine that subject. The study of deviance, Goode maintains, has focused not so much on **why** people commit deviant acts, but more on "how others condemn and punish them," and on what deviant behavior is really like.

Society is on shaky ground, in a way. What is taught as "the right way" is not the only way, and it is necessary to try to establish and reestablish the rules on a more than casual basis. Authorities establish fictions to protect the rules. Goode points out, "The fact is, we are not always successfully socialized into believing that our society is always right in everything it teaches. We are not robots." Some people will question the rules and even the social order itself. Goode, therefore, introduces the human being who fails to assume the positions in structure waiting for him or her, who questions the culture, who seems to assume "that the rules are a lie, a hoax, and are invalid or ineffective." To be labeled "deviant" is to represent to the defenders of society "a heresy against the said order."

Throughout this selection, Goode looks at why some people are labeled deviant and condemned. Although he does not really show why some people are able to reject the game of society, he does introduce two important points about individuality:

1. Societies punish individuals in order to discourage what are perceived as threats to the moral order. Individuality is not something that is safe for the actor.
2. Despite all of society's attempts to control, to socialize, to gain commitment, to get the individual to accept the culture and the structure, some people, for reasons not

*explained, escape and become individuals or join with others into groups that also do not accept society's rules.*

*Goode describes the human as more alive, more active, and more challenging than do the authors of earlier selections in this book: Norms are not as exact as other sociologists describe; humans are not as conformist; society is not so much the puppet theater. Yet Goode does not try to analyze where individuality comes from. Are we naturally rebellious? Is individuality an accident? Or can we trace individuality, like most other things, to socialization and social structure?*

On October 13, 1972, 45 Uruguayans, including 15 members of an amateur rugby team, took off from Mendoza, Argentina, in a Fairchild F-227 across the Andes Mountains toward Santiago, Chile. At 3:30 in the afternoon, the aircraft crashed, ploughing into a desolate region of the snowy range at an altitude of 11,500 feet. The crash left 17 dead and a number of others mortally wounded. A dozen more were to die before the party was rescued 72 days later. There were only 16 survivors. On the eighth day after the crash, word came over their transistor radio that the search party looking for them had been called off. Their food supplies consisted of some candy, jam, dates and plums, one packet of crackers, and a can of salted almonds. By the tenth day, even these skimpy supplies, although parsimoniously rationed, were gone. There was no living creature within miles of them — not even a blade of grass. They were in the center of the Andes, in one of the most inaccessible and inhospitable regions of the earth. Without food, death was absolutely certain.

For some days, several of the boys had realized that if they were to survive they would have to eat the bodies of those who had died in the crash. It was a ghastly prospect. The corpses lay around in the snow, preserved by the intense cold…. While the thought of cutting flesh from those who had been their friends was deeply repugnant to them all, a lucid appreciation of their predicament led them to consider it…. Most of the bodies were covered by the snow, but the buttocks of one protruded…. With no exchange of words, Canessa knelt, bared the skin, and cut into the flesh with a

From *Deviant Behavior: An Interactionist Approach*, by Erich Goode. Copyright © 1978. Reprinted by permission of Prentice-Hall, Inc., Englewood Cliffs, NJ.

piece of broken glass. It was frozen hard and difficult to cut, but he persisted until he had cut away twenty slivers the size of matchsticks…. He prayed to God to help him do what he knew to be right and then took a piece of meat in his hand. He hesitated. Even with his mind so firmly made up, the horror of the act paralyzed him. His hand would neither rise to his mouth nor fall to his side while the revulsion that possessed him struggled with his stubborn will. The will prevailed. The hand rose and pushed the meat into his mouth. He swallowed it. He felt triumphant. His conscience had overcome a primitive, irrational taboo. He was going to survive (Read 1974: 82, 85–86).

When they emerged into the world of civilization, many of their parents were horrified by the revelation of how they had survived. One mother "could not control the aghast expression on her face" when her son told her "of the extremes to which they had gone" to keep alive. Another mother "gave an involuntary grimace of horror" when her son informed her what their source of nourishment had been. "Like many of the other mothers who still had faith in their sons' survival, she had not thought, in detail, of how this miracle might be achieved; she assumed that there would be woods to shelter them, with rabbits running over the pine needles and fish swimming in the streams" (Read 1974: 312–313). Later, when the world had gotten used to the idea that cannibalism was absolutely necessary for survival, the young men were treated everywhere they went as heroes.

On June 26, 1968, a New York City policeman, Frank Serpico, began testifying in a series of appearances before a grand jury inquiry investigating the acceptance of payoffs by gamblers to police officers. By January 1969, the grand jury had completed its hearings. Theoretically, these hearings were secret, but word leaked out that Serpico had been testifying against his fellow officers. Transferred to another borough, "Serpico was elaborately ignored. No one said anything to him or even looked at him. And then it happened":

As Serpico stood alone, a plainclothesman…walked up to him. He stopped about three feet from Serpico, and reached into his pocket and took out a knife…. The others in the room fell silent. Out of the corner of his eye, Serpico could see some of them smirking. The plainclothesman with the knife said, "We know how to handle guys like you." He extended his right hand, the one with the knife in it, pressed a button in the handle with his thumb, and five inches of steel blade leaped out, pointing up. "I ought to cut your tongue out," the plainclothesman said (Maas 1974: 227).

After disarming him, Serpico pulled out a nine-millimeter Browning automatic and trained it on his assailant as the other men watched in horror. "How many rounds does it hold?" one of them asked, mesmerized by the enormous size of the weapon. "Fourteen," Serpico replied. "Fourteen? What do you need fourteen rounds for?" "How many guys you got in this office?" (1974: 228).

After his confrontation with the officer with the switchblade, "everyone figuratively tiptoed around" Serpico, but "he remained completely ostracized" (1974: 235).

James Morris served five years in one of Britain's most elite and military-minded cavalry regiments, including a stint in World War II. At 26, in 1953, he climbed three-quarters of the way up the world's highest mountain and scooped all other reporters on the story that Edmund Hillary and Tenzing Norkay had conquered Mount Everest. His entire life was like that: flamboyant, adventurous, romantic. While in Cairo as a reporter for *The Times* of London, Morris lived in a houseboat on the Nile. He had married at 22 and eventually fathered five children. Once, after quitting a reporting job, he bought an old Rolls-Royce and "moved his growing family in stately progress across the southern counties of England, and into France, Italy, and Spain, renting houses along the way that seemed to possess some vaguely superior quality of age or distinction."

Neither in life nor work did he shirk risks or plead caution, and in his writing he always responded sympathetically to the most manly images. Soldiers and adventurers brought out the best in him, and in his own way he seemed to belong to their brotherhood, displaying the discipline of the one and the carefree spirit of the other (Holden 1974: 19).

There was only one thing wrong: During his entire life, James Morris wanted to be a woman. "Please God, make me a girl," he would plead night after night in his childhood. This desire grew stronger as he grew older. "In the end, I couldn't go on as a man any longer because I really believed I *was* a woman, anyway — so I was living a lie, wasn't I?" In the early 1960s, Morris consulted with Dr. Harry Benjamin, an endocrinologist who conducted a pioneering research on (and first gave a name to) transsexuals. In 1963, Morris began taking female hormones. His body and face began to change; he acquired softer, more rounded features. He began to appear on the streets of Oxford, where he had a country home, dressed in women's clothing. He registered for research at one of Oxford's libraries under the name of a woman. Morris was, in fact, experimenting with passing as a woman. At first, only his wife knew; then a few close friends; eventually it became public knowledge. By 1972, James Morris began writing book reviews under the "suitably androgynous" name of Jan Morris. That year, he flew to Casablanca and underwent a sex change operation. The transition from James Morris, the man, to Jan Morris, the woman, was complete. His prayers had been answered (Morris 1974).

In the early morning hours just after midnight on Saturday, August 9, 1969, four young Charles Manson followers — Susan Atkins, Patricia Krenwinkel, Linda Kasabian, and Charles Watson — drove up a hill in a fashionable neighborhood of Beverly Hills, stopping in front of a residence located at 10050 Cielo Drive. Watson cut the telephone wires to the house, and the group climbed the fence surrounding the house. While they were hiding a change of clothes in the bushes, the headlights of a car in the driveway attracted their attention. Watson went to the car, ordered the driver, Steven Parent, 18 years old, to halt. Over the young man's pleas for mercy. Watson shot Parent four times. Watson then returned to the three young women and, together, they pushed Parent's Rambler back up the driveway away from the gate.

The party then walked down the driveway toward the house. Watson crawled into the dining room window and opened the front door, letting two of the women inside; Kasabian remained outside. There were four occupants of the house at the time – Voytek Frykowski, Abigail Folger, Jay Sebring, and Sharon Tate. Watson, Atkins, and Krenwinkel brutally murdered all four and wrote the word *PIG* on the front door with Sharon Tate's blood. Then they rejoined the waiting Kasabian, left by the front gate, and hurried down the hill to the car. The three killers changed their bloody clothes and drove off.

These four, it turns out, lived in a kind of commune headed by 34-year-old Charles Manson, who believed himself to be Jesus Christ. Manson had spent half of his life behind prison bars. Released in 1967, Manson gravitated to the Haight-Ashbury area of San Francisco and quickly established himself as something of a prophet among the area's young and often homeless street people. He developed a philosophy, "Helter Skelter," which was to be launched by the murder of affluent whites and to be climaxed by Manson becoming the "ruler of the world." The Tate-Frykowski-Folger-Sebring murders were simply part of a large but undetermined number of killings engineered or actually performed by Manson (Bugliosi, with Gentry, 1974, 1975).

What do cannibalism, testifying against one's fellow police officers, changing one's sex, and mass murder have in common? We would search in vain for similarities if we tried to understand the motives of the people involved, if we tried to determine the causes of their actions. We would also search in vain for some sort of internal consistency in these actions – if they all harmed others, if they were uniformly self-destructive, or if they broke some religious or natural law. The only thing that they have in common, really, is that they are all examples of deviant behavior....

## THE SOCIAL CONSTRUCTION OF REALITY

If, by "instincts," we mean behavioral impulses that are with us at birth, that do not have to be learned, humans have some instincts that "wire" us for some forms of behavior. Infants grasp and suckle. When presented with a smiling face, they smile back. Harlow showed that infant monkeys deprived of tactile nurturance do not grow up to do the sorts of things that other monkeys do. Humans, probably much more than monkeys, "need" warmth and affection; this, too, might be considered analogous to an instinct.

However, these few instincts do not take us very far. They do not dictate any specific or complex forms of behavior. We could not survive, at birth, on our instincts alone. In order to survive, we need one another. All the peoples of the world depend on, and have to devise, a culture – a system of rules and regulations that takes the place of instincts. Our world, then, has to be *humanly constructed*. This necessitates a social construction of reality (Berger and Luckmann 1966). Our relationship with our physical environment, unlike that of animals, is not fixed. The necessity for invention is almost absolute. Luckily, our capacity for invention is equally prodigious.

Not only must humans create a social order that protects its members from annihilation, but we must also infuse the world with meaning. We have to convince ourselves that certain things matter. No civilization could continue if large numbers of its members saw life and everything in it as a matter of emotional indifference. It would be impossible for a society to exist if all people met every situation with a shrug of the shoulders and a grunt that said, "What's the difference?"

Thus, it is the job of all societies to convince their members – large numbers of them at any rate – that there *is* meaning in life and in the universe. Consequently, we are, as existentialist philosopher Merleau-Ponty puts it, "*condemned* to meaning."

Although we are *theoretically* capable of creating a multiplicity of worlds, still, as a people, we are "compelled to impose a meaningful order on reality" (Berger 1967: 22). Every socially constructed universe "is an area of meaning carved out of a vast mass of meaninglessness, a small clearing of lucidity in a formless, dark, always ominous jungle" (Berger 1967: 29). "*All* societies are constructed in the face of chaos" (Berger and Luckmann 1966: 103). One major job of every civilization, then, is *universe maintenance* (Berger and Luckmann 1966: 105). A culture offers a kind of "protective cocoon" against chaos and death.

To be effective, these social constructions we call a society have to appear to be "natural," inevitable, and God-given — not artificially, symbolically, and humanly constructed. Members of the society have to be convinced of the ultimate reality of their culture, and have to remain ignorant of their mere expediency, their artificiality. We have to "forget" our own role in the creation of meaning. We have to see the rules of society as "something other than a human product" (Berger and Luckmann 1966: 61). We have to believe that they are right in some larger sense. The humanly made rules of society "are given a cosmic status" (Berger 1967: 36). We have to accept the social world, its views of right and wrong, of true and false, of good and bad, as taken for granted, as self-evident. Successful socialization is the internalization of society's rules such that they are not questioned, but rather seen as inevitable, in the nature of things. "The humanly-made world is explained in terms that deny its human production;" a kind of "fictitious inexorability" is placed on the rules of a culture (Berger 1967: 89, 95). This means that the "socially created" aspect of human existence has an authoritarian side to it as well as a side that inclines us toward freedom.

Once large numbers of the members of a society begin questioning the validity and the legitimacy of the social order and its rules, their foundation and their grip on people becomes shaky. The fact is, we are not always successfully socialized into believing that our society is always right in everything it teaches. We are not robots. We are not sponges that simply "soak up" rules. There will always be a certain number of people who question the rules, even the entire social order. In fact, it is often difficult to determine just what "the rules of society" are because there may be many competing sets of rules that are believed by different sets of people in that society. However, it is often the case that a majority believes in the validity of one set of rules. And those who believe otherwise, or who do things that seem to contradict these rules, will be regarded with suspicion. These people are often seen as troublemakers who threaten the social order. They seem to offer an alternative way of looking at reality, at the world, at the rules. They are engaged (or so some think) in an active denial of the social order.

Deviance is often seen as a kind of alternative world view. It announces that the rules are a lie, a hoax, and are invalid or ineffective. Hostility is directed at deviants in large part because they challenge the very basis of what most of us have been taught from the cradle. Once a set of rules is historically institutionalized and legitimated, many members of that society have a great emotional investment in protecting the status quo from any onslaught from those whom they consider barbarians. Because the rules have taken on a kind of semi-sacred status, deviance is a heresy against the social order. Hostility toward the deviant, relegating deviants to the status of inferior beings, is an outgrowth of the need to protect the symbolic universe that one sees as protective and nurturant.

[The roots of this hostility, then] may lie in the extremely significant function that the symbolic universe serves in making social life possible…. [Human] life is by its nature disorderly and the symbolic universe helps to create for us a kind of certainty and anchorage. Anything that threatens to strip us of this protective cocoon will inevitably be seen as evil…. [The] deviant is a person whose existence does threaten to inundate with chaos the symbolic system by which order and meaning are given to human existence (Scott 1972: 30, 31).

Probably the classic case of this perceived threat to the social universe created by conventional society is the world view ascribed to witches in the Middle Ages, and the deviant image they acquired. Hostility and outrage seemed at that time to be the only reasonable reaction to such heresy. There existed, writes Norman Cohn, author of *Europe's Inner Demons*, "somewhere in the midst of the great society, another society, small and clandestine, which not only threatened the existence of the great society but was also addicted to practices that were felt to be wholly abominable in the literal sense of anti-human." There was, consequently, an "urge to purify the world through the annihilation of some category of human beings imagined as agents of corruption and incarnation of evil" (Cohn 1975: xiv).

There are, of course, different types of deviants and different reasons for conventional people to condemn them. Clearly, one major type are deviants who deny or challenge (or seem to) the validity of the institutional order with which we are comfortable. Communists and political revolutionaries fit this description for many conventionals. So do atheists, "swingers," users of illegal drugs, and women's liberationists. Many members of our society denounce them because they fear what they stand for, they fear the contamination of their world, they fear that the basis of their own reality will be undermined.

Sometimes people do not fear the specific threat that the deviant's world view offers to theirs; they even may feel smugly superior and righteous face to face with certain deviants. But they may fear that people around them — or even they themselves — will become, or secretly *are*, the deviant they see, interact with, or imagine. Certainly, many "straight" men react in a hostile way to homosexuals for this reason: Their own sense of security in being heterosexual (what they see as their own "masculinity") is shaky. Many men look down on prostitutes (even though they may make use of their services) because they fear that their wives, daughters (or even mothers) are, were, or could become prostitutes. Conventional people are contemptuous of many deviants because they are seen as pitiable. They do not so much challenge the legitimacy of the social order as demonstrate that its downfall is entirely possible. We, too, and those we care about, in fact *anyone*, could become a poor, unfortunate creature — an alcoholic, a suicide, a drug addict, an insane person.

In addition, people fear and hate deviants because they threaten our well-being, perhaps our very physical existence. They are thought, actually or potentially, to visit violence on us, or on those we are close to, or on the social body as a whole. Many "criminals" would fit this description. So would juvenile delinquents. On the other hand, there are perpetrators of damage and violence that conventional people rarely condemn — politicians who start wars for patriotic reasons, for instance. Most deviants commit no damage of any kind on conventional people, ever. This "damage" reason is usually cited for a society's opposition to deviance and deviants; it is, in fact, the weakest reason of all. People see deviants as dangerous because they are already condemned; they do not condemn deviants because they are dangerous.

Many deviants also threaten powerful, established interests. Hostility toward deviance does not arise spontaneously out of society's "culture." In every society, certain members have more power to shape public opinion and the legal structure than others do. These more influential members may see in certain behavior a potential threat to what they have. It often happens that what they have was obtained at the expense of less powerful members of their society. The powerful want to maintain the status quo — and try to convince the less advantaged that this is for the best. When the behavior of a threatening group comes too close for comfort, adverse public opinion alone is not sufficient; the powerful have their ideology translated into the criminal code. Thus, deviant behavior often becomes illegal behavior as well. Deviants may divert attention from the sources of inequality in a society — they may serve a kind of "scapegoating" function. Or the social control and punishment of deviance may serve to isolate and immobilize those who are too threatening (or are perceived as too threatening) to the most affluent and powerful members of society. This does not account for hostility toward all deviant behavior, but it does illuminate a great deal of the condemnation of deviance.

More general than the threat to powerful established interests is the fact that deviant behavior is widely seen as a challenge to the established hierarchical order — the ranking system of a society. The moral order (notions of right and wrong) rests on making invidious comparisons between people. Some are elevated and others lowered by what they do. When people do things we disapprove of, our sense of our own position in this stratificational system is threatened. Conventional people feel that they deserve a higher position in the moral hierarchy because they have followed the rules, and that others should be placed lower because they have not. Deviance may be seen as an "attack on an existing arrangement of ranked statuses." "Anyone who successfully promotes a new convention in which he is skilled and I am not attacks...my position in the world.... When new people successfully create a new world that defines other conventions as embodying...value, all the participants in the old world who cannot make a place in the new lose out" (Becker 1974: 774).[1] Deviance, in short, is seen by many members of a society as challenging a moral order that is the basis for a ranking system. People fear that a new moral order will be one in which their own ranking will be low. Consequently, they wish to punish those who seem to be trying to take their existing privileges and position away. They need not even rank very high in the existing system. All that is necessary is that they feel that their position will be lowered. This may be enough to generate fear, insecurity, and hostility toward the offending party.

## THE UNIVERSALITY OF DEVIANCE

Deviance is universal. Not only do people everywhere set rules detailing what constitutes appropriate and inappropriate — or conventional and deviant — behavior, but groups of people everywhere experience deviance in their midst. And everywhere, some sort of punishment is meted out for nonconformity. No society experiences absolute conformity from all its members. *Deviance is implicit in social organization.* In order to render human existence viable and workable, rules have to be set. And when rules are set, it is inevitable that they will be broken by some people at some time. The social organization of the condemnation of deviant behavior is universal. And the behavior itself — that is, some sort of behavior that touches off condemnation — is also universal. *The only universal in deviance is its very existence.* There are no actions that are literally condemned everywhere, but the condemnation of some actions does exist everywhere. Exactly what it is that upsets people is enormously variable. And exactly how flexible "the rules" are is also highly variable. But the fact that large numbers of the members of a society will and do become upset at something others do is everywhere the case.

It has been claimed that socially disapproved or "deviant" behavior is only characteristic of (or widespread in) complex, industrialized, urbanized societies — that illiterate, tribal folk societies experience little or no significant deviance. They are perceived as homogeneous, with everyone living in harmony and conformity. People in these societies, some say, tend to act pretty much alike,

to believe more or less the same things. It turns out that these claims are grossly exaggerated. In fact, "troublesome behavior is frequent and varied in the world's small and simple societies" (Edgerton 1973: 25). In all societies, large and small, industrialized or agrarian, some degree of individuality among members exists. It is, of course, measurably greater in some societies than others; but it may not be *experienced* as lesser in the small societies, where small differences may take on greater subjective importance. And in all societies, there is a point at which "individuality" becomes deviance....

## ENDNOTES

1. Becker's argument here applies specifically to artistic convention, and it is based on an unpublished paper by Everett C. Hughes, who in turn borrowed the idea from William Graham Sumner's *Folkways.*

## REFERENCES

Becker, Howard S. "Art as Collective Action." *American Sociological Review,* Vol. 39 (December 1974): 767–776.

Berger, Peter L. *The Sacred Canopy.* Garden City, NY: Doubleday, 1967.

— — and Thomas Luckmann. *The Social Construction of Reality.* Garden City, NY: Doubleday, 1966.

Bugliosi, Vincent, with Curt Gentry. *Helter Skelter.* New York: Norton, 1974; New York: Bantam, 1975.

Cohn, Norman. *Europe's Inner Demons: An Enquiry Inspired by the Great Witch Hunt.* New York: Basic Books, 1975.

Edgerton, Robert B. "Deviant Behavior and Cultural Theory." Reading, MA: Addison-Wesley, *Module in Anthropology* no. 37, 1973.

Holden, David. "James and Jan." *The New York Times Magazine,* March 17, 1974: 18–19, 78ff. Reprinted by permission, New York Times Company.

Maas, Peter. *Serpico.* New York: Bantam. 1974.

Morris, Jan. *Conundrum.* New York: New American Library, 1975.

Read, Piers Paul. *Alive: The Story of the Andes Survivors.* Philadelphia: Lippincott, 1974. Reprinted by permission of J. B. Lippincott Company.

Scott, Robert A. "A Proposed Framework for Analyzing Deviance as a Property of Social Order." In Robert A. Scott and Jack D. Douglas (eds.), *Theoretical Perspectives on Deviance.* New York: Basic Books, 1972.

# 42. THE SOCIAL CREATION OF STIGMA

ERICH GOODE

*"In contemporary America, obesity is stigmatized. Fat people are considered less worthy human beings than thin people are.... Men and women of average weight tend to look down on the obese, feel superior to them, reward them less, punish them, make fun of them.... What is more, thin people will feel that this treatment is just...."*

By examining our reaction to obesity, Erich Goode illustrates very well what **stigma** means and why it occurs. He challenges all of us to examine our reactions to other people, and to ask ourselves how we have come to believe what we do.

Bertha was a massive woman. She weighed well over 400 pounds. Still, people enjoyed her company, and she had an active social life. One Friday night, Bertha and several of her friends stopped in a local Burger and Shake for a quick snack. Bertha disliked fast-food restaurants with good reason: Their seats were inadequate for her size. But she was a good sport and wanted to be agreeable, so she raised no objection to the choice of an eating establishment. Bertha squeezed her huge body into the booth and enjoyed a shake and burger. A typical Friday night crowd stood waiting for tables, so Bertha and her companions finished their snack and began to vacate the booth so that others could dine. But Bertha's worst fears were realized: She was so tightly jammed in between the table and the chair that she was stuck.

Bertha began struggling to get out of the booth, without success. Her friends pulled her, pushed her, and twisted her — all to no avail. She was trapped. Soon, all eyes in the Burger and Shake were focused on the hapless Bertha and her plight. Onlookers began laughing at her. Snickers esca-

lated to belly laughs, and the restaurant fairly rocked with raucous laughter and cruel, taunting remarks, "Christ, is she fat." "What's the matter, honey — one burger too many?" "Look at the trapped whale!" "How could anyone get that fat!" Bertha's struggles became frenzied; she began sweating profusely. Every movement became an act of desperation to free herself from her deeply humiliating situation. Finally, in a mighty heave, Bertha tore the entire booth from its bolts and she stood in the middle of the floor of the Burger and Shake, locked into the booth as if it had been a barrel. The crowd loved it, and shrieked with laughter that intensified in volume and stridency, as Bertha staggered helplessly, squatting in the center of the room.

One of Bertha's friends ran to his car, grabbed a hammer and a wrench, came back in, and began smashing at the booth. He broke it into pieces that fell to the floor, freeing the woman from her torture chamber. Bertha lumbered and pushed her way through the laughing, leering crowd, and ran to her car, hot tears in her eyes and burning shame in her throat. The friend who freed her limply placed the pieces of the chair and table onto the counter. The employees, now irritated, demanded that he pay for the damaged booth, but he and Bertha's other companions simply left the restaurant.

After that incident, Bertha rarely left her house. Two months later, she died of heart failure. She was 31 years old.

In contemporary America, obesity is stigmatized. Fat people are considered less worthy human beings than thin people are. They receive less of the good things that life has to offer, and more of the bad. Men and women of average weight tend to look down on the obese, feel superior to them, reward them less, punish them, make fun of them. The obese are often an object of derision and harassment for their weight. What is more, thin people will feel that this treatment is just, that the obese deserve it, indeed, that it is even something of a humanitarian gesture because such humiliation will supposedly inspire them to lose weight. The stigma of obesity is so intense and so persuasive that eventually the obese will come to see themselves as deserving of it, too.

The obese, in the words of one observer, "are a genuine minority, with all the attributes that a corrosive social atmosphere lends to such groups: poor self-image, heightened sensitivity, passivity, withdrawal, a sense of isolation and rejection." They are subject to relentless discrimination, they are the butt of denigrating jokes, they suffer from persecution; it would not be an exaggeration to say that they attract cruelty from the thin majority. Moreover, their friends and family rarely give the kind of support and understanding they need to deal with this cruelty; in fact, it is often friends and family who are themselves meting out the cruel treatment. The social climate has become "so completely permeated with anti-fat prejudice that the fat themselves have been infected by it. They hate other fat people, hate themselves when they are fat, and will risk anything—even their lives—in an attempt to get thin.... Anti-fat bigotry...is a psychic net in which the overweight are entangled every moment of their lives" (Louderback 1970, pp. v, vi, vii). The obese typically accept the denigration thin society dishes out to them because they feel, for the most part, that they deserve it. And they do not defend other fat people who are being criticized because they are a mirror of themselves; they mirror their own defects—the very defects that are so repugnant to them. Unlike the members of most other minorities, they don't fight back; in fact, they feel that they can't fight back. Racial, ethnic and religious minorities can isolate themselves to a degree from majority prejudices; the obese cannot. The chances are, most of the people they meet will be average size, and they live in a physical world built for individuals with much smaller bodies. The only possibilities seem to be to brace themselves—to cower under the onslaught of abuse—or to retreat and attempt to minimize the day-to-day disgrace.

Our hostility toward the overweight runs up and down the scale, from the grossly obese to men and women of average weight. If the hugely obese are persecuted mightily for their weight, the slightly overweight are simply persecuted proportionally less—they are not exempt. We live in a weight-obsessed society. It is impossible to escape nagging reminders of our ideal weight. Standing at the checkout counter in a supermarket, we are confronted by an array of magazines, each with its own special diet designed to eliminate those flabby pounds. Television programs (and advertising even more so) display actresses and models who are considerably slimmer than average, setting up an almost impossibly thin ideal for the viewing public. If we were to gain ten pounds, our friends would all notice it, view the gain with negative feelings, and only the most tactful would not comment on it.

These exacting weight standards not surprisingly fall more severely on the shoulders of women than on men. In a survey of the 33,000 readers of *Glamour* who responded to a questionnaire placed in the August 1983 issue of the magazine, 75 percent said that they were "too fat," even though only one-quarter were overweight according to the stringent 1959 Metropolitan Life Insurance Company's height-weight tables. (According to Metropolitan's current standards, even fewer of *Glamour's* readers are deemed overweight.) Still more surprising, 45 percent who were *under*weight according to Metropolitan's figures felt that they were "too fat." Only 6 percent of the respondents felt "very happy" about their bodies; only 15 percent described their bodies as "just right." When looking at their nude bodies in the mirror, 32 percent said that they felt "anxious," 12 percent felt "depressed," and 5 percent felt "repulsed."

Commenting on the *Glamour* survey, one of the researchers who analyzed its results, Susan Wooley, professor of psychiatry at the University of Cincinnati's medical school, stated, "What we see is a steadily growing cultural bias — almost no woman of whatever size feels she's thin enough" (*Glamour* 1984, p. 199). When asked which of the following would make them happiest, 22 percent chose success at work, 21 percent said having a date with a man they admired, and 13 percent said hearing from an old friend. However, the alternative that attracted the highest proportion of the sample was losing weight — 42 percent. The overwhelming majority (80 percent) said that they have to be slim to be attractive to men. A substantial proportion had "sometimes" or "often" used the potentially dangerous weight-loss methods of diet pills (50 percent), liquid formula diets (27 percent), diuretics (18 percent), laxatives (15 percent), fasting or starving (45 percent), and self-induced vomiting (15 percent). Judging from the results of this survey, it is safe to say that the readers of *Glamour* who responded to it are obsessed about being thin.

Evidence suggests that the standards for the ideal female form have gotten slimmer over the years. Women whose figures would have been comfortably embraced by the norm a generation or more ago are now regarded as overweight, even fat. The model for the White Rock Girl, inspired by the ancient Greek goddess Psyche, was 5'4" tall in 1894 and she weighed 140; her measurements were 37"-27"-38". Over the years, the woman who was selected to depict the White Rock Girl has gotten taller, slimmer, and has weighed less. In 1947, she was 5'6", weighed 125 pounds. and measured 35"-25"-35". And today, she's 5'8", weighs 118, and measures 35"-24"-34". Commenting on this trend in an advertising flyer, the executives of White Rock explain: "Over the years the Psyche image has become longer legged, slimmer hipped, and streamlined. Today — when purity is so important — she continues to symbolize the purity of all White Rock products." The equation of slenderness with purity is a revealing comment on today's obsession with thinness: Weighing a few pounds over some mythical ideal is to live in an "impure" condition. Interestingly, today's American woman averages 5'4" and weighs 140 pounds, the same as 1894's White Rock Girl.

Advertising models represent one kind of ideal; they tend to be extremely thin. They are not, however, the only representation of the ideal female form depicted by the media. There are, it may be said, several ideals, not only one. Photographs appear to add between five and ten pounds to the subject; clothes add a few more in seeming bulk. (White Rock's Psyche, however, wears very little in the way of clothes.) Consequently, fashion models typically border on the anorexic, and women who take them as role models to be emulated are subjecting themselves to an almost unattainable standard. It would be inaccurate to argue that all American women aspire to look like a fashion model, and it would be inaccurate to assert that women in all media are emaciated. Still, it is entirely accurate to say that the ideal woman's figure as depicted in the media is growing slimmer over the years. Even in settings where women were once fairly voluptuous, today's version has slimmed them down significantly.

Before 1970, contestants in Miss America pageants weighed 88 percent of the average for American women their age; after 1970, this declined somewhat to 85 percent. More important, before 1970, pageant *winners* weighed the same as the other contestants; after 1970, however, winners weighed significantly *less* than the contestants who didn't win — 82.5 percent of the average for American women as a whole. Similarly, the weight of women who posed for *Playboy* centerfolds also declined between 1959 and 1978. Centerfolds for 1959 were 91 percent of the weight for an average American woman in her 20s; this declined to 84 percent in 1978. The measurements of the 1959 *Playboy* were 37"-22"-36". In 1978, they were 35"-24"-34 1/2" indicating a growing preference for a less voluptuous, and a slimmer and more angular, or "tubular" ideal appearance. Interestingly, during this same period, the American woman under 30 *gained* an average of five pounds (which was entirely caused by an increase in height during this time, not an increase in bulk). The number of diet articles published in six popular women's magazines nearly doubled between 1959 and 1979 (Garner et al. 1980). Thus, American women suffer from what might be described as a triple whammy — they are evaluated more severely on the basis of looks than is true of men, the standards of ideal weight for them falls within a far narrower range than it does for men, and these standards are becoming more rigid over time.

The increasingly slim standards of feminine beauty represent the most desirable point on a scale. The opposite end of this scale represents undesirable territory — obesity. If American women have been evaluated by standards of physical desirability that have shifted from slim to slimmer over the years, it is reasonable to assume that, during this same period, it has become less and less socially acceptable to be fat. In tribal and peasant societies, corpulence was associated with affluence. An abundant body represented a corresponding material abundance. In a society in which having enough to eat is a mark of distinction, heaviness will draw a measure of respect. This is true not only for oneself but also for one's spouse or spouses, and one's children as well. With the coming of mature industrialization, however, nutritional adequacy becomes sufficiently widespread as to cease being a sign of distinction; slenderness rather than corpulence comes to be adopted as the prevailing esthetic standard among the affluent (Powdermaker 1960; Cahnman 1968, pp. 287–288). In fact, what we have seen is a gradual adoption of the slim standard of attractiveness in all economic classes for both men and women, but much more strongly and stringently for women. And although it is more firmly entrenched in the upper socioeconomic classes, the slim ideal has permeated all levels of society.

Not only is obesity unfashionable and considered unesthetic to the thin majority, it is also regarded as "morally reprehensible," a "social disgrace" (Cahnman 1968, p. 283). Fat people are *set apart* from men and women of average size; they are isolated from "normal" society (Millman 1980). Today, being obese bears something of a *stigma*. In the words of sociologist Erving Goffman, the stigmatized are "disqualified from full social acceptance." They have been reduced "from a whole and usual person to a tainted, discounted one." The bearer of stigma is a "blemished person…to be avoided, especially in public places." The individual with a stigma is seen as "not quite human" (Goffman 1963, pp. i. 1, 3, 5).

Over the centuries, the word *stigma* has hidden two meanings — one good and the second, very bad. Among the ancient Greeks, a stigma was a brand on the body of a person, symbolizing that the bearer was in the service of the temple. In medieval Christianity, *stigmata* were marks resembling the wounds and scars on the body of Jesus, indicating that the bearer was an especially holy individual. It is, however, the negative meaning of the word that is dominant today. In ancient times,

criminals and slaves were branded to identify their inferior status; the brand was a stigma. Lepers were said to bear the stigma of their loathsome disease. As it is currently used, stigma refers to a stain or reproach on one's character or reputation, or a symbol or sign of this inferiority or defect. Anything that causes someone to look down on, condemn, denigrate, or ignore another can be said to be *stigmatizing*.

A stigmatizing trait is rarely isolated. Hardly anyone who possesses one such characteristic is thought to have only one. A single sin will be regarded as housing a multitude of others as well, to be the "tip of the iceberg." The one stigmatizing trait is presumed to hide "a wide range of imperfections" (Goffman 1963, p.5). To be guilty of one sin automatically means to be thought of as being guilty of a host of others along with it. The one negative trait is a *master status* — everything about the individual is interpreted in light of the single trait. "Possession of one deviant trait may have a generalized symbolic value, so that people automatically assume that its bearer possesses other undesirable traits allegedly associated with it." Thus, the question is raised when confronting someone with a stigma: "What kind of person would break such an important rule?" The answer that is offered is typically: "One who is different from the rest of us, who cannot or will not act as a moral human being and therefore might break other important rules." In short, the stigmatizing characteristic "becomes the controlling one" (Becker 1963, pp. 33, 34).

To be stigmatized is to possess a *contaminated* identity. Interaction with nonstigmatized individuals will be strained, tainted, awkward, inhibited. Although the nonstigmatized may, because of the dictates of polite sociability, attempt to hide their negative feelings toward the stigmatized trait specifically, or the stigmatized individual as a whole, and act normally, they are, nonetheless, intensely *aware* of the other's blemish. Likewise, the stigmatized individual remains self-conscious about his or her relations with "normals," believing (often correctly) that the stigma is the exclusive focus of the interaction.

I am always worried about how Jane judges me because she is the real beauty queen and the main gang leader. When I am with her, I hold my breath hard so my tummy doesn't bulge and I pull my skirt down so my fat thighs don't show. I tuck in my rear end. I try to look as thin as possible for her. I get so preoccupied with looking good enough to get into her gang that I forget what she's talking to me about…. I am so worried about how my body is going over that I can hardly concentrate on what she's saying. She asks me about math and all I am thinking about is how fat I am (Allon 1976, p. 18).

Highly stigmatized individuals, in the face of hostility on the part of the majority to their traits and to themselves as bearers of those traits, walk along one of two paths in reacting to stigma. One is to fight back by forming subcultures or groups of individuals who share the characteristics the majority rejects, and to treat this difference from the majority as a badge of honor — or at least, as no cause for shame. Clearly, the homosexual subculture provides an example of the tendency to ward off majority prejudices and oppression. This path is trod by those who feel that the majority's opinion of them and of the characteristic the majority disvalues is illegitimate or invalid — just plain wrong. Here, the legitimacy of the stigma is rejected. A trait, characteristic, a form of behavior that others look down on, they say, is no cause for invidiousness. You may put us down, those who travel this path say, but you have no right to do so. What we are or do is every bit as blameless, indeed, honorable, as what you are or do.

The second path the stigmatized take in reacting to stigma from the majority is *internalization*. Here, stigmatized individuals hold the same negative attitudes toward themselves as the majority does. The stigmatized individual is dominated by feelings of self-hatred and self-derogation. Thus, those who are discriminated against are made to understand that they *deserve* it; they come to accept their negative treatment as just (Cahnman 1968, p. 294). They feel that the majority has a right to stigmatize them. They may despise themselves for being who or what they are, for doing what they do or have done. As we see in testimony from fat people themselves, there is a great deal of evidence to suggest that the obese are more likely to follow the second path than the first. In fact, it might be said that in comparison with the possessors of all stigmatized characteristics or behavior, the obese most strongly agree with the majority's negative judgment of who they are….

Overweight individuals are "stigmatized because they are held responsible for their deviant status, presumably lacking self-control and will power. They are not merely physically deviant as are physically disabled or disfigured persons, but they [also] seem to possess characterological stigma. Fat people are viewed as 'bad' or 'immoral'; supposedly, they do not want to change the error of their ways" (Allon 1982, p. 131):

The obese are presumed to hold their fate in their own hands; if they were only a little less greedy or lazy or yielding to impulse or oblivious of advice, they would restrict excessive food intake, resort to strenuous exercise, and as a consequence of such deliberate action, they would reduce…. While blindness is considered a misfortune, obesity is branded as a defect…. A blind girl will be helped by her agemates, but a heavy girl will be derided. A paraplegic boy will be supported by other boys, but a fat boy will be pushed around. The embarrassing and not infrequently harassing treatment that is meted out to obese teenagers by those around them will not elicit sympathy from onlookers, but a sense of gratification; the idea is that they have got what was coming to them (Cahnman 1968, p. 294).

The obese are overweight, according to the popular view, because they eat immodestly and to excess. They have succumbed to temptation and hedonistic pleasure seeking, where other, more virtuous and less self-indulgent individuals have resisted. It is, as with behavioral deviance, a matter of a struggle between vice and virtue. The obese must therefore pay for the sin of overindulgence by attracting well-deserved stigma (Cahnman 1968; Maddox et al. 1968). The obese suffer from what the public sees as "self-inflicted damnation" (Allon 1973, 1982). In one study of the public's rejection of individuals with certain traits and characteristics, it was found that the stigma of obesity was in between that of physical handicaps such as blindness, and behavioral deviance such as homosexuality (Hiller 1981, 1982). In other words, the public stigmatized the obese *more* than possessors of involuntarily acquired undesirable traits but *less* than individuals who engage in unpopular, unconventional behavior.

This introduces a *moral* dimension to obesity that is lacking in other physical characteristics. The stigma of obesity entails three elements or aspects: (1) The overweight attract public scorn; (2) they are told that this scorn is deserved; (3) they come to accept this negative treatment as just (Cahnman 1968, p. 293). A clear-cut indication that the obese are derogated because of their presumed character defects can be seen in the fact that if obesity is seen to be caused strictly by a physical abnormality, such as hormonal imbalance, the individual is condemned by the public almost not at all, whereas if the etiology of the obesity is left unexplained (and therefore is presumed to be a result of a lack of self-control, resulting in overeating), the individual is, indeed, severely stigmatized (DeJong 1980). A trait that is seen as beyond the individual's control, for which he or she is held to be not responsible, is seen as a misfortune. In contrast, character flaws are regarded in a much harsher light. Obesity is seen as the outward manifestation of an undesirable character; it therefore invites retribution, in much of the public's eyes.

So powerfully stigmatized has obesity become that, in a *New York Times* editorial (Rosenthal 1981), one observer argues that obesity has replaced sex and death as our "contemporary pornography." We attach some degree of shame and guilt to eating. Our society is made up of "modern puritans" who tell one another how "*repugnant* it is to be fat"; "what's really disgusting," we feel, "is not sex, but fat." We are all so humorless, "so relentless, so determined to punish the overweight…. Not only are the overweight the most stigmatized group in the United States, but fat people are expected to participate in their own degradation by agreeing with others who taunt them."

## REFERENCES

Allon, Natalie. 1976. *Urban Life Styles.* Dubuque, IA: W. C. Brown.

Becker, Howard S. 1963. *Outsiders: Studies in the Sociology of Deviance.* New York: Free Press.

Cahnman, Weiner J. 1968. "The Stigma of Obesity." *The Sociological Quarterly,* 9 (Summer), 283–299.

DeJong, William. 1980. "The Stigma of Obesity: The Consequences of Naive Assumptions Concerning the Causes of Physical Deviance." *Journal of Health and Social Behavior,* 21, 75–87.

Garner, David M., Paul E. Garfinkel, D. Schwartz, and M. Thompson. 1980. "Cultural Expectations of Thinness in Women." *Psychological Reports,* 47, 483–491.

Goffman, Erving. 1963. *Stigma: Notes on the Management of Spoiled Identity.* Englewood Cliffs, NJ: Prentice-Hall/Spectrum.

Louderback, Llewellyn. 1970. *Fat Power: Whatever You Weigh Is Right.* New York: Hawthorn Books.

Maddox, George L., Kurt W. Back, and Veronica Liederman. 1968. "Overweight as Social Deviance and Disability." *Journal of Health and Social Behavior,* 9 (December 1968), 287–298.

Millman, Marxia. 1980. *Such a Pretty Face: Being Fat in America.* New York: W. W. Norton.

Powdermaker, Hortense. 1960. "An Anthropological Approach to the Problem of Obesity." *Bulletin of the New York Academy of Medicine,* 36, 286–295.

# 43.  THE SAINTS AND THE ROUGHNECKS

WILLIAM J. CHAMBLISS

*"Selective perception and labeling—finding, processing, and punishing some kinds of criminality and not others—means that visible, poor, nonmobile, outspoken, undiplomatic, 'tough' kids will be noticed, whether their actions are seriously delinquent or not. Other kids, who have established a reputation for being bright (even though underachieving), disciplined, and involved in respectable activities, who are mobile and moneyed, will be invisible when they deviate from sanctioned activities."*

*This article is fascinating. It is, on one hand, about deviance—more specifically, how deviance is defined. Deviance always exists in a social context: Other people define it; other people punish it.*

*It is, on the other hand, about social class. It is a comparison of two groups of boys: One group is working class, and the other is middle class. It shows how class influences behavior, but more importantly, how class influences adult perception of that behavior.*

*The point of the author is simple: Deviance defined by middle-class people is biased against those who are working class. Perceptions are selective. A further point is also important here: Labeling someone as deviant may in fact encourage further deviance.*

Eight promising young men—children of good, stable, white, upper-middle-class families, active in school affairs, good pre-college students—were some of the most delinquent boys at Hanibal High School. Although community residents and parents knew that these boys occasionally sowed a few wild oats, they were totally unaware that sowing wild oats completely occupied the daily routine of these young men. The Saints were constantly occupied with truancy, drinking, wild driving, petty theft, and vandalism. Yet not one was officially arrested for any misdeed during the two years I observed them.

This record was particularly surprising in light of my observations during the same two years of another gang of Hanibal High School students, six lower-class white boys known as the Roughnecks. The Roughnecks were constantly in trouble with police and community even though their rate of delinquency was about equal with that of the Saints. What was the cause of this disparity? The result? The following consideration of the activities, social class, and community perceptions of both gangs may provide some answers.

## THE SAINTS FROM MONDAY TO FRIDAY

The Saints' principle daily concern was with getting out of school as early as possible. The boys managed to get out of school with minimum dan-

ger that they would be accused of playing hookey through an elaborate procedure for obtaining "legitimate" release from class. The most common procedure was for one boy to obtain the release of another by fabricating a meeting of some committee, program or recognized club. Charles might raise his hand in his 9:00 chemistry class and ask to be excused—a euphemism for going to the bathroom. Charles would go to Ed's math class and inform the teacher that Ed was needed for a 9:30 rehearsal of the drama club play. The math teacher would recognize Ed and Charles as "good students" involved in numerous school activities and would permit Ed to leave at 9:30. Charles would return to his class, and Ed would go to Tom's English class to obtain his release. Tom would engineer Charles' escape. The strategy would continue until as many of the Saints as possible were freed. After a stealthy trip to the car (which had been parked in a strategic spot), the boys were off for a day of fun.

Over the two years I observed the Saints, this pattern was repeated nearly every day. There were variations on the theme, but in one form or another, the boys used this procedure for getting out of class and then off the school grounds. Rarely did all eight of the Saints manage to leave school at the same time. The average number avoiding school on the days I observed them was five.

Having escaped from the concrete corridors, the boys usually went either to a pool hall on the other (lower-class) side of town or to a cafe in the suburbs. Both places were out of the way of people the boys were likely to know (family or school officials), and both provided a source of entertainment. The pool hall entertainment was the generally rough atmosphere, the occasional hustler, the sometimes drunk proprietor and, of course, the game of pool. The cafe's entertainment was provided by the owner. The boys would "accidentally" knock a glass on the floor or spill cola on the counter—not all the time, but enough to be sporting. They would also bend spoons, put salt in sugar bowls, and generally tease whoever was working in the cafe. The owner had opened the cafe recently and was dependent on the boys' business, which was, in fact, substantial because in between the horsing around and the teasing, they bought food and drinks.

## THE SAINTS ON WEEKENDS

On weekends, the automobile was even more critical than during the week, for on weekends the Saints went to Big Town—a large city with a population of over a million 25 miles from Hanibal. Every Friday and Saturday night, most of the Saints would meet between 8:00 and 8:30 and would go into Big Town. Big Town activities included drinking heavily in taverns or nightclubs, driving drunkenly through the streets, and committing acts of vandalism and playing pranks.

By midnight on Fridays and Saturdays, the Saints were usually thoroughly high, and one or two of them were often so drunk they had to be carried to the car. Then the boys drove around town, calling obscenities to women and girls; occasionally trying (unsuccessfully so far as I could tell) to pick girls up; and driving recklessly through red lights and at high speeds with their lights out. Occasionally they played "chicken." One boy would climb out the back window of the car and across the roof to the driver's side of the car while the car was moving at high speed (between 40 and 50 miles an hour); then the driver would move over and the boy who had just crawled across the car roof would take the driver's seat.

Searching for "fair game" for a prank was the boys' principal activity after they left the tavern. The boys would drive alongside a foot patrolman and ask directions to some street. If the policeman leaned on the car in the course of answering the question, the driver would speed away, causing him to lose his balance. The Saints were careful to play this prank only in an area where they were

not going to spend much time and where they could quickly disappear around a corner to avoid having their license plate number taken.

Construction sites and road repair areas were the special province of the Saints' mischief. A soon-to-be-repaired hole in the road inevitably invited the Saints to remove lanterns and wooden barricades and put them in the car, leaving the hole unprotected. The boys would find a safe vantage point and wait for an unsuspecting motorist to drive into the hole. Often, although not always, the boys would go up to the motorist and commiserate with him about the dreadful way the city protected its citizenry.

Leaving the scene of the open hole and the motorist, the boys would then go searching for an appropriate place to erect the stolen barricade. An "appropriate place" was often a spot on a highway near a curve in the road where the barricade would not be seen by an oncoming motorist. The boys would wait to watch an unsuspecting motorist attempt to stop and (usually) crash into the wooden barricade. With saintly bearing, the boys might offer help and understanding.

A stolen lantern might well find its way onto the back of a police car or hang from a street lamp. Once a lantern served as a prop for a reenactment of the "midnight ride of Paul Revere" until the "play," which was taking place at 2:00 A.M. in the center of a main street of Big Town, was interrupted by a police car several blocks away. The boys ran, leaving the lanterns on the street, and managed to avoid being apprehended.

Abandoned houses, especially if they were located in out-of-the-way places, were fair game for destruction and spontaneous vandalism. The boys would break windows, remove furniture to the yard and tear it apart, urinate on the walls, and scrawl obscenities inside.

Through all the pranks, drinking, and reckless driving, the boys managed miraculously to avoid being stopped by police. Only twice in two years was I aware that they had been stopped by a Big Town policeman. Once was for speeding (which they did every time they drove, whether they were drunk or sober), and the driver managed to convince the policeman that it was simply an error. The second time they were stopped they had just left a nightclub and were walking through an alley. Aaron stopped to urinate and the boys began making obscene remarks. A foot patrolman came into the alley, lectured the boys, and sent them home. Before the boys got to the car, one began talking in a loud voice again. The policeman, who had followed them down the alley, arrested this boy for disturbing the peace and took him to the police station where the other Saints gathered. After paying a $5.00 fine, and with the assurance that there would be no permanent record of the arrest, the boy was released.

The boys had a spirit of frivolity and fun about their escapades. They did not view what they were engaged in as "delinquency," although it surely was by any reasonable definition of that word. They simply viewed themselves as having a little fun and who, they would ask, was really hurt by it? The answer had to be no one, although this fact remains one of the most difficult things to explain about the gang's behavior. Unlikely though it seems, in two years of drinking, driving, carousing, and vandalism, no one was seriously injured as a result of the Saints' activities.

## THE SAINTS IN SCHOOL

The Saints were highly successful in school. The average grade for the group was B, with two of the boys having close to a straight A average. Almost all the boys were popular, and many of them held offices in the school. One of the boys was vice-president of the student body one year. Six of the boys played on athletic teams.

At the end of their senior year, the student body selected ten seniors for special recognition as the "school wheels"; four of the ten were Saints. Teachers and school officials saw no problem with any of these boys and anticipated that they would all "make something of themselves."

How the boys managed to maintain this impression is surprising in view of their actual behavior while in school. Their technique for covering truancy was so successful that teachers did not even realize that the boys were absent from school much of the time. Occasionally, of course, the system would backfire and then the boy was on his own. A boy who was caught would be most contrite, would plead guilty and ask for mercy. He inevitably got the mercy he sought.

Cheating on examinations was rampant, even to the point of orally communicating answers to exams as well as looking at one another's papers. Because none of the group studied and because they were primarily dependent on one another for help, it is surprising that grades were so high. Teachers contributed to the deception in their admitted inclination to give these boys (and presumably others like them) the benefit of the doubt. When asked how the boys did in school, and when pressed on specific examinations, teachers might admit that they were disappointed in John's performance, but would quickly add that they "knew that he was capable of doing better," so John was given a higher grade than he had actually earned. How often this happened is impossible to know. During the time I observed the group, I never saw any of the boys take homework home. Teachers may have been "understanding" very regularly....

## THE POLICE AND THE SAINTS

The local police saw the Saints as good boys who were among the leaders of the youth in the community. Rarely, the boys might be stopped in town for speeding or for running a stop sign. When this happened, the boys were always polite, contrite, and pled for mercy. As in school, they received the mercy they asked for. None ever received a ticket or was taken into the precinct by the local police.

The situation in Big Town, where the boys engaged in most of their delinquency, was only slightly different. The police there did not know the boys at all, although occasionally the boys were stopped by a patrolman. Once they were caught taking a lantern from a construction site. Another time they were stopped for running a stop sign, and on several occasions they were stopped for speeding. Their behavior was as before: contrite, polite, and penitent. The urban police, like the local police, accepted their demeanor as sincere. More important, the urban police were convinced that these were good boys just out for a lark.

## THE ROUGHNECKS

Hanibal townspeople never perceived the Saints' high level of delinquency. The Saints were good boys who just went in for an occasional prank. After all, they were well dressed, well mannered, and had nice cars. The Roughnecks were a different story. Although the two gangs of boys were the same age, and both groups engaged in an equal amount of wild-oat sowing, everyone agreed that the not-so-well-dressed, not-so-well-mannered, not-so-rich boys were heading for trouble. Townspeople would say, "You can see the gang members at the drugstore, night after night, leaning against the storefront (sometimes drunk) or slouching around inside buying cokes, reading magazines, and probably stealing old Mr. Wall blind. When they are outside and girls walk by, even respectable girls, these boys make suggestive remarks. Sometimes their remarks are downright lewd."

From the community's viewpoint, the real indication that these kids were in for trouble was that they were constantly involved with the police. Some of them had been picked up for stealing, mostly small stuff, of course, "but still, it's stealing small stuff that leads to big-time crimes." "Too bad," people said. "Too bad that these boys couldn't behave like the other kids in town; stay out of trouble, be polite to adults, and look to their future."

The community's impression of the degree to which this group of six boys (ranging in age from 16 to 19) engaged in delinquency was somewhat distorted. In some ways, the gang was more delinquent than the community thought; in other ways, they were less.

The fighting activities of the group were fairly readily and accurately perceived by almost everyone. At least once a month, the boys would get into some sort of fight, although most fights were scraps between members of the group or involved only one member of the group and some peripheral hanger-on. Only three times in the period of observation did the group fight together: once against a gang from across town, once against two blacks, and once against a group of boys from another school. For the first two fights, the group went out "looking for trouble"—and they found it both times. The third fight followed a football game and began spontaneously with an argument on the football field between one of the Roughnecks and a member of the opposition's football team.

Jack had a particular propensity for fighting and was involved in most of the brawls. He was a prime mover of the escalation of arguments into fights.

More serious than fighting, had the community been aware of it, was theft. Although almost everyone was aware that the boys occasionally stole things, they did not realize the extent of the activity. Petty stealing was a frequent event for the Roughnecks. Sometimes they stole as a group and coordinated their efforts; other times they stole in pairs. Rarely did they steal alone.

The thefts ranged from very small things like paperback books, comics, and ballpoint pens to expensive items like watches. The nature of the thefts varied from time to time. The gang would go through a period of systematically shoplifting items from automobiles or school lockers. Types of thievery varied with the whim of the gang. Some forms of thievery were more profitable than others, but all thefts were for profit, not just thrills.

Roughnecks siphoned gasoline from cars as often as they had access to an automobile, which was not very often. Unlike the Saints, who owned their own cars, the Roughnecks would have to borrow their parents' cars, an event which occurred only eight or nine times a year. The boys claimed to have stolen cars for joy rides from time to time....

The Roughnecks, then, engaged mainly in three types of delinquency: theft, drinking, and fighting. Although community members perceived that this gang of kids was delinquent, they mistakenly believed that their illegal activities were primarily drinking, fighting, and being a nuisance to passersby. Drinking was limited among the gang members, although it did occur, and theft was much more prevalent than anyone realized.

Drinking would doubtless have been more prevalent had the boys had ready access to liquor. Because they rarely had automobiles at their disposal, they could not travel very far, and the bars in town would not serve them. Most of the boys had little money, and this, too, inhibited their purchase of alcohol. Their major source of liquor was a local drunk who would buy them a fifth if they would give him enough extra to buy himself a pint of whiskey or a bottle of wine.

The community's perception of drinking as prevalent stemmed from the fact that it was the most obvious delinquency the boys engaged in. When one of the boys had been drinking, even a casual observer seeing him on the corner would suspect that he was high.

There was a high level of mutual distrust and dislike between the Roughnecks and the police. The boys felt very strongly that the police were unfair and corrupt. Some evidence existed that the boys were correct in their perception.

The main source of the boys' dislike for the police undoubtedly stemmed from the fact that the police would sporadically harass the group. From the standpoint of the boys, these acts of occasional enforcement of the law were whimsical and uncalled for. It made no sense to them, for example, that the police would come to the corner occasionally and threaten them with arrest for loitering when the night before the boys had been out siphoning gasoline from cars and the police had been nowhere in sight. To the boys, the police were stupid on the one hand, for not being where they should have been and catching the boys in a serious offense, and unfair on the other hand, for trumping up "loitering" charges against them.

From the viewpoint of the police, the situation was quite different. They knew, with all the confidence necessary to be a policeman, that these boys were engaged in criminal activities. They knew this partly from occasionally catching them, mostly from circumstantial evidence ("the boys were around when those tires were slashed"), and partly because the police shared the view of the community in general that this was a bad bunch of boys. The best the police could hope to do was to be sensitive to the fact that these boys were engaged in illegal acts and arrest them whenever there was some evidence that they had been involved. Whether or not the boys had in fact committed a particular act in a particular way was not especially important. The police had a broader view: Their job was to stamp out these kids' crimes; the tactics were not as important as the end result.

Over the period that the group was under observation, each member was arrested at least once. Several of the boys were arrested a number of times and spent at least one night in jail. Although most were never taken to court, two of the boys were sentenced to six months' incarceration in boys' schools.

## THE ROUGHNECKS IN SCHOOL

The Roughnecks' behavior in school was not particularly disruptive. During school hours, they did not all hang around together, but tended instead to spend most of their time with one or two other members of the gang who were their special buddies. Although every member of the gang attempted to avoid school as much as possible, they were not particularly successful, and most of them attended school with surprising regularity. They considered school a burden — something to be gotten through with a minimum of conflict. If they were "bugged" by a particular teacher, it could lead to trouble. One of the boys, Al, once threatened to beat up a teacher and, according to the other boys, the teacher hid under a desk to escape him.

Teachers saw the boys the way the general community did, as heading for trouble, as being uninterested in making something of themselves. Some were also seen as being incapable of meeting the academic standards of the school. Most of the teachers expressed concern for this group of boys and were willing to pass them despite poor performance, in the belief that failing them would only aggravate the problem.

The group of boys had a grade point average just slightly above C. No one in the group failed either grade, and no one had better than a C average. They were very consistent in their achievement or, at least, the teachers were consistent in their perception of the boys' achievement.

Two of the boys were good football players. Herb was acknowledged to be the best player in the school, and Jack was almost as good. Both boys were criticized for their failure to abide by training rules, for refusing to come to practice as often as they should, and for not playing their best during practice. What they lacked in sportsmanship they made up for in skill, apparently, and played every game no matter how poorly they had performed in practice or how many practice sessions they had missed.

## TWO QUESTIONS

Why did the community, the school, and the police react to the Saints as though they were good, upstanding, nondelinquent youths with bright futures but to the Roughnecks as though they were tough, young criminals who were headed for trouble? Why did the Roughnecks and the Saints in fact have quite different careers after high school

—careers which, by and large, lived up to the expectations of the community?

The most obvious explanation for the differences in the community's and law enforcement agencies' reactions to the two gangs is that one group of boys was "more delinquent" than the other. Which group *was* more delinquent? The answer to this question will determine in part how we explain the differential responses to these groups by the members of the community and, particularly, by law enforcement and school officials.

In sheer number of illegal acts, the Saints were the more delinquent. They were truant from school for at least part of the day almost every day of the week. In addition, their drinking and vandalism occurred with surprising regularity. The Roughnecks, in contrast, engaged sporadically in delinquent episodes. Although these episodes were frequent, they certainly did not occur on a daily or even a weekly basis.

The difference in frequency of offenses was probably caused by the Roughnecks' inability to obtain liquor and to manipulate legitimate excuses from school. Because the Roughnecks had less money than the Saints, and teachers carefully supervised their school activities, the Roughnecks' hearts may have been as [evil] as the Saints', but their misdeeds were not nearly as frequent.

There are really no clear-cut criteria by which to measure qualitative differences in antisocial behavior. The most important dimension of the difference is generally referred to as the "seriousness" of the offenses.

If seriousness encompasses the relative economic costs of delinquent acts, then some assessment can be made. The Roughnecks probably stole an average of about $5.00 worth of goods a week. Some weeks, the figure was considerably higher, but these times must be balanced against long periods when almost nothing was stolen.

The Saints were more continuously engaged in delinquency, but their acts were not for the most part costly to property. Only their vandalism and occasional theft of gasoline would so qualify. Perhaps once or twice a month, they would siphon a tankful of gas. The other costly items were street signs, construction lanterns, and the like. All these acts combined probably did not quite average $5.00 a week, partly because much of the stolen equipment was abandoned and presumably could

be recovered. The difference in cost of stolen property between the two groups was trivial, but the Roughnecks probably had a slightly more expensive set of activities than did the Saints.

Another meaning of seriousness is the potential threat of physical harm to members of the community and to the boys themselves. The Roughnecks were more prone to physical violence; they not only welcomed an opportunity to fight, they went seeking it. In addition, they fought among themselves frequently. Although the fighting never included deadly weapons, it was still a menace, however minor, to the physical safety of those involved.

The Saints never fought. They avoided physical conflict both inside and outside the group. At the same time, however, the Saints frequently endangered their own and other people's lives. They did so almost every time they drove a car, especially if they had been drinking. Sober, their driving was risky; under the influence of alcohol, it was horrendous. In addition, the Saints endangered the lives of others with their pranks. Street excavations left unmarked were a very serious hazard.

Evaluating the relative seriousness of the two gangs' activities is difficult. The community reacted as though the behavior of the Roughnecks was a problem, and they reacted as though the behavior of the Saints was not. But the members of the community were ignorant of the array of delinquent acts that characterized the Saints' behavior. Although concerned citizens were unaware of much of the Roughnecks' behavior as well, they were much better informed about the Roughnecks' involvement in delinquency than they were about the Saints'.

## VISIBILITY

Differential treatment of the two gangs resulted in part because one gang was infinitely more visible than the other. This differential visibility was a direct function of the economic standing of the families. The Saints had access to automobiles and were able to remove themselves from the sight of the community. In as routine a decision as to where to go to have a milkshake after school, the Saints stayed away from the mainstream of community life. Lacking transportation, the Roughnecks could not make it to the edge of town. The center of town was the only practical place for them to meet because their homes were scattered throughout the town and any noncentral meeting place put an undue hardship on some members. Through necessity, the Roughnecks congregated in a crowded area where everyone in the community passed frequently, including teachers and law enforcement officers. They could easily see the Roughnecks hanging around the drugstore.

The Roughnecks, of course, made themselves even more visible by making remarks to passersby and by occasionally getting into fights on the corner. Meanwhile, just as regularly, the Saints were either at the cafe on one edge of town or in the pool hall at the other edge of town. Without any particular realization that they were making themselves inconspicuous, the Saints were able to hide their time-wasting. Not only were they removed from the mainstream of traffic, but they were almost always inside a building.

On their escapades, the Saints were also relatively invisible because they left Hanibal and traveled to Big Town. Here, too, they were mobile, roaming the city, rarely going to the same area twice.

## DEMEANOR

To the notion of visibility must be added the difference in the responses of group members to outside intervention with their activities. If one of the Saints was confronted with an accusing policeman, even if he felt he was truly innocent of a wrongdoing, his demeanor was apologetic and penitent. A Roughneck's attitude was almost the polar opposite. When confronted with a threatening adult authority, even one who tried to be pleasant, the Roughneck's hostility and disdain were clearly observable. Sometimes he might attempt to put up a veneer of respect, but it was thin and was not accepted as sincere by the authority.

School was no different from the community at large. The Saints could manipulate the system by reigning compliance with the school norms. The availability of cars at school meant that once free from the immediate sight of the teacher, the boys could disappear rapidly. And this escape was well-enough planned that no administrator or teacher

was nearby when the boys left. A Roughneck who wished to escape for a few hours was in a bind. If it were possible to get free from class, downtown was still a mile away, and even if he arrived there, he was still very visible. Truancy for the Roughnecks meant almost certain detection, while the Saints enjoyed almost complete immunity from sanctions.

## BIAS

Community members were not aware of the transgressions of the Saints. Even if the Saints had been less discreet, their favorite delinquencies would have been perceived as less serious than those of the Roughnecks.

In the eyes of the police and school officials, a boy who drinks in an alley and stands intoxicated on the street corner is committing a more serious offense than is a boy who drinks to inebriation in a nightclub or a tavern and drives around afterwards in a car. Similarly, a boy who steals a wallet from a store will be viewed as having committed a more serious offense than a boy who steals a lantern from a construction site.

Perceptual bias also operates with respect to the demeanor of the boys in the two groups when they are confronted by adults. It is not simply that adults dislike the posture affected by boys of the Roughneck ilk; more important is the conviction that the posture adopted by the Roughnecks is an indication of their devotion and commitment to deviance as a way of life. The posture becomes a cue, just as the type of the offense is a cue, to the degree to which the known transgressions are indicators of the youths' potential for other problems.

Visibility, demeanor, and bias are surface variables that explain the day-to-day operations of the police. Why do these surface variables operate as they do? Why did the police choose to disregard the Saints' delinquencies while breathing down the backs of the Roughnecks?

The answer lies in the class structure of American society and the control of legal institutions by those at the top of the class structure. Obviously, no representative of the upper class drew up the operational chart for the police that led them to look in the ghettoes and on street corners—which led them to see the demeanor of lower-class youth as troublesome and that of upper-middle-class youth as tolerable. Rather, the procedures simply developed from experience — experience with irate and influential upper-middle-class parents insisting that their son's vandalism was simply a prank and his drunkenness only a momentary "sowing of wild oats" — experience with cooperative or indifferent, powerless, lower-class parents who acquiesced to the laws' definition of their son's behavior.

## ADULT CAREERS OF THE SAINTS AND THE ROUGHNECKS

The community's confidence in the potential of the Saints and the Roughnecks apparently was justified. If anything, the community members underestimated the degree to which these youngsters would turn out "good" or "bad."

Seven of the eight members of the Saints went on to college immediately after high school. Five of the boys graduated from college in four years. The sixth one finished college after two years in the army, and the seventh spent four years in the air force before returning to college and receiving a B.A. degree. Of these seven college graduates, three went on for advanced degrees: One finished law school and is now active in state politics, one finished medical school and is practicing near Hanibal, and one boy is now working for a Ph.D. The other four college graduates entered sub-managerial, managerial, or executive training positions with larger firms.

The only Saint who did not complete college was Jerry. Jerry had failed to graduate from high school with the other Saints. During his second senior year, after the other Saints had gone on to college, Jerry began to hang around with what several teachers described as a "rough crowd" — the gang that was heir apparent to the Roughnecks. At the end of his second senior year, when he did graduate from high school, Jerry took a job as a used car salesman, got married, and quickly had a child. Although he made several abortive attempts to go to college by attending night school, when I last saw him (ten years after high school), Jerry was unemployed and had been living on unemployment for almost a year. His wife worked as a waitress.

Some of the Roughnecks have lived up to community expectations. A number of them were headed for trouble. A few were not.

Jack and Herb were the athletes among the Roughnecks, and their athletic prowess paid off handsomely. Both boys received unsolicited athletic scholarships to college. After Herb received his scholarship (near the end of his senior year), he apparently did an about-face. His demeanor became very similar to that of the Saints. Although he remained a member in good standing of the Roughnecks, he stopped participating in most activities and did not hang on the corner as often.

Jack did not change. If anything, he became more prone to fighting. He even made excuses for accepting the scholarship. He told the other gang members that the school had guaranteed him a C average if he would come to play football — an idea that seems far-fetched, even in this day of highly competitive recruiting.

During the summer after graduation from high school, Jack attempted suicide by jumping from a tall building. The jump would certainly have killed most people trying it, but Jack survived. He entered college in the fall and played four years of football. He and Herb graduated in four years, and both are teaching and coaching in high schools. They are married and have stable families. If anything, Jack appears to have a more prestigious position in the community than does Herb, though both are well respected and secure in their positions.

Two of the boys never finished high school. Tommy left at the end of his junior year and went to another state. That summer he was arrested and placed on probation on a manslaughter charge. Three years later, he was arrested for murder; he pleaded guilty to second-degree murder and is serving a 30-year sentence in the state penitentiary.

Al, the other boy who did not finish high school, also left the state in his senior year. He is serving a life sentence in a state penitentiary for first-degree murder.

Wes is a small-time gambler. He finished high school and "bummed around." After several years, he made contact with a bookmaker who employed him as a runner. Later he acquired his own area and has been working it ever since. His position among the bookmakers is almost identical to the position he had in the gang; he is always around, but no one is really aware of him. He makes no trouble, and he does not get into any. Steady, reliable, capable of keeping his mouth closed, he plays the game by the rules, even though the game is an illegal one.

That leaves only Ron. Some of his former friends reported that they had heard he was "driving a truck up north," but no one could provide any concrete information.

## REINFORCEMENT

The community responded to the Roughnecks as boys in trouble, and the boys agreed with that perception. Their pattern of deviancy was reinforced, and breaking away from it became increasingly unlikely. Once the boys acquired an image of themselves as deviants, they selected new friends who affirmed that self-image. As that self-conception became more firmly entrenched, they also came willing to try new and more extreme deviances. With their growing alienation came freer expression of disrespect and hostility for representatives of the legitimate society. This disrespect increased the community's negativism, perpetuating the entire process of commitment to deviance. Lack of a commitment to deviance works the same way. In either case, the process will perpetuate itself unless some event (like a scholarship to college or a sudden failure) external to the established relationship intervenes. For two of the Roughnecks (Herb and Jack), receiving college athletic scholarships created new relations and culminated in a break with the established pattern of deviance. In the case of one of the Saints (Jerry), his parents' divorce and his failing to graduate from high school changed some of his other relations. Being held back in school for a year and losing his place among the Saints had sufficient impact on Jerry to alter his self-image and virtually ensure that he would not go on to college as his peers did. Although the experiments of life can rarely be reversed, it seems likely in view of the behavior of the other boys who did not enjoy this special treatment by the school that Jerry, too, would have "become something" had he graduated as anticipated. For Herb and Jack, outside intervention worked to their advantage; for Jerry it was his undoing.

Selective perception and labeling—finding, processing, and punishing some kinds of criminality and not others—means that visible, poor, nonmobile, outspoken, undiplomatic, "tough" kids will be noticed, whether their actions are seriously delinquent or not. Other kids, who have established a reputation for being bright (even though underachieving), disciplined, and involved in respectable activities, who are mobile and moneyed, will be invisible when they deviate from sanctioned activities. They'll sow their wild oats—perhaps even wider and thicker than their lower-class cohorts—but they won't be noticed. When it's time to leave adolescence, most will follow the expected path, settling into the ways of the middle class, remembering fondly the delinquent but unnoticed fling of their youth. The Roughnecks and others like them may turn around, too. [But] it is more likely that their noticeable deviance will have been so reinforced by police and community that their lives will be effectively channeled into careers consistent with their adolescent background.

# 44. CRIME, FEAR, AND SOCIAL DISORDER

CHARLES E. SILBERMAN

*"Ultimately, the whole fabric of urban life is based on trust: trust that others will act predictably, in accordance with generally accepted rules of behavior, and that they will not take advantage of that trust."*

*What are the effects of crime on society? The effects of violent crime? The effects of random violent crime? Society begins with trust; everyday life between strangers relies on trust; social order is possible only through trust. The erosion of interpersonal trust is the real cost of violent crime, and with it the erosion of social order. The result is fear, unpredictability, and helplessness in everyday life. That is the central point in this selection by Charles E. Silberman.*

Life in metropolitan areas involves a startling paradox: we fear strangers more than anything else, and yet we live our lives among strangers. Every time we take a walk, ride a subway or bus, shop in a supermarket or department store, enter an office building lobby or elevator, work in a factory or large office, or attend a ball game or the movies, we are surrounded by strangers. The potential for fear is as immense as it is unavoidable.

We cope with this paradox in a number of ways. The equation whereby *strange* means *dangerous* has an obverse, in which *familiar* means *safe*. The longer something is present in the environment without causing harm, the more favorably we regard it and the warmer our feelings are likely to be. People who live near a glue factory become oblivious to the smell; city dwellers come to love the noise, often finding it hard to sleep in the countryside because of the unaccustomed quiet. In psychological experiments, people who were shown nonsense syllables and Chinese ideograms for a second time judged them "good" as opposed to "bad" in comparison with other nonsense syllables and ideograms they were shown, later on, for the first time. The more often people were shown photographs of strangers, the warmer their feelings became toward them.

In cities, familiarity breeds a sense of security. People who know that they have to be on guard in a strange neighborhood, especially at night, feel more secure in their own neighborhood and come to believe that they have a moral right to count on its being safe. This tendency helps explain a phenomenon that has puzzled social scientists: The fact that people's assessment of the safety of the neighborhood in which they live seems to bear little relationship to the actual level of crime there. In one survey, 60 percent of those queried con-

sidered their own neighborhoods to be safer than the rest of the community in which they lived; only 14 percent thought their neighborhood was more dangerous. What was striking was that people felt this way no matter how much crime there was in the neighborhood: In Washington, D.C., in precincts with crime rates well above the average for the city, only 20 percent of respondents thought the risks of being assaulted were greater in their neighborhood than in other parts of the city.[1]

This same phenomenon makes crime a terribly bewildering, as well as fear-evoking, event when it is experienced on one's own turf. "Casual conversations with urban citizens or regular reading of the newspapers in recent years would indicate that many, if not most, inner-city residents live with the fatalistic expectation that sooner or later they will be mugged," Robert LeJeune and Nicholas Alex write in their richly informative study of the experiences of mugging victims. "But closer examination reveals that most of these fear-laden accounts are not associated with a corresponding mental frame necessary to develop the appropriate precautionary behavior."[2]

To the contrary, the mugging victims studied by LeJeune and Alex had all assumed before they were mugged that, however dangerous *other* neighborhoods might be, they were reasonably safe from attack in their own. "I never felt afraid," said one victim, a widowed secretary. "Well, I'm not willing to say that I wasn't afraid at all," she added. "Everybody has a little bit of a feeling of fear." What she meant, it turned out, was that she had always been afraid of the neighborhood in which her daughter lived. "Because I heard things of that neighborhood —and it wasn't safe. I heard of people being mugged. And there I didn't feel secure." Her own neighborhood was something else again. As she explained, "Here I wasn't afraid.... In my neighborhood, there are police cars, there are people walking. How can anybody be afraid?... And on *my* block—I'm not going to be afraid on Post Avenue."

But city dwellers rarely stay cooped up in their own neighborhoods; most adults have to venture elsewhere to go to work, to shop, to visit relatives and friends, or to use the cultural and entertainment facilities that make cities cities. When we enter any environment, whether familiar or strange, we automatically take a quick "reading" or "sounding" in order to decide whether to be on guard or not. If things are as they should be, if appearances are normal, we can be off guard; we can concentrate on the task at hand, confident of our ability to predict what will happen from the cues we pick up out of the corner of the eye. The result is the sense of safety that comes from feeling in control of one's own fate. For if we can predict danger in advance, we can avoid it—if only by retreating in time to some safer haven.

The process is extraordinarily fragile. We can predict danger only if the subtle cues on which we depend—for example, people's dress or attitude or demeanor—are accurate, which is to say, only if things are as they appear. Ultimately, the whole fabric of urban life is based on trust: Trust that others will act predictably, in accordance with generally accepted rules of behavior, and that they will not take advantage of that trust. For life to go on in public places—in city streets, building lobbies, elevators, and hallways—people must put themselves in other people's hands.

Consider the elaborate etiquette pedestrians employ to avoid bumping into one another. The American pedestrian maintains a scanning or check-out range of about three or four sidewalk squares, assuming that people beyond this range—whether in front or behind—can be ignored. As other people enter the scanning range, they are glanced at briefly and then ignored if their distance, speed, and direction imply that neither party has to change course to avoid a collision. When people have been checked out in this manner, Goffman writes, they can be allowed to come quite close without evoking concern. Moreover, pedestrians ignore oncomers who are separated from them by other people; thus someone may walk in dense traffic and be completely unconcerned about people just a few feet away.[3] As Goffman observes, "City streets, even in times that defame them, provide a setting in which mutual trust is routinely displayed between strangers...."

Crime does more than expose the weakness in social relationships; it undermines the social order itself by destroying the assumptions on which it is based. The need to assume that familiar environments are safe is so great that until they have become victims themselves, many people rationalize that newspaper and television accounts of crime are greatly exaggerated. "This kind of thing happens on television, but not in real life," a college student exclaimed after she and a friend had been held up on the Ellipse, an area adjacent to the White House. (Although the two students were not injured, a migrant worker sitting on a nearby bench was shot in the face and blinded when he told the robbers—correctly—that he had no money.) "You just don't shoot someone in the back like in a Western movie," a young woman who had been shot and seriously injured in a D.C. robbery attempt told a *Washington Post* reporter.

Even when they admit that crime does occur, people comfort themselves with the assumption that it won't happen to them—in much the same way we assume our own immortality, or our invulnerability to earthquake or flood.[4] It is only in retrospect, as LeJeune and Alex explain, that victims realize they should have been more aware of their own vulnerability. "Of course, the conditions have been getting worse and worse," one of their respondents observed. "Uh, someone thinks that accidents happen to other people but they don't happen to me. Then when it did happen, I was very upset because I didn't think it could happen to me."[5]

The need to feel safe is so powerful that people routinely misread cues that should signal danger. They may simply delay responding to a stranger, to give him a chance to explain or apologize; intuitive knowledge of this tendency on the part of pickpockets, assassins, and saboteurs makes it possible for them to carry out their missions.[6] People also may redefine a danger signal as a normal event—for example, by assuming that a mugger is merely panhandling or playing a practical joke. Consider these explanations by three of LeJeune and Alex's respondents:

"I was walking down the street. Four young men approached me. I say, 'Oh, cut this fooling out.' And then they put their hands in my pocket."

"When I got into the elevator, I felt a hand, you know, and I thought the fellow was joking. But then I started feeling the pain. He was very strong. It was no joke."

Similarly, a victim may perceive a threatening stranger as a friendly neighbor who forgot his keys:

"I thought: it's one of my neighbors waving to me not to close the door. He must have forgotten his key. Just then somebody grabbed me in the back of the neck and held my head in both his arms."

Or the victim may interpret a robber's demand for money as a request for a loan:

"When we started getting off the elevator, he turned around and he said: 'Give me ten dollars.' I thought he wanted to borrow ten dollars. He said, 'I don't want any trouble. Give me ten dollars.' And I looked him up and down, and I see he has a knife in his hand. So I didn't let myself get knifed. I gave him the ten dollars and he got off."[7]

People *need* to be able to make sense out of their environment; otherwise, life would be intolerable. To "live with fear," as victims call it — to be suspicious of every sound and every person — converts the most elementary and routine aspects of life into an exercise in terror. It is to avoid such terror that people who have not been victimized (and some who have) interpret threatening gestures and events in terms that are more understandable and comfortable.

Thus the emotional impact of being attacked by a stranger transcends the incident itself; it reaches a primordial layer or fear unlike anything evoked by an equally damaging encounter with an automobile or other inanimate object, or even by a crime that does not involve a direct encounter with another person. A criminal attack is disorienting as well, evoking traumatic reactions similar to those the sociologist Kai T. Erikson found among the survivors of the Buffalo Creek flood.[8] Victims of criminal violence, like victims of earthquake or flood, develop what Erikson describes as "a sense of vulnerability, a feeling that one has lost a certain natural immunity to misfortune, a growing conviction, even, that the world is no longer a safe place to be." Because they previously had underestimated the peril in which they lived, the survivors of a disaster lose confidence in their ability to monitor their environment; as a result, they live in constant fear that something terrible will happen again.[9]

Crime victims are affected in much the same way; the inability to tell friend from foe — the sense that they no longer know how to monitor their environment — can turn the most ordinary encounter into a nightmare. Until the attack in which he was blinded, James Martin, a nineteen-year-old former handyman, never worried about crime. In the Washington, D.C., ghetto where he lived, talk about crime was a constant, but Martin recalls, "I never paid any attention…. I felt safe. I thought people would look at me and say, 'the dude ain't got nothing.'" He was wrong. The men who held him up at a bus stop were enraged when Martin told them he had only $6 on his person; they knocked him down, beat his head against the sidewalk, then smashed a soda bottle on the curb and rammed the jagged edge into his right eye, completely destroying his vision. Although the robbers were convicted and imprisoned, Martin found that there was no way he could continue to live in Washington. Afraid to go out alone and equally afraid to stay home, he could not sleep, either, for fear his assailants would break out of prison and return to attack him again. He and his family moved back home to a small town in North Carolina, to live in a trailer on his mother-in-law's farm.[10]

This sense of vulnerability and fear seems to be a universal feeling, regardless of whether the person attacked is injured or not. Instead of familiar environments being automatically defined as safe, they now are perceived as uniformly dangerous because of the victim's inability to rely on the old cues. Asked whether being mugged had changed their outlook on life in any way, respondents in LeJeune and Alex's survey replied as follows:

"I am just so much more frightened wherever I turn, and it seems as though the entire city has turned into an incredible jungle…. It's incredible that I think that way, that I feel that way; it's so unlike me."

"Yes. It's made the city more of a jungle to me. Yes it has. And I haven't got too long to retire. And where I had really thought I would stay in the city, you believe it, I'll get out."

"Well, it has. I mean I don't feel free, like to do things. You feel you like to go to the movies or something. You don't feel you could do it. You always fear that there's somebody, uh, even if you go to the movies and you're safe — you're inside — coming out you'll always have that fear, oh my God, somebody's passing or something."

The worst fear is felt in the area in which the person was attacked, particularly if it is his own neighborhood. "I've been living here for three and a half years, and I've never had any real fear of it," a mugging victim who decided to move out of her neighborhood told LeJeune and Alex. "It's like it's my home. I know the block. I recognize people. It's all very familiar to me. Now it's become very unfamiliar to me, very threatening, very, very much like a jungle. I trust nobody. You know, I'm constantly looking around me…. I will never walk on *that* block again."

The most disorienting aspect of all is the senselessness of the whole experience, which shatters victims' belief that cause and effect have some relationship. They no longer can view the world as a rational, hence predictable, place over which they have some control. "The thing that bothers me, and always will, is why they shot me," says Sally Ann Morris, a twenty-six-year-old woman badly injured in a holdup attempt. "I didn't pose any threat to them; I was running away…."[11] Tommy Lee Harris, a sixty-two-year-old man who was badly beaten by two young muggers after he had given them all his money, says in obvious bewilderment, "I don't know why it happened; I didn't know the men." After beating Harris to the ground, breaking four ribs, the muggers put him in the trunk of his own car, which they proceeded to drive away. Harris' life was saved when a policeman saw the muggers run through a red light and pursued them in his patrol car.[12]

The victim's bewilderment is compounded by the realization of how large a role coincidence and chance had played. For the first week after the shooting, Ms. Morris blamed the friend who had been with her at the time:

"I thought why couldn't it have been him, he could have taken it better. Why me?" she recalls. "Isn't that just terrible to think like that? …And then I spent a long time thinking: if it had just taken longer to park, or if we had gone down another street…."

The discovery that life is irrational and unpredictable makes victims feel completely impotent. This, in turn, exacerbates their fear: Whether or not we feel in control of a situation directly affects the way we respond to it. Indeed, psychological experiments indicate that fear is substantially reduced if people merely *believe* they have some control over a stimulus, even if their response has no effect….

In violent crime, there is a direct intrusion on the self that produces anger and shame, in addition to fear. "My whole life has been invaded, violated—and not just by the act itself," says a forty-seven-year-old woman who was raped in her apartment. "It didn't happen just to me but to my husband and children." The rape so totally shattered her sense of self, leaving her with a feeling of having been defiled, of being "stained and different," that, ten months later, her husband's love and understanding had not been able to overcome it. "She says, 'You don't want anything to do with me because I am so dirty,'" the husband reports, and the wife wonders if she can ever put her life together again. "There have been times when I wish [the rapist] had killed me—it would have been kinder…. It was as though there were something lacking in dignity in still being alive." At times, to be sure, she feels a glimmer of hope: "I know that somehow we will work it out…." But she adds: "I have changed and the world has changed. I don't see things the way I used to." In the best of moods, in fact, she is besieged by fear, afraid to go out alone and afraid to stay home, obsessed, as so many victims are, that the attacker will come back to seek revenge on her or on her two younger children.[13]

Although the sense of shame and defilement is most evident (and most understandable) in instances of rape, robbery and assault victims have similar, if less intense, reactions. Our sense of self is bound up with our ability to control the personal space in which we live. As administrators of prisons and concentration camps well know, stripping people of their clothes serves to strip them of the normal defenses of their egos, leaving them far more compliant and docile. Victims of muggings, robberies, and assaults also experience a diminishment in their ego defenses. Male victims feel stripped of some portion of their masculinity as well; hence, they often display a compulsive need to explain why it was impossible for them to resist or prevail. This need is strongest of all in men who have been the victims of homosexual rape.

Crimes such as homicide and rape deprive both victims and their relatives of the protective mantle of privacy, converting their intensely private agony and pain into public experiences. "It's impossible for somebody who hasn't been through it to understand the difference between a father dying of natural causes and being murdered," the married daughter of a murdered Bronx pharmacist told a *New York Post* reporter a year after the event. "If I had to name one thing that I hate [the murderer] for the most, it is that he made my father's death — which you should have to cope with privately — a very public thing."[14]

Burglary, too, evokes considerable fear, even though there is no confrontation with a stranger. For one thing, burglary victims are highly conscious of the fact that there might have been a confrontation had they come home earlier; hence, they often are afraid to be home alone. Children whose homes have been burglarized sometimes need psychiatric help to cope with the fear.

More important, forced entry into one's home is an invasion of the self, for our homes are part of the personal space in which we live. We express our individuality in the way we furnish and decorate and in the artifacts we collect; we may view some of our possessions in a casual manner, but others are invested with layers of meaning that bear no relationship to their monetary value. I can still feel the rage that overcame me when I discovered that the person who had burglarized my home had taken a set of cuff-links and studs worn by my father on his wedding day. The fact that they were covered by insurance was irrelevant; their value lay in their power to evoke my father's physical presence seventeen years after his death. I remember, too, the enormous relief my wife and I felt when we discovered that the burglar had been interrupted before he had a chance to take the candlesticks my mother had used to usher in the Sabbath every week of her life.

Because our homes are psychological extensions of our selves, burglary victims often describe their pain in terms strikingly similar to those used by victims of rape — and in a symbolic sense, burglary victims *have* been violated. The saying that one's home is a sanctuary is no mere epigram; it expresses a profound psychological truth. One of the oldest and most sacred principles of Anglo-Saxon law held that no matter how humble a person's cottage might be, not even the King could enter without his consent. The principle is recog-

nized, after a fashion, by totalitarian regimes. The dramatic symbol of totalitarianism is the harsh knock on the door in the middle of the night; as Goffman points out, the fact that even stormtroopers knock implies their acknowledgment of the territorial rights of the residents. It is not too much to conclude that crime threatens the social order in much the same way as does totalitarianism.

## ENDNOTES

1. Jennie McIntyre, "Public Attitudes Toward Crime and Law Enforcement," *Annals of the American Academy of Political and Social Science*, Vol. 374 (November, 1967), pp. 38–39. See also *Crimes and Victims: A Report on the Dayton–San Jose Pilot Survey of Victimization* (Washington, D.C.: U.S. Department of Justice, Law Enforcement Assistance Administration, 1974), Table 13.

2. Robert LeJeune and Nicholas Alex, "On Being Mugged: The Event and Its Aftermath," *Urban Life and Culture*, Vol. 2, No. 3 (October, 1973), reprinted in *The Aldine Crime and Justice Annual*, 1973 (Chicago, Ill.: Aldine Publishing Co., 1974), pp. 161–89.

3. Erving Goffman, *Relations in Public* (New York: Harper Colophon Books, 1971), pp. 11–12.

4. "In this respect, as in many others, the man of prehistoric age survives unchanged in our unconscious," Sigmund Freud wrote. "Thus, our unconscious does not believe in its own death; it behaves as if immortal...." We really believe that "nothing can happen to me. On the other hand, for strangers and for enemies, we do acknowledge death...." Sigmund Freud, "Thoughts on War and Death," in *Freud, On War, Sex, and Neurosis*, reprinted in Richard D. Donnelly et al., *Criminal Law* (New York: The Free Press, 1962), p. 347.

5. LeJeune and Alex, "On Being Mugged," p. 171.

6. Goffman, *Relations in Public*, pp. 265 ff. On pickpockets, see David W. Maurer, *Whiz Mob* (Gainesville, FL: American Dialect Society, November 1955), especially Chapter 5.

7. LeJeune and Alex, "On Being Mugged," p. 171.

8. On February 26, 1976, 132 million gallons of mud and debris broke through a faulty mining company dam in Buffalo Creek, West Virginia, killing 125 and leaving 4,000 of the hollow's 5,000 residents homeless.

9. Kai T. Erikson, *Everything in Its Path* (New York: Simon and Schuster, 1976), p. 234.

10. John Saar, "Attack at Bus Stop Wrecks Man's Life, Denies Ambition." *Washington Post* (March 9, 1975).

11. Ron Shaffer, "Tormented Gun Victim Asks Why," *Washington Post* (November 29, 1975).

12. Shaffer and Alfred E. Lewis, "You Go Out...and Might Not Get Back," *Washington Post* (August 23, 1975).

13. John Saar, "Rape Victim's Memories Haunt Her," *Washington Post* (April 20, 1975).

14. Barry Cunningham, "Murder Victim's Family: One Year Later," *New York Post* (September 12, 1974), p. 54.

# 45. THE JAIL AS DEGRADATION

JOHN IRWIN

*"The jail…is not trying to cure persons or engage them in any complex enterprises.…*
*What is needed and wanted in a jail are prisoners who will wait obediently wherever they*
*are placed.… Generally the method used to convert free adults into this compliant and*
*passive state is to give commands—either short and polite orders or shouted threats—*
*and to back them up by applying whatever force is required to immobilize a person."*

Most of us will never be arrested; likewise, most of us will not spend time in jail. It seems that jail is like a strange, foreign land meant for others.

However, real people go to jails—some innocent, some guilty. All face degradation, and that has an effect on most. Whatever else we might think about crime in society, in a democracy, it is imperative that we all realize the human consequences of jailing people. If we want to **understand** human behavior, it is important for us to critically evaluate jailing policies.

This is the spirit of John Irwin's description of the jail. This description is one chapter from Irwin's book on the jail, a book based on a very extensive research study.

Prisoners receive much more than the treatment required to introduce them to the jail and hold them there. They are impersonally and systematically degraded by every step in the criminal justice process, from arrest through detention to court appearance. They are also degraded personally by the hostility and contempt directed at them by police officers, deputies, and other criminal justice functionaries.

## PROCESS DEGRADATION

Even when police officers act in a polite and professional manner, an arrest is degrading to all but the seasoned rabble. In making an arrest, officers occasionally invade a person's private space—a home, office, or workplace—and remove him or her from the presence of shocked acquaintances or

From *Jail: Managing the Underclass in American Society*, by John Irwin. Copyright © 1985 by The Regents of the University of California. Reprinted by permission of the University of California Press.

friends. Most often, however, the police arrest persons in public places where most of the witnesses are strangers; but even this remains humiliating to all but the most hardened and frequently arrested disreputables. Arrests are unusual public events, and those who witness them often express shock, dismay, or revulsion—reactions that further humiliate and degrade the person being arrested.

When arresting officers believe that danger is involved, they often take standard precautions that increase the humiliation. …When police fear that suspects may be armed, they make them stand spread-eagle against a wall or hunched over a car hood until they search them. Occasionally, they may go even further. For example, in December 1983, three members of the Harlem Globetrotters basketball team were shopping in downtown Santa Barbara. They left an ice cream store, cones in hand, and hailed a taxi. After traveling for a few blocks through the heart of the business district, their cab was stopped by policemen who ordered them out of the car and commanded them to lie on the ground, face down. A jewelry store had been robbed an hour before, and the police suspected these men — even though their only physical similarity to the robbers was that they were black. Their terrifying and humiliating ordeal, which had drawn a large crowd, lasted until the store owner arrived and saw that they were not the robbers.[1]

Sometimes persons who are inexperienced or less experienced with arrest and anxious about their suddenly powerless position will argue, joke, or even resist the police, who then respond with tougher tactics.[2] The total subjugation and immobility that continue through arrest and transportation to jail are deeply mortifying to persons who have never experienced this condition as adults. (Those who have been in the armed services may have experienced something that resembles it in their first weeks after induction.) Erving Goffman stated it well:

First, total institutions disrupt or defile precisely those actions that in civil society have the role of attesting to the actor and those in his presence that he has some command over his world — that he is a person with "adult" self-determination, autonomy, and freedom of action. A failure to retain this kind of adult executive competency, or at least the symbols of it, can produce in the inmate the terror of feeling radically demoted in the age-grading system.[3]

Degradation increases during the time a person is being introduced to the jail. In his study of "total institutions" (of which the jail is a type), Goffman explored at length the numerous mortifying rituals — such as searching, stripping, bathing, spraying, and the taking of personal property — that are conducted with the institutional purpose of converting newcomers into manageable inmates.[4] In the jail, because it is conceived by its operators as a short-term holding facility, no elaborate conception of a desired inmate is at work. The jail, unlike other total institutions, is not trying to cure persons or engage them in any complex enterprises, such as running a prison with convict labor. What is needed and wanted in a jail are prisoners who will wait obediently wherever they are placed (in a cell, on a bench, or against a wall), who will make no demands (or few), and who will willingly perform the few required jail procedures, such as returning to their cells, standing for a count, coming to the front when called (for a visit, release, bail, or transfer), and follow-

ing the procedures required when being delivered to court. Generally, the method used to convert free adults into this compliant and passive state is to give commands — either short and polite orders or shouted threats — and to back them up by applying whatever force is required to immobilize a person. This often means removing a prisoner to an isolation cell (sometimes padded) where he can engage in any behavior the surroundings permit without bothering anyone else or damaging any jail property....

The routine demands for compliance, the excessive attention to security, and the general lack of concern for the welfare of the rabble, whom the jail employees understand to be the jail's major clients, result in a painfully harsh introduction to the jail. As we have seen, the fish are herded here and there, crowded together to wait in small, bare cells for unexplained periods of time, and ignored or rebuffed when they make requests; besides being sternly ordered to do whatever is required in the entrance process, they may be commanded to strip naked and bend over with buttocks spread in front of many other fish and deputies.

The degrading experiences and conditions continue during the time prisoners spend in the tanks.[5] Their loss of self-determination becomes only slightly less painful as they learn the official limits and the informal mechanisms for bypassing them. In most jails, they discover that their managers are interested in little more than their name, charge, bail, and court date. Recently, many jail systems, such as those in Los Angeles and San Francisco, have also begun to classify incoming prisoners according to a set of custody concerns. Potential troublemakers and "weak" prisoners (those seen as potential victims of exploitation, particularly sexual exploitation) are selected for special placement in tanks set aside for them. Deputies look for any serious medical conditions that might cause a problem while the prisoners are in jail. And sometimes deputies are interested in identifying new prisoners who seem likely candidates for trusty status. Beyond these managerial concerns, the deputies and jail employees have virtually no interest in the individuality of the prisoners.[6]

In addition, the jail routine makes it virtually impossible for a prisoner to maintain his normal physical appearance, which is a crucial factor in sustaining his conception of self.[7] Immediately on entering the jail, all clothing is taken from the prisoners, and they are supplied with ill-fitting, conspicuous jail uniforms, such as the baggy, bright orange jumpsuits worn by San Francisco County jail pretrial detainees. Most of the other things they use to manage their appearance — the set of tools Goffman refers to as an "identity kit" — are taken from them, and they are allowed to keep only a few (such as a toothbrush, toothpaste, hairbrush, comb, and soap) during incarceration.[8] (In San Francisco and Los Angeles, the toothbrush and toothpaste are supplied by the jail, and the other items must be purchased from the canteen.)

It is very often difficult for prisoners to keep clean. A man who had been in several small city and county jails in California told me: "If you wanted to wash, you had to wash in the toilet. The whole place was so filthy that I just stayed in my clothes. After a week I got out and took off my shoes. Whew, the smell. I had the worst case of athlete's foot you ever saw. Two toes looked like they were going to fall off." In large, relatively humane county jails, such as those in San Francisco County, prisoners are scheduled to receive a change of clothing about once a week. But to many, this provision has not been reliable or sufficient; the files of the San Francisco jail ombudsman contain complaints like these: "We have not had a clothes change in three weeks. We want a full set of clean clothes once a week." And: "We should be allowed to change underwear twice a week — and have two pairs, so that we will not be naked while we wash underwear." Furthermore, it is virtually impossible to be "well groomed" in jail. Shaving is difficult because prisoners are not allowed to keep razor blades, and the deputies usually supply one razor blade a day to be used by many prisoners; in San Francisco, up to twenty prisoners must use one blade for their morning shave. Prisoners have no fingernail clippers. Most jails have no barbers, and prisoners either cut one another's hair with razor blades or let their hair grow....

As we have seen, prisoners live in tanks containing crowds of strangers. The human density and total lack of privacy expose them to one another in ways that can occur only in total institutions. They inspect one another's genitals, scars, rashes, and deformities. They smell one another's breath, sweat, gases, and feces. They hear one another's snoring, breaking wind, and masturbating.

Most people depend on a variety of shields, such as clothing, private rooms, and deodorants, to disguise certain aspects of themselves and to hide their publicly offensive practices. These efforts are more than attempts to "look one's best" or to conform to social standards; they help maintain basic conceptions of self, of individuality. The degradation caused by all jail processes is summed up in the relatively uniform appearance of prisoners — plain, sallow, unclean, disheveled.

## ATTITUDINAL DEGRADATION

Many criminal justice functionaries express contempt and hostility toward suspects and defendants, and this fact compounds the degradation experienced by prisoners. This contempt is not idiosyncratic, however. It stems from values shared by police officers, deputies, prosecutors, and many judges. These values are rooted in a theory of crime and society that Herbert Packer has identified as the "crime control model." He writes: "The crime control model is based on the proposition that the repression of criminal conduct is by far the most important function to be performed by the criminal process. The failure of law enforcement to bring criminal conduct under tight control is viewed as leading to the breakdown of public order and thence to the disappearance of an important condition of human freedom."[9]

The majority of police officers and deputies accept this theory, but they do not see crime control as simply or mainly a practical endeavor. In their view, what threatens the public order is not crime itself but immorality, and the major threat lies in the immorality of certain classes or types of people, most of them belonging to the rabble.

### Arresting Officers

The police, who make the initial and highly discretionary arrest decisions, tend to believe that street people or disreputables — the people they arrest most frequently — are the primary source of trouble in society. As Officer C. of the San Francisco police told me in an interview: "It's the people who are hanging around on the corner. They're unemployed and don't have anything else to do. Like the guys on Eighteenth and Mission.

They don't act like other people. They don't know when to stop. They're ready to do anything. People who have jobs, live in apartments or houses, they don't cause us any trouble."

Most police officers are not dispassionate toward the rabble. Their personal class prejudices and cultural distaste (to use the mildest term) are strengthened by the irritating and time-consuming task of policing a class of people who have always posed the most visible and offensive problem of social order in big cities.[10] In the neighborhoods where there are significant contingents of the rabble, most police work is directed toward managing them. Officer C. told me: "If you don't keep on top of them, then they get out of hand. If you let too big a crowd of them form, it will get out of control. They bother people who have to pass them and the business in the area. You have to keep them moving."

Some rabble types consistently show disrespect toward the police and threaten their authority. This failure to show respect often stems from a moral contest between disreputables and police. Most disreputables (as we should expect) operate according to beliefs and values that bolster their dignity and justify their position and behavior as morally correct. These beliefs usually also define police officers as lowly and despicable human beings. So instead of passively or obsequiously submitting to an officer's commands, disreputables may engage the police in a moral contest, objecting and arguing from their own moral position. When police officers who are already hostile toward the rabble are confronted with such hostility and moral condemnation, an invidious dynamic is set in motion. Anything less than complete obedience by the rabble can be seen as a moral or physical threat that must be countered with immediate force.

The hostility of police officers is clearly expressed in the names they use to label the rabble category. Officer C. explained the epithets now in use: "Some guys use *slime balls* and *pukes*. I like *dirt ball*. Now *kronks* is popular. *Assholes* is still the most common term." The hostility is also evident in the way police handle disreputable types when they arrest them and take them to jail. Approximately half the persons in our felony sample reported that the arresting officers were verbally abusive to them. For example, "They talked to me

like a dog." Or "They talked to me like I was an asshole. I'm not a criminal, I wasn't even high." Seven persons in the sample reported that they were handled in a physically abusive manner. One of them, a twenty-two-year-old Nicaraguan corner boy, said: "I was playing football with my cousin in a field. This cop came up to me with his gun drawn. He pushed me down on the ground. He was shaking. I was petrified. He jerked my hands way up my back and put on the cuffs." In addition, seven others stated that they were struck or kicked by the arresting officers. For example: "They hit me in the face and the stomach when they got me in the car." And this: "He was pushing me in the car and gave me a big kick in the stomach when I was bent over getting in."[11]

## Deputies

Like police officers, jail deputies (employees of the sheriff who run the jail) tend to hold strongly negative attitudes toward most persons who are arrested and held in jail. These attitudes stem largely from their work with prisoners, which is in many ways more annoying than police work. They must constantly handle repulsive, difficult, and even violent prisoners, some of whom are drunk, high, enraged, belligerent, or insane. Many prisoners hate deputies, and a few openly express this hate. For example, I once heard a prisoner who was being booked loudly threaten the booking room deputies as follows: "You rotten motherfuckers, if I catch you on my turf you're in trouble." (The response from one deputy was: "You haven't *got* any turf, asshole.")[12]

Besides occasionally expressing such hostility, prisoners regularly try to combat their deprivation by beseeching deputies for help. Deputies who do not immediately and emphatically rebuff these entreaties are inundated with pleas. New deputies who have not yet acquired the deputies' culture and may have some sympathy for prisoners are especially vulnerable. Roger Martin, a temporary deputy, described his experience in this way:

Earlier on the job, the inmates conned me often. I learned this is standard procedure with a new deputy. He usually begins as a relatively nice guy before the jail brutalizes him. The inmates try to take advantage of this, to ask for favors and get the deputy to do things for them. I was gullible enough to be conned at first, but I quickly learned they were taking advantage of me and laughing at me behind my back.[13]

These supplications from prisoners confront deputies with a constant moral dilemma. They must work closely with other humans (prisoners) who are in a state of deprivation and visibly suffering. (If the deputies do not notice, the prisoners will remind them.) If the deputies remain committed to a philosophy of humanity and egalitarianism, or even to a basic sense of fairness, the plight of the needy and the suffering around them will eventually take a heavy toll on their peace of mind and personality organization. To avoid this, most deputies embrace and help sustain the theory that prisoners are worthless and deserve their deprivation. For some, who have operated all their lives on similar concepts (stereotypical thinking or racial prejudice), this is relatively easy. Others, however, must consciously reject more humane and tolerant conceptions of prisoners before they can accept the cynical viewpoint. In most cases, they cannot accomplish this without some strain, and this strain and their lingering ambivalence often make them *more* expressive of hate and brutality. As in other situations, the convert is very often the extremist.[14]

Deputies openly refer to prisoners by derogatory names. As Martin described the practice: "The deputies routinely called the inmates *asshole* or *motherfucker* to their faces or just out of their hearing. The terms were so commonly used that they literally became the inmate's name…. They look on Mexicans and Blacks as scum. *Spic, greaser, jungle bunny, nigger* — the names flow effortlessly from the deputy's lips."[15]

The hostility of deputies is by no means exhausted in name calling. It is also expressed in their routine discretionary decisions: Whether to allow entering prisoners to make phone calls, or to keep some items on their person, or to eat, or to retrieve money taken from them during arrest. For example, I once asked a deputy who was temporarily in charge of the property room if he could transfer a prisoner's money to his "books" so that he could spend it in jail. His answer was: "Fuck the asshole. If it was up to me, the assholes wouldn't get anything. If they want to spend their money, let 'em stay out of jail." It is expressed in their decisions to ignore prisoners' visible medical needs; to punish them on the spot for talking, shouting, talking back, or having a "bad attitude"; to place them in cells or tanks where they will be in danger from other prisoners; to keep them locked in cells; to withhold their mail or money sent to them through the mail; to ransack their cells in cell searches; and to subject them to humiliating and painful experiences….

Sometimes special events or processes inhibit the strong tendencies of deputies to develop or express malevolent attitudes. For example, several court actions apparently have restrained deputies in Los Angeles. Many prisoners and ex-prisoners have reported to me that during the middle 1970s at the Los Angeles County jail, deputies became exceptionally abusive to prisoners. One of them said: "Man, someone should do something about that jail. I mean those cops will get on people for nothing. A guy doesn't have to get out of line to get mistreated there. I watched it many times. Young guys who didn't know what was happening, and the cops would yank them out of line and treat 'em like dogs. It made me sick. I haven't seen anything like it in all my years of being in these places." Prisoners at the jail in 1983 suggested to me that a series of lawsuits and court injunctions against the jail had significantly reduced the verbal and physical abuse. As one of them put it: "Yeah, they used to be bad here, but the courts have been on them, and most of that really rough stuff has stopped."

At the Yolo County jail, the friendlier rural atmosphere and the efforts of a relatively humanitarian jail supervisor, who is able to control his small staff effectively, have apparently prevented the normal deputy culture from developing. As one prisoner put it: "This place is a piece of cake. You should look at Sacramento. There it's mean. This place is a playground. Everyone treats you like a human being."

At the San Francisco County jails, two humanitarian sheriffs, Richard Hongisto (1972–1978) and Michael Hennessey (1980 to the present), have systematically promoted a humane approach. They have fired or transferred many deputies who were involved in abusive practices and have hired and promoted persons who demonstrate more humanity and tolerance for prisoners. In spite of these efforts, which are still continuing, many deputies at the San Francisco County jails openly revealed their hatred for prisoners during the time I was observing there. They regularly called the prisoners *assholes* and stubbornly resisted the attempts of outsiders, such as the prisoner services caseworkers, to help them.

## JUDICIAL DEGRADATION

As Malcolm Feeley has noted in his study of the New Haven court system, court proceedings are conducted as a *moral* enterprise: "Many observers of the courts have become preoccupied with procedural justice and have consequently failed to appreciate the intensity of the normative concern that informs the decisions of so many officials in the criminal process."[16] More concretely, this means that prisoners are judged not solely or even primarily for their crimes but rather for their character, and that they are often profoundly degraded during their court appearances.

Degradation is built into the court routines, which are planned and executed to dignify reputability (and condemn disreputability). Usually the judge is introduced by the bailiff, who orders those present to stand while the judge whisks in to assume his high station. From his lofty seat, which is the largest and most luxurious in the room, he directs the proceedings with virtually absolute official power—including the power to summarily jail anybody in the room for contempt of court. The bailiff attempts to enforce the rigid code of courtroom decorum, which goes far beyond the rules necessary to maintain order and to speed the court process (men must remove their hats, no one may read a newspaper, and so on). The attorneys, clerks, and bailiff address the court, make requests and motions, and generally perform their roles in a practiced manner that shows respect for the judge....

Besides appearing out of place, most defendants fail to perform properly and skillfully, and they often disturb or disrupt the routine. When they approach the bench to take their position behind "the bar," some of them meander awkwardly forward with small unsteady steps, hands groping for some comfortable position, head lowered. Others stride forward in an arrogant street gait, arms swinging, body swaying, and head bobbing. Whereas the attorneys are at ease and poised before the bench, most defendants bend and slant their bodies, shift their weight from one foot to the other, fiddle with their hands or perhaps stick them into their front or back pockets. When they sit at the defense table, they slouch and fidget in their seats, jut their legs far out in front of them, and appear to be either too ill-at-ease or too relaxed.

During the hearings, many of them fail to respond to the judge's commands or to understand essential information. The more aggressive defendants occasionally pierce the courtroom decorum with disruptive commands, requests, and opinions. Thus, for example, a young man accused of grabbing a radio from another man on the street and then knocking him down—a robbery—loudly protested against his attorney's request to be removed from the case, which would result in a delay: "I've already been here forty-one days and I want to go out and get to work. My birthday is January 26, I sure don't want to be in jail for my birthday." And another defendant argued with the judge over his attorney's motion to have him ruled incompetent. Defendant (loudly): "Certainly I'm competent!" Judge: "Your attorney is not in agreement with you." Defendant (shouting): "How could my attorney not be in agreement with me? He's supposed to defend me. What's crazy about wanting to get out of jail!"

Such behavior by poorly dressed defendants, besides being personally offensive, serves to remind the judge and his court of the importance of observing social properties and respecting society's status systems. In a sense, the court is a microcosm and a symbol of society's formal and stratified aspects. The behavior of defendants here is taken as a demonstration of their general social weaknesses and as evidence that they are truly *moral inferiors*. Thus, the court functionaries—particularly the prosecutor and the judge, but also the bailiff, the court reporter, and even the defense counsel—openly or indirectly display their contempt for most defendants, who are thereby humiliated and degraded....

## LOSS OF COMMITMENT

One basic premise behind the practice of law enforcement as a moral enterprise is the idea that persons will respond to contempt and castigation with apology, contrition, and alteration of their character and conduct. The tenacity of this belief is peculiar in the face of so much contradictory evidence. Under some conditions, of course, some defendants bow and conform when they are degraded, condemned, and disciplined. But under other conditions, which are just as common if not more so, they squirm away from the disapprobation, avoid the punishment, and refuse to follow prescriptions for future conduct. Such conditions are not hard to imagine. The disapprobation meted out to them may be severe, contemptuous, and unmitigated by any positive attitudes. Realistically, there may be no clear paths to their "rehabilitation," that is, to their achievement of dignified social status and economic self-sufficiency. And they may have contact with the deviant viewpoints that characterize the official deliverers of disapprobation and punishment as morally inferior and the "offender" as honorable.

When these conditions apply, many marginal persons lose or relax their commitment to conventional society. This is more understandable when we consider the tremendous effort it can take to maintain that commitment when one is poor and of low social status. It means struggling to meet all the obligations required of a conventional citizen, such as paying rent, bills, taxes, fines, fees, alimony, and child support. It means avoiding deviant habits, such as stealing or excessive drinking and drug use. And it means observing society's pervasive and subtle definitions of respectability, which define in rather narrow terms just how to comport oneself in public. To many persons, the prospect of giving up this struggle looks appealing.

Rejection of conventional values and loss of commitment to society are even more likely to occur when defendants believe that those who punish them in the name of the law are hypocrit-ical and unfair. Due process values — such as "all persons are innocent until proven guilty" and "every person has the right to a fair and impartial trial" — are widely and proudly celebrated in conventional society and often ceremoniously repeated during the judicial process. Yet what the defendants actually experience are the practices that stem from law enforcement conceived as a moral enterprise, practices that involve systematic violations of due process values. Moreover, they believe that they are being intentionally punished during all stages of the judicial process, regardless of its eventual outcome. And in this, they are correct.[17] The great majority of persons arrested do not receive jail or prison sentences; but all of them, including many whose charges are dismissed, are subjected to some punishment. The experience of harsh and unfairly delivered punishment frequently enrages or embitters defendants and makes it easier for them to reject the values of those who have dealt with them in this way.

With their commitment to conventional values damaged or destroyed, and their ties to the dominant culture shaken loose, many persons — particularly those who are already living on the margins of conventional society and having difficulty conforming — "drop out": They migrate to deviant worlds and the rabble status. The jail experience prepares them for an acceptance of the rabble life.

## ENDNOTES

1. See *Los Angeles Times*, December 14, 1983, pt. 1, p. 2, and December 15, 1983, pt. 1, pp. 3, 17; and *People Weekly*, February 13, 1984, pp. 30–31.
2. In 1982, F. Lee Bailey, a well-known criminal attorney, was arrested in San Francisco for driving under the influence of alcohol. He pleaded not guilty, and at his trial he testified that he was trying to keep his humor during the arrest by joking in a friendly manner with the police; he said that they became verbally and then physically abusive toward him and that one officer knocked a cigarette out of his hand with a "vicious karate chop." The police officers testified that Bailey was insulting and combative. He was acquitted in a lengthy jury trial. See *San Francisco Chronicle*, April 14, 1982, p. 14, and April 16, 1982, p. 1.
3. Erving Goffman, *Asylums* (Chicago: Aldine Pub. Co., 1961), p. 43.
4. Goffman, "On the Characteristics of Total Institutions," in ibid.

5. Most of these have been recognized and analyzed by Goffman in *Asylums*.

6. Some deputies, if they work in a jail for a long time, get to know some of the jail regulars and interact with them on a broader set of characteristics; and a few prisoners who are known to possess skills and knowledge that are useful to the jail operation may be dealt with almost as if they were real people. But most prisoners never see this sort of treatment.

7. One of Goffman's major contributions to sociology is his convincing analysis of how persons "present" themselves through behavior and how important this presentation is in their definitions of self. See his *Presentation of Self in Everyday Life*.

8. Goffman, *Asylums*, p. 20.

9. Herbert Packer, *The Limits of the Criminal Sanction* (Stanford: Stanford University Press, 1968), p. 158. Packer contrasts this model with the due process model, which is dominated by other concerns: seeing that the system does not err in convicting persons of crime, restraining the extension of government power, and ensuring equality of treatment for the defendant.

10. The police were first introduced in London as a response to the rabble, who were then spoken of as "the dangerous classes." See Alan Silver, "The Demand for Order in Civil Society," in *The Police*, ed. David Bordua.

11. I have only the prisoners' accounts of these acts and do not know what actually happened or what, if anything, had provoked the officers' actions. However, four of the seven prisoners had facial bruises. In his study of police behavior, *The Police and the Public*, Albert Reiss found that in the majority of cases in which the persons arrested were "violent or aggressive" or "disgruntled or sullen," the police used "gross force" or "firm handling, generally moving the offender about by holding him by the arm, prodding him with a nightstick, or surrounding him with several police officers" (p. 54). This suggests that the expression of hostility is interactive. Nevertheless—and this is what is important for this analysis of degradation—many arrested persons in my sample *believed* that police officers had unnecessarily abused them, physically or verbally, and this made them feel both angry and degraded.

12. Many similar verbal attacks on the deputies occurred while I was observing in the booking room. If the prisoner persisted, he was firmly warned, and if he still persisted, the deputies roughly removed him to an isolation cell. In the Los Angeles County jail, such outbursts were not tolerated; they precipitated either a severe warning or instant removal to an isolation cell.

13. Roger Martin, *Pigs and Other Animals* (Myco Publishing House, 1980), p. 57. Personal observation has persuaded me that the vast majority of prisoner requests are motivated by nothing more than a desire to improve on reduced circumstances. Martin's conclusion that prisoners intended to take advantage of him made it easier for him to turn down their requests and accept the collective cynicism.

14. I witnessed this process not only in deputies, some of whom I had known as students before they became deputies, but in myself and my fellow prisoner services caseworkers. We were constantly beseeched for more help than we could deliver, and we had to cope with feelings that we were not doing enough. (One knows he can always do more.) In compensation for these feelings, we began to develop a more cynical view of our work and a more derogatory conception of the prisoner. We used the common term *burnout* to describe this process.

15. Roger Martin, *Pigs and Other Animals*, pp. 54, 75.

16. Malcolm Feeley, *The Process Is the Punishment* (New York: Russell Sage, 1979), p. 15.

17. This is Malcolm Feeley's important thesis: The primary purpose of the court process is not to determine legal guilt through due process or, as many critics have argued, to run an efficient system through plea bargaining, but rather to punish most defendants through the court process. He suggests that the sanctioning powers are distributed among several people—the arresting officers, bail bondsmen, defense attorneys, prosecutors, and judges—and that punishment is contained in the arrest, jail experience, and court appearances; see *Process Is the Punishment*, pp. 31–32. In the samples I followed in my research, slightly less than half of the felony charges and more than 50 percent of the misdemeanor charges were dismissed. Another 18 percent of those arrested for a felony and more than 31 percent of those arrested for a misdemeanor were diverted, fined, or granted probation without jail sentences. The vast majority of misdemeanor charges were dismissed or otherwise disposed of within forty-eight hours of arrest, and half of the persons arrested for a felony were released from jail within seventy-two hours. However, the process of arrest, booking, and being jailed is extremely punitive. Moreover, some categories of people were held longer before having their cases dismissed or disposed of through diversion or probation. Thirteen of the petty hustlers (46 percent) had their cases dismissed, but they waited an average of 5.3 days to be released. Among the rabble or marginal rabble types, forty-two out of the 100 arrested for a felony had their cases dismissed, but eleven of them were held for more than three days, and four were held more than fifteen days. In some other counties, persons are held much longer before dismissal. In a "tracking sample" of 2,255 persons arrested for misdemeanors and felonies in San Mateo County from November 1981 to October 1982, the eighty-two persons who had their cases dismissed by the court or the district attorney had remained in jail for an average of thirteen days; see Institute for Law and Police Planning, *San Mateo County Needs Assessment* (Oakland, CA, 1983). In Miami in 1981 and 1982, over 66 percent of all felony charges were dismissed, and those who waited in jail for dismissal spent an average of fifty days there; the median stay was twenty-one days; see James Austin, Barry Krisberg, and Paul Litsky, *Supervised Pretrial Release Test Design Evaluation*.

# Part X

## SOCIAL INSTITUTIONS: POLITICAL AND ECONOMIC

Institutions are the various accepted means by which society is able to operate. They are the patterns by which we solve ongoing problems. For society to continue, institutions must work. If they do not, services will not be adequately provided for people, social problems will become increasingly serious, and problems of order will arise more regularly.

Part X focuses on economic and political institutions. **Economic** institutions are those patterns created in society that deal with producing, distributing, and consuming goods and services. **Political** institutions are those patterns that deal with governing society. Both types of institutions have a lot to do with social power; in sociology, there almost always are attempts to show how political and economic institutions are linked.

The first selection by Peter L. Berger and Thomas Luckmann examines the meaning of institutions and how they are developed in social interaction. The second selection by Seymour Martin Lipset describes the economic, social, and cultural conditions necessary for democratic institutions to develop; Laird Wilcox examines the nature of **extremism** in society, a form of thinking and acting that threatens the continuation of democratic institutions.

In his selection, John Kenneth Galbraith attempts to tie economics to politics by examining the politics of the affluent and how that politics perpetuates great inequalities in society. The last selection, by S. Aronowitz and W. Di Fazio, is about economic institutions, more specifically, the future of jobs in a society increasingly driven by technological change.

# 46. THE ORIGINS OF INSTITUTIONS

PETER L. BERGER AND THOMAS LUCKMANN

"An institutional world, then, is experienced as an objective reality. It has a history
that antedates the individual's birth and is not accessible to his biographical recollection. It was there before he was born, and it will be there after his death."

Social patterns arise in interaction. They come to be objective forces—institutions
—that confront and control the individual. How do they arise? What are their
qualities? Here, Peter Berger and Thomas Luckmann examine the process of "institutionalization," how social patterns become an integral part of organization,
and how they acquire an independent existence from specific actors. It might
be useful to keep in mind the following outline:

1. Interaction and habituation
2. Transmission and historicity
3. Objectivity
4. Legitimation
5. Social controls

...As A and B interact, in whatever manner, typifications will be produced quite quickly. A watches B perform. He attributes motives to B's actions
and, seeing the actions recur, typifies the motives
as recurrent. As B goes on performing, A is soon
able to say to himself, "Aha! There he goes again."
At the same time, A may assume that B is doing the
same thing with regard to him. From the beginning, both A and B assume this reciprocity of typification. In the course of their interaction, these
typifications will be expressed in specific patterns
of conduct. That is, A and B will begin to play roles
vis-à-vis each other. This will occur even if each
continues to perform actions different from those
of the other. The possibility of taking the role of
the other will appear with regard to the same actions performed by both. That is, A will inwardly
appropriate B's reiterated roles and make them the
models for his own role-playing. For example, B's

From *The Social Construction of* Reality, by Peter L. Berger and
Thomas Luckmann. Copyright © 1966 by Peter L. Berger and
Thomas Luckmann. Used by permission of Doubleday, a di-
vision of Bantam Doubleday Dell Publishing Group, Inc.

role in the activity of preparing food is not only
*typified* as such by A, but enters as a constitutive element into A's own food-preparation role. Thus a
collection of reciprocally typified actions will
emerge, *habitualized* for each in roles, some of
which will be performed separately and some in
common.[1] Although this reciprocal typification is
not yet institutionalization (there being only two
individuals, there is no possibility of a typology of
actors), it is clear that institutionalization is already
present *in nucleo*.

At this stage, one may ask what gains accrue to
the two individuals from this development. The
most important gain is that each will be able to
predict the other's actions. Concomitantly, the interaction of both becomes predictable. The "there
he goes again" becomes a "there *we* go again."
This relieves both individuals of a considerable
amount of tension. They save time and effort, not
only in whatever external tasks they might be engaged in separately or jointly, but in terms of their
respective psychological economies. Their life together is now defined by a widening sphere of
taken-for-granted routines....

Let us push our paradigm one step further and imagine that A and B have children. At this point, the situation changes qualitatively. The appearance of a third party changes the character of the ongoing social interaction between A and B, and it will change even further as additional individuals continue to be added.[2] The institutional world, which existed in statu nascendi in the original situation of A and B, is now passed on to others. In this process, institutionalization perfects itself. The habitualizations and typifications undertaken in the common life of A and B – formations that until this point still had the quality of ad hoc conceptions of two individual – now become historical institutions. With the acquisition of historicity, these formations also acquire another crucial quality, or, more accurately, perfect a quality that was incipient as soon as A and B began the reciprocal typification of their conduct: This quality is objectivity. This means that the institutions that have now been crystallized (for instance, the institution of paternity as it is encountered by the children) are experienced as existing over and beyond the individuals who "happen to" embody them at the moment. In other words, the institutions are now experienced as possessing a reality of their own, a reality that confronts the individual as an external and coercive fact.[3]

As long as the nascent institutions are constructed and maintained only in the interaction of A and B, their objectivity remains tenuous, easily changeable, almost playful, even while they attain a measure of objectivity by the mere fact of their formation....

A and B alone are responsible for having constructed this world. A and B remain capable of changing or abolishing it. What is more, because they themselves have shaped this world in the course of a shared biography that they can remember, the world thus shaped appears fully transparent to them. They understand the world that they themselves have made. All this changes in the process of transmission to the new generation. The objectivity of the institutional world "thickens" and "hardens," not only for the children, but (by a mirror effect) for the parents as well. The "there we go again" now becomes "this is how these things are done." A world so regarded attains a firmness in consciousness; it becomes real in an ever more massive way, and it can no longer be changed so readily. For the children, especially in the early phase of their socialization into it, it becomes *the* world. For the parents, it loses its playful quality and becomes "serious." For the children, the parentally transmitted world is not fully transparent. Because they had no part in shaping it, it confronts them as a given reality that, like nature, is opaque in places at least.

Only at this point does it become possible to speak of a social world at all, in the sense of a comprehensive and given reality confronting the individual in a manner analogous to the reality of the natural world. Only in this way, *as* an objective world, can the social formations be transmitted to a new generation....

The process of transmission simply strengthens the parents' sense of reality; ...to put it crudely, if one says, "this is how these things are done," often enough, one believes it oneself.[4]

An institutional world, then, is experienced as an objective reality. It has a history that antedates the individual's birth and is not accessible to his biographical recollection. It was there before he was born, and it will be there after his death. This history itself, as the tradition of the existing institutions, has the character of objectivity. The individual's biography is apprehended as an episode located within the objective history of the society. The institutions, as historical and objective facticities, confront the individual as undeniable facts. The institutions are *there*, external to him, persistent in their reality, whether he likes it or not. He cannot wish them away. They resist his attempts to change or evade them. They have coercive power over him, both in themselves, by the sheer force of their facticity, and through the control mechanisms that are usually attached to the most important of them. The objective reality of institutions is not diminished if the individual does not understand their purpose or their mode of operation. He may experience large sectors of the social world as incomprehensible, perhaps oppressive in their opaqueness, but real nonetheless. Because institutions exist as external reality, the individual cannot understand them by introspection. He must "go out" and learn about them, just as he must to learn about nature. This remains true even though the social world, as a humanly produced reality, is potentially understandable in a way not possible in the case of the natural world.[5]

At the same point, the institutional world requires *legitimation*, that is, ways by which it can be "explained" and justified. This is not because it appears less real. As we have seen, the reality of the social world gains in massivity in the course of its transmission. This reality, however, is a historical one that comes to the new generation as a tradition rather than as a biographical memory. In our paradigmatic example, A and B, the original creators of the social world, can always reconstruct the circumstances under which their world and any part of it was established. That is, they can arrive at the meaning of an institution by exercising their powers of recollection. A and B's children are in an altogether different situation. Their knowledge of the institutional history is by way of "hearsay." The original meaning of the institutions is inaccessible to them in terms of memory. Therefore, it becomes necessary to interpret this meaning to them in various legitimating formulas. These will have to be consistent and comprehensive in terms of the institutional order if they are to carry conviction to the new generation. The same story, so to speak, must be told to all the children. It follows that the expanding institutional order develops a corresponding canopy of legitimations, stretching over it a protective cover of both cognitive and normative interpretation. These legitimations are learned by the new generation during the same process that socializes them into the institutional order....

The development of specific mechanisms of social controls also becomes necessary with the historicization and objectivation of institutions. Deviance from the institutionally "programmed" courses of action becomes likely once the institutions have become realities divorced from their original relevance in the concrete social processes from which they arose. To put this more simply, it is more likely that one will deviate from programs set up for one by others than from programs one has helped establish oneself. The new generation posits a problem of compliance, and

its socialization into the institutional order requires the establishment of sanctions. The institutions must and do claim authority over the individual, independently of the subjective meanings he may attach to any particular situation. The priority of the institutional definitions of situations must be consistently maintained over individual temptations at redefinition. The children must be "taught to behave" and, once taught, must be "kept in line." So, of course, must the adults. The more conduct is institutionalized, the more predictable and thus the more controlled it becomes. If socialization into the institutions has been effective, outright coercive measures can be applied economically and selectively. Most of the time, conduct will occur "spontaneously" within the institutionally set channels. The more (on the level of meaning) conduct is taken for granted, the more possible alternatives to the institutional "programs" will recede, and the more predictable and controlled conduct will be.

## ENDNOTES

1. The term "taking the role of the other" is taken from Mead. Here, we are taking Mead's paradigm of socialization and applying it to the broader problem of institutionalization. The argument combines key features of both Mead's and Gehlen's approaches.
2. Simmel's analysis of the expansion from the dyad to the triad is important in this connection. The following argument combines Simmel's and Durkheim's conceptions of the objectivity of social reality.
3. In Durkheim's terms, this means that, with the expansion of the dyad into a triad and beyond, the original formations become genuine "social facts," that is, they attain *choséité*.
4. For an analysis of this process in the contemporary family, cf. Peter L. Berger and Hansfried Kellner, "Marriage and the Construction of Reality," *Diogenes* 46 (1964), 1 ff.
5. The preceding description closely follows Durkheim's analysis of social reality. This does *not* contradict the Weberian conception of the meaningful character of society. Because social reality always originates in meaningful human actions, it continues to carry meaning even if it is opaque to the individual at a given time. The original may be *reconstructed*, precisely by means of what Weber called *Verstehen*.

# 47. THE SOCIAL BASES OF DEMOCRACY

SEYMOUR MARTIN LIPSET

*"Democracy is an international cause. A host of democratic governments and parties, as well as various nongovernmental organizations dedicated to human rights, are working and providing funds to create and sustain democratic forces in newly liberalized governments and to press autocratic ones to change…. The outside world can help, but the basis for [democratic institutions]…must come from within."*

In 1960, Seymour Martin Lipset wrote **Political Man: the Social Bases of Politics**, a work dedicated to understanding the links between social conditions and the development of democratic political institutions. This selection is a follow-up to that book, a speech he gave as president of the American Sociological Association in 1993. The theme is the same: Democracy is difficult to establish, and it is created and maintained only through certain economic and social conditions. The article attempts to show the link between democratic political institutions and the following:

1. Social and economic equality
2. Capitalism and the rise of a strong middle class as well as a strong working class
3. Supportive cultural ideas and values
4. The active involvement of groups, media, and networks of people in politics

The recent expansion of democracy, what Huntington (1991) has called "the third wave," began in the mid-1970s in Southern Europe. Then, in the early and mid-1980s, it spread to Latin America and to Asian countries like Korea, Thailand, and the Philippines, and then, in the late 1980s and early 1990s, to Eastern Europe, the Soviet Union, and parts of sub-Saharan Africa. Not long ago, the overwhelming majority of the members of the United Nations had authoritarian systems. As of the end of 1993, over half—107 out of 186 countries—have competitive elections and various guarantees of political and individual rights—that is more than twice the number two decades earlier in 1970 (Karatnycky 1994:6: *Freedom Review* 1993:3-4, 10)…. The move toward democracy is not a simple one. Countries that previously have had authoritarian regimes may find it difficult to set up a legitimate democratic system because their traditions and beliefs may be incompatible with the workings of democracy.

In his classic work *Capitalism, Socialism, and Democracy*, Schumpeter (1950) defined democracy as "that institutional arrangement for arriving at political decisions in which individuals acquire the power to decide by means of a competitive struggle for the people's vote" (p. 250).[1] This definition is quite broad, and my discussion here cannot hope to investigate it exhaustively[2]….

Excerpt from "The Social Requisites of Democracy Revisited," (1993 ASA presidential address) by Seymour Martin Lipset, in *American Sociological Review*, February 1994, Vol. 59, pp. 1–22.

## HOW DOES DEMOCRACY ARISE?

### Politics in Impoverished Countries

In discussing democracy, I want to clarify my biases and assumptions at the outset. I agree with the basic concerns of the founding fathers of the United States – that government, a powerful state, is to be feared (or *suspected*, to use the lawyer's term), and that it is necessary to find means to control governments through checks and balances. In our time, as economists have documented, this has been particularly evident in low-income nations. The "Kuznets curve" (Kuznets 1955, 1963, 1976), although still debated, indicates that when a less developed nation starts to grow and urbanize, income distribution worsens, but then becomes more equitable as the economy industrializes (Olson 1963, Weede and Tiefenbach 1981, Todaro 1981:134, Bollen and Jackman 1985, Muller 1988, Chan 1989, Weede 1993).[3] Before development, the class income structure resembles an elongated pyramid, very fat at the bottom, narrowing or thin toward the middle and top (Lipset 1981:51). Under such conditions, the state is a major, usually *the* most important, source of capital, income, power, and status. This is particularly true in statist systems, but also characterizes many so-called free market economies. For a person or governing body to be willing to give up control because of an election outcome is astonishing behavior, not normal, not on the surface a "rational choice," particularly in new, less stable, less legitimate polities.

Marx frequently noted that intense inequality is associated with scarcity, and therefore that socialism, which he believed would be an egalitarian and democratic system with a politically weak state, could only occur under conditions of abundance (Marx 1958:8–9). To try to move toward socialism under conditions of material scarcity would result in sociological abortions and in repression. The Communists proved him correct. Weffort (1992), a Brazilian scholar of democracy, has argued strongly that, although "the political equality of citizens…is…possible in societies marked by a high degree of [economic] inequality," the contradiction between political and economic inequality "opens the field for tensions, institutional distortions, instability, and recurrent

violence…[and may prevent] the consolidation of democracy" (p. 22). Contemporary social scientists find that greater affluence and higher rates of well-being have been correlated with the presence of democratic institutions (Lipset, Seong, and Torres 1993: 156–58; see also Diamond 1992). Beyond the impact of national wealth and economic stratification, contemporary social scientists also agree with Tocqueville's analysis that social equality, perceived as equality of status and respect for individuals regardless of economic condition, is highly conducive for democracy (Tocqueville 1976: vol. 2, 162–216; Lipset 1981: 439–50; Dahl 1971:85–104; Sartori 1987: 343–345; Dogan 1988:11–12). But as Weffort (1992) emphasized, "such a 'minimal' social condition is absent from many new democracies…[that can] help to explain these countries' typical democratic instability" (p. 18).

### The Economy and the Polity

In the nineteenth century, many political theorists noted the relationship between a market economy and democracy (Lipset 1992: 2). As Glassman (1991) has documented, "Marxists, classical capitalist economists, even monarchists accepted the link between industrial capitalism and parliamentary democracy" (p. 65). Such an economy, including a substantial independent peasantry, produces a middle class that can stand up against the state and provide the resources for independent groups, as many twentieth-century scholars such as Weber (1906: 346 ff), Schumpeter (1950), Moore (1966), Skocpol (1979), and Berger (1986; 1992) have also concluded. Schumpeter (1950) held that "modern democracy is a product of the capitalist process" (p. 297). Moore (1966), noting his agreement with the Marxists, concluded, "no bourgeois, no democracy" (p. 418)….

But although the movement toward a market economy and the growth of an independent middle class have weakened state power and enlarged human rights and the rule of law, it has been the working class, particularly in the West, that has demanded the expansion of suffrage and the rights of parties (Therborn 1977; Rueschemeyer, Stephens, and Stephens 1992: 59, 97–98, 140–43). As John Stephens (1993) noted, "Capitalist development is associated with the rise of democracy in part because it is associated with a transformation of the class structure strengthening the working class" (p. 438)....

## The Centrality of Political Culture

Democracy requires a supportive culture, the acceptance by the citizenry and political elites of principles underlying freedom of speech, media, assembly, religion, of the rights of opposition parties, of the rule of law, of human rights, and the like (Almond 1956: 34–42; Pye 1965: 3–26; Dahl 1971: 1–16; Bobbio 1987: 63–78; Diamond, Linz, and Lipset, 1990: 16–18). Such norms do not evolve overnight. Attempts to move from authoritarianism to democracy have failed after most upheavals from the French Revolution in 1789 to the February Revolution in Russia in 1917, from those in most new nations in Latin America in the nineteenth century to those in Africa and Asia after World War II. Linz (1988) and Huntington (1991) noted that the two previous waves of democratization were followed by "reverse waves" that witnessed the revival of authoritarianism. "Only four of the seventeen countries that adopted democratic institutions between 1915 and 1931 maintained them throughout the 1920s and 1930s.... One-third of the 32 working democracies in the world in 1958 had become authoritarian by the mid-1970s" (Huntington 1991: 17–21).

These experiences do not bode well for the current efforts in the former Communist states of Eastern Europe or in Latin America and Africa. And the most recent report by Freedom House concludes: "As 1993 draws to a close, freedom around the world is in retreat while violence, repression, and state control are on the increase. The trend marks the first increase in five years..." (Karatnycky 1994: 4). A "reverse wave" in the making is most apparent in sub-Saharan Africa, where "9 countries showed improvement while 18 registered a decline" (p. 6). And in Russia, a proto-fascist movement led all other parties, albeit with 24 percent of the vote, in the December 1993 elections, while the Communists and their allies secured over 15 percent.

Almost everywhere that the institutionalization of democracy has occurred, the process has been a gradual one in which opposition and individual rights have emerged in the give and take of politics (Sklar 1987: 714). As I, and my then-students Martin Trow and James Coleman, wrote almost 40 years ago:

Democratic rights have developed in societies largely through the struggles of various groups — class, religious, sectional, economic, professional, and so on — against one another and against the group that controls the state. Each interest group may desire to carry out its own will, but if no one group is strong enough to gain complete power, the result is the development of tolerance. In large measure, the development of the concept of tolerance, of recognition of the rights of groups with whom one disagrees to compete for adherents or power, arose out of conflicts among strong and indestructible groups in different societies. There were a number of processes through which tolerance became legitimate. In some situations, groups such as the Catholic and the Protestant churches attempted to destroy the opposing faction, but finally recognized that the complete victory of one group was impossible or could occur only at the risk of destroying the very fabric of society. In these conflicts, minority or opposition groups developed a democratic ideology, an insistence on specific minority rights, as a means of legitimating their own right to exist. These groups might then force the dominant power group to grant these rights in order to prevent a revolutionary upsurge or achieve power themselves. For them to reject their own program may then mean a considerable loss of support from adherents who have come to hold the democratic values. (Lipset, Trow, and Coleman 1956: 15–16)

As a result, democratic systems developed gradually, at first with suffrage, limited by and linked to property and/or literacy. Elites yielded slowly in admitting the masses to the franchise and in tolerating and institutionalizing opposition rights (Almond and Verba 1963: 7–8; Rustow 1970:357). As Dahl (1971: 36–37) has emphasized, parties such as the Liberals and Conservatives in nineteenth-century Europe, formed for the purpose of securing a parliamentary majority rather than to win the support of a mass electorate, were not pressed to engage in populist demagoguery.

Comparative politics suggest that the more the sources of power, status, and wealth are concentrated in the state, the harder it is to institutionalize democracy. Under such conditions, the political struggle tends to approach a zero-sum game in which the defeated lose all. The greater the importance of the central state as a source of prestige and advantage, the less likely it is that those in power – or the forces of opposition – will accept rules of the game that institutionalize party conflict and could result in the turnover of those in office. Hence, once again it may be noted, the chances for democracy are greatest where, as in the early United States and to a lesser degree in other Western nations, the interaction between politics and economy is limited and segmented. In Northern Europe, democratization let the monarchy and the aristocracy retain their elite status, even though their powers were curtailed. In the United States, the central state was not a major source of privilege for the first half-century or more, and those at the center thus could yield office easily.

Democracy has never developed anywhere by plan, except when it was imposed by a democratic conqueror, as in post–World War II Germany and Japan. From the United States to Northern Europe, freedom, suffrage, and the rule of law grew in a piecemeal, not in a planned, fashion. To legitimate themselves, governmental parties, even though they did not like it, ultimately had to recognize the right of oppositions to exist and compete freely. Almost all the heads of young democracies, from John Adams and Thomas Jefferson to Indira Gandhi, attempted to suppress their opponents. As noted before, most new democracies are soon overthrown, as in France before 1871, in various parts of Europe after 1848, in Eastern, Central, and Southern Europe after World War I, and repeatedly in Latin America and Africa. Democratic successes have reflected the varying strengths of minority political groups and lucky constellations, as much or more than commitments by new office holders to the democratic process.

Cross-national historical evaluations of the correlates of democracy have found that cultural factors appear even more important than economic ones (Lipset et al. 1993: 168–70; see also Huntington 1991: 298–311). Dahl (1970: 6), Kennan (1977: 41–43), and Lewis (1993: 93–94) have emphasized that the first group of countries that became democratic in the nineteenth century (about 20 or so) were Northwest European or settled by Northwest Europeans. "The evidence has yet to be produced that it is the natural form of rule for peoples outside these narrow perime-

ters" (Kennan 1977: 41–43).[4] Lewis (1993), an authority on the Middle East, has reiterated Kennan's point: "No such [democratic] system has originated in any other cultural tradition; it remains to be seen whether such a system transplanted and adapted in another culture can long survive" (pp. 93–94).

More particularly, recent statistical analyses of the aggregate correlates of political regimes have indicated that having once been a British colony is the variable most highly correlated with democracy (Lipset et al. 1993: 168). As Weiner (1987) has pointed out, beyond the experiences in the Americas and Australasia in the nineteenth century, "every country with a population of at least 1 million (and almost all the smaller countries as well) that has emerged from colonial rule and has had a continuous democratic experience is a former British colony" (p. 20). The factors underlying this relationship are not simple (Smith 1978). In the British/non-British comparison, many former British colonies, such as those in North America before the revolution or India and Nigeria in more recent times, had elections, parties, and the rule of law before they became independent. In contrast, the Spanish, Portuguese, French, Dutch, and Belgian colonies, and former Soviet-controlled countries did not allow for the gradual incorporation of "out groups" into the polity. Hence democratization was much more gradual and successful in the ex-British colonies than elsewhere; their pre-independence experiences were important as a kind of socialization process and helped to ease the transition to freedom.

## Religious Tradition

Religious tradition has been a major differentiating factor in transformations to democracy (Huntington 1993: 25–29). Historically, there have been negative relationships between democracy and Catholicism, Orthodox Christianity, Islam, and Confucianism; conversely, Protestantism and democracy have been positively interlinked. These differences have been explained by the much greater emphasis on individualism in Protestantism and the traditionally close links between religion and the state in the other four religions. Tocqueville (1976) and Bryce (1901) emphasized that democracy is furthered by a separation of religious and po-

litical beliefs so that political stands are not required to meet absolute standards set down by
the church....

Conversely, Moslem (particularly Arab) states
have not taken part in the third wave of democratization. Almost all remain authoritarian. Growth
of democracy in the near future in most of these
countries is doubtful because "notions of political
freedom are not held in common...they are alien
to Islam" (Vatikiotis 1988: 118).

Kazancigil (1991) has offered parallel explanations of the weakness of democracy in Islam with
those for Orthodox Christian lands as flowing from
their failures "to dissociate the religious from the
political spheres" (p. 345). In Eastern Europe, particularly Russia, the Orthodox Church has closely linked the two. As Guroff and Guroff (1993)
emphasized: "The Church has always been an
organ of the Russian state, both under the Tsar
and under the Soviet Union.... Neither in Tsarist
Russia nor in the Soviet Union has the Orthodox
Church played an active role in the protection of
human rights or religious tolerance" (pp. 10–11).

Noting that in Confucian China "no church
or cultural organization...existed independently
of the state" (p. 25), and that "Islam has emphasized the identity between the religious and political communities," Eisenstadt (1968) stressed the
resultant "important similarity between the Chinese and Islamic societies" (p. 27). Huntington
(1993) reported that "no scholarly disagreement
exists regarding the proposition that traditional
Confucianism was either undemocratic or anti-
democratic" (p. 15; see also Whyte 1992: 60).

These generalizations about culture do not
augur well for the future of the third wave of
democracy in the former Communist countries.
The Catholic Church played a substantial role in
Poland's move away from Soviet Communism. But
as noted previously, historically deeply religious
Catholic areas have not been among the most
amenable to democratic ideas. Poland is now troubled by conflicts flowing from increasing Church
efforts to affect politics in Eastern Europe even as
it relaxes its policies in Western Europe and most
of the Americas. Orthodox Christianity is hegemonic in Russia and Belarus. The Ukraine is dominated by both the Catholic and Orthodox
Churches. And fascists and Communists are strong
in Russia and the Ukraine. Moslems are a signifi-

cant group in the Central Asian parts of the former Soviet Union, the majority in some – these
areas are among the consistently least democratic
of the successor Soviet states. Led by the Orthodox
Serbians, but helped by Catholic Croats and Bosnian Moslems, the former Yugoslavia is being torn
apart along ethnic and religious lines with no
peaceful, much less democratic, end in sight. We
are fooling ourselves if we ignore the continuing
dysfunctional effects of a number of cultural values and the institutions linked to them.

But belief systems change; and the rise of Capitalism, a large middle class, an organized working class, increased wealth, and education are
associated with secularism and the institutions of
civil society that help create autonomy for the state
and facilitate other pre-conditions for democracy.
In recent years, nowhere has this been more apparent than in the economically successful Confucian states of East Asia – states once thought of
as nearly hopeless candidates for both development and democracy. Tu (1993) noted their totally "unprecedented dynamism in democratization and marketization. Singapore, South
Korea, and Taiwan all successfully conducted
national elections in 1992, clearly indicating that
democracy in Confucian societies is not only possible but also practical" (p. viii). Nathan and Shi
(1993), reporting on "the first scientifically valid
national sample survey done in China on political
behavior and attitudes," stated: "When compared
to residents of some of the most stable, long-
established democracies in the world, the Chinese
population scored lower on the variables we
looked at, but not so low as to justify the conclusion that democracy is out of reach" (p. 116). Surveys done in Russia offer similar positive
conclusions (Gibson and Duch 1993), but the
December 1993 election in which racist nationalists and pro-Communists did well indicate that
much more is needed. Democracy is not taking
root in much of the former Soviet Union, the less
industrialized Moslem states, or many nations in
Africa. The end is not in sight for many of the efforts at new democracies; the requisite cultural
changes are clearly not established enough to justify the conclusion that the "third wave" will not
be reversed. According to the Freedom House survey, during 1993 there were "42 countries regis-
tering a decline in their level of freedom [political

rights and civil liberties] and 19 recording gains" (Karatnycky 1994: 5).[5]

## CIVIL SOCIETY AND POLITICAL PARTIES

### Civil Society as a Political Base

More important than electoral rules in encouraging a stable system is a strong civil society—the presence of myriad "mediating institutions," including "groups, media, and networks" (Diamond 1993: 4) that operate independently between individuals and the state. These constitute "subunits, capable of opposing and countervailing the state" (Gellner 1991: 500). Forty years ago, my first major effort to analyze "the conditions that favor democracy" (Lipset, Trow, and Coleman 1956: 15) focused on civil societies, noting that "in a large complex society, the body of the citizenry is unable to affect the policies of the state. If citizens do not belong to politically relevant groups, if they are atomized, the controllers of the central power apparatus will completely dominate the society" (p. 15).

Citizen groups must become the bases of—the sources of support for—the institutionalized political parties that are a necessary condition for—part of the very definition of—a modern democracy. As Merkl (1993) reiterating Schumpeter (1950) correctly emphasized, "The major device for facilitating the formation of the popular will, its generation of meaningful choices, and its impact on government, has been political parties" (pp. 257–258). Or as Weffort (1992) puts it: "Democracy-building is a process of…institutionalizing conflict" (p. 111).

We owe our awareness of the importance of civil society to Tocqueville (1976) who, in the early nineteenth century, saw in the widespread existence of civil associations the secret to why Americans did so well politically and economically when compared to the European nations of his day.[6] He noted:

…[People] cannot belong to these associations for any length of time without finding out how order is maintained among a large number of people and by what contrivance they are made to advance, harmoniously and methodically, to the same object…. Political associations may therefore be considered as large free schools, in which all the members of the community go to learn the general theory of association…. (vol. 2:116)

In their political associations, the Americans, of all conditions, minds, and ages, daily acquire a general taste for association and grow accustomed to the use of it…. They are mutually stimulated to all sorts of undertakings. They afterwards transfer to civil life the notions they have thus acquired and make them subservient to a thousand purposes. (vol. 2, 119)

A fully operative civil society is likely to also be a participant one. Organizations stimulate interests and activity in the larger polity; they can be consulted by political institutions about projects that affect them and their members, and they can transfer this information to the citizenry. Civil organizations reduce resistance to unanticipated changes because they prevent the isolation of political institutions from the polity and can smooth over, or at least recognize, interest differences early on.

In a twist on Schumpeter's (1950) definition of political parties as the basis of democracy, certain democratic values and rights have evolved primarily through conflict among groups in society. Instead of struggling to attain elite political power, various groups—class, religious, economic, professional, and the like—compete with one another and the state for popular attention, for the power to carry out their own agendas. As noted earlier, such opposition groups must legitimate themselves by encouraging the rights of other groups to oppose them, thus providing a basis for democracy. Through these conflicts and their differing ideologies, these groups form an alternative to the state and its control of society.

Totalitarian systems, however, do not have effective civil societies. Instead, they either seek to eliminate groups mediating between the individual and the state or to control these groups so that there is no competition. And although by so doing they may undermine the possibility for *organized* opposition, they also reduce group effectiveness generally, and reduce the education of individuals for innovative activities (that is, Tocqueville's "civil partnerships" [1976, vol. 2: 124]). In the West, polities are based on a wide diversity of groups that form the basis for parties (for example, unions, ethnic and religious groups, farm associations, veterans' organizations, and so on). Fortunately, most of the new democracies outside of the ex-

Communist bloc, such as Argentina, Chile, South Korea, Taiwan, and Spain, were not totalitarian and had institutionalized some of the pluralistic institutions of civil society while under autocratic rule (Scalapino 1989). The new democracies must be encouraged to form more of these civil groups. Yet the "newly created" leaders of these interest groups more often than not only have "become…[favorable to democracy] during the transition period" (Weffort 1992: 12).

The countries of Eastern Europe and the former Soviet Union, however, are faced with the consequences of the absence of modern civil society, a lack that makes it difficult to institutionalize democratic polities. These countries have not had the opportunity to form the civil groups necessary to coalesce into stable political parties, except through churches in some nations, such as Poland, and assorted small autonomous illegal networks (Sadowski 1993: 171–80). Instead, they have had to create parties "from scratch." Ideologically splintered groups must oppose the former Communists, who have been well organized for many years and have constructed their own coalitions. "Instead of consolidation, there is fragmentation: 67 parties fought Poland's most recent general election, 74 [fought] Romania's" (*Economist* 1993a: 4). As a result, the former Communists (now "socialists") have either been voted in as the majority party in parliament, as in Lithuania, or have become the largest party heading up a coalition cabinet, as in Poland. In January 1992, the Communist-backed candidate for president in Bulgaria garnered 43 percent of the vote (Malia 1992: 73). These situations are, of course, exacerbated by the fact that replacing command economies by market processes is difficult; frequently, conditions worsen before they begin to improve….

as the European Community, NATO, the World Bank, and the International Monetary Fund (IMF) are requiring a democratic system as a condition for membership or aid. A diffusion, a contagion, or demonstration effect seems operative, as many have noted, one that encourages democracies to press for change and authoritarian rulers to give in. It is becoming both uncouth and unprofitable to avoid free elections, particularly in Latin America, East Asia, Eastern Europe, and to some extent in Africa (Ake 1991: 33). Yet the proclamation of elections does not ensure their integrity. The outside world can help, but the basis for institutionalized opposition, for interest and value articulation, must come from within.

Results of research suggest that we be cautious about the long-term stability of democracy in many of the newer systems given their low level of legitimacy. As the Brazilian scholar Francisco Weffort (1992) has reminded us, "In the 1980s, the age of new democracies, the processes of political democratization occurred at the same moment in which those countries suffered the experience of a profound and prolonged economic crisis that resulted in social exclusion and massive poverty…. Some of those countries are building a political democracy on top of a minefield of social apartheid…" (p. 20). Such conditions could easily lead to breakdowns of democracy as have already occurred in Algeria, Haiti, Nigeria, and Peru, and to the deterioration of democratic functioning in countries such as Brazil, Egypt, Kenya, the Philippines, the former Yugoslavia, and some of the trans-Ural republics or "facade democracies" — as well as the revival of anti-democratic movements on the right and left in Russia and in other formerly Communist states….

## CONCLUSION

Democracy is an international cause. A host of democratic governments and parties, as well as various nongovernmental organizations (NGOs) dedicated to human rights, are working and providing funds to create and sustain democratic forces in newly liberalized governments and to press autocratic ones to change (*Economist* 1993c: 46). Various international agencies and units such

## ENDNOTES

1. For elaborations, see Lipset (1981: 27); Dahl (1970: 78; 1971: 150–62; 1982: 11); Huntington (1991: 5–13); and Schmitter and Karl (1993: 40–46).
2. For a discussion of the way definitions affect analyses of democracy, see Sartori (1983: 28–34; 1987: 257–77).
3. These generalizations do not apply to the East Asian NICS, South Korea, Taiwan, and Singapore.
4. That evidence, of course, has emerged in recent years in South and East Asia, Latin America, and various countries descended from Southern Europe.

5. In the Freedom House survey, a country may move up or down with respect to measures of freedom without changing its status as a democratic or authoritarian system.

6. Gramsci, a leading Marxist scholar, writing in the '20s, also emphasized the need for a "dense civil society" arising out of Capitalism, which made democratic discourse possible (Stephens 1993: 414), as more recently did Lipset (1981: 52–53) and Huntington (1984: 202–3).

# REFERENCES

Ake, Claude. 1991. "Rethinking African Democracy." *Journal of Democracy* 2(1): 32–47.

Almond, Gabriel. 1956. "Comparative Political Systems." Pp. 34–42 in *Political Behavior: A Reader in Theory and Research*, edited by H. Eulau, S. J. Eldersveld, and M. Janowitz. Glencoe, IL: Free Press.

Almond, Gabriel and Sidney Verba. 1963. *Civic Culture: Political Attitudes and Democracy in Five Nations*. Princeton, NJ: Princeton University.

Berger, Peter. 1986. *The Capitalist Revolution*. New York: Basic Books.

——. 1992. "The Uncertain Triumph of Democratic Capitalism." *Journal of Democracy* 3(3): 7–17.

Bobbio, Norberto. 1987. *The Future of Democracy: A Defense of the Rules of the Game*. Minneapolis, MN: University of Minnesota.

Bollen, Kenneth and Robert Jackman. 1985. "Political Democracy and the Size Distribution of Income." *American Sociological Review* 50: 438–57.

Bryce, James. 1901. *Study in History and Jurisprudence*. New York: Oxford University.

Calhoun, John. 1947. *A Disquisition on Government*. New York: Political Science Classics.

Chan, Steve. 1989. "Income Inequality Among LDCs: A Comparative Analysis of Alternative Perspectives." *International Studies Quarterly* 33: 45–65.

Dahl, Robert. 1970. *After the Revolution: Authority in a Good Society*. New Haven, CT: Yale University.

——. 1971. *Polyarchy: Participation and Opposition*. New Haven, CT: Yale University.

Diamond, Larry. 1992. "Economic Development and Democracy Reconsidered." Pp. 93–139 in *Reexamining Democracy: Essays in Honor of Seymour Martin Lipset*, edited by G. Marks and L. Diamond. Newbury Park, CA: Sage.

——. 1993. "Ex-Africa, a New Democratic Spirit Has Loosened the Grip of African Dictatorial Rule." *Times Literary Supplement*, 2 July (no. 4709), pp. 3–4.

——. Juan Linz, and Seymour Martin Lipset, eds. 1990. *Politics in Developing Countries, Comparing Experiences with Democracy*. Boulder, CO: Lynne Rienner.

Dogan, Mattei, ed. 1988. *Comparing Pluralist Democracies: Strains on Legitimacy*. Boulder, CO: Westview.

*Economist*. 1993a. Survey on Eastern Europe. March 13: 1–22.

——. 1993b. "Russia Into the Swamp." May 22: 59–60.

——. 1993c. "Aid for Africa: If You're Good." May 29: 46.

Eisenstadt, Shmuel N. 1968. "The Protestant Ethic Theses in the Framework of Sociological Theory and Weber's Work." Pp. 3–45 in *The Protestant Ethic and Modernization: A Comparative View*, edited by S. N. Eisenstadt. New York: Basic Books.

*Freedom Review* 24(1) (Special Issue). 1993. "Freedom Around the World." Pp. 3–67.

Garton Ash, Timothy. 1990. "Eastern Europe: The Year of Truth." *New York Review of Books*, 15 February, pp. 17–22.

Gellner, Ernest. 1991. "Civil Society in Historical Context." *International Social Science Journal* 43: 495–510.

Gibson, James L. and Raymond M. Duch. 1993. "Emerging Democratic Values in Soviet Political Culture." Pp. 69–94 in *Public Opinion and Regime Change*, edited by A. A. Miller, W. M. Reisinger, and V. Hesli. Boulder, CO: Westview.

Glassman, Ronald. 1991. *China in Transition: Communism, Capitalism and Democracy*. Westport, CT: Praeger.

Guroff, Gregory and A. Guroff. 1993. "The Paradox of Russian National Identity." (Russian Littoral Project, Working Paper No. 16). College Park and Baltimore, MD: University of Maryland–College Park and The Johns Hopkins University SAIS.

Huntington, Samuel. 1984. "Will More Countries Become Democratic?" *Political Science Quarterly* 99: 193–218.

——. 1991. *The Third Wave: Democratization in the Late Twentieth Century*. Norman, OK: University of Oklahoma.

——. 1993. "The Clash of Civilizations." *Foreign Affairs* 72(3): 22–49.

Karatnycky, Adrian. 1994. "Freedom in Retreat." *Freedom Review* 25(1): 4–9.

Kazancigil, Ali. 1991. "Democracy in Muslim Lands: Turkey in Comparative Perspective." *International Social Science Journal* 43: 343–60.

Kennan, George. 1977. *Clouds of Danger: Current Realities of American Foreign Policy*. Boston, MA: Little, Brown.

Kuznets, Simon. 1955. "Economic Growth and Income Inequality." *American Economic Review* 45: 1–28.

——. 1963. "Quantitative Aspects of the Economic Growth of Nations: VIII, The Distribution of Income by Size." *Economic Development and Cultural Change* 11: 1–80.

——. 1976. *Modern Economic Growth: Rate, Structure and Spread*. New Haven, CT: Yale University.

Lewis, Bernard. 1993. "Islam and Liberal Democracy." *Atlantic Monthly*. 271(2): 89–98.

Linz, Juan J. 1988. "Legitimacy of Democracy and the Socioeconomic System." Pp. 65–97 in *Comparing Pluralist Democracies: Strains on Legitimacy*, edited by M. Dogan. Boulder, CO: Westview.

Lipset, Seymour Martin [1960] 1981. *Political Man: The Social Bases of Politics*. Expanded ed. Baltimore, MD: Johns Hopkins.

——. 1992. "Conditions of the Democratic Order and Social Change: A Comparative Discussion." Pp. 1–14 in *Studies in Human Society: Democracy and Modernity*, edited by S. N. Eisenstadt. New York: E. J. Brill.

——. 1993. "Reflections on Capitalism, Socialism, and Democracy." *Journal of Democracy* 4(2): 43–53.

——. Kyoung-Ryung Seong, and John Charles Torres. 1993. "A Comparative Analysis of the Social Requisites of Democracy." *International Social Science Journal* 45: 155–75.

——. Martin Trow, and James Coleman. 1956. *Union Democracy: The Inside Politics of the International Typographical Union*. New York: Free Press.

Malia, Martin. 1992. "Leninist Endgame." *Daedalus* 121(2): 57–75.

Marx, Karl. 1958. *Capital*. Vol. 1. Moscow, Russia: Foreign Languages, Publishing House.

Merkl, Peter H. 1993. "Which Are Today's Democracies?" *International Social Science Journal* 45: 257–70.

Moore, Barrington. 1966. *Social Origins of Dictatorship and Democracy: Lord and Peasant in the Making of the Modern World*. Boston, MA: Beacon.

Muller, Edward N. 1988. "Democracy, Economic Development, and Income Inequality." *American Sociological Review* 53: 50–68.

Nathan, Andrew J. and Tao Shi. 1993. "Cultural Requisites for Democracy in China: Findings from a Survey." *Daedalus* 122: 95–124.

Olson, Mancur, Jr. 1963. "Rapid Growth as a Destabilizing Force." *Journal of Economic History* 23: 453–72.

Pye, Lucian W. 1965. "Introduction: Political Culture and Political Development." Pp. 3–26 in *Political Culture and Political Development*, edited by L. Pye and S. Verba. Princeton, NJ: Princeton University.

Rueschemeyer, Dietrich, Evelyne Huber Stephens, and John D. Stephens. 1992. *Capitalist Development and Democracy*. Chicago, IL: University of Chicago.

Rustow, Dankwart. 1970. "Transitions to Democracy." *Comparative Politics*. 2: 337–66.

Sadowski, Christine M. 1993. "Autonomous Groups as Agents of Democratic Change in Communist and Post-Communist Eastern Europe." Pp. 163–95 in *Political Culture and Developing Countries*, edited by L. Diamond. Boulder, CO: Lynne Rienner.

Sartori, Giovanni. ed. 1983. *Social Science Concepts: A Systemic Analysis*. Beverly Hills, CA: Sage.

———. 1987. *The Theory of Democracy Revisited*. Chatham, NJ: Chatham House.

Scalapino, Robert H. 1989. *The Politics of Development: Perspectives on Twentieth-Century Asia*. Cambridge, MA: Harvard University.

Schmitter, Philippe C. and Terry Lynn Karl. 1993. "What Democracy Is...and Is Not." Pp. 39–52 in *The Global Resurgence of Democracy*, edited by L. Diamond and M. F. Plattner. Baltimore, MD: Johns Hopkins.

Schumpeter, Joseph. 1950. *Capitalism, Socialism, and Democracy*. 3d ed. New York: Harper and Row.

Sklar, Richard. 1987. "Developmental Democracy." *Comparative Studies in Society and History* 29: 686–714.

Skocpol, Theda. 1979. *States and Social Revolutions*. Cambridge, England: Cambridge University.

Smith, Tony. 1978. "A Comparative Study of French and British Decolonization." *Comparative Studies in Society and History* 20(1): 70–102.

Stephens, John D. 1993. "Capitalist Development and Democracy: Empirical Research on the Social Origins of Democracy." Pp. 409–47 in *The Idea of Democracy*, edited by D. Copp, J. Hampton, and J. Roemer. Cambridge, England: Cambridge University.

Therborn, Göran. 1977. "The Rule of Capital and the Rise of Democracy." *New Left Review* 103: 3–41.

Tocqueville, Alexis de. 1976. *Democracy in America*. Vols. 1 and 2. New York: Knopf.

Todaro, Michael P. 1981. *Economic Development in the Third World*. New York: Longman.

Tu, Wei-ming. 1993. "Introduction: Cultural Perspectives." *Daedalus* 122: vii–xxii.

Vatikiotis, Panayiotis J. 1988. *Islam and the State*. London, England: Croom Helm.

Weber, Max. 1906. "Zur Lage der bürgerlichen Demokratie in Russland" *Archiv für Sozialwissenschaft und Sozialpolitik* 22: 234–353.

———. 1946. *From Max Weber: Essays in Sociology*. Edited and translated by H. H. Gerth and C. W. Mills. New York: Oxford University.

Weede, Erich. 1993. "The Impact of Democracy or Repressiveness on the Quality of Life, Income Distribution, and Economic Growth Rates." *International Sociology* 8: 177–95.

——— and Heinrich Tiefenbach. 1981. "Some Recent Explanations of Income Inequality." *International Studies Quarterly* 25: 255–82.

Weffort, Francisco C. 1992. "New Democracies, Which Democracies?" (Working Paper #198). The Woodrow Wilson Center, Latin American Program, Washington, DC.

Weiner, Myron. 1987. "Empirical Democratic Theory." Pp. 3–34 in *Competitive Elections in Developing Countries*, edited by M. Weiner and E. Ozbudun. Durham, NC: Duke University.

Whyte, Martin King. 1992. "Prospects for Democratization in China." *Problems of Communism* 42(3): 58–70.

# 48.  WHAT IS EXTREMISM?

LAIRD WILCOX

> "...*Mere advocacy of 'fringe' positions gives our society the variety and vitality it needs to function as an open democracy, to discuss and debate all aspects of an issue, and to deal with problems that otherwise have been ignored. The extremist style is another issue altogether, however, in that it hampers our understanding of important issues, muddies the waters of discourse,...and impairs our ability to make intelligent, well-informed choices."*

This selection systematically describes **extremism**, a certain way of thinking about politics and political opposition. Understanding this kind of thought will help us examine both ourselves and others with whom we interact or to whom we listen. Extremism is a style of thinking and acting that threatens democratic institutions. It is the **style** rather than the positions advocated that describes extremists.

*If it's a despot you would dethrone, see first that his throne erected within you is destroyed.*

Kahlil Gibran, 1923

In *A Dictionary of Political Thought* (1982), Roger Scruton defines "extremism" as:

1. Taking a political idea to its limits, regardless of unfortunate repercussions, impracticalities, arguments, and feelings to the contrary, and with the intention not only to confront, but to eliminate opposition.
2. Intolerance toward all views other than one's own.
3. Adoption of means to political ends that show disregard for the life, liberty, and human rights of others.[1]

This definition basically reflects my own experience, that extremism is more an issue of style than of content. In the twenty-five years I have been investigating political groups of the left and right, I have found that most people can hold radical or unorthodox views and still entertain them in a more or less reasonable, rational, and non-

dogmatic manner. On the other hand, I have met people whose views were fairly close to the political mainstream but were presented in a shrill, uncompromising, bullying, and distinctly authoritarian manner. The latter demonstrated a starkly extremist mentality while the former demonstrated only ideological unorthodoxy, which is hardly to be feared in a relatively free society such as ours.

This view of extremism, which may seem novel to many people because in today's climate the term is usually used as an epithet, is held by many writers and authorities, especially those who approach the issue from a relatively evenhanded and nonideological point of view. Milton Rokeach, whose book *The Open and Closed Mind* is a classic in the field of dogmatic thinking, prejudgment, and authoritarianism, has this to say about it:

To study the organization of belief systems, we find it necessary to concern ourselves with the structure rather than the content of beliefs. The relative openness or closedness of a mind cuts across specific content; that is, it is not uniquely restricted to any particular ideology, or religion, or philosophy, or scientific viewpoint. A person may adhere to communism, existentialism, Freudianism, or the "new conservatism" in a relatively open or relatively closed manner. Thus, a basic requirement is that concepts to be employed in the description of belief systems must not be tied to any one particular belief system; they must be constructed to apply equally to all belief systems.[2]

Rokeach goes on to say "authoritarianism and intolerance in belief and interpersonal relations are surely not a monopoly of fascists, anti-Semites, Ku Klux Klanners, or conservatives."[3] I agree and would add that the same behaviors merely take different forms and use different vocabulary on the "left" side of the political spectrum. The essential characteristics remain quite similar. The choice of adjectives used to describe the behavior in question often derives more from the biases and interests of the observer than from the objective facts of the situation. Daniel Bell, the eminent sociologist, tends to support this view. He says:

The way you hold beliefs is more important than what you hold. If somebody's been a rigid Communist, he becomes a rigid anti-Communist—the rigidity being constant.[4]

In my opinion, most strident opponents of right-wing or left-wing "extremism" exhibit significant ideological bias, and many are actually representatives of the opposing extreme. The fact that an extremist hates and agitates against other extremists doesn't mitigate his or her own character in this regard. In fact, opposing extremists often form a vague bond or symbiotic relationship with one another, each justifying the other's existence in a peculiar kind of way.

In focusing on the style rather than the content of a belief system, I don't mean to imply that content is entirely irrelevant. People who tend to adopt the extremist style most often champion causes and adopt ideologies that are essentially "fringe" positions. But mere advocacy of "fringe" positions gives our society the variety and vitality it needs to function as an open democracy, to discuss and debate all aspects of an issue, and to deal with problems that otherwise have been ignored. The extremist style is another issue altogether, however, in that it hampers our understanding of important issues, muddies the waters of discourse with invective, defamation, self-righteousness, fanaticism, and hatred, and impairs our ability to make intelligent, well-informed choices.

Another point is that the extremist style is not only found at the fringes of the political or reli-

gious spectrum, but sometimes in the "middle" as well. An individual who is uncompromisingly, intolerantly "centrist" may be far more dogmatic and prejudiced than someone who adopts more radical views but does so in an open and tolerant manner. Consequently, a guarded middle-of-the-road position doesn't necessarily provide a solution to extremism, and in some cases may only serve as a mask to conceal it. In fact, it could be argued that those beliefs that are accorded legitimacy by consensus, which is to say that everyone unthinkingly accepts them, may be even more prone to appear on the extremist agenda and more difficult to challenge or effectively debate.

When the word *extremist* is used as an epithet, it usually represents points of view with which we disagree, advocated by someone we dislike (but usually don't know) and whose interests are contrary to our own. Political ideologues and special interests often attempt definitions of "extremism" that specifically condemn the views of their critics and opponents while leaving their own equally strident and intolerant behavior untouched. In the debate over abortion, for example, one side or the other will condemn opponents as "extremists" while describing themselves as valiant defenders of human life or champions of freedom. In fact, *bona fide* extremist elements exist on both sides of this controversy, as do relatively calm, fair-minded, honest, evenhanded, and rational advocates. It is not the position they take, but *how* they take it that matters. The ability to define the terms, as Milton Rokeach suggests, goes a long way in deciding how a particular belief system or set of values is viewed. The use of loaded terms including slogans, buzzwords, and cliches, and selective vocabulary that is biased toward certain forms of authoritarianism, bigotry, and prejudice and that exempts others from criticism is but an example of the pervasive double standards one encounters in this area.

## THE TRAITS OF "EXTREMISTS"

The late Senator Robert F. Kennedy wrote:

What is objectionable, what is dangerous about extremists is not that they are extreme, but that they are intolerant. The evil is not what they say about their cause, but what they say about their opponents.[5]

In analyzing the rhetoric and propaganda of several hundred militant "fringe" political and social groups across the political spectrum, I have identified a number of specific traits or behaviors that tend to represent the extremist "style." Other writers have delineated various extremist traits; where their criteria have been objective, I have included them. I am especially indebted to Dr. John George and also to Gordon Hall for their suggestions. Please let me caution you with the admonition that we are all fallible human beings, and anyone, without bad intentions, may resort to some of these behaviors from time to time. With *bona fide* extremists, however, these lapses are not occasional. Rather, they are a habitual and strongly established part of their repertoire, so much so that in some cases their entire belief system is expressed in these terms, including a political style that is fairly easy to identify.

1. *Character assassination.* Extremists often attack the character of an opponent rather than deal with the facts or issues raised. They will question motives, qualifications, past associations, alleged values, personality, looks, and mental health as a diversion from the issues under consideration. Some of these matters are not entirely irrelevant, but they should not serve to avoid the real issues. Extremists object strenuously when this is done to them, of course!

2. *Name calling and labeling.* Extremists are quick to resort to epithets (such as *subversive, pervert, racist, hatemonger, nut, crackpot, degenerate, un-American, anti-Semite, Red, commie, Nazi, kook, fink, liar, bigot,* and so on) to label and condemn opponents in order to divert attention from their arguments and to discourage others from hearing them out. These epithets don't have to be proved to be effective; the mere fact that they have been said is often enough.

3. *Irresponsible sweeping generalizations.* Extremists tend to make sweeping claims or judgments on the basis of little or no evidence, and they have a tendency to confuse similarity with sameness. That is, they assume that because two (or more) things, persons, or events are alike in some respects, they must be alike in most or all respects. The sloppy use of analogy is a treacherous form of logic and has a high potential for false conclusions.

4. *Inadequate proof for assertions.* Extremists tend to be very fuzzy about what constitutes proof, and they also tend to get caught up in logical fallacies, such as *post hoc ergo propter hoc* (assuming that a prior event explains a subsequent occurrence simply because of

their before-and-after relationship). They tend to project wished-for conclusions and to exaggerate the significance of information that confirms their beliefs while derogating or ignoring information that contradicts them. They tend to be motivated by feelings more than facts, what "ought to be" rather than what is. Extremists do a lot of wishful and fearful thinking.

5. *Advocacy of double standards.* Extremists generally tend to judge themselves or their interest group in terms of their intentions, which they tend to view generously, and their critics and opponents by their acts, which they tend to view very critically. They would like you to accept their assertions on faith, but they demand proof for yours. They tend to engage in special pleading on behalf of themselves or their interests, usually because of some alleged special status, past circumstance, or present disadvantage.

6. *Tendency to view opponents and critics as essentially evil.* To the extremist, opponents hold opposing positions because they are bad, immoral, dishonest, unscrupulous, mean-spirited, hateful, cruel, prejudiced, or whatever, and not merely because they simply disagree, see matters differently, or are mistaken.

7. *Manichaean world view.* Extremists have a tendency to see the world in terms of absolutes of good and evil, for them or against them, with no middle ground or intermediate positions. All issues are ultimately moral issues of right and wrong, good and bad, with the "right" and "good" position coinciding with their interests. Their slogan is often "those who are not with me are against me."

8. *Advocacy of some degree of censorship or repression of their opponents and/or critics.* This may include a very active campaign to keep opponents from media access and a public hearing, as in the case of blacklisting, banning, or "quarantining" dissident spokespersons. It may include lobbying for legislation against speaking, writing, teaching, or instructing "subversive" or forbidden information or opinions. It may even include attempting to keep offending books out of stores or off of library shelves, discouraging advertising with threats of reprisals, and keeping spokespersons for "offensive" views off the airwaves or certain columnists out of newspapers. In each example, the goal is some kind of information control. Extremists would prefer that you listen only to them. They feel threatened if someone talks back or challenges their views.

9. *Tendency to identify themselves in terms of who their enemies are.* Accordingly, extremists may become emotionally bound to their opponents, who may be competing extremists themselves. Because they tend to view their enemies as evil and power-

ful, they tend, perhaps subconsciously, to emulate them, adopting the same tactics to a certain degree. For example, anti-Communist and anti-Nazi groups often behave surprisingly like their opponents. Anti-Klan rallies often take on much of the character of the stereotype of Klan rallies themselves, including an orgy of emotion, bullying, screaming epithets, and even acts of violence. To behave the opposite of someone is to actually surrender your will to them, and "opposites" are often more like mirror images that, although they have "left" and "right" reversed, look and behave amazingly alike.

10. *Tendency to use argument by intimidation.* Extremists tend to frame their arguments in such a way as to intimidate others into accepting their premises and conclusions. To disagree with them is to "ally oneself with the devil" or to give aid and comfort to the enemy. They use a lot of moralizing and pontificating, and tend to be very judgmental. This shrill, harsh rhetorical style allows them to keep their opponents and critics on the defensive, cuts off troublesome lines of argument, and allows them to define the parameters of debate.

11. *Use of slogans, buzzwords, and thought-stopping clichés.* For many extremists, shortcuts in thinking and in reasoning matters out seem necessary in order to avoid troublesome facts and compelling counter-arguments. Extremists generally behave in ways that reinforce their prejudices and alter their own consciousness in a manner that bolsters their false confidence and sense of self-righteousness.

12. *Assumption of moral superiority over others.* Most obvious would be claims of general racial or ethnic superiority—a master race, for example. Less obvious are claims of ennoblement because of alleged victimhood, a special relationship with God, membership in a special "elite" or "class" with the accompanying entitlements, and a kind of aloof "high-minded" snobbishness that accrues because of the weightiness of their preoccupations, their altruism, and their willingness to sacrifice themselves (and others) to their cause. (After all, who can bear to deal with common people and their petty concerns when one is trying to save the world!) Extremists can show great indignation when one is "insensitive" enough to challenge these claims.

13. *Doomsday thinking.* Extremists often predict dire or catastrophic consequences from a situation or from a failure to follow a specific course, and they tend to exhibit a kind of "crisis mindedness." It can be a Communist takeover, a Nazi revival, nuclear war, earthquakes, floods, or the wrath of God. Whatever, it's just around the corner unless we follow their program and listen to their special insight and

wisdom, to which only the truly enlightened have access. For extremists, any setback or defeat is "the beginning of the end!"

14. *Belief that it's okay to do bad things in the service of a "good" cause.* Extremists may deliberately lie, distort, misquote, slander, defame, or libel their opponents and/or critics, engage in censorship or repression, or undertake violence in "special cases." This is done with little or no remorse as long as it's in the service of defeating the Communists or Fascists or whomever. Defeating an "enemy" becomes an all-encompassing goal to which other values are subordinate. With extremists, the end justifies the means.

15. *Emphasis on emotional responses and, correspondingly, a de-emphasis on reasoning and logical analysis.* Extremists have an unspoken reverence for propaganda, which they may call "education," "sensitivity training," or "consciousness-raising." Symbolism plays an exaggerated role in their thinking, and they tend to think imprecisely and metaphorically. Harold D. Lasswell, in his book *Psychopathology and Politics*, says, "The essential mark of the agitator is the high value he places on the emotional response of the public."[6] Effective extremists tend to be effective propagandists. Propaganda differs from education in that the former teaches one what to think, and the latter teaches one how to think clearly.

16. *Hypersensitivity and vigilance.* Extremists perceive hostile innuendo in even casual and innocuous comments, imagine rejection and antagonism concealed in honest disagreement and dissent, and see "latent" subversion, anti-Semitism, perversion, racism, disloyalty, and so on in innocent gestures and ambiguous behaviors. Although few extremists are actually clinically paranoid, many of them adopt a paranoid style with its attendant projective mechanisms, hostility, and distrust.

17. *Use of supernatural rationales for beliefs and actions.* Some extremists, particularly those involved in "cults" and religious movements—such as fundamentalist Christians, militant Zionist extremists, and members of mystical and metaphysical organizations—claim some kind of supernatural rationale for their beliefs and actions. Their movement or cause, they believe, is ordained or looked on favorably by God. In this case, stark extremism may become reframed in a "religious" context, which can have a legitimizing effect for some people. It's surprising how many people are reluctant to challenge "religiously" motivated extremism because it represents "religious belief" or because of the sacred-cow status of some religions in our culture.

18. ***Problems tolerating ambiguity and uncertainty.***
Indeed, the ideologies and belief systems to which
extremists tend to attach themselves often represent
grasping for certainty in an uncertain world, or an
attempt to achieve absolute security in an environment that is naturally unpredictable or perhaps populated by people with agendas and interests opposed
to their own. Extremists exhibit a kind of risk-
aversiveness that compels them to engage in controlling and manipulative behavior, both on a
personal level and in a political context, to protect
themselves from the unforeseen and unknown. The
more laws or rules there are that regulate the behavior of others — particularly their "enemies" — the
more secure extremists feel.

19. ***Inclination toward "groupthink."*** Extremists, their
organizations, and their subcultures are prone to a
kind of inward-looking group cohesiveness that
leads to what Irving Janis describes as "groupthink."
Groupthink involves a tendency to conform to
group norms and to preserve solidarity and con-
currence at the expense of distorting members' observations of facts, conflicting evidence, and
disquieting observations that would call into question the shared assumptions and beliefs of the
group. Right-wingers (or left-wingers), for example,
talk mostly to one another, read only material that
reflects their own views, and can be almost phobic
about the "propaganda" of the "other side." The result is a deterioration of reality-testing, rationality, a
sense of perspective and moral judgment. With
groupthink, shared illusions of righteousness, superior morality, and persecution remain intact, and
those who challenge them are viewed with skepticism and hostility.[7]

20. ***Tendency to personalize hostility.*** Extremists often
wish for the personal bad fortune of their "enemies,"
and celebrate when it occurs. When a critic or an
adversary dies or has a serious illness, a bad accident, or personal legal problems, extremists often
rejoice and chortle about how he or she "deserved"
it. I recall seeing right-wing extremists celebrate the
assassination of Martin Luther King and leftists ag-
onizing because George Wallace survived an assassination attempt. In each instance, their hatred
was not only directed against ideas, but also against
individual human beings.

21. ***Extremists often feel that the system is no good
unless they win.*** For example, if they lose an election, the election was "rigged." If public opinion
turns against them, it is because of "brainwashing."
If their followers become disillusioned, it's because
of "sabotage." The test of the rightness or wrongness of the system is how it has an impact on them.

22. ***Extremists tend to believe in far-reaching conspiracy theories.*** Many extremists claim that there

is a secret conspiracy by some hidden elite to control the world. Both leftists and rightists have their
own versions of conspiracy theories. Sometimes
claims by extremists may have an element of truth
to them, however tenuous and ephemeral, and
every claim must be judged on the basis of its evidence. However, extremists are prone to jump to
conclusions, disregard evidence to the contrary, and
grasp at the most insubstantial and elusive facts and
theories to support their case.

Thus, extremists tend to have these things in
common:

1. Extremists represent some attempt to distort reality for
themselves and others. Extremism tends to be "feeling-
based" rather than "evidence-based," although the selective use of evidence may obscure that fact.
2. Extremists try to discourage critical examination of
their beliefs by a variety of means, usually by false
logic, rhetorical trickery, or some kind of censorship,
intimidation, or repression.
3. Extremism usually represents some attempt to act
out private personal grudges or to rationalize the pursuit of special interests in the name of public welfare, morality, duty, or social consciousness.
Extremists often have motives they themselves do
not recognize.

Human beings are imperfect and fallible. Even
an honest, rational, and well-intentioned person
may resort to some of these tactics from time to
time. Everyone has strong feelings about some issues and anyone can become excited and "blow
up" once in a while. Most of us still retain our
basic common sense, good will, and sense of
humor. My purpose is not to establish some impossible standard that almost no one can meet,
but simply to suggest a better direction. The difference between true extremists and others is that
this general kind of behavior is the extremist's normal and usual way of relating their values and feelings, and they usually feel no guilt or sense that
anything is wrong when they behave this way. The
extremist subculture, such as it is, rewards and reinforces these behaviors, while the society of
thoughtful and fair-minded people discourages it.

## ONE FINAL NOTE

The truth of a proposition cannot be inferred merely from the manner in which arguments are pre-

sented in its behalf, from the fact that its adherents may censor or harass their opponents, or because they practice any other behavior or combination of behaviors suggested in this article. Ultimately, the truth of any proposition or claim must rest on the evidence for it. Moreover, the intensity of a conviction has nothing whatsoever to do with whether or not it is true. To dismiss a proposition out of hand merely because it is advocated by obvious extremists is to dismiss it *ad hominem*, that is, because of *who* advocates it and not on its merits.

Extremists sometimes fulfill a "watchdog" function in society in that they're especially sensitive to issues concerning their particular interests. They often deal with the "hot" issues, the controversial issues many people choose to avoid. Many social problems were first identified by extremists, whose agitating and propagandizing forced society to take a closer look and then apply more moderate and realistic solutions. In point of fact, extremists are sometimes correct. Before you write people off as extremists, take a look at their evidence. However unlikely it may seem, it might be that they're actually on to something important after all.

## ENDNOTES

1. Roger Scruton, *A Dictionary of Political Thought* (New York: Hill & Wang, 1982), 164.
2. Milton Rokeach, *The Open and Closed Mind: Investigations Into the Nature of Belief Systems and Personality Systems* (New York: Basic Books, 1969), 6.
3. Rokeach, 13.
4. Daniel Bell, quoted in Rushworth M. Kidder, "A Lifetime of Looking at Life," *The Christian Science Monitor* (March 12, 1991), 14.
5. Theodore J. Lowe, ed., *The Pursuit of Justice* (New York: Harper & Row, 1964).
6. Harold D. Lasswell, *Psychopathology and Politics* (New York: Viking Press, 1960), 78.
7. Irving L. Janis, *Victims of Groupthink* (Boston: Houghton-Mifflin, 1972).

# 49.  THE POLITICS OF THE CONTENTED

JOHN KENNETH GALBRAITH

"*[The Contented Majority] rule under the rich cloak of democracy, a democracy in which the less fortunate do not participate…they are [not] silent in their contentment. They can be…very angry and very articulate about what seems to invade their state of self-satisfaction.*"

Americans pride themselves on a set of political institutions they call democracy. However, can a democracy exist when large numbers of people are excluded from the process (or exclude themselves from the process), especially if they are the most discontented and the most disadvantaged in the society? In this critique of American democracy, Galbraith describes the views of those who are active in and have come to control our political system. They are not a few rich people, but instead a large diversity of contented people who work together to keep what they have and protect themselves through action and through a set of principles they claim to be democratic. Galbraith's book describes these contented people, and this selection is an analysis worth serious attention if we are to understand the working of our political institutions.

...In past times, the economically and socially fortunate were, as we know, a small minority — characteristically a dominant and ruling handful. They are now a majority, though...a majority not of all citizens but of those who actually vote. A convenient reference is needed for those so situated and who so respond at the polls. They will be called the *Contented Majority*, the *Contented Electoral Majority*, or more spaciously, the *Culture of Contentment*. There will be adequate reiteration that this does not mean they are a majority of all those eligible to vote. They rule under the rich cloak of democracy, a democracy in which the less fortunate do not participate. Nor does it mean — a most important point — that they are silent in their contentment. They can be, as when this book goes to press, very angry and very articulate about what seems to invade their state of self-satisfaction.

• • •

Although income broadly defines the contented majority, no one should suppose that that majority is occupationally or socially homogeneous. It includes the people who manage or otherwise staff the middle and upper reaches of the great financial and industrial firms, independent businessmen and women, and those in lesser employments whose compensation is more or less guaranteed. Also the large population — lawyers, doctors, engineers, scientists, accountants and many others, not excluding journalists and professors — who make up the modern professional class. Included also are a certain, if diminishing, number who once were called *proletarians* — those with diverse skills whose wages are now, with some frequency, supplemented by those of a diligent wife. They, like others in families with dual paychecks, find life reasonably secure.

Further, although they were once a strongly discontented community, there are the farmers, who, when buttressed by government price supports, are now amply rewarded.[1] Here, too, there is a dominant, if not universal, mood of satisfaction. Finally, there is the rapidly increasing number of the aged who live on pensions or other retirement allowance and for whose remaining years of life there is adequate or, on occasion, ample financial provision.

---

None of this suggests an absence of continuing personal aspiration or a unanimity of political view. Doing well, many wish to do better. Having enough, many wish for more. Being comfortable, many raise vigorous objection to that which invades comfort. What is important is that there is no self-doubt in their present situation. The future for the contented majority is thought effectively within their personal command. Their anger is evident — and, indeed, can be strongly evident — only when there is a threat or possible threat to present well-being and future prospect — when government and the seemingly less deserving intrude or threaten to intrude their needs or demands. This is especially so if such action suggests higher taxes.

As to political attitude, there is a minority, not small in number, who do look beyond personal contentment to a concern for those who do not share in the comparative well-being. Or they see the more distant dangers that will result from a short-run preoccupation with individual comfort. Idealism and foresight are not dead; on the contrary, their expression is the most reputable form of social discourse. Although self-interest, as we shall see, does frequently operate under a formal cover of social concern, much social concern is genuinely and generously motivated.

Nonetheless, self-regard is, predictably, the dominant — indeed the controlling — mood of the Contented Majority. This becomes wholly evident when public action on behalf of those outside this electoral majority is the issue. If it is to be effective, such action is invariably at public cost. Accordingly, it is regularly resisted as a matter of high, if sometimes rather visibly contrived, principle. Of this, more later.

• • •

In the recent past, much has been held wrong with the performance of the United States government as regards both domestic and foreign policy. This has been widely attributed to the inadequacy, incompetence, or generally perverse performance of individual politicians and political leaders. Mr. Reagan and his now accepted intellectual and administrative detachment, and Mr. Bush, his love of travel and his belief in oratory as the prime instrument of domestic action, have been often cited. Similarly criticized have been leaders and members of the Congress, and, if less stridently, governors and other politicians throughout the Republic.

This criticism, or much of it, is mistaken or, at best, politically superficial. The government of the United States in recent years has been a valid reflection of the economic and social preferences of the majority of those voting—the electoral majority. In defense of Ronald Reagan and George Bush as Presidents, it must be said and emphasized that both were, or are, faithful representatives of the constituency that elected them. We attribute to politicians what should be attributed to the community they serve.

• • •

The first and most general expression of the Contented Majority is its affirmation that those who compose it are receiving their just deserts. What the individual member aspires to have and enjoy is the product of his or her personal virtue, intelligence, and effort. Good fortune being earned or the reward of merit, there is no equitable justification for any action that impairs it— that subtracts from what is enjoyed or might be enjoyed. The normal response to such action is indignation or, as suggested, anger at anything infringing on what is so clearly deserved.

There will be, as noted, individuals—on frequent occasion in the past, some who have inherited what they have—who will be less certain that they merit their comparative good fortune. And more numerous will be those scholars, journalists, professional dissidents, and other voices who will express sympathy for the excluded and concern for the future, often from positions of relative personal comfort. The result will be political effort and agitation in conflict with the aims and preferences of the contented. The number so motivated is, to repeat, not small, but they are not a serious threat to the electoral majority. On the contrary, by their dissent, they give a gracing aspect of democracy to the ruling position of the fortunate. They show in their articulate way that "democracy is working." Liberals in the United States, Labour politicians and spokesmen in Britain, are, indeed, vital in this regard. Their writing and rhetoric give hope to the excluded and, at a minimum, ensure that they are not both excluded *and* ignored.

Highly convenient social and economic doctrine also emerges in defense of contentment, some of which is modern and some ancient. As will be seen, what once justified the favored position of the few— a handful of aristocrats or capitalists—has now become the favoring defense of the comfortable many.

• • •

The second, less conscious but extremely important characteristic of the Contented Majority, one already noted, is its attitude toward time. In the briefest word, short-run public inaction, even if held to be alarming as to consequence, is always preferred to protective long-run action. The reason is readily evident. The long run may not arrive; that is the frequent and comfortable belief. More decisively important, the cost of today's action falls or could fall on the favored community; taxes could be increased. The benefits in the longer run may well be for others to enjoy. In any case, the quiet theology of laissez faire holds that all will work out for the best in the end.

Here, too, there will be contrary voices. These will be heard, and often with respect, but not to the point of action. For the Contented Majority, the logic of inaction is inescapable. For many years, for example, there has been grave concern in the northeastern United States and extending up to Canada over acid rain caused by sulphurous emissions from the power plants of the Midwest. The long-run effects will, it is known, be extremely adverse—on the environment, the recreational industries, the forest industry, maple sugar producers, and on the general benignity of local life and scene. The cost of corrective measures to the electric power plants and their consumers will be immediate and specific; the longer-term conservation reward will, in contrast, be diffuse, uncertain, and debatable as to specific incidence. From this comes the policy avowed by the contented. It does not deny the problem, this not being possible; rather, it delays action. Notably, it proposes more research, which very often provides a comforting, intellectually reputable gloss over inaction. At the worst, it suggests impaneling a commission, the purpose of which would be to discuss and recommend action or perhaps postponement thereof. At the very worst, there is limited, perhaps symbolic, action, as in recent times. Other long-run environmental dangers—global warming and the dissipation of the ozone layer— invite a similar response.

Another example of the role of time is seen in attitudes toward what is called, rather formidably, the *economic infrastructure of the United States*— its highways, bridges, airports, mass transportation facilities, and other public structures. These are now widely perceived as falling far below future need and even present standards of safety. Nonetheless, expenditure and new investment in this area are powerfully and effectively resisted. Again the very plausible reason: Present cost and taxation are specific; future advantage is dispersed. Later and different individuals will benefit; why pay for persons unknown? So again the readily understandable insistence on inaction and the resulting freedom from present cost. Contentment is here revealed to be of growing social influence, more decisive than in the past. The interstate highway system, the parkways, the airports, even perhaps the hospitals and schools of an earlier and financially far more astringent time but one when the favored voters were far fewer, could not be built today.

In the 1980s, the preference for short-run advantage was dramatically evident, as will later be noted, in the continued deficits in the budget of the United States and in the related and resulting deficits in the international trade accounts. Here, the potential cost to the favored voting community, the Contented Electoral Majority, was highly specific. To reduce the deficit meant more taxation or a reduction in expenditures, including those important to the comfortable. The distant benefits seemed, predictably, diffuse and uncertain as to impact. Again, no one can doubt that Presidents Reagan and Bush were or are in highly sympathetic response to their constituency on this matter. Although criticism of their action or inaction has been inevitable, their instinct as to what their politically decisive supporters wanted has been impeccable.

• • •

A third commitment of the comfortably situated is to a highly selective view of the role of the state – of government. Broadly and superficially speaking, the state is seen as a burden; no political avowal of modern times has been so often reiterated and so warmly applauded as the need "to get government off the backs of the people." The albatross was not hung more oppressively by his shipmates around the neck of the Mariner. The need to lighten or remove this burden and therewith, agreeably, the supporting taxes is an article of high faith for the comfortable or Contented Majority.

But although government in general has been viewed as a burden, there have been, as will be seen, significant and costly exceptions from this broad condemnation. Excluded from criticism,

needless to say, have been Social Security, medical care at higher income levels, farm income supports, and financial guarantees to depositors in ill-fated banks and savings and loan enterprises. These are strong supports to the comfort and security of the Contented Majority. No one would dream of attacking them, even marginally, in any electoral contest.

Specifically favored also have been military expenditures, their scale and fiscally oppressive effect notwithstanding. This has been for three reasons. These expenditures, as they are reflected in the economy in wages, salaries, profits, and assorted subsidies to research and other institutions, serve to sustain or enhance the income of a considerable segment of the Contented Electoral Majority. Weapons expenditure (unlike, for example, spending for the urban poor) rewards a very comfortable constituency.

More important, perhaps, [is that] military expenditures – and those for the associated operations of the CIA and (to a diminishing extent) the Department of State – have been seen in the past as vital protection against the gravest perceived threat to continued comfort and contentment. That threat was from Communism, with its clear and overt, even if remote, endangerment of the economic life and rewards of the comfortable. This fear, in turn, extending on occasion to clinical paranoia, ensured support to the military establishment. And American liberals, no less than conservatives, felt obliged, given their personal commitment to liberty and human rights, to show by their support of defense spending that they were not "soft on Communism."

The natural focus of concern was the Soviet Union and its once seemingly stalwart satellites in Eastern Europe. Fear of the not-inconsiderable competence of the Soviets in military technology and production provided the main pillar of support for American military spending. However, the alarm was geographically comprehensive. It supported expenditure and military action against such improbable threats as those from Angola, Afghanistan, Ethiopia, Grenada, El Salvador, Nicaragua, Laos, Cambodia, and, massively, tragically, and at great cost, from Vietnam. From being considered a source of fear and concern, only Communist China was, from the early 1970s on, exempt. Turning against the Soviet Union and forgiven for its earlier role in Korea and Vietnam, it became an honorary bastion of democracy and free enterprise, which, later repressive actions notwithstanding, it rather substantially remains.

The final reason that military expenditures have continued to be favored is the self-perpetuating power of the military and weapons establishment itself — its control of the weaponry it is to produce, the missions for which it is to be prepared, and in substantial measure the funds that it receives and dispenses.

Until World War II, the fortunately situated in the United States, the Republican Party in particular, resisted military expenditures, as they then resisted all government spending. In the years since, the presumed worldwide Communist menace, as frequently it was designated, brought a major reversal: Those with a comfortable concern for their own economic position became the most powerful advocates of the most prodigal of military outlays. With the collapse of Communism, an interesting question arises as to what the attitude of the contented will now be. That the military establishment, public and private, will continue on its own authority to claim a large share of its past financial support is not, however, seriously in doubt.

• • •

Such are the exceptions that the Contented Majority makes to its general condemnation of government as a burden. Social expenditure favorable to the fortunate, financial rescue, military spending and, of course, interest payments — these constitute in the aggregate by far the largest part of the federal budget and that which in recent times has shown by far the greatest increase. What remains — expenditures for welfare, low-cost housing, health care for those otherwise unprotected, public education, and the diverse needs of the great urban slums — is what is now viewed as the burden of government. It is uniquely that which serves the interests of those outside the Contented Electoral Majority; it is, and inescapably, what serves the poor. Here again, Mr. Reagan and now Mr. Bush showed or now show a keen sense of their constituency. So also they do with regard to one further tendency of the Contented Majority.

• • •

The final characteristic here to be cited and stressed is the tolerance shown by the contented of great differences in income. These differences have already been noted, as has the fact that the disparity is not a matter that occasions serious dispute. A general and quite plausible convention is here observed: The price of prevention of any aggression against one's own income is tolerance of the greater amount for others. Indignation at, and advocacy of, redistribution of income from the very rich, inevitably by taxes, opens the door for consideration of higher taxes for the comfortable but less endowed. This is especially a threat given the position and possible claims of the least favored part of the population. Any outcry from the fortunate half could only focus attention on the far inferior position of the lower half. The plush advantage of the very rich is the price the Contented Electoral Majority pays for being able to retain what is less but what is still very good. And, it is averred, there could be solid social advantage in this tolerance of the very fortunate: "To help the poor and middle classes, one must cut the taxes on the rich."[2]

Ronald Reagan's single-most celebrated economic action (the acceptance of the related budget deficit possibly apart) was his tax relief for the very affluent. Marginal rates on the very rich were reduced from a partly nominal 70 percent to 50 percent in 1981; then, with tax reform, the rate on the richest fell to 28 percent in 1986, although this was partly offset by other tax changes. The result was a generous increase in the after-tax income in the higher income brackets. That part of Mr. Reagan's motivation was his memory of the presumptively painful tax demands on his Hollywood pay seems not in doubt. He was also influenced by the economic ideas that had been adapted to serve tax reduction on the rich — broadly, the doctrine that if the horse is fed amply with oats, some will pass through to the road for the sparrows. But once again there was also the sense of what served his larger constituency, as well as that of the concurring Congress. This constituency accepted the favor to the very rich in return for protection for itself.

• • •

In summary, we see that much that has been attributed in these past years to ideology, idiosyncrasy, or error of political leadership has deep roots in the American polity. It has been said, and often, in praise of Ronald Reagan as President that he gave the American people a good feeling about themselves This acclaim is fully justified as regards the people who voted for him, and even perhaps as regards that not inconsiderable number who, voting otherwise, found themselves in silent approval of the very tangible personal effect of his tax policies.

In past times in the United States, under government by either of the major parties, many experienced a certain sense of unease, of troubled conscience and associated discomfort when contemplating those who did not share the good fortune of the fortunate. No such feeling emanated from Ronald Reagan; Americans were being rewarded as they so richly deserved. If some did not participate, it was because of their inability or by their choice. As it was once the privilege of Frenchmen, both the rich and the poor, to sleep under bridges, so any American had the undoubted right to sleep on street grates. This might not be the reality, but it was the presidentially ordained script. And this script was tested by Ronald Reagan, out of his long and notable theatrical training, not for its reality, not for its truth, but, as if it were a motion picture or a television commercial: for its appeal. That appeal was widespread; it allowed Americans to escape their consciences and their social concerns and thus to feel a glow of self-approval.

Not all, of course, could so feel, nor, necessarily, could a majority of all citizens of voting age. And there was a further and socially rather bitter circumstance, one that has been conveniently, neglected: the comfort and economic well-being of the Contented Majority was being supported and enhanced by the presence in the modern economy of a large, highly useful, even essential class that does not share in the agreeable existence of the favored community.

## ENDNOTES

1. "The average 1988 income of farm operator households was $33,535, compared with $34,017 for all U.S. households. However, 5 percent of farm operator households had incomes above $100,000, compared to 3.2 percent of all U.S. households." *Agricultural Income and Finance: Situation and Outlook Report* (Washington, D.C.: U.S. Department of Agriculture Economic Research Service, May 1990), p. 26.
2. George Gilder, *Wealth and Poverty* (New York: Basic Books, 1981), p. 188. He is quoted by Kevin Phillips in *The Politics of Rich and Poor: Wealth and the American Electorate in the Reagan Aftermath* (New York: Random House, 1990), p. 62.

# 50.  JOBS — AND JOBLESSNESS — IN A TECHNOLOGICAL AMERICA

S. ARONOWITZ AND W. DI FAZIO

*"...The shape of things to come — as well as those already in existence — signals the emerging proletarianization of work at every level below top management and a relatively few scientific and technical occupations."*

There is a revolution going on in society concerning our economic institutions. Specifically, it has to do with work. This selection examines that revolution and ties it to a scientific-technological revolution. Aronowitz and Di Fazio show us what is happening and why. Jobs will never be the same as they were; incomes and standard of living for most people will be considerably lower than they are now; mobility will become more difficult, and a greater gap will be created between those at the top of the economic order and everyone else. This selection deserves careful examination and debate. It will probably happen in the classroom more than it will in the political order.

## OVERVIEW

In 1992, the long-term shifts in the nature of paid work became painfully visible not only to industrial workers and those with technical, professional, and managerial credentials and job experience but also to the public. During that year, "corporate giants like General Motors and IBM announced plans to shed tens of thousands of workers." General Motors, which at first said it would close twenty-one U.S. plants by 1995, soon disclaimed any definite limit to the number of either plant closings or firings and admitted that the numbers of jobs lost might climb above the predicted 70,000, even if the recession led to increased car sales. IBM, which initially shaved about 25,000 blue- and white-collar employees, soon increased its estimates to possibly 60,000, in effect reversing the company's historic policy of no layoffs. Citing economic conditions, Boeing, the world's largest airplane producer, and Hughes Aircraft, a major parts manufacturer, were poised for substantial cuts in their well-paid workforces. In 1991 and 1992, major retailers, including Sears, either shut down stores or drastically cut the number of employees; in late January 1993, Sears announced that it was letting about 50,000 employees go. The examples could be multiplied. Millions, worldwide, were losing their jobs in the industrialized West and Asia. Homelessness was and is growing....

...The scientific-technological revolution of our time, which is not confined to new electronic processes but also affects organizational changes in the structure of corporations, has fundamentally altered the forms of work, skill, and occupation. The whole notion of tradition and identity of persons with their work has been radically changed.

From *The Jobless Future: Sci-Tech and the Dogma of Work*, by S. Aronowitz and W. DiFazio. Copyright © 1994 by the Regents of the University of Minnesota. Reprinted by permission of the University of Minnesota Press.

Scientific and technological innovation is, for the most part, no longer episodic. Technological change has been routinized. Not only has abstract knowledge come to the center of the world's political economy, but there is also a tendency to produce and trade in symbolic significations rather than concrete products. Today, knowledge rather than traditional skill is the main productive force. The revolution has widened the gap between intellectual, technical, and manual labor, between a relatively small number of jobs that, owing to technological complexity, require more knowledge and a much larger number that require less; because the mass of jobs are "de-skilled," there is a resultant redefinition of occupational categories that reflects the changes in the nature of jobs. As these transformations sweep the world, older conceptions of class, gender, and ethnicity are called into question. For example, on the New York waterfront (until 1970, the nation's largest), Italians and blacks dominated the Brooklyn docks and the Irish and Eastern Europeans worked the Manhattan piers. Today, not only are the docks vanishing as sites of shipping, the workers are gone as well. For those who remain, the traditional occupation of longshoreman – dangerous, but highly skilled – has given way, as a result of containerization of the entire process, to a shrunken workforce that possesses knowledge but not the old skills[1] ...This is just an example of a generalized shift in the nature and significance of work.

As jobs have changed, so have the significance and duration of joblessness. Partial and permanent unemployment, except during the two great world depressions (1893–1898 and 1929–1939) largely episodic and subject to short-term economic contingencies, has increasingly become a mode of life for larger segments of the populations not only of less industrially developed countries, but for those in "advanced" industrial societies as well. Many who are classified in official statistics as "employed" actually work at casual and part-time jobs, the number of which has grown dramatically over the past fifteen years. This phenomenon, once confined to freelance writers and artists, laborers and clerical workers, today cuts across all occupations, including the professions. Even the once buoyant "new" profession of computer programmer is already showing signs of age after barely a quarter of a century. We argue that the shape of things to come—as well as those already in existence—signals the emerging proletarianization of work at every level below top management and a relatively few scientific and technical occupations.

At the same time, because of the permanent character of job cuts starting in the 1970s and glaringly visible after 1989, the latest recession has finally and irrevocably vitiated the traditional idea that the unemployed are an "industrial reserve army" awaiting the next phase of economic expansion. Of course, some laid-off workers, especially in union workplaces, will be recalled when the expansion, however sluggish, resumes. Even if one stubbornly clings to the notion of a reserve army, one cannot help but note that its soldiers in the main now occupy the part-time and temporary positions that appear to have replaced the well-paid full-time jobs.

Because of these changes, the "meaning" (in the survival, psychological, and cultural senses) of work—occupations and professions—as forms of life is in crisis. If the tendencies of the economy and the culture point to the conclusion that work is no longer significant in the formation of the self, one of the crucial questions of our time is what, if anything, can replace it. When layers of qualified—to say nothing of mass—labor are made redundant, obsolete, *irrelevant*, what, after five centuries during which work remained a, perhaps *the*, Western cultural ideal, can we mean by the "self"? Have we reached a large historical watershed, a climacteric that will be as devastating as natural climacterics of the past that destroyed whole species?

…Science and technology (of which organization is an instance) alter the nature of the labor process, not only the rationalized manual labor but also intellectual labor, especially the professions. Knowledge becomes ineluctably intertwined with, even dependent on, technology. Even so-called labor-intensive work becomes increasingly mechanized and begins to be replaced by capital- and technology-intensive—*capitech-intensive*—work. Today, the regime of world economic life consists of scratching every itch of every-

day life with sci-tech: eye glasses, underarm deodorant, preservatives in food, braces on pets. Technology has become the universal problem solver, the postmodern equivalent of *deus ex machina*, the ineluctable component of education and play as much as of work. No level of schooling is spared: Students interact with computers to learn reading, writing, social studies, math, and science in elementary school through graduate school. Play, once and still the corner of the social world least subject to regimentation, is increasingly incorporated into computer software, especially the products of the Apple corporation. More and more, we, the service and professional classes, are chained to our personal computers; with the help of the modem and the fax, we can communicate, in seconds, to the farthest reaches of the globe. We no longer need to press the flesh: By e-mail, we can attend conferences, gain access to library collections, and write electronic letters to perfect strangers. And, of course, with the assistance of virtual reality, we can engage in electronic sex. The only thing the computer cannot deliver is touch, but who needs it, anyway?[2]

…The new electronic communication technologies have become the stock-in-trade of a relatively few people because newspapers, magazines, and television have simply refused to acknowledge that we live in a complex world. Instead, they have tended to *simplify* news, even for the middle class. Thus, an "unintended" consequence of the dissemination of informatics to personal use is a growing information gap already implied by the personal computer. A relatively small number of people—no more than ten million in the United States—will, before the turn of the century, be fully wired to world sources of information and new knowledge: libraries, electronic newspapers and journals, conferences and forums on specialized topics, and colleagues, irrespective of country or region around the globe. Despite the much-heralded electronic highway, which will be largely devoted to entertainment products, the great mass of the world's population, already restricted in its knowledge and power by the hierarchical division of the print media into tabloids and newspapers of record, will henceforth be doubly disadvantaged.

Of course, the information gap makes a difference only if one considers the conditions for a democratic—that is, a participatory—society. If popular governance even in the most liberal-democratic societies has been reduced in the last several decades to *plebiscitary* participation, the potential effect of computer-mediated knowledge is to exacerbate exclusion of vast portions of the underlying populations of all countries....

New uses of knowledge widen the gap between the present and the future; new knowledge challenges not only our collectively held beliefs but also the common ethical ground of our "civilization." The tendency of science to dominate the labor process, which emerged in the last half of the nineteenth century but attained full flower only in the last two decades, now heralds an entirely new regime of work in which almost no production *skills* are required. Older forms of technical or professional knowledge are transformed, incorporated, superseded, or otherwise eliminated by computer-mediated technologies — by applications of physical sciences intertwined with the production of knowledge: expert systems — leaving new forms of knowledge that are *inherently* labor-saving. But, unlike the mechanizing era of pulleys and electrically powered machinery, which retained the "hands-on" character of labor, computers have transferred most knowledge associated with the crafts and manual labor and, increasingly, intellectual knowledge, to the machine. As a result, although each generation of technological change makes some work more complex and interesting and raises the level of training or qualification required by a (diminishing) fraction of intellectual and manual labor force, for the overwhelming majority of workers, this process simplifies tasks or eliminates them, and thus eliminates the worker....

## THINGS FALL APART

...Of course, the introduction of computer-mediated technologies in administrative services — especially banks and insurance companies and retail and wholesale trades — preceded that in goods production. From the early days of office computers in the 1950s, there has been a sometimes acrimonious debate about their effects. Perhaps the Spencer Tracy–Katharine Hepburn comedy *Desk Set* best exemplifies the issues: When a mainframe computer is introduced into the library of a large corporation, its professional and technical staff is at first alarmed, precisely because of their fear of losing their jobs. The film reiterates the prevailing view of the period (and ours?) that, far from posing a threat, computers promise to increase work by expanding needs. Significantly, the film asserts that the nearly inexhaustible desire for information inherent in human affairs will provide a fail-safe against professional and clerical redundancy. In contradistinction to these optimistic prognostications, new information technologies have enabled corporations, large law firms, and local governments to reduce the library labor force, including professional librarians. In turn, several library science schools have closed, including the prestigious library school at Columbia University.

By the 1980s, many if not most large and small businesses used electronic telephone devices to replace the live receptionist. A concomitant of these changes has been the virtual extinction of the secretary as an occupational category for all except top executives and department heads, if by that term we mean the individual service provided by a clerical worker to a single manager or a small group of managers. Today, at the levels of line and middle management, the "secretary" is a word-processing clerk; many middle managers have their own answering machines or voice mail and do their own word processing. They may have access to a word-processing pool only for producing extensive reports. Needless to say, after a quarter of a century during which computers displaced nearly all major office machines — especially typewriters, adding machines, and mechanical calculators — and all but eliminated the job category of file clerk, by the 1980s, many major corporations took advantage of the information "revolution" to decentralize their facilities away from cities to suburbs and exurbs. Once concentrated in large urban areas, data processing now can be done not only in small rural communities but also in satellite- and wire-linked, underdeveloped offshore sites. This has revived the once-scorned practice of working at home. Taken together, new forms of corporate organization, aided by the computer, have successfully arrested and finally reversed the steady expansion of the clerical labor force and have transferred many of its functions from the office to the bedroom.

Visiting a retail food supermarket in 1992, President George Bush was surprised to learn that the inventory label on each item enabled the checkout clerk to record the price by passing it through an electronic device, a feature of retailing that has been in place for at least fifteen years. This innovation has speeded the checkout process but has also relieved the clerk of punching the price on the register, which, in turn, saves time by adding the total bill automatically. The clerk in retail food and department stores works at a checkout counter and has been reduced to handling the product and observing the process, but intervenes only when it fails to function properly. Supermarket employers require fewer employees and, perhaps equally important, fewer workers in warehouses: An operator sits at a computer and identifies the quantity and location of a particular item rather than having to search for its location and count the numbers visually. The goods are loaded onto a vehicle by remote control and a driver operating a forklift takes them to the trucking dock, where they are mechanically loaded again. Whereas once the warehouse worker required a strong back, most of these functions are now performed mechanically and electronically.

Some of the contraction of clerical and industrial employment is, of course, a result of the general economic decline since the late 1980s. But given the astounding improvements in productivity of the manual industrial and clerical work force attributable to computerization, as we argued earlier, there is no evidence that a general economic recovery would restore most of the lost jobs in office and production sites—which raises the crucial issue of the relationship between measures designed to promote economic growth and job creation in the era of computer-mediated work....

The American cultural ideal is tied not only to consumer society but also to the expectation that, given average abilities, with hard work and a little luck almost anyone can achieve occupational and even social mobility. Professional, technical, and managerial occupations perhaps even more than the older aspiration of entrepreneurial success are identified with faith in American success, and the credentials acquired through postsecondary education have become cultural capital, the necessary precondition of mobility. Put another way, if

scientifically based technical knowledge has become the main productive force, schooling becomes the major route to mobility. No longer just places where traditional culture is disseminated to a relatively small elite, universities and colleges have become the key repositories of the cultural and intellectual capital from which professional, technical, and managerial labor is formed.

For the first quarter century after World War II, the expansion of these categories in the labor force was sufficient to absorb almost all of those trained in the professional and technical occupations. In some cases—notably education, the health professions, and engineering—there were chronic shortages of qualified professionals and managers. Now there is growing evidence of permanent redundancy within the new middle class....

In the two decades beginning in the mid-1960s, the United States experienced the largest-scale restructuring and reforming of its industrial base in more than a century. Capital flight, which extended beyond U.S. borders, was abetted by technological change in administration and in production. Millions of workers, clerical and industrial, lost their high-paying jobs and were able to find employment only at lower wages. Well-paid union jobs became more scarce, and many, especially women, could find only part-time employment. But the American cultural ideal, buttressed by ideological—indeed, sometimes mythic—journalism and social theory, was barely affected in the wake of the elimination of millions of blue- and white-collar jobs. As C. Wright Mills once remarked in another context, these public issues were experienced as private troubles.

The persistence, if not so much the real and exponential growth, of poverty amid plenty was publicly acknowledged, even by mainstream politicians, but, like alienated labor, it was bracketed as a discrete "racial problem" that left the mainstream white population unaffected. Job creation precluded serious consideration of the old Keynesian solutions; these had been massively defeated by the state-backed, yet ideologically antistatist, free-market ideologies. We were told that deregulation would free up the market and ensure economic growth that eventually would employ the jobless, provided they cleaned up their act. Even in the halcyon days of the Great Society programs of the war-inflated Johnson years, the antipoverty crusade offered the long-term unemployed only literacy and job training and, occasionally, the chance to finish high school and enter college or technical school. The Great Society created few permanent jobs and relied on the vitality of the private sector to employ those trained by its programs....

The question now is not only what the consequences of the closing of routes to mobility of a substantial fraction of sons and daughters of manual and clerical workers may be, but also whether the professional and technical middle class can expect to reproduce itself at the same economic and social level under the new, deregulated conditions. For...the older and most prestigious professions of medicine, university teaching, law, and engineering are in trouble: Doctors and lawyers and engineers are becoming like assembly-line clerks... proletarians. Although thus far there are only scattered instances of long-term unemployment among them, the historical expectation, especially among doctors and lawyers, that they will own their own practices, has for most of them been permanently shattered. More than half of each profession (and a substantially larger proportion of recent graduates) have become salaried employees of larger firms, hospitals, or group practices; with the subsumption of science and technology under large corporations and the state, engineers have not, typically, been self-employed for over a century.

Similarly, the attainment of a Ph.D. in the humanities or the social or natural sciences no longer ensures an entry-level academic position or a well-paid research or administrative job. Over the past fifteen years, a fairly substantial number of Ph.D.s have entered the academic proletariat of part-time and adjunct faculty. Most full-time teachers have little time and energy for the research they were trained to perform. Of course, the reversal of fortune for American colleges and universities is overdetermined by the stagnation and, in some sectors, decline of some professions; by the long-term recession; by organizational and technological changes; and by twenty years of conservative hegemony, which often takes the cultural form of anti-intellectualism. Since the 1960s, universities have been sites of intellectual as well as political

dissent and even opposition. A powerful element in the long-term budget crises, that many private as well as public institutions have suffered is at least partially linked to the perception among executive authorities that good money should not be thrown after bad.

And, with the steep decline in subprofessional and technical jobs, universities and colleges, especially the two-year community colleges, are re-examining their "mission" to educate virtually all who seek postsecondary education. In the past five years, we have seen the reemergence of the discourse of faculty "productivity," the reimposition of academic "standards," and other indicators that powerful forces are arrayed to impose policies of contraction in public education....

In the subprofessions of elementary and secondary school teaching, social work, nursing, and medical technology, to name only the most numerically important, salaries and working conditions have deteriorated over the past decade so that the distinction, both economically and at the workplace, between the living standards of skilled manual workers and these professionals has sharply narrowed. Increasingly, many in these categories have changed their psychological as well as political relationship to the performance of the job. The work of a classroom teacher, line social worker, or nurse is, despite efforts by unions and professional organizations to shore up their professional status, no longer seen as a "vocation" in the older meaning of the term. Put succinctly, many in these occupations regard their work as does any manual worker: They take the money and run. More and more, practicing professionals look toward management positions to obtain work satisfaction as well as improvements in their living standard because staying "in the trenches" is socially unappreciated and financially appears to be a dead end. Consequently, in addition to a mad race to obtain more credentials in order to qualify for higher positions, we have seen a definite growth in union organization among these groups even as union membership in the private sector, especially as a proportion of the manual labor force, has sharply declined....

The economic and technological revolutions of our time notwithstanding, work is of course not disappearing. Nor should it. Rebuilding the cities, providing adequate education and child care, and saving the environment are all labor-intensive activities. The unpaid labor of housekeeping and child rearing remain among the major social scandals of our culture. The question is whether work as a cultural ideal has not already been displaced by its correlates: status and consumption. Except for a small proportion of those who are affected by technological innovation — those responsible for the innovations, those involved in developing their applications, and those who run the factories and offices — most workers, including professionals, are subjugated by labor-saving, work-simplification, and other rationalizing features of the context within which technology is introduced. For the subjugated, paid work has already lost its intrinsic meaning. It has become, at best, a means of making a living and a site of social conviviality.

## ENDNOTES

1. William Di Fazio, *Longshoremen: Community and Resistance on the Brooklyn Waterfront* (South Hadley, MA: Bergin and Garvey, 1985).
2. Phillip K. Dick, *The Three Stigmata of Palmer Eldritch* ( London: Jonathan Cape and Granada Books, 1978). First published in 1964, Dick's novel foreshadows the development of virtual reality technology, linking it to a future when most people can no longer live on Earth but are afforded the means to simulate a life on this planet from a position somewhere in the galaxy.

# Part XI

# SOCIAL INSTITUTIONS: KINSHIP, RELIGIOUS, EDUCATIONAL

Institutions are most easily understood by dividing them into the areas of life they regulate. Part X of this book examined political and economic institutions; Part XI briefly looks at three more institutional areas.

Two selections are studies of **marriage and the family** in the United States. Arlene and Jerome Skolnick give us an excellent overview of the changes that have taken place in the American family, asking us always to consider the complexity, causes, and consequences of these changes. Richard Gelles and Murray Straus examine violence in the family and give us some unusual, interesting, and important reasons for this.

Two selections introduce **religious institutions**. The first by Bryan Wilson emphasizes the importance of studying religious institutions scientifically. The second by Robert Wuthnow introduces us to a trend that his research supports: the turning to small groups for purposes of community and spirituality.

Two selections examine **educational institutions**. Harry Gracey takes one institution—kindergarten—and shows its importance to becoming a citizen in the schools and in society at large. Jonathan Kozol reports on New York public schools, educational institutions characterized by "savage inequalities."

# 51. FAMILY IN TRANSITION, 1997

ARLENE AND JEROME SKOLNICK

*"A knowledge of family history reveals that the solution to contemporary problems will not be found in some lost golden age. Families have always struggled with outside circumstances and inner conflict. Our current troubles inside and outside the family are genuine, but we should never forget that many of the most vexing issues confronting us derive from benefits of modernization few of us would be willing to give up."*

To understand the history of the family in society is to become aware of the many ways it has changed. It is the product of change, and it is responsible for change. It adjusts to modern society, and it contributes to what modern society becomes. It is, the Skolnicks warn us, not something that used to be wonderful and no longer is, but something that is no longer what it used to be. For good or bad—and it depends on one's perspective—we have witnessed a very basic transformation. There are many themes that the Skolnicks highlight in this selection that are worth paying attention to: the diversity of family structures, nostalgia for a past that never was, the Victorian model of the family that emerged during the industrial revolution, the companionate model that eventually replaced the Victorian model in the early twentieth century, and a triple revolution in the mid-twentieth century that brought significantly new patterns—including a lot more choices for young people, changing female roles, and more emphasis on the ideals of emotional satisfaction in the family and democratic structure. The family is alive and well as we enter the twenty-first century; it has, however, undergone very important changes we need to understand.

It was one of the oddest episodes in America's political history—a debate between the vice president of the United States and a fictional television character. During the 1992 election campaign, former Vice President Dan Quayle set off a firestorm of debate with a remark denouncing a fictional television character for choosing to give birth out of wedlock. The *Murphy Brown* show, according to Quayle, was "mocking the importance of fathers." It reflected the "poverty of values" that was responsible for the nation's ills. From the talk shows to the front pages of newspapers to dinner tables across the nation, arguments broke out about the meaning of the vice president's remarks.

Comedians found Quayle's battle with a TV character good for laughs. But others saw serious issues being raised. Many people saw Quayle's comments as a stab at single mothers and working women. Some saw them as an important statement about the decline of family values and the importance of the two-parent family. In the opening show of the fall season, *Murphy Brown* fought back by poking fun at Quayle and telling the audience that families come in many different shapes and sizes. After the election, the debate seemed to fade away. It flared up again in the spring of 1993, after the *Atlantic Monthly* featured a cover story entitled "Dan Quayle was Right."

Why did a brief remark in a political speech set off such a heated and long-lasting debate? The Dan Quayle-Murphy Brown affair struck a nerve because it touched a central predicament in American society: the gap between the everyday realities of family life and our cultural images of how families ought to be. Contrary to the widespread notion that some flaw in American character or culture is to blame for these trends, comparable shifts are found throughout the industrialized world. All advanced modern countries have experienced shifts in women's roles, rising divorce rates, lower marriage and birth rates, and an increase in single-parent families. In no other country, however, has family change been so traumatic and divisive as ours.

The transformation of family life has been so dramatic that, to many Americans, it has seemed as if "an earthquake had shuddered through the American family" (Preston 1984). Divorce rates first skyrocketed, then stabilized at historically high levels. Women have surged into the workplace. Birth rates have declined. The women's movement has changed the way men and women think and act toward one another, both inside the home and in the world at large. Furthermore, social and sexual rules that once seemed carved in stone have crumbled away: Unmarried couples can live together openly; unmarried mothers can keep their babies. Abortion has become legal. Remaining single and remaining childless, once thought to be highly deviant (although not illegal), have both become acceptable lifestyle options.

Today, most people live in ways that do not conform to the cultural ideal that prevailed in the 1950s. The traditional breadwinner/housewife family with minor children today represents only a small minority of families. The "typical" American family in the last two decades of the twentieth century is likely to be one of four other kinds: the two-wage-earner family, the single-parent family, the "blended" family of remarriage, or the "empty nest" couple whose children have grown up and moved out. Indeed, in 1984, fully half of American families had no children under age 18 (Norton and Glick 1986: 9). Apart from these variations, large numbers of people will spend part of their lives living apart from their families—as single young adults, as divorced singles, as older people who have lost a spouse.

The changes of recent decades have affected more than the forms of family life; they have been psychological changes as well. A major study of American attitudes over two decades revealed a profound shift in how people think about family life, work, and themselves (Veroff, Douvan, and Kulka 1981). In 1957, four-fifths of respondents thought that a man or woman who did not want to marry was sick, immoral, and selfish. By 1976, only one-fourth of respondents thought that choice was bad. Two-thirds were neutral, and one-seventh viewed the choice as good. Summing up many complex findings, the authors conclude that America underwent a "psychological revolution" in the two decades between surveys. Twenty years earlier, people defined their satisfaction and problems—and indeed themselves—in terms of how well they lived up to traditional work and family roles. More recently, people have become more introspective, more attentive to inner experience. Fulfillment has come to mean finding intimacy, meaning, and self-definition, rather than satisfactory performance of traditional roles.

## A DYING INSTITUTION?

All these changes, occurring as they did in a relatively short period of time, gave rise to fears about the decline of the family. Since the early 1970s, anyone watching television or reading newspapers and magazines would hear again and again that the family is breaking down, falling apart, disintegrating, and even becoming "an endangered species." There also began a great nostalgia for the "good old days" when Mom was in the kitchen, families were strong and stable, and life was uncomplicated. This mood of nostalgia mixed with anxiety contributed to the rise of the conservative New Right and helped propel Ronald Reagan into the White House.

In the early 1980s, heady with victory, the conservative movement hoped that by dismantling the welfare state and overturning the Supreme Court's abortion decision, the clock could be turned back and the "traditional" family restored. As the 1990s began, it became clear that such hopes had failed. Women had not returned to full-time homemaking; divorce rates had not returned to the levels of the 1950s. The "liberated" sexuality of the 1960s and 1970s had given way to greater restraint, largely because of fear of AIDS, although the norms of the 1950s did not return.

Despite all the changes, however, the family in America is "here to stay" (Bane 1976). The vast majority of Americans—at least 90 percent—marry and have children, and surveys repeatedly show that family is central to the lives of most Americans. They find family ties their deepest source of satisfaction and meaning, as well as the source of their greatest worries (Mellman, Lazarus, and Rivlin 1990). In sum, family life in America is a complex mixture of both continuity and change.

Although the transformations of the past three decades do not mean the end of family life, they have brought a number of new difficulties. For example, most families now depend on the earnings of wives and mothers, but the rest of society has not caught up to the new realities. There is still an earnings gap between men and women. Employed wives and mothers still bear most of workload in the home. For both men and women, the demands of the job are often at odds with family needs. Debates about whether or not the family is "in decline" do little to solve these dilemmas.

During the same years in which the family was becoming the object of public anxiety and political debate, a torrent of new research on the family was pouring forth. The study of the family had come to excite the interest of scholars in a range of disciplines—history, demography, economics, law, psychology. As a result of this research, we now have much more information available about the family than ever before. Ironically, much of the new scholarship is at odds with the widespread assumption that the family had a long, stable history until hit by the social "earthquake" of the 1960s and 1970s. We have learned from historians that the "lost" golden age of family happiness and stability we yearn for never actually existed....

## THE STATE OF THE
## CONTEMPORARY FAMILY

Part of the confusion surrounding the current status of the family arises from the fact that the family is a surprisingly problematic area of study; there are few if any self-evident facts, even statistical ones. Researchers have found, for example, that when the statistics of family life are plotted for the entire twentieth century, or back into the nineteenth century, a surprising finding emerges:

Today's young people—with their low marriage, high divorce, and low fertility rates—appear to be behaving in ways consistent with long-term historical trends (Cherlin 1981; Masnick and Bane 1980). The recent changes in family life appear deviant only when compared to what people were doing in the 1940s and 1950s. But it was the postwar generation that married young, moved to the suburbs, and had three, four, or more children that departed from twentieth-century trends. As one study put it, "Had the 1940s and 1950s not happened, today's young adults, would appear to be behaving normally" (Masnick and Bane 1980: 2).

Thus, the meaning of "change" in a particular indicator of family life depends on the time frame in which it is placed. If we look at trends over too short a period of time—say ten or twenty years—we may think we are seeing a marked change, when, in fact, an older pattern may be reemerging. For some issues, even discerning what the trends are can be a problem. Whether or not we conclude that there is an "epidemic" of teenage pregnancy depends on how we define adolescence and what measure of illegitimacy we use. Contrary to the popular notion of skyrocketing teenage pregnancy, teen-aged childbearing has actually been on the decline during the past two decades (Luker). It is possible for the *ratio* of illegitimate births to all births to go up at the same time as there are declines in the *absolute number* of births and in the likelihood that an individual will bear an illegitimate child. This is not to say that concern about teenage pregnancy is unwarranted; but the reality is much more complex than the simple and scary notion an "epidemic" implies.

Given the complexities of interpreting data on the family, it is little wonder that, as Joseph Featherstone observes (1979: 37), the family is a "great intellectual Rorschach blot." One's conclusions about the current state of the family often derive from deeper values and assumptions one holds in the first place about the definition and role of the family in society....

## THE MYTH OF A STABLE,
## HARMONIOUS PAST

Laments about the current state of decay of the family imply some earlier era in which the family was more stable and harmonious. But unless we can agree what "earlier time" should be chosen as a baseline and what characteristics of the family should be specified, it makes little sense to speak of family decline. Historians have not, in fact, located a golden age of the family.

Recent historical studies of family life also cast doubt on the reality of family tranquillity. Historians have found that premarital sexuality, illegitimacy, generational conflict, and even infanticide can best be studied as a part of family life itself rather than as separate categories of deviation. For example, William Kessen (1965), in his history of the field of child study, observes:

Perhaps the most persistent single note in the history of the child is the reluctance of mothers to suckle their babies. The running war between the mother who does not want to nurse and the philosopher-psychologists who insist she must stretches over two thousand years (pp. 1–2).

The most shocking finding of the recent wave of historical studies is the prevalence of infanticide throughout European history. Infanticide has long been attributed to primitive peoples or assumed to be the desperate act of an unwed mother. It now appears that infanticide provided a major means of population control in all societies lacking reliable contraception, Europe included, and that it was practiced by families on legitimate children. Historians now believe that increases and decreases in recorded birth rates may actually reflect variations in infanticide rates.

Rather than being an instinctive trait, having tender feelings toward infants — regarding a baby as a precious individual — seems to emerge only when infants have a decent chance of surviving and adults experience enough security to avoid feeling that children are competing with them in a struggle for survival. Throughout many centuries of European history, both of these conditions were lacking.

Another myth about the family is that of changelessness — the belief that the family has been essentially the same over the centuries, until recently, when it began to come apart. Family life has always been in flux; when the world around them changes, families change in response. At periods when a whole society undergoes some major transformation, family change may be especially rapid and dislocating.

In many ways, the era we are living through today resembles two earlier periods of family crisis and transformation in American history (Skolnick 1991). The first occurred the early nineteenth century, when the growth of industry and commerce moved work out of the home. Briefly, the separation of home and work disrupted existing patterns of daily family life, opening a gap between the way people actually lived and the cultural blueprints for proper gender and generational roles (Ryan 1981). In the older pattern, when most people worked on farms, a father was not just the head of the household, but also the boss of the family enterprise. Mother and children and hired hands worked under his supervision. But when work moved out, father — along with older sons and daughters — went with it, leaving behind mother and the younger children. These dislocations in the functions and meaning of family life unleashed an era of personal stress and cultural confusion.

Eventually, a new model of family emerged that not only reflected the new separation of work and family, but glorified it. No longer a workplace, the household now became idealized as "home sweet home," an emotional and spiritual shelter from the heartless world outside. Although father remained the head of the family, mother was now the central figure in the home. The new model celebrated the "true woman's" purity, virtue, and selflessness. Many of our culture's most basic ideas about the family in American culture, such as "women's place is in the home," were formed at this time. In short, the family pattern we now think of as traditional was in fact the first version of the modern family. Historians label this model of the family "Victorian" because it became influential in England and Western Europe as well as in the United States during the reign of Queen Victoria. It reflected, in idealized form, the nineteenth-century middle-class family. However, the Victorian model became the prevailing cultural definition of family. Few families could live up to the ideal in all its particulars; working-class, black, and ethnic families, for example, could not get by without the economic contributions of wives, mothers, and daughters. And even for middle-class families, the Victorian idea prescribed a standard of perfection that was virtually impossible to fulfill (Demos 1986).

Eventually, however, social change overtook the Victorian model. Beginning around the

1880s, another period of rapid economic, social, and cultural change unsettled Victorian family patterns, especially their gender arrangements. Several generations of so-called "new women" challenged Victorian notions of femininity. They became educated, pursued careers, became involved in political causes — including their own — and created the first wave of feminism. This ferment culminated in the victory of the women's suffrage movement. It was followed by the 1920s' jazz age era of flappers and flaming youth — the first, and probably the major, sexual revolution of the twentieth century.

To many observers at the time, it appeared that the family and morality had broken down. Another cultural crisis ensued, until a new cultural blueprint emerged — the companionate model of marriage and the family. The new model was a revised, more relaxed version of the Victorian family; companionship and sexual intimacy were now defined as central to marriage.

This highly abbreviated history of family and cultural change forms the necessary backdrop for understanding the family upheavals of the late twentieth century. As in earlier times, major changes in the economy and society have destabilized an existing model of family life and the everyday patterns and practices that have sustained it. We have experienced a triple revolution: First, the move toward a postindustrial service and information economy; second, a life course revolution brought about the reductions in mortality and fertility; and third, a psychological transformation rooted mainly in rising educational levels.

Although these shifts have profound implications for everyone in contemporary society, women have been the pacesetters of change. Most women's lives and expectations over the past three decades, inside and outside the family, have departed drastically from those of their own mothers. Men's lives today also are different from their fathers' generation, but to a much lesser extent.

## THE TRIPLE REVOLUTION

### The Postindustrial Family

The most obvious way the new economy affects the family is in its drawing women, especially married women, into the workplace. A service and information economy produces large numbers of jobs that, unlike factory work, seem suitable for women. Yet as Jessie Bernard (1982) once observed, the transformation of a housewife into a paid worker outside the home sends tremors through every family relationship. It creates a more "symmetrical" family, undoing the sharp contrast between men's and women's roles that marks the breadwinner/housewife pattern. It also reduces women's economic dependence on men, thereby making it easier for women to leave unhappy marriages.

Beyond drawing women into the workplace, shifts in the nature of work and a rapidly changing globalized economy have unsettled the lives of individuals and families at all class levels. The well-paying industrial jobs that once enabled a blue-collar worker to own a home and support a family are no longer available. The once-secure jobs that sustained the "organization men" and their families in the 1950s and 1960s have been made shaky by downsizing, an unstable economy, corporate takeovers, and a rapid pace of technological change.

The new economic climate has also made the transition to adulthood increasingly problematic. The reduction in job opportunities is in part responsible for young adults' lower fertility rates and for women flooding into the workplace. Further, the family formation patterns of the 1950s are out of step with the increased educational demands of today's postindustrial society. In the post-war years, particularly in the United States, young people entered adulthood in one giant step — going to work, marrying young, moving to a separate household from their parents, and having children quickly. Today, few young adults can afford to marry and have children in their late teens or early twenties. In an economy where a college degree is necessary to earn a living wage, early marriage impedes education for both men and women.

Those who do not go on to college have little access to jobs that can sustain a family. Particularly in the inner cities of the United States, growing numbers of young people have come to see no future for themselves at all in the ordinary world of work. In middle-class families, a narrowing opportunity structure has increased anxieties about downward mobility for offspring and parents as well. The "Hamlet syndrome" or the "incompletely launched young adult syndrome" has become common: Young adults deviate from their parents' expectations by failing to launch careers and become successfully independent adults, and may even come home to crowd their parents' empty nest (Schnaiberg and Goldenberg 1989).

## The Life Course Revolution

The demographic transformations of the twentieth century are no less significant than the economic ones. We cannot hope to understand current predicaments of family life without understanding how radically the demographic and social circumstances of twentieth-century Americans have changed. In earlier times, mortality rates were highest among infants, and the possibility of death from tuberculosis, pneumonia, or other infectious diseases was an ever-present threat to young and middle-aged adults. Before the turn of this century, only 40 percent of women lived through all the stages of a normal life course — growing up, marrying, having children, and surviving with a spouse to the age of 50 (Uhlenberg 1980).

Demographic and economic change has had a profound effect on women's lives. Women today are living longer and having fewer children. When infant and child mortality rates fall, women no longer have to have five or seven or nine children to make sure that two or three will survive to adulthood. After rearing children, the average woman can look forward to three or four decades without maternal responsibilities. Because traditional assumptions about women are based on the notion that they are constantly involved with pregnancy, child rearing, and related domestic concerns, the current ferment about women's roles may be seen as a way of bringing cultural attitudes in line with existing social realities.

As people live longer, they can stay married longer. Actually, the biggest change in twentieth-century marriage is not the proportion of marriages disrupted through divorce, but the potential length of marriage and the number of years spent without children in the home. By the 1970s, the statistically average couple would spend only 18 percent of their married lives raising young children, compared with 54 percent a century ago (Bane 1976). As a result, marriage is becoming defined less as a union between parents raising a brood of children and more as a personal relationship between two individuals.

## A Psychological Revolution

The third major transformation is a set of psychocultural changes that might be described as "psychological gentrification" (Skolnick 1991). That is, cultural advantages once enjoyed only by the upper classes — in particular, education — have been extended to those lower down on the socioeconomic scale. Psychological gentrification also involves greater leisure time, travel, and exposure to information, as well as a general rise in the standard of living. Despite the persistence of poverty, unemployment, and economic insecurity in the industrialized world, far less of the population than in the historical past is living at the level of sheer subsistence.

Throughout Western society, rising levels of education and related changes have been linked to a complex set of shifts in personal and political attitudes. One of these is a more psychological approach to life — greater introspectiveness and a yearning for warmth and intimacy in family and other relationships (Veroff, Douvan, and Kulka 1981). There is also evidence of an increasing preference on the part of both men and women for a more companionate ideal of marriage and a more democratic family. More broadly, these changes in attitude have been described as a shift to "postmaterialist values," emphasizing self-expression, tolerance, equality, and a concern for the quality of life (Inglehart 1990).

The multiple social transformations of our era have brought both costs and benefits: Family relations have become both more fragile and more emotionally rich; mass longevity has brought us a host of problems as well as the gift of extended life. Although change has brought greater opportunities for women, persisting gender inequality means women have borne a large share of the costs of these gains. But we cannot turn the clock back to the family models of the past.

Paradoxically, after all the upheavals of recent decades, the emotional and cultural significance of the family persists. Family remains the center of most people's lives and, as numerous surveys show, a cherished value. Although marriage has become more fragile, the parent-child relationship — especially the mother-child relationship — remains a core attachment across the life course (Rossi and Rossi 1990). The family, however, can be both "here to stay" and beset with difficulties. There is widespread recognition that the massive social and economic changes we have lived through call for public and private sector policies in support of families. Most European countries have recognized for some time that governments must play a role in supplying an array of supports to families — health care, children's allowances, housing subsidies, support for working parents and children (such as child care, parental leave, and shorter workdays for parents), as well as an array of services for the elderly.

Each country's response to these changes...has been shaped by its own political and cultural traditions. The United States remains embroiled in a cultural war over the family; many social commentators and political leaders have promised to reverse the recent trends and restore the "traditional" family. In contrast, other Western nations, including Canada and the other English-speaking countries, have responded to family change by establishing policies aimed at mitigating the problems brought about by economic and social changes. As a result of these policies, these countries have been spared much of the poverty and social disintegration that has plagued the United States in the last decade (Edgar 1993, Smeeding 1992).

## LOOKING AHEAD

The world at the end of the twentieth century is vastly different from what it was at the beginning, or even in the middle. Families are struggling to adapt to new realities. The countries that have been at the leading edge of family change still find themselves struggling with yesterday's norms, today's new realities, and an uncertain future. As we have seen, changes in women's lives have been a pivotal factor in recent family trends. In many countries, there is a considerable difference between men's and women's attitudes and expectations of one another. Even where both partners accept a more equal division of labor in the home, there is often a gap between attitudes and behavior. In no country have employers, the govern-

ment, or men fully caught up to the changes in women's lives.

But a knowledge of family history reveals that the solution to contemporary problems will not be found in some lost golden age. Families have always struggled with outside circumstances and inner conflict. Our current troubles inside and outside the family are genuine, but we should never forget that many of the most vexing issues confronting us derive from benefits of modernization few of us would be willing to give up — for example, longer, healthier lives, and the ability to choose how many children to have and when to have them. There was no problem of the aged in the past, because most people never aged — they died before they got old. Nor was adolescence a difficult stage of the life cycle when children worked, education was a privilege of the rich, and a person's place in society was determined by heredity rather than choice. And when most people were hungry illiterates, only aristocrats could worry about sexual satisfaction and self-fulfillment.

In short, there is no point in giving in to the lure of nostalgia. There is no golden age of the family to long for, nor even some past pattern of behavior and belief that would guarantee us harmony and stability if only we had the will to return to it. Family life is bound up with the social, economic, and ideological circumstances of particular times and places. We are no longer peasants, Puritans, pioneers, or even suburbanites circa 1955. We face conditions unknown to our ancestors, and we must find new ways to cope with them.

## REFERENCES

Bane, M. J. 1976. *Here to Stay.* New York: Basic Books.

Bernard, J. 1982. *The Future of Marriage.* New York: Bantam.

Blake, J. 1978. "Structural Differentiation and the Family: A Quiet Revolution." Presented at American Sociology Association, San Francisco.

Cherlin, A. J. 1981. *Marriage, Divorce, Remarriage.* Cambridge, MA: Harvard University Press.

Demos, John. 1986. *Past, Present, and Personal.* New York: Oxford University Press.

Featherstone, J. 1979. "Family Matters." *Harvard Educational Review* 49, no. 1: 20–52.

Gagnon, J. H., and W. Simon. 1970. *The Sexual Scene.* Chicago: Aldine/Transaction.

Inglehart, Ronald. 1990. *Culture Shift.* New Jersey: Princeton University Press.

Keller, S. 1971. "Does the Family Have a Future?" *Journal of Comparative Studies* Spring.

Kessen, E. W. 1965. *The Child.* New York: John Wiley.

Masnick, G., and M. J. Bane. 1980. *The Nation's Families: 1960–1990.* Boston: Auburn House.

Mellman, A., E. Lazarus, and A. Rivlin. 1990. "Family Time, Family Values." In *Rebuilding the Nest*, edited by D. Blankenhorn, S. Bayme, and J. Elshtain. Milwaukee: Family Service America.

Norton, A. J. and P. C. Glick. 1986. "One-Parent Families: A Social and Economic Profile." *Family Relations* 35: 9–17.

Preston, S. H. 1984. "Presidential Address to the Population Association of America." Quoted in *Family and Nation* by D. P. Moynihan (1986). San Diego: Harcourt Brace Jovanovich.

Rossi, A. S. and P. H. Rossi. 1990. *Of Human Bonding: Parent-Child Relations Across the Life Course.* Hawthorne, New York: Aldine de Gruyter.

Ryan, M. 1981. *The Cradle of the Middle Class.* New York: Cambridge University Press.

Schnaiberg, A. and S. Goldenberg. 1989. "From Empty Nest to Crowded Nest: The Dynamics of Incompletely Launched Young Adults." *Social Problems* 36, no. 3 (June) 251–69.

Skolnick, A. 1991. *Embattled Paradise: The American Family in an Age of Uncertainty.* New York: Basic Books.

Uhlenberg, P. 1980. "Death and the Family." *Journal of Family History* 5, no. 3: 313–20.

Veroff, J., E. Douvan, and R. A. Kulka. 1981. *The Inner American: A Self-Portrait from 1957 to 1976.* New York: Basic Books.

# 52. PROFILING VIOLENT FAMILIES

## RICHARD GELLES AND MURRAY STRAUS

*"Sometimes, the very characteristics that make the family a warm, supportive, and intimate environment also lead to conflict and violence."*

This is indeed a very interesting approach to understanding family violence. It focuses not on the personality traits of violent offenders, but on the structural factors that affect the likelihood of family violence. In a typical sociological fashion, the authors ask us to look closely at the way our structures and institutions work in order to become more aware of the complexities of this problem in society— and also to become more alert to characteristics of own relationships.

## VIOLENCE AND THE SOCIAL ORGANIZATION OF THE FAMILY

The myth that violence and love do not coexist in families disguises a great irony about intimacy and violence. There are a number of distinct organizational characteristics of the family that promote intimacy, but at the very same time contribute to the escalation of conflict to violence and injury. Sometimes, the very characteristics that make the family a warm, supportive, and intimate environment also lead to conflict and violence.

Excerpt from *Physical Violence in American Families: Risk Factors and Adaptations to Violence in 8,145 Families*, by Richard J. Gelles and Murray A. Straus. By permission of Transaction Publishers, © 1990.

The time we spend with our family almost always exceeds the time we spend at work or with nonfamily members. This is particularly true for young children, men and women who are not in the work force, and the very old. From a strictly quantitative point of view, we are at greater risk in the home simply because we spend so much time there. But, time together is not sufficient to lead to violence. What goes on during these times is much more important than simply the minutes, hours, days, weeks, or years spent together.

Not only are we with our parents, partners, and children, but we interact with them over a wide range of activities and interests. Unless you live (and love) with someone, the total range of activities and interests you share are much narrower than intimate, family involvements. Although the range of intimate interactions is great, so is the intensity. When the nature of intimate involvement is deep, the stakes of the involvement rise. Failures are more important. Slights, insults, and affronts hurt more. The pain of injury runs deeper. A cutting remark by a family member is likely to hurt more than the same remark in another setting.

We know more about members of our family than we know about any other individuals we ever deal with. We know their fears, wants, desires, frailties. We know what makes them happy, mad, frustrated, content. Likewise, they know the same about us. The depth of knowledge that makes intimacy possible also reveals the vulnerabilities and frailties that make it possible to escalate conflict. If, for instance, our spouse insults us, we know in an instant what to say to get even. We know enough to quickly support a family member, or to damage him. In no other setting is there a greater potential to support and help, or hurt and harm, with a gesture, a phrase, or a cutting remark. Over and over again, the people we talk to point to an attack on their partner's vulnerabilities as precipitating violence:

If I want to make her feel real bad, I tell her how stupid she is. She can't deal with this, and she hits me.

We tear each other down all the time. He says things just to hurt me—like how I clean the house. I complain about his work—about how he doesn't make enough money to support us. He gets upset, I get upset, we hit each other.

If I really want to get her, I call her dirty names or call her trash.

We found, in many of our interviews with members of violent families, that squabbles, arguments, and confrontations escalate rapidly to violence when one partner focused on the other's vulnerabilities. Jane, a thirty-two-year-old mother, found that criticizing her husband's child-care skills often moved an argument to violence:

Well, we would argue about something, anything. If it was about our kids I would say, "But you shouldn't talk, because you don't even know how to take care of them." If I wanted to hurt him I would use that. We use the kids in our fights and it really gets bad. He [her husband] doesn't think the baby loves him. I guess I contribute to that a bit. When the baby start's fussin' my husband will say "Go to your mom." When I throw it up to him that the baby is afraid of him, that's when the fights really get goin'."

It is perhaps the greatest irony of family relations that the quality that allows intimacy—intimate knowledge of social biographies—is also a potential explosive, ready to be set off with the smallest fuse.

The range of family activities includes deciding what television program to watch, who uses the bathroom first, what house to buy, what job to take, how to raise and discipline the children, or what to have for dinner. Whether the activities are sublime or ridiculous, the outcome is often "zero-sum" for the participants. Decisions and decision making across the range of family activities often mean that one person (or group) will win, while another will lose. If a husband takes a new job in another city, his wife may have to give up her job, while the children may have to leave their friends. If her job and the children's friends are more important, then the husband will lose a chance for job advancement or a higher income. Although the stakes over which television station to watch or which movie to go to may be smaller, the notion of winning and losing is still there. In fact, some of the most intense family conflicts are over what seem to be the most trivial choices. Joanne, a twenty-five-year-old mother of two toddlers, remembers violent fights over whether she and her husband would talk or watch television:

When I was pregnant the violence was pretty regular. John would come home from work. I would want to talk with him, 'cause I had been cooped up in the house with the baby and being pregnant. He would just want to watch the TV. So he would have the TV on and he didn't want to listen to me. We'd have these big fights. He pushed me out of the way. I would get in front of the TV and he would just throw me on the floor.

We talked to one wife who, after a fight over the television, picked the TV up and threw it at her husband. For a short time at least, they did not have a television to fight over.

Zero-sum activities are not just those that require decisions or choices. Less obvious than choices or decisions, but equally or sometimes more important, are infringements of personal space or personal habits. The messy wife and the neat husband may engage in perpetual zero-sum conflict over the house, the bedroom, and even closet space. How should meals be served? When should the dishes be washed? Who left the hairbrush in the sink? How the toothpaste should be squeezed from the tube and a million other daily conflicts and confrontations end with a winner and a loser.

Imagine that you have a co-worker who wears checkered ties with striped shirts, who cannot spell, and whose personal hygiene leaves much to be desired. How likely are you to: (1) tell him that he should change his habits; (2) order him to change; (3) spank him, send him to his room, or cut off his paycheck until he does change? Probably never. Yet, were this person your partner, child, or even parent, you would think nothing of getting involved and trying to influence his behavior. Although the odd behavior of a friend or co-worker may be cause for some embarrassment, we typically would not think of trying to influence this person unless we had a close relationship with him. Yet, family membership carries with it not only the right, but sometimes the obligation, to influence other members of the family. Consequently, we almost always get involved in interactions in the home that we would certainly ignore or make light of in other settings.

Few people notice that the social structure of the family is unique. First, the family has a balance of both males and females. Other settings have this quality — coeducational schools, for instance. But many of the social institutions we are involved in have an imbalance of males and females. Some settings — automobile assembly lines, for instance — may be predominantly male, while other groups — a typing pool, for instance — may be almost exclusively female. In addition to the fact that intimate settings almost always include males and females, families also typically include a range of ages. Half of all households have children under eighteen years of age in them. Thus the family, more so than almost any other social group or social setting, has the potential for both generational and sex differences and conflicts. The battle between the sexes and the generation gap have long been the source of intimate conflict.

Not only is the family made up of males and females with ages ranging from newborn to elderly,

but the family is unique in how it assigns tasks and responsibilities. No other social group expects its members to take on jobs simply on the basis of their age or their sex. In the workplace, at school, and in virtually every other social setting, roles and responsibilities are primarily based on interest, experience, and ability. In the home, duties and responsibilities are primarily tied to age and gender. There are those who argue that there is a biological link between gender and task — that women make better parents than men. Also, the developmental abilities of children certainly preclude their taking on tasks or responsibilities they are not ready for. But, by and large, the fact that roles and responsibilities are age and gender linked is a product of social organization and not biological determinism.

When someone is blocked from doing something he or she is both interested in and capable of doing, this can be intensely frustrating. When the inequality is socially structured and sanctioned within a society that at the same time espouses equal opportunity and egalitarianism, it can lead to intense conflict and confrontation. Thus, we find that the potential for conflict and violence is especially high in a democratic and egalitarian society that sanctions and supports a male-dominated family system. Even if we did not have values that supported democracy and egalitarianism, the linking of task to gender would produce considerable conflict because not every man is capable of taking on the socially prescribed leadership role in the home; and not every woman is interested in and capable of assuming the primary responsibility for child care.

The greater the inequality, the more one person makes all the decisions and has all the power, the greater the risk of violence. Power, power confrontations, and perceived threats to domination, in fact, are underlying issues in almost all acts of family violence. One incident of nearly deadly family violence captures the meaning of power and power confrontations:

My husband wanted to think of himself as the head of the household. He thought that the man should wear the pants in the family. Trouble was, he couldn't seem to get his pants on. He had trouble getting a job and almost never could keep one. If I didn't have my job as a waitress, we would have starved. Even though he didn't make no money, he still wanted to control the house and the kids. But it was my money, and I wasn't about to let him spend it on booze or gambling. This really used to tee him off. But he would get the maddest when the kids showed him no respect. He and I argued a lot. One day we argued in the kitchen and my little girl came in. She wanted to watch TV. My husband told her to go to her room. She said, "No, I don't have listen to you!" Well, my husband was red. He picked up a knife and threw it at my little girl. He missed. Then he threw a fork at her and it caught her in the chin. She was bloody and crying, and he was still mad and ran after her. I had to hit him with a chair to get him to stop. He ran out of the house and didn't come back for a week. My little girl still has a scar on her cheek.

You can choose whom to marry, and to a certain extent you may chose to end the marital relationship. Ending a marital relationship, even in the age of no-fault divorce, is not neat and simple. There are social expectations that marriage is a long-term commitment—"until death do us part." There are social pressures that one should "work on a relationship" or "keep the family together for the sake of the children." There are also emotional and financial constraints that keep families together or entrap one partner who would like to leave.

You can be an ex-husband or an ex-wife, but not an ex-parent or an ex-child. Birth relationships are quite obviously involuntary. You cannot choose you parents or your children (with the exception of adoption, and here your choices are still limited).

Faced with conflict, one can fight or flee. Because of the nature of family relations, it is not easy to choose the flight option when conflict erupts. Fighting, then, becomes a main option for resolving intimate conflict.

The organization of the family makes for stress. Some stress is simply developmental—the birth of a child, the maturation of children, the increasing costs of raising children as they grow older, illness, old age, and death. There are also voluntary transitions—taking a new job, a promotion, or moving. Stress occurring outside of the home is often brought into the home—unemployment, trouble with the police, trouble with friends at school, trouble with people at work. We expect a great deal from our families: love, warmth, understanding, nurturing, intimacy, and financial support. These expectations, when they cannot be fulfilled, add to the already high level of stress with which families must cope.

Privacy is the final structural element of modern families that makes them vulnerable to conflict, which can escalate into violence.... The nuclear structure of the modern family, and the fact that it is the accepted norm that family relations are private relations, reduces the likelihood that someone will be available to prevent the escalation of family conflict to intimate violence.

We have identified the factors that contribute to the high level of conflict in families. These factors also allow conflicts to become violent and abusive interchanges. By phrasing the discussion differently, we could have presented these factors as also contributing to the closeness and intimacy that people seek in family relations. People who marry and have families seek to spend large amounts of time together, to have deep and long-lasting emotional involvement, to have an intimate and detailed knowledge of another person, and to be able to create some distance between their intimate private lives and the interventions of the outside world.

There are a number of conclusions one can draw from the analysis of the structural factors that raise the risk of conflict and violence in the family. First, there is a link between intimacy and violence. Second is the classic sociological truism— structures affect people. Implicit in the discussion of these factors is that one can explain part of the problem of violence in the home without focusing on the individual psychological status of the perpetrators of violence and abuse. Violence occurs, not just because it is committed by weird, bad, different, or alien people, but because the structure of the modern household is conducive to violent exchanges.

## FAMILY CHARACTERISTICS RELATED TO INTIMATE VIOLENCE

The structural arrangement of the family makes it possible for violence to occur in all households. However, not all homes are violent....

Economic adversity and worries about money pervade the typical violent home. Alicia, the 34-year-old wife of an assembly-line worker, has beaten, kicked, and punched both her children. So has her husband, Fred. She spoke about the economic problems that hung over their heads:

He worries about what kind of a job he's going to get, or if he's going to get a job at all. He always worries about supporting the family. I think I worry about it more than he does.... It gets him angry and frustrated. He gets angry a lot. I think he gets angry at himself for not providing what he feels we need. He has to take it out on someone, and the kids and me are the most available ones.

We witnessed a more graphic example of the impact of economic stress during one of our in-home interviews with a violent couple. When we entered the living room to begin the interview, we could not help but notice the holes in the living room walls. During the course of the interview, Jane, the 24–year-old mother of three children, told us that her husband had been laid off from his job at a local shipyard and had come home, taken out his shotgun, and shot up the living room. Violence had not yet been directed at the children, but as we left and considered the family, we could not help but worry about the future targets of violent outbursts.

Stressful life circumstances are the hallmark of the violent family. The greater the stress individuals are under, the more likely they are to be violent toward their children. Our 1976 survey of violence in the American family included a measure of life stress. Subjects were asked whether they had experienced any of a list of 18 stressful events in the last year, ranging from problems at work, to death of a family member, to problems with children. Experience with stress ranged from households that experienced no stressful event to homes that had experienced 13 of the 18 items we discussed.

The average experience with stress, however, was modest — about two stressful life events each year. Not surprisingly, the greater the number of stressful events experienced, the greater the rate of abusive violence toward children in the home. More than one out of three families that were unfortunate enough to encounter ten or more stressful events reported using abusive violence toward a child in the previous year. This rate was 100 percent greater than the rate for households experiencing only one stressful incident.

Violent parents are likely to have experienced or been exposed to violence as children. Although this does not predetermine that they will be violent (and likewise, some abusive parents grew up in nonviolent homes), there is the heightened risk that a violent past will lead to a violent future.

A final characteristic of violent parents is that they are almost always cut off from the community they live in. Our survey of family violence found that the most violent parents have lived in their community for less than two years. They tend to belong to few, if any, community organizations and have little contact with friends and relatives. This social isolation cuts them off from any possible source of help to deal with the stresses of intimate living or economic adversity. These parents are not only more vulnerable to stress, their lack of social involvement also means that they are less likely to abandon their violent behavior and conform to community values and standards. Not only are they particularly vulnerable to responding violently to stress, they tend not to see this behavior as inappropriate.

---

# 53. THE SOCIOLOGICAL STUDY OF RELIGION

## BRYAN WILSON

*"[We are not saying that] a sociologist of religion cannot be personally a religiously committed man; clearly that is a possibility. But in his sociological work, he must adopt the professional stance of the detached, neutral, and objective investigator; and this we may take as a necessary qualification."*

*There are some things about society many people would prefer not to study objectively. One such area is religion. Religious institutions are defined as sacred to the believer; they are a central part of society to the sociologist. Bryan Wilson reminds us to maintain objectivity if we are to understand religion. He skillfully shows us the difficulties inherent in the scientific study of religion.*

...The sociology of religion is committed, as is any branch of sociology, to the maintenance of a scientific orientation. In this respect, it becomes important to recognize just what the sociology of religion seeks to do and what lies beyond its range of possibilities. In the first place, the sociology of religion takes the formulations of a religious movement, or the religious dispositions of a people, as its points of departure. The statement of beliefs, the prescriptions of ritual, and their basis of legitimation are all taken as basic data—as phenomena existent at the emergent level from which the sociology of religion must proceed. The sociologist is not concerned to test the "truth" of belief. He is not concerned with the efficacy of rituals. He does not attempt to judge between divergent interpretations of a tradition. He does not challenge the claimed legitimation for practices and ideas that religionists endorse. All of these things he must accept as part of the data. He proceeds at the emergent social level, with a body of information that must, in the first instance, come from the believers themselves. Whether his interest is in the nature of religious belief, in the appeal of religious teachings or rituals, in the processes of conversion, in the character of organization, in the regularity of religious practice, in the consequences of becoming religiously committed, in the relation of priests to laymen, in the style and function of religious legitimation, or whatever else it may be, the sociologist must first take the self-interpretation of religious individuals and groups as the point of departure from which his study begins. He does not, of course, seek to learn the doctrines of a religion in the same way in which believers seek to learn. He is not going to become a disciple. Were he to do so, he would necessarily cease to be a sociologist. But he should at least seek to understand

exactly what it is that a disciple learns, and as far as possible, he should seek to understand what *they* understand and should do so in *their* terms. Now clearly, because he is to remain detached and apart, there will inevitably be a gap between the ultimate meaning for him and the meaning for the believer of the same formulations. But he can, and indeed must, seek to acquire an empathic understanding of *their* commitment and *their* beliefs. Only if he can gain some apprehension of what it means to be a believer can he say anything useful about the religious movement he studies; and yet, in gaining that understanding, he must not actually become a believer.[1]

It will be apparent that the cultivation of what I call "sympathetic detachment" will always remain a matter of difficulty, and between sympathy and detachment there is a frontier of tension. Mixing with a religious group, a sociologist may feel deeply drawn to them and to their activities, and this may be necessary for the fullest understanding of them. But he must also remember that his brief is to interpret religion sociologically; his values lie in a scientific discipline and, in consequence, he must always maintain appropriate distance. It is sometimes objected by religious people that to properly understand a religion one must belong to it. Scholars in any of the disciplines that make religion their object of study cannot accept that. One does not need to be a medieval man to study medieval society, nor a tribesman to understand a tribal group. Indeed, this objection to the sociological study of religion is an objection to the detached and objective approach of any academic discipline. We may, of course, concede the obvious fact that, at one level, the sociologist will never understand as much as does a believer of equal intelligence and perspicacity. At another level, however, because he sees from the outside, he may acquire a much sharper perspective about a religion and about the practices of its adherents than is possible for those who are committed and who can see only from the inside. Thus, at best, the sociologist should be able to add a whole dimension to the understanding of a religious movement that believers themselves could not obtain from their own perspective. In certain ways, he will know less than they do; in other ways, he will know more. Part of his way of knowing "more" will of course come not only from his objectivity and detachment, but also from the fact that he has access, or should have access, to a wider body of information about other comparable religious movements. Comparison is a fundamental requirement of sociological method. From comparisons arise hypotheses of wider generality, and formulations that can transcend, in their abstraction, the circumstances of given cases. Without betraying the peculiarities and particularities of any given movement or any given cultural context, the sociologist should be able to gain some useful interpretative insight from an examination of comparable cases, and from the generalizations that his colleagues and teachers have already established with respect to them.

A number of problems arise from the distinctive stance adopted by the sociologist of religion, not all of which can be easily resolved. The basic problem for the investigator is implicit in his role: sympathy and detachment are not easily balanced....

There are other problems that are often closely associated with one another in practice, but that, for analytical purposes, we may treat separately. First, the application of scientific procedures to human phenomena presents difficulties. The religious participants feel deeply about their faith. In some respects, it is for them not only the true interpretation of life, but it is also inextricably part of life itself. Life is lived according to the dictates of the truth as they see it, and, in consequence, their religion becomes, for seriously committed people, what life is about. Obviously, for the sociologist of religion, the religious movement and its members are a subject matter that constitute sociological phenomena. But no sociologist would succeed in studying religion were he not to appreciate the profound seriousness of religion to its adherents. He cannot therefore be casually clinical in the way that, for example, medical men sometimes appear to be casual in their clinical view of their cases. Furthermore, the measure of his seriousness, in a

sense his dedication (even though it is dedication to his discipline — the sociology of religion — and not to religion *per se*), is quickly appraised by those whom he seeks as informants and respondents.

Arising from this problem is the fact that scientific procedures may easily appear profane in the context of religion. Usually, people will much more readily discuss their leisure-time pursuits — their work and industrial relations, their problems arising from ecological and urban development, their political opinions, and even their familial, kinship, and sexual relationships and activities — than their religious dispositions and beliefs. This very sensitivity of the area of enquiry — which is perhaps more evident in some respects in the West — presents the sociologist of religion with a delicate problem in the conduct of his research. Not only must his attitude be much more delicately attuned to the expectations of his respondents than is the case in most other sociological research, but it is likely that many of the methods of enquiry used by sociologists in other fields are unavailable to him, or are usable only with great circumspection. Above all, he must avoid the impression of using methods that appear to trivialize, disparage, or relativize the activities of his respondents....

Quite apart from the attempt to convey the distinctive character of a religious movement and its believers, there are problems that arise between sociologists and believers in the analysis by which sociologists seek to explain religious phenomena. To take only one important example, the sociologist will necessarily have in mind comparative cases when considering the development, general belief system, social composition, and social activities of any religious movement. He will wish to examine each movement in the light of the implicit understanding that is derived from the knowledge of other movements and other cultures. This is an implicit element of sociological procedure; comparison is vital to it. But there is a sense in which comparison must be odious to the committed adherents of any religion. Each religion is claimed as the most complete system and expression of ultimate truth, with warranted and necessary practices, and complete legitimation. This is more emphatically the case in the West, where religions have arisen in hostility to each other, and where exclusivism has been the norm. Adherents know, of course, that their own faith is not the only one that has claimed to possess the unique and universal truth, or at least to present a full expression of the truth that, in other religions, is understood at best partially; nonetheless, the idea that different movements might be examined in impartial comparison is not one that commends itself to religious believers. Here the divergent value orientations of the adherent and the sociologist become apparent, and the adherent is called on to display a tolerance about sociological investigation that his own religious commitment may make difficult. There is no final solution to this problem for exclusivistic religions, even though in practice the point is not always pressed.

The intrinsic claims of a religion cannot be represented by the sociologist as direct first-order statements to his own public. He must say, "the members of religion X claim so-and-so." If he is careless in his formulation of their self-claim, he may find himself in difficulty — and regarded as in some sense hostile to the movement he has been studying. Some years ago, I had to write a short *Encyclopedia* article about Mormonism.[2] I said that the movement began in the United States in about 1830. That proposition is accepted by all non-Mormons, and might be tolerated even by Mormons, but to some very deeply committed Mormons, it was a misstatement: They claimed that their religion was at that time simply "re-founded" after its extinction for centuries. Clearly, if adherents are adamant that the movement's self-claims are the absolute truth and are beyond compromise, even for the benefit of a public that is uninstructed in it, the sociologist of religion will find himself in a position of insurmountable difficulty....

The scientific orientation of the sociology of religion is deliberate. The steady consolidation of this position among those who investigate religion in its social implications has created a sense of distinction between this explicitly professional commitment and the work of religiously committed commentators that is necessarily regarded as amateur. This is not to say that a sociologist of religion cannot be *personally* a religiously committed man; clearly that is a possibility. But in his sociological work, he must adopt the professional stance of the detached, neutral, and objective investigator; and this we may take as a necessary qualification....

For his religious public, the professional sociologist of religion is something of a curiosity. Here is a man seen to be deeply interested in religion and (one may hope) seen to be widely informed about it. And yet he is not, and quite deliberately not, a religiously committed man — at least, while practicing his sociology. The religious people with whom he works know that his values are not their values. And yet he clearly knows a great deal about the religion he is studying. Sometimes respondents say, as they have said to me, "You know a lot about us; you know about the truth: Why do you not join us?" It is a difficult — a fundamental — question; but it is an understandable question and a perfectly proper question. The sociologist cannot say, "I know what you think is the truth, but I do not accept it." Indeed, it would be professionally wrong to discuss what one accepted or rejected as "the truth." The respondents know that one is not committed to their perspective. They ask because they have a genuine concern for another human being — and if they are concerned, this is an indication that they perceive the sympathy that a sociologist of religion must feel for his respondents. To be asked is to be paid a compliment. But it is also a dilemma. The best answer I can give to such a question is to say, as I have said on occasions, "You must regard me as a photographer. Because I am taking pictures of what I find, I cannot be in the picture myself." It is not a perfect reply, and it does not solve the serious implications of the question, but it maintains the investigator's detachment and the integrity of the professional nature of his commitment; it sustains the necessary sympathetic relationship of investigator and respondent; and it provides some analogous justification for the meeting point of their different set of values.

## ENDNOTES

1. This methodological position may be supported in considerable measure from Max Weber's writings: See two discussions as translated into English, Max Weber, *The Methodology of the Social Sciences* (translated by Edward A. Shils and Henry A. Finch), Glencoe, IL: The Free Press, 1949; and Max Weber, *Basic Concepts in Sociology* (translated by H. P. Secher), London: Peter Owen, 1962.

2. This article appears in the current edition of the *Encyclopedia Britannica*.

# 54. RELIGION, COMMUNITY, AND THE SMALL-GROUP MOVEMENT

ROBERT WUTHNOW

*"As people try to rediscover the sacred, they are led to ask questions about community. And as they seek community, they are led to ask questions about the sacred. Both quests are propelling their interest in small, intimate groups."*

Robert Wuthnow's study of religion in the United States has identified a very important trend: Increasingly, people are turning away from large established traditional churches for spiritual fulfillment and toward small groups in which both spirituality and a sense of community are likely to meet their religious and social needs. Wuthnow, like many sociologists and philosophers, is concerned about what happens to people without strong ties to a larger community. What happens to us when we draw further and further into ourselves? He believes that one way we deal with this in modern society is to seek support in small groups.

From whence does the small-group movement originate? Why has it arisen at this particular moment in history? To answer these questions, we must turn directly to the role of spirituality in American culture, to the quest for community, and to the complex interplay between the two. It is in this vortex that the small-group movement has emerged and acquired its distinctive appeal. The movement is a response both to the intense yearning for the sacred that characterizes the American people and to the breakdown of communities, neighborhoods, families, and other sources of personal support. As people try to rediscover the sacred, they are led to ask questions about community. And as they seek community, they are led to ask questions about the sacred. Both quests are propelling their interest in small, intimate groups. The current strength of the movement is thus a function of the fact that it arises from two prevailing characteristics of American society. The

Excerpt from *Sharing the Journey,* by Robert Wuthnow (Free Press, 1994).

fragmented lives that many of us lead provide an *incentive* to seek community in support groups. But the religious traditions that are so much a part of American culture *legitimate* this quest by telling us that community is important, and, indeed, by leading us to believe that community is also the way to find spirituality and transcendence. A brief examination of these two features of our society will help us understand the forces currently propelling the small-group movement.

## YEARNING FOR THE SPIRITUAL

The contemporary quest for the sacred is not new. Americans always have been intense seekers of spirituality. The first settlers prayed for divine guidance and beseeched God to bless their journey to the New World. Subsequent generations found spirituality to be as essential to their lives as the bread they ate. They read the Bible, prayed, and sought God's blessings as they planted their crops, bore their children, experienced the joy of living, and faced illness and death.[1] They pursued the sacred in their private — and vastly differing — ways because the spiritual then, as now, was a matter of individual conscience.

But this personal faith was only part of the story: Americans have always expressed their religious convictions in communities as well as individually. The Puritans may have sought spirituality deep within their own souls, but they were a communal people who met regularly in corporate acts of worship. The pioneers who journeyed westward were known for their rugged individualism, yet they planted churches everywhere they went. As the nation grew, popular piety grew apace, fostered by Methodist class meetings and Baptist Bible studies.[2] People may have been converted individually in the revival meetings that swept through farming areas and cities alike, but they started fellowship groups, attended ladies' aid societies, and swelled the ranks of Sunday school classes.[3]

Spirituality went hand in hand with group life for historic, theological, and practical reasons. The historic reason was that personal piety had been expressed in this way for as long as anyone could remember. Even the earliest Christians met in groups, forming churches in their homes and subjecting their interests in spirituality to the authority of their fellow believers.[4] The theological reason was that Christianity encouraged believers to come together and form bonds of love and fellowship like those taught by their Lord. The practical reason was that believers found they needed one another for support. Without the affirmation of others, their faith was weakened.

We are still a deeply spiritual people. Despite all the material progress that was supposed to take our minds off God, and despite all the scientific advancement that was going to undermine our faith that God even existed, most Americans continue to express a need in one way or another for spirituality in their lives. Some people realize this need when they struggle to understand themselves and feel drawn to the spiritual insights of poets and religious writers. Many people see it when they are caught up in anxiety and find comfort in uttering a prayer. Others may be drawn to spirituality by the beauty of nature or by the cry of a newborn baby.

Opinion surveys show just how widespread the search for spirituality is in our society. In a recent study, 79 percent of the American public said they think about their relation to God "a lot" or "a fair amount" of the time. In the same study, 82 percent gave the same answers to questions about how much they think about the basic meaning and value of their life. And 68 percent said they think this much about developing their faith. In this study, as in other studies, only about one person in twenty seemed to consider the sacred unimportant.[5]

Other evidence demonstrates that the search for spirituality is more than a casual response to the latest public opinion pollster. As a nation, we purchase more Bibles per capita than in any other industrialized society. The market for religious and devotional books is a billion-dollar-a-year industry. So is religious television. Virtually everyone claims to believe in God, and the vast majority pray to this God regularly.[6] Philosophers who once were content to write that life had no inherent meaning are now devoting increasing attention to questions about the meaning and purpose of human existence. Hundreds of thousands of college students flock each year to courses in religious studies departments.[7] Meditation appears to be at an all-time high. Even political figures and business leaders claim to seek divine guidance in making important decisions.

## THE LOSS OF COMMUNITY?

This interest in spirituality is, in many ways, like that of our ancestors. But the deep ties with community that sustained people in their faith and in their lives over the centuries, argue many social observers, may now be on the verge of collapse.[8] The villages and farming communities where most people lived at the start of the twentieth century have become virtually extinct. A century ago, nearly three-quarters of the American population lived in small towns and in rural areas. Today, fewer than one-quarter reside in these locales. Nationally, the vast majority of people live in metropolitan areas. If the South is excluded, these areas now include more than 80 percent of the population. The composition of urban areas has also changed dramatically over the past century. At one time, urban neighborhoods — reinforced by a common ethnic heritage, language, customs, local shops, and schools — provided community, but these, too, mostly have been lost. People now live anonymous lives in suburban housing developments or in high-rise apartment buildings. Instead of feeling a common bond with our neighbors, we fear them.[9]

To be sure, the situation has not become as bad as some gloomy forecasts predicted. In the 1950s, when television first became popular, many commentators worried that Americans would simply retreat into their living rooms, watch sitcoms with abandon, and never come out again. Harvard sociologist David Riesman, in his widely read book *The Lonely Crowd*, envisioned a society in which people were thrown together in shallow ways but had neither the courage to be themselves nor the desire to share intimately with anyone else.[10] Others predicted the rise of widespread mental illness because people would be isolated and have no friends. Most of these forecasts have failed to come true. People do not sit at home watching television all the time (although they spend an enormous amount of time doing so). They still go to work, make sure that their children go to school, and find time on weekends to attend ball games and go shopping. People have not become nameless faces in the crowd. Instincts to blend into the herd notwithstanding, people still jealously guard their individuality, and often do so by cherishing their family heritage, their ethnic identity, and their national origins.[11] Instead of being entirely isolated, most people still have close friends, and many of these friends live in the same community.[12]

But genuine community entails more than simply having friends with the same zip code. We may know some of our neighbors well enough to wave as they whiz by on their way to work in the morning. We may stop to chat once in a while or take them pumpkin bread at Christmas as a neighborly gesture. We may even consider them our friends. It is more doubtful that we have ever discussed our most cherished values with these neighbors. It is equally doubtful that these neighbors can help us recover from addictions or dysfunctional family backgrounds or that they can help mentor us when we are uncertain about the core of our identity. The same may be true of the people we know at church. Sitting together in the pews on Sunday morning, we may feel that there is much in common among us. But do we know that? Skeptics, at least, ask: Have we ever opened up to these people by admitting our fears, discussing our deepest anxieties, or sharing our most basic dreams and aspirations?

In other ways, personal experience in contemporary society often leads us to see evidence all around us of the breakdown of community. The smile and "hello" that used to greet us at the grocery store have been replaced by the pallid face of an automaton who busily passes our items across a bar-code scanner. Work was once a place where people did the same things, knew the same skills, and shared a common destiny. Now the boss may be miles away, linked to us by satellite and computer networks, and our coworkers may have become our most bitter competitors. If we are lucky, we may have some close friends at work — after all, we spend an increasing share of our waking hours in the workplace. But we also know that the hectic pace of everyday life makes it harder to keep up with our friends, and we know that the large-scale institutions that make up our society do not make the quest for community any easier. Faced with impersonality, bureaucratic red tape, and incessant competition, we may be sorely tempted to launch a full-scale retreat from public life.

Social observers worry that we may be making these conditions worse, rather than better, by retreating more and more into our private lives. Individualism, they remind us, once meant being responsible for ourselves *and* our neighbors. But we have replaced this traditional concept with a more radical individualism that looks out for number one at the expense of everyone else.[13] In the 1970s, this radical individualism came to be associated with the Me Generation, as people struggled to find themselves and turned inward. This period was followed by the Decade of Greed: Failing to find anything deep within themselves, people seemed to give up and merely opted for the chance to collect as many toys for themselves as they could before dying.

Most people, however, seem to believe at some level that this self-centered individualism is no way to live. They may not have the security of a tight-knit neighborhood, but they want it. They may not enjoy the comfort of a warm family, but they wish they could. They value their individual freedom, but they go through life feeling lonely. They desire intimacy and wonder how to find it. They cling to the conviction that they have close friends who care about them, but they frequently feel distant from these friends. They worry what would happen if they were truly in need.[14] Wanting community, and not being able to find it, they turn to other solutions, some of which become their worst enemies.

In the case of Betty, a young woman at the Alcoholics Anonymous group...the intense loneliness in her first year away from home at college led her to drink. For a time she was able to tell herself that she would never be lonely again. The bottle would always be her friend. Others tell themselves the same thing about their work. As long as they can stay head-over-heels in love with their projects, they will never need anyone else.

Religious leaders, sensing the dysfunctional behavior and pain that come when people lack the care and support they need, are increasingly pointing out how desperately the American public needs to rediscover community. As the rector of a church populated mostly by busy suburban professionals lamented recently, "What community we used to enjoy has slowly been taken away as people are off commuting to work in another city, and the children are all in different school districts, and the whole family is following a different schedule." Even the church, he felt, was being undermined by these centrifugal forces. "Before, you already knew people from your neighborhood, and therefore you would know them in church. But now we have to reinvent ways to get [community] back."

Rebuilding community, then, is the challenge, at least according to many religious leaders and social observers alike. For each of us, as individuals, can we find the caring and supportive communities we so deeply desire, and can these communities nurture us on our spiritual journeys in the ways they have done in the past? Or must people of our time go the distance alone, facing the ultimate questions of their existence in the lonely solitude of their hearts? And for us, as community and religious leaders or simply as responsible citizens, can we reinvent ways to find community? Or must we see our society driven ever more by the fragmenting forces of the marketplace, the mass media, and the impersonal demands of bureaucratic organizations? Certainly, this yearning for community is one of the significant forces behind the recent rise of the small-group movement.

## THE TURN INWARD

The lack of community may be serious in its own right, but it is even more serious when we consider how closely spirituality has always been linked to community. Indeed, many observers wonder if spirituality can survive the challenges of our society if it is not connected again in some meaningful way with the power and support of caring communities. Spirituality, they fear, will retreat so far inside the individual that it may never come out again. And if it does not, is it really spirituality?

Even to suggest this possibility is likely to arouse some disagreement. Isn't spirituality, after all, fundamentally a matter of the heart? Mustn't it be the individual who seeks the sacred, explores the mysteries of life, and comes up with answers that are uniquely and individually satisfactory? How genuine can a conviction be if it doesn't touch the inner being of the individual?

We can answer all these questions in a way that upholds the value of the individual and of a deep inner spirituality. And yet we can still ask whether spirituality is becoming such a private affair in our time that it loses much of its power. We can certainly question a spirituality that fails to result in any love of neighbor. We can also ask how well a purely inward spirituality may function for the individual as a person. Doesn't that person still need encouragement to engage in this inner quest? Aren't there times when people run into dead ends in their search for spirituality and need to talk about it with others? Isn't the connection between spirituality and basic human needs likely to be closer when intimacy and caring are part of a person's experience? And isn't it likely that his or her spirituality will be enriched by the chance to express it in public or to see it acted out and reaffirmed by trusted loved ones?

Certainly it is unnecessary to look far to find strong statements about the inherent connections between a commitment to healthy, caring communities and spirituality. Philosopher Robert Fuller, reviewing the recent literature in a number of academic disciplines, concludes: "Wholeness or fulfillment is…necessarily a collective rather than a personal issue. In the complex web of life, individuality is important, but never final."[15] In a similar vein, Gordon Kaufman asserts: "Life itself has a structure of interdependence, and unless human living and thinking and working can become increasingly oriented accordingly, and we learn to subordinate our particular interests and desires as individuals and communities…to this wider loyalty to on-going life—both human and other—we shall certainly all perish."[16]

The possibility that spirituality is becoming a victim of the loss of community was suggested some years ago in Thomas Luckmann's book *The Invisible Religion.*[17] Luckmann argued that fundamental religious convictions and world views in modern societies are increasingly separated from our dominant institutions—namely, the political and economic institutions that govern so much of our lives. As a result, spirituality is becoming more a matter of personal choice and private belief. But, he asked, can these choices ever carry the weight once associated with the God of heaven whose existence was independent of ours? Don't we need to live in community with others in order to see that the hand of God is not simply a figment of our imaginations?[18]

In a more recent book, some anecdotal evidence of how much religious faith may have retreated into the inner life is provided by Robert N. Bellah and his co-authors in their widely read volume *Habits of the Heart.*[19] They interviewed a woman named Sheila who had invented her own religion and named it after herself (Sheilaism). This woman, they argued, represents only the latest of a long history of pietists in our society who have looked inside themselves to find evidence of the divine. What is different, they suggest, is that this woman's faith is contained entirely inside herself. It is not an inner light planted in her conscience by a transcendent God, but an inner strength that comes from knowing herself and resolving to be good. Faith of this kind, said Bellah and his co-authors, "involves a kind of radical individualism that tends to elevate the self to a cosmic principle."[20]

Certainly a person's faith must be personal, a matter of conviction, a belief that is part of that person's fundamental outlook on life. When we say that religious beliefs are personal and private, though, we may ignore the importance of their public dimension. Throughout history, men and women of faith have declared their convictions in public, taken a stand on what they believed to be right, and sometimes given their lives for those convictions. In our society, it has become much more common to believe that people should keep their religious convictions to themselves lest they offend someone by speaking out. Even among devout believers, a norm of polite civility that turns even absolute truth into a matter of personal opinion seems to prevail.[21]

It is also partially correct to say that personal spirituality does not depend on being involved in any religious organization. The prevalence of this view first became evident in a 1978 survey in which 78 percent of the American public agreed that "a person can be a good Christian or Jew if he or she doesn't attend church or synagogue." Ten years later, a follow-up study found that an equally high proportion (76 percent) still held this view.[22]

For the last few years of his life, my grandfather lived in a nursing home in a different town from the one where he had gone to church all his life. He was a man of deep faith, and this faith remained central to his life until his death, even though he was unable to be part of a religious community. He was living proof of the validity of the statement asked about in the poll. Some of the men who were held as hostages in the Middle East during the 1980s kept themselves going through the long days and nights of their captivity by cultivating their relationship with God. They were able to do so despite being thousands of miles away from the religious organizations with which they were formally affiliated. Our culture, however, has taken this partial truth and extended it. Millions of Americans claim to believe in God and say spirituality is important among their values, but they do not belong to any religious community and do not participate in the services of any religious organization. In the survey just cited, 80 percent of the public agreed that "an individual should arrive at his or her own religious beliefs independent of any churches or synagogues."

Many people in our society have turned inward to find God because they have become disillusioned with the clergy and the churches. People of faith have always recognized the dangers of pledging too much unthinking loyalty to religious authorities. The Protestant Reformation, for example, asserted explicitly that people should be their own priests rather than thinking that the clergy had more direct access to God than they did. It also criticized the established church for being badly out of step with the times, if not morally and spiritually corrupt. These attitudes have reappeared in new guise in our own culture in recent decades. At an earlier time, clergy were regarded with respect for having heard a special call from God and having devoted their lives to that calling, including gaining extensive knowledge of the scriptures and of theology. In our time, though, many clergy are uncertain of their calling, and their authority seems fairly ordinary compared with the vast knowledge commanded by other professionals, such as scientists and physicians.[23] The church has become but one among many ways in which people can pursue their spirituality. If they disagree with the church's position on issue X, they can merely stay home, watch a religious program on television, read an inspirational book, or meditate to their favorite devotional tape.

Observers of American religion also believe the turn inward has been encouraged by the pluralism and relativism so widely evident in our culture. With a thousand and one different denominations to choose from, it has been easy for many people to conclude that all churches must be alike. Just going to one that you like is the important criterion. But it is an easy step from there, once you become dissatisfied at that church, to say that it doesn't make much difference whether you attend at all. The important goal is to believe something firmly and to behave yourself when you are around other people whose views are different. As evidence, one survey found that more than half the American public (57 percent) agreed that "it doesn't matter what church a person attends — one church is as good as another."[24]

For all these reasons, the communal dimension of spirituality has suffered. Many people in our society are so withdrawn into themselves that they find it difficult to seek help from others when their convictions start to unravel. They many find it equally difficult to give support when other people seek answers. The result is a privatized faith that may leave the individual feeling alone and alienated. Even if such faith remains strong for the individual, it may prove difficult to transmit to one's children, and it may do little to address the wider ills that beset our society.

## SMALL GROUPS

The small-group movement has emerged as a serious effort to combat the forces of fragmentation and anonymity in our society and to reunite spirituality with its roots in human community. The movement developed on a national scale in the 1960s as a result of a wide variety of local efforts that proved to have increasing value to those involved in them. Training groups, or "T-groups" as they were called, emerged in business settings to give people experience in discussing personal and work-related problems with their peers. Encounter groups grew out of the more specialized group therapy sessions that began in the 1950s and then spread quickly, especially on college campuses and among young professionals who found that these groups offered ways to overcome their isolation in large urban settings.[25] Religious organizations soon realized that small groups could play a vital role in their programs. Retreat centers found that small groups were an effective way of encouraging spiritual renewal. Youth ministries adopted the small group as a favorite style of teaching and fellowship, and new religious movements among young people often followed suit. But it was in the established churches and synagogues that small groups became especially prominent....[26]

### Distinctive Features

The small-group movement that emerged in the late 1960s and 1970s built on the precedents long established by these classes and other specialized meetings, but it also differed from these more traditional gatherings in significant ways:

- Small groups were initiated deliberately as additions to the more traditional classes and church meetings, often by clergy and lay leaders who were convinced that these traditional gatherings were not entirely effective in meeting their own needs or the needs of others in their congregations.

- As a supplement to the instructional, administrative, or task-oriented activities of the established classes and meetings (which were often retained, especially in the form of Bible lessons and prayer sessions), the new small groups were often consciously oriented toward the cultivation of community, support, and relationships; activities such as eating together, playing games, sharing problems, and having time for informal conversation were specifically encouraged.
- The new groups often drew explicitly on ideas from the 1960s about group dynamics and group process, and they paid special attention to mutual interaction rather than following the earlier didactic models. They often borrowed heavily from the emerging literature on expressiveness, thus taking as an end in itself the goal of giving members a chance to express themselves and discover new insights through group discussions. Medical and therapeutic models increasingly influenced the thinking of group leaders and members and encouraged them to believe that greater self-awareness, healing, and the realization of deeper life goals could be nurtured by talking about themselves. There was thus a new epistemology: Knowledge was not something that already existed, needing to be transmitted to an audience of learners by someone in authority; it was something to be generated by the group itself by discussing the personal views of its individual members.
- The basis for forming specific groups generally expanded beyond gender and age-grading as well, often taking into account the centrifugal social forces affecting contemporary urban and suburban congregations. Thus groups were created on the basis of members' geographic location, lifestyle attributes (such as singles, young marrieds, and parents-without-partners groups), and more specialized concerns, such as racial integration, experimental worship, in-depth spiritual knowledge, or social action. Small groups thus became a way for established churches and synagogues to respond to the growing cultural diversity of the society. They also focused increasingly on specific personal needs, such as recovery from addictions.

## Continuing Growth

During the 1980s, the small-group movement grew rapidly, especially as religious leaders began to recognize its potential as a way of revitalizing declining congregations and of achieving rapid growth in new congregations. The movement spread widely in other settings as well, particularly as therapists began to recommend group participation as a way

in which individuals who could not afford high-priced fees for professional counseling or psychotherapy could at least help one another in small ways, and as alcoholism and other forms of drug addiction forced growing numbers of people to seek group support as a means of recovery.[27]

In the 1990s, this growth has, if anything, accelerated. Increasing numbers of religious congregations are experimenting with small groups of ever-widening variety. Catholic parishes that were involved in the Renew movement have often turned to small groups as a way of maintaining some of their momentum. Jewish communities are experimenting with *havurot* and other small, informal, gatherings in homes.[28] Protestant pastors are encouraging small groups as a way of securing church growth. Therapy groups and various support groups modeled after the twelve steps of recovery developed by Alcoholics Anonymous appear to be increasingly popular. Many small, supportive groups have sprung up in the workplace and in volunteer organizations. Some of these groups gather simply to discuss issues of common interest; others meet primarily to accomplish specific tasks but in the process give emotional and spiritual support as well. In addition, countless varieties of self-help groups have been formed to meet more specialized interests in the populations. From job-seekers groups, to weight-control groups, to support groups for the dying and the bereaved, the small-group movement shows signs of enormous and continuing vitality.

## THE EXTENT OF INVOLVEMENT

Many estimates of the scope of the small-group movement have been made, generally drawing on whatever means happened to be available: mailing lists, numbers of study guides distributed, telephone directories, leaders' impressions. But such estimates are notoriously unreliable. Although there is a widespread impression that the small-group movement has grown, it has been difficult for anyone to say with certainty whether the movement was indeed pervasive or whether it was limited to a very small proportion of the total American population.

To find out how many people are actually involved, we commissioned a nationally representative survey of adults age 18 and over living in the continental United States…. According to this survey, exactly 40 percent of the adult population of the United States claims to be involved in "a small group that meets regularly and provides caring and support for those who participate in it." This is an extraordinary figure. It does not include all the children and teenagers who are also in groups. It means that approximately 75 million adult Americans are meeting regularly for some kind of small-group interaction and support….

The majority of groups, though, meet at least once a week. Virtually all the rest meet at least once a month. Group members do admit that getting people to attend is sometimes a problem, but perhaps not as much of a problem as one would think. Two people in three say that almost everyone in their group attends every time, while only a third say a lot of the members of their group do not attend. As for themselves, about half say they attend every week, while virtually everyone else attends at least once a month. In other words, attendance patterns pretty much reflect how often the group actually meets. Indeed, 78 percent of all group members attend as frequently as their group meets: 82 percent of those whose groups meet weekly attend that often, 73 percent of those whose groups meet biweekly attend biweekly, and 86 percent of those whose groups meet monthly attend that often.

On balance, these figures suggest that small groups command a very serious level of commitment from their members. Most members attend faithfully and often, the norm being several hours each week. They do so over extended periods of time in groups that somehow enjoy a great deal of stability. The subjective assessments people give also suggest a high level of commitment to their groups. Nearly three-quarters say their group is very important to them (30 percent say it is extremely important). Almost everyone else says the group is fairly important. Scarcely anyone admits it is not very important….

ment's relationship to people's desire for community. In the survey, members of small groups were posed some questions about such needs as having neighbors with whom one can interact freely and comfortably and being able to share one's deepest feelings with people….

Virtually everyone who is currently in a small group has experienced these needs at one time or another. The figures range from 98 percent who say they have felt the need for friends who value the same things in life that they do and who have felt the need for people who can give them deep emotional support to 83 percent who say they have felt the need for people who are never critical of them. It is not surprising that so many people have experienced these needs. The fact that these needs are so widespread, though, is clearly one of the bases from which the current interest in small groups has sprung. It is, of course, not the only one. People who are not in small groups probably experience these needs as well. But the desire for intimacy, support, sharing, and other forms of community involvement is certainly an essential precondition of the small-group movement….

What [does this study] tell us about small groups and community? [It] suggests that nearly everyone in our society desperately wants community, but that most people have trouble finding it in all the ways they would like it to be present in their lives. Neighborhoods and the workplace provide opportunities for interaction, but for most people these arenas do not yield the sharing and caring they desire. Small groups are an alternative. They do not necessarily tie people in better with their neighbors and coworkers. These groups do, however, give other chances for people to become acquainted and to share their basic values. Enough of those who participate in small groups receive enough fulfillment there to keep going back. Quite a number keep going back, too, because their needs for community are still in the process of being met….

## SMALL GROUPS AND COMMUNITY

With this information in mind, we can now return to the question of community. …We can gain an initial sense of why small groups have become so important in our society by considering the move-

## SMALL GROUPS AND SPIRITUALITY

Before going any further, we must now turn directly to the question that probably already has emerged in many readers' minds. Maybe what people were thinking about when they said they belonged to a small group was their Tuesday night bowling team, or their Wednesday lunch with fellow used-car dealers, or their Friday evening bridge club. Maybe there is very little connection between these kinds of groups and spirituality.

...Here, it suffices to say that the majority of these groups, whatever their make-up or auspices, are perceived by their members as having contributed to their spiritual development. Specifically, 61 percent of all group members say their "faith or spirituality" has been influenced by being involved in their group. And more than half of these people (57 percent) say their faith has been "deepened a lot" by their involvement. These proportions are also higher among persons who say their group is very important to them: 73 percent say their faith has been influenced; of these, 63 percent say it has deepened a great deal.

Several other preliminary indications of the extent to which small groups and the quest for spirituality go together are worth considering as well. One is that among people who have been involved in any kind of small group in the past, 63 percent say they were in a group that focused on religious or spiritual matters. Another sign is that among current group members, 65 percent say their interest in spiritual matters has increased in the past five years; only 4 percent say it has decreased. And still another indication is that approximately half of all group members (46 percent) say "wanting to become more disciplined in my spiritual life" was a reason why they became involved. We also saw...that 53 percent of all group members say they have fully met their need to be in a group that helps them grow spiritually; another 35 percent say they have partially met this need; only 10 percent say they have never experienced it.

So, even if some of what we are tapping consists of nothing more than a bowling team or a bridge club, we are for the most part dealing with something that is of major significance to the spiritual lives of many Americans. Indeed, what else in our society might we think of that is influencing the spirituality of so many of those who participate in it?

Certainly it is their potential contribution to spiritual development – and, indeed, to the redefinition of spirituality – that makes small groups especially interesting. Were we just interested in how small groups work, we could read the vast literature that social psychologists have written on this topic. The groups we are interested in here are not ends in themselves. They are the settings in which millions of Americans are currently trying to find themselves and to discover what it means to be more fully human and more fully in tune with their own spirituality and with God.

We considered earlier the question of whether spirituality has become such a private matter in our society that its communal dimension needs to be rediscovered. We suggested that a number of characteristics of our culture have worked together to drive spirituality inward and to erode the authority of established religious institutions. We can now ask what the relationship of small groups is to these cultural trends. Do people involved in small groups regard spirituality as a private matter and do they have misgivings about large religious organizations? Is that why they are turning to small groups? Or is their involvement in small groups a counter-trend, turning spirituality once again into a more communal enterprise?

These are complex questions and demand closer examination...but we can suggest their importance by considering briefly how small-group members nationally respond to some statements about the nature of spirituality and the role of churches. These responses are shown in Table 54.1. Two patterns are particularly worthy of emphasis. First, small-group members are by no means devoid of privatized views of spirituality and critical views of the churches. A majority, for ex-

TABLE 54.1   VIEWS OF SPIRITUALITY AND THE CHURCHES

*Percent of Group Members Who Mostly Agree with Each Statement Among Those Saying the Importance of Their Group Is High or Low*

|  | High | Low |
|---|---|---|
| My religious beliefs are very personal and private | 57 | 63 |
| My spirituality does not depend on being involved in a religious organization | 55 | 71 |
| The clergy are generally no more spiritual than other people | 46 | 47 |
| A lot of churches are out of date | 37 | 47 |
| All churches are pretty much alike | 19 | 24 |
| It doesn't matter what you believe, as long as you are a good person | 47 | 68 |

ample, say that their own religious beliefs are personal and private, agree that their spirituality does not depend on being involved in a religious organization, and assert that it makes no difference what you believe as long as you are a good person. Their views of the churches are mixed: Only one in five believe all churches are alike, but two in five think that churches are badly out of date. Second, the responses of group members who say their group is very important in their lives differ systematically from those of members whose groups are less important. The former appear to be less privatized in their view of spirituality, somewhat less relativistic, and somewhat less critical of the churches. To this extent, small groups may be stemming the tide of privatization in American religion for at least some of their members. And yet, the differences are not great, and there are other ways in which small groups are influencing spirituality as well. Although they draw people back to the churches, they also do so, as we shall see, by making spirituality more palatable. Their members are often faced with the dilemma of wanting a more solid, communal form of religious commitment and at the same time picking up the privatized, relativistic messages that infuse their groups from the wider culture. Indeed, this conflict is why the small-group movement is now at a critical juncture in its development.

...For now, the important point is that small groups are clearly a phenomenon in our society to be reckoned with if we want to understand better how spirituality is nurtured—an aim that millions of Americans share, whether they are in groups or not. The small-group movement is clearly linked to a long tradition of collective quests for the sacred. It is not at all unusual for Americans to band together as they pursue their interests in the sacred. That they are banding together is nevertheless important to realize, especially in view of the fact that so much emphasis has been placed on the ways in which faith is becoming more private. With the changes that have been taking place in traditional forms of community, it is also not surprising that new forms of banding together have had to be invented. Why these forms have become so widespread in our society is the question to which we must now turn.

## ENDNOTES

1. Mark A. Noll, Nathan O. Hatch, George M. Marsden, David F. Wells, and John D. Woodbridge (eds.), *Eerdmans' Handbook to Christianity in America* (Grand Rapids, MI: Eerdmans, 1983). One of the most useful overviews of the role of religion in American history.

2. This part of the story is captured magnificently in Nathan O. Hatch, *The Democratization of American Christianity* (New Haven, CT: Yale University Press, 1989).

3. Even the traditional image of revival meetings focusing chiefly on individual piety is being challenged by new historical studies emphasizing its links to the corporate rites and services of churches; see for example Leigh Eric Schmidt, *Holy Fairs: Scottish Communions and American Revivals in the Early Modern Period* (Princeton, NJ: Princeton University Press, 1989).

4. Justo L. Gonzalez, *The Story of Christianity*, 2 vols (New York: Harper & Row, 1984). A readable history of Christianity (volume 1 focuses on the early Christian church through the Middle Ages, volume 2 on the Protestant Reformation to the present) that demonstrates repeatedly how small groups sustained and revitalized individuals' commitment to their faith.

5. George Gallup, Jr., *Faith Development and Your Ministry* (Princeton, NJ: Princeton Religion Research Center, 1985). Based on an extensive national survey carried out in cooperation with the Religious Education Association of the United States and Canada, this 78-page report documents the extent to which people are currently interested in developing their faith and some of the practical ways in which religious organizations might help to meet these needs. Available from the Princeton Religion Research Center, P.O. Box 628, Princeton, NJ 08542.

6. For an overview of the role of religion in contemporary U.S. society, see my book *The Restructuring of American Religion: Society and Faith Since World War II* (Princeton, NJ: Princeton University Press, 1988). Comparisons between the U.S. and other advanced industrial societies can be found in David Harrington Watt, "United States: Cultural Challenges to the Voluntary Sector," in *Between States and Markets: The Voluntary Sector in Comparative Perspective*, edited by Robert Wuthnow (Princeton, NJ: Princeton University Press, 1991), pp. 243–287. Other chapters in the same volume provide evidence on the strength of religion in Japan, England, Germany, France, and other countries.

7. On the recent rise of interest in religion as an academic topic, see Ellen K. Coughlin, "Social Scientists Again Turn Attention to Religion's Place in the World," *Chronicle of Higher Education* (April 1, 1992), A6-A8.

8. The decline of community has been a perennial theme in the social sciences at least since Ferdinand Tönnies, *Community and Society*, trans. by Charles P. Loomis (New York: Harper & Row, 1963, originally published in 1887). For a dispassionate empirical discussion of the ways in which community is and is not changing in American society, see Claude S. Fischer, "Ambivalent Communities: How Amer-

icans Understand Their Localities," in *America at Century's End*, edited by Alan Wolfe (Berkeley and Los Angeles: University of California Press, 1991), pp. 79-91.

9. These points are emphasized in Paul Leinberger and Bruce Tucker, *The New Individualists: The Generation After the Organization Man* (New York: Harper Collins, 1991). Based on hundreds of qualitative interviews, this is a major study providing contrasts between social patterns in the 1950s and the 1980s. It is, however, written for a popular audience and many of its claims would require further substantiation.

10. David Riesman, Nathan Glazer, and Reuel Denney, *The Lonely Crowd: A Study of the Changing American Character* (New Haven, CT: Yale University Press, 1950). See also David Riesman, *Individualism Reconsidered* (Glencoe, IL: Free Press, 1954).

11. For a recent empirical study, see David Hummon, *Commonplaces: Community Ideology and Identity in American Culture* (Albany: State University of New York Press, 1990); the literature on urbanism and its impact on social life more generally is reviewed in Suzanne Keller, *The Urban Neighborhood* (New York: Random House, 1968), and Claude S. Fischer, *The Urban Experience*, 2d ed. (San Diego, CA: Harcourt Brace Jovanovich, 1984).

12. Robert J. Sampson, "Friendship Networks and Community Attachment in Mass Society: A Multilevel Systemic Model," *American Sociological Review* 53 (1988), 766-779; Charles E. Connerly, "The Community Question: An Extension of Wellman and Leighton," *Urban Affairs Quarterly* 20 (1985), 537-556; and Carol J. Silverman, "Neighboring and Urbanism: Commonality Versus Friendship," *Urban Affairs Quarterly* 22 (1986), 312-328.

13. Herbert J. Gans, *Middle American Individualism: Political Participation and Liberal Democracy* (New York: Oxford University Press, 1988). Clearly written exposition by a former president of the American Sociological Association of the social sources and consequences of the emphasis on individualism and the breakdown of community in American society.

14. In my research on caring, I found in a national survey I conducted in 1989 that 37 percent of the public feel they could not count on their immediate neighbors if someone in their family became ill and they needed help; about the same proportions said they could not count on relatives in their extended family or members of a church or synagogue; see *Acts of Compassion: Caring for Others and Helping Ourselves* (Princeton, NJ: Princeton University Press, 1991), p.11.

15. Robert C. Fuller, *Ecology of Care: An Interdisciplinary Analysis of the Self and Moral Obligation* (Louisville, KY: Westminster/John Knox, 1992), p. 92.

16. Gordon Kaufman, *Theology for a Nuclear Age* (Philadelphia: Westminster Press, 1985), p. 60.

17. Thomas Luckmann, *The Invisible Religion: The Transformation of Symbols in Industrial Society* (New York: Macmillan, 1967). A classic discussion that examines the major social forms of contemporary religion, how these forms are being challenged by modern society, and the ways in which religious convictions are increasingly becoming matters of private belief.

18. The same point was forcefully argued about the same time in Peter L. Berger, *The Sacred Canopy: Elements of a Sociological Theory of Religion* (Garden City, NY: Doubleday, 1967).

19. Robert N. Bellah, Richard Madsen, William M. Sullivan, Ann Swidler, and Steven M. Tipton, *Habits of the Heart: Individualism and Commitment in American Life* (Berkeley: University of California Press, 1985). Based on indepth interviews with middle-class persons in several regions of the country, this widely praised book examines the extent to which utilitarian individualism and expressive individualism have eroded public commitment in many areas of our lives. For a counter-argument, see Andrew M. Greeley, "Review of *Habits of the Heart*, by Robert N. Bellah et al.," *Sociology and Social Research* 70 (1985), 114. See also the essays in Charles H. Reynolds and Ralph V. Norman (eds.), *Community in America: The Challenge of Habits of the Heart* (Berkeley and Los Angeles: University of California Press, 1988).

20. Bellah, et al., *Habits of the Heart*, p. 236.

21. James Davison Hunter, *Evangelicalism: The Coming Generation* (Chicago: University of Chicago Press, 1987), especially Chapter 5. Hunter makes this point with reference to young evangelicals in the United States. His discussion draws heavily from the insightful work of John Murray Cuddihy, *No Offense: Civil Religion and Protestant Taste* (New York: Seabury, 1978).

22. George Gallup, Jr., *The Unchurched American — 10 Years Later* (Princeton, NJ: Princeton Religion Research Center, 1988).

23. Among the many analyses of changes in the clergy and in perceptions of clergy authority, see John Seidler and Katherine Meyer, *Conflict and Change in the Catholic Church* (New Brunswick, NJ: Rutgers University Press, 1989).

24. Ibid.

25. See Kurt W. Back, *Beyond Words: The Story of Sensitivity Training and the Encounter Movement*, 2d ed. (New Brunswick, NJ: Transaction Books, 1987). Recently updated, this book (originally published in 1972) remains one of the best introductions to the history of the small-group movement in secular settings during the 1960s.

26. Steve Barker, *Good Things Come in Small Groups: The Dynamics of Good Group Life* (Downers Grove, IL: InterVarsity Press, 1985), especially Chapter 1. One of the most useful brief introductions to the role that small groups can play in nurturing spirituality.

27. A brief history of the recent growth of the self-help and recovery movement is given in John Steadman Rice, *A Disease of One's Own: Psychotherapy, Addiction, and the Emergence of "Co-Dependency"* (Princeton, NJ: Princeton University Press, 1993), Chapter 1.

28. Riv-Ellen Prell, *Prayer and Community: The Havurah in American Judaism* (Detroit: Wayne State University Press, 1989).

# 55. KINDERGARTEN AS ACADEMIC BOOT CAMP

HARRY L. GRACEY

*"By the end of the school year, the successful kindergarten teacher has a well-organized group of children. They follow classroom routines automatically, having learned all the command signals and the expected responses to them. They have, in our terms, learned the student role."*

Kindergarten is preparation for school, and school is preparation for living in society. Gracey links citizenship in the bureaucratic school to taking on positions in a highly bureaucratic society—both expect obedience to rules. To make his point, Gracey describes one afternoon in a kindergarten class. The student learns routine, submission, and discipline. It is, according to Gracey, a preparation for life.

Education must be considered one of the major institutions of social life today. Along with the family and organized religion, however, it is a "secondary institution," one in which people are prepared for life in society as it is presently organized. The main dimensions of modern life, that is, the nature of society as a whole, is determined principally by the "primary institutions," which today are the economy, the political system, and the military establishment. Education has been defined by sociologists, classical and contemporary, as an institution that serves society by socializing people into it through a formalized, standardized procedure. At the beginning of this century Emile Durkheim told student teachers at the University of Paris that education "consists of a methodical socialization of the younger generation." He went on to add:

It is the influence exercised by adult generations on those that are not ready for social life. Its object is to arouse and to develop in the child a certain number of physical, intellectual, and moral states that are demanded of him by the political society as a whole and by the special milieu for which he is specifically des-

Reprinted by permission of Harry L. Gracey, Cambridge, MA.

tined…. To the egotistic and asocial being that has just been born, [society] must, as rapidly as possible, add another, capable of leading a moral and social life. Such is the work of education.[1]

The education process, Durkheim said, "is, above all, the means by which society perpetually re-creates the conditions of its very existence."[2] The contemporary educational sociologist, Wilbur Brookover, offers a similar formulation in his recent textbook definition of education:

Actually, therefore, in the broadest sense, education is synonymous with socialization. It includes any social behavior that assists in the induction of the child into membership in the society or any behavior by which the society perpetuates itself through the next generation.[3]

The educational institution is, then, one of the ways in which society is perpetuated through the systematic socialization of the young, while the nature of the society being perpetuated — its organization and operation, its values, beliefs, and ways of living — are determined by the primary institutions. The educational system, like other secondary institutions, *serves* the society that is *created* by the operation of the economy, the political system, and the military establishment.

Schools, the social organizations of the educational institution, are today for the most part large bureaucracies run by specially trained and certified people. There are few places left in modern societies in which formal teaching and learning is carried on in small, isolated groups, like the rural, one-room schoolhouses of the last century. Schools are large, formal organizations that tend to be parts of larger organizations, local community School Districts. These School Districts are bureaucratically organized, and their operations are supervised by state and local governments. In this context, as Brookover says:

The term *education* is used...to refer to a system of schools, in which specifically designated persons are expected to teach children and youth certain types of acceptable behavior. The school system becomes a...unit in the total social structure and is recognized by the members of the society as a separate social institution. Within this structure, a portion of the total socialization process occurs.[4]

Education is the part of the socialization process that takes place in the schools; and these are, more and more today, bureaucracies within bureaucracies.

Kindergarten is generally conceived by educators as a year of preparation for school. It is thought of as a year in which small children, five or six years old, are prepared socially and emotionally for the academic learning that will take place over the next twelve years. It is expected that a foundation of behavior and attitudes will be laid in kindergarten on which the children can acquire the skills and knowledge they will be taught in the grades. A booklet prepared for parents by the staff of a suburban New York school system says that the kindergarten experience will stimulate the child's desire to learn and cultivate the skills he will need for learning in the rest of his school career. It claims that the child will find opportunities for physical growth, for satisfying his "need for self-expression," acquire some knowledge, and provide opportunities for creative activity. It concludes, "The most important benefit that your five-year-old will receive from kindergarten is the opportunity to live and grow happily and purposefully with others in a small society." The kindergarten teachers in one of the elementary schools in this community, one we shall call the Wilbur Wright School, said their goals were to see that the children "grew" in all ways: physically, of course, emotionally, socially, and academically. They said they wanted children to like school as a result of their kindergarten experiences and that they wanted them to learn to get along with others.

None of these goals, however, is unique to kindergarten; each of them is held to some extent by teachers in the other six grades at Wright School. And growth would occur, but differently, even if the child did not attend school. The children already know how to get along with others, in their families and their play groups. The unique job of the kindergarten in the educational division of labor seems rather to be teaching children the *student role*. The student role is the repertoire of behavior and attitudes regarded by educators as appropriate to children in school. Observation in the kindergartens of the Wilbur Wright School revealed a great variety of activities through which children are shown and then drilled in the behavior and attitudes defined as appropriate for school and thereby induced to learn the role of student. Observations of the kindergartens and interviews with the teachers both pointed to the teaching and learning of classroom routines as the main element of the student role. The teachers expended most of their efforts, for the first half of the year at least, in training the children to follow the routines the teachers created. The children were, in a very real sense, *drilled* in tasks and activities created by the teachers for their own purposes and beginning and ending quite arbitrarily (from the child's point of view) at the command of the teacher. One teacher remarked that she hated September because during the first month "everything has to be done rigidly, and repeatedly, until they know exactly what they're supposed to do." However, "by January," she said, "they know exactly what to do [during the day] and I don't have to be after them all the time." Classroom routines were introduced gradually from the beginning of the year in all the kindergartens, and the children were drilled in them as long as was necessary to achieve regular compliance. By the end of the school year, the successful kindergarten teacher has a well-organized group of children. They follow classroom routines automatically, having learned all the command signals and the expected responses to them. They have, in our terms, learned the student role. The following observation shows one such classroom operating at optimum organization on an afternoon late in May. It is the class of an experienced and respected kindergarten teacher.

## AN AFTERNOON IN KINDERGARTEN

At about 12:20 in the afternoon on a day in the last week of May, Edith Kerr leaves the teachers' room where she has been having lunch and walks to her classroom at the far end of the primary wing of Wright School. A group of five- and six-year-olds peers at her through the glass doors leading from the hall cloakroom to the play area outside. Entering her room, she straightens some material in the "book corner" of the room, arranges music on the piano, takes colored paper from her closet and places it on one of the shelves under the window. Her room is divided into a number of activity areas through the arrangement of furniture and play equipment. Two easels and a paint table near the door create a kind of passageway inside the room. A wedge-shaped area just inside the front door is made into a teacher's area by the placing of "her" things there: her desk, file, and piano. To the left is the book corner, marked off from the rest of the room by a puppet stage and a movable chalkboard. In it are a display rack of picture books, a record player, and a stack of children's records. To the right of the entrance are the sink and clean-up area. Four large round tables with six chairs at each for the children are placed near the walls about halfway down the length of the room, two on each side, leaving a large open area in the center for group games, block building, and toy truck driving. Windows stretch down the length of both walls, starting about three feet from the floor and extending almost to the high ceilings. Under the windows are long shelves on which are kept all the toys, games, blocks, paper, paints, and other equipment of the kindergarten. The left rear corner of the room is a play store with shelves, merchandise, and cash register; the right rear corner is a play kitchen with stove, sink, iron-

ing board, and bassinette with baby dolls in it. This area is partly shielded from the rest of the room by a large standing display rack for posters and children's art work. A sandbox is found against the back wall between these two areas. The room is light, brightly colored, and filled with things that adults feel five- and six-year-olds will find interesting and pleasing.

At 12:25, Edith opens the outside door and admits the waiting children. They hang their sweaters on hooks outside the door and then go to the center of the room and arrange themselves in a semi-circle on the floor, facing the teacher's chair, which she has placed in the center of the floor. Edith follows them in and sits in her chair checking attendance while waiting for the bell to ring. When she has finished attendance, which she takes by sight, she asks the children what the date is, what day and month it is, how many children are enrolled in the class, how many are present, and how many are absent.

The bell rings at 12:30 and the teacher puts away her attendance book. She introduces a visitor, who is sitting against the wall taking notes, as someone who wants to learn about schools and children. She then goes to the back of the room and takes down a large chart labeled "Helping Hands." Bringing it to the center of the room, she tells the children it is time to change jobs. Each child is assigned some task on the chart by placing his name, lettered on a paper "hand," next to a picture signifying the task — for example, a broom, a blackboard, a milk bottle, a flag, and a Bible. She asks the children who wants each of the jobs and rearranges their "hands" accordingly. Returning to her chair, Edith announces, "One person should tell us what happened to Mark." A girl raises her hand, and when called on says, "Mark fell and hit his head and had to go to the hospital." The teacher adds that Mark's mother had written saying that he was in the hospital.

During this time, the children have been interacting among themselves in their semi-circle. Children have whispered to their neighbors, poked one another, made general comments to the group, waved to friends on the other side of the circle. None of this has been disruptive, and the teacher has ignored it for the most part. The children seem to know just how much of each kind of interaction is permitted — they may greet in a soft voice someone who sits next to them, for example, but may not shout greetings to a friend who sits across the circle, so they confine themselves to waving and remain well within understood limits.

At 12:35, two children arrive. Edith asks them why they are late and then sends them to join the circle on the floor. The other children vie with each other to tell the newcomers what happened to Mark. When this leads to a general disorder, Edith asks, "Who has serious time?" The children become quiet and a girl raises her hand. Edith nods and the child gets a Bible and hands it to Edith. She reads the Twenty-third Psalm while the children sit quietly. Edith helps the child in charge begin reciting the Lord's Prayer; the other children follow along for the first unit of sounds, and then trail off as Edith finishes for them. Everyone stands and faces the American flag hung to the right of the door. Edith leads the pledge to the flag, with the children again following the familiar sounds as far as they remember them. Edith then asks the girl in charge what song she wants and the child replies, "My Country." Edith goes to the piano and plays "America," singing as the children follow her words.

Edith returns to her chair in the center of the room and the children sit again in the semi-circle on the floor. It is 12:40 when she tells the children, "Let's have boys' sharing time first." She calls the name of the first boy sitting on the end of the circle, and he comes up to her with a toy helicopter. He turns and holds it up for the other children to see. He says, "It's a helicopter." Edith asks, "What is it used for?" and he replies, "For the army. Carry men. For the war." Other children join in, "For shooting submarines." "To bring back men from space when they are in the ocean." Edith sends the boy back to the circle and asks the next boy if he has something. He replies "No" and she passes on to the next. He says "Yes" and brings a bird's nest to her. He holds it for the class to see, and the teacher asks, "What kind of bird made the nest?" The boy replies, "My friend says a rain bird made it." Edith asks what the nest is made of and different children reply, "mud," "leaves" and "sticks." There is also a bit of moss woven into the nest and Edith tries to describe it to the children. They, however, are more interested in seeing if anything is inside it, and Edith lets the boy carry it around the semi-circle showing the children its

insides. Edith tells the children of some baby robins in a nest in her yard, and some of the children tell about baby birds they have seen. Some children are asking about a small object in the nest which they say looks like an egg, but all have seen the nest now and Edith calls on the next boy. A number of children say, "I know what Michael has, but I'm not telling." Michael brings a book to the teacher and then goes back to his place in the circle of children. Edith reads the last page of the book to the class. Some children tell of books they have at home. Edith calls the next boy, and three children call out, "I know what David has." "He always has the same thing." "It's a bang-bang." David goes to his table and gets a box which he brings to Edith. He opens it and shows the teacher a scale-model of an old-fashioned dueling pistol. When David does not turn around to the class, Edith tells him, "Show it to the children" and he does. One child says, "Mr. Johnson [the principal] said no guns." Edith replies, "Yes, how many of you know that?" Most of the children in the circle raise their hands. She continues, "That you aren't supposed to bring guns to school?" She calls the next boy on the circle and he brings two large toy soldiers to her which the children enthusiastically identify as being from "Babes in Toyland." The next boy brings an American flag to Edith and shows it to the class. She asks him what the stars and stripes stand for and admonishes him to treat it carefully. "Why should you treat it carefully?" she asks the boy. "Because it's our flag," he replies. She congratulates him, saying, "That's right."

"Show and Tell" lasted twenty minutes and during the last ten, one girl in particular announced that she knew what each child called on had to show. Edith asked her to be quiet each time she spoke out, but she was not content, continuing to offer her comment at each "show." Four children from other classes had come into the room to bring something from another teacher or to ask for something from Edith. Those with requests were asked to return later if the item wasn't readily available.

Edith now asks if any of the children told their mothers about their trip to the local zoo the previous day. Many children raise their hands. As Edith calls on them, they tell what they liked in the zoo. Some children cannot wait to be called on, and they call out things to the teacher, who asks them to be quiet. After a few of the animals are mentioned, one child says, "I liked the spooky house," and the others chime in to agree with him, some pantomiming fear and horror. Edith is puzzled, and asks what this was. When half the children try to tell her at once, she raises her hand for quiet, then calls on individual children. One says, "The house with nobody in it"; another, "The dark little house." Edith asks where it was in the zoo, but the children cannot describe its location in any way she can understand. Edith makes some jokes, but they involve adult abstractions the children cannot grasp. The children have become quite noisy now, speaking out to make both relevant and irrelevant comments, and three little girls have become particularly assertive.

Edith gets up from her seat at 1:10 and goes to the book corner, where she puts a record on the player. As it begins a story about the trip to the zoo, she returns to the circle and asks the children to go sit at the tables. She divides them among the tables in such a way as to indicate that they don't have regular seats. When the children are all seated at the four tables, five or six to a table, the teacher asks, "Who wants to be the first one?" One of the noisy girls comes to the center of the room. The voice on the record is giving directions for imitating an ostrich and the girl follows them, walking around the center of the room holding her ankles with her hands. Edith replays the record, and all the children, table by table, imitate ostriches down the center of the room and back. Edith removes her shoes and shows that she can be an ostrich too. This is apparently a familiar game, for a number of children are calling out, "Can we have the crab?" Edith asks one of the children to do a crab "so we can all remember how," and then plays the part of the record with music for imitating crabs by. The children from the first table line up across the room, hands and feet on the floor and faces pointing toward the ceiling. After they have "walked" down the room and back in this posture, they sit at their table and the children of the next table play "crab." The children love this; they run from their tables, dance about on the floor waiting for their turns and are generally exuberant. Children ask for the "inch worm" and the game is played again with the children squirming down the floor. As a conclusion, Edith shows them a new animal

imitation, the "lame dog." The children all hobble down the floor on three "legs," table by table, to the accompaniment of the record.

At 1:30, Edith has the children line up in the center of the room; she says, "Table one, line up in front of me," and children ask, "What are we going to do?" Then she moves a few steps to the side and says, "Table two over here, line up next to table one," and more children ask, "What for?" She does this for table three and table four and each time the children ask, "Why, what are we going to do?" When the children are lined up in four lines of five each, spaced so that they are not touching one another, Edith puts on a new record and leads the class in calisthenics, to the accompaniment of the record. The children just jump around every which way in their places instead of doing the exercises, and by the time the record is finished, Edith, the only one following it, seems exhausted. She is apparently adopting the President's new "Physical Fitness" program in her classroom.

At 1:35, Edith pulls her chair to the easels and calls the children to sit on the floor in front of her, table by table. When they are all seated she asks, "What are you going to do for work time today?" Different children raise their hands and tell Edith what they are going to draw. Most are going to make pictures of animals they saw in the zoo. Edith asks if they want to make pictures to send to Mark in the hospital, and the children agree to this. Edith gives drawing paper to the children, calling them to her one by one. After getting a piece of paper, the children go to the crayon box on the right-hand shelves, select a number of colors, and go to the tables, where they begin drawing. Edith is again trying to quiet the perpetually talking girls. She keeps two of them standing by her so they won't disrupt the others. She asks them, "Why do you feel you have to talk all the time," and then scolds them for not listening to her. Then she sends them to their tables to draw.

Most of the children are drawing at their tables, sitting or kneeling in their chairs. They are all working very industriously and, engrossed in their work, very quietly. Three girls have chosen to paint at the easels, and having donned their smocks, they are busily mixing colors and intently applying them to their pictures. If the children at the tables are primitives and neo-realists in their animal depictions, these girls at the easels are the class abstract-expressionists, with their broad-stroked, colorful paintings.

Edith asks of the children generally, "What color should I make the cover of Mark's book?" Brown and green are suggested by some children "because Mark likes them." The other children are puzzled as to just what is going on and ask, "What book?" or "What does she mean?" Edith explains what she thought was clear to them already, that they are all going to put their pictures together in a "book" to be sent to Mark. She goes to a small table in the play-kitchen corner and tells the children to bring her their pictures when they are finished and she will write their message for Mark on them.

By 1:50, most children have finished their pictures and given them to Edith. She talks with some of them as she ties the bundle of pictures together — answering questions, listening, carrying on conversations. The children are playing in various parts of the room with toys, games, and blocks they have taken off the shelves. They also move from table to table, examining each other's pictures, offering compliments and suggestions. Three girls at a table are cutting up colored paper for a collage. Another girl is walking about the room in a pair of high heels with a woman's purse over her arm. Three boys are playing in the center of the room with the large block set, with which they are building walk-ways and walking on them. Edith is very much concerned about their safety and comes over a number of times to fuss over them. Two or three other boys are pushing trucks around the center of the room, and mild altercations occur when they drive through the block constructions. Some boys and girls are playing at the toy store, two girls are serving "tea" in the play kitchen, and one is washing a doll baby. Two boys have elected to clean the room, and with large sponges they wash the movable blackboard, the puppet stage, and then begin on the tables. They run into resistance from the children who are working with construction toys on the tables and do not want to dismantle their structures. The class is like a room full of bees, each intent on pursuing some activity, occasionally bumping into one another, but just veering off in another direction without serious altercation. At 2:05, the custodian arrives pushing a cart loaded with half-pint milk containers. He places a tray of cartons on the counter next to the sink, then leaves. His coming and going is unnoticed in the room (as, incidentally, is the presence of the observer, who is completely ignored by the children for the entire afternoon).

At 2:15, Edith walks to the entrance of the room, switches off the lights, and sits at the piano and plays. The children begin spontaneously singing the song, which is "Clean up, clean up. Everybody clean up." Edith walks around the room supervising the clean-up. Some children put their toys, the blocks, puzzles, games, and so on back on their shelves under the windows. The children making a collage keep right on working. A child from another class comes in to borrow the 45-rpm adaptor for the record player. At more urging from Edith, the rest of the children shelve their toys and work. The children are sitting around their tables now and Edith asks, "What record would you like to hear while you have your milk?" There is some confusion and no general consensus, so Edith drops the subject and begins to call the children, table by table, to come get their milk. "Table one," she says, and the five children come to the sink, wash their hands and dry them, pick up a carton of milk and a straw, and take it back to their table. Two talking girls wander about the room interfering with the children getting their milk and Edith calls out to them to "settle down." As the children sit, many of them call out to Edith the name of the record they want to hear. When all the children are seated at tables with milk, Edith plays one of these records called "Bozo and the Birds" and shows the children pictures in a book that goes with the record. The record recites, and the book shows the adventures of a clown, Bozo, as he walks through a woods meeting many different kinds of birds who, of course, display the characteristics of many kinds of people or, more accurately, different stereotypes. As children finish their milk, they take blankets or pads from the shelves under the windows and lie on them in the center of the room, where Edith sits on her chair showing the pictures. By 2:30, half the class is lying on the floor on their blankets, the record is still playing and the teacher is turning the pages of the book. The child who came in previously returns the 45-rpm adaptor, and one of the kindergartners tells Edith what the boy's name is and where he lives.

The record ends at 2:40. Edith says, "Children, down on your blankets." All the class is lying on blankets now, Edith refuses to answer the various questions individual children put to her because, she tells them, "it's rest time now." Instead, she talks very softly about what they will do tomorrow. They are going to work with clay, she says. The children lie quietly and listen. One of the boys raises his hand and when called on tells Edith, "The animals in the zoo looked so hungry yesterday." Edith asks the children what they think about this and a number try to volunteer opinions, but Edith accepts only those offered in a "rest-time tone," that is, softly and quietly. After a brief discussion of animal feeding, Edith calls the names of the two children on milk detail and has them collect empty milk cartons from the tables and return them to the tray. She asks the two children on clean-up detail to clean up the room. Then she gets up from her chair and goes to the door to turn on the lights. At this signal, the children all get up from the floor and return their blankets and pads to the shelf. It is raining (the reason for no outside play this afternoon), and cars driven by mothers clog the school drive and line up along the street. One of the talkative little girls comes over to Edith and pointing out the window says, "Mrs. Kerr, see my mother in the new Cadillac?"

At 2:50, Edith sits at the piano and plays. The children sit on the floor in the center of the room and sing. They have a repertoire of songs about animals, including one in which each child sings a refrain alone. They know these by heart and sing along through the ringing of the 2:55 bell. When the song is finished, Edith gets up and coming to the group says, "Okay, rhyming words to get your coats today." The children raise their hands and as Edith calls on them, they tell her two rhyming words, after which they are allowed to go into the hall to get their coats and sweaters. They return to the room with these and sit at their tables. At 2:59 Edith says. "When you have your coats on, you may line up at the door." Half of the children go to the door and stand in a long line. When the three o'clock bell rings, Edith returns to the piano

and plays. The children sing a song called "Goodbye," after which Edith sends them out.

## TRAINING FOR LEARNING AND FOR LIFE

The day in kindergarten at Wright School illustrates both the content of the student role as it has been learned by these children and the processes by which the teacher has brought about this learning, or, "taught" them the student role. The children have learned to go through routines and to follow orders with unquestioning obedience, even when these make no sense to them. They have been disciplined to do as they are told by an authoritative person without significant protest. Edith has developed this discipline in the children by creating and enforcing a rigid social structure in the classroom through which she effectively controls the behavior of most of the children for most of the school day. The "living with others in a small society" which the school pamphlet tells parents is the most important thing the children will learn in kindergarten can be seen now in its operational meaning, which is learning to live by the routines imposed by the school. This learning appears to be the principal content of the student role.

Children who submit to school-imposed discipline and come to identify with it, so that being a "good student" comes to be an important part of their developing identities, *become* the good students by the school's definitions. Those who submit to the routines of the school but do not come to identify with them will be adequate students who find the more important part of their identities elsewhere, such as in the play group outside school. Children who refuse to submit to the school routines are rebels who become known as "bad students" and often "problem children" in the school, for they do not learn the academic curriculum and their behavior is often disruptive in the classroom. Today, schools engage clinical psychologists in part to help teachers deal with such children.

In looking at Edith's kindergarten at Wright School, it is interesting to ask how the children learn this role of student—come to accept school-imposed routines—and what, exactly, it involves in terms of behavior and attitudes. The most prominent features of the classroom are its physical and social structures. The room is carefully furnished and arranged in ways adults feel will interest children. The play store and play kitchen in the back of the room, for example, imply that children are interested in mimicking these activities of the adult world. The only space left for the children to create something of their own is the empty center of the room, and the materials at their disposal are the blocks, whose use causes anxiety on the part of the teacher. The room, being carefully organized physically by the adults, leaves little room for the creation of physical organization on the part of the children.

The social structure created by Edith is a far more powerful and subtle force for fitting the children to the student role. This structure is established by the very rigid and tightly controlled set of rituals and routines through which the children are put during the day. There is first the rigid "locating procedure" in which the children are asked to find themselves in terms of the month, date, day of the week, and the number of the class who are present and absent. This puts them solidly in the real world as defined by adults. The day is then divided into six periods whose activities are for the most part determined by the teacher. In Edith's kindergarten, the children went through Serious Time, which opens the school day, Sharing Time, Play Time (which, in clear weather, would be spent outside), Work Time, Clean-Up Time, after which they have their milk, and Rest Time, after which they go home. The teacher has programmed activities for each of these Times.

Occasionally, the class is allowed limited discretion to choose between proffered activities, such as stories or records, but original ideas for activities are never solicited from them. Opportunity for free individual action is open only once in the day, during the part of Work Time left after the general class assignment has been completed (on the day reported, the class assignment was drawing animal pictures for the absent Mark). Spontaneous interests or observations from the children are never developed by the teacher. It seems that her schedule just does not allow room

for developing such unplanned events. During Sharing Time, for example, the child who brought a bird's nest told Edith, in reply to her question of what kind of bird made it, "My friend says it's a rain bird." Edith does not think to ask about this bird, probably because the answer is "childish," that is, not given in accepted adult categories of birds. The children then express great interest in an object in the nest, but the teacher ignores this interest, probably because the object is uninteresting to her. The soldiers from "Babes in Toyland" strike a responsive note in the children, but this is not used for a discussion of any kind. The soldiers are treated in the same way as objects that bring little interest from the children. Finally, at the end of Sharing Time, the child-world of perception literally erupts in the class with the recollection of "the spooky house" at the zoo. Apparently, this made more of an impression on the children than did any of the animals, but Edith is unable to make any sense of it for herself. The tightly imposed order of the class begins to break down as the children discover a universe of discourse of their own and begin talking excitedly with one another. The teacher is effectively excluded from this child's world of perception and for a moment she fails to dominate the classroom situation. She reasserts control, however, by taking the children to the next activity she has planned for the day. It seems never to have occurred to Edith that there might be a meaningful learning experience for the children in re-creating the "spooky house" in the classroom. It seems fair to say that this would have offered an exercise in spontaneous self-expression and an opportunity for real creativity on the part of the children. Instead, they are taken through a canned animal imitation procedure, an activity that they apparently enjoy, but that is also imposed on them rather than created by them.

Although children's perceptions of the world and opportunities for genuine spontaneity and creativity are being systematically eliminated from the kindergarten, unquestioned obedience to authority and rote learning of meaningless material are being encouraged. When the children are called to line up in the center of the room they ask "Why?" and "What for?" as they are in the very process of complying. They have learned to go smoothly through a programmed day, regardless of whether parts of the program make any sense to them or not. Here the student role involves what might be called "doing what you're told and never mind why." Activities that might "make sense" to the children are effectively ruled out and they are forced or induced to participate in activities that may be "senseless," such as the calisthenics.

At the same time, the children are being taught by rote meaningless sounds in the ritual oaths and songs, such as the Lord's Prayer, the Pledge to the Flag, and "America." As they go through the grades, children learn more and more of the sounds of these ritual oaths, but the fact that they have often learned meaningless sounds rather than meaningful statements is shown when they are asked to write these out in the sixth grade; they write them as groups of sounds rather than as a series of words, according to the sixth grade teachers at Wright School. Probably much learning in the elementary grades is of this character, that is, having no intrinsic meaning to the children, but rather being tasks inexplicably required of them by authoritative adults. Listening to sixth grade children read social studies reports, for example, in which they have copied material from encyclopedias about a particular country, an observer often gets the feeling that he is watching an activity that has no intrinsic meaning for the child. The child who reads, "Switzerland grows wheat and cows and grass and makes a lot of cheese" knows the dictionary meaning of each of these words but may very well have no conception at all of this "thing" called Switzerland. He is simply carrying out a task assigned by the teacher *because* it is assigned, and this may be its only "meaning" for him.

Another type of learning that takes place in kindergarten is seen in children who take advantage of the "holes" in the adult social structure to create activities of their own, during Work Time or out-of-doors during Play Time. Here the children are learning to carve out a small world of their own within the world created by adults. They very quickly learn that if they keep within permissible limits of noise and action, they can play as much as they please. Small groups of children formed during the year in Edith's kindergarten who played

together at these times, developing semi-independent little groups in which they created their own worlds in the interstices of the adult-imposed physical and social world. These groups remind the sociological observer very much of the so-called "informal groups" adults develop in factories and offices of large bureaucracies.[5] Here too, within authoritatively imposed social organizations, people find "holes" to create little subworlds that support informal, friendly, unofficial behavior. Forming and participating in such groups seems to be as much part of the student role as it is of the role of bureaucrat.

The kindergarten has been conceived of here as the year in which children are prepared for their schooling by learning the role of student. In the classrooms of the rest of the school grades, the children will be asked to submit to systems and routines imposed by the teachers and the curriculum. The days will be much like those of kindergarten, except that academic subjects will be substituted for the activities of the kindergarten. Once out of the school system, young adults will more than likely find themselves working in large-scale bureaucratic organizations, perhaps on the assembly line in the factory, perhaps in the paper routines of the white-collar occupations, where they will be required to submit to rigid routines imposed by "the company" that may make little sense to them. Those who can operate well in this situation will be successful bureaucratic functionaries. Kindergarten, therefore, can be seen as preparing children not only for participation in the bureaucratic organization of large modern school systems, but also for the large-scale occupational bureaucracies of modern society.

## ENDNOTES

1. Emile Durkheim, *Sociology and Education* (New York: The Free Press, 1956), pp. 71–72.

2. Ibid., p. 123.

3. Wilbur Brookover, *The Sociology of Education* (New York: American Book Company, 1957), p. 4.

4. Ibid., p. 6.

5. See, for example, Peter M. Blau, *Bureaucracy in Modern Society* (New York: Random House, 1956), Chapter 3.

# 56. AMERICAN EDUCATION: SAVAGE INEQUALITIES

JONATHAN KOZOL

*"In effect, a circular phenomenon evolves: The richer districts…have more revenue, de-rived from taxing land and homes, to fund their public schools. The reputation of the schools, in turn, adds to the value of their homes, and this, in turn, expands the tax base for their public schools…. Few of the children [in the poorer districts will] be likely to com-pete effectively with kids [in the wealthier districts] for admissions to the better local col-leges and universities of New York state. Even fewer will compete for more exclusive Ivy League admissions. And few of the graduates or dropouts of those poorer systems, as a consequence, are likely ever to earn enough to buy a home in [the wealthier districts]…."*

Jonathan Kozol's work, **Savage Inequalities**, is a detailed examination of the public schools in several American cities. The theme was the same wherever he looked: Some districts provide the very best opportunities; others barely get by. This selection is an excerpt from his description of schools in New York City. Most of us probably have a hunch that public education is characterized by great in-equalities; Kozol's description confirms these suspicions.

"In a country where there is no distinction of class," Lord Acton wrote of the United States 130 years ago, "a child is not born to the station of its parents, but with an indefinite claim to all the prizes that can be won by thought and labor. It is in conformity with the theory of equality…to give as near as possible to every youth an equal state in life." Americans, he said, "are unwilling that any should be deprived in childhood of the means of competition."[1]

It is hard to read these words today without a sense of irony and sadness. Denial of "the means of competition" is perhaps the single most consis-tent outcome of the education offered to poor chil-dren in the schools of our large cities; and nowhere

is this pattern of denial more explicit or more ab-solute than in the public schools of New York City.

Average expenditures per pupil in the city of New York in 1987 were some $5,500. In the high-est spending suburbs of New York (Great Neck or Manhasset, for example, on Long Island) funding levels rose above $11,000, with the highest districts in the state at $15,000. "Why," asks the city's Board of Education, "should our students receive less" than do "similar students" who live elsewhere? "The inequity is clear…."[2,3]

New York City's public schools are subdivided into 32 school districts. District 10 encompasses a large part of the Bronx but is, effectively, two sep-arate districts. One of these districts, Riverdale, is in the northwest section of the Bronx. Home to many of the city's most sophisticated and well-ed-ucated families, its elementary schools have rela-tively few low-income students. The other section, to the south and east, is poor and heavily nonwhite.

The contrast between public schools in each of these two neighborhoods is obvious to any visitor. At Public School 24 in Riverdale, the principal speaks enthusiastically of his teaching staff. At Public School 79, serving poorer children to the south, the principal says that he is forced to take the "tenth-best" teachers. "I thank God they're still breathing," he remarks of those from whom he must select his teachers....

Sometimes a school principal, whatever his background or his politics, looks into the faces of the children in his school and offers a disarming statement that cuts through official ambiguity. "These are the kids most in need," says Edward Flanery, the principal of one of the low-income schools, "and they get the worst teachers." For children of diverse needs in his overcrowded rooms, he says, "you need an outstanding teacher. And what do you get? You get the worst."

In order to find Public School 261 in District 10, a visitor is told to look for a mortician's office. The funeral home, which faces Jerome Avenue in the North Bronx, is easy to identify by its green awning. The school is next door, in a former roller-skating rink. No sign identifies the building as a school. A metal awning frame without an awning supports a flagpole, but there is no flag.

In the street in front of the school is an elevated public transit line. Heavy traffic fills the street. The existence of the school is virtually concealed within this crowded city block.

In a vestibule between the outer and inner glass doors of the school is a sign with these words: "All children are capable of learning."

Beyond the inner doors, a guard is seated. The lobby is long and narrow. The ceiling is low. There are no windows. All the teachers I see at first are middle-aged white women. The principal, who is also a white woman, tells me that the school's "capacity" is 900, but that there are 1,300 children here. The size of classes for fifth and sixth grade children in New York, she says, is "capped" at 32, but she says that class size in the school goes "up to 34." (I later see classes, however, as large as 37.) Classes for younger children, she goes on, are "capped at 25," but a school can go above this limit if it puts an extra adult in the room. Lack of space, she says, prevents the school from operating a pre-kindergarten program.

I ask the principal where her children go to school. They are enrolled in private school, she says.

"Lunch time is a challenge for us," she explains. "Limited space obliges us to do it in three shifts, 450 children at a time."

Textbooks are scarce and children have to share their social studies books. The principal says there is one full-time pupil counselor and another who is here two days a week: A ratio of 930 children to one counselor. The carpets are patched and sometimes taped together to conceal an open space. "I could use some new rugs," she observes.

To make up for the building's lack of windows and the crowded feeling that results, the staff puts plants and fish tanks in the corridors. Some of the plants are flourishing. Two boys, released from class, are in a corridor beside a tank, their noses pressed against the glass. A school of pinkish fish inside the tank are darting back and forth. Farther down the corridor a small Hispanic girl is watering the plants.

Two first-grade classes share a single room without a window, divided only by a blackboard. Four kindergartens and a sixth-grade class of Spanish-speaking children have been packed into a single room in which, again, there is no window. A second-grade bilingual class of 37 children has its own room, but again there is no window.

By eleven o'clock, the lunchroom is already packed with appetite and life. The kids line up to get their meals, then eat them in ten minutes. After that, with no place they can go to play, they sit and wait until it's time to line up and go back to class.

On the second floor, I visit four classes taking place within another undivided space. The room has a low ceiling. File cabinets and movable blackboards give a small degree of isolation to each class. Again, there are no windows.

The library is a tiny, windowless, and claustrophobic room. I count approximately 700 books. Seeing no reference books, I ask a teacher if encyclopedias and other reference books are kept in classrooms.

"We don't have encyclopedias in classrooms," she replies. "That is for the suburbs."

The school, I am told, has 26 computers for its 1,300 children. There is one small gym, and children get one period, and sometimes two, each week. Recess, however, is not possible because there is no playground. "Head Start," the principal says, "scarcely exists in District 10. We have no space."

The school, I am told, is 90 percent black and Hispanic; the other 10 percent are Asian, white, or Middle Eastern.

In a sixth-grade social studies class, the walls are bare of words or decorations. There seems to be no ventilation system, or, if one exists, it isn't working.

The class discusses the Nile River and the Fertile Crescent.

The teacher, in a droning voice: "How is it useful that these civilizations developed close to rivers?"

A child, in a good loud voice: "What kind of question is that?"

In my notes, I find these words: "An uncomfortable feeling—being in a building with no windows. There are metal ducts across the room. Do they give air? I feel asphyxiated…."

On the top floor of the school, a sixth grade of 30 children shares a room with 29 bilingual second graders. Because of the high class size, there is an assistant with each teacher. This means that 59 children and four grown-ups—63 in all—must share a room that, in a suburban school, would hold no more than 20 children and one teacher. There are, at least, some outside windows in this room—it is the only room with windows in the school—and the room has a high ceiling. It is a relief to see some daylight.

I return to see the kindergarten classes on the ground floor and feel stifled once again by lack of air and the low ceiling. Nearly 120 children and adults are doing what they can to make the best of things: 80 children in four kindergarten classes, 30 children in the sixth-grade class, and about eight grown-ups who are aides and teachers. The kindergarten children, sitting on the worn rug, which is patched with tape, look up at me and turn their heads to follow me as I walk past them.

As I leave the school, a sixth-grade teacher stops to talk. I ask her, "Is there air conditioning in warmer weather?"

Teachers, while inside the building, are reluctant to give answers to this kind of question. Out-side, on the sidewalk, she is less constrained: "I had an awful room last year. In the winter, it was 56 degrees. In the summer, it was up to 90. It was sweltering."

I ask her, "Do the children ever comment on the building?"

"They don't say," she answers, "but they know."

I ask her if they see it as a racial message.

"All these children see TV," she says. "They know what suburban schools are like. Then they look around them at their school. This was a roller-rink, you know…. They don't comment on it, but you see it in their eyes. They understand."

On the following morning, I visit P.S. 79, another elementary school in the same district. "We work under difficult circumstances," says the principal, James Carter, who is black. "The school was built to hold one thousand students. We have 1,550. We are badly overcrowded. We need smaller classes but, to do this, we would need more space. I can't add five teachers. I would have no place to put them."

Some experts, I observe, believe that class size isn't a real issue. He dismisses this abruptly. "It doesn't take a genius to discover that you learn more in a smaller class. I have to bus some 60 kindergarten children elsewhere, since I have no space for them. When they return next year, where do I put them?"

"I can't set up a computer lab. I have no room. I had to put a class into the library. I have no librarian. There are two gymnasiums upstairs, but they cannot be used for sports. We hold more classes there. It's unfair to measure us against the suburbs. They have 17 to 20 children in a class. Average class size in this school is 30."

"The school is 29 percent black, 70 percent Hispanic. Few of these kids get Head Start. There is no space in the district. Of 200 kindergarten children, 50 maybe get some kind of preschool."

I ask him how much difference preschool makes.

"Those who get it do appreciably better. I can't overestimate its impact but, as I have said, we have no space."

The school tracks children by ability, he says. "There are five to seven levels in each grade. The highest level is equivalent to 'gifted,' but it's not a full-scale gifted program. We don't have the funds.

We have no science room. The science teachers carry their equipment with them."

We sit and talk in the nurse's room. The window is broken. There are two holes in the ceiling. About a quarter of the ceiling has been patched and covered with a plastic garbage bag.

"Ideal class size for these kids would be 15 to 20. Will these children ever get what white kids in the suburbs take for granted? I don't think so. If you ask me why, I'd have to speak of race and social class. I don't think the powers that be in New York City understand, or want to understand, that if they do not give these children a sufficient education to lead healthy and productive lives, we will be their victims later on. We'll pay the price someday—in violence, in economic costs. I despair of making this appeal in any terms but these. You cannot issue an appeal to conscience in New York today. The fair-play argument won't be accepted. So you speak of violence and hope that it will scare the city into action."

While we talk, three children who look six or seven years old come to the door and ask to see the nurse, who isn't in the school today. One of the children, a Puerto Rican girl, looks haggard. "I have a pain in my tooth," she says. The principal says, "The nurse is out. Why don't you call your mother?" The child says, "My mother doesn't have a phone." The principal sighs. "Then go back to your class." When she leaves, the principal is angry. "It's amazing to me that these children ever make it with the obstacles they face. Many *do* care and *they do* try, but there's a feeling of despair. The parents of these children want the same things for their children that the parents in the suburbs want. Drugs are not the cause of this. They are the symptom. Nonetheless, they're used by people in the suburbs and rich people in Manhattan as another reason to keep children of poor people at a distance."

I ask him, "Will white children and black children ever go to school together in New York?"

"I don't see it," he replies. "I just don't think it's going to happen. It's a dream. I simply do not see white folks in Riverdale agreeing to cross-bus with kids like these. A few, maybe. Very few. I don't think I'll live to see it happen."

I ask him whether race is the decisive factor. Many experts, I observe, believe that wealth is more important in determining these inequalities.

"This," he says—and sweeps his hand around him at the room, the garbage bag, the ceiling—"would not happen to white children...."

Two months later, on a day in May, I visit an elementary school in Riverdale. The dogwoods and magnolias on the lawn in front of P.S. 24 are in full blossom on the day I visit. There is a well-tended park across the street, another larger park three blocks away. To the left of the school is a playground for small children, with an innovative jungle gym, a slide, and several climbing toys. Behind the school are two playing fields for older kids. The grass around the school is neatly trimmed.

The neighborhood around the school, by no means the richest part of Riverdale, is nonetheless expensive and quite beautiful. Residences in the area—some of which are large, free-standing houses, others condominiums in solid red-brick buildings—sell for prices in the region of $400,000, but some of the larger Tudor houses on the winding and tree-shaded streets close to the school can cost up to $1 million. The excellence of P.S. 24, according to the principal, adds to the value of these homes. Advertisements in the *New York Times* will frequently inform prospective buyers that a house is "in the neighborhood of P.S. 24."

The school serves 825 children in the kindergarten through sixth grade. This is approximately half the student population crowded into P.S. 79, where 1,550 children fill a space intended for 1,000, and a great deal smaller than the 1,300 children packed into the former skating rink; but the principal of P.S. 24, a capable and energetic man named David Rothstein, still regards it as excessive for an elementary school.

The school is integrated in the strict sense that the middle- and upper-middle-class white children here occupy a building that contains some Asian and Hispanic and black children; but there is little integration in the classrooms because the vast majority of the Hispanic and black children are assigned to "special" classes on the basis of evaluations that have classified them EMR—"educable mentally retarded"—or else, in the worst of cases, TMR—"trainable mentally retarded."

I ask the principal if any of his students qualify for free-lunch programs. "About 130 do," he says. "Perhaps another 35 receive their lunches at reduced price. Most of these kids are in the special classes. They do not come from this neighborhood."

The very few nonwhite children that one sees in mainstream classes tend to be Japanese or of other Asian origins. Riverdale, I learn, has been the residence of choice for many years to members of the diplomatic corps.

The school therefore contains effectively two separate schools: one of about 130 children, most of whom are poor, Hispanic, black, assigned to one of the 12 special classes; the other of some 700 mainstream students, almost all of whom are white or Asian.

There is a third track also — this one for the students who are labeled "talented" or "gifted." This is termed a "pull-out" program because the children who are so identified remain in mainstream classrooms but are taken out for certain periods each week to be provided with intensive and, in my opinion, excellent instruction in some areas of reasoning and logic often known as "higher-order skills" in the contemporary jargon of the public schools. Children identified as "gifted" are admitted to this program in first grade and, in most cases, will remain there for six years. Even here, however, there are two tracks of the gifted. The regular gifted classes are provided with only one semester of this specialized instruction yearly. Those very few children, on the other hand, who are identified as showing the most promise are assigned, beginning in the third grade, to a program that receives a full-year regimen.

In one such class, containing ten intensely verbal and impressive fourth-grade children, nine are white and one is Asian. The "special" class I enter first, by way of contrast, has twelve children of whom only one is white and none is Asian. These racial breakdowns prove to be predictive of the schoolwide pattern.

In a classroom for the gifted on the first floor of the school, I ask a child what the class is doing. "Logic and syllogisms," she replies. The room is fitted with a planetarium. The principal says that all the elementary schools in District 10 were given the same planetariums ten years ago, but that certain schools, because of overcrowding, have been forced to give them up. At P.S. 261, according to my notes, there was a domelike space that had been built to hold a planetarium, but the plane-

tarium had been removed to free up space for the small library collection. P.S. 24, in contrast, has a spacious library that holds almost 8,000 books. The windows are decorated with attractive, brightly colored curtains and look out on flowering trees. The principal says that it's inadequate, but it appears spectacular to me after the cubicle that holds a meager 700 books within the former skating rink.

The district can't afford librarians, the principal says, but P.S. 24, unlike the poorer schools of District 10, can draw on educated parent volunteers who staff the room in shifts three days a week. A parent organization also raises independent funds to buy materials, including books, and will soon be running a fund-raiser to enhance the library's collection.

In a large and sunny first-grade classroom that I enter next, I see 23 children, all of whom are white or Asian. In another first grade, there are 22 white children and two others who are Japanese. There is a computer in each class. Every classroom also has a modern fitted sink.

In a second-grade class of 22 children, there are two black children and three Asian children. Again, there is a sink and a computer. A sixth-grade social studies class has only one black child. The children have an in-class research area that holds some up-to-date resources. A set of encyclopedias (World Book, 1985) is in a rack beside a window. The children are doing a Spanish language lesson when I enter. Foreign languages begin in sixth grade at the school, but Spanish is offered also to the kindergarten children. As in every room at P.S. 24, the window shades are clean and new, the floor is neatly tiled in gray and green, and there is not a single light bulb missing.

Walking next into a special class, I see twelve children. One is white. Eleven are black. There are no Asian children. The room is half the size of mainstream classrooms. "Because of overcrowding," says the principal, "we have had to split these rooms in half." There is no computer and no sink.

I enter another special class. Of seven children, five are black, one is Hispanic, one is white. A little black boy with a large head sits in the far corner and is gazing at the ceiling.

"Placement of these kids," the principal explains, "can usually be traced to neurological damage."

In my notes: "How could so many of these children be brain damaged?"

Next door to the special class is a woodworking shop. "This shop is only for the special classes," says the principal. The children learn to punch in time cards at the door, he says, in order to prepare them for employment.

The fourth-grade gifted class, in which I spend the last part of the day, is humming with excitement. "I start with these children in the first grade," says the teacher. "We pull them out of mainstream classes on the basis of their test results and other factors such as the opinion of their teachers. Out of this group, beginning in third grade, I pull out the ones who show the most potential, and they enter classes such as this one."

The curriculum they follow, she explains, "emphasizes critical thinking, reasoning, and logic." The planetarium, for instance, is employed not simply for the study of the universe as it exists. "Children also are designing their own galaxies," the teacher says.

A little girl sitting around a table with her classmates speaks with perfect poise: "My name is Susan. We are in the fourth-grade gifted program."

I ask them what they're doing, and a child says, "My name is Laurie, and we're doing problem-solving."

A rather tall, good-natured boy who is half-standing at the table tells me that his name is David. "One thing that we do," he says, "is logical thinking. Some problems, we find, have more than one good answer. We need to learn not simply to be logical in our own thinking but to show respect for someone else's logic even when an answer may be technically incorrect."

When I ask him to explain this, he goes on, "A person who gives an answer that is not 'correct' may nonetheless have done some interesting thinking that we should examine. 'Wrong' answers may be more useful to examine than correct ones."

I ask the children if reasoning and logic are innate or if they're things that you can learn.

"You know some things to start with when you enter school," Susan says. "But we also learn some things that other children don't."

I ask her to explain this.

"We know certain things that other kids don't know because we're *taught* them."

She has braces on her teeth. Her long brown hair falls almost to her waist. Her loose white T-shirt has the word *TRI-LOGIC* on the front. She tells me that Tri-Logic is her father's firm.

Laurie elaborates on the same point: "Some things, you know. Some kinds of logic are inside of you to start with. There are other things that someone needs to teach you."

David expands on what the other two have said: "Everyone can think and speak in logical ways unless they have a mental problem. What this program does is bring us to a higher form of logic."

The class is writing a new "Bill of Rights." The children already know the U.S. Bill of Rights and they explain its first four items to me with precision. What they are examining today, they tell me, is the very *concept* of a "right." Then they will create their own compendium of rights according to their own analysis and definition. Along one wall of the classroom, opposite the planetarium, are seven Apple II computers on which children have developed rather subtle color animations that express the themes—of greed and domination, for example—that they also have described in writing.

"This is an upwardly mobile group," the teacher later says. "They have exposure to whatever New York City has available. Their parents may take them to the theater, to museums...."

In my notes: "Six girls, four boys. Nine white, one Chinese. I am glad they have this class. But what about the others? Aren't there ten black children in the school who could enjoy this also?"

The teacher gives me a newspaper written, edited, and computer-printed by her sixth-grade gifted class. The children, she tells me, are provided with a link to kids in Europe for transmission of news stories.

A science story by one student asks whether scientists have ever falsified their research. "Gregor Mendel," the sixth grader writes, "the Austrian monk who founded the science of genetics, published papers on his work with peas that some experts say were statistically too good to be true. Isaac Newton, who formulated the law of gravitation, relied on unseemly mathematical sleight of hand in his calculations.... Galileo Galilei, founder of modern scientific method, wrote about experiments that were so difficult to duplicate that colleagues doubted he had done them."

Another item in the paper, also by a sixth-grade student, is less esoteric: "The Don Cossacks dance company, from Russia, is visiting the United States. The last time it toured America was 1976.... The Don Cossacks will be in New York City for two weeks at the Neil Simon Theater. Don't miss it!"

The tone is breezy – and so confident! That phrase – "Don't miss it!" – speaks a volume about life in Riverdale.

"What makes a good school?" asks the principal when we are talking later on. "The building and teachers are part of it, of course. But it isn't just the building and the teachers. Our kids come from good families and the neighborhood is good. In a three-block area, we have a public library, a park, a junior high.... Our typical sixth grader reads at eighth-grade level." In a quieter voice he says, "I see how hard my colleagues work in schools like P.S. 79. You have children in those neighborhoods who live in virtual hell. They enter school five years behind. What do they get?" Then, as he spreads his hands out on his desk, he says: "I have to ask myself why there should be an elementary school in District 10 with fifteen hundred children. Why should there be an elementary school within a skating rink? Why should the Board of Ed allow this? This is not the way that things should be...."

The differences *between* school districts and *within* school districts in the city are, however, almost insignificant compared to those between the city and the world of affluence around it – in Westchester County, for example, and in largely prosperous Long Island.

Even in the suburbs, nonetheless, it has been noted that a differential system still exists, and it may not be surprising to discover that the differences are once again determined by the social class, parental wealth, and sometimes race, of the schoolchildren. A study, a few years ago, of 20 of the wealthiest and poorest districts of Long Island, for example, matched by location and size of enrollment, found that the differences in per-pupil spending were not only large but had approximately doubled in a five-year period. Schools, in Great Neck, in 1987, spent $11,265 for each pupil. In affluent Jericho and Manhasset, the figures were, respectively, $11,325 and $11,370. In Oyster Bay, the figure was $9,980. Compare this to Levittown, also on Long Island but a town of most-

ly working-class white families, where per-pupil spending dropped to $6,900. Then compare these numbers to the spending level in the town of Roosevelt, the poorest district in the county, where the schools are 99 percent nonwhite and where the figure dropped to $6,340. Finally, consider New York City, where, in the same year, $5,590 was invested in each pupil – less than half of what was spent in Great Neck. The pattern is almost identical to that which we have seen outside Chicago.

Again, look at Westchester County, where, in the same year, the same range of discrepancies was found. Affluent Bronxville, an attractive suburb just north of the Bronx, spent $10,000 for each pupil. Chappaqua's yearly spending figure rose above $9,000. Studying the chart again, we locate Yonkers – a blue-collar town that is predominantly white but where over half the student population is nonwhite – and we find the figure drops to $7,400. This is not the lowest figure, though. The lowest-spending schools within Westchester, spending a full thousand dollars less than Yonkers, serve the suburb of Mount Vernon, where three quarters of the children in the public schools are black.[+]

"If you're looking for a home," a realtor notes, "you can look at the charts for school expenditures and use them to determine if your neighbors will be white and wealthy or, conversely, black or white but poor...."

In effect, a circular phenomenon evolves: The richer districts – those in which the property lots and houses are more highly valued – have more revenue, derived from taxing land and homes, to fund their public schools. The reputation of the schools, in turn, adds to the value of their homes, and this, in turn, expands the tax base for their public schools. The fact that they can levy lower taxes than the poorer districts but exact more money, raises values even more; and this, again, means further funds for smaller classes and for higher teacher salaries within their public schools. Few of the children in the schools of Roosevelt or Mount Vernon will, as a result, be likely to compete effectively with kids in Great Neck and Manhasset for admissions to the better local colleges and universities of New York state. Even fewer will compete for more exclusive Ivy League admissions. And few of the graduates or dropouts of those poorer systems, as a consequence, are likely ever to earn enough to buy a home in Great Neck or Manhasset....

The point is often made that, even with a genuine equality of schooling for poor children, other forces still would militate against their school performance. Cultural and economic factors and the flight of middle-income blacks from inner cities still would have their consequences in the heightened concentration of the poorest children in the poorest neighborhoods. Teen-age pregnancy, drug use, and other problems still would render many families in these neighborhoods all but dysfunctional. Nothing I have said...should leave the misimpression that I do not think these factors are enormously important. A polarization of this issue, whereby some insist on the primacy of school, others on the primacy of family and neighborhood, obscures the fact that both are elemental forces in the lives of children.

The family, however, differs from the school in the significant respect that government is not responsible, or at least not directly, for the inequalities of family background. It *is* responsible for inequalities in public education. The school is the creature of the state; the family is not. To the degree, moreover, that destructive family situations may be bettered by the future acts of government, no one expects that this could happen in the years immediately ahead. Schools, on the other hand, could make dramatic changes almost overnight if fiscal equity were a reality.

If the New York City schools were funded, for example, at the level of the highest-spending suburbs of Long Island, a fourth-grade class of 36 children such as those I visited in District 10 would have had $200,000 more invested in their education during 1987.[5] Although a portion of this extra money would have gone into administrative costs, the remainder would have been enough to hire two extraordinary teachers at enticing salaries of $50,000 each, divide the class into *two classes* of some 18 children each, provide them with computers, carpets, air conditioning, new texts and reference books, and learning games—indeed, with everything available today in the most affluent school districts—and also pay the costs of extra counseling to help those children cope with the dilemmas that they face at home. Even the most skeptical detractor of "the worth of spending fur-

ther money in the public schools" would hesitate, I think, to face a grade-school principal in the South Bronx and try to tell her that this "wouldn't make much difference."

It is obvious that urban schools have other problems in addition to their insufficient funding. Administrative chaos is endemic in some urban systems. (The fact that this in itself is a reflection of our low regard for children who depend on these systems is a separate matter.) Greater funding, if it were intelligently applied, could partially correct these problems—by making possible, for instance, the employment of some very gifted, high-paid fiscal managers who could ensure that money is well used—but it probably is also true that major structural reforms would still be needed. To polarize these points, however, and to argue, as the White House has been claiming for a decade, that administrative changes are a "better" answer to the problem than equality of funding and real efforts at desegregation is dishonest and simplistic. The suburbs have better administrations (sometimes, but not always), and they also have a lot more money in proportion to their children's needs. To speak of the former and evade the latter is a formula that guarantees that nothing will be done *today* for children who have no responsibility for either problem.

To be in favor of "good families" or of "good administration" does not take much courage or originality. It is hard to think of anyone who is opposed to either. To be in favor of redistribution of resources and of racial integration would require a great deal of courage—and a soaring sense of vision—in a president or any other politician. Whether such courage or such vision will someday become transcendent forces in our nation is by no means clear....

Until 1983, Mississippi was one of the few states with no kindergarten program and without compulsory attendance laws. Governor William Winter tried that year to get the legislature to approve a $60-million plan to upgrade public education. The plan included early childhood education, higher teacher salaries, a better math and science program for the high schools, and compulsory attendance with provisions for enforcement. The state's powerful oil corporations, facing a modest increase in their taxes to support the plan, lobbied vigorously against it. The Mid-Continent Oil and Gas Association began a television advertising campaign to defeat the bill, according to a *Newsweek* story.[6]

"The vested interests are just too powerful," a state legislator said. Those interests, according to *Newsweek*, are "unlikely" to rush to the aid of public schools that serve poor children.

It is unlikely that the parents or the kids in Rye or Riverdale know much about realities like these; and, if they do, they may well tell themselves that Mississippi is a distant place and that they have work enough to do to face inequities in New York City. But, in reality, the plight of children in the South Bronx of New York is almost as far from them as that of children in the farthest reaches of the South.

All of these children say the Pledge of Allegiance every morning. Whether in the New York suburbs, Mississippi, or the South Bronx, they salute the same flag. They place their hands across their hearts and join their voices in a tribute to "one nation indivisible" which promises liberty and justice to all people. What is the danger that the people in a town like Rye would face if they resolved to make this statement true? How much would it really harm their children to compete in a fair race?

## ENDNOTES

1. Lord Acton cited: George Alan Hickrod, "Reply to the 'Forbs' Article," *Journal of School Finance*, vol. 12 (1987).

2. Per-pupil Spending, New York City and Suburbs: Office for Policy Analysis and Program Accountability, New York State Board of Education, "Statistical Profiles of School Districts," (Albany: 1987).

3. Question Asked by New York City Board of Education and Response of Community Service Society: Community Service Society of New York, "Promoting Poverty: The Shift of Resources Away from Low-Income New York City School Districts," (New York: 1987).

4. Per-pupil Spending in Long Island and Westchester County: New York State Department of Education, "Statistical Profiles of School Districts," cited above. Also see *Newsday*, May 18, 1986. According to Sandra Feldman, President of the United Federation of Teachers in New York City, "the average per-pupil expenditure is nearly $2,500 higher" in the suburbs "right outside the city." (*The School Administrator*, March 1991.) According to the *New York Times* (May 4, 1991), New York City now spends $7,000 for each pupil. The wealthiest suburbs spend approximately $15,000.

5. $200,000 More Each Year: In the school year ending in June 1987, per-pupil funding was $5,585 in New York City, about $11,300 in Jericho and Manhasset. For 36 children, the difference was over $200,000.

6. Mississippi Data: *Time*, November 14, 1988; *Newsweek*, December 13, 1982; *Governing Magazine*, January 1990.

# Part XII

# SOCIAL CHANGE

Individuals must be understood within the context of social organization. We are located in structure, learn culture, are socialized, and are subject to institutions and social controls.

However, human beings also act back on society, and in those actions, they sometimes change society. Society is not simply a static entity; it is ever changing.

What causes society to change? Does violence produce change? According to William Gamson in the first selection, sometimes it does. Michel Crozier warns us that it is very difficult for any individual to change as complex a system as society. In the third selection by William G. Flanagan, the important role of the city is examined; and in the fourth selection by David Ashley and David Michael Orenstein, the trends that they identify as "postmodern" alert us to some very recent changes in society as we approach the twenty-first century.

Lewis Killian writes a very personal view of social change as it relates to race relations. This selection is part of the final chapter in his autobiography as a sociologist, and his conclusions question how much has really changed when it comes to race relations in society.

# 57. VIOLENCE AND POLITICAL POWER: THE MEEK DON'T MAKE IT

WILLIAM A. GAMSON

*"The successful group is one that is ready and willing to fight like hell for goals that can be met without overturning the system."*

There are always some in society who refuse to accept the way things are. Sometimes, such people perform individual acts of protest (such as refusing to pay that part of their income tax earmarked for war), and sometimes they join together with others to work for change. Americans have had a long tradition of protest movements, and it seems that in the 1960s, such movements were very influential in effecting change. Sometimes, social movements are diffuse and only slightly structured (such as the anti-Vietnam War movement) but are able to influence change through marches, demonstrations, boycotts, or acts of violence by individual protesters or authorities.

William A. Gamson's article discusses organized protest groups and their attempts to alter society. It asks a simple question: Do groups that end up using violence to achieve their ends succeed or are they doomed to fail? The answer is not a simple one, and it may be surprising.

Besides being a good introduction to social change, the article is also an example of how a sociologist might scientifically study this complex topic. One does not have to just **think** that violence works or that it does not. Here is a beginning to that long and difficult process of gathering evidence carefully and without serious bias. As in all good scientific reporting, the technique used by the researcher is carefully laid out for the reader, so that the reader has the necessary information to criticize the study or to do one of his or her own to show that the researcher is wrong.

Most political scientists view the American system as a pluralist democracy. The image is of a contest carried out under orderly rules. "You scratch my back and I'll scratch yours"; "If you want to get along, go along"; "Don't make permanent enemies because today's adversary may be your ally next time around."

It's a contest for power and recognition that any number can play. If you've got a problem, get organized, play the game, and work for change. Don't expect to win every time or to win the whole pot; compromise is the lifeblood of pluralist politics. More likely than not, you'll find some allies who are willing to help you because they think you can help them, now or in the future.

Of course, some people won't play by the rules. Instead of bargaining for advantages, forming coalitions with the powerful, writing peaceful propaganda, and petitioning, some groups get nasty. Contestants who misbehave, who resort to violence and, perish the thought, try to eliminate other contestants, must be excluded from the game.

In such a calculus, the Tobacco Night Riders should have failed. They began as a secret fraternal order, officially called the "Silent Brigade," whose purpose was to force tobacco growers to join the Planters Protective Association, hold tobacco off the market, and bargain collectively with the huge tobacco companies.

## WHEN VIOLENCE PAID

The Night Riders didn't play by the rules of pluralist politics. On December 1, 1906, 250 masked and armed men swarmed into Princeton, Kentucky, and took control. They disarmed the police, shut off the water supply, and captured the courthouse and telephone offices. They patrolled the streets, ordered citizens to keep out of sight, and shot at those who disobeyed. Then they dynamited and burned two large tobacco factories and rode off singing "the fire shines bright in my old Kentucky home."

A year later, they struck again, at Hopkinsville, Kentucky. They occupied strategic posts and dragged a buyer from the Imperial Tobacco Company from his home to pistol-whip him. As usual, they marched out singing, but this time the sheriff organized a posse to pursue the raiders and attacked their rear. The pursuers killed one man and wounded another before the raiders drove the posse back into Hopkinsville.

Violence, we are told, doesn't pay, but the Night Riders enjoyed a considerable measure of success. By 1908, the Planters Protective Association was handling nine-tenths of the crop produced in its area. The power of the big tobacco companies was broken, and they were buying their tobacco through the association at substantially increased prices. From the depressed conditions of a few years earlier, the black patch area of Kentucky and Tennessee prospered. Mortgages were paid off and new homes, new buggies, and new barns appeared everywhere. The state of Kentucky even passed a law providing a penalty of "triple damages" for any association member who sold his tobacco "outside."

## FLAWS IN THE PLURALIST HEAVEN

In recent years, the body of criticism about the assumptions of pluralist theory has grown. Critics such as C. Wright Mills, whose *The Power Elite* was one of the earliest and most vocal attacks on the theory, deny the pluralist premise that America has no single center of power. "The flaw in the pluralist heaven," writes political scientist E. E. Schattschneider, "is that the heavenly chorus sings with a strong upper-class accent. Probably about 90 percent of the people cannot get into the pressure system."

To know who gets into the system, and how, is to understand the central issue of American politics. In the last 200 years, hundreds of previously unorganized groups here challenged the existing powers. Many of them collapsed quickly and left no trace; some died and rose again from the ashes. Some were pre-empted by competitors, some won the trappings of influence without its substance. Some shoved their way into the political arena yelling and screaming, some walked in on the arms of powerful sponsors, some wandered in unnoticed. The fate of these challenging groups reveals just how permeable the American system is.

To see which groups make it, and what factors contribute to their success, I picked a random sample from the hundreds of challenging groups that surfaced in America between 1800 and 1945. I drew the line after World War II because the outcomes for current protest groups are still unclear. I defined a *challenging group* by its relationship to two targets: its *antagonist* (the object of actual or planned attempts at influence) and its *constituency* (the individuals or organizations whose resources and energy the group seeks to organize and mobilize).

A challenging group must meet two problems at the same time. Unlike an established interest group such as the American Medical Association, its membership is not already organized. A challenging group cannot send out a call to action and expect that most of its loyal members will follow it into battle; it must create this loyalty from scratch. Of course, many of today's established groups went through a period of challenge and we studied some of them during their early years.

Second, a challenging group must demand some change that its own membership cannot provide. A messianic group that offered salvation to members would not qualify unless the group wanted changes in laws or social institutions as well.

A challenge ends when one of three events occurs: The group disbands; the group stops trying to win friends and influence people, even though it continues to exist; or the group's major antagonists accept it as a legitimate spokesman for its constituency.

I drew my sample from an exhaustive list of social movements and formal organizations. After eliminating those that did not fit the definition of a challenging group, we were left with 64 valid groups, and of these we were able to get sufficient information on 53.

## CHALLENGES FROM BICYCLES TO BIRTH CONTROL

The 53 groups are a representative sample of challenging groups in American history.... Some failed, some won. Some had quite humble goals: The League of American Wheelmen formed in 1880 to get the right to bicycle on public highways. Others sought nothing less than revolution. Some groups, such as the American Birth Control League, started radical and became establishment. Others, like the Night Riders, appear more disreputable today than they probably seemed then.

Twenty of the groups were occupationally based, such as the American Federation of Teachers; 17 were reform oriented, such as the Federal Suffrage Association; 10 were socialist, such as the International Workingmen's Association (the First International); and 6 were some brand of right-wing or nativist group, such as the Christian Front Against Communism or the German-American Bund.

Definitions of success are complicated. We tried many and settled on two summary measures. The first focuses on whether other power holders came to accept the group as a valid representative of legitimate interests. The second measure focuses on whether the group gained new advantages for its constituents and beneficiaries and accomplished its goals.

The combination of these two definitions of success means that a group's efforts may have four possible outcomes. It may win many new advantages and full acceptance from its antagonists (complete success); no advantages but acceptance (co-optation); many advantages but no acceptance (preemption); or neither advantages nor acceptance (failure). More than half of the groups, 58 percent, were successful on one measure or the other; only 38 percent were successful in both meanings.

Next, I explored the strategies and characteristics of the groups to see why some succeeded and others failed. I began with the touchiest issue of all, violence.

Most of the groups had no violence at all in their history, but 15 of them participated in some kind of violent exchange. It is misleading, however, to assume that these groups used violence as a tactic. In some cases, they were attacked by the police or by mobs with little or no provocation; in other cases, pitched battles took place but it is no easy matter to know who started in. Rather than trying to make that judgment, we divided the groups into two types — eight activist groups that, whether or not they initiated a fight, were willing to give and take if one started. The other seven were passive recipients; they were attacked and could not, or simply did not, fight back.

## THE SUCCESS OF THE UNRULY

In the case of violence, it appears better to give than to receive if you want to succeed in American politics. The activist groups that fought back or, in some cases, initiated violence had a higher-than-average success rate; six of the eight won new advantages and five of the six were eventually accepted as well. The nonviolent recipients of attack, however, lost out completely. None of them met their goals, although one, the Dairymen's League, was co-opted.

Violence is even more certain to reap benefits when the group's goals are limited and when the group does not aim to displace its antagonists but rather to coexist with them. When I eliminated revolutionary groups that aimed to displace the opposition, I found that *every* violence user was successful in winning new advantages and *every* violence recipient was unsuccessful.

Several groups tried a strategy that we might call speaking loudly and carrying a small stick. They advocated violence but never actually used it. The Communist Labor Party, the Revolutionary Workers League, and the German-American Bund roared a good deal, but they never bit. This is the least effective strategy of all, for such groups pay the cost of violence without gaining its benefits. They are threatening but they are weak, which makes them an easy target for repression.

Violence is not the only kind of high-pressure tactic that brings success. Ten groups used other unruly strategies on their opposition; such as strikes, boycotts, and efforts to humiliate or embarrass their antagonists. For example, A. Philip Randolph's March on Washington Committee threatened a mass march on the Capitol in the spring of 1941 to push President Franklin D. Roosevelt into a more active role in ending racial discrimination in employment. The government was then arousing the country for war with appeals that contrasted U.S. democracy with Nazi racism, so such a march would have been a considerable embarrassment to the administration. A week before the march was scheduled to happen, President Roosevelt promised a policy of nondiscrimination in all federal hiring and, by executive order, created a Fair Employment Practices Committee to carry out this policy.

The League of Deliverance used the boycott against businesses that hired Chinese workers. They threatened worse. They notified "offenders" that after six days of non-compliance, their district would be declared "dangerous.... Should the Chinese remain within the proclaimed district after the expiration of...30 days, the General Executive Committee will be required to abate the danger in whatever manner seems best to them." The league, however, never had call to go beyond the boycott tactic. By firing its Chinese employees, a business could buy peace with the league; many did just that.

Forceful tactics are associated with success, as violence is. Eight out of the ten groups that applied such pressures were accepted and won new advantages, a percentage that is twice as great as the percentage for groups that avoided such tactics.

## VIOLENCE COMES FROM CONFIDENCE

These data undermine the pluralist argument that violence is the product of frustration, desperation, and weakness, that it is an act of last resort by those who are unable to attract a following and achieve their goals. Violence, pluralists assume, is unsuccessful as a tactic because it simply increases the hostility around it and invites the legitimate action of authorities against it.

My interpretation is nearly the opposite. Violence grows from an impatience born of confidence and a sense of rising power. It occurs when the challenging group senses that the surrounding community will condone it, when hostility toward the *victim* renders it a relatively safe strategy. In this sense, violence is as much a symptom of success as a cause.

Groups use violence to prevent being destroyed and to deter authorities from attack; less often, they use violence to gain a specific objective. Successful groups almost never used it as a primary tactic. Typically, the primary means of influence were strikes, bargaining, and propaganda. Violence, in short, is the spice of protest, not the meat and potatoes.

The size of the violent groups supports this interpretation. The active groups tend to be large; only one of the eight, the Night Riders, had fewer than 10,000 members, while five of the seven recipients of violence were this small. Such numbers seem more likely to breed confidence and impatience than desperation.

The successful group in American politics is not the polite petitioner who carefully observes all the rules. It is the rambunctious fighter, one with limited goals, that can elbow its way into the arena. But the willingness to fight is not enough. A group must be *able* to fight; it needs organization and discipline to focus its energies.

A challenging group faces antagonists that have control over their members, as established bureaucracies do. Challenging groups can overcome this disadvantage by adopting the structure of established organizations. They can deal on more equal terms if they are able to create their own apparatus of internal control — if they can turn *members* into *agents*.

Even when challenging groups have a committed membership, however, they may still lack unity of command. It is not enough to have agents if they have no direction, if some factions shout, "March!" and others cry, "Wait!"

## THE READINESS IS ALL

One may convert members into soldiers, but soldiers fight civil wars as well as foreign ones. Thus a group needs a bureaucratic structure to help become ready for action, and centralized power to help it reach unified decisions.

I considered a group *bureaucratic* if it had three characteristics. It must have a constitution or charter that states the purposes of the group and rules for its operation; an ideological manifesto is not enough. It must keep a formal list of its members, which it distinguishes from mere sympathizers. And it must have at least three internal divisions; for example, executives, chapter heads, and the rank and file.

Twenty-four of the groups met all three criteria, and these were more likely than nonbureaucratic groups to win acceptance (71 percent to 28 percent) and new advantages (62 percent to 38 percent).

I defined a group as *centralized* if power resided in a single leader or central committee and local chapters had little autonomy. Slightly more than half of the groups, 28, had such a centralized structure; 19 of these had a single, dominant leader, and 9 had some form of collective leadership such as a national board or an executive committee. The rest of the groups had no one center of power.

Centralization is unrelated to bureaucracy as defined above; half of the bureaucratic groups and half of the nonbureaucratic groups had centralized power structures. Bureaucracy and centralization each contribute something to success, but it is the combination that really does the trick. Groups that were both bureaucratic *and* centralized had the best chance of achieving their goals; 75 percent of them were successful. Groups that were neither bureaucratic nor centralized had very little chance of winning anything. Only one, the

Federal Suffrage Association, defied the odds and won both acceptance and advantages. The FSA was only one, and hardly the most important, of the groups that fought for women's suffrage. It achieved its objective, but it was neither alone nor always in the center of the struggle.

Thus modern protest groups that attempt to distribute authority among all their members and avoid hierarchy should take heed. If they are going to be involved with struggles with the authorities, they will have a difficult time avoiding factions in their ranks and reaching their goals.

## JUNGLE LAWS VERSUS POLITE POLITICS

The pluralist image of orderly contest is a half-truth. It fits well enough into the bargaining and give-and-take that goes on inside the political arena. But there is another kind of contest going on at the same time between those outside the arena and those already inside. This conflict is a great deal less orderly than what happens in the lobbies, the board rooms, and the other corridors of established power.

This second locus of conflict has its own rules too, but they are more like the laws of the jungle. Whatever differences the powerful may have among themselves, they are on the same team in the struggle between insiders and outsiders. Challengers who try to play by the rules that members observe among themselves should realize two things. Insiders won't apply their rules to outsiders; and outsiders, being poor in resources, have little to offer the powerful in an alliance.

Challengers do better when they realize that they are in a political combat situation. They don't need to look for a fight, but they had better be ready to participate in one if the occasion arises. They must therefore be organized like a combat group — with willing, committed people who know what to do, and a command structure that can keep its people out of the wrong fight at the wrong time.

But this advice really only applies to groups with limited goals. I included revolutionary groups in my sample, but it should come as no surprise that none of them were successful. I can't say what makes for success among such groups because I had no successes to compare with the failures. A more complete picture of the successful group is one that is ready and willing to fight like hell for goals that can be met without overturning the system.

Perhaps it is disconcerting to discover that the meek do not inherit the earth — or at least that part of it presided over by the American political system. But those rambunctious groups that fight their way into the political arena escape misfortune because they are prepared to withstand counterattack, and to make it costly to those who would keep them out.

# 58. SOCIETY AND CHANGE

## MICHEL CROZIER

*"We will never succeed in changing society the way we want…. Every society is a complex system, and this is why it cannot be changed or renewed simply by a decision, even one arrived at democratically by majority rule."*

Michel Crozier, a French sociologist, regards social change as very complex. Although we may think that society changes because someone is successful in doing so, it rarely changes because of the will of the individual. Our efforts may bring unintended consequences and even have the opposite effect of what we intended. Yet it is still important to try to make change because retreat from attempting change will bring even worse problems.

We will never succeed in changing society the way we want. Even if we were to persuade the majority of our fellow citizens to follow our lead, we would not succeed in enacting a plan for society because society, human relations, and social systems are too complex. We would have succeeded in mobilizing nothing but an abstract and unsubstantial agreement, the awakened dreams of our fellow men. This desire, this fantasy, never determines how people really act.

It is possible to work within a system only by understanding its characteristics. This assertion is not as self-evident as it may appear because all too often we are not willing to understand society as it is. Instead, we spend our time making social blueprints that do not have the slightest chance of success because they do not take into account the complex working of human relationships and everyday social interaction.

Every society is a complex system, and this is why it cannot be changed or renewed simply by a decision, even one arrived at democratically by majority rule. This is not to say that there are fixed laws of society, imposed on humanity like a sort of divine will. This all-too-human construction is the product of human history, and so it can be shaped, reworked, and changed. But at the same time, it is a system, an interdependent framework of relations that is beyond the conscious will of individual people.

Of course, neither these relations nor the whole system are unalterable. They do change as a result of human action, but the overall result of this action is different from the wishes of individual people. It is possible to bring about change more consciously and effectively, but it is not possible to impose a specific program simply through the

From "The Future of French Society," by Michel Crozier, in *Strategies for Change*, MIT Press, Trans. William R. Beer, 1982. English translation copyrighted © 1982 by the Massachusetts Institute of Technology.

agreement of individual people. This may seem contradictory, particularly if the profound difference that exists between people's individual preferences and their real behavior toward others is not appreciated.

Behavior in social relationships is like a game in which each person depends on the other. To win, or simply not to lose, you have to take the possible reactions of others into account. The games of social life make us obey rules that are independent of us. These games are regulated, commanded, corrected, and maintained by mechanisms to which we do not have direct access. These games are the building blocks of systems that organize every one of our activities, including the biggest and most complex, society itself.

When a warehouse worker sets aside a special supply of goods to meet unexpected requests of production workers, while at the same time politely refusing to provide for the maintenance workers, he is neither obeying his boss nor hoping for the final victory of the working class. It is not because of some personal character trait that he is easy-going with his old assistant and strict with his new one. This is the only way he can succeed in keeping the wheels turning in the department that is his world of work, while at the same time keeping the respect of his peers and influencing events that affect him. This is as true at the level of society as it is at the level of a business.

Games, systems, and society are the necessary mediators of all human action, but they are structured in such a way that this mediation can have an effect opposite to what most participants want or think they want. The road to hell, as everyone knows, is paved with good intentions. To set up the rule of virtue, hypocrisy and eavesdropping are brought in, and have been from the time of Savonarola to Mao; the control of excess profits strengthens the black market. And very often in the attempt to free people, new chains are forged for them. Every organized human action, every collective effort, and even ideological movements lead to what can be called the *perverse effect*, effects that are the opposite of what the participants wanted. These perverse effects cannot be blamed on some force of evil — neither on the powerful at the top of the social scale nor on agitators at the bottom. They are the necessary consequence of interdependent relationships among people.

This will come as a surprise to those who still believe in the myth of the social contract, who believe that the collective will of people, the sum of their individual wishes, naturally produces rational decisions. The use of opinion polls has given new respectability and weight to this idealistic view of democracy. In fact, we are prisoners of our social situation, of our relationships, of our need to exist for, with, and against other people. Outside of this situation and these interactions, we cannot decide what we want because we literally do not know. This is why abstract opinion, cut off from the real context of social relations, only partially indicates what our real behavior is. In the spring of 1968, opinion polls registered satisfaction in France, and the pollsters said that the students had never been so happy.

It would be tempting to conclude that it is better not to try to intervene at all because every social action leads to a series of effects that can be the exact opposite of what was intended. This is the temptation of pessimism that has recently reappeared among the "new philosophers." It must be resisted, not simply because it leads people to give up but also because it leads to an even worse state of affairs. Every situation in which we do not intervene tends to deteriorate. Every analysis of businesses or institutions that are not working reveals that the same rules and principles that were successful twenty or thirty years ago are the cause of disorder and failure today.

So it is not a question of choosing between action and retreat but of finding the means and direction of the action that cannot be avoided. In everyday life, we continually make choices on the basis of tested rules based on our experience. Unfortunately, we cannot transpose this principle to a broader area because individually we are helpless against large-scale organizations, nationwide societies, and the world order. The inescapable recognition of our limitations leads us to examine two principles of action.

The first principle is that of giving priority to the understanding of real systems, not to the discussion of aims and ideals. We can find out what we want only if we know what we are doing. As long as we are not aware of what is really going on, our ideals and goals are nothing but projections of our inadequacies and inabilities. We can progress only by bringing the ideal back to earth, by putting the system of relations on its feet: reality first, ideals later.

The second principle, a consequence of understanding the perverse effect, is that we have to get away from the guesswork of everyday activity. We have to spend as much energy on the ongoing operation of the system as we do on utopian projects for changing the whole system radically and idealistically. We cannot do our job as responsible people and citizens unless we go beyond the sort of blind empiricism that led an English minister of foreign affairs to declare shortly before the war in 1914, "You know, nothing really ever happens."

# 59. THE CITY AND SOCIAL CHANGE

### WILLIAM G. FLANAGAN

*"People use cities in different ways, pursue different routines and interests. Each of us uses only part of the city we live in, we experience the urban environment from our own perspectives. These perspectives, in turn, are affected by social class, age, gender, occupation, and many other factors. Because each of us occupies a unique space with respect to all others, our particular image of the city will be unique. In this sense…each of us lives in our own city. Yet the city belongs to no one of us, and we experience it as a world of strangers."*

There is probably nothing so identified with change in the twentieth century as the increasing dominance of the city in people's lives. There are many different ways sociologists have thought about and researched how society and individuals change as we become increasingly urban. Typically, sociologists have seen the city as a place in which the individual is transformed into a stranger without a sense of community. Yet, as Flanagan points out, we must see city life as far more complex than this. As we focus on the life of the individual in the city, we begin to recognize neighborhoods and networks, interdependence and interrelationships, both estrangement and intimacy.

Urban sociology emerged at the end of the nineteenth century, at about the same time that sociology itself was achieving a greater measure of distinction among the social sciences. The same features of the changing world provided the impetus for the development of both general sociological principles and for the development of a branch of social science devoted to the study of cities. The social consequences of the industrial revolution raised important philosophical questions about the future condition or humanity: Foremost among these was the question of how the massing of people in cities would affect the social order. It was largely the growth of the eighteenth- and nineteenth-century city, within the wider economic changes that were taking place in the world, that fostered the development of sociology and encouraged the development of urban sociology in particular.

Excerpt from *Contemporary Urban Sociology*, by William G. Flanagan, Cambridge, England: Cambridge University Press, 1993, pp. 13–23, 39–40.

The central question for the precursors of contemporary urban sociology was what would become of the cohesive mechanisms that had maintained the rural social order. In a word, what would become of "community" in a new urban world? What impact would urbanization have on the integrity of pre-existing forms of social organization? The tension between city and community has remained a central issue in urban sociology. Although the last two or three decades witnessed a significant expansion of the scope of the discipline…there is still a substantial share of urban sociology devoted to the question of how the urban setting modifies the way people think and behave. This is the tradition from which urban sociology has evolved, both in the sense that the tradition has provided a foundation for the development of various interpretations of "urbanism," and in the sense that it provides a target for criticism from various quarters today….

## THE TENSION BETWEEN CITY AND COMMUNITY

During the nineteenth century, rapid change, including the growth of cities, inspired social philosophers to speculate about how the emerging social order would differ from that of the past. Their conclusions have furnished some of sociology's most basic, classic generalizations. Tönnies's ([1887] 1940) well-known observations regarding *Gemeinschaft* and *Gesellschaft* have provided generations of social scientists with a basis for distinguishing between the essences of rural and urban life. Rural life is dominated by group identity, *Gemeinschaft*, the condition of being subordinate to the group. It is a challenge to the imagination of the contemporary student to envision the individual primarily as a fragment of a solidarity. *Gesellschaft*, the opposite condition of being on one's own in the world appears, on the other hand, to be a description of the familiar, the taken for granted. The observations that people operate as individuals, on the basis of self-interest, that each person seeks to profit from interaction, appear today no more than simple descriptive statements, not theoretical speculations. The aspect of

Tönnies's thesis that we doubt today is his extrapolation: The dominant motive of self-interest ensures that each person is truly alone. Like many who followed him, Tönnies did not provide individuals with a private sphere in which they might cultivate meaningful and rich social ties.

Durkheim's (1893) classical formulation, contrasting *mechanical* and *organic solidarity*, has for a century reinforced the spirit of Tönnies's bipolar distinction. For Durkheim, rural or peasant life is characterized by a unity of values and vision, because the members of every peasant household experience roughly the same set of circumstances and cycles during the course of their lives. The result of common experience is the unity of ideas expressed in a collective consciousness, in a mechanical solidarity. This social condition cannot be obtained in the city. In the city, the density of population demands occupational specialization; it hence breaks down the unity formed of common experience and creates in its place an order based on functional interdependence among people engaged in specialized work. People don't identify with each other, instead they depend on one another to serve the many needs of the populace. In the case of both Tönnies and Durkheim, the moral order of common values in a preurban society is replaced by an instrumental order in an urban society.

Max Weber (1905) is prominent among those who have pointed out that cities are, above all else, marketplaces. Yet, for him, market relations did not undermine social cohesion, but accentuated it. What sets Weber's work apart is that he chose the preindustrial city as most closely approximating the ideal-typical model of urban life and organization. For Weber, what distinguished truly urban life was that all the city's residents were dependent for their very existence on the marketplace and the daily exchange of goods and services. The city was an elaborate system of exchange, residents naturally acquired a sense of allegiance to that economic arena, were prepared to contribute to its defense (literally) against outsiders, and true cities were at least partially autonomous political units. The city, through the consciousness of its citizens (burghers), had a sense of itself, was constituted to regulate and administer on behalf of the interests of its business classes; it was a rational, corporate unity.

Weber thought that such cities captured the potential of human achievement and gave it expression. Yet he saw the promise of the city fading in his own time. The characteristic rationalism of the twentieth century pushed aside the spiritual and cultural essence of the urban promise as cities became the dense and frantic manifestations of the bureaucratic organization of industrial society. The cities of the Renaissance might be called true urban communities, engines of culture and learning: The industrial city represented the simple massing of populations, human aggregations, where efficient administration according to the bureaucratic model was the goal. All that was left of the ideal city was the unifying self-interest of the marketplace. This idea is at the core of the legacy of classical theory for urban sociology.

## Life in the Faceless Metropolis

The rapid growth of cities during the industrial revolution had intensified the misgivings that social and moral commentators in Western nations had long felt about the impact of living in cities. In both the popular imagination and in social theory, the city was understood to undermine moral values and to weaken social ties.

During the first half of the twentieth century, popular writers and critics were divided over the question of the impact of urbanization on the quality of life. This division of opinion and the changing conditions of the cities themselves contrasted with the best-known commentaries of the last century. The dreary images of nineteenth-century coketowns in Dickens's fiction are more than matched by the descriptions of Manchester from Engels (1845) and Tocqueville (1835). By the turn of the century, the image of the city had not improved much. Lincoln Steffens (1904) warned of the moral evils rooted in the political power and economic temptations of the cities in the United States, and Charles Booth (1902) chronicled the desperate conditions of the poor in England. In the decades that followed, there continued to be much critical writing that dwelt on the negative consequences of living in cities, but it was not so single-minded as the social criticisms that had appeared earlier. Despite Weber's indictment of the deadening rationalization of urban life, the evolving cities of the twentieth century had, after all, become more hospitable environments, at least with regard to the material conditions under which most people lived.

The generations of social scientists and social commentators that came of age in the twentieth century were the products of an urban environment. Many had lost the capacity to be awed by that sheer physical presence. Yet the social impact of the city remained an issue for probably just as many others. British writers worried about the potential for political and social revolution, the breathless pace of life, the monotony and the squalor that some associated with cities. George Orwell, for example, commented on the festering, planless chaos of the city, on the one hand, and on what he saw as the prisonlike atmosphere that resulted from planning to control the urban environment and make it more orderly, on the other. For many French writers, Paris in the first decades of the 1900s may have been a modern-day Athens, only on a grander scale; yet others raised the question of whether Paris had grown too large, an arrogant monster that devoured resources that rightfully belonged to the rest of the country. German writers during the 1920s and 1930s regarded favorably the cultural achievements that attached to the great cities, but split along political lines in their concern about the social implications of continued growth. Artists and writers on the political left pointed to injustice, corruption, and the focused excesses of capitalism that were found in cities. Moderates worried about growing congestion and housing shortages. The ascendant National Socialist right was concerned about political drift to the Marxist left in urban areas, remarking ominously about the "biological decline" that they saw resulting from the mixing of "races" in cities (Lees 1985: 259-88).

Sociologists working in the first half of the twentieth century on theories of city life emphasized the alienating aspects of the urban environment. The two outstanding examples of this position were, in Germany, Georg Simmel's (1905) essay "The Metropolis and Mental Life," and, in the United States, Louis Wirth's (1938) essay "Urbanism as a Way of Life."

Simmel is important because he distinguished between the two basic features of urban life that were understood to shape human behavior. First, the crowded and bustling social environment itself caused people to retreat within themselves, to develop a capacity to ignore what went on around them. He argued that it was necessary for people who lived in cities to develop this capacity in order to maintain their sanity. The second compelling feature of the urban environment was the reduction of human motives to a question of cost. In Simmel's view, urban life is a series of exchanges in which each person asks, "What will I get out of this? How much will it cost me?" The consequences of emotional strain and impersonal interaction are that aversion and calculation are the distinguishing social features of the metropolis. In every sense, people cannot afford to care about one another.

Wirth (1938) incorporated Simmel's point of view as well as those of Tönnies, Durkheim, Weber, and others in his effort to develop a full "theory" of urban life. His much-criticized essay on the combined sociological effects of the *size*, *density*, and *heterogeneity* of urban populations remains an elegant attempt to model the gross consequences of the urban environment. Together, those three factors conditioned the nature of social interaction. An increase in the size of a given population means that relationships become segmented and specialized — and remain superficial. Second, the high population densities that characterize urban life mean that not only people's roles, but also the various physical areas within the city, become specialized. Wirth's teacher, Robert Park (1915; 1929), had described the ecology of urban space as a mosaic of isolated social or moral worlds, each with its own distinctive code of conduct. The principle of heterogeneity was based on the fact that cities contained a wide variety of cultural and class characteristics, and generated or reinforced social differences by promoting occupational specialization. People who lived in cities found it hard to identify with one another and were more than content to allow relationships to remain at the superficial and instrumental level.

Together, Simmel and Wirth, but especially Wirth, set the tone for subsequent sociological interpretations of the consequences of urban life. People in the city are wary, alienated, manipulative, and aversive. Relationships tend to be predominantly superficial and secondary in nature. Urbanites lead isolated existences. This vision squared with much of the popular interpretation of what cites did to people. Contemporary social scientists are largely wary of the one-dimensional character of these early anti-urban formulations. Yet, as we will see in the section "Current Trends in Urban Community Research," classical assumptions regarding alienated urbanites both guide and are supported by contemporary investigation. However, they provide only a partial picture of the urban experience.

## The Urban Community Studies Tradition

The image of the urban way of life reflected in sociological theory was contradicted, almost from the beginning, by the evidence uncovered by researchers doing fieldwork in cities. Wirth (1927) himself had described close ties and a richly communal social life that characterized Chicago's Jewish ghetto in the 1920s. William Foote Whyte's (1943) study of the close-knit Italian-American community in Boston's North End followed close of the heels of Wirth's urbanism essay, and came to enjoy a prominent place in urban sociology roughly equivalent to Wirth's famous essay, their contrary emphases notwithstanding.

Study after study in the emerging tradition of "urban community studies" during the 1950s showed that cities contained neighborhoods where people felt a strong sense of place, where they felt they belonged, and where they were involved with their neighbors, especially with family members who lived close by. These studies focused on working-class areas of the city. Gans's (1962) *The Urban Villagers* depicted second- and third-generation Italians living in a soon-to-be-razed neighborhood, enjoying a set of close social relationships centered on kin. Members of these "peer groups" expressed a strong sense of attachment to other group members and their local place of residence. Kinship also provided the main channel for social life in East London. Young and Wilmott (1957) uncovered a matrifocal system of social cohesiveness among this working-class population. Adult daughters with families of their own were closely tied to their mothers. Families tended to remain locally based, generation after generation.

Suttles (1968) has argued that it is the locality, itself, the provides a basis for social cohesion and neighborhood identification in the city. Although the "Addams Area" (a fictitious name) that he studied in Chicago contained a number of different ethnic groups (Blacks, Italians, Mexicans, and Puerto Ricans), and although there were tensions among these groups within the area, a common sense of "turf" or a proprietary sentiment caused these groups to unite in response to any threat from outside the area....

## IS URBAN SPACE AN IMPORTANT SOCIOLOGICAL VARIABLE?

To this point wer have reviewed two kinds of argument about the capacity of physical space to affect social llife. First, there is the position that environmental factors, such as population size and density, attenuate social ties that are characteristic of smaller and more dispersed populations. Second, there is the contrary, empirically derived argument that community ties of various sorts are capable of withstanding the disintegrating effects of large, dense population centers.

Herbert Gans (1962) suggested a third possibility. This is that the nature of the urban environment is not so important as other, established sociological factors, such as social class, in determining the life experiences of people who happen to live in cities. He maintains that the urbanism proposition is weakened by the fact that there are not one but a number of conditions of urban living. There are a large number of alienated and isolated souls in the city, but the urban population also includes artists and intellectuals who live in the city because they love it, as well as other categories of persons attracted by urban living. The most isolated and alienated people of the city are the poor, the trapped, and the downwardly mobile segments of the urban population. Their alienation and isolation has more to do with their economic place in society than it does with the fact that they live in cities. An analysis of the size, density, and heterogeneity of their surroundings adds little to an understanidng of their condition.

A second line of argument that questions whether urban *space* is an important independent variable is directed at the udrban community studies contention that urban neighborhoods continue to be an important focus of social life. What basis is there for assuming that residential neighborhood provides the key organizing force for urban social relationships? It is reasonable to assume that people will have some social contact with their neighbors and will also be involved with people outside of the neighborhood with whom they share common interests.

This important assunmption is made in Claude fischer's (1975, 1984) "subcultural theory of urbanism." Fischer finds in the city a vital force for amplifying cultural experience and human creativity, for generating both genius and deviance. It is the sheer size of urban populations, their "critical mass," that provides a fertile soil for the cultivation of ideas. The critical mass hypothesis says that larger populations provide individuals who have a shared interest with a base for establishing rewarding social ties for collectively pursuing, enhancing, and articulating those interests. In large population pools, individuals can find otthers of like mind with whom to share their ideas, to accompany and encourage them as they indulge their particular (or peculiar) tastes, together to experiment, expand, and innovate their esoteric, unconventional, avant-garde interests.

Fischer's observations reflect an important change in the way students of the city have come to see urban social organizaiton. We may accept that Wirth and the empirical community studies tradition have told us something important about the nature of the urban experience, but it is time to move beyond these limited views of urban life. Recent studies have proceeded in the direction of the "community liberated" model (Wellman and Leighton 1979) or urban social relations, where community is liberated from the confinements of local space. In this view people's social relationships are drawn from the city at large, the total metropolitan area. People sleep in their neighborhood, they identify with it to a greater or lesser extent as being their own special place in the city, but they live their daily social lives within a spatially diffuse and more heterogenous social network.

### Social Networks

The conceptual development of the social networks perspective in contemporary sociology is traceable to the work of J. A. Barnes (1954), although some trace recent developments back to Moreno's sociometric studies during the 1930s and 1940s (Rogers 1987: 287). At its simplest level, the network metaphor asks that we visualize individuals as embedded in a set of social relationships that encompass the individual's various group memberships (e.g., family, peers, work, formal group memberships). The social networks imagery urges us to appreciate the fact that an ividual lives within no particular group, or even within a set of groups, but that people live within a complex set of social relationships. This complex set of social relationships links individuals, as individuals, with specific other individuals. Thus at any time a given person is subject to influence in his or her thinking and behavior from the full range of his or her contacts with others: These others are people who are personally known to the individual in question. Every person knows some number of other people, and that individual's friends and acquaintances know others, and so on. So, each of us can be pictured as standing at the center of a set of ties that radiate outward from us to and through others. This is our social network.

The imagery of the social network provides a useful metaphor for distinguishing between the structural characteristics of personal ties in urban and rural places. Rural networks tend to be densely structured, which is to say that in relatively small places, like a very small town, everyone knows everyone else. It is appropriate to picture a very highly interconnected web of relationships among residents. In the city, it is rare for all of one person's friends, acquaintances, and other contacts to know and be in regular contact with one another. So, urban networks are said to be loosely structured, or "open." Of course, within the city some individual's networks may be more dense, others more open, as a matter of degree. An urban villager, who life is circumscribed pretty fully by the territory of the neighborhood, or a woman in London's East End, who is closely attuned to the happenings in her particular street, will have networks more closed than will Gans's cosmopolites. Frankenberg's (1966) edited collection of community studies from England, Ireland, and Wales remains a very useful illustration of the relevance of the social networks concept for contrasting the difference in social structure between small-and large-scale population centers.

Networks may be seen as resource structures. They provide a reservoir of aid and information that the individual may call upon under particular circumstances. They also link the individual directly or indirectly to well-placed others who can influence outcomes favorable to the person in question. Theoretically, the more open an individual's network, the more varied and heterogenous that person's set of relationships, the more valuable will be that set of ties under a wide variety of circumstances. This is what is meant by Granovetter's (1973, 1982) wonderfully precise reference to the "strength of weak ties." An urban villager may enjoy the warmth of a small, but close, network of friends and relatives, all of them with roughly the same background and experience, but the resources contained in such a network of strong ties are limited and redundant. This is especially evident if that network is contrasted with the network of an individual who is linked by relatively weak ties to a wide spectrum of others: Weak ties are valuable because they tie an individual to a variety of reference points and thereby potentially link the actor to information that is novel and not otherwise accessible (Campbell, Marsden, and Hurlbert 1986: 98–9).

The social network concept has ultimately contributed in an important way to our ability to create a mental image of the social structure of the city. One begins with a mental image of a single social network, an egocentric structure (based on the relationships and point of view of a single individual). At the center stands that person, surrounded by all the persons with whom he or she can be said to have a relationship. Next, each of the persons in this mental image can be seen to be standing at the center of their own set of relationships, as can each of the individuals they are related to, and so on. Although the diagram soon becomes too intricate to hold in one's mind, it suggests something of the structure of any population, such as that of a particular city. Following the implications of the network image, it can be seen that one important dimension of urban structure is that the city is a network of social networks (Craven and Wellman 1973).

## CURRENT TRENDS IN URBAN COMMUNITY RESEARCH

The imageries of the community lost, community saved, and community liberated perspectives continue to operate side by side in urban sociology. Current research indicates that people who live in cities sometimes suffer the alienating effects of life in the urban arena, sometimes live in urban villages of various types, and inevitably stand at the center of their own social networks. The productive questions that should guide contemporary research are these: To what extent and under which circumstances do these features of urban experience and organization operate? Can we determine how important residence is in anchoring the urban network? Under what conditions do people feel comfortably at home in the city, and under what conditions are they stressed by the urban environment?

The question of the fate and shape of urban community yields a variety of answers. Contemporary urban sociologists employ a number of perspectives in researching these questions. It is important to ask what each of these points of view contributes to an overall understanding of social cohesion in the city. It is important, as well, to recognize that each of the perspectives has limitations as well as something valuable to say about the manner in which people live urban life, and about the way they believe they and others live in cities. Fundamental to any understanding of the nature of the urban community, local identification, and interaction in the urban arena is the perception and experience of people themselves. At the level of experience, cities are socially constructed images. People use cities in different ways, pursue different routines and interests. Each of us uses only part of the city we live in, we experience the urban environment from our own perspectives. These perspectives, in turn, are affected by social class, age, gender, occupation, and many other factors. Because each of us occupies a unique space with respect to all others, our particular image of the city will be unique. In this sense, because each of us has his or her own mental map of the city we use, each of us lives in our own city (Lynch 1973). Yet, the city belongs to no one of us, and we experience it as a world of strangers.

Lofland's (1973) little book, *World of Strangers*, helps make sense of much that we have reviewed here. Following Lynch, Lofland points out that the city must be seen in part in terms of individual internalizations, because each one of us performs cognitive operations on the urban space, making the parts of it we know our own. The city exists in the individual's experience as a series of places within which that person is to some degree comfortable. The more we use a place, all other things being equal, the more comfortable we are in it, the more we make it ours. It is interesting that Lofland chooses terms that reflect the primarily commercial nature of urban space to describe the three degrees of familiarity found among space users. The "customer" is a person who is in a particular place intermittently, who has firsthand but "casual" knowledge of that particular slice of public space. The "patron" has developed "semipersonal" relationships with the regulars and employees always found there. The "resident" has carved out a "home territory" through regular use and identification, and has developed a proprietary sense.

These labels are intended to convey an impression of gradations of personal mastery of particular settings. Beyond the familiar places still exists the vast remainder of the cityscape that the individual has little knowledge of or personal claim to. That is the world of strangers....

## REFERENCES

Barnes, J. A. 1954. "Class an dCommittees in a Norwegian Island Parish." *Human Relations* 7:39–58.

Booth Charles. 1902–3. *Life and Labour of the People in London*. Vols. 1–17. London: Macmillan Press.

Campbell, Kren E., Peter V. Marsden, and Jean S. Hurlbert. 1986. "Social Resources and Socioeconomic Status." *Social Networks* 8: 97–117.

Craven, P., and Barry Wellman. 1973. "The Network City." *Social Inquiry* 43: 57–8.

Durkheim, Emile. [1893] 1933. *The Division of Labor in Society*. Translated by George Simpson. New York: Free Press.

Engels, Fredrick. [1845] 1970. "Early Slum Conditions: Manchester in 1844." In A. R. Desai and S. Devadas Pillai (eds.), *Slums and Urbanization*, 24–33. Bombay: Popular Prakashan. Reprint of Fedrick Engels. 1936. *The Condition of the Working Class*. Translated by Florence Kelley Wischnewetsky. London: Unwin Hyman Ltd.

Fischer, Claude S. 1975. "Toward a Subcultural Theory of Urbanism." *American Journal of Sociology* 80: 1,319–41. 1982. *To Dwell Among Friends: Personal Networks in Town and City.* Chicago; University of Chicago Press. 1984. *The Urban Experience.* Second Edition. New York: Harcourt, Brace, Jovanovich.

Frankenberg, Ronald. 1966. *Communities in Britain: Social Life in Town and Country.* Baltimore: Penguin.

Gans, Herbert J. 1962. "Urbanism and Suburbanism As Ways of Life: A Reevaluation of Definitions." In Arnold M. Rose (ed.), *Human Behavior and Social Processes: An Interactionist Approach,* 625–48. Boston: Houghton Mifflin.

Granovetter, Mark S. 1973. "The Strength of Weak Ties." *American Journal of Sociology* 78: 1,360–80. 1982. "The Strength of Weak Ties: A Network Theory Revisited." In Peter D. Massden and Nan Lin (eds.), *Social Structure and Network Analysis,* 105–30. Beverly Hills, Calif.: Sage.

Lees, Andrew. 1985. *Cities Perceived: Urban Society in European and American Thought, 1820–1940.* New York: Columbia University Press.

Lofland, Lyn. [1973] 1985. *A World of Strangers.* Prospect Heights, Ill: Waveland Press.

Lynch, Kevin. 1973. *The Image of the City.* Cambridge, Mass.: MIT Press.

Park, Robert E. 1915. "The City: Suggestions for the Investigation of Human Behavior in the City." *American Journal of Sociology* 20: 577–612. [1929] 1952. "Sociology, Community, and Society." In Robert E. Park (ed.), *Human Communities: The City and Human Ecology,* 178–209. Glencoe, Ill.: Free Press.

Rogers, Everett M. 1987. "Progress, Problems, and Progress for Network Research: Investigating Relationships in the Age of Electronic Communication Technologies." *Social Networks* 9: 285–310.

Simmel, Georg. [1905] 1950. "The Metropolis and Mental Life." In Kurt H. Wold (ed.), *The Sociology of Georg Simmel,* 409–24. New York: Free Press.

Steffens, Lincoln. 1904. *The Shame of Citites.* Cambridge, Mass.: McClure Phillips.

Suttles, Gerald D. 1968. *The Social Order of the Slum: Ethnicity and Territory in the Inner City.* Chicago: University of Chicago Press.

Tocqueville, Alexis de. [1835] 1958. *Journeys to England and Ireland.* Translated by G. Lawrence and K. P. Mayer. London.

Tönnies, Ferdinand. (1887) 1940. *Fundamental Concepts of Sociology (Gemeinschaft und Gelleschaft).* Translated by Charles P. Loomis. new York: American Book Company.

Weber, Max. [1905] 1958. *The City.* Translated and edited by Don Martindale and Gertrud Neuwirth. New York: Free Press.

Wellman, Barry, and Barry Leighton. 1979. "Networks, Neighborhoods, and Communities: Approaches to the Study of the Community Question." *Urban Affairs Quarterly* 14: 363–90.

Whyte, William Foote. 1943. *Street Corner Society.* Chicago: University of Chicago Press.

Wirth, Lewis. 1927. *The Ghetto.* Chicago: University of Chicago Press. 1938. "Urbanism as a Way of Life." *American Journal of Sociology* 4: 1–24.

Young, Michael, and Peter Willmott. 1957. *Family and Kinship in East London.* Baltimore: Penguin.

# 60. POSTMODERN SOCIETY

## DAVID ASHLEY AND DAVID MICHAEL ORENSTEIN

*"Some theorists have argued that the rapid social change that has occurred in the advanced capitalist societies since 1945 and that accelerated after the 1960s has created mostly cultural transformations that seem to take humans beyond a recognizably modern stage of development."*

This brief selection is a fine summary of what some social scientists have come to describe as "postmodern society," a society that no longer shares the same features of what was once called "modern society."

In the last couple of decades, there has been increasing debate in sociology about the significance of "postmodernism."[1] Some theorists have argued that the rapid social change that has occurred in the advanced capitalist societies since 1945 and that accelerated after the 1960s has created mostly cultural transformations that seem to take humans beyond a recognizably *modern* stage of development. In fact, some theorists suggest that, if you were born in the West after about 1965, you do not even know what it is like to live in an old-fashioned modern society—the world as it used to exist before Elvis, the Beatles, shopping malls, prosthetic bodies (think of Michael Jackson's), and MTV.

Advanced capitalist societies today can no longer be described, primarily, as *industrial* societies. In the United States, for instance, the production of consumers seems at least as important for economic growth as the production of goods and services, and contemporary U.S. presidents see nothing wrong in urging citizens to help *spend* the country out of a recession. In the last decade or so, the leisure and entertainment sectors of the economy, and not the manufacturing sector, have been the most profitable. It has become increasingly difficult for many contemporary theorists to argue that economic growth today is rational or instrumentally adaptive in some sense. Rather, consumerism seems to be an end in itself. Capitalists now develop new and highly profitable markets by selling consumers new needs, new experiences, and new forms of meaning, all of which are defined exclusively by the marketplace.

In the early modern period, it was assumed that economic development would make people wiser, stronger, and more, rather than less, human. Yet, in contemporary capitalist societies, the relationship between economic growth *per se* and human "progress" no longer seems as obvious as it was a century ago. For one thing, most of the truly impressive products of the industrial era (for example, the steam engine, the internal combustion engine, the jet engine, the airplane, artificial fabrics, plastics, radio, television, and so on) were invented and merchandised before most people alive today were even born. For another, in the most developed capitalist societies, economic growth now seems to rely on entrepreneurs' ability to sell symbols or culture, and not on their capacity to develop new industrial products or market technological breakthroughs. Perhaps it's not surprising that people today have less faith than they used to in science and technology's ability to create a better world. In a modern society, technology and economic development went hand in hand. In a postmodern society, economic and cultural domains of activity become increasingly difficult to separate—a development that was, to some extent, anticipated by Veblen in his *Theory of the Leisure Class.* The great increase in the number of people in postmodern societies who sell information, knowledge, or credentials to the masses has led some sociologists to talk about the rise of a New Class—a class that specializes in the development and sale of culture.[2] This New Class is neither bourgeois nor proletarian in Victorian terms.

Postmodern societies are relatively more dependent on knowledge and information than modern societies, and they are less immediately involved in producing material artifacts. As people become "consumers" rather than "citizens," they also tend to become politically indifferent. To the extent that individuals can access, or enjoy, symbolic meaning only by having it sold to them, postmodern culture becomes increasingly self-absorbed and self-enclosed—claustrophobic even.

Ronald Reagan has been described as the first postmodern president because his office was so transparently a victory of style over substance. His 1984 "Morning in America" election campaign dispensed with modern versions of political will formation and wooed voters by selling them feel-good images that they could either like or not like. These images, of course, had no connection with "reality." They might just as well have been McDonald's commercials, which, like political commercials, are not intended to give consumers reliable information about real people. The voters were not supposed to test Reagan's advertise-

From David Ashley and David Michael Orenstein, *Social Theory: Classical Statements,* 4th Edition. Copyright © 1996. Allyn and Bacon. Reprinted/Adapted by permission.

ments or subject them to any kind of critical scrutiny. Of course, the kind of messages that sold Reagan to a large portion of the United States can work only when consumers lose the capacity to use criteria or standards that are *extrinsic* to a message to evaluate its meaning – in other words, when they lose the ability to exercise critical judgment.

Successful versions of postmodern symbolism are less representational than modern symbolism and more obviously self-referential or self-contained. Although U.S. presidential candidates have always used rhetoric and images to get themselves elected, Reagan's handlers took the "selling of the president" to new and unprecedented levels. For instance, they *relied* on surveys to find out what consumers would buy – just as any manufacturer might want to poll its customers to discover what images will encourage them to purchase a certain type of pantyhose. In a postmodern society, the "modern" emphasis on the responsibilities of political leaders and on the duties of citizens disappears. Commercial and political activities become almost indistinguishable. Thought is folded into emotion and feeling.

Postmodernism is also linked to the "death of the subject" or to the "end of the individual." Modern versions of individuality emerged with the Reformation and, as we have seen, with the Enlightenment. In a postmodern society, individuality (or the relatively autonomous reproduction of the self) is undermined in at least two ways. First of all, whereas early modern societies required and rewarded self-mastery and self-control, postmodern culture emphasizes and encourages hedonism, self-indulgence, and an obsession with "personal" image or self, as opposed to an "old-fashioned" (modern) reliance on character or vocation. Second, the transcendental, or generalizable theologies that were so important during the Enlightenment and in the early modern era now seem to have lost their power. The postmodern subject is besieged by an endless jumble of messages, codes, and ideas, most of which are incompatible, inconsistent, and quite infantile. Many people respond to the current cacophony of mostly commercial messages that bombard them daily by abandoning all hope that they ever could attain some kind of rational understanding of the world.

Whatever its merits, or lack of merits, Marxism, for instance (or traditional religion, come to that), did give people some overarching guidelines or standards that enabled them to participate in a common and supposedly *universal* program of human or spiritual development. Postmodern belief systems (such as "New Age" religions) lack a transcendental perspective. The postmodern deity turns out to be consumer friendly, and most people today see nothing wrong with putting together a "personal philosophy" using precisely the same methodology they would adopt to select new clothes or decide on a new hair style. At the end of the twentieth century, humans are much less optimistic about the future and less sure about their grip on the present than they were 150 years ago. They appear to have fewer "inner" resources. The postmodern subject is a feather for each wind that blows.

Unless humans are able to internalize some kind of moral code or learn some kind of generalizable philosophy on which they can rely in diverse circumstances, it is difficult to see how they can be categorized as "individuals" in the modern or Enlightenment sense of the term. Some contemporary postmodernists – Jean Baudrillard, for instance – see the postmodern subject as an empty shell that is incapable of exercising any kind of critical judgment.[3] This picture is quite at odds with the idea of human potential developed by eighteenth-century philosophers like Immanuel Kant or by nineteenth-century theorists like Marx.

Postmodern transformations can usually be understood as an extension of cultural modernism (classically defined by Simmel), not as unique developments in their own right. Perhaps the best way to approach postmodernism is to see it as "the cultural logic of late capitalism," the description favored by the critic Fredric Jameson.[4] In any case, before the meaning of postmodernism can be grasped, modernization and modernism have to be understood in their own right as conditions that postmodernism supposedly has surpassed. For the most part, postmodernism is what happens to modern societies once they reach a certain level of maturity and development. It is a tribute to theorists like Nietzsche, Simmel, Weber, Marx, and Veblen that they managed to anticipate many of the cultural trends that are today being labeled postmodern.

## ENDNOTES

1. See Jean-François Lyotard, *The Postmodern Condition* (Minneapolis: University of Minnesota Press, 1984); Mark Poster (Ed.), *Jean Baudrillard: Selected Writings* (Stanford, CA: Stanford University Press, 1988); David Harvey, *The Condition of Postmodernity* (Oxford: Basil Blackwell, 1989); Fredric Jameson, *Postmodernism or the Cultural Logic of Late Capitalism* (Durham, NC: Duke University Press, 1991); Steven Best and Douglas Kellner, *Postmodern Theory: Critical Interrogations* (New York: Guilford Press, 1991); and Stephen Crook, Jan Pakulski, and Malcolm Waters, *Postmodernization: Change in Advanced Society* (London: Sage, 1992). Also see Alex Callinicos, *Against Postmodernism: A Marxist Critique* (New York: St. Martin's Press, 1989).

2. See Alvin W. Gouldner, *The Future of Intellectuals and the Rise of the New Class* (New York: Oxford University Press, 1979), and Hansfried Kellner and Frank W. Heuberger (Eds.), *Hidden Technocrats: The New Class and New Capitalism* (New Brunswick, NJ: Transaction Books, 1992).

3. See, for instance, Jean Baudrillard, *In the Shadows of the Silent Majorities* (New York: Semiotext[e], Foreign Agent Press, 1983).

4. Frederic Jameson, "Postmodernism, or the Cultural Logic of Late Capitalism," *New Left Review, 146* (1984), 5-93.

# 61. SOCIAL CHANGE AND RACE RELATIONS

### LEWIS M. KILLIAN

*"I rejoice that black citizens are so much freer than they were in my childhood and that I have been released from the bonds of a Jim Crow society. But my joy turns to despair when I must confront the fact that behind the facade of freedom in public places exists a structure of inequality that is in some aspects more hideous than that of the past, offering less hope of salvation to the victims."*

Lewis Killian, a sociologist who has spent much of his professional career studying race relations in the United States, describes what he sees as he looks back at the mixed record of change as it relates to inequality between African Americans and whites.

The South I came home to was very different from the one I had left in 1968. The changes since my childhood introduction to race relations in Georgia were even vaster. It is an urban South, swept out of its rural past by the same winds that have changed the rest of the nation. The rural charm disappeared along with the rural problems that, during the

From *Black and White: Reflections of a White Southern Sociologist*, by Lewis M. Killian. Dix Hills, NY: General Hall, 1994.

Great Depression, seemed to epitomize the South — according to FDR, "the nation's economic problem number one." The people are far more heterogeneous than was the two-toned population in which I grew to manhood; Latinos of various sorts, Southeast Asians, Koreans, and Asian Indians are familiar compatriots, particularly in a navy community such as Pensacola. So are transplanted Yankees, born anywhere from Boston to California but long since retired to the Sunbelt. It is dismaying to me, a born-and-bred southern Democrat who rejoiced in Jimmy Carter's election and am still angry over his subsequent defeat, that now so many southerners are Republicans. Even by the time I published the first edition of my book, *White Southerners*, in 1970, white voters living in the South had become one of the bulwarks of Republican strength in presidential contests.

Sociologists and historians who have devoted much study to the South as a region now debate whether there remains a distinctive southern culture. I stay out of the discussion but feel personally that there is still enough different about the South and many of its people to make me feel that I have indeed come home. There is always a "new South," but enough of the old persists to remind me of the one I once knew and have always loved in spite of its faults.

Along with the growth of the crowded cities, the most visible evidence of change in the region is in race relations. As a Cracker who knew and accepted segregation when it was at its cruelest and most extensive, I now suffer from culture shock when I see the changes that were so violently resisted during the civil rights movement. The "Colored" restrooms and drinking fountains are gone. A few, very few, black families worship regularly in my parish church; there is still a black Episcopal parish in Pensacola. Blacks appear to shop freely with whites, and both are often served by stylishly dressed black salespeople and cashiers. In the past two years, I have formed a close friendship with a black man of about my age. Henry Burrell, who grew up in the slums of Detroit, is a veteran of the U.S. Air Force and now is a permanent deacon in the Roman Catholic church. We work together as members of the Human Rights Advocacy Committee in northwest Florida. When, after a meeting, Henry and I want to have lunch together, we don't have to wonder where it will be safe for us to go. All we have to decide is what kind of food we want.

As an adjunct professor at the University of West Florida, I have occasionally taught classes in minority relations. Rarely have I encountered a student, even one raised in the South, who retains even the dimmest memory of segregation. These students, white and black, are as intrigued and shocked by my lecture describing "the way it was" as were the audiences to whom I gave the same lecture in Massachusetts. I, in turn, experienced a bit of shock one day when a beautiful young white woman casually informed the class that her husband was a black air force pilot on duty in Korea. I still am subject to a twinge of anxiety when I see an interracial couple on Pensacola Beach, remembering how blacks were beaten when they tried to desegregate the beaches near St. Augustine, Florida, in the early 1960s.

I rejoice that black citizens are so much freer than they were in my childhood and that I have been released from the bonds of a Jim Crow society. But my joy turns to despair when I must confront the fact that behind the facade of freedom in public places exists a structure of inequality that is in some aspects more hideous than that of the past, offering less hope of salvation to the victims.

The statistics sociologists and economists present in their endless outpouring of books and articles tell a story of persistent residential segregation, the resegregation of public schools, and an almost invariant gap between the incomes of white and black families. They confirm the reality of disproportionate rates of delinquency, illegitimacy, and welfare dependence among minority ethnic groups, even though the rates are also increasing in the white population and the white poor still outnumber the black.

But I do not have to study the tables and graphs to find evidence of the enduring consequences of slavery, segregation, and exploitation. As I drive along the freeway that bisects Pensacola from south to north, there are places where I can see black slum dwellings on either side. Only a few blocks away I can find the all-black public housing projects where the poor but decent residents live in fear of the drug dealers who prey on their children. With Henry Burrell, I visit the juvenile detention center and see children as young as twelve years old awaiting trial for armed robbery, car theft, or worse felonies. There are young white felons there, too, but I know that society still offers more opportunities for whites if they are reformed than for the blacks. I see machines, from mechanical cottonpickers and ditchdiggers to my wife's washing machine, doing the work that once provided employment for many blacks who, though underpaid, enjoyed the dignity of a job. At the same time, I know that despite nearly a quarter of a century of affirmative action, only a well-qualified minority of black workers have been able to move into the professional and high-tech jobs that each year become more important in our economy. Although the small city of Pensacola is far removed in space and population from Chicago, I can see in my new home in the South the same trends toward greater segregation and inequality that Bill Wilson and his students are discovering in the northern industrial metropolis.

Worse yet, I am condemned by the fact that in spite of the dismantling of *de jure* segregation, I still live in a white world that is, in a way, more segregated than was my environment in Macon. With the disappearance of domestic servants and black yardmen such as "Black Lewis," I do not have the daily close contact with blacks that I once knew. The domestics have not been replaced by black neighbors, although the law says that they could be. Only once in our lives have we enjoyed the fellowship of a black family in an American neighborhood. That was in Amherst, where an army officer whom I knew at the University of Massachusetts, James Faison, bought a house on our little cul-de-sac. He and his wife, Martha, lived there for a few years before building a grander house in another part of the town. Kay and I would welcome neighbors such as the Faisons again and would go to great lengths to defend their exercise of their rights. But we are not about to embark on a quixotic crusade that would entail inviting a black friend, or a stranger, to endure the tribulations of being a test case.

In the early days of my professional study of race relations, my theoretical views were quite clear to me, and my faith in progress was firm. Once awakened to the dangers of the myth of race and the evils of segregation, I cherished the naive belief that the tide of history was flowing slowly but inexorably toward erasing them. The very concept of race and the divisions rationalized by it were, I had learned, relatively recent developments in the long history of human culture. Although I did not anticipate their immediate demise, I was confident that every move, scientific, theological, or legal, to destroy them would be a sure step in the direction of racial democracy, to be realized perhaps even in my lifetime. In my teaching at the University of Oklahoma and at Florida State University, I preached a simple but powerful gospel of assimilation.

Then the mixed and inadequate accomplishments of the civil rights movement and the unmasking of the deep economic problems that remain little affected by civil rights laws all thrust a haze of doubt into my theoretical view and cast a pall of gloom over my hopes for progress. I still preferred an assimilationist outcome, but I no longer had faith that it would come in my lifetime, if ever. The ethnic divisions and the hostilities that were revived and magnified in the 1960s, not only in the United States but throughout the world, suggested that the tide flowed toward unending conflict, not assimilation or even peaceful, harmonious pluralism.

My record of theoretical and personal devotion to assimilation suggests that I should be an enthusiastic advocate of affirmative action in the form of compensatory discrimination. I cannot, however, join the ranks of my friends who believe that it will lead eventually to the disappearance of color consciousness. The evidence I have assiduously examined leads me to conclude that such a program leads only to a form of "supertokenism" benefiting a fortunate few but changing neither the distribution of power nor the concentration of wealth that together keep poor blacks outside the mainstream and even increase their numbers. At the same time, the issue, wielded as a political weapon, perpetuates and deepens the rift between white and black Americans. I see no inclination on the part of white voters and their elected representatives to support or even propose the radical economic reforms that would be necessary to reverse the decades-long trend for the rich to get richer and the poor, poorer. It is easier for politicians to unite white voters in opposition to new taxes, to welfare programs, and to "quotas" than to inspire them with a vision of a society in which the vast wealth of the nation is distributed more equally.

Equally confusing and discouraging is the disarray among black Americans. There are no contemporary counterparts of Washington and Du Bois or of Martin Luther King, Jr., and Malcolm X, with opposing but inspiring philosophies and calls to action. The current "black establishment," the NAACP, the Urban League, and the greatly shrunken Southern Christian Leadership

Conference, year after year advocate measures that have proven inadequate and that depend on the goodwill of whites, a goodwill that is diminishing. A small but growing number of black intellectuals — hardly "leaders" — criticize the shopworn solutions proposed by the established "leaders" and advocate self-help programs reminiscent of the Black Power era. No contemporary social movement has emerged, however. Although there are frequent cries of anguish from black Americans, the black protest movement that stretches back to the slave revolts and the Underground Railroad appears to be moribund or, at the least, quiescent....

# Part XIII

# THE IMPORTANCE OF SOCIOLOGY

In this final part, we turn our attention to three selections that deal with the reasons why sociology should be important to the student. Of what use is it? Why bother with it? In the first selection, Peter Berger argues that it is a liberating perspective; in the second selection, he argues that it is a humanistic perspective. In the final chapter, Joel Charon argues that sociology is important for anyone who is interested in democracy in society and in their own relationships.

# 62. SOCIOLOGY AND FREEDOM

## PETER L. BERGER

*"Sociology is subversive.... Sociology is conservative...."*

The sociological perspective brings to the serious student a "transformation of consciousness." Peter Berger seems to put his finger on the importance of thinking sociologically in this short essay.

I would like to look at the theoretical question at issue. To wit: *In what sense, if at all, can sociology be called a liberating discipline?*

I will approach the question by way of two seemingly contradictory propositions: *Sociology is subversive of established patterns of thought. Sociology is conservative in its implications for the institutional order.* I would like to suggest that both propositions are correct, and that an understanding of this also entails grasping the relation of sociology and freedom, at least on the level of politics....

Every human society rests on assumptions that, most of the time, are not only unchallenged but not even reflected on. In other words, in every society, there are patterns of thought that most people accept without question as being of the very nature of things. Alfred Schutz called the sum of these "the world-taken-for-granted," which provides the parameters and the basic programs for our everyday lives. Robert and Helen Lynd, in their classic studies of *Middletown*, pointed to the same phenomenon with their concept of "of-course statements" — statements that people take for granted to such a degree that, if questioned about them, they will preface their answer with "of course." These socially established patterns of thought provide the individual with what, paraphrasing Erving Goffman, we might call his *basic reality kit* — the cognitive and normative tools for the construction of a coherent universe in which to live. It is difficult to see how social life would be possible without this. But specific institutions and specific vested interests are also legitimated by such taken-for-granted patterns of thought. Thus a threat to the taken-for-granted quality of the legitimating thought patterns can very quickly become a threat to the institutions being legitimated and to the individuals who have a stake in the institutional status quo.

Sociology, by its own intrinsic logic, keeps generating such threats. Simply by doing its cognitive job, sociology puts the institutional order *and* its legitimating thought patterns under critical scrutiny. Sociology has a built-in debunking effect. It shows up the fallaciousness of socially established interpretations of reality by demonstrating that the facts do not gibe with the "official" view, or, even more simply, by relativizing the latter (by showing that it is only one of several possible views of society). *That* is already dangerous enough and would provide sufficient grounds for sociologists to become what the Prussian authorities used to call *polizeibekannt* — of interest, that is, to the cognitive if not to the actual police. (Every society has its cognitive policemen who administer the "official" definitions of reality.) But sociology, at least in certain situations, is more directly subversive. It unmasks vested interests and makes visible the manner in which the latter are served by social fictions. At least in certain situations, then, sociology can be political dynamite....

Anyone who pursues the sociological perspective to its logical consequences will find himself undergoing a transformation of his consciousness of society. At least potentially, this makes him unsafe from the viewpoint of the guardians of law and order. It also produces unsafety (sometimes with catastrophic effects) for his own peace of mind.

"Bringing to consciousness," in this sense, does indeed have a liberating quality. But the freedom to which it leads, apart from its possible political effects, can be a rather terrible thing. It is the freedom of ecstasy, in the literal sense of *ek-statis* — stepping or standing outside the routine ways and assumptions of everyday life — which, let us recall, also includes routine comforts, routine security. Thus, if there is a relation between "bringing to consciousness" and the ecstasy of liberation, there is also a relation between that ecstasy and the possibility of desperation. Toward the end of his life, Max Weber was asked by a friend to whom he had been explaining the pessimistic conclusions of his sociological analysis: "But if you think this way, why do you continue doing sociology?" Weber's reply is one of the most chilling statements I know in the history of Western thought: "Because I want to know how much I can stand...."

But let me go on to my second proposition: *Sociology is conservative in its implications for the institutional order....*

After a lecture of mine on sociological theory, a perceptive student remarked to me: "You sure have a hang-up on order, don't you?" I had to concede the description. But I also added that my "hang-up" was not arbitrary or inadvertent. Behind it is the conviction that sociology leads to the understanding that order is *the* primary imperative of social life....

*Every* social institution, no matter how "non-repressive" or "consensual," is an imposition of order — beginning with language, which is the most basic institution of all. If this is understood, there will then also be the understanding that social life abhors disorder as nature abhors a vacuum.

This has the directly political implication that, except for rare and invariably brief periods, the forces of order are always stronger than those of disorder, and, further, that there are fairly narrow limits to the toleration of disorder in any human society....

If all this adds up to a conservative propensity, it should be emphasized that the conservatism in question is of a peculiar kind. It is *not* based on the conviction that the institutions of the status quo are sacred, inexorably right, or empirically inevitable. The aforementioned subversive impulse of sociology precludes this type of conservatism. Rather, it is based on skepticism about the status quo in society *as well as* about various programs for new social orders. It is...*the stance of a man who thinks daringly but acts prudently.* This, of course, is exactly the kind of man our young revolutionaries will call a fink. So be it. It is probably one of the unavoidable blindnesses of youth to fail to see that acting prudently in society, while it may be the simple result of wanting to preserve one's little applecarts, may also be motivated quite differently — namely, by carefully thought — through concern to avoid senseless pain and to protect the good things of ordinary life....

Sociology, therefore, is a liberating discipline in a very specific way. There can be no doubt about its liberating effects on consciousness. At least potentially, sociology may be a prelude to liberation not only in thought but in action. At the same time, however, sociology points up the social limits of freedom — the very limits that, in turn, provide the social space for any empirically viable expression of freedom. This perspective, alas, is not simple. It requires intellectual effort and is not too easily harnessed to political passions. I would contend that the effort is worth it and that it will serve well precisely those political purposes that come from a concern for living men rather than for abstract doctrines of liberation.

# 63.  SOCIOLOGY AS A HUMANISTIC DISCIPLINE

PETER L. BERGER

*"We contend that it is part of a civilized mind in our age to have come in touch with the peculiarly modern, peculiarly timely form of critical thought that we call sociology."*

In this closing to his book, **Invitation to Sociology**, Peter Berger tackles a question that many teaching sociologists ask: Why bother teaching sociology—does it do anyone any good? Berger here describes a faith many of us have come to share.

…A sociologist teaching in many an average college, looking over his classes of young men and women desperately intent on social mobility, seeing them fight their way upward through the credit system and argue over grades with pertinacity, understanding that they could not care less if he read the phone directory to them in class as long as three credit hours could be added to the ledger at the end of the semester—such a sociologist will have to wonder sooner or later what sort of vocation it is that he is exercising. Even a sociologist teaching in a more genteel setting, providing intellectual pastime to those whose status is a foregone conclusion and whose education is the privilege rather than the instrumentality of such status, may well come to question what point there is to sociology, of all fields, in this situation. Of course, in state universities as well as in Ivy League colleges, there are always the few students who really care, really understand, and one can always teach with only those in mind. This, however, is frustrating in the long run, especially if one has some doubts about the pedagogic usefulness of what one is teaching. And that is precisely the question a morally sensitive sociologist ought to ask himself in an undergraduate situation.

The problem of teaching students who come to college because they need a degree to be hired by the corporation of their choice or because this is what is expected of them in a certain social position is shared by the sociologist with all his colleagues in other fields. We cannot pursue it here. There is, however, a peculiar problem for the sociologist that is directly related to the debunking, disenchanting character of sociology that we discussed before. It may well be asked with what right he peddles such dangerous intellectual merchandise among young minds that, more likely than not, will misunderstand and misapply the perspective he seeks to communicate. It is one thing to dispense the sociological poison to such graduate students as have already committed themselves to full-time addiction and who, in the course of intensive study, can be led to understand the therapeutic possibilities present in that poison. It is another thing to sprinkle it liberally among those who have no chance or inclination to proceed to that point of deeper understanding. What right does any man have to shake the taken-for-granted beliefs of others? Why educate young people to see the precariousness of things they had assumed to be absolutely solid? Why introduce them to the subtle erosion of critical thought? Why, in sum, not leave them alone?

Evidently, at least part of the answer lies in the responsibility and the skill of the teacher. One will not address a freshman class as one would a graduate seminar. Another partial answer could be given by saying that the taken-for-granted structures are far too solidly entrenched in consciousness to be that easily shaken by, say, a couple of sophomore courses. "Culture shock" is not induced that readily. Most people who are not prepared for this sort of relativization of their taken-for-granted world view will not allow themselves to face its implications fully and will instead look on it as an interesting intellectual game to be played in their sociology class, very much as one may play the game of discussing whether an object is there when one is not looking at it in a philosophy class—that is, one will play the game without for a moment seriously doubting the ultimate validity of one's previous commonsense perspective. This partial answer has its merits too, but it will hardly do as a justification of the sociologist's teaching, if only because it applies only to the degree that this teaching fails to achieve its purpose.

We maintain that the teaching of sociology is justified insofar as a liberal education is assumed to have a more than etymological connection with intellectual liberation. Where this assumption does not exist, where education is understood in purely technical or professional terms, let sociology be eliminated from the curriculum. It will only interfere with the smooth operation of the latter, provided, of course, that sociology has not also been emasculated in accordance with the educational ethos prevailing in such situations. Where, however, the assumption still holds, sociology is justified by the belief that it is better to be conscious than unconscious, and that consciousness is a condition of freedom. To attain a greater measure of awareness, and with it of freedom, entails a certain amount of suffering and even risk. An educational process that would avoid this becomes simple technical training and ceases to have any relationship to the civilizing of the mind. We contend that it is part of a civilized mind in our age to have come in touch with the peculiarly modern, peculiarly timely form of critical thought that we call sociology. Even those who do not find in this intellectual pursuit their own particular demon, as Weber put it, will by this contact have become a little less stolid in their prejudices, a little more careful in their own commitments, and little more skeptical about the commitments of others—and perhaps a little more compassionate in their journeys through society.

Let us return once more to the image of the puppet theater that our argument conjured up before. We see the puppets dancing on their miniature stage, moving up and down as the strings pull them around, following the prescribed course of their various little parts. We learn to understand the logic of this theater and we find ourselves in its motions. We locate ourselves in society and thus recognize our own position as we hang from its subtle strings. For a moment, we see ourselves as puppets indeed. But then we grasp a decisive difference between the puppet theater and our own drama. Unlike the puppets, we have the possibility of stopping in our movements, looking up and perceiving the machinery by which we have been moved. In this act lies the first step towards freedom. And in this same act, we find the conclusive justification of sociology as a humanistic discipline.

# 64.  SOCIOLOGY AND DEMOCRACY

JOEL M. CHARON

*"…The theme of democracy stands out. One might, in truth, argue that the study of sociology is the study of issues relevant to understanding democratic society."*

*The study of sociology is important if democratic society is going to thrive. The issues that matter in a democratic society are studied in sociology. This is the point of view of this selection.*

In the final analysis, it may be true that ignorance is bliss. It may be true that people should be left alone with the myths they happen to pick up in interaction with one another. It may be true that a liberal arts education that does not have immediate practical value is worthless.

## SOCIOLOGY AND A LIBERAL ARTS EDUCATION

I do not believe any of these ideas, but I wonder about them a lot. One can more easily make a case for mathematics, foreign languages, writing, speech, psychology, and economics on the level of practical use. "The student needs to know these if he or she is to get along in life," the argument goes. It is far more difficult to make a case for sociology on the basis of practical use — unless, of course, by *practical use* one means *thinking about and understanding the world*. If a college education is ultimately an attempt to encourage people to wonder, investigate, and carefully examine their lives, then sociology is one of the most important disciplines.

Note its purpose: To get students to examine an aspect of life carefully and systematically that most people only casually and occasionally think about. It is to get people to understand what culture is and to recognize that what they believe is largely a result of their culture. It is to get them to see that they are born into a society that has a long history, that they are ranked and given roles in that society, and that ultimately they are told who they are, what to think, and how to act. It is to get them to see that the institutions they follow and normally accept are not the only ways in which society can function — that there are always alternatives. It is to get them to realize that those whom they regard as sick, evil, or criminal are often simply different. It is to get them to see that those they

Excerpt from *Ten Questions: A Sociological Perspective*, 3rd Edition, by Joel M. Charon. Belmont, CA: Wadsworth Publishing Co., 1998.

hate are often a product of social circumstances that should be understood more carefully and objectively.

In short, the purpose of sociology is to get people to examine objectively their lives and their society. This process is uncomfortable and sometimes unpleasant. I keep asking myself, as I teach the insights of sociology, "Why not just leave those students alone?" And, quite frankly, I do not usually know how to answer this question. We are socialized into society. Shouldn't we simply accept that which we are socialized to believe? Isn't it better for society if people believe myth? Isn't it better for people's happiness to let them be?

I usually come back to what many people profess to be one primary purpose of a university education: "liberal arts." To me, the liberal arts should be "liberating." A university education should be liberating: It should help the individual escape the bonds of his or her imprisonment by bringing an understanding of that prison. We should read literature, understand art, and study biology and sociology in order to break through what those who defend society want us to know to reach a plane from which we can see reality in a more careful and unbiased way. In the end, sociology probably has the greatest potential for liberation in the academic world: At its best, it causes individuals to confront their ideas, actions, and being. We are never the same once we bring sociology into our lives. Life is scrutinized. Truth becomes far more tentative.

## SOCIOLOGY AND DEMOCRACY

### The Meaning of Democracy

Liberation, as you probably realize, has something to do with democracy. Although democracy is clearly an ideal that Americans claim for themselves, it is not usually clearly defined or deeply explored.

Sociology, however, explores democracy, and it asks rarely examined questions about the possibility for democracy in this — or any — society. To many people, democracy simply means "majority rule," and we too often superficially claim that if people go to a voting booth, then democracy has been established and the majority does, in fact, rule. Democracy, however, is far more than majority rule, and majority rule is far more than the existence of voting booths.

Democracy is very difficult to achieve. No society can become perfectly democratic; few societies really make much progress in that direction. Alexis de Tocqueville, a great French social scientist who wrote *Democracy in America* (1840) after traveling throughout much of the United States in 1831, believed that here was a thriving democracy, one with great future potential. Tocqueville pointed out many of our shortcomings — most important, the existence of slavery — but he believed that we probably had a more democratic future than any other society in the world. What Tocqueville did was examine the nature of our society — our structure, culture, and institutions — and then show what qualities of our society encouraged the development of democracy. For example, he identified our willingness to join voluntary associations that would impact government, strong local ties, and the little need we had for a central government. Although much has changed since Tocqueville wrote, his lasting importance was to remind us that democracy is a very difficult social state to achieve, that certain social conditions make it possible and certain patterns support its continued existence. It is also, he wrote, very easy to lose.

Democracy is difficult to define. When I try, I usually end up listing four qualities. These describe a whole society, not just the government in that society. Although everyone will not agree that these are the basic qualities of a democracy, I think they offer a good place to begin:

1. *A democratic society is one in which the individual is free in both thinking and action.* People are in control of their own lives. To the extent that a society encourages freedom, we can call it a democratic society.
2. *A democratic society is one in which the government is effectively limited.* Those who control government do not do what they choose to do. Voting, law, organizations of people, and constitutions effectively limit

their power. To the extent that government is effectively limited, we call it a democratic society.
3. *A democratic society is one in which human differences are respected and protected.* There is a general agreement that no matter what the majority favors, certain rights are reserved for the individual and for minorities who are different from the majority. Diversity is respected and even encouraged. To the extent that diversity and individuality is respected and protected, we call it a democratic society.
4. *A democratic society is one in which all people have an equal opportunity to live a decent life.* That is, privilege is not inherited, people have equality before the law, in educational opportunity, in opportunity for material success, and in whatever is deemed to be important in society. To the extent that real equality of opportunity exists, we call it a democratic society.

These four qualities that make up the definition of democracy described here must be tentative descriptions, and people should debate their relative significance. Some will regard other qualities to be more important, and some will regard only one or two of these qualities as necessary. I am only trying here to list four qualities that make sense to me and that guide my own estimate of whether the United States and other societies are democratic.

If these qualities do capture what democracy means, however, it should be obvious by now that the questions and thinking [that sociologists investigate]…are relevant to both the understanding of and the working toward a democratic society. Because sociology focuses on social organization, structure, culture, institutions, social order, social class, social power, social conflict, socialization, and social change, *sociology must continually examine issues that are relevant to understanding a democratic society.* And, on top of this, because *sociology critically examines people and their society, it encourages the kind of thinking that is necessary for people living in and working for a democratic society....* One might, in truth, argue that the study of sociology is the study of issues relevant to understanding democratic society.

## Sociology: An Approach to Understanding Democratic Society

[Sociology deals] with the nature of the human being and the role of socialization and culture in what we all become. To ask questions about human nature is to ask simultaneous questions about the possibility for democratic society, a society built on qualities that are not often widespread in society: respect for individual differences, compromise, and concern over inequality and lack of freedom. The sociological approach to the human being makes no assumption of fixed qualities, but it has a strong tendency to see human beings as living within social conditions that are responsible for forming many of their most important qualities. A society tends to produce certain types of people and certain social conditions, encouraging one value or another, one set of morals or another, one way of doing things or another. Conformity, control of the human being, tyranny, and pursuit of purely selfish interests can be encouraged; but so, too, can freedom, respect for people's rights, limited government, and equality. *The possibilities for and the limits to a human being who can live democratically are part of what sociology investigates through its questions concerning culture, socialization, and human nature.*

Those who think about society must inevitably consider the central problem of social order: How much freedom and how much individuality can we allow and still maintain society…? Those who favor greater freedom will occasionally wonder: How can there really be meaningful freedom in any society? As long as society exists, how much freedom can we encourage without destroying the underlying order? Are there limits? If so, how can we discover them? What are the costs, if any, of having a democratic society? Those who fear disorder and the collapse of society might ask: How much does the individual owe to society? Such questions are extremely difficult to answer, but they are investigated with the discipline of sociology, and they push the serious student to search for a delicate balance between order and freedom. Too often, people are willing to sell out freedom in the name of order; too often, people claim so much freedom that they do not seem to care about the continuation of society. The sociologist studies these problems and causes the student to reflect again and again on this dilemma inherent in all societies, especially those that claim to be part of the democratic tradition. There can be no freedom without society, Emile Durkheim reminds us, because a basic agreement over rules must precede the exercise of freedom. *But the problem is, How many rules? How much freedom? There is no more basic question for those who favor democracy, and there is no question more central to the discipline of sociology.*

The question of social order also leads us to the questions of what constitutes a nation and what constitutes a society…. These issues may not seem at first to have much relevance to democracy, but they surely do. It is easy for those who profess democracy to favor majority rule. It is much more difficult for any nation to develop institutions that respect the rights of all societies within its borders. A nation is a political state that rules over one – or more – societies. If it is democratic, the nation does not simply rule these societies but responds to their needs and rights, from true political representation to a decent standard of living. If it is democratic, the question the nation faces is *not* "How can we mold that society to be like the dominant society?" but "How can we create an order in which many societies can exist?" If it is democratic, the nation must balance the needs of each society's push for independence with the need for maintaining social order. *The whole meaning of what it is to be a society, as well as the associated problems of order and independence, are central sociological – and democratic – concerns.*

It is the question of control by social forces over the human being that places sociology squarely within the concerns of democracy. Much of sociology questions the possibility for substantial freedom. Democracy teaches that human beings should and can think for themselves. Much of the purpose of sociology, however, is to show us that our thinking is created by our social life; that, although we may claim that our ideas are our own, they really result from our cultures, from our positions in social structure, and from powerful and wealthy people…. Even to claim that "we are a democracy" can simply be part of an ideology, an exaggeration we accept because we are victims of various social forces. Our actions, too, result from a host of social forces that few of us understand or appreciate: institutions, opportunities, class, roles, social controls – to name only some – that quietly work on the individual, pushing him or her in directions not freely chosen…. Sociology seems to make democracy an almost impossible dream, and to some extent, the more sociology one knows, the more difficult democracy seems. *Indeed, sociology tends to simply uncover more and more ways in which human beings are shaped and controlled. This, in itself, makes sociology very relevant for understanding the limits of democracy. It causes one to seriously wonder whether human beings can be free in any sense.*

As I said earlier in this chapter, however, *sociology as a part of a liberal education is an attempt to liberate the individual from many of these controls.* The first step in liberation is understanding: It is really impossible to think for oneself or to act according to free choice unless one understands the various ways in which we are controlled. For example, it is only when I begin to see that my ideas of what it means to be a "man" have been formed through a careful and calculated process throughout society that I can begin to act in the way I choose. Only when I begin to understand how powerful advertising has become in developing my personal tastes as well as my personal values can I begin to step back and direct my own life. And even then, an important sociological question continuously teases the thoughtful person: Can society exist if people are truly liberated? If people question everything, can there still be the unity necessary for order?

The study of social inequality—probably the central concern within all sociology—is, of course, an issue of primary importance to understanding the possibility for a democratic society.... It seems that it is the nature of society to be unequal. Many forces create and perpetuate inequality. Indeed, even in our groups and our formal organizations, great inequalities are the rule. Why? Why does it happen? And what are its implications for democracy? If society is characterized by great inequalities of wealth and power, then how can free thought and free action prevail among the population? If a society—in name, a democracy—has a small elite that dominates the decision making, what difference does going to the polls make? If large numbers of people must expend all their energy to barely survive because of their poverty, where is their freedom, their opportunity to influence the direction of society, their right to improve their lives? If society is characterized by racist and sexist institutions, how is democracy possible for those who are victims? *More than any other perspective, sociology makes us aware of many problems standing in the way of a democratic society,* not the least of which are social, economic, and political inequality.

This focus on social inequality will cause many individuals to look beyond the political arena to understand democracy. A democratic society requires not only limited government but also a limited military, a limited upper class, limited corporations, and limited interest groups. Limited government may bring freedom to the individual, but it also may simply create more unlimited power for economic elites in society, which is often an even more ruthless tyranny over individual freedom. *Sociology, because its subject is society, broadens our concerns, investigates the individual not only in relation to political institutions but also in relation to many other sources of power that can and do limit real democracy and control much of what we think and do.*

The democratic spirit cares about the welfare of all people. It respects life, values individual rights, encourages quality of life, and seeks justice for all. Sociology studies social problems.... Many people live lives of misery, characterized by poverty, crime, bad jobs, exploitation, lack of self-worth, stress, repressive institutions, violent conflict, inadequate socialization, and alienation of various kinds. These are more than problems caused by human biology or human genes; these are more than problems caused by the free choices of individual actors. Something social has generally caused misery to occur. *Although it is impossible for sociology—or a democratic society—to rid the world of such problems, it is part of the spirit of both to understand them, to suggest and to carry out ways to deal with them.* Democracy is shallow and cold if large numbers of people continue to live lives of misery.

...Ethnocentrism, although perhaps inevitable and even necessary to some extent, is a way of looking at one's own culture and others in a manner antagonistic to a basic principle of democracy: respect for human diversity and individuality. To claim that our culture is superior to others is to treat other cultures without respect, to reject them for what they are, to believe that everyone must be like us. Such ideas encourage violent conflict and war and justify discrimination, segregation, and exploitation. Sociology challenges us to be careful with ethnocentrism. We must understand what it is, what its causes are, and how it functions. An understanding of ethnocentrism will challenge us to ask: "When are my judgments of others simply cultural and when are they based on some more defensible standards (such as democratic standards)?" "When are my judgments narrow and intolerant; when are they more careful and thought out?" Even then, an understanding of ethnocentrism will not allow us to judge people who are different without seriously questioning our judgments. *Sociology and democracy are perspectives that push us to understand human differences and to be careful in condemning those differences.*

[Sociology also examines] social change and the power of the individual. This discussion, too, challenges many of our taken-for-granted "truths" concerning democracy. The sociologist's faith in the individual as an agent of change is not great. Democracy is truly an illusion if it means that the individual has an important say in the direction of society. But if sociology teaches us anything about change that has relevance for democracy, it is that intentionally created change is possible only through a power base. If a democracy is going to be more than a description in a book, people who desire change in society — ideally, toward more freedom, limited government, equality of opportunity, and respect for individual rights — must work together and act from a power base, recognizing that the existing political institutions are usually fixed against them. And before we go off armed with certainty, we should remember that our certainty was probably also socially produced and that, through our efforts, we may bring change we never intended and may even lose whatever democracy we now have. Social change is complex, depends on social power, and is difficult to bring about in a way we would like. *The sociologist will examine the possibility for intentional social change in a democratic society and will be motivated to isolate the many barriers each society establishes to real social change.*

should understand the nature of all society, the nature of power, ethnocentrism, inequality, change, and all the other concepts discussed and investigated in sociology. Whereas other disciplines may study issues relevant to understanding democracy and encourage people to think democratically, in a very basic sense, this study is the heart of sociology.

...Democracy means that one must understand reality not by accepting authority but by careful, thoughtful investigation. It is through evidence, not bias, that one should understand. It is through open debate, not a closed belief system, that one should try to understand. *The principles of science and democracy are similar. There is no greater test of those principles than the discipline of sociology: an attempt to apply scientific principles to that for which we are all taught to feel a special reverence.*

Because it is a critical perspective that attempts to question what people have internalized from their cultures, sociology is a threat to those people who claim to know the truth. It punctures myth and asks questions that many of us would rather not hear. To see the world sociologically is to wonder about all things human. To see the world sociologically is to see events in a much larger context than the immediate situation, to think of individual events in relation to the larger present, to the past, and to the future. To see the world sociologically is to be suspicious of what those in power do (in our society and in our groups), and it is constantly to ask questions about what is and what can be.

The sociologist wonders about society and asks questions that get at the heart of many of our most sacred ideas. Perhaps this is why it seems so threatening to "those who know"; and perhaps this is why it is so exciting to those who take it seriously.

## SUMMARY AND CONCLUSION

Democracy exists at different levels. For some, it is a simplistic, shallow idea. For others, however, it is a complex and challenging idea to investigate and a reality worthwhile to create. If it is going to be more than a shallow idea, however, people